THE MEANING OF FREEDOM

THE
MEANING
OF FREEDOM

Philip Drew

ABERDEEN UNIVERSITY PRESS

First published 1982
Aberdeen University Press
A member of the Pergamon Group

© Philip Drew 1982

British Library Cataloguing in Publication Data
Drew, Philip
 The meaning of freedom
 1. Free will and determinism in literature
 2. English literature—history and criticism
 I. Title
 820'.9'38   PR149.F/

ISBN 0-08-025743-7

PRINTED IN GREAT BRITAIN
AT THE UNIVERSITY PRESS
ABERDEEN

Contents

Plates

Acknowledgments

I wish to acknowledge the support of the Publications Board of the University of Glasgow and of the Carnegie Trust for the Universities of Scotland.

I am happy also to take this opportunity to express my gratitude to a number of people whose kindness has helped and heartened me. Valerie Eden, Ingrid Swanson and, in particular, Irene Elsey produced an immaculate final typescript and have given unfailingly cheerful and efficient assistance in many other ways. My daughters have devoted much time and thought to making the index, for which I am most grateful to them. The labour of seeing the book through the press has been lightened by the helpfulness and experience of the officers of AUP: I am especially indebted to Colin MacLean for his encouragement and advice. My last and largest debt is acknowledged in the dedication.

PHILIP DREW
Glasgow 1981

Abbreviations

BJHS	British Journal for the History of Science
ELH	Journal of English Literary History
E&S	Essays and Studies
ES	English Studies
JEGP	Journal of English and Germanic Philology
JHI	Journal of the History of Ideas
MLQ	Modern Language Quarterly
MLR	Modern Language Review
NC	The Nineteenth Century
NCF	Nineteenth-Century Fiction
PMLA	Publications of the Modern Language Association of America
PQ	Philological Quarterly
RES	Review of English Studies
ShS	Shakespeare Survey
SIR	Studies in Romanticism (Boston U.)
SP	Studies in Philology
UTQ	University of Toronto Quarterly
VS	Victorian Studies

To M.L.D.

One Word More, line 4

Introduction

I could never think the study of wisdom confined only to the philosopher: or of piety to the divine: or of state to the politic. But that he which can feign a commonwealth (which is the poet), can govern it with councils, strengthen it with laws, correct it with judgements, inform it with religion, and morals; is all these. We do not require in him mere elocution; or an excellent faculty in verse; but the exact knowledge of all virtues, and their contraries; with ability to render the one loved, the other hated, by his proper embattling them.—BEN JONSON, *Discoveries*.

I

My object in writing this book is to recommend a change of proceeding, or more accurately a change of emphasis, in literary criticism. I begin from the premise that when we speak of greatness in a literary work we normally do so because we recognize that it has enlarged our knowledge of the nature and capacities of man: understanding and explaining what a writer says or takes for granted about human nature is thus very often an essential part of the critic's task. To demonstrate what I have in mind I have chosen a topic which has been for many centuries particularly prominent in major works of literature—in its broadest definition human freedom and the forces which limit it or are thought to limit it. I offer a number of studies of poems, plays and novels with the intention of showing the central part that is played in their organization by the assumptions the writer adopts about the freedom of the human will and the possibility of human freedom in general.

These ten studies cover widely different periods, and are set out in chronological order, with four short linking chapters placing the major texts in a context of changing views of the nature of freedom. Without implying that any inevitable historical forces were at work, I suggest that the differences I notice between individual authors who lived at different times are not simply a matter of personal idiosyncrasy but part of a larger process of intellectual change, in which the agents of change were ideas and arguments about ideas. I do not think that we need be disturbed by the knowledge that the writers themselves often played an important part in these arguments. As is normally the case, the individual authors were shaped by the general forces of their age and recorded them with particular sensitivity while at the same time they took part in the dialogue of the leading minds of the day which most decisively altered the direction and pressure of these forces.

It follows that much of my attention in the central chapters of the book will be given to features of my chosen texts which are at present seldom candidates for extended study and will no doubt, to critics of many persuasions, appear improper subjects for literary inquiry. Nothing however could more seriously misrepresent my purpose than to suppose that I intend to enforce an artificial opposition between form and content with the object of ignoring the first and offering an abstract account of the second. On the contrary, since I propose an approach which depends equally on a formal and a conceptual understanding of a work, I assume a willingness on the part of the reader to cooperate in the detailed reading of particular passages but with the continual awareness that scrutiny, however discriminating, of the words a writer uses does not mark the end of critical activity. If our period of literary criticism is, as I believe, distinguished for the subtlety of its close reading of poetry and prose, the question must sooner or later be asked, 'What is this close reading for?'

In my case it is to allow me to display as clearly as I am able the complex and often contradictory interweavings in my chosen texts of theory, superstition, tradition and speculation about the nature of human freedom. The general justification of criticism of this kind has been put many times, but nowhere I think more clearly and simply than by Jerome Schneewind:

> If the work portrays human life, it cannot but portray it as existing in some form or other; and, consequently, it must embody at least some of the data from which moral philosophers start. . . . To describe a work [presenting a rich and complex world] in philosophical terms is to point up something in the work, and something essential to its being the work it is. And if the work presents or reflects problems which have analogs among the conceptual difficulties of philosophy, it can only add a level to our understanding of what is in the work if we see the moral problems in the light of the conceptual ones (p. 39).[1]

I hope that it will not be necessary for me to say too much in justification of the use of imaginative works in the history of ideas: this is in the tradition of Burckhardt, who has rightly been praised as 'the first to understand that the history of art and literature is the historian's index for understanding the transformation of senti-ment, those ill-understood processes by which men come to feel about the world in new ways and to see it differently'.[2]

But were this to be considered the chief value of a work of literature it need amount to no more than Byron's reductive comment, 'Troy owes to Homer what whist owes to Hoyle.'[3] It will be an important part of my case that the close study of literary texts is justified not only because they are documents of unique value in the history of ideas but also because they add to our current understanding of the nature of man. As Conrad puts it, 'Moral discovery . . . should be the object of every tale.' What I have in mind is not so much Racine's preface to *Phèdre*, where he proposes specific moral instruction as part of the artist's duty, as Boccaccio's observation that Dante was known in his lifetime variously as a poet and a philosopher and a theologian. Without imposing a narrowly didactic role on imaginative writers one may still agree with Mill that 'every great poet, every poet who has extensively or permanently influenced mankind, has been a great thinker'[4] and with Arnold that poetry interprets the world not only by 'natural magic' but also 'by expressing, with inspired conviction, the ideas and laws of the inward world of man's moral and spiritual nature'.[5]

It is plain that what is necessary to illustrate this is a way of talking about books which, far from making an artificial separation between form and content, deals with both simultaneously. I put forward and demonstrate a method of literary criticism which offers a possible solution to the problem. It requires the critic to bear in mind a wide range of scientific, political, religious, philosophical and historical ideas, many of which, because life is short and the human mind limited, will have to be approached by way of secondary sources. I must therefore at this point acknowledge how much I owe to the authors whose books I have rummaged through in the attempt to borrow their understanding of a subject not my own. There are obvious dangers in this, and I cannot hope to have avoided them all. I can only plead that interdisciplinary studies of any kind are bound to force a writer beyond his own special province: it is the price to be paid for trying to connect different areas of scholarship.

There are, however, two compensations. First, an approach of this kind helps to move literary criticism out of the preserve of the professional, where scholasticism always threatens, into the realm of informed general discussion. 'The first distemper of learning is when men study words and not matter,' as Bacon said, '. . . for words are but the images of matter; and except they have life of reason and invention, to fall in love with them is all one as to fall in love with a picture.'[6] Secondly, it presents the great poets, dramatists and novelists as engaged in a continuous debate about a matter of fundamental human importance, in company with philosophers, politicians and scientists. The claim they make on our attention is not on the grounds of technical excellence, impressive though that may be, but on the grounds of having something of value to say to man. 'It exceeds all imagination to conceive what would have been the moral condition of the world if [the poets] had never been born.'[7] If this is true it follows that the poet's works are not mere structures, not *vides*, but full of matter: they are of effect on the life of the reader and on the course of human history. It is, in short, my concern to promote a view of literature in which we see

> Poets, even as Prophets, each with each
> Connected in a mighty scheme of truth.[8]

II

My argument to this point has been that if a critic asks himself a question in some such form as 'What assumptions about the nature of man are present, implicitly or explicitly, in the work under examination?' he can produce an adequate answer only by devoting equal attention to the form and the content and by refusing to consider either in isolation. To illustrate this general argument I take as an example the related topics of free will, fate, fortune, foreknowledge, divine providence, the reality of the self, chance, determinism, the nature of freedom, social and political liberty, and so on, and I ask therefore what assumptions about the freedom of the human will and the extent of human freedom the author requires his readers to accept.

It may be asked why the free will question should be considered particularly suitable for this purpose. While it is true that many other topics would lend themselves to a similar enquiry, free will has the following special advantages. First, it is vague and varied as a concept, but in some form is an active issue in almost every period of our literature: thus some sort of continuous history of an idea is possible and is available for provisional confirmation or falsification by other disciplines. Secondly, it is pervasive, in that it underlies a wide selection of philosophical problems, and yet it is not itself a problem of which there is any generally accepted analysis. Thirdly, it enables us to compare, most obviously in the novel, an author's explicit accounts of the general question of human freedom with his presentation of his own characters, thus bringing into the argument the theoretical problems engendered by a consideration of the nature of fiction. And finally, as I show in the concluding chapters, the difficulty of defining a free action has particularly disturbing consequences in the literature and political theory of our own time.

What then briefly is the free will problem, and in what terms is it most easily discussed? (Those who are familiar with the issues will find nothing new in their presentation here and may safely turn to p. 17.) As usual, Dr Johnson provides the starting-point: 'All theory is against the freedom of the will; all experience for it.'[9] As the second part of this statement implies, it is very difficult and perhaps unnecessary to set out rational arguments in favour of the freedom of the will: the appeal is always to shared experience. 'We *know* our will is free.'[10] To show why Johnson was so impressed by the theoretical case on the other side even though it contradicts the common sense of mankind, I shall list a number of straightforward definitions of the terms most frequently used in the discussion. All the definitions are preliminary, in the sense that their very naïveté is enough to suggest at once further questions which cannot be answered in such simple terms.

I begin with two attempts to explain briefly what is meant by Liberty. The first is by Hobbes, the second by Harold Laski.

Liberty, or Freedome, signifieth (properly) the absence of Opposition; (by Opposition, I mean externall Impediments of motion;)[11]

Liberty is essentially an absence of restraint. . . . [Men] are free when the rules under which they live leave them without a sense of frustration in realms they deem significant.[12]

The relation of this physical or political view of liberty to the freedom of the will is clearly put by David Raphael:

'Freedom' means the absence of restraint. A man is free in so far as he is not restrained from doing what he wants to do or what he would choose to do if he knew that he could. The idea of choice itself implies a kind of freedom. Choice is the selection of one possibility among others. More than one possibility must be open to us before we can be said to have a choice. If we were always bound to do the one thing that we in fact do, we should not be free to choose; there would be no freedom of the will.[13]

A definition in the same clear but non-technical language of 'will' comes conveniently from the eighteenth century American divine Jonathan Edwards:

And therefore I observe, that the *Will* (without any metaphysical refining) is *That by which the mind chooses anything*. The faculty of the *Will*, is that power, or principle of mind, by which it is capable of *choosing*: an act of the *Will* is the same as an act of *choosing* or *choice*. . . . So that by whatever names we call the act of the Will, choosing, refusing, approving, disapproving, liking, disliking, embracing, rejecting, determining, directing, commanding, forbidding, inclining or *being* averse, *being* pleased or displeased with; all may be reduced to this of *choosing*.[14]

Why then, since all our experience, as Johnson says, disposes us to recognize that our wills are in this sense free, are there any difficulties? The answer lies in our attempts to do two things—first to understand and explain why our wills, though free *ex hypothesi*, are often thwarted, and secondly, to arrive at an account of the operation of a free will which does not contradict some other equally important article of belief. It is my argument that so far all attempts to do these things have led to a series of antinomies,[15] of which the six following are, for my purposes, the most important.

(i) If, in order to explain our own creation or our own inability to impose our wills on the rest of the world we postulate an Omnipotent Power, or set of superior powers, an immediate problem is to reconcile its operation with the existence of our own desires. What implants the desires if not the power? If it is responsible for them why does it thwart them? It is to soften these contradictions that such subordinate powers as the Fates and Furies, or Fate and Fortune, are employed. The difficulties to which this device leads are clearly shown by Burckhardt's comment on Dante:

> His God leaves all the details of the world's government to a deputy, Fortune, whose sole work is to change and change again all earthly things, and who can disregard the wailings of men in unalterable beatitude.[16]

Burckhardt adds, apparently without any sense of awkwardness, 'Nevertheless, Dante does not for a moment loose his hold on the moral responsibility of man; he believes in free will.'

Ralegh, in his *History of the World*, devotes many pages to explaining the puzzling relationship between Nature and God and Fate and Fortune. He declares in his Preface, 'Certainly there is no other account to be made of this ridiculous world, than to resolue, That the change of fortune on the great Theater, is but as the change of garments on the lesse,' but he is not prepared to agree that it is a world of meaningless change:

> The same power which they called *animam mundi, the soule of the world*, was no other than that incomprehensible wisedome, which we expresse by the name of God, gouerning euery being aswell in heauen as in earth; to which wisdome and power they sometime gaue the title of necessitie or Fate, because it bindeth by ineuitable ordinance: sometime, the stile of Fortune, because of many effects there appeare vnto vs no certaine causes.[17]

Plate 1. Title page of the first edition of Sir Walter Ralegh's HISTORY OF THE WORLD (1614), engraved by Renold Elstracke from a design by Ralegh. *By courtesy of Glasgow University Library*

Thus while he accepts Fortune as a rather capricious agent of the divine purpose he sets his face firmly against 'that kind of Idolatrie, or God of fooles, called *Fortune*, or Chance' (p. 114). In this repudiation of chance he is at one with Boethius.[18] In Book V Prosa 1 of the *De Consolatione* Philosophy insists that, since God governs all, there is no such thing as chance, if you define it like this: 'Hap is a bytydynge ibrought forth by foolissh moevynge and by no knyttynge of causes.' There are *no* uncaused events. There *are* unexpected coincidences, 'But forsothe it nis nat of naught, for it hath his propre causes, of whiche causes the cours unforseyn and unwar semeth to han makid hap' . . . 'Now mai I thus diffinysshen "hap": hap is an unwar betydinge of causes assembled in thingis that ben doon for som oothir thing.' But *this* 'hap' is caused just like everything else: in spite of appearances, what men term chance is only a name for their own ignorance. There are no uncaused events. *Ex nihilo nihil fit.*

(ii) The same doctrine is of force even if we eliminate the idea of an omnipotent power. Our experience suggests to us that the Universe is so constructed as not to admit of causal progenitors. A causal progenitor is defined as 'an event not itself dependent on a previous event, which stands at the beginning of a chain of acts and consequences'.[19] That there are no uncaused events in the Universe is the assumption which underlies the classical determinist view of the world. John Stuart Mill gives a clear account of the basic position:

> The Law of Causation, the recognition of which is the main pillar of inductive science, is but the familiar truth, that invariability of succession is found by observation to obtain between every fact in nature and some other fact which has preceded it.[20]

I introduce here a short digression on the subject of predictability, not because I think that it represents an important line in the argument, but because it is a common and forceful way of presenting the implication of universal causality and because it is of some literary interest especially in the reading of Chaucer, Shakespeare and Milton. When Augustine writes 'The first morning of Creation wrote what the last Dawn of Reckoning shall read' or observes that in the mind of God 'Futura iam facta sunt' he says only what a mechanical determinist would be prepared to express in secular terms, that, the Universe being determined, a total knowledge of the system and its laws at any time would in theory enable accurate predictions to be made of all future states of the system. The point to note is that such a prediction would not, as is sometimes implied, be the final achievement of a determinist but simply one theoretical property of a determined system. If then it is argued that prediction *per se* does not constrain there is no need to disagree, for the determinist case is that the nature of the Universe constrains, just as the nature of the Universe theoretically enables its future states to be predicted. When in a celebrated passage Laplace writes

> We ought then to regard the present state of the universe as the effect of its antecedent state and the cause of the state that is to follow. An intelligence knowing at a given instant of time, all forces acting in nature, as well as the momentary positions of all things of which the universe consists, would be able to comprehend the motions of the largest bodies of the world and those of the lightest atoms in one single formula, provided his intellect were sufficiently powerful to subject all data to analysis; to him nothing would be uncertain, both past and future would be present to his eyes.[21]

the first sentence is essential, the second is a purely theoretical consequence. Thus if I plant a cabbage seed and say 'That will come up as a cabbage' it is not the prediction that determines the future plant but the nature of the seed.[22]

It is immaterial for the purposes of the argument whether we are dealing with Laplace's Supreme Intelligence or Boethius' 'devyne prescience': the essence of the argument is that in a world from which causal progenitors have been eliminated the past inevitably determines, indeed contains, the future.

> It [i.e. determinism] professes that those parts of the Universe already laid down absolutely appoint and decree what other parts shall be. The future has no ambiguous possibilities hidden in its womb: the part we call the present is compatible with only one totality. Any other future complement than the one fixed from eternity is impossible. The whole is in each and every part, and welds it with the rest into an absolute unity, an iron block, in which there can be no equivocation or shadow of turning.[23]

There are no uncaused events. *Ex nihilo nihil fit.* It is therefore necessary to classify all events that appear to arise by chance as simply manifestations of incomplete knowledge.

(iii) When Mill's 'law of causality' is applied to the whole of the Universe, that is to thinking substances as well as to those having extension only,[24] we are confronted by a world in which human free will is no longer possible. Tolstoy gives a clear description of such a world:

> Freewill is for history only an expression connoting what we do not know about the laws of human life. . . .

The recognition of man's freewill as a force capable of influencing his-toricial events, that is, as not subject to laws, is the same for history as the recognition of a free force moving the heavenly bodies would be for astronomy.

Such an assumption would destroy the possibility of the existence of laws, that is, of any science whatever. If there is even one heavenly body moving freely then the laws of Kepler and Newton are negated and no conception of the movement of the heavenly bodies any longer exists. If there is a single human action due to freewill then not a single historical law can exist, nor any conception of historical events.[25]

One of the plainest descriptions of the chain of reasoning which leads from a belief in the universality of natural law to a willing abandonment of any claims for the freedom of the will is given in Shelley's Notes to *Queen Mab*. Commenting on line 198 of Section VI—'Necessity! thou mother of the world'—he begins on familiar enough lines:

He who asserts the doctrine of Necessity means that, contemplating the events which compose the moral and material universe, he beholds only an immense and uninterrupted chain of causes and effects, no one of which could occupy any other place than it does occupy, or act in any other place than it does act. The idea of necessity is obtained by our experience of the connection between objects, the uniformity of the operations of nature, the constant conjunction of similar events, and the consequent inference of one from the other.

He then proceeds to make, with some satisfaction, the transition from physical to psychological necessity:

Motive is to voluntary action in the human mind what cause is to effect in the material universe. The word liberty, as applied to mind, is analo-gous to the word chance as applied to matter: they spring from an ignorance of the certainty of the conjunction of antecedents and conse-quents. Every human being is irresistibly impelled to act precisely as he does act: in the eternity which preceded his birth a chain of causes was generated, which, operating under the name of motives, make it impos-sible that any thought of his mind, or any action of his life, should be otherwise than it is. Were the doctrine of Necessity false, the human mind would no longer be a legitimate object of science; from like causes it would be in vain that we should expect like effects; the strongest motive would no longer be paramount over the conduct; all knowledge would be vague and undeterminate; we could not predict with any certainty that we might not meet as an enemy to-morrow him with whom we have parted in friendship to-night; the most probable induce-ments and the clearest reasonings would lose the invariable influence they possess.... History, politics, morals, criticism, all grounds of reasonings, all principles of science, alike assume the truth of the doctrine of Necessity.... But, whilst none have scrupled to admit necessity as influencing matter, many have disputed its dominion over mind. Independently of its militating with the received ideas of the justice of God, it is by no means obvious to a superficial inquiry. When the mind observes its own operations, it feels no connection of motive and action.

When we try to describe in simple terms what happens in the act of volition it is difficult to avoid using metaphors from the mechanical world such as 'weight' or 'balance' or 'strength' or 'equilibrium'. Consider Jonathan Edwards once more

> I trust it will be allowed by all, that in every act of *will* there is an act of *choice*; that in every *volition* there is a *preference*, or a prevailing inclination of the soul, whereby, at that instant, it is out of a state of perfect indifference, with respect to the direct object of the volition. So that in every act, or going forth of the Will, there is some preponderation of the mind, one way rather than another; and the soul had rather *have* or *do* one thing, than another, or than *not* to have or do that thing; and that where there is absolutely no preferring or choosing, but a perfect, continuing equilibrium, there is no volition. (I, end)

> It is that motive, which, as it stands in the view of the mind, is the strongest, that determines the Will. (II)

> If it be so, that the Will is always determined by the strongest motive, then it must always have an Inability, in this latter sense, to act otherwise than it does; it not being possible, in any case, that the Will should, at present, go against the motive which has now, all things considered, the greatest advantage to introduce it. (IV)

Shelley writes in similar but more forceful terms and with very different objects:

> The advocates of free-will assert that the will has the power of refusing to be determined by the strongest motive: but the strongest motive is that which, overcoming all others, ultimately prevails; this assertion therefore amounts to a denial of the will being ultimately determined by that motive which does determine it, which is absurd. But it is equally certain that a man cannot resist the strongest motive as that he cannot overcome a physical impossibility.

The argument is clearly presented, and is of an obvious cogency. The principal objection to acknowledging its truth is that to do so entails a series of consequences which most people find unacceptable.

Shelley tries to meet the obvious objection that it is hard to explain what meaning 'responsibility' and 'morality' would have in a completely determined world:

> The doctrine of Necessity tends to introduce a great change into the established notions of morality, and utterly to destroy religion. Reward

and punishment must be considered, by the Necessarian, merely as motives which he would employ in order to procure the adoption or abandonment of any given line of conduct. Desert, in the present sense of the word, would no longer have any meaning; and he who should inflict pain upon another for no better reason than that he deserved it, would only gratify his revenge under pretence of satisfying justice. . . . At the same time, the doctrine of Necessity does not in the least diminish our disapprobation of vice. . . . A Necessarian is inconsequent to his own principles if he indulges in hatred or contempt; the compassion which he feels for the criminal is unmixed with a desire of injuring him: he looks with an elevated and dreadless composure upon the links of the universal chain as they pass before his eyes; whilst cowardice, curiosity, and inconsistency only assail him in proportion to the feebleness and indistinctness with which he has perceived and rejected the delusions of free-will.

Shelley is thus able to contemplate with equanimity a world from which free will has been banished. A contemporary behaviourist, B. F. Skinner, takes a similarly composed view of a much more drastic set of limitations on human activity:

Science has probably never demanded a more sweeping change in a traditional way of thinking about a subject, nor has there ever been a more important subject. In the traditional picture a person perceives the world around him, selects features to be perceived, discriminates among them, judges them good or bad, changes them to make them better (or, if he is careless, worse), and may be held responsible for his action and justly rewarded or punished for its consequences. In the scientific picture a person is a member of a species shaped by evolutionary contingencies of survival, displaying behavioural processes which bring him under the control of the environment in which he lives, and largely under the control of a social environment which he and millions of others like him have constructed and maintained during the evolution of a culture. The direction of the controlling relation is reversed: a person does not act upon the world, the world acts upon him.[26]

Skinner discloses and bravely faces the difficult question which arises if we accept the existence of a universal law of causation and follow the implications of this to a conclusion—in a world from which free will has been banished what could be meant by 'personality' or 'self'?

If it is agreed that in a determined world all events (and *a fortiori* human decisions) are the results of pre-existing events, all the elements of the human personality that come into play in decision-making must themselves be the products of heredity or environment. What then remains for the 'self' to be? It must represent simply the sum of all the relevant factors and cannot therefore be something set over against them and choosing between them *sua sponte*. When Forster writes in 'What I believe', 'For the purpose of living one has to assume that the personality is solid, and the 'self' an entity, and to ignore all contrary evidence',[27] his insistence on 'self' is a corollary of his belief in free will, an entity designed to explain the origin of uncaused impulses and to give a point of reference to what would otherwise seem an unrelated series of responses. Part of its job then is to make volitions seem not arbitrary choices or mere acts of caprice but rational and consistent decisions.

It is possible to argue, with Hume, that, far from destroying the character of man as a moral being, material necessity 'is so essential to religion and morality, that without it there must ensue an absolute subversion of both, and that every other supposition is entirely destructive to all laws, both *divine* and *human*'. Yet many writers are, like Macneile Dixon, unwilling or unable to contemplate the replacement of *homo sapiens* by a puppet with a memory, since they see this as leading directly to the disintegration of the self and the loss of any sanction for ethical judgements:

> The universe has, by modern thought, been weighed in the balances and found wanting. Modern thought declares that we are but parts of a stupendous mechanism, a theatre of marionettes, in which all men speak their previously allotted parts, that every movement of our bodies and our minds is as strictly controlled as the wheeling of the planets and the swinging of the tides; that every hope springing up in the breast, every tear that falls from the eye, is a result not less rigidly determined than the tick of the clock, or the movement of its hands upon the dial. We puppets within the gigantic grasp of necessity emit sighs like the doll pressed by the fingers of the child, the beats of our hearts were numbered from the beginning, and the pulses of our emotions already counted a million million years ago. As regards ourselves, then, the teaching of modern knowledge is easily summarized. It proclaims our complete unimportance.[28]

(iv) Macneile Dixon is of course presenting the 'New Thought' ironically and rejecting its mechanical view of man. Tolstoy goes further and moves to the heart of the problem when he states plainly the impossibility of conceiving how any action can be either completely free or completely determined:

> If we study one man by himself, if we isolate him from his environment, every action of his seems free to us. But if we see any relation of his whatever to what surrounds him, if we see any connexion with anything whatever—with another man talking to him, a book read by him, the work in which he is engaged, even with the air he breathes or the light that falls on the objects about him—we see that each of these circumstances has its influence on him and orders at least one side of his activity. . .

However clear we may make to ourselves the connexion between our man and the external world or however hopelessly we fail to trace any such connexion, however much we lengthen or shorten the period of time involved, however intelligible or incomprehensible the causes of the action may be to us, we can never conceive of either complete freedom or complete necessity of action.[29]

If then external circumstances are continually shaping a man's behaviour, can he ever be said to act authentically? Even the most powerful impulses and the most deep-seated principles of judgement, since they must have been acquired directly or indirectly from others, are tainted by their origins. It is but a short step from this conclusion to maintaining, like Sartre's Daniel, that freedom consists in doing the opposite of what you want to do.

Paradoxes of this kind naturally provoke enquiry into what might be meant by a completely unconstrained action and what value such an action, if we could imagine it, might be supposed to have. A line of argument follows from this which denies any virtue to freedom in itself: it has been strikingly put by Ruskin in *The Cestus of Aglaia* (1865–6). The first quotation refers particularly to drawing:

> All freedom is error. Every line you lay down is either right or wrong: it may be timidly and awkwardly wrong, or fearlessly and impudently wrong: the aspect of the impudent wrongness is pleasurable to vulgar persons; and is what they commonly call 'free' execution: the timid, tottering, hesitating wrongness is rarely so attractive; yet sometimes, if accompanied with good qualities, and right aims in other directions, it becomes in a manner charming, like the inarticulateness of a child: but, whatever the charm or manner of the error there is but one question ultimately to be asked respecting every line you draw, Is it right or wrong? If right, it most assuredly is not a 'free' line, but an intensely continent, restrained, and considered line; and the action of the hand in laying it is just as decisive, and just as 'free' as the hand of a first-rate surgeon in a critical incision. (Ch. VI, §72)

The second deals with the value of freedom in general:

> I believe we can nowhere find a better type of a perfectly free creature than in the common house fly. Nor free only, but brave; and irreverent to a degree which I think no human republican could by any philosophy exalt himself to. There is no courtesy in him; he does not care whether it is king or clown whom he teases; and in every step of his swift mechanical march, and in every pause of his resolute observation, there is one and the same expression of perfect egotism, perfect independence and self-confidence, and conviction of the world's having been made for flies. . . . You cannot terrify him, nor govern him, nor persuade him, nor convince him. He has his own positive opinion on all matters; not an

unwise one, usually, for his own ends; and will ask no advice of yours. He has no work to do—no tyrannical instinct to obey. The earthworm has his digging; the bee her gathering and building; the spider her cunning network; the ant her treasury and accounts. All these are comparatively slaves, or people of vulgar business. But your fly, free in the air, free in the chamber—a black incarnation of caprice—wandering, investigating, flitting, flirting, feasting at his will, with rich variety of choice in feast, from the heaped sweets in the grocer's window to those of the butcher's back-yard, and from the galled place on your cab-horse's back, to the brown spot in the road, from which, as the hoof disturbs him, he rises with angry republican buzz—what freedom is like his? (§74)

If 'pure' freedom is worthless, some qualifications must clearly be introduced which will stipulate that freedom shall be used only for worthy ends and is to be valued accordingly.

Freedom can consist only in the power of doing *what we ought to will.*— MONTESQUIEU

Free will is not the liberty to do whatever one likes, but the power of doing *whatever one sees ought to be done,* even in the face of otherwise overwhelming impulse. There lies freedom, indeed.—GEORGE MACDONALD

By liberty I mean the assurance that every man shall be protected in *doing what he believes his duty* against the influence of authority and majorities, custom and opinion.—ACTON

My italics show how the key terms are heavily modified, first in order to prevent 'freely willed' from meaning merely 'without motive or reason' and secondly to ensure that the motive or reason shall not be a purely selfish one. Generations of philosophers have insisted on the need for the individual to commit himself to some larger loyalty if he is to give meaning and value to his actions. T. H. Green, for example, defines 'freedom in the positive sense' as 'the liberation of the powers of all men equally for contributions to a common good'.[30]

(v) But if, in order to preserve for actions a quality beyond the purely gratuitous we accept that all actions of value must be to some extent determined (if only by a necessary commitment to the Good) what becomes of personal freedom as an ideal to be defended at all costs? In particular, if freedom is not *per se* valuable, on what grounds can one object to the totalitarian state which offers to ensure that all its citizens shall act from a thoroughly sufficient motive at all times? This question is particularly acute for any writer who begins from the premise that governments are at present the forces which most oppressively limit the freedom of their subjects. What is he to set in his work against the values of the state if not the untrammelled will of the individual?

(vi) This brings me to the final paradox which I wish to demonstrate. It arises from a consideration of the representation of human beings and their decisions in a work of literature. Lukàcs has rightly said

> The key question is: what is meant by 'chance' in fiction? Without chance all narration is dead and abstract. No writer can portray life if he eliminates the fortuitous.[31]

Yet a novel is shaped not fortuitously but under control: once it is finished the outcomes are determined. What part is there for chance to play? Equally once a book is completed there is no room for the characters to exercise their will: Ahab cannot suddenly change his mind about hunting the white whale, head for home and spend a happy old age in Nantucket. How then is a writer to represent free choice on the part of his characters? Is it even possible, or must he rely on a convention by which characters are through the co-operation of the reader, assumed to be acting freely, rather as actors in the theatre are supposed to be reacting spontaneously to the situation on the stage, although everybody knows that they are in fact repeating words that someone else has written and they have learned by heart? Is the first reading of a work of fiction, where the end is still unknown to the reader and the result of all deliberations is in doubt, of a different order from subsequent readings, where the illusion of multiple possibilities can no longer be sustained by his ignorance of the outcome?

Again, suppose that Spinoza is right when he says, 'Those who believe they do anything from the free decision of the mind dream with their eyes open.'[32] And suppose also that when Basil Willey says, 'The conclusion of most of the disputes on this problem has been, in effect, that we must in any case go on behaving *as if* we were free,'[33] he is directing our attention to a generally accepted resource: suppose, that is, that the strongest argument in favour of the existence of free will is that it is the least inconvenient assumption. Does this mean that a novelist, for example, can at best show his characters as pretending to be free when in fact they are not, or assuming that they are free when they may not be? If it *is* an assumption can the novelist afford to share it? Can an omniscient narrator fairly decline to disclose whether the assumption is well-founded or not? In short, if the writer wishes to represent the actual conditions of human life with the greatest possible fidelity, how is he to do so if the basic mechanism of human decisions is either unknown or such that any hypothesis about its operation leads to an antinomy? So thickly do the paradoxes throng that it sometimes seems as though the inconsistencies which beset even the subtlest representation of freely acting human characters were not failures in art but faithful reflections, uniquely available from a study of literature, of the confusions in which most of us labour.

Such then is an outline, in the most elementary terms, of the free will problem, with most of the leading positions indicated by quotations deliberately chosen for their unproblematic and non-rigorous statements of a point of view, without any attempt to allow for or even admit the difficulties which such a position would encounter if more comprehensively stated.

III

The free will problem, considered in its widest sense, is related to many other departments of philosophical enquiry. For example in questions of the status of inductive reasoning as soon as we ask 'Why do we expect the future to be like the past?' we must at least consider the answer 'Because the future is in some way contained in and determined by the past.' Again if we are prepared to consider the possibility of a Universe which is completely determined we must contemplate also a solid block Universe of which Time is merely a dimension. We have to ask whether this is an adequate view of the nature of Time, one of the most fruitful areas of modern speculation. Alternatively if we wish to examine the consequences of postulating a random Universe we shall have to consider a suitable theory of causality, which will certainly involve some consideration of probability, another topic of great interest at present.

I need hardly mention the importance of a study of the free will problem for questions of morality and human responsibility for actions and for questions of political philosophy, rights, liberty, consent and obligation. As Hobbes puts it 'The true and perspicuous explication of the elements of laws natural and politic . . . dependeth upon the Knowledge of what is human nature'.[34] No more fundamental question can be asked about the nature of man than whether he initiates actions or whether everything that he does is part of a sequence of events which he cannot control. Such a question calls out for answer in many other branches of philosophy, such as the philosophy of law.[35] Almost the only topics that are not obviously involved are questions of meaning, though even here it might be relevant if you take the view that all human development is controlled by men's linguistic capacities; questions of perception, though even here the free will issues raises itself, as I show when I discuss Wordsworth; and questions of belief such as 'How do we know what we believe to be true?', though even here, as I show in the chapter on Milton, we may fairly ask whether we can choose whether or not to believe. The fact that these three topics of meaning, perception and belief are of particular interest to contemporary philosophers may explain, if not excuse, the present neglect of the free will question.

That it has been neglected, or at least relegated by tacit agreement to the status of an unprofitable controversy, is not open to question. Even the most general histories make the point explicitly. I have already quoted Basil Willey, and Alban Widgery closes his additional chapter to Sidgwick's *History of Ethics* with this comment:

> The attitude of writers on ethics towards the problem of human freedom has changed during the last fifty years. In earlier times the notion of moral responsibility received much more attention than now, and was thought to be closely bound up with the idea of freedom. It is now generally thought sufficient to recognise the fact of moral choice. It may with some reason be objected that this method of description in terms of emergent evolution simply ignores ultimate problems which nevertheless continue to press themselves on human thought. However that may be, it is regarded as sufficient in ethics to recognise the reality of human activity and the element of spontaneity in moral advance.

C. A. Campbell remarked pointedly, 'We do know of one traditional problem that is definitely on the black list of the *avant garde*—the problem of "Free Will",'[36] and it is notable that in A. J. Ayer's *The Central Questions of Philosophy* (1973) the question of free will is given only a section a few pages long in the last chapter, 'The Claims of Theology': it comes immediately before the final section, called 'The Meaning of Life'.

It will be evident that I do not share the opinion that the topic is without further interest. On the contrary I feel about it as Pascal felt about the immortality of the soul:

> It is beyond a doubt that the mortality or immortality of the soul must make an entire difference in morals; yet philosophers have treated morality as independent of the question. They discuss to pass the time.[37]

Two final quotations from Tolstoy make the point with notable clarity:

> The presence of the problem of man's freewill, though unexpressed, is felt at every step in history.

> If only one man out of millions once in a thousand years had the power of acting freely, i.e. as he chose, it is obvious that one single free act of

that man in violation of the laws would be enough to prove that laws governing all human action cannot possibly exist.

Again, if there is a single law controlling the actions of men, free will cannot exist, for man's will will then be subject to that law.

In this contradiction lies the problem of free will, which from earliest times has occupied the best intellects of mankind and has from earliest times appeared in all its colossal significance.[38]

Nor is this a purely mid-nineteenth century point of view. William James, for example, commented:

A common opinion prevails that the juice has ages ago been pressed out of the free-will controversy, and that no new champion can do more than warm up stale arguments which everyone has heard. This is a radical mistake. I know of no subject less worn out, or in which inventive genius has a better chance of breaking open new ground.

Nearer our own time Isaiah Berlin concluded his introductory remarks to his *Four Essays on Liberty* with the observation:

I am well aware of how much more needs to be done, especially on the issue of free will, the solution of which seems to me to require a set of new conceptual tools, a break with traditional terminology, which no one, so far as I know, has yet been able to provide. (lxiii)

As testimony to the neglect of the free will question, especially in its political aspect, and at the same time to its literary importance I cannot do better than quote Croce:

I confess that I am not a little alarmed at the scant attention, if any at all, that is being paid to the problem of freedom in the philosophical literature of our time, and at the little interest that is being shown in the vicissitudes and destinies of freedom throughout the world. One can say the same, for that matter, of literature in general—of the drama, of the novel, of historical writing.[39]

The specifically literary side of this complaint finds an echo in Sartre, 'The writer, a free man addressing free men, has only one subject—freedom.'

IV

These then are the positions from which I begin, that the free will problem, though neglected at present, is of fundamental importance; that its expression in literature is equally important; that whenever a writer treats of the human will or human choice explicitly, or whenever he creates fictional characters who are supposed to live in a world like our own we can ask what assumptions he makes about the operation of the human will; and that an understanding of these assumptions cannot fail to illuminate his work. Since, as I have suggested, at no time between 1300 and today has there been available to writers a theory of the human will which has been free from some unacceptable consequences, or internal contradictions, or at least severe anomalies and paradoxes, we shall normally expect to find such inconsistencies in their works, or signs of a conscious attempt to resolve them. To put the matter briefly:

The writer must make some assumptions.
The assumptions are never consistent.
The rhetoric disguises or exploits the flaws in the assumptions.
The assumptions determine the rhetoric.

I examine therefore a number of works by authors of the first importance in order to show what assumptions, conscious or unconscious, the author has made, and how far they have dictated his strategy in the work. In the intercalary chapters I attempt to go beyond the individual texts and suggest a continuous pattern of change in the general idea of human freedom and its limitations. It is therefore to my interest at this point to secure a provisional agreement that the texts and authors I have chosen are in some relevant sense representative. I do not expect that there will be much disagreement with the choice of Chaucer, Marlowe, Shakespeare, Milton, Pope, Wordsworth and Byron. After 1830 the procedure of the book changes slightly, since it is more difficult to devote each chapter to a single major text. Instead of finding great central works I find a network of important and interesting works, and therefore after 1830 I deal with a group of works in each chapter. Even so certain texts, such as *In Memoriam*, *The Mill on the Floss*, *Little Dorrit*, *The Mayor of Casterbridge* and *The Picture of Dorian Gray*, bear special emphasis.

In addition it is much more difficult to point to a single line of development after 1830. Thus although Dickens and Tennyson were contemporary, as were Hardy and Wilde, they do not work from shared assumptions about the nature and extent of human freedom. My conclusions are therefore necessarily tentative, especially after 1830, since the evidence from which they are drawn is limited by shortage of space and human frailty, but they may nevertheless be true. As for the possibility of writing a collective intellectual history at all, 'they are ill discoverers that think there is no land, when they can see nothing but sea'.[40]

My argument in essence is that in the period under discussion there has been a continual shifting in the idea of what freedom is, and that in order to give some definition to this it is not just convenient but essential to think as specifically as possible in terms of what force or forces in any age are felt to *limit* freedom.[41] I make also the unexamined assumption that the necessary information is available from works of art. As Hegel puts it, 'It is in works of art that nations have deposited their profoundest intuitions, and ideas of their hearts; and fine art is often the key—with many nations there is no other key—to the understanding of their wisdom and of their religion.' In particular I venture the suggestion that by taking a chronological view of English literature it is possible to chart the varying emphasis placed at different periods on the primacy of the freely choosing self, or conversely on the sense of some overriding constraining power or circumstance which determines human life. I offer, that is, the hypothesis that there has been a significant though untidy correspondence between the general movement of mind and the central works of literature in Britain from 1320 to the present time and that the works I examine in the body of the book provide sufficient evidence for determining the broad pattern of this correspondence. In practical terms this involves asking of each author in turn, 'Did he believe that free actions were possible? If so what would be for him a clear example of a free action? Is there any evidence that he shared this idea of the nature of free action with his contemporaries?' and similarly 'Did he believe that some power lying beyond the control of the individual made free actions difficult or impossible? If so, what was that power? Is there any evidence that he shared his idea of the nature of such a power with his contemporaries?' If a pattern emerges it can be identified and made available for testing by other readers or through other disciplines.

I realize that I lie open to the charge that I am trying to construct a literary and intellectual history of Britain on no firmer basis than a few quotations, which I have myself selected because they produce the result I am looking for; and that I have necessarily chosen the texts that I think significant and have thus already assumed and incorporated the pattern of which I shall later triumphantly announce the discovery.

Although I see the justice of the complaint, it is not altogether true. The quotations are offered as illustration, not as the only evidence. They are clear expressions of the various points of view which I put forward as dominant from time to time, and thus help to define and bring out the implications of the attitudes which I describe. I rely of course on the reader's willingness to measure my conclusions against his own experience of the period. In addition I have set among the studies of the major texts four chapters designed to show how other writers, of imaginative literature and of other kinds, might be held to sustain the general pattern. It is at these points that the production of sufficient contrary examples can most readily modify or overturn my hypothesis.

V

To summarize, by the end of the book I shall have offered three different sorts of study, all overlapping—first, a series of critical accounts of particular literary texts, secondly a historical sketch of the movement of an idea over six hundred years, and finally a general discussion of the issues involved in a major philosophical question. Of these the first is the most important, in that my primary purpose is to encourage a broader critical approach to literature. If in even one chapter the technique of freedom-analysis is found to be helpful I shall consider the general point established. To avoid misunderstanding I should perhaps say at this point that I claim no particular originality for the method or the conclusions. In many chapters, especially those on Shakespeare, Milton and Wordsworth, I have been conscious of traversing some familiar territory and arriving at destinations that others had reached before me, though by a rather different route. I have not found this worrying: at least it suggests that my conclusions have a certain degree of independent corroboration. In passing I may mention that many works which I have not had time or space to examine in detail would, I have reason to believe, respond well to this kind of analysis. I have only to mention the names of Cervantes, Molière, Scott, Balzac, Melville, James and Conrad to indicate the possible scope. There are also many other topics which might be made the basis for a similar kind of analysis. Jerome Schneewind has demonstrated how effectively an enquiry may be pursued into the basis of the ethical theory which is implicit in a work[42] and I have no doubt that similarly revealing questions could be asked about, for example, ideas of progress and perfectibility, following Frank Manuel and John Passmore.[43]

The second or historical field of study leads me to offer two very tentative suggestions. First that one way of describing a historical period is by identifying the force or forces which are thought to limit or thwart the will of the individual, and that a sequence of these dominant constraining forces can be presented, showing not indeed a neat timetable with every change precisely dated but at least a large, continuous process of intellectual development, in which the principal agents of change are ideas and arguments about ideas. Secondly that in this sequence the period 1590–1660 stands out as an irregularity. This can be described retrospectively by saying that towards the end of the sixteenth century there was,

for whatever reason, a 'premature' burst of interest in the individual, producing seventy years of 'aberrant' literature and
thought. This culminated in our own country in *Paradise Lost*,
which is deeply ambiguous in its presentation of human freedom.
In the event one side of the poem was emphasized far more than
the other, marking the return to the more 'orthodox' tradition
which persisted until 1800, when there was another violent shift of
sentiment, individuality being once again admired at the expense of
homogeneity, with all the excitement and anguish that such a
choice entails. In so far as the Romantic impulse persists into our
own day we look back to 1590–1660 as an extraordinarily congenial period, feeling that Donne and Webster and Bacon and Ford
are more modern or closer to us than their successors. The details
are open to argument: I shall be satisfied with an agreement that
some such historical account is possible, that its general outline is
not unlike my description of it, and that it is of use in arriving at a
general understanding of successive periods.

Finally, I do not suggest that the great philosophical tangle of free
will has been unravelled. To adapt Tennyson, if these unsystematic
speculations

> Were taken to be such as closed
> Grave doubts and answers here proposed
> Then these were such as men might scorn.

But I am not unwilling to believe that an increased understanding
of the deepest intuitions of generations of poets will at least make
plainer what is at stake in the debate. 'By setting things in their
right point of view/Knowledge at least is gain'd.'

When asked what this book is about I have often been tempted to
vary Coleridge's reply when asked the subject of his great work,
and to say *De omne scribibile quibusdamque aliis*. The protean
nature of the subject and the approach I have chosen have made it
very difficult for me to prevent the argument from wandering and
to avoid repetition. In general I have more willingly run the risk of
repeating an argument than that of confronting the reader with an
ellipsis. Some defects of organization are due to my own lack of
skill and knowledge, others to the intractable nature of much of
the material. For both kinds I offer my apologies, and conclude
with the words of Ruskin, from the Preface to volume five of
Modern Painters:

> As the work changed like a tree, it was also rooted like a tree—not
> where it would, but where need was; on which, if any fruit grow such
> as you can like, you are welcome to gather it without thanks; and so far
> as it is poor or bitter, it will be your justice to refuse it without reviling.

1

Chaucer

I *KNIGHT'S TALE*

When we encounter the discussion of the predisposing power of dreams in the *Nun's Priest's Tale*, or learn from the *Legend of Good Women* that Hypermnestra did not kill her husband because of the disposition of the planets at her birth, or read the following passage in the *Man of Law's Tale*:

> Paraventure in thilke large book
> Which that men clepe the hevene ywriten was
> With sterres, whan that he his birthe took,
> That he for love sholde han his deeth, allas!
> For in the sterres, clerer than is glas,
> Is writen, God woot, whoso koude it rede,
> The deeth of every man, withouten drede.
>
> In sterres, many a wynter therbiforn,
> Was writen the deeth of Ector, Achilles,
> Of Pompei, Julius, er they were born;
> The strif of Thebes; and of Ercules,
> Of Sampson, Turnus, and of Socrates
> The deeth; but mennes wittes ben so dulle
> That no wight kan wel rede it atte fulle. (190–203)[1]

we have to decide whether Chaucer is offering us a fanciful or a serious account of the world, just as we have to decide whether to treat his interest in the humours and in physiognomy as superstitious or scientific.[2] Every reader of his narratives will have observed his repeated use, at crucial points, of the materials of astrology, a study which, if its claims are taken literally, has the most far-reaching implications in any consideration of fate, fortune, divine providence and the freedom of the human will.

Nowhere is this more obvious than in the *Knight's Tale*. The central action is the contest of two young men, Palamon and Arcite, for the love of Emily, the sister of Hippolyta. Theseus decrees that their rival claims shall be decided by a tournament. Palamon prays to Venus, while Arcite prays to Mars. Arcite is given victory in the tournament, as Mars had promised him, but Venus has appealed to a stronger god, Saturn, on behalf of Palamon. Saturn sends a fury who causes Arcite to fall from his horse in the moment of victory. He dies painfully and Emily is given in marriage to Palamon. It is evident that the crucial actions of this tale, including the chances that bring Palamon and Arcite into rivalry for Emily, are not the outcome of human choices but are to be attributed to Fortune or to the direct intervention of the gods in human affairs. The peculiar powers of the planets are emphasized repeatedly in the poem, notably in the descriptions of the temples of the gods and in Saturn's chill statement of his own influence:

> 'My deere doghter Venus,' quod Saturne,
> 'My cours, that hath so wyde for to turne,
> Hath moore power than woot any man.
> Myn is the drenchyng in the see so wan;
> Myn is the prison in the derke cote;
> Myn is the stranglyng and hangyng by the throte,
> The murmure and the cherles rebellyng,
> The groynynge, and the pryvee empoysonyng;
> I do vengeance and pleyn correccioun,
> Whil I dwelle in the signe of the leoun.
> Myn is the ruyne of the hye halles,
> The fallynge of the toures and of the walles
> Upon the mynour or the carpenter.
> I slow Sampsoun, shakynge the piler;
> And myne be the maladyes colde,
> The derk tresons, and the castes olde;
> My lookyng is the fader of pestilence.' (2453-69)

Many accounts of the poem have tried to show that the human agents are not as helpless as they seem: the most interesting of these is that of R. Neuse.[3] The crucial step in his argument is taken when he says, 'The divine presences sum up certain ways of life to which men dedicate themselves. In another sense, they have a psychological function: the god a person serves is his ruling passion. The gods are man's wills and appetites writ large.' Later he says, 'But despite appearances, it may be argued that the real causality of events lies in the human will or appetite. As we have seen, the gods ultimately function as metaphors of man's will.'

There is nothing impossible in this argument, but the objections to it are strong. In the first place there is no evidence that it is true. Neuse suggests for example that the man who wants violence wills himself into the service of Mars, who personifies the cause to which the man has chosen to bind himself. The text nowhere supports this: the few occasions when Mars is used as a metaphor for war are clearly distinguished from his other appearances, when he is a powerful god. Secondly there is the obvious difficulty that the gods do not simply give men what they ask for. Saturn, for example, can by no stretch of the imagination be held to be a manifestation of Arcite's will. In the Temple of Mars the fates of men yet unborn were already recorded 'as is depeynted in the sterres above.' Similarly Juno and Mercury play their parts quite independently of human volition.

If then men are not in control of their destinies how are we to regard the human lot? We must presume that Chaucer did not expect his readers to believe that Venus's grandfather personally intervened in human affairs. But to concede this is not to admit that Chaucer depicts men as free agents with full responsibility for and power over their own destiny. In the course of the tale he is careful to introduce a number of comments on the human situation which point fairly explicitly to the realities which the pagan gods represent.

After the death of Arcite Theseus, who is presented throughout the tale as absolutely in command of the temporal situation, speaks to Emily and Palamon offering them consolation for the loss of their friend 'brent to asshen colde'. His aged father Aegeus, 'that knew the worldes transmutacioun', had earlier proposed an irrefutable if unoriginal account of human existence:

> 'Right as ther dyed never man,' quod he,
> 'That he ne lyvede in erthe in som degree,
> Right so ther lyvede never man,' he seyde,
> 'In al this world, that som tyme he ne deyde.
> This world nys but a thurghfare ful of wo,
> And we been pilgrymes, passynge to and fro.
> Deeth is an ende of every worldly soore.' (2843–9)

Theseus begins as if to place the whole matter in a more scientific light by discussing the nature of the world and the constituents of all matter (2987), explaining that the 'Firste Moevere of the cause above' has set fire, air, water and earth 'in certeyn boundes, that they may nat flee', and also

> Hath stablissed in this wrecched world adoun
> Certeyne dayes and duracioun
> To al that is engendred in this place.

He proceeds to argue, appealing repeatedly to the common experience of man, that although 'thilke Moevere stable is and eterne', what he has created is by definition derivative and therefore less perfect. Thus the entire creation is necessarily 'corrumpable'. In this sense all things are subject to necessity:

> Loo the ook, that hath so long a norisshynge
> From tyme that it first bigynneth to sprynge,
> And hath so long a lif, as we may see,
> Yet at the laste wasted is the tree.
> Considereth eek how that the harde stoon
> Under oure feet, on which we trede and goon,
> Yet wasteth it as it lyth by the weye.
> The brode ryver somtyme wexeth dreye;
> The grete tounes se we wane and wende.
> Thanne may ye se that al this thyng hath ende.

This moving account of the world's mutability must, of force, encompass the fate of man also: his only choice is to die 'in youthe or elles age'. Theseus has now arrived at a position not far removed from that reached earlier by Aegeus. Although he is careful to insist that the ultimate responsibility lies with Jupiter, this is hardly enough to dispel the effects of his earlier argument that the imperfections of the human condition are entailed by the nature of the universe:

> What maketh this but Juppiter, the kyng,
> That is prince and cause of alle thyng,
> Convertynge al unto his propre welle
> From which it is dirryved, sooth to telle?
> And heer-agayns no creature on lyve,
> Of no degree, availleth for to stryve. (3035–40)

At this point Theseus, as A. C. Spearing neatly puts it, 'abandons the attempt to make the universe rational, and turns to an attempt to give advice about how to live in an irrational universe'.[4]

> Thanne is it wysdom, as it thynketh me,
> To maken vertu of necessitee,
> And take it weel that we may nat eschue.

The comfort which Theseus finally offers is that Arcite has departed at the height of his fame 'out of this foule prisoun of this lyf'. Having reached this conclusion to his 'longe serye' he blandly counsels his listeners to 'thanken Juppiter of al his grace'. The reader can hardly avoid remembering that it is not the grace of Jupiter but the malevolence of Saturn which has determined the course of events. In some ways it seems that Arcite at the very beginning of the poem has a clearer notion than Theseus of the real causes of things:

Fortune hath yeven us this adversitee.
Som wikke aspect or disposicioun
Of Saturne, by som constellacioun,
Hath yeven us this, although we hadde it sworn;
So stood the hevene whan that we were born.
We moste endure it; this is the short and playn. (1086–91)

When we reach the end of the poem we can see in retrospect how truly Arcite described man's delusive faith in his own powers:

We witen nat what thing we preyen heere:
We faren as he that dronke is as a mous.
A dronke man woot wel he hath an hous,
But he noot which the righte wey is thider,
And to a dronke man the wey is slider.
And certes, in this world so faren we;
We seken faste after felicitee,
But we goon wrong ful often, trewely. (1260–7)

We may even feel that Palamon is not altogether wide of the mark when he demands of the 'crueel goddes that governe/This world with binding of youre word eterne'

What is mankynde moore unto you holde
Than is the sheep that rouketh in the folde? (1307–8)

What is especially notable is that the narrator of the story, the Knight who has fought in a series of wars for Christianity, makes little attempt to mitigate the harshness of this picture. The death of Arcite, for example, is described in painful detail, but the narrator pointedly refuses to offer the traditional Christian consolations:

His spirit chaunged hous and wente ther,
As I cam nevere, I kan nat tellen wher.
Therefore I stynte, I nam no divinistre;
Of soules fynde I nat in this registre,
Ne me ne list thilke opinions to telle
Of hem, though that they writen wher they dwelle.
Arcite is coold, ther Mars his soule gye!
Now wol I speken forth of Emelye. (2809–16)

And in his most obvious comment on the world of the poem the Knight leaves little room for human freedom:

The destinee, ministre general,
That executeth in the world over al
The purveiaunce that God hath seyn biforn,
So strong it is that, though the world had sworn
The contrarie of a thyng by ye or nay,
Yet somtyme it shal fallen on a day
That falleth nat eft withinne a thousand yeer.
For certeinly, oure appetites heer,
Be it of werre, or pees, or hate, or love,
Al is this reuled by the sighte above. (1663–72)

It requires great determination to see the *Knight's Tale* as a comedy simply because it finishes with a wedding, or to feel, as Neuse does, that its 'geometric design' functions as a 'comic mechanism'. It seems to me that the only way to read the poem is as a fable about man in a condition of strictly limited freedom and to accept the introduction of the planets as gods as an emphatic symbol of this limitation. This reading accords exactly with the stiff, almost ritualistic movement of the narrative, which is not intended to be free in any sense.

When, at the end of the poem, Theseus rests his case on an appeal to his hearers to acknowledge their littleness and helplessness, his argument, like those elsewhere in the Tale, derives directly from Boethius' *De Consolatione Philosophiae*, a work which Chaucer translated (*c.* 1380) and which deeply influenced his approach to metaphysical questions. Yet, as I have said, it is the consolations of the Christian philosopher which are so conspicuously withheld after the death of Arcite. Boethius similarly furnishes the philosophical ideas and vocabulary of *Troilus and Criseyde*: again Chaucer does not follow him to his comforting theoretical conclusion. The reader who wishes to do so has first to overcome the powerful countervailing force of Chaucer's austerely unhopeful narrative.

II DESTINY IN *TROILUS*

Speculation about human destiny and how it is controlled is so prominent in the *Troilus* that detailed references are unnecessary: Curry gives an extensive but not exhaustive summary.[5] Chaucer forces the question on the reader's attention in many of the major incidents of the poem, such as Calchas' foreseeing of the future, Troilus' long soliloquy on foreknowledge, Cassandra's interpretation of Troilus' dream, and repeatedly in the 'sorrows' of Troilus. It is equally evident in minor details of imagery and casual conversation. Similarly the references to the gods, to planetary influences

and to astronomical occurrences are frequent and closely linked.[6]
The planets are not only the means by which time is reckoned but
are personified as gods with a direct personal interest in human
affairs: thus, as in the *Knight's Tale*, the gods superintend the destinies of mortals, especially by means of the planetary influences
ruling at their birth. This destiny is irrevocable; prayers to the
Gods are, strictly speaking, nonsense, since future events have
been determined by a planetary conjunction which is already past
and therefore not to be altered by intercession. Troilus recognizes
this in his prayer for success in love (III. 712–35). He begins by addressing Venus,

> And if ich hadde, O Venus ful of myrthe,
> Aspectes badde of Mars or of Saturne,
> Or thow combust or let were in my birthe,
> Thy fader prey al thilke harm disturne
> Of grace. . . .

works through all the planet-gods with the notable exception of
Saturn, but concludes by acknowledging that the Fates have long
ago decided his destiny:

> O fatal sustren, which, er any cloth
> Me shapen was, my destine me sponne. . . .[7]

All these direct discussions of and casual allusions to destiny may
be explained either as a medieval commonplace or as an attempt to
impart a Classical or archaic flavour to the tale, but there are many
signs that Chaucer fully realized the particular appropriateness to
his story of this omnipresent system. The frequent references to
Fate and Fortune are not conventional flourishes but point directly
to one of the major themes of the poem.

For example, in the proems Chaucer is speaking directly to his
readers and at the same time dedicating each of the five books and
invoking supernatural help. In the proem to the first book he calls
on Thesiphone, 'thow cruwel Furie, sorwynge evere yn peyne'; in
that to the second book on 'Cleo', the Muse of history; in that to the
third book on Venus, 'Joves doughter deere', and on Calliope, Muse
of epic poetry; that to the fourth book opens with a description of
Fortune and her capriciousness and then calls on all three Furies
and on 'cruel Mars'; to the fifth book there is no formal proem,
merely a brief invocation of the three angry Fates, the executors of
Jove's destiny. The 'patrons' of the last three books are easily seen
to be appropriate and to determine the mood of the books they

introduce. The first two proems are equally significant, but in a different way.

In the first Chaucer says 'For now wil I gon streght to my matere', and in the first three stanzas of the poem proper (I, 57–77) proceeds to describe briefly, as something which was common knowledge, the occasion of the siege of Troy and to state explicitly that its outcome was to be the destruction of the city by the Greeks. Thus at the outset any reader or listener who did not know the story of the Trojan war (and these cannot have been many) was informed that Troy was doomed.

Not only does the besieged city provide a particularly enclosed and concentrated setting for the action but, in addition, as more than one critic has remarked, the inevitability of the destruction of Troy hangs over the story, giving additional weight to the tragedy of Troilus. In the earlier books Chaucer continually reminds his readers both of the siege and its outcome, and the fact of living in a besieged city is never far from the minds of his characters; in the fourth and fifth books the fortunes of Troy wane as the sorrows of the lovers increase. At the beginning of the fourth book Calchas, knowing 'be astronomye,/By sort, and by augurye ek' that Troy is fated to be destroyed in a short while, persuades the Greeks to exchange the captured Trojan Antenor for his daughter Criseyde. This scene (IV. 50–140) at once serves to show the imminence of the burning of the city and unites the fate of Troy with that of Troilus, since Antenor, for whom the Trojan people willingly surrender Criseyde, has a vital part to play in the undermining of Troy. Chaucer makes explicit the irony of the exchange:

> This folk desiren now deliveraunce
> Of Antenor, that brought hem to meschaunce.
>
> For he was after traitour to the town
> Of Troye; allas, they quytte hym out to rathe!
> O nyce world, lo, thy discrecioun!
> Criseyde, which that nevere dide hem scathe,
> Shal now no lenger in hire blisse bathe;
> But Antenor, he shal com hom to towne,
> And she shal out; thus seyden here and howne. (IV. 202–10)

He refers, again ironically, to the transaction at IV. 553, when Troilus says that he will not try to hinder the transfer, 'Syn she is chaunged for the townes goode'. Similarly when Chaucer comments (V. 71–77) that all the Trojans welcomed Antenor and even Troilus embraced him, the reader is reminded again that once Antenor is within the gates there is no hope for Troy:[8] the victory of the Trojans is incompatible with the reader's 'purveyaunce' of their inevitable defeat. The outcome of the story is determined, with the reader sharing the prescience of the foreknowing God.

Precisely this argument is used by Diomed in his assault on Criseyde:

> The folk of Troie, as who seyth, alle and some
> In prisoun ben, as ye youreselven se;
> Nor thennes shal not oon on-lyve come
> For al the gold atwixen sonne and se . . . (v. 883–6)
> What! wene ye youre wise fader wolde
> Han yeven Antenor for yow anon,
> If he ne wiste that the cite sholde
> Destroied ben? (v. 904–7)

Criseyde soon sees the force of Diomed's practical determinism, but the Trojans continue to fight and Troilus continues to hope, each equally in ignorance of the future. By his use of a story of which the end is known Chaucer directly involves the reader at every turn in his progress through the poem with the paradoxes of freedom.

Troilus and Criseyde, under the domination of Love, Fate and Fortune are no more able to avoid their destiny than Troy is, and what their destiny is to be is equally well known to the reader. The story was, of course, widely distributed, but Chaucer allows nobody to be surprised. In the first lines of the first book the matter of the whole poem is made plain:

> The double sorwe of Troilus to tellen,
> That was the kyng Priamus sone of Troye,
> In lovynge, how his aventures fellen
> Fro wo to wele, and after out of joie,
> My purpos is, er that I parte fro ye.
> Thesiphone, thow help me for t'endite
> Thise woful vers, that wepen as I write.

> . . . For now wil I gon streght to my matere,
> In which ye may the double sorwes here
> Of Troilus in lovynge of Criseyde,
> And how that she forsook hym er she deyde. (I. 53–6)

The reader's foreknowledge is perhaps most obviously exploited at the end of Book III, where, after Troilus has won Criseyde, he takes Pandarus into the garden and sings a hymn to Love, celebrating not its joys but its permanence and its stabilising effect on the world. The third book thus ends with the lovers 'in lust and

quiete', a Paradise which the reader knows is destined not to endure. Chaucer has significantly said farewell to Venus, Cupid, and
the Muses, who have been his companions thus far, for his theme
thereafter is to be that second sorrow which has been ordained for
Troilus since the first stanza of the poem. Book IV begins:

> But al to litel, weylaway the whyle,
> Lasteth swich joie, ythonked be Fortune,
> That semeth trewest whan she wol bygyle,
> And kan to fooles so hire song entune,
> That she hem hent and blent, traitour comune!
> And whan a wight is from hire whiel ythrowe,
> Than laugheth she, and maketh hym the mowe.

> From Troilus she gan hire brighte face
> Awey to writhe, and tok of hym non heede,
> But caste hym clene out of his lady grace,
> And on hire whiel she sette up Diomede; . . .

Similarly Chaucer is setting up Diomede in the reader's mind as the
successful lover. Again, when he comments on Criseyde's departure 'But Troilus, now far-wel al thi joie,/For shaltow nevere sen
hire eft in Troie!' (V. 27–8), he is once more laying down well in advance the lines on which the story must inevitably run, and thus
restricting his characters' possible courses of action.

Another familiar instance of dramatic irony is Criseyde's repeated declaration that she will always be faithful to Troilus.
Chaucer obtains similar effects at IV. 1345, where Criseyde talks
hopefully of a truce between the two armies, and at III. 372 where
Troilus swears to keep secret his love for Criseyde:

> But natheles, by that God I the swere,
> That, as hym list, may al this world governe,—
> And, if I lye, Achilles with his spere
> Myn herte cleve, al were my lif eterne. . . .

Less obvious perhaps is the contrast between the doctrines of
Courtly Love, which depend on the freedom of the lovers, and the
actual course of love in a world where nobody is free. The reader,
of course, knows that in this particular case the love of Troilus is
doomed since it is involved inextricably in the fall of Troy, but the
irony which Chaucer most forcibly brings home to the reader is
that of general human helplessness in the face of unknown destiny. Troilus' long soliloquy in Book IV, in which he reaches the
conclusion

> And over al this, yet sey I more herto,
> That right as whan I wot there is a thyng,
> Iwys, that thyng moot nedfully be so;
> Ek right so, whan I woot a thyng comyng,
> So mot it come; and thus the bifallyng
> Of thynges that ben wist bifore the tyde,
> They mowe nat ben eschued on no syde. (IV. 1072–8)

is thus an epitome of the whole poem. The foreknowledge is the reader's either because he knows the story in advance or because he has observed Chaucer's careful indications of the end that must come. The characters in the poem illustrate the doctrines of foreknowledge and fate which Troilus states.

Part of the poem's power comes from the reader's sympathy with the characters' groping attempts to understand how destiny works, and with their powerlessness to resist their own fates. As the emphasis of the poem shifts from Fortune as the inconstant goddess to Fortune as the 'executrice of wyrdes', and finally to the angry Fates themselves as agents of 'the fatal destyne', so the characters in the poem find less and less freedom to choose their own destinies, and we as omniscient readers see them moving to their ordained terminus. This provision of a reader-as-Jove has clear implications all pointing to the necessity that governs human actions.

But the paradox is not left at quite this stage of resolution, for there is another character in the poem, Chaucer as narrator. He is at pains in many places to point out that his own freedom in this capacity is as limited as that of one of his own creations and in a very similar way. He cannot vary the outcome of the story any more than they can. As God knows the fate of his creatures and executes it by the agency of Fortune, so the reader knows the end of the story, and this knowledge is what compels Chaucer to bring the story to its appointed ending. Chaucer is also the executor of 'wyrd'; he is the 'hierde' and his characters the 'bestes' whose free will is only apparent. But while they preserve the illusion of free choice Chaucer knows that do what he will he cannot give his story a new ending. He cannot make Troy survive the siege or Criseyde return to Troilus, but must proceed to the inevitable foreknown conclusion. Hence the significance of the dedication of the second book to Clio:

> Me nedeth here noon other art to use.
> Forwhi to every lovere I me excuse,
> That of no sentement I this endite,
> But out of Latyn in my tonge it write.

> Wherefore I nyl have neither thank ne blame
> Of al this werk, but prey yow mekely,
> Disblameth me, if any word be lame,
> For as myn auctor seyde, so sey I. (II. 11–18)

It is the Muse of history who is to guide him, and he must therefore
tell the story as it actually happened, not as he would like to make it
happen. He represents himself not only as unable to avert the
ending of his story but as unable even to mitigate its painfulness
(e.g. III. 1816–17). When the pivotal point of the story is reached at
the end of the third book and Troilus' fortunes begin to decline,
Chaucer says

> And now my penne, allas! with which I write,
> Quaketh for drede of that I moste endite.
>
> For how Criseyde Troilus forsook,
> Or at the leeste, how that she was unkynde,
> Moot hennesforth ben matere of my book,
> As writen folk thorugh which it is in mynde. (IV. 13–18)

Especially towards the end of the poem he is careful to stress the
compulsion under which he labours, not only diverting responsibility for many episodes on to 'olde bokes' or 'the storie' or 'som
men', but attributing other episodes to the imaginary author
Lollius. Clearly he wished to make a point of his own lack of 'fre
chois' in shaping the story.

One obvious result of this apparent renunciation of the author's
power over his own work and acceptance of the role of a 'sorwful
instrument' is that Chaucer is unable (or, to put it another way,
enables himself to refuse) to make moral judgements on his characters: clearly any consistent representation of characters as powerless to avert an already determined future entails the suspension of
all such judgements, which are appropriate only to those responsible for their actions.[9] (Note that Chaucer calls both Troilus and
Criseyde *sely* 'innocent'.) Criseyde in particular is not judged.
Throughout the poem Chaucer shows her as a woman prepared to
play any part for which she is cast by Fortune. As a widow she is
devout, as a niece dutiful, as a mistress she is no less eager than
Troilus to embrace the ideals of courtly love, as a daughter she is
submissive ('muwet, milde and mansuete'), as a wanton coopera-
tive. Chaucer does not condemn her for her lack of self-assertion,
since he recognises that, 'born in corsed constellacioun', she is
bound to fulfil her destiny just as he is bound to record her story in
the form in which it has reached him. 'But execut was al bisyde

hire leve/The goddes wil' (III. 621–2). He presents her with un-varying tolerance, or rather impartiality: it is especially notable that he does not even put points in her favour as his own, for example IV. 1415–21, where he assures the reader that he has good authority for saying that she was sincere in her declaration that she would return to Troilus.

Eventually she realises her own helplessness. She says before she has falsed Troilus:

> To late is now to speke of that matere.
> Prudence, allas, oon of thyne eyen thre
> Me lakked alwey, er that I come here!
> On tyme ypassed wel remembred me,
> And present time ek koud ich wel ise,
> But future tyme, er I was in the snare,
> Koude I nat sen; that causeth now my care. (V. 743–9)

Her fault is only that of humanity in general. When Chaucer de-scribes her final capitulation to Diomede he does so in terms notably free from any condemnation. After a barrage of 'the sothe for to seyn', 'the sothe for to telle', 'gostly for to speke' and 'the sothe for to seyne', Chaucer says of Diomede 'He refte hire of the grete of al hire peyne', a finely ambiguous phrase which he does not elaborate. He continues to represent himself as a faithful recorder of what his originals tell him:

> And after this the storie telleth us
> That she hym yaf the faire baye stede,
> The which he ones wan of Troilus;
> And ek a broche—and that was litel nede—
> That Troilus was, she yaf this Diomede. (V. 1037–41)

The remark 'and that was litel nede' is the only comment Chaucer permits himself on Criseyde's behaviour. Thereafter he reassumes his role of the impartial and powerless instrument of history—'I fynde ek in the stories elleswhere': 'And for to helen hym of his sorwes smerte,/Men seyn—I not—that she yaf hym hire herte.//But trewely, the storie telleth us . . .' (V. 1049–51).[10] Finally he refuses entirely to judge her, much less to condemn her, yet insists once more that he is powerless to exculpate her (V. 1093–9).

Chaucer thus resists any moral ordering of his characters: he places them in another way by ascribing to them carefully differ-entiated attitudes to the paradoxes of free will and foreknowledge. Diomede, as we have seen, uses predestination, laying it before Criseyde as a reason for evading her obligations. If the Greeks are bound to take Troy what is the sense of remaining faithful to a Trojan lover? Criseyde attempts a not very original meditation on the topic, concluding that neither knowledge of Fortune's mutability nor ignorance of it can really conduce to lasting happiness. Otherwise she is content to shape her demeanour to circumstances, especially to the company she finds herself in. In the end she reaches an almost fatalistic resignation—'But al shal passe; and thus take I my leve.'

Pandarus adopts an opportunist attitude to Fortune, whom he regards as a woman to be won. If she were constant she would not be fortune (I. 841⁻54); if you fail to win her the fault is not hers but your own (II. 281⁻7). In the second and third books Pandarus takes over some of the functions of Destiny:

> But God and Pandare wiste al what this mente. (II. 1561)

> For he with gret deliberacioun
> Hadde every thyng that herto myght availle
> Forncast and put in execucioun . . . (III. 519⁻21)

But at the end of the poem his confidence has gone. Fate has overreached him and left him speechless (V. 1728⁻9, 1742⁻3).

Troilus' approach to the problem is more complex and more interesting. At times he is inclined to pity himself as the victim of a cruel destiny. At others he makes a resolute attempt to understand what destiny is and whether it is irrevocable. The most notable example of this is in his long soliloquy in Book Four after it has been decided that Criseyde shall leave Troy: his argument covers ground which will be familiar enough to readers of Boethius. He begins by saying

> For al that comth, comth by necessitee:
> Thus to ben lorn, it is my destinee,

and then proceeds to speculate about the meaning of 'necessity' in that sentence. Clearly if God foresees, he must foresee accurately (985), which seems to entail that what is foreseen will necessarily happen. Some men say that this means not that God causes things to happen by foreknowing them but that he foresees the events because they are going to happen. Troilus, as he says, 'labours' to discover whether God's prescience is the result or the cause of the necessity. He admits that he is unable to determine 'how the ordre of causes stant', but knows that if an event is certainly foreseen it must happen. To explain this he observes that if you see a man sitting he must be sitting: you have not made him sit, 'yet necessite/

Is entrechaunged both in hym and the' (1042–3). Troilus then
transfers this notion of mutual necessity to the original discussion
of God's foreknowledge;

> By which resoun men may wel yse
> That thilke thinges that in erthe falle,
> That by necessite they comen alle.

Since he rejects the 'fals sentence' that earthly things can cause
God's foreknowledge (1060–78), he is driven to the unwelcome
conclusion that

> the bifallyng
> Of thynges that ben wist bifore the tyde,
> They mowe nat ben eschued on no syde.

The arguments are drawn from Boethius V, proses 3 and 4. But
in prose 6 of the *De Consolatione* Philosophie proposes a distinction
between simple and conditional necessity and on this basis claims
triumphantly *'syn that necessite nis nat in thinges by the devyne
prescience*, thanne is ther fredom of arbitrie, that duelleth hool and
unwemmed to mortal men'.[11] It is notable that Troilus omits this extension of the argument and is unable to move past the much less
sanguine conclusion that

> This suffiseth right ynough, certeyn,
> For to destruye oure fre chois every del.

He arrests his argument, that is to say, at the position that offers
him least personal comfort.

   The relevance of this long soliloquy to the other main themes of
the poem is not hard to see, especially if we recollect the proem to
Book III (1–49). This hymn to love, which had appeared in *Il
Filostrato* as a song by Troilus, was adopted by Chaucer for the
introduction to the book over which Venus presides. He talks of
love not simply as a human passion but as the universal principle
by which the entire world is permeated and sustained:

> And in this world no lyves creature
> Withouten love is worth, or may endure.

Her powers are almost unlimited, especially over human sympathies:

Ye holden regne and hous in unitee;
Ye sothfast cause of frendshipe ben also;
Ye knowe al thilke covered qualitee
Of thynges, which that folk on wondren so,
Whan they kan nought construe how it may jo
She loveth hym, or whi he loveth here,
As whi this fissh, and naught that, comth to were. (29–35)

She does not spare those who attempt to resist her:

Ye folk a lawe han set in universe,
And this knowe I by hem that lovers be,
That whoso stryveth with yow hath the werse.

The divine power of love is even more strongly stated in Troilus'
song at the end of the same book (1744–71). This replaces the song
which Chaucer adopted as the proem and is an extremely close
paraphrase of Book II metrum 8 of Boethius, which is a celebration
of Divine Love, 'Love, that of erthe and se hath governaunce . . .'.

That that the world with feith, which that is stable,
Diverseth so his stowndes concordynge,
That elementz that ben so discordable
Holden a bond perpetuely durynge. . . .

This passage refers the reader back to Troilus' earlier hymn of
thanksgiving to Venus 'the wel-willy planete' (III. 1254–74), in
which echoing the *Paradiso*, he addresses 'Benigne Love, thow holy
bond of things'.

Two points emerge clearly from this. First, that in the *Troilus* the
sort of Love that Book III celebrates is not mere carnal delight but a
deep bond between humans, so deep that it can without absurdity
be compared to the divine love which gave the world being and is
now its vital principle. Secondly, that love in all its aspects, whether
it is thought of as a powerful goddess or as the master-principle of
creation, acts irresistibly. Like Fate, it is an 'uneschuable byndinge
togidre':

For evere it was, and evere it shal byfalle,
That Love is he that alle thing may bynde,
For no man may fordon the laws of kynde. (I. 236–8)

Troilus himself, looking back over the course of his love and addressing Cupid, sees that the 'myghty god, and dredefull for to

greve' has been too powerful for him throughout and comments ruefully, 'Men myght a book make of it, like a storie'. At this point he sees, more clearly than any of the other characters in the poem, his own part in a complicated pattern that has been created by some larger power.

III THE EPILOGUE

As might be expected, the complexity of *Troilus* has engendered a multitude of conflicting interpretations. Most critics agree that there are difficult passages in the poem and deal with them by various means, such as suggesting that Chaucer refers ironically to the operations of Fortune whereas the real action of the poem is Troilus' voluntary perversion of his original freedom of will into his ultimate thraldom to Love: others make a distinction between Chaucer and the narrator, ascribing inconsistencies to the ineptness of the latter.[12]

The problem is particularly acute at the end of the poem. When Troilus at last accepts that Criseyde will never return and has tarnished her own good name he determines to die in battle and is killed by Achilles. His spirit goes to the eighth sphere: from there he sees the planets moving harmoniously on their appointed courses and, in the other direction, 'this litel spot of erthe'. He despises 'this wrecched world' and its transitory pleasures. The narrator (or Chaucer) comments

> Swich fyn hath, lo, this Troilus for love!
> Swich fyn hath al his grete worthynesse!
> Swich fyn hath his estat real above,
> Swich fyn his lust, swich fyn hath his noblesse!
> Swich fyn false worldes brotelnesse!
> And thus bigan his lovyng of Criseyde,
> As I have told, and in this wise he deyde.

There follows an epilogue of five stanzas which has caused much critical perturbation. It calls on 'yonge, fresshe folkes' to love Christ and to think of the world as no more than a passing show:

> Lo here, of payens corsed olde rites,
> Lo here, what alle hire goddes may availle;
> Lo here, thise wrecched worldes appetites;
> Lo here, the fyn and guerdon for travaille
> Of Jove, Appollo, of Mars, of swich rascaille! (1849–53)

Of course this can be taken at face value as Chaucer's final comment on the poem and one can agree with Kemp Malone's verdict, 'It was part of the tragedy of Troilus that he lived in a time and place far from the grace of God, the gift of Jesus Christ to mankind.'[13] Alternatively it can be argued that the epilogue contradicts the whole spirit of the poem and should be rejected.[14] Finally there is a body of criticism well represented by A. C. Spearing, E. T. Donaldson and Charles Muscatine which takes the poem as a subtle and exceedingly complex structure, not free from inconsistencies but able to contain them, since it presents human existence itself as founded on contradictions.[15]

My own opinion is that the last five stanzas cannot simply be discarded: they are there and are part of the text of the poem. On the other hand their connection with the rest of the poem is tenuous in the extreme. They seem to me to stand to the rest of the poem as a moral tag does to its fable when it is not specially appropriate. For example one could add at the end of *Hamlet* 'Moral: Revenge is sweet,' or to the end of *The Merchant of Venice* 'A bird in the hand is worth two in the bush.' These sentiments bear some distant relation to the fable and offer in part an acceptable, if trite and nonspecific, example of a maxim that might be derived from one strand of the play: in part they are irrelevant, and if they were taken to represent a constant moral positive in the interests of which the entire fable was narrated they would rapidly lead to an absurd conclusion.

The epilogue is not quite so unintegrated as these examples. It is easy to accept that Troilus' translation to the eighth sphere, like that of Scipio at the beginning of *The Parliament of Fowls*, induces a violent shift of perspective. When one regards 'the lytel erthe that here is,/At regard of the hevenes quantite' it is natural to attach less importance to everything 'that in this world is don of al mankynde'. One can accept therefore the injunction to regard the world as mutable, and the comparison between the constant love of Jesus and the inconstancy of Criseyde. But they are not specific; that is, the first could be applied to any story about the death of a man, and the second derived from any measuring of human love against divine. The prayer to the Trinity in the last stanza of all is in itself equally unexceptionable, yet it can hardly be given any direct application to the rest of the poem. The divine forces in the poem which the comparison with the Trinity seems designed to disparage are not Jove, Apollo, Mars and 'swich rascaille', nor is Troilus shown as acting through primitive superstition. As we have seen, the major divinity in the poem is Venus, the Goddess of Love, and love is represented as beneficent, natural and an essential principle of the Universe. The epilogue can only be preserved if it is not brought into contact with Book III. Similarly the praise of divine love in the epilogue will stand, but only if we deliberately refrain from interpreting this praise as implying that Troilus was rightly punished for choosing as he did.[16] As I have devoted this chapter to demonstrating, Chaucer repeatedly insists that Troilus did not in any real sense choose his destiny. The epilogue then, like Malcolm's last speech in *Macbeth*, is sound within its own terms of reference. If it can exist in isolation from the rest of the poem it can be accepted, but if we try to treat it on equal terms with the rest of the poem it leads to profound contradictions. If it is argued that this is not out of place in a poem which is so deeply concerned with the inconsistencies of men's actions in an unexplainable world, I do not deny that Chaucer is prepared to confront his readers with a series of ironic paradoxes in the fields of human behaviour, moral judgements and the responsibilities of the poet, but the whole poem is rendered pointless if we are invited to suppose that there really is a simple resolution of all these paradoxes and that it has simply been withheld from the characters and the reader alike until the last few lines.

I am arguing in short that the poem's continual investigation of the forces that constrain human actions is not something accidental or erroneous but an essential part of its nature. It provides the foundation for the distinctive tone of tolerance and understanding and heightens the tragic power of the central situation by emphasising its pathos. I turn now to consider whether *Troilus* is in fact a tragedy.

IV CHANCE IN *TROILUS*

> And forth he wente, shortly for to telle,
> Ther as Mercurye sorted hym to dwelle.

This is the final episode in the history of Troilus. It is worth noting that he is to the last under the care of the pagan gods, not transported to a Christian heaven. It has been my contention that he has been shown throughout the poem as acting under the domination of mighty powers, which constitute a determining force in the universe or may be taken as symbols of such a determining force. The question is whether tragedy is possible in a world so constituted. I discuss medieval ideas of tragedy at some length in the following chapter. At present I will say only that the *Troilus* as we have it falls within the broad formula for tragedy given in Chaucer's own gloss on *De Consolatione* II, prose 2: 'Tragedye is to seyn a dite of a prosperite for a tyme, that endeth in wrecchidnesse.' Pandarus' words, spoken when Troilus is at the height of his happiness, aptly foreshadow his future misery:

> For of fortunes sharpe adversitee
> The worste kynde of infortune is this,
> A man to han ben in prosperitee,
> And it remembren, whan it passed is. (III. 1625–8)

If we look once more at Troilus' long soliloquy at the point in the story where his prosperity is threatened it is hard not to admire him as he pursues the argument with dogged honesty to the conclusion that he does not wish to reach. He would naturally prefer to convince himself that Criseyde was perfectly free to stay in Troy, or that she would be perfectly free to return to him if she went away. But if men are not really free then the matter is out of Criseyde's power: Troilus, being unable to rely on Criseyde's love for him, is thus left with no comfort but hope, hope which is powerless to avert a fate which has already been determined. ('O fatal sustren, which, er any cloth/Me shapen was, my destine me sponne. . . .') The last two thousand five hundred lines of the poem are devoted to a slow analysis of Troilus' hopes as, encouraged by Criseyde at first and by Pandarus for much longer, they gradually find less and less to feed on and finally die. As his hopes of future happiness fade Troilus lives more and more in the past, visiting the places where he had been happy with Criseyde, even though the sight of them causes him great pain. Chaucer spares us nothing of the agonizing fluctuations between hope and despair—the hope doomed, as we know, to bitter disappointment, the despair finally driving Troilus to welcome death. This careful analysis of increasing wretchedness is what C. S. Lewis calls 'the prolonged and sickening process' of Troilus' suffering.[17]

> For mannes hed ymagynen ne kan,
> N'entendement considere, ne tonge telle
> The cruele peynes of this sorwful man,
> That passen every torment down in helle. (IV. 1695–8)

Lewis rightly comments, 'All is to be endured and nothing to be done,' an observation which must be true of any determinist tragedy. But his argument that this state is too familiar to be tragic implies that tragedy is unable to depict any situation common to human experience. Jealousy is no doubt a vulgar enough torment, but *Othello* is still a tragedy. If Troilus' fate is painful as well as terrible this increases rather than diminishes its tragic power.

As I have repeatedly suggested, Troilus struggles in the toils of destiny with additional anguish because he is conscious of his own impotence, and the reader feels the pain of Troilus' suffering with additional acuteness because the inevitable end of the story has been known to him from the first lines of the poem.

Chaucer does not try to diminish Troilus' distress, nor does he try to make it more acceptable by suggesting that he is in some way to blame for his own suffering. He consistently locates the responsibility elsewhere, and does not conceal that this bleak view of human destiny offers little hope or cheer to mankind. Theseus' sober advice 'to maken vertu of necessitee' finds an echo in Chaucer's own presentation and commentary. In what is almost his last mention of Fortune in the poem he offers his own view of the world:

> Gret was the sorwe and pleynte of Troilus;
> But forth hire cours Fortune ay gan to holde.
> Criseyde loveth the sone of Tideüs,
> And Troilus moot wepe in cares colde.
> Swich is this world, whoso it kan byholde:
> In ech estat is litel hertes reste.
> God leve us for to take it for the beste! (V. 1744–50)

The final point that has to be considered is the nature of the forces that manipulate and finally destroy Troilus. Curry gives a reasonably clear exposition of the conventional view of the relationship between Providence, Destiny, the planets, Fortune and Nature.[18] Chaucer obviously follows this up to a point, but with significant variations. The critical question is the role of Fortune in men's affairs. Chaucer takes a line that is perfectly consonant with Boethius when he rapidly shifts the emphasis from Fortune as an arbitrary and capricious goddess to Fortune as an inexorable force. Compare, for example, the following stanzas:

> Approchen gan the fatal destyne
> That Joves hath in disposicioun,
> And to yow, angry Parcas, sustren thre,
> Committeth, to don execucious;
> For which Criseyde moste out of the town,
> And Troilus shal dwellen forth in pyne
> Til Lachesis his thred no lenger twyne. (V. 1–7)

> But O Fortune, executrice of wyrdes,
> O influences of thise hevenes hye!
> Soth is, that under God ye ben oure hierdes,
> Though to us bestes ben the causes wrie.
> This mene I now, for she gan homward hye,
> But execut was al bisyde hire leve
> The goddes wil; for which she moste bleve. (III. 617–22)

Fortune is here hardly to be distinguished from the Fates. The same presentation of Fortune is found later in Book V:

> Fortune, which that permutacioun
> Of thynges hath, as it is hire comitted
> Thorugh purveyaunce and disposicioun
> Of heighe Jove, as regnes shal be flitted
> Fro folk in folk, or when they shal be smytted,
> Gan pulle awey the fetheres brighte of Troie
> Fro day to day, til they ben bare of joie. (1541–7)

The imagery seems deliberately designed to bring to mind the earlier description of Troilus after his first sight of Criseyde—'For love bigan his fetheres so to lyme.' Especially in the realms of love and marriage Fortune is not light and variable but despotic: love, as we have seen, operates as irresistibly as Fate.

Love, Fate and Fortune are all names for the power that overcomes Troilus. Specifically he falls in love, a process which he is powerless to resist, love being a universal principle. But the partner of his love, being subject to the instability of all sublunary things, is removed from him: his grief proves mortal. This seems to be sheer ill-luck but is in fact part of his fate. It is not hard to see why Fate and Fortune coalesce in this way. If we start from a view of the world such as that expressed by Theseus in Part Four of the *Knight's Tale*, the one thing that we can say for certain about the world is that it is not unchangeable: since all things change mutability is the one constant principle in the universe. It follows that all living things will die and that no joy can endure.

> But litel while it lasteth, I yow heete,
> Joye of this world, for tyme wol nat abyde;
> Fro day to nyght it changeth as the tyde.[19]

Thus it is the very instability of Fortune, 'traitour comune', which becomes in the end the constant element in the affairs of man. Chaucer is often at pains to present Fortune as something more than an agency, as an independent force which may be actively hostile to men, and is at best indifferent.[20] In a tragedy of the general pattern of the *Troilus* there will normally be a shift of emphasis from Fortune as 'cas' or 'aventure' or simply 'good luck' to Fortune as the mistress of the turning wheel which inexorably brings the prosperous to wretchedness.

We have then a poem in which chance and destiny are brought so close together that they are virtually identified. All this is to be found in Boethius, who proceeds to argue that there is no 'fortuit

hap' since all that happens has its proper cause. One might reasonably come to the same conclusion from a reading of *Troilus*. Yet it is
notable that although Chaucer seems to be following some such
system here and in the *Knight's Tale* and reinforces the idea by his
frequent astrological references he does not offer any consolation
based on it, by saying, for instance, that the apparently arbitrary
injustices of Fortune must be accepted and even welcomed as part
of some larger plan. To identify Fortune and Destiny may be to say
that there is nothing ruling the world but chance.[21] It is interesting
that Chaucer leaves this possibility open.

This view of Fortune as haphazard in detail but operating to an
inevitable pattern over a period of time is not unlike a more
modern view of chance occurrences taken in bulk exhibiting a
statistical regularity. It explains why the general name Fortune can
be used for all the forces lying outside a man's control which determine the events of his life. In the following chapter I discuss how
far it is possible to write a tragedy set in a world dominated by
Fortune and whether it is more accurate to say that the hero of a
love-tragedy chooses Love or that he is sought out and smitten by
Love.

In addition to the works cited in the notes the following have useful
material on *Troilus*: Ann B. Gill, *Paradoxical Patterns in Chaucer's Troilus*
(Washington D.C.: Catholic U.P., 1960); J. P. McCall, 'Five-book Structure in
Troilus and Criseyde', *MLQ,* 23 (1962), 297–308; Elizabeth Salter, '*Troilus
and Criseyde*: a Reconsideration', in *Patterns of Love and Courtesy: Essays in
Memory of C. S. Lewis,* ed. John Lawlor (Arnold, 1966), pp. 86–106; Ida L.
Gordon, *The Double Sorrow of Troilus: a Study of the Ambiguities of Troilus
and Criseyde* (O.U.P. 1970); Harriett Hawkins, *Poetic Freedom and Poetic
Truth* (O.U.P. 1976) chs. I and II.

2

Elizabethan and Jacobean Tragedy

I TRAGEDY BEFORE MARLOWE

Chaucer, undoubtedly, did excellently in his *Troilus and Cressida*; of whom truly, I know not whether to marvel more, either that he in that misty time could see so clearly, or that we in this clear age walk so stumblingly after him.—SIDNEY, *Apology for Poetry* (1595)

To return from *Troilus* into the world of medieval literature is a curious experience. The poem is a sport, a literary achievement quite without parallel at that period in our literature: when we look beyond it what strikes us most is the naïveté of almost every other poem and every other statement about literature. Even Chaucer is content elsewhere to present a much simpler account of the nature of tragedy. *The Monk's Prologue* and *Tale* offer three passages which are almost too hackneyed to bear repetition:

> Tragedie is to seyn a certeyn storie,
> As olde bookes maken us memorie,
> Of hym that stood in greet prosperitee,
> And is yfallen out of heigh degree
> Into myserie, and endeth wrecchedly. (*Prologue* 85–9)[1]

> I wol biwaille, in manere of tragedie,
> The harm of hem that stoode in heigh degree,
> And fillen so that ther nas no remedie
> To brynge hem out of hir adversitee.
> For certein, whan that Fortune list to flee,
> Ther may no man the cours of hire withholde.
> Lat no man truste on blynd prosperitee;
> Be war by thise ensamples trewe and olde. (*Tale* 1–8)

> Tragediës noon oother maner thyng
> Ne kan in syngyng crie ne biwaille
> But that Fortune alwey wole assaille
> With unwar strook the regnes that been proude;
> For whan men trusteth hire, thanne wol she faille,
> And covere hire brighte face with a clowde. (*Tale* 770–6)

It is worth noting that in all but four of the seventeen examples of tragic history given by the Monk the agent of the hero's downfall is Fortune.

47

I do not wish to trace in detail the line from Chaucer to Marlowe especially as the theatrical practice and literary theory of the time were equally inconsistent. But I offer a brief account of the persistence of the apparently primitive definition of tragedy which we find in the Monk's Tale. It is at once evident that it is a description of a tragedy almost entirely in terms of the shape of the action. This fitted in well enough with such Classical ideas of the form as eventually percolated, chiefly through knowledge of Seneca.[2] Madeleine Doran has well illustrated the persistence of what may for convenience be called the parabolic definition of tragedy, that is, one which is described by the rise and fall of the hero.[3] This parabolic definition coalesces illogically and somewhat uneasily with the idea of literature as primarily a medium of moral instruction, and as deriving its main justification and part of its value from this function. Tragedy here had a particular role to play, and this role was influenced by a number of non-dramatic works all using a parabolic career of the kind I have described as an instrument of moral edification.

The works in question are not of enduring interest: I describe them briefly here as a preliminary to discussing what was new in the tragedies of Marlowe. A rapid review of Boccaccio's *De Casibus Illustrium Virorum* indicates the standard procedure for uniting tragic events and moral injunctions. This compilation, which had originally a tincture of political satire, is in essence a series of brief narratives of noble careers (from Adam to the time of writing) terminated by death. It is thus in part in the tradition of the *Danse Macabre* or the *Memento Mori*. However celebrated or virtuous the man, his career assumed a tragic shape, and this trajectory was, however awkwardly, made the vehicle of, or pretext for, a lesson in right conduct. Perhaps the most helpful explanation of how this was done is given by Puttenham in his *Arte of English Poesie* (1589):

> But after that some men among the moe became mighty and famous in the world, soueraignetie and dominion hauing learned them all manner of lusts and licentiousness of life, by which occasions also their high estates and felicities fell many times into most lowe and lamentable fortunes: whereas before in their great prosperities they were both feared and reuerenced in the highest degree, after their deathes, when the posteritie stood no more in dread of them, their infamous life and tyrannies were laid open to all the world, their wickednes reproched, their follies and extreme insolencies derided, and their miserable ends pointed out in playes and pageaunts, to shew the mutabilitie of fortune, and the just punishment of God in reuenge of a vicious and euill life.

This then is the *De Casibus* tradition of moral tragedy.[4] The essential element is the fall from prosperity of some great personage: if this person was virtuous the moral lesson, if it deserves the name of morality, is not to trust Fortune. But, since power corrupts, great men will hardly ever be righteous men. The lesson then is to observe and beware of the doom that lies in wait for the wicked.[5]

The *De Casibus* tradition had many ways into English—partly by obvious imitations such as Chaucer's *Monk's Tale*, but more notably in the work of John Lydgate. A few quotations will serve to illustrate the general tenor of his massive work, *The Fall of Princes* (written 1430–8, printed 1494), based on a French adaptation of Boccaccio. He announces his theme:

> Sodeyne departyng out of felicite
> Into miserie and mortal hevynesse,
> Unwar depryvyng of our prosperite,
> Chaung off gladnesse into wrechchidnesse

In the Prologue he pays due tribute to Boccaccio and sets out the essential qualities of tragedy of this pattern, stressing repeatedly the trajectory of tragedy, the rise to the top of Fortune's wheel and the inevitable fall when her favours are withdrawn:

> And haue a maner contemplacioun,
> That thynges all, wher Fortune may atteyne,
> Be transitory of condicioun;
> For she off kynde is hasti & sodeyne,
> Contrarious hir cours for to restreyne,
> Off wilfulnesse she is so variable,
> When men most truste, than is she most chaungable. . . .
>
> Among, this Bochas writith off suetnesse
> And off materes that lusti been and glade,
> And sumwhile he writt off wrechidnesse,
> And how Fortune kan floure and afftir fade—
> Ioie vndir cloude, prosperite in the shade,
> Entirchaungyng off euery maner thyng,
> Which that men feele, heer in this world lyvyng. (i. 106–12, 120–6)

That the tragic figure must be that of a 'prince' or man of great importance is assumed from the outset:

> And to pryncis, for thei be nat stable,
> Fortune ful offte, for al ther gret estat,
> Vnwarli chaungith & seith to hem chekmat. (i. 180–2)

This pattern of tragedy is so simple that it is tempting to accept as a sufficient definition of tragedy in general some such description of it in terms of the status and trajectory of the hero. What stands in the way is a question which Lydgate himself raises when he says, 'Reading off bookis bryngeth in vertu' (I. 416), and 'All that is write, is write to our doctrine' (IX. 3271), for it is by no means evident that a simple account of the turning of Fortune's wheel has any bearing on the moral life of the reader. This is a point which recurs constantly in any discussion of the themes of this book. Just as one of the great difficulties of the determinist position is that it seems to entail dismissing as an illusion all human moral activity, so the problem for the writer who presents in his work a world in which the crucial events in the life of his characters are determined by an agency, such as Fortune, which is quite independent of and in-accessible to the will of man, is to show how such a presentation has any beneficial moral effect on his readers. Lydgate began to tackle the problem in his Prologue, but lines 213–17 clearly show how intractable he found it:

> And when the suerd off vengaunce eek doth bite
> Vpon pryncis for ther transgressioun,
> The Comon peeple in ther opynyoun,
> For verray dreede tremble don & quake,
> And bi such mene ther vices thei forsake.

The issues are made explicit at the beginning of Book VI. Lines 1–985 are of the first interest. Fortune herself appears in the poem—'a monstrous ymage,/Partid on tweyne of colour &. corage,/Her rihte side ful of somer flours,/The tothir oppresssid with wintris stormy shours' (VI. 18–21). She proclaims her power to 'Bochas', who replies starkly, pointing out that Fortune has no power over the virtuous life. The seven virtues, he says, can defy Fortune and her wheel: she isn't even a planet. Similarly gifts of grace and gifts of nature, and meritorious actions done with humility, love and compassion are out of her province. However he concludes by asking her to favour his book, and Fortune herself does not seem much put down by what he has said, even agreeing to narrate a number of stories to him in which she herself figures as the agent of disaster. She finally summons up the dead and dis-figured body of Pompey as a proof of her power, a proof which Bochas seems to accept. This episode, taken in conjunction with Book IX 3239–302—'A chapitle of Fortune', in which Lydgate re-affirms in the strongest possible terms the universal dominion of Fortune,[6] leaves the reader with the impression that Lydgate did not really dispute the supremacy of the arbitrary goddess and had no more complicated moral message to put forward than this:

And for to sette a short conclusioun,
In a breeff somme this book to comprehende:
Fortunis wheel bi reuolucioun
Doth oon clymbe up, another to discende.

This conclusion receives some support from the haphazard arrangement of the book itself, since the absence of any consistent narrative line, or indeed of any determining pattern of episodes whatever, suggests by analogy a world at the mercy of chance. This point, I think, occurs to Lydgate himself, for the final words of his final envoy are

Blak be thi weede of compleynt and moornynge,
Callid Fall of Princis from ther felicite,
Lik chaunteplure, now singyng now weeping,
Wo afftir merthe, next ioie aduersite,
So entermedlid ther is no seurete,
Lik as this book doth preise and reprehende,—
Now on the wheel, now set in louh degre;
Who wil encrece bi vertu must ascende. (IX. 3621–8)

No reader can fail to see how cursory and contradictory the last line is, and I am confident that no real injustice is done by classifying *Fall of Princes* as a work which pivots on a recognition of the unpredictability and capriciousness of Fortune. But as I have said, Lydgate does show himself conscious from time to time of a possible system in which men's prosperity would in some way be related to their deserts, or at least their downfall in some way seen as a retribution for their vices. The most obvious example is the succession of Roman emperors who cruelly persecuted the Christians and themselves came to a bad end (Book VIII).

It is not hard to see how a suitable lesson can be drawn from such a career, but we are then faced with the difficulty of explaining why a narrative of this pattern should be tragic, since *prima facie* the 'punishment' of a wicked man should occasion satisfaction, possibly tempered by compassion. This difficulty is even more acute when we consider the works which are explicitly presented as a vehicle of instruction. The text I have particularly in mind is *A Mirror for Magistrates* (1559, 1563, 1571, 1578, 1587 etc.), which was originally designed to bring *Fall of Princes* up to date and teach lessons suitable for the troubled reigns of the Tudors. Its ambiguity is well displayed on the title page of the 1587 edition:

The Mirror for Magistrates, wherein may be seene, by examples passed in this Realme, with how greeuous plagues vices are punished in great Princes and Magistrates, and how fraile and vnstable worldly prosperity is found, where Fortune seemeth most highly to favour.[7]

Fortune is, as one would expect, much in evidence as we read these chronicles of 'the ryders of the rollyng wheele'. Sackville's Induction corroborates the previous evidence. Lines 57–70 and 113–19 are obvious examples, and lines 526–53 make the point, which must by now be fairly familiar:

> Lo here (quod Sorowe) Prynces of renowne,
> That whilom sat on top of Fortune wheele
> Nowe layed ful lowe, like wretches whurled downe,
> Even with one frowne, that stayed but with a smyle,
> And nowe behold the thing that thou erewhile,
> Saw only in thought, and what thou now shalt heare,
> Recompt the same to Kesar, King, and Peer.

As in *The Fall of Princes*, there are among the 'Fortune tragedies' some 'tragedies of villainy', such as those of Lord Mowbray and Lord Clifford. Here the operations of chance are explicitly ruled out: these men were wicked and *therefore* died wretchedly.

> I blame not Fortune though she dyd her parte,
> And true it is she can doo lytell harme,
> She gydeth goods, she hampereth not the harte.
> A virtuous mynde is safe from euery charme.
> Vyce, onely vyce, with her stoute strengthles arme,
> Doth cause the harte to euyll to enclyne,
> Whiche I alas, doo fynde to true by myne. ∴ . . (Ld. Mowbray 8–14)

> An headles arrow strake me through the throte
> Wherthrough my soule forsooke his filthy coate.
> Was this a chaunce? no suer, gods iust award,
> Wherein due iustice playnly doth appere:
> An headles arrowe payed me my reward,
> For heading Richard lying on the bere. (Lord Clifford 55–60)

Once again the problem is to show why 'due justice' is matter for a tragedy.

(It is worth noting in passing that the authors of *Mirror for Magistrates* occasionally confront the questions which at other times they are content to ignore. For example, Jack Cade begins his account of his own career by asking, 'Shal I cal it Fortune or my frouard folly/That lifted me, and layed me down below?' But, by the end of the stanza, he has, like all the villains, concluded that 'Our lust and wils our evils chefely warke'. Then in an intensely interesting passage of argument he reasons that although every man has the power to control his baser impulses—'lust and will'—too few men exercise this power.

Now if this happe wherby we yelde our mynde
To lust and wyll, be fortune, as we name her,
Than is she iustly called false and blynde,
And no reproche can be to much to blame her:
Yet is the shame our owne when so we shame her,
For sure this hap if it be rightly knowen,
Cummeth of our selves, and so the blame our owne. (*Jack Cade* 29–35)

This is a comparatively ingenious and sophisticated attempt to escape from the dilemma I have described: Cade, as a rebel, must accept full responsibility for his treasonable and impious actions.)

If then we look at the history of *De Casibus* tragedy from Chaucer to the 1580s we can obtain a rough idea of the difficulties of formulating a tragic theory at this time. Such a theory would have (1) to define a tragedy, (2) account for the fact that it is pleasurable to its readers or audience, and (3) justify the existence of tragedy. Further, if this last point involves claiming tragedy as a medium of moral instruction there seems to be an insoluble dilemma. For if the characters do not act freely (but are, for example, under the domination of Fortune) then the narrative can have only limited moral implications. If the characters act freely, it would be possible to represent some tragedies as vehicles of moral instruction. But now the difficulty is to satisfy conditions (1) and (2) simultaneously, for it seems reasonable to accept that the first condition will require the main character to end in suffering more than he did at some other point. Since Aristotle it has been pointed out that the spectacle of a man who chooses to act rightly but nevertheless suffers cannot be supposed to give pleasure, while a man who chooses to act wickedly and thereby comes to a bad end is justly punished. A play with an action of this kind thus comes to a very proper conclusion and could indeed be more accurately described as a comedy than a tragedy.[8]

If tragedy neighboured with comedy on one side, on the other it was scarcely to be distinguished from history. The whole *De Casibus* pattern chimed in precisely with the political philosophy that would be most readily deduced from the vicissitudes of public life in those troubled centuries. Perlin, for example, commenting on England in 1558, remarked, 'One day sees a man as a great lord, the next he is in the hands of the executioner,' while Sir Robert Naunton observed in his *Fragmenta Regalia* (1641)

> *Sir Walter Rawleigh* was one that it seems fortune had picked out of purpose, of whom to make an example, or to use as her Tennis-Ball, thereby to shew what she could do; for she tossed him up of nothing, and to and fro to greatnesse, and from thence down to little more than to that wherein she found him, a bare gentleman. (p. 33)

Further, if tragedy was to be of the largest possible amplitude it had to deal not with the fall of a man in a humble station but with what Rosencrantz called 'the cease of majesty'.[9] Thus writers of Tragedy, verse, prose, or drama, found a series of subjects ready to their hands in the rulers of Greece and Rome, the tyrants of Asia Minor, and the mythical or actual rulers of Britain. Clearly the use of a well-known story or episode from history will foster a sense of inevitability. The reader's concern, that is to say, is not with whether or not the hero will make a certain decision: we know that he can decide only in one way, and that way is common knowledge to the writer and the reader. The interest lies in the working out of the destined events. Fortune is apparently capricious, yet she is an agent of Fate and therefore inevitable, while Fate in turn is an agent of Time.

If we try to express as favourably as possible the effect of tragedy of the *De Casibus* pattern we must lay particular stress on the idea of Time. 'Injurious Time, now with a robber's haste/Crams his rich thievery up, he knows not how.' Time is the force which draws man inevitably but mysteriously towards the grave. The Fates, like the Icelandic Norns, spin the rope which is each man's fortune: indeed the names of the Norns—Verdandi, Urdi (Wyrd), and Skuld—mean simply Past, Present (Becoming), and Future.[10] Hence the combination of predictability and incomprehensibility, which we experience also in our own lives, arouses pity and awe when we encounter it in a tragedy, and, as Swift says, 'No preacher is listened to, but Time.'

All this is theoretically true, but the practice was less impressive. Chaucer, in his *Troilus*, by refusing to acknowledge the necessity for obvious moral instruction, had been able to present a world in the grip of destiny and yet to achieve effects to which it would be pointless to deny the name of tragedy. The *De Casibus* writers, unwilling to renounce their declared didactic purpose, found themselves deeply confused about the standing of the central characters and thus committed simultaneously to two incompatible world views. This makes the vast *De Casibus* collections tedious in the extreme, indeed almost impossible to read as a connected work, and leads to precisely the sort of questions which are most destructive of their claim to offer moral instruction. In particular one notices that the virtuous characters are normally the hapless victims of Fortune, while the only characters to bring about their own destiny are the villains. In time this not surprisingly suggested the idea of presenting a hero who was not merely a pawn of Fortune but had a will of his own, which he exerted against other men and against his own fate.

II MARLOWE

There is little that is new and, I think, nothing that is contentious in my description of the progress of tragedy from the time of Chaucer to that of Elizabeth. It is more difficult to offer an uncontroversial account of the profound changes in the idea of tragedy which occurred in the 1580s. The traditional view of these changes is most simply expressed by saying that instead of contemplating a tragic trajectory the audience is involved in the downfall of a tragic hero. This apparent drastic shift in the entire idea of what constitutes a tragedy is frequently explained by pointing to the influence of Seneca's dramas and Machiavelli's political philosophy. Kyd and Marlowe are, on this view, the first to write the new 'heroic' tragedy: Shakespeare obviously continues in the same vein, and Ford and Webster take it to and beyond its permissible limits.

This view has the merits of being clear and uncomplicated, and it might be better to leave it undisturbed; it leads, however, to a number of distortions when we try to formulate a general theory of tragedy and these distortions involve an erroneous reading of a number of important plays. The difficulties are obvious as soon as we consider the two influences mentioned in the previous paragraph. What had Seneca to add to the pattern of *De Casibus* tragedy? No more perhaps than such devices as ghosts and physical atrocities, and a number of stoic tags, of which 'O nos dura sorte creatos' is the best known.[11] But in addition the tragedies conveyed into the English theatre a particularly acute form of the doubleness of vision which I have noticed in the *De Casibus* tragedies. As one can see from Heywood's original dedication to the translators Seneca was often put forward as a great moralist.[12] It is hard to see how this claim can be sustained unless Seneca represents his characters as responsible moral agents, yet it is common form in Seneca for the play to pivot on the theme of revenge. The whole argument of a revenge tragedy is that 'blood will have blood' or 'blood is a beggar': it stresses, that is, the inevitability of a chain of vengeful murders, and hence suggests the working out of fate by a series of hapless participants.

Apart from revenge, ambition is almost the only independent motive recognised by a Senecan hero. But ambition leads, by a familiar path, to wretchedness. The final chorus of *Jocasta* is especially revealing:

> Example here, loe take by Oedipus,
> You Kings and Princes in prosperitie,
> And euery one that is desirous
> To sway the seate of worldlie dignitie,
> How fickle tis to trust in Fortune's wheele.

It is hardly necessary to point out what total confusion is indicated by portraying Oedipus, of all tragic heroes, not just as a victim of the fickleness of Fortune but as a man properly punished for ambition.

Machiavelli leads equally rapidly to an equally awkward paradox. What he actually wrote in *The Prince* (1513) is of no moment. The work was not translated into English until 1640, and a debased version of his teaching held the field. According to this Machiavelli said that all rulers were absolute rulers, who were not merely entitled but obliged to use any means whatever to retain their power, the subtler and more cunning the better. In particular ruthless punishments, torture and oppression were held to be recommended. In short Machiavelli was supposed to have compounded a recipe for the ideal stage villain—ambitious, powerful, unscrupulous, vindictive, and fertile in diabolical contrivance, free from all restraints of conscience, decency, law and religion, and convinced that simply because he was free he was of finer quality than other men. Of course this is a travesty of Machiavelli, but it has elements of truth. Machiavelli's political advice draws its cogency, its 'realism', from the boldness of his assumptions, in particular that the great abstractions of conduct are superstitions, that a man can free himself from all unreal restraints simply by deciding to be free, and that he will get only what he is strong or clever enough to take.

It is clear that the Machiavellian man could fuse very easily with the Senecan tyrant to give a new kind of character, one with no respect for traditional restraints and continuously active to satisfy his own desires. It is equally plain that if this view of the history of tragedy is broadly correct, free will enters tragedy and asserts itself in the person of the villain. It is convenient to look at this proposition with the plays of Marlowe in mind, especially as Machiavel himself speaks the Prologue to *The Jew of Malta*.

It is a commonplace of criticism that the plays of Marlowe furnish some of the most fervent celebrations in literature of the aspirations of the individual man towards dominance over his environment, over his fellows, over his own nature, and over Fate. One of Marlowe's soundest critics, Harry Levin, puts the matter strongly but justly in his admirable book *The Overreacher*[13]. Marlowe, he says, was 'the most eloquent spokesman in England for the complex of attitudes and the sequence of undertakings that we vaguely term the Renaissance'. And again, 'His [Marlowe's] protagonist . . . is *l'uomo singolare*, the exceptional man who becomes king because he is a hero, not hero because he is a king: the private individual who remains captain of his fate, at least until his ambition o'erleaps itself; the overreacher whose tragedy is more of an action than a passion, rather an assertion of man's will than an acceptance of God's.' This seems to me a fair general account of Marlovian tragedy. What remains to do is first to demonstrate this, and secondly to explain why tragic pleasure should be derived from it.

Tamburlaine provides a conveniently uncomplicated example. In the opening scenes of the play the hero has shown himself as the typical architect of his own career. One of his earliest vaunts is in Act I Scene ii

> Forsake thy king, and do but join with me,
> And we will triumph over all the world;
> I hold the Fates bound fast in iron chains,
> And with my hand turn Fortune's wheel about;
> And sooner shall the sun fall from his sphere
> Than Tamburlaine be slain or overcome.

Menaphon (II i) describes Tamburlaine with particular emphasis on his purely human strength,—'his piercing instruments of sight,/ Whose fiery circles bear encompassèd/A heaven of heavenly bodies in their spheres' and 'His lofty brows in folds do figure death/And in their smoothness amity and life'. Tamburlaine's expression has taken the place of the planets. Cosroe comments with admiration

> Nature doth strive with Fortune and his stars
> To make him famous in accomplished worth;
> And well his merits show him to be made
> His fortune's master and the king of men.   (II. i)

Tamburlaine is thus established as the man who is in command of his world and who is not subject to the caprices of Fortune or the domination of Fate. If then he is free to do what he chooses why does he choose to do what he in fact does? He attempts an explanation in II. vii when he confronts the wounded Cosroe:

> Nature that framed us of four elements,
> Warring within our breasts for regiment,
> Doth teach us all to have aspiring minds:
> Our souls, whose faculties can comprehend
> The wondrous architecture of the world,
> And measure every wandering planet's course,
> Still climbing after knowledge infinite,
> And always moving as the restless spheres,
> Will us to wear ourselves, and never rest,
> Until we reach the ripest fruit of all,
> That perfect bliss and sole felicity,
> The sweet fruition of an earthly crown.

Plate 2. Andrea del Verrocchio: equestrian monument to Bartolomeo Colleoni, Venice. From VERROCCHIO: SCULPTURES, PAINTINGS AND DRAWINGS by G Passavant. London 1969. *By courtesy of Phaidon Press Ltd and of Soprintendenze alle Gallerie, calle Ca'd'Oro, Cannaregio, Venice*

This speech expresses the central concern of *Tamburlaine* with great clarity. Challenged to justify his ravening ambition, Tamburlaine replies that it is only natural—nature has made all men ambitious by the very constitution of their being. He seizes on the idea of the unbounded potentialities of man and links it with the new knowledge in a leaping panegyric of human achievement. But if we examine what he actually says it is plain that he has not really cut mankind loose. The 'Nature' he has so carelessly invoked as explanation can only explain if it is indeed a prime cause of human activity. Tamburlaine holds the Fates in chains, but is in turn bound by a Nature that is located in the very heart of the process of creation and has framed mankind of four elements which, of course, act only as they must act.[14] Water cannot burn or fire drown.

Tamburlaine proceeds through the double play, confident in his absolute dominion. He commits acts which would surely, if the orthodox tragic mechanism were in operation at all, bring about his downfall.

Techelles	What shall be done with their wives and children, my lord?
Tamburlaine	Techelles, drown them all, man, woman, and child. Leave not a Babylonian in the town.
Techelles	I will about it straight. Come, soldiers. (*Tamb.* 2 v. i)

Yet his wickedness and impiety alike go without dramatic reprisal. At the end of Part Two what brings him to death has no connection with his career as conqueror, but is simply what he has in common with other men, the frailty of his body. At once his friends try to bring his illness back into the sphere of Fortune. In v iii they call upon the 'heavens', the 'stars that govern his nativity', the 'powers that sway eternal seats/And guide this massy substance of the earth', and surmise that the thrones of the angels have been usurped by devils. But the attempts to invest Tamburlaine's illness with the dignity of a singular divine visitation collapse in face of the plain speech of the physician:[15]

> I viewed your urine, and the hypostasis
> Thick and obscure, doth make your danger great;
> Your veins are full of accidental heat,
> Whereby the moisture of your blood is dried.
> The humidum and calor, which some hold
> Is not a parcel of the elements,
> But of a substance more divine and pure,
> Is almost clean extinguished and spent;
> Which, being the cause of life, imports your death.

The matter is now simply one of cause and effect—the elements, being as they are, will act as they must. After their brief compounding they will return to themselves. As Nature has brought us up in the first place, so Nature (i.e. the natural course of events) will bring us down again. Death, as Tamburlaine has already conceded, is not to be halted for long by an act of will:

> See, where my slave, the ugly monster, Death,
> Shaking and quivering, pale and wan for fear,
> Stands aiming at me with his murdering dart,
> Who flies away at every glance I give,
> And, when I look away, comes stealing on.

Thus the key word of the last speeches of the play is 'necessity':

Tamburlaine	Let not thy love exceed thine honour, son,
	Nor bar thy mind that magnanimity
	That nobly must admit necessity. . . .
Theridamas	My lord, you must obey his majesty,
	Since fate commands and proud necessity. (v. iii)

In the end Tamburlaine yields up his empire in precisely the manner of one of Lydgate's Princes. I see no reason, apart from convention, why *Tamburlaine* should not be classified as a pure *De Casibus* tragedy, with the additional circumstance that the hero as he rises on Fortune's wheel is totally persuaded that he is rising by his own efforts and in response to his own will and can maintain himself at the top of the wheel by the same means. This new element finds expression in all the ways to which commentators have drawn attention for centuries—the hyperbole, the rhetoric, the surging blank verse, the emphasis on verbs of climbing and flying (though it is worth remembering that Marlowe's favourite images for this are Phaethon and Icarus) and the constant exaltation of the human by disparaging comparison with the Classical divinities. One may point also to the structure of the play. It can hardly have any very tight mechanism of cause and effect. All that can happen is that the hero continues to find more and more confirmation of his own sense of boundless power until he learns at last that his will is subject to the nature of things. In *Tamburlaine* Marlowe adopted something very close to the *De Casibus* formula, yet, since he charged the language of the play with the full force of his poetic energy, transformed that tradition so radically that we can hardly recognise it.

This reductionist account of the Marlovian tragic pattern can be applied in varying degrees to his other plays: *Edward II* shows how easily this may be done. Edward himself, as has often been remarked, speaks in the very accents of *Mirror for Magistrates*:

> Stately and proud, in riches and in train,
> Whilom I was, powerful, and full of pomp:
> But what is he whom rule and empery
> Have not in life or death made miserable? . . .   (IV. vi)[16]

Young Mortimer, on the other hand, introduces the extra element which I have pointed out in *Tamburlaine*, the rising man's confidence that he is himself supreme over Fortune,

> As thou intend'st to rise by Mortimer,
> Who now makes Fortune's wheel turn as he please . . .   (V. ii)

> And what I list command who dare control?
> *Major sum quam cui possit fortuna nocere.*   (V. iv)

only to discover that the general laws persist and all men are subject to them:

> Base Fortune, now I see, that in thy wheel
> There is a point, to which when men aspire,
> They tumble headlong down: that point I touched,
> And seeing there was no place to mount up higher,
> Why should I grieve at my declining fall?—   (V. vi)

The application to *The Jew of Malta* is plain when we note Barabas' progression from the expansive opening speech designed to embody his desire for 'infinite riches in a little room', and his confidence that a divine power is at work on his behalf:

> What more may Heaven do for earthly men
> Than thus to pour out plenty in their laps,
> Ripping the bowels of the earth for them,
> Making the seas their servants, and the winds
> To drive their substance with successful blasts?   (I. i)

When he loses his wealth his confidence is in his own unique qualities:

> No, Barabas is born to better chance,
> And framed of finer mould than common men,
> That measure naught but by the present time.
> A reaching thought will search his deepest wits,
> And cast with cunning for the time to come: (I. ii)

Patience and submission are the virtues which are barred to him. If his 'luckless stars' think to oppress him with misfortune he will defy them, and trust not fortune but his own devices:

> No, I will live; nor loathe I this my life:
> And, since you leave me in the ocean thus
> To sink or swim, and put me to my shifts,
> I'll rouse my senses and awake myself.   (I. ii)

His course through the play is essentially that of an initiator—the ideas of Machiavelli define his means and the Vice of medieval plays defines his dramatic function. In the end he is brought down, not because of presumption or indeed through any necessary consequence of his own acts, but because he meets in Ferneze someone who outmatches him in policy. At this point the play's source of dramatic energy is disposed of and the play ends. The barrenness of a life based on betrayal and deception might be deduced from this, but I do not think that such a conclusion would be immediately apparent in the theatre, especially since the play ends with the triumph of the Christian intriguers, nor should I expect an audience to feel the emotions of pity and terror by which tragedy is traditionally recognized. The tragic force of the play is insignificant in comparison with the enormous power with which Barabas asserts his own will.

When we turn to *Faustus* the case is altered, for there the primary fact on which criticism must build is the dreadful tragic impact of the play in the theatre. Once again the protagonist in an early speech makes clear the poles between which the action is to move. In the very first scene Faustus deliberately examines the ends of every profession, and dismisses them precisely because they profess attainable and therefore limited ends. He disdains Philosophy, Medicine, and the Law and then in a crucial passage examines the claims of Divinity:

> When all is done divinity is best;
> Jerome's Bible, Faustus, view it well.
> *Stipendium peccati mors est.* Ha! *Stipendium* etc.   [*Reads*
> The reward of sin is death. That's hard.   [*Reads*
> *Si peccasse negamus fallimur et nulla est in nobis veritas.*
> If we say that we have no sin we deceive ourselves, and
> there's no truth in us. Why then, belike we must sin,
> and so consequently die.
> Ay, we must die an everlasting death.
> What doctrine call you this, *Che sera sera,*
> What will be shall be? Divinity, adieu!

The grounds of his rejection is thus that Divinity tells him that the life of man is subject to universal law. Necromancy on the other hand promises unlimited power to the individual:

> All things that move between the quiet poles
> Shall be at my command; emperors and kings
> Are but obeyed in their several provinces,
> Nor can they raise the wind or rend the clouds;
> But his dominion that exceeds in this
> Stretcheth as far as does the mind of man.
> A sound magician is a demi-god.

A simple framework is thus set up: its likeness to *Tamburlaine* is obvious. Faustus acts on his conviction that the mind of man is free and capable of authentic action without any necessary consequence. Having made a bargain on this basis he has two tasks in the play—first to convince himself that he is a free agent, secondly to convince himself that he will not have to abide the necessary consequences of his own acts. Thus he addresses himself as follows, 'The God thou serv'st is thine own appetite,/Wherein is fixed the love of Belzebub', and shortly afterwards tries again to reassure himself:

> What might the staying of my blood portend?
> Is it unwilling I should write this bill?
> Why streams it not that I may write afresh?
> Faustus gives to thee his soul. Ah, there it stayed.
> Why should'st thou not? Is not thy soul thy own?   (I. v)

When he speaks to Mephistopheles and attempts to deny the very existence of Hell, the irony is plain. Mephistopheles has already made it clear that Hell is real: his role in the play is to be Hell, to demonstrate that necessity which Faustus vainly attempts to deny

Faustus	Why, think'st thou then that Faustus shall be damned?
Mephistophilis	Ay, of necessity, for here's the scroll Wherein thou hast given thy soul to Lucifer.
Faustus	Ay, and body too; but what of that? Think'st thou Faustus is so fond to imagine That, after this life, there is any pain? Tush; these are trifles, and mere old wives' tales.

The irony is complicated by a device which we have observed in Chaucer's *Troilus*—the author's exploitation of the audience's knowledge that Faustus is deluding himself, a knowledge derived partly from the fact that they are watching what purports to be a

History play and is thus bound by the actual outcome of the Faustus story, partly by the careful explanation of the Prologue with its familiar imagery of inevitable downfall:

> Till swollen with cunning of a self-conceit,
> His waxen wings did mount above his reach,
> And, melting, Heavens conspired his overthrow.

Thus to the audience the unreality of the freedom in which Faustus trusts is always plain. (Similarly the choice which he is apparently free to make between the Good Angel and the Evil Angel presents itself to the audience in other terms than it does to Faustus.) He has no freedom, nor is there any way in which the descent to Hell can be averted. So the play continues its scarcely tolerable course, each minute that passes bringing us nearer to the inevitable catastrophe. Faustus himself at last must feel the pressure of time:

> Now, Mephistophilis, the restless course
> That Time doth run with calm and deadly foot,
> Shortening my days and thread of vital life,
> Calls for the payment of my latest years. . . .

His final cry 'Ah Mephistophilis' is a recognition of the character who has embodied doom in its physical and metaphysical aspects.[17]

It is tempting at this point to accept a widely held view that Marlowe's plays are explicitly designed to celebrate the triumph of virtú (or the qualities of human endeavour) over Fortune, in much the same way as Dekker's *Old Fortunatus*, in which the reverence paid to Fortune at the beginning of the play is by the end of the play transferred *in identical terms* to Virtue.[18] Even in *Edward II*, which is the most traditional of his plays, in that Edward's fate is precisely in the *De Casibus* tradition and Fortune is still the agent of Young Mortimer's fall, the principal interest lies in Mortimer's defiance of Fortune and confidence that he is in control of his Fate. While a similar confidence is the dominant characteristic of Marlowe's other heroes, the crucial point is that their downfall is not ascribed to Fortune. What was most original in Marlowe was the parts of his plays in which he celebrated the freedom and scope of the individual who is no longer clogged by superstition or convention. When we hear the speech of Guise in *The Massacre at Paris*

> That like I best that flyes beyond my reach.
> Set me to scale the high Peramides,
> And thereon set the diadem of Fraunce,
> Ile either rend it with my nayles to naught,
> Or mount the top with my aspiring winges,
> Although my downfall be the deepest hell.   (99–104)[19]

we seem at a bound to be in the realm of the new man and are conscious that a new dimension of human experience is receiving
immediate reflection on the stage. There is no doubt that this magnificent asssertion of human capacity is what comes first to mind
when we think of Marlowe. But even with the assertion comes the
questioning. Prometheus is immediately compromised by his association with Phaethon and Icarus. A complete reading of
Marlowe's plays must recognize the constancy with which he sets
his abounding sense of freedom in a trajectory which eventually
subjects it to inexorable law. Marlovian man has perhaps learned
not to be intimidated by the fictitious Fates or Dame Fortune, but
in their place he finds Nature, the laws which govern the world
and admit no exceptions. It is not perhaps far-fetched to see the
mechanism of the plays, in which a given set of circumstances
leads inevitably to the death of the hero, as a figure for all human
aspirations which are brought low not because of an unlucky combination of chances but because of some contradiction inherent in
the idea of human freedom. One thing Marlowe's plays are about is
what it is like to feel free, and what it is like to lose that feeling. The
tragedy of the Marlovian hero is the tragedy of all men who think
they are free, and it is a tragedy of delusion.

The plays can thus be reduced without undue distortion to a *De
Casibus* formula as long as we do not lose sight of two points. First
that complex ironic effects are available to a writer who is
prepared to exploit the incongruity of a character who asserts his
freedom in a fictional world where there is ultimately no room for
freedom. The second point is most clearly brought out in *Faustus*.
The final speech of the Chorus, although it gives full weight to the
exemplary nature of Faustus' fall, is also at pains to emphasize his
qualities:

> Cut is the branch that might have grown full straight,
> And burnèd is Apollo's laurel bough,
> That sometime grew within this learnèd man.

It is the value of Faustus which contributes to the tragedy: if he
were worthless, or vicious like Barabas, our pity would be less.

The Marlovian heroes are so by virtue of the very qualities that
bring about their ruin. It is impossible to dissolve their characters
into general virtues, which are to be emulated, and specific failings,
which are to be avoided, for their virtú is at once ἀρετη and
ἁμαρτια. Marlowe expresses their boundless ambition with unprecedented power while leaving the spectators in no doubt of the
course it must take. Thus we simultaneously admire the hero for
making the assertion of his own freedom and recognize that he
must suffer for asserting himself in this way. We contemplate his

tragic trajectory, not with an impartial or aesthetic regard, not simply with awe, but with compassion. We feel for him in part as a deposed king but more keenly as a disappointed man, whose aspirations have been frustrated, and frustrated inevitably by his human composition.

> [*Faustus*] Tell me where is the place that men call hell?
> *Mephistophilis* Under the Heavens.
> *F.* Ay, but whereabout?
> *M.* Within the bowels of these elements,
> Where we are tortured and remain for ever;
> Hell hath no limits, nor is circumscribed
> In one self place; for where we are is hell,
> And where hell is there must we ever be.

III SHAKESPEARE

> *Lafeu*
> They say miracles are past; and we have our philosophical persons, to make modern and familiar, things supernatural and causeless. Hence it is that we make trifles of terrors; ensconcing ourselves into seeming knowledge, when we should submit ourselves to an unknown fear. Why, 'tis the rarest argument of wonder that hath shot out in our latter times.　　　　　　　　　　　　　　　　　　　　　(*All's Well* II. iii)

One way to approach the tragedies of Shakespeare is to set aside for the moment the influence of individual genius such as that of Marlowe and to consider rather how far Shakespeare took advantage of all the kinds of tragic effect which were open to him in, say, 1595. Willard Farnham, for example, has argued very strongly for the importance of Shakespeare's use of his inheritance of Gothic tragedy.[20] If he is right one would expect the power of the plays to lie in part in a feeling of awe at the mysterious but inexorable workings of fate. Yet only in part, for there was also available to Shakespeare a version of the tragic pattern in which the hero was not simply a helpless victim of time, fate's instrument, which inevitably bears all men away, do what they will, but was also wilfully at war with order, the natural principle on which the universe is framed and which is inevitably stronger than any individual who presumes to assert himself against it. A further development beyond the *De Casibus* pattern is open when the hero, as well as the audience, comes to recognize the inevitability of his fate. The dramatist can thus exploit for example the audience's reaction to a display of stoic fortitude or of vain defiance or simply to the spectacle of the hero's grief at his own unhappy lot.

Most of Shakespeare's history plays have a *De Casibus* shape, with historical inevitability as the determining influence on the incidents and the conclusion of the story. Shakespeare's consciousness of the pattern is clearest in *Richard II*:

> For God's sake let us sit upon the ground
> And tell sad stories of the death of kings:
> How some have been depos'd, some slain in war,
> Some haunted by the ghosts they have depos'd,
> Some poison'd by their wives, some sleeping kill'd,
> All murder'd—for within the hollow crown
> That rounds the mortal temples of a king
> Keeps Death his court; and there the antic sits,
> Scoffing his state and grinning at his pomp;
> Allowing him a breath, a little scene,
> To monarchize, be fear'd, and kill with looks;
> Infusing him with self and vain conceit,
> As if this flesh which walls about our life
> Were brass impregnable; and, humour'd thus,
> Comes at the last, and with a little pin
> Bores through his castle wall, and farewell, king! (III. ii)

This is the pulse of all the history plays, right through to *Henry VIII*. Richard is especially conscious of himself as a *De Casibus* hero:

> Here, cousin, seize the crown. Here, cousin,
> On this side my hand, and on that side thine.
> Now is this golden crown like a deep well
> That owes two buckets, filling one another;
> The emptier ever dancing in the air,
> The other down, unseen, and full of water.
> That bucket down and full of tears am I,
> Drinking my griefs, whilst you mount up on high.   (IV. i)

The fact that Richard sees himself in this role endows him with more interest and more complexity than the ordinary *De Casibus* hero, and thus shifts part of the interest from his fate to his motives. Of course as we move into the realm of the invented plot we are less likely to encounter unchangeable historical facts, and therefore less likely to encounter the kinds of inevitability that depend on the irrevocability of the past. Its place is taken by our feeling with the central character: an admiration for his largeness of spirit, not dependent on moral approval of his end or means, and if anything accentuated by his lack of success. What we seem to be approving is simply assertion of his will, without reference to the ends for which he exerts it. The central character refuses to be the victim of Fortune or a subject of Fate, at least for a spell, and this refusal makes him the hero of the play even if his behaviour is, ethically regarded, villainous. On a simple level one can illustrate this from *Richard III* and on a more complex level from *Macbeth*.

How is this to be reconciled with Aristotle's stipulation that tragedy is not an imitation of persons, but of action? According to Aristotle the characters are there for the sake of the action. The story of a tragedy should be tragic *in itself* so that even hearing it narrated stirs our pity and awe. So that there shall be no doubt about what he means Aristotle recommends writing out the plot first and only then giving the characters names and inventing episodes. It appears that Shakespeare is defying or proving false Aristotle's principles, for he seems a clear case of a dramatist whose handling of the action is perfunctory while his real interest lies in character and its complexities. *Hamlet* is an obvious example: a bare summary of the plot omits the vitally important illumination of Hamlet's mind and motives. Yet there is a little to be said on the other side. Presumably Shakespeare himself was first attracted by the story as he found it, a diagram of action. It seems possible therefore that certain sequences of events impressed Shakespeare as intrinsically tragic, regardless of the character of the participants. Take the following story, for instance.

The world of the play is divided into two halves, each bitterly opposed to the other to the point of civil war. The hero belongs to one half by birth, the heroine to the other. In spite of this the hero, who has been in love before, visits the heroine, disregarding the danger and warnings of danger. As the play proceeds the division between the two camps grows deeper and feelings become increasingly bitter. The hero has one particular friend who dies before him. The hero is separated from the heroine and by mischance hears that she is dead, although she is in fact alive. On receiving the false news he kills himself. When the heroine learns that he is dead she kills herself. The play ends with the divided parties reconciled and a funeral oration from the Prince.

It will be observed that this description applies both to *Romeo and Juliet* and to *Antony and Cleopatra*.[21] If this suggests that Shakespeare felt that there was something intrinsically tragic about such a series of pathetic situations, it is perhaps worth looking at the plays in question to see whether they share other qualities, in particular whether they agree in their presentation of the status of human free will.

The point can be briefly put by asking the following question: 'Since in each play the hero and heroine meet a fate which they are powerless to avert, must we not conclude that Shakespeare places human activity in the context of a larger determining power?' In *Romeo and Juliet* we observe what we have already noticed in

Chaucer—the deliberate setting-out of the story in advance. The Prologue allows no doubt about the outcome:

> From forth the fatal loins of these two foes
> A pair of star-cross'd lovers take their life;
> Whose misadventur'd piteous overthrows
> Doth with their death bury their parents' strife.

With the audience thus forewarned of the determined end of the story, which was in any case very well-known, Shakespeare exploits many of the devices which Chaucer used in *Troilus*. The beginning of the play is full of premonitions. Romeo, for example, foresees 'some consequence, yet hanging in the stars' which will end 'by some vile forfeit of untimely death' (I. iv). After the death of Mercutio and immediately before his fight with Tybalt, he again laments 'This day's black fate on moe days doth depend;/This but begins the woe others must end' (III. i. 118–19). Perhaps the point is made most clearly in III. v. Romeo is about to leave for exile in Mantua:

Juliet	O, think'st thou we shall ever meet again?
Romeo	I doubt it not; and all these woes shall serve For sweet discourses in our times to come.
Juliet	O God, I have an ill-divining soul! Methinks I see thee, now thou art below, As one dead in the bottom of a tomb; Either my eyesight fails or thou look'st pale.
Romeo	And trust me, love, in my eye so do you; Dry sorrow drinks our blood. Adieu, adieu!
Juliet	O Fortune, Fortune! all men call thee fickle. If thou art fickle, what dost thou with him That is renown'd for faith? Be fickle, Fortune; For then, I hope, thou wilt not keep him long, But send him back.

(51–64)

Later in the same scene Juliet pleads

> O, sweet my mother, cast me not away!
> Delay this marriage for a month, a week;
> Or, if you do not, make the bridal bed
> In that dim monument where Tybalt lies.

(198–201)

In a precisely similar vein she speaks to the Friar. 'Rather than force me to marry Paris', she says,

> chain me with roaring bears,
> Or hide me nightly in a charnel house,
> O'er-covered quite with dead men's rattling bones,
> With reeky shanks and yellow chapless skulls;
> Or bid me go into a new-made grave,
> And hide me with a dead man in his shroud—
> Things that, to hear them told, have made me tremble—
>
> (iv. i. 80–6)

Sometimes the premonitions take the form of an absurdly hopeful misreading of the situation:

Friar   In one respect I'll thy assistant be;
       For this alliance may so happy prove
       To turn your households' rancour to pure love.   (ii. iii. 90–2)

This cheerful forecast would not fail of its ironic effect on an audience which knew what the outcome was to be and by what means hidden from the Friar the feud was to be at last composed.

    To encounter these repeated glimpses into the future—obscure to the characters but plain to the audience—is not unlike the experience of talking to children, who only half understand what is being said to them and do not know the full implications of what they reply:

> For even the day before, she broke her brow;
> And then my husband—God be with his soul!
> 'A was a merry man—took up the child.
> 'Yea', quoth he 'dost thou fall upon thy face?
> Thou wilt fall backward when thou hast more wit,
> Wilt thou not, Jule?' and, by my holidam,
> The pretty wretch left crying, and said 'Ay'.
> To see, now, how a jest shall come about!   (i. iii. 39–46)

It is hard not to borrow a line here from *All For Love*, and comment 'Men are but children of a larger growth.'

    As the play wears on the awareness of the tragic ending is no longer confined to the audience. The characters, especially Romeo, become increasingly conscious of the forces which limit their freedom and drive them willy-nilly to their destiny. 'O, I am Fortune's fool,' he realizes when he has killed Tybalt. Friar Lawrence tells him, 'Affliction is enamoured of thy parts,/And thou art wedded to calamity.' Juliet comments ambiguously to Paris, 'What must be, shall be.' At this point in the play, when she has determined on Friar Lawrence's plan, almost everything she says bears a triple meaning—one for the other characters, one for herself, and yet another for the audience. In v. i Romeo hears of Juliet's death and concludes that Fate can do him no more injury—'Is it e'en so? Then I defy you, stars.' After he has killed Paris he describes him as 'one writ with me in sour misfortune's book'. And when he meets his own death it is to him simply shaking 'the yoke of inauspicious stars/From this world-wearied flesh'. Friar Lawrence finally comments, 'A greater power than we can contradict/Has thwarted our intents.'

It is the miscarrying of human plans, the crossing of the high will of the heavens bringing its own prompt retribution, which is the mainspring of the play. When Escalus speaks the final couplet

> For never was a story of more woe
> Than this of Juliet and her Romeo

there is no sense of hyperbole: he is truly expressing the stature of the play which was, in Shakespeare's lifetime and long afterwards, the tragedy *par excellence*. Yet if we try to account for its tragic force in terms of some disabling defect in the hero or heroine the results fall absurdly short of the play. This is, to sum up, because the doctrine of the tragic flaw applies only to characters who may be conceived of as making meaningful choices—that is it implies that their fate at the end of the play is a consequence of decisions they make during the play. Yet in *Romeo* the lovers are star-crossed from the beginning. How then are we to explain the tragic elements?

Antony and Cleopatra offers a slightly different version of the same problem. Once again the story is known in advance, primarily through Plutarch, but also as part of medieval tradition.[22] As in *Romeo*, there are frequent references to Fate, Fortune and Destiny, most notably in the person of the Soothsayer. The short scene, II. iii, placed immediately after Enobarbus' description of Antony's first meeting with Cleopatra, begins with a brief exchange between Antony and Octavia. His central choice, on which the whole action of the play must depend, is thus put before the audience in the space of a few minutes. One would perhaps at this point expect a soliloquy in which Antony weighed the arguments for staying in Rome with Octavia against those for returning to Egypt and Cleopatra. Instead there comes a dialogue between Antony and the Soothsayer, who has previously made true but ambiguous predictions to Charmian and Iras and has no other part in the play.

Antony	Say to me,
	Whose fortunes shall rise higher, Caesar's or mine?
Sooth	Caesar's. Therefore, O Antony, stay not by his side.
	Thy daemon, that thy spirit which keeps thee, is
	Noble, courageous, high, unmatchable,
	Where Caesar's is not; but near him thy angel
	Becomes a fear, as being o'erpowr'd. Therefore
	Make space enough between you.

Antony   Speak this no more.

Sooth   To none but thee; no more but when to thee.
           If thou dost play with him at any game,
           Thou art sure to lose; and of that natural luck
           He beats thee 'gainst the odds. Thy lustre thickens
           When he shines by. I say again, thy spirit
           Is all afraid to govern thee near him;
           But, he away, 'tis noble.

Antony   Get thee gone
           Say to Ventidius I would speak with him.
                              (*Exit Soothsayer*)
           He shall to Parthia.—Be it art or hap,
           He hath spoken true. The very dice obey him;
           And in our sports my better cunning faints
           Under his chance. If we draw lots, he speeds;
           His cocks do win the battle still of mine,
           When it is all to nought, and his quails ever
           Beat mine, inhoop'd, at odds. I will to Egypt;

In place of rational deliberation is set a mysterious message from
'Nature's infinite book of secrecy'.[23] J. F. Danby describes *Antony
and Cleopatra* as a play which pre-eminently makes 'use of deliberate choice as a means of characterization',[24] but Antony's
crucial decision to desert Octavia for Cleopatra is presented without deliberation. We do not even witness his return. We can only
assume that the compulsion to be with Cleopatra has proved
stronger than all the opposing arguments. Indeed many characters
in the play question the reality of human choices. For example:

Caesar   . . . You shall find there
            A man [Antony], who is the abstract of all faults
            That all men follow.

Lepidus   I must not think there are
            Evils enow to darken all his goodness.
            His faults, in him, seem as the spots of heaven,
            More fiery by night's blackness; hereditary
            Rather than purchas'd; what he cannot change
            Than what he chooses.   (I. iv. 8–15)

Enobarbus comments on Antony's decision to challenge Caesar to
single combat:

                         I see men's judgements are
            A parcel of their fortunes, and things outward
            Do draw the inward quality after them, (III. xiii. 31–3)

and later in the same scene Antony comments

> But when we in our viciousness grow hard—
> O misery on't!—the wise gods seel our eyes,
> In our own filth drop our clear judgements, make us
> Adore our errors, laugh at's while we strut
> To our confusion.   (111–15)

As in *Romeo*, the end of the play brings a sense of inevitable narrowing of scope: the choices, for whatever reason, have been made and all that remains is the working out of the consequences. Cleopatra, after Antony's death, again like Romeo, defies 'the false housewife, Fortune', and in the closing scene repeatedly expresses the paradox that death alone gives complete freedom. Of the clown who brings the fatal snake she says 'He brings me liberty.'

> My desolation does begin to make
> A better life. 'Tis paltry to be Caesar:
> Not being Fortune, he's but Fortune's knave,
> A minister of her will; and it is great
> To do that thing that ends all other deeds,
> Which shackles accidents and bolts up change.   (v. ii. 1–6)[25]

Cleopatra escapes from destiny or the randomness of life, whichever man is really subject to: this is her triumph. Caesar comments with admiration, 'Bravest at the last,/She levell'd at our purposes, and being royal,/Took her own way' (332–4), and, like Escalus, has a final word on the quality of the story:

>   Take up her bed,
> And bear her women from the monument.
> She shall be buried by her Antony;
> No grave upon the earth shall clip in it
> A pair so famous. High events as these
> Strike those that make them; and their story is
> No less in pity than his glory which
> Brought them to be lamented.   (354–60)

An interpretation of *Antony and Cleopatra* in terms of the tragic flaw is not impossible—one can say that Antony should have recognized his political responsibilities and his duty to Octavia, that Cleopatra should have been inspecting the rigging of her fleet instead of playing billiards, and so on. It seems not wrong, but simply irrelevant to the catastrophe. As Lepidus points out so lucidly, the tragedy is that Antony is the man he was. This eliminates the notion of human responsibility, in the sense that Nemesis is now not the power that waits to punish a weakness, but takes the form of the daimon, the power that afflicts man with such weaknesses in the first place.

It is a view commonly held that Romeo and Antony are tragic heroes, responsible for their own fates, because, in the words of Othello, they 'loved not wisely but too well'. It is possible however to see Love Tragedy in general as pivoting not on some defect in the lovers but on some quality in love itself. Perhaps, as Lysander suggests, love provokes the hostility of the rest of the world:

> Or, if there were a sympathy in choice,
> War, death, or sickness, did lay siege to it,
> Making it momentary as a sound,
> Swift as a shadow, short as any dream,
> Brief as the lightning in the collied night
> That, in a spleen, unfolds both heaven and earth,
> And ere a man hath power to say 'Behold!'
> The jaws of darkness do devour it up;
> So quick bright things come to confusion.

Hermia   If then true lovers have been ever cross'd,
It stands as an edict in destiny.   (*M.N.D.* I. i)

Perhaps, as Claudius tells Hamlet, love itself must change and degenerate:

> There lives within the very flame of love   (IV. vii. 114–16)
> A kind of wick or snuff that will abate it;
> And nothing is at a like goodness still;   (IV. vii. 114–16)

Perhaps love, being 'a certain inborn suffering derived from the sight of and excessive meditation upon the beauty of the opposite sex', is itself an affliction, which may be fatal.

The tradition of this double view of love as at once 'a tempest and a haven'[26] is very strong, especially in English, particularly when love is personified as Cupid (or Desire) or as what Chaucer calls 'the lover's maladye/Of Hereos [Eros]'.[27] Obvious examples are *Parlement of Foules* 1–7:

> The lyf so short, the craft so long to lerne,
> Th'assay so hard, so sharp the conquerynge,
> The dredful joye, alwey that slit so yerne:
> Al this mene I by Love, that my felynge
> Astonyeth with his wonderful werkynge
> So sore iwis, that whan I on hym thynke,
> Nat wot I wel wher that I flete or synke.

and *Troilus* V. 582–5:

> Thanne thoughte he thus, 'O blisful lord Cupide,
> Whan I the proces have in my memorie,
> How thow me hast wereyed on every syde,
> Men mygght a book make of it, lik a storie.'

Similarly in Book III of the *Faerie Queene* Spenser addresses Love as at once the inspiration of noble actions in men and the instrument by which fate operates:

> The fatall purpose of diuine foresight,
> Thou doest effect in destined descents,
> Through deepe impression of thy secret might,
> And stirredst vp th'Heroes high intents,
> Which the late world admyres for wondrous moniments.   (III. 2)

Romeo and Juliet do not meet their doom in the vault of the Capulets, with death as their punishment for loving: the whole course of their love is their doom. Yet 'there is no good thing in the world, and no courtesy, which is not derived from love as from its fountain'.[28] The paradox that love is at once a source of good and a fatal affliction lies at the root of *Romeo* and of *Antony*. 'And God knows what, when love is all,/The end will be.'[29] The love tragedies present one terrible illustration of Hardy's double-edged lines, and in so doing point once again to a cardinal element in Shakespearean tragedy in general—the questioning of the reality of acts of the will.

The corollary of this is the scrutiny of the meaning of freedom. The play in which this is most systematically carried out is *Timon of Athens*. At the very outset the bearings of the old morality play are, as it were, formally marked out in the dialogue between the Poet and the Painter. First Timon is presented emblematically: his portrait is displayed and commented on and endowed with an independent power. But in the subsequent exchanges Timon's fortune, in the simple financial sense, is expressly equated with his Fortune, in the mythological sense. With extraordinary skill and sureness of touch Shakespeare incorporates in the action and persons of the play an equally firm emblematic diagram of Fortune:

Poet   I will unbolt to you.
>   You see how all conditions, how all minds—
>   As well of glib and slipp'ry creatures as
>   Of grave and austere quality, tender down
>   Their services to Lord Timon. His large fortune,
>   Upon his good and gracious nature hanging,
>   Subdues and properties to his love and tendance
>   All sorts of hearts; . . .
>   Sir, I have upon a high and pleasant hill
>   Feign'd Fortune to be thron'd. The base o' th' mount
>   Is rank'd with all deserts, all kind of natures
>   That labour on the bosom of this sphere
>   To propagate their states. Amongst them all
>   Whose eyes are on this sovereign lady fix'd
>   One do I personate of Lord Timon's frame,

> Whom Fortune with her ivory hand wafts to her;
> Whose present grace to present slaves and servants
> Translates his rivals. . . .
> All those which were his fellows but of late—
> Some better than his value—on the moment
> Follow his strides, his lobbies fill with tendance,
> Rain sacrificial whisperings in his ear,
> Make sacred even his stirrup, and through him
> Drink the free air.

Painter   Ay, marry, what of these?

Poet   When Fortune in her shift and change of mood
> Spurns down her late beloved, all his dependants,
> Which labour'd after him to the mountain's top
> Even on their knees and hands, let him slip down,
> Not one accompanying his declining foot.

Painter   'Tis common.
> A thousand moral paintings I can show
> That shall demonstrate these quick blows of Fortune's
> More pregnantly than words. Yet you do well
> To show Lord Timon that mean eyes have seen
> The foot above the head.   (I. i. 54 . . . 97)

The audience must, at this early point in the play, be fully aware that Timon's prosperity is a thing which cannot last, although I do not see that its reality at the beginning of the play is called in question, as is sometimes suggested. Timon is to be seen in Act I at the top of Fortune's wheel, and it is an essential part of the dramatic structure that when the play opens he is seen at the height of his expansive liberality.

The interest of the play lies in the fact that it continues to follow the hero for two acts after his fall from prosperity. Flavius' speech at the end of IV. ii reads almost as if it were the final verdict on Timon:

> O the fierce wretchedness that glory brings us!
> Who would not wish to be from wealth exempt,
> Since riches point to misery and contempt?   (30–2)

This sounds as though Flavius were classifying Timon's fall as simple *De Casibus*. But he continues

> Poor honest lord, brought low by his own heart,
> Undone by goodness! Strange, unusual blood,
> When man's worst sin is he does too much good!   (37–9)

It seems now as though *Timon* were now being put forward as a textbook illustration of a tragedy based on *hamartia*. But the next scene shows that something subtler is being attempted, for the play continues, and the hero himself is still present to comment on his own downfall and on the experience of sustaining good fortune and great wealth:

> Not nature,
> To whom all sores lay seige, can bear great fortune
> But by contempt of nature. (6–8)

This seems to me one of the crucial moments of the play and to direct our attention to one of its chief concerns. J. C. Maxwell in his Introduction to the New Cambridge edition of *Timon* rightly observes that '"free" is a word that meets with keen criticism in the course of the play'. But, as his examples show, 'free' is most sharply scrutinised in this way in the first half of the play, and becomes progressively less important. The word which takes its place in the second half of the play is 'nature'. Timon in IV. 3 becomes master of Fortune: gold is put in his way, but he returns it to the earth saying 'I will make thee do thy right nature.' We now have a hero who has learned the perils of Fortune's wheel and is able to refuse her treacherous gifts. Is he now free, as the Timon of Acts I–III was not? Or is he, as a man, infected with all the weaknesses of his human nature? If so, he is free from the caprices of Fortune only to meet the more enduring constraints of Nature.

In Timon's long scene with Apemantus (IV. iii. 196–394) the whole argument pivots on the idea of nature in its double meaning of 'that which is' and 'human nature'. If the word 'nature' means the same in both expressions then the strong implication is that man is by his own nature not free but constrained to act in a particular way, a way which is, as every commentator on the bestial imagery of the play has remarked, different only in intensity from the behaviour of animals. Timon himself has made the point shortly before in his address to nature

> Common mother, thou,
> Whose womb unmeasurable and infinite breast
> Teems and feeds all; whose self-same mettle,
> Whereof thy proud child, arrogant man, is puff'd,
> Engenders the black toad and adder blue,
> The gilded newt and eyeless venom'd worm,
> With all th' abhorred births below crisp heaven
> Whereon Hyperion's quick'ning fire doth shine— (IV. iii. 178–85)

The final comment on 'nature' in all its meanings comes at the end of v. i. After Timon's superb farewell speech—

> Come not to me again; but say to Athens
> Timon hath made his everlasting mansion
> Upon the beached verge of the salt flood,
> Who once a day with his embossed froth
> The turbulent surge shall cover. Thither come,
> And let my gravestone be your oracle.
> Lips, let sour words go by and language end:
> What is amiss, plague and infection mend!
> Graves only be men's works and death their gain!
> Sun, hide thy beams. Timon hath done his reign.   (v. i. 212–21)

the First Senator comments, 'His discontents are unremovably/ Coupled to nature.' The focus of definition then shifts from freedom and how it is to be rightly used to nature and how far it determines the life of man as well as of the beasts. In addition there is a double movement also associated with the ideas of liberty and bondage.

Everybody who has read the play must have noticed the growing constriction—from the lordly generosity and amplitude of the opening scenes, to the shifts and dilemmas of Acts II and III as resource after resource is stopped to Timon, to the woods and at last to the cave. Timon has progressively less room for manoeuvre and a progressively clearer knowledge of the limitations on his own actions:

> What, are my doors oppos'd against my passage?
> Have I been ever free, and must my house
> Be my retentive enemy, my gaol?   (III. iv. 80–82)

Finally he comments, 'Nothing brings me all things,' and then, 'Graves only be men's works, and death their gain.' The constriction is complete.

Yet there is also an equally clear process by which Timon becomes progressively freer in the course of the play. That this should be possible is a consequence of the paradoxical nature of the term 'freedom'. As I have said, when Timon is at his 'freest' at the beginning of the play, freedom is not what he wants. He uses his position expressly to create bonds between himself and the society of Athens—'O, what a precious comfort 'tis to have so many like brothers commanding one another's fortunes!'—thus showing that freedom, which is so often praised as a desirable end in itself, is really to be valued only for allowing people to form attachments. Timon's catastrophe is not that he loses his money but that he loses his friends. He finds, that is, that he has money, which gives him freedom, but that he cannot use this freedom to bind himself to others, try as he will. In the second half of the play he has money once more, but now he no longer has any desire to unite himself with anyone. Indeed the process of the central part of the play is a progressive severing of ordinary human obligations. First (III. vi) he turns on his false friends, then (IV. i) on the whole city of Athens, then (IV. iii) on mankind in general. When all his ties with the rest of the world are severed he has total freedom, but, since he does not know what to do with it it is useless to him. It is not 'natural' to be completely without ties. Since he has nothing to live for he dies—he does not even commit suicide.

> I am sick of this false world, and will love nought
> But even the mere necessities upon't.
> Then, Timon, presently prepare thy grave;   (IV. iii. 373–5)

Increasing constraint and increasing freedom have led to the same spot. There are loose ends and inconsistencies, but the main argument is developed on both levels with a power and consistency not easy to match elsewhere in Shakespeare.

Timon is, it may at once be conceded, not typical of Shakespearean tragedy, but it does illustrate very clearly one general proposition about tragedy—that the traditional contrast between the tragedy of character and the tragedy of determined fate is not an absolute one. For the cliché, 'Character is destiny,' has particular application to the character of the tragic hero. Even if he has brought about his own destruction there remains the sense of pity and terror that he should be the kind of man who is fated to destroy himself. His character is more aptly described by a stronger term, such as daimon, which the Soothsayer used of Antony. This means simply the force that makes a man what he is. It is thus both the power which is operating when he feels himself to be acting most authentically and the force which determines his conduct. It is arete and hamartia and nemesis. It is most easily isolated when it can be thought of as an obsession, as in *Othello*, or, even more clearly, in *The Winter's Tale*, where Leontes does not choose to be jealous. He is not even beguiled, as Othello was: jealousy simply descends on him without cause or choice. It is his daimon. Hermione says

> There's some ill planet reigns.
> I must be patient till the heavens look
> With an aspect more favourable.   (II. i. 105–7)[30]

Similarly Mamilius, Perdita, and Hermione meet a fate which they have done nothing to cause. The contrasted careers of Antigonus and Autolycus show that it is not his own moral worth which determines whether a man shall come to misery or prosperity.

Moreover Time, introduced to speak a Chorus before Act IV, represents himself as the dominant mover of human affairs:

> it is in my pow'r
> To o'erthrow law, and in one self-born hour
> To plant and o'erwhelm custom.   (7–9)

That this is true is shown in the world of the play, since Time is a
principal agent in the radical change between the Leontes of Act III
and the Leontes of Act V. Grace, like Corruption, is depicted as
simply visiting Leontes, not as having been earned or chosen by
him. Perhaps we should even think of Time as casting out Leontes'
daimon. In particular the side of the play that deals with the oracle
serves to suggest that the characters are not free but are closely
observed and schooled by some larger power. The instant that
Leontes attempts to assert his own will by refusing to believe the
oracle he learns that his young son has died. 'Apollo's angry, and
the heavens themselves/Do strike at my injustice.' It may indeed be
made a point of criticism that the characters are not presented as
in charge of their destinies or as deliberating in any very consistent
way about the choices open to them or as changing interestingly in
the course of the play.

Yet, even if the point is granted, it is not necessarily a fault in the
play, since one element of the Romance is necessarily the marvellous and surprising. Coincidences and incredible survivals are part
of the apparatus for arousing wonder and awe at the unpredictability of the world. So too are violent and unexpected changes of
character. Fortune is bound to be the dominant figure in a
Romance—'Fortune, visible an enemy' (v. i. 214)—over-shadowing
the human agents, who seem in consequence flat and character-
less. What is perhaps surprising is to find so much emphasis in *The
Winter's Tale* on Fate. As we have seen from *Troilus*, the two are
not incompatible, but to dwell on Fate rather than on Fortune normally entails a darkening of tone, which is in fact what we find.

From a play in which one character is shown as dominating all
the rest one would normally expect to derive a picture of a limited
and rather grim world.[31] Although this is not true of *The Tempest*,
principally because the figure of Prospero is inside the action of
the play and is seen to be benevolent, the equally powerful figure
of Time in *The Winter's Tale* is at best neutral. Though not positively hostile, he must inevitably bear everything away: Acts IV and
V of the play juggle continually with the idea of time. The young
people, as is often remarked, bring promise of regeneration. When
Perdita first meets Leontes it is almost as if he were looking again
on Hermione. Yet what is past is past and cannot be restored:

Leontes has still lost his queen. Then in the great *coup de théâtre* in the last scene it is as if Time had really been set at nothing, for Hermione reappears, miraculously and preposterously, to show that Fortune's wheel can, at rare times, turn back again. Yet Time is not completely overthrown—

> But yet Paulina ,
> Hermione was not so much wrinkled, nothing
> So aged as this seems. (v. iii. 27–9)[32]

Shakespeare's characteristic achievement in *The Winter's Tale* is the marrying of the world of Romance to a world of reality. Hope and honesty are kept at their maximum.

If we ask whether the idea of the daimon can be extended to Shakespearean tragedy in general the first point in the reply is to observe that Shakespeare seems to show very little sympathy to those who assert their own independence of action. The characters who most arrogantly proclaim the power of the will are villains like Richard III, Aaron, Iago, Cassius and Edmund, or morally ambiguous like Parolles. Conversely Shakespeare makes us far more aware than Marlowe does of human helplessness.

Hamlet is, it is a commonplace to remark, a play of deliberation. Yet by the end of the play Hamlet can say

> Our indiscretion sometime serves us well,
> When our deep plots do pall; and that should learn us
> There's a divinity that shapes our ends,
> Rough-hew them how we will. (v. ii. 8–11)

There is a cutting ambiguity in his last speech to Horatio before the fatal duel—

> We defy augury: there is a special providence in the fall of a sparrow. If it be now, 'tis not to come; if it be not to come, it will be now; if it be not now, yet it will come—the readiness is all. Since no man knows aught of what he leaves, what is't to leave betimes? Let be.
> (v. ii. 211–17)

Horatio does not give a complete account of the tragedy at the end of the play, but what he describes is an important part of the tragedy:

> And let me speak to th' yet unknowing world
> How these things came about. So shall you hear
> Of carnal, bloody, and unnatural acts;
> Of accidental judgments, casual slaughters;
> Of deaths put on by cunning and forc'd cause;
> And, in this upshot, purposes mistook
> Fall'n on th' inventors' heads—all this can I
> Truly deliver. (v. ii. 371–8)

As in the love tragedies, simple pity and terror are provoked equally by man's bewilderment in the face of unpredictable misfortunes and by his helplessness in the hands of an inexorable destiny. In Hamlet's words we 'look pale and tremble at this chance/ That are but mutes or audience to this act'.

Thus when towards the end of their lives Othello says, 'Who can control his fate?' or Macbeth says, 'Life's but a walking shadow; a poor player,/That struts and frets his hour upon the stage,/And then is heard no more: it is a tale/Told by an idiot, full of sound and fury,/Signifying nothing,' or Gloster says, 'As flies to wanton boys, are we to the gods,—/They kill us for their sport,' or Lear says, 'When we are born, we cry that we are come/To this great stage of fools' or 'You do me wrong to take me out o' the grave:—/Thou art a soul in bliss; but I am bound/Upon a wheel of fire, that mine own tears/Do scald like molten lead,' or Coriolanus says, 'Behold, the heavens do ope,/The gods look down, and this unnatural scene/ They laugh at,' it would be an error to suppose that what they say is Shakespeare's final account of a universe which, arbitrary or determined, indifferent or malign, mocks the impotence of mankind. But it would be equally wrong to try to explain away these passages as momentary weaknesses or obvious absurdities. The malice, the arbitrariness, the indifference are all elements of our field of action and are all inscrutable by man, who is as he is through no choice of his own and is moved to an end that there is no evading. What Gloster says is a vital part of the fabric of *Lear*, but points also to a dreadful truth in a larger fabric.

In brief the sense of men driven to shape their own destinies in a universe which allows no permanent powers to the human will is never absent from the extraordinary world of Shakespearean tragedy—that world, which, for all its journeyings, its madnesses, its disguises, its ghosts and its tempests (that is, all the elements which mark it as theatrical), we can enter with a feeling of understanding and familiarity, because we meet there more powerfully than anywhere else in our experience of art an image of the riddling world in which we live.

IV REVENGE TRAGEDY

> Public revenges are for the most part fortunate . . . But in private revenges it is not so; nay, rather vindictive persons live the life of witches: who, as they are mischievous, so end they unfortunate.—BACON, *Of Revenge*

I have suggested that Shakespeare in his tragedies did not consciously select an exclusively determinist or libertarian basis, any more than most people do in their own lives, but allows elements of both to combine to produce an unprecedentedly full account of man's efforts to understand his own destiny. The playwrights who succeeded him had clearly learned the lesson that the world of Shakespeare's tragedies owed something of its power to its darkness, its violence, its inscrutability, and its searching of man in situations of peculiar suffering and at the limits of his reason. These elements they used to build their own world, less varied than Shakespeare's, with a more limited understanding of the possible greatness of men, and consequently with a heavier and more insistent emphasis on the helplessness of the individual in the power of his daimon and exposed to the malice of Fate.

I have mentioned in the introductory chapter (pp. 13–15) the extraordinary difficulty of defining and exemplifying a free action. This problem has its counterpart for the dramatist, for if he wishes to present to his audience characters who purport to be acting freely it appears that they must either reach decisions capriciously—that is, not because the motives on one side are stronger than those on the other—or act irrationally—that is, deliberately choose to do what is against their own best interests—or act perversely—that is, act in a way that does violence to their own moral feelings or their own sense of human nature—or, perhaps, act pointlessly. In brief the more convincingly an author supplies a character with adequate motives the more difficult it is to convince an audience that the character is acting freely; conversely the more pointedly a character is, by definition or position, presented to the audience as free the more difficult it is to suggest any reason at all why he should act, and thus the more likely it becomes that his demonstration of freedom will lie in some unnecessary, irrational or 'carnal, bloody and unnatural' act.

In the world of revenge tragedy much the clearest example is Domitian in Massinger's *The Roman Actor.*[33] From the beginning of the play he is established as exercising absolute power and as being conscious of this:

Parthenius   When power puts in its plea the laws are silenc'd.
             The world confesses one Rome, and one Caesar,
             And, as his rule is infinite, his pleasures
             Are unconfin'd; this syllable, his will,
             Stands for a thousand reasons.   (I. ii. 44–9)

Domitian   Shall we be circumscrib'd? Let such as cannot
             By force make good their actions, though wicked,
             Conceal, excuse, or qualify their crimes.
             What our desires grant leave and privilege to,
             Though contradicting all divine decrees,
             Or laws confirm'd by Romulus, and Numa,
             Shall be held sacred.   (II. i. 143–9)

Domitian   Mankind lives
          In few, as potent monarchs and their peers;
          And all those glorious constellations
          That do adorn the firmament, appointed,
          Like grooms, with their bright influence to attend
          The actions of kings, and emperors,
          They being the greater wheels that move the less.
                                        (III. ii. 34–40)

But of course absolute power corrupts, since it has to prove its
own absolute nature by actions which are unnatural, such as
having people tortured. His most conspicuous act of this kind is to
take Domitia from her husband Lamia, whom he taunts and finally
executes. But this again demonstrates the difficulty of defining
freedom. He seems in his imperious commandeering of the women
of his choice to be acting with total freedom: in fact, as the rest of
the play makes clear, the action is that of a man in thrall to desire.
Before the end of the play he realizes his total subjection.

                                          I am lost;
          Nor am I Caesar. When I first betray'd
          The freedom of my faculties and will
          To this imperious siren [Domitia], I laid down
          The empire of the world, and of myself,
          At her proud feet.   (v. i. 81–6)

In parallel, as it were, with this theme Massinger handles another
of the topics raised by the form of revenge tragedy. As we shall see,
the desire for vengeance is normally represented as self-defeating.
The implied recommendation to a wronged man is to wait patiently
until the duly constituted authority in the state acts with the
powers of law. The good old Aëcius in Beaumont and Fletcher's
Valentinian, almost echoing the Good Counsellor in *Gorboduc*, puts
the orthodox point of view very plainly:

          We are but subjects, Maximus; obedience
          To what is done, and grief for what is ill done
          Is all we can call ours. The hearts of princes
          Are like the temples of the gods; pure incense,
          Until unhallowed hands defile those offerings,
          Burns ever there; we must not put 'em out,
          Because the priests that touch those sweets are wicked;
          We dare not, dearest friend, nay, more, we cannot,—
          While we consider who we are, and how,
          To what laws bound, much more to what lawgiver;
          Whilst majesty is made to be obeyed,
          And not to be inquired into.   (I. iii. 425–36)

But an obvious difficulty arises when, as in *The Roman Actor*, the centre of government is incurably corrupt. Massinger's answer to this problem is not clear—on the one hand he presents the various conspirators against Domitian with a fair degree of sympathy but without ever actually suggesting that what they do is right: on the other he allows rather more prominence to the sort of inevitable retribution for pride that we have noticed in some of the Falls of Princes stories. Thus Domatilla comments

> The immortal Powers
> Protect a prince, though sold to impious acts,
> And seem to slumber, till his roaring crimes
> Awake their justice; but then, looking down,
> And with impartial eyes, on his contempt
> Of all religion and moral goodness,
> They, in their secret judgements, do determine
> To leave him to his wickedness, which sinks him
> When he is most secure.   (III. i. 58–66)

Just before an astrologer accurately predicts his death Domitian defies augury in a familiar manner:

> Though all the sky were hung with blazing meteors,
> Which fond astrologers give out to be
> Assur'd presages of the change of empires
> And deaths of monarchs, we, undaunted yet,
> Guarded with our own thunder, bid defiance
> To them and fate, we being too strongly arm'd
> For them to wound us.   (IV. i. 104–10)

and finally points out himself the exact correspondence of the trajectory of his career with the classic *De Casibus* pattern:

> Oh no, it cannot be; it is decreed
> Above, and by no strengths here to be alter'd.
> Let proud mortality but look on Caesar,
> Compass'd of late with armies, in his eyes
> Carrying both life and death, and in his arms
> Fadoming the earth; that would be styl'd a god,
> And is for that presumption cast beneath
> The low condition of a common man,
> Sinking with mine own weight.   (v. i. 271–9)

It is an interesting irony, and one which suggests the extent of Massinger's understanding of what he was doing, that by the end of the play Domitian is so terrified by the astrologer's prophecies that he is completely in thrall to superstitious fears.

Other examples of the difficulty of presenting men who are free and rational are Ferdinand and the Cardinal in *The Duchess of*

Malfi. They point directly to the central paradox of plays of this kind—that the characters who most prominently assert their wills are all seen to be in the very act of assertion no longer free but under the domination of their daimon. This is most obvious in the treatment of revenge. Tourneur's careful study in *The Revenger's Tragedy* of the way in which a wronged man can be corrupted first by the desire for vengeance and then by his own ingenuity in devising his revenge is the most comprehensive statement, but the same idea is common elsewhere.

Francisco's words in Massinger's *Duke of Milan* show how the desire for revenge becomes an overpowering obsession:

> all my plots
> Turn back upon myself; but I am in,
> And must go on: and, since I have put off
> From the shore of innocence, guilt be now my pilot!
> Revenge first wrought me; murder's his twin brother:
> One deadly sin, then, help to cure another.   (II. i)

> It is enough;
> Nay, all I could desire, and will make way
> To my revenge, which shall disperse itself
> On him, on her, and all.   (III. iii)

> And let my plots produce this longed-for birth,
> In my revenge I have my heaven on earth.   (IV. ii)

Towards the end of the play he expresses the enduring power of the passion for revenge—'For injuries are writ in brass, kind Graccho,/And not to be forgotten' (V. i). Meanwhile he has in turn incurred the enmity of Graccho, who says

> And if I now outstrip him not, and catch him,
> And by a new and strange way too, hereafter
> I'll swear there are worms in my brains.   (V. i)

The emphasis on the wittiness and ingenuity of the means of revenge is typical.[34] In *'Tis Pity* the Spanish servant Vasques sets out to goad his master Soranzo:

Why, this is excellent and above expectation—her own brother! O, horrible! to what height of liberty in damnation hath the devil trained our age! her brother, well! there's yet but a beginning; I must to my lord, and tutor him better in his points of vengeance.   (IV. iii)

He succeeds so well that Soranzo, who has already declared, 'I carry hell about me; all my blood/Is fired in swift revenge' (IV. iii), goes on to say, 'O, my soul/Runs circular in sorrow for revenge' (IV. iii), and 'Revenge is all the ambition I aspire;/To that I'll climb or fall: my blood's on fire' (V. ii). Meanwhile Hippolita and Giovanni have been seized in the same remorseless grip:

Hippolita	On this delicious bane my thoughts shall banquet;
	Revenge shall sweeten what my griefs have tasted. (II. ii)

Giovanni	Yes, father; and, that times to come may know
	How, as my fate, I honoured my revenge,
	List, father; to your ears I will yield up
	How much I have deserved to be your son. (V. vi)

The idea of revenge as fate is particularly interesting. It must bring to mind Greek tragedy and the unbreakable chain of offence and revenge and retaliation which shackles the hapless victims. Yet if we think of Orestes on the one hand and on the other Vasques, who survives until the end of the play and sees most of the other characters killed, the differences are plain. Vasques' final remark is not that of a man condemned by fate to pay a debt in blood—'Tis well: this conquest is mine, and I rejoice that a Spaniard outwent an Italian in revenge' (V. vi). The idea of a sort of Davis Cup for Vengeance is an expressly non-tragic one, and it is true that there are non-tragic elements in many of these plays. They are in some ways close to the Comedy of Humours, which is not unexpected: both sorts of play are studies in obsessive behaviour, and find common ground in the premise that 'almost/All the wide world is little else in nature,/But parasites or sub-parasites'.[35] The potentially comic spectacle of a world reduced to a series of selfish squabbles among bloodsuckers, and the potentially comic spectacle of a man whose determined behaviour is at variance with his own loudly proclaimed ideas of freedom, are important elements in the picture of man's nature that emerges from these obsessional tragedies.

The pattern that one finds repeated again and again is the bold stroke designed to demonstrate freedom which ironically proves the opposite. In *The Changeling* Beatrice-Joanna seems the most emancipated of Renaissance heroines when she hires De Flores to kill Alonso. Yet the path is swift from that to the admission—'I'm in a labyrinth;/What will content him? I would fain be rid of him.' De Flores, an unpitying realist, confronts her with brutal facts:

> Push, fly not to your birth, but settle you
> In what the act has made you, y'are no more now;
> You must forget your parentage to me:
> Y'are the deed's creature.

His power over her in this scene (III. iv) is derived from his readiness to put bluntly before her the truth about her own situation, a truth which she recognises almost with relief:

De Flores	Let this silence thee:
	The wealth of all Valencia shall not buy
	My pleasure from me;
	Can you weep fate from its determined purpose?
	So soon may you weep me.
Beatrice	Vengeance begins;
	Murder I see is followed by more sins.

She finally realizes how her own actions have brought her to her destined end:

> Beneath the stars, upon yon meteor
> Ever hung my fate, 'mongst things corruptible;
> I ne'er could pluck it from him: my loathing
> Was prophet to the rest, but ne'er believ'd;
> Mine honour fell with him, and now my life.   (v. iii)

Orgilus in *The Broken Heart* travels the full course also. At the beginning of the play he exalts in the freedom which he has won by setting aside conventional restraints in his pursuit of revenge:

> Inspire me, Mercury, with swift deceits.
> Ingenious Fate has leapt into mine arms,
> Beyond the compass of my brain. Mortality
> Creeps on the dung of earth, and cannot reach
> The riddles which are purposed by the gods.   (I. ii)

Halfway through the play Tecnicus makes the following comment on Orgilus:

> Much mystery of fate
> Lies hid in that man's fortunes; curiosity
> May lead his actions into rare attempts:—
> But let the gods be moderators still;
> No human power can prevent their will.   (III. i)

Then at the end of the play Orgilus, his guilt revealed, opens his veins. As he dies he speaks as follows:

> O Tecnicus, inspired with Phoebus' fire!
> I call to mind thy augury, 'twas perfect;
> 'Revenge proves its own executioner.'
> When feeble man is bending to his mother,
> The dust he first was framed on, thus he totters.

Bassanes	Life's fountain is dried up.
Orgilus	So falls the standard Of my prerogative in being a creature! A mist hangs o'er mine eyes, the sun's bright splendour Is clouded in an everlasting shadow; Welcome, thou ice, that sitt'st about my heart No heat can ever thaw thee. (*Dies*)
Nearchus	Speech hath left him.
Bassanes	He has shook hands with time. (v. ii)

The last remark of Bassanes is especially revealing. It expresses another quality that has often been noticed in these plays, that after the brutality and perversity, the obsessions and the extravagances of the early part of the play, pushed almost as I have said to a comic pitch of grotesqueness, there is an abrupt change of tone when the characters are confronted with death. The action of the plays, that is, offers a study in the pathology of a damaged mind; the interest is the doubtful and uneasy one of exploring the more bizarre recesses of human behaviour. Dramatically the action expresses the paradox that life is full of irresistible impulses which lead inevitably to death. But at the climax the characters seem to be confronting in an altered mood a related but different question—what of death itself? Will it solve the mystery of life, or is it an even greater riddle? Death stands in all the plays as a dark but alluring doorway into the unknown. It is terrifying to go through it, yet those who do perhaps know more than the cowards who remain behind.

> O, that it were possible we might
> But hold some two days' conference with the dead!
> From them I should learn somewhat, I am sure,
> I never shall know here.   (*Duchess of Malfi*, IV. ii)

Thus at the end of the plays the characters who have confidently asserted their freedom begin to lose their certainty. Either they say with Orgilus, 'So falls the standard/Of my prerogative in being a creature,' or they are reduced like Francisco in *The Duke of Milan* to a blank assertion of identity.

The poles between which their ideas on death move are indicated in the following exchange from Beaumont and Fletcher's *Thierry and Theodoret*. Thierry is attempting to terrify Ordella with the prospect of imminent death: she is declaring her readiness to die if it will do good to the kingdom:

[*Thierry*]   . . . And endless parting
          With all we can call ours, with all our sweetness,
          With youth, strength, pleasure, people, time, nay, reason?
          For in the silent grave, no conversation,
          No joyful tread of friends, no voice of lovers,
          No careful father's counsel; nothing's heard
          Nor nothing is, but all oblivion,
          Dust and an endless darkness; and dare you, woman,
          Desire this place?

Ordella   'Tis of all sleeps the sweetest:
          Children begin it to us, strong men seek it,
          And kings from height of all their painted glories
          Fall like spent exhalations to this centre:
          And those are fools that fear it, or imagine
          A few unhandsome pleasures or life's profits
          Can recompense this place; and mad that stay it,
          Till age blow out their lights, or rotten humours
          Bring them dispersed to the earth.   (IV. i)

Later Thierry himself shows the characteristic preoccupations of
those about to meet death in these plays. First he talks in some
detail about his own sufferings:

                                        Tell me,
          Can ever these eyes more, shut up in slumbers,
          Assure my soul there is sleep? is there night
          And rest for human labours? do not you
          And all the world, as I do, out-stare Time,
          And live, like funeral lamps, never extinguished?
          Is there a grave? (and do not flatter me,
          Nor fear to tell me truth,) and in that grave
          Is there a hope I shall sleep? can I die?
          Are not my miseries immortal? Oh,
          The happiness of him that drinks his water,
          After his weary day, and sleeps for ever!   (V. ii)

and then in a notably simpler tone and with a touch of conscious
pathos he exclaims as he dies, 'Love, I must die; I faint:/Close up my
glasses!' Beaumont and Fletcher are clearly fond of this sudden
access of clarity at the last; clarity, of course, in a verbal sense only.
Often a vivid physical detail, perhaps a medical one, gives a sense of
solidity, as if it were too late for rhetoric: but the mystery loses
none of its darkness for being alluded to in a simple metaphor. A
few examples illustrate the point. Beaumont and Fletcher's are
plain but not particularly interesting:

Hengo	I grow cold;
	Mine eyes are going. (*Bonduca* v. v)

Valentinian   If ye be anything but dreams and ghosts,
                  And truly hold the guidance of things mortal;
                  Have in yourselves times past, to come, and present;
                  Fashion the souls of men, and make flesh for 'em,
                  Weighing our fates and fortunes beyond reason;
                  Be more than all, ye gods, great in forgiveness!
                  Break not the goodly frame ye build in anger,
                  For you are things, men teach us, without passions:
                  Give me an hour to know ye in; oh, save me!
                  But so much perfect time ye make a soul in,
                  Take this destruction from me!—No; ye cannot;
                  The more I would believe, the more I suffer.
                  My brains are ashes! now my heart, my eyes!—friends,
                  I go, I go! more air, more air!—I am mortal!   (*Dies*)
                                                  (*Valentinian* v. ii)

Evadne   Thy hand was welcome, but it came too late.
             Oh, I am lost! the heavy sleep makes haste.   (*Dies*)
                                         (*Maid's Tragedy* v. iv)

Amintor   This earth of mine doth tremble, and I feel
              A stark affrighted motion in my blood;
              My soul grows weary of her house, and I
              All over am a trouble to myself . . .
              There's something yet, which I am loath to leave:
              There's man enough in me to meet the fears
              That death can bring; and yet would it were done.
              I can find nothing in the whole discourse
              Of death, I dare not meet the boldest way.   (ibid. v. iv)

Aspatia   Give me thy hand; mine hands grope up and down,
              And cannot find thee; I am wondrous sick:
              Have I thy hand, Amintor?   (ibid. v. iv)

Of a similar kind is the death of D'Amville in *The Atheist's Tragedy*:

> O! the lust of death commits
> A rape upon me as I would ha' done
> On Castabella.   (*Dies*)   (v. ii)[36]

The master of this particular effect is Webster: indeed the fifth act of both of his greatest tragedies is, it is hardly too strong to say, expressly constructed to give the greatest possible reverberation to the amazingly concrete yet riddling remarks with which the main actors encounter their death.

The last act of *The White Devil* gives Flamineo ample opportunity to explore attitudes. The key is set by Brachiano's remark in v. iii—'On pain of death, let no man name death to me:/It is a word infinitely terrible.' Then Flamineo pretends to be facing death:

> Whether I resolve to fire, earth, water, air,
> Or all the elements by scruples, I know not,
> Nor greatly care.—Shoot, shoot:
> Of all deaths the violent death is best;
> For from ourselves it steals so fast,
> The pain, once apprehended, is quite past.   (v. vi)

When he is confronted with imminent death in the person of Lodovico he first offers a fairly conventional stoic resignation:

> Fate's a spaniel,
> We cannot beat it from us. What remains now?
> Let all that do ill, take this precedent,—
> Man may his fate foresee but not prevent:
> And of all axioms this shall win the prize,—
> 'Tis better to be fortunate than wise.

Then in response to Lodovico's taunts he replies with the abstraction of a man engaged in a supremely absorbing activity: dying requires all his concentration.

Lodovico	Naught grieves but that you are too few to feed
The famine of our vengeance. What dost think on?
Flamineo	Nothing; of nothing: leave thy idle questions.
I am i' the way to study a long silence:
To prate were idle. I remember nothing.
There's nothing of so infinite vexation
As man's own thoughts.

Vittoria, having been stabbed, picks up the precise idiom:

Vittoria	My soul, like to a ship in a black storm,
Is driven, I know not whither.
Flamineo	Then cast anchor.
Prosperity doth bewitch men, seeming clear;
But seas do laugh, show white, when rocks are near.
We cease to grieve, cease to be fortune's slaves,
Nay, cease to die, by dying. Art thou gone? . . .
I do not look
Who went before, nor who shall follow me;
No, at myself I will begin and end.
While we look up to heaven, we confound
Knowledge with knowledge. O, I am in a mist.

Flamineo's last words are

> 'Tis well yet there's some goodness in my death;
> My life was a black charnel. I have caught
> An everlasting cold; I have lost my voice
> Most irrecoverably. Farewell, glorious villains!
> This busy trade of life appears most vain,
> Since rest breeds rest, where all seek pain by pain. (*Dies*)

The Duchess of Malfi is equally full of these probing ambiguities. Antonio's reply to his servant just after he has been stabbed by Bosola is typical. The servant asks 'Where are you, sir?' and Antonio answers, 'Very near my home.' The remaining principal actors die in succession. Ferdinand is first mad—

> Give me some wet hay; I am broken-winded.
> I do account this world but a dog-kennel:
> I will vault credit and affect high pleasures
> Beyond death.   (v. v)

—and then dies with the words

> Whether we fall by ambition, blood, or lust,
> Like diamonds we are cut with out own dust.   (*Dies*)

followed by his brother

> *Cardinal*   And now, I pray, let me
>   Be laid by and never thought of.   (*Dies*)

and *Bosola*

> O, I am gone! . . .
>   Fare you well.
> It may be pain, but no harm, to me to die
> In so good a quarrel. O, this gloomy world!
> In what a shadow, or deep pit of darkness,
> Doth womanish and fearful mankind live!
> Let worthy minds ne'er stagger in distrust
> To suffer death or shame for what is just:
> Mine is another voyage.   (*Dies*)

This speech brings to the surface something which is implicit in all these dying riddles, that these desperately late conjectures about the experience of death are a particular way of expressing a general uncertainty about life. 'He seems to come to himself,/Now he's so near the bottom' (*D of M* v. v).[37] Bosola himself has brilliantly given voice to these doubts:

Thou art a box of worm-seed, at best but a salvatory of green mummy. What's this flesh? a little crudded milk, fantastical puff-paste. Our bodies are weaker than those paper-prisons boys use to keep flies in; more contemptible, since ours is to preserve earth-worms. Didst thou ever see a lark in a cage? Such is the soul in the body; this world is like her little turf of grass, and the Heaven o'er our heads, like her looking-glass, only gives us a miserable knowledge of the small compass of our prison. (IV. ii)

He speaks similarly after he has stabbed Antonio:

> Antonio!
> The man I would have saved 'bove mine own life!
> We are merely the stars' tennis-balls, struck and bandied
> Which way please them. (V. iv)[38]

And Antonio echoes him:

> In all our quest of greatness,
> Like wanton boys, whose pastime is their care,
> We follow after bubbles blown in the air.
> Pleasure of life, what is't? only the good hours
> Of an ague; merely a preparative to rest,
> To endure vexation.

Observations of this kind carry far more weight in the plays than conventional expressions of hope or piety. Florio in *'Tis Pity* says, 'Great men may do their wills, we must obey;/But Heaven will judge them for't another day,' and Ricardetto in the same play says, 'All human worldly courses are uneven;/No life is blessed but the way to Heaven.' Giovanni concludes *The White Devil* by saying 'Let guilty men remember, their black deeds/Do lean on crutches made of slender reeds.' And Lysippus brings the *Maid's Tragedy* to a close with these words:

> May this a fair example be to me,
> To rule with temper; for on lustful kings
> Unlooked-for sudden deaths from Heaven are sent;
> But cursed is he that is their instrument.

but the sentiments quite fail to measure up to the action of the plays. In contrast the whole weight of the dramas comes to bear on speeches like Penthea's in *The Broken Heart*:

> In vain we labour in this course of life
> To piece our journey out a length, or crave
> Respite of breath: our home is in the grave

or Bosola's in *The Duchess of Malfi*: 'We are only like dead walls or vaulted graves,/That, ruined, yield no echo.'

It is not of great importance whether we call these plays tragedies of blood, tragedies of infection, or tragedies of revenge. From my point of view the interesting thing about all of them is the way in which an assertion of freedom is made and instantly shown to be fallacious. With Webster in particular and the other playwrights in their degree, the result is a presentation of the human condition which is bleak in the extreme—freedom is a mockery, self-assertion is the first step to bondage, yet nobody could live contented in the violent and treacherous world of the plays themselves.

V TRAGIC KINDS AND TRAGIC PLEASURES

The variety of kinds of tragedy in the period covered by this chapter suggests the possibility of setting up some kind of tragic spectrum, in which plays would be placed according to the extent to which the hero's own willed acts were responsible for his downfall. Thus at one extreme we should place those plays in which disasters simply overwhelm the hero, although he has done nothing to deserve them. Fate is predominant, or unlucky chance, and the main elements arousing pity and awe are the suffering of the characters and the spectator's sense of their ultimate helplessness in the face of capricious, inscrutable or inexorable powers. It is hard to say when the representation of human distress is tragic and when it is simply painful or disgusting, but this difficulty should not lead us to deny the name of tragedy to *The Trojan Women* of Euripides, to the play of the same title by Seneca, to Chaucer's *Troilus*, to Racine's *Andromaque*, to *The Woodlanders*, to *The Plough and the Stars*, to films such as *The Ox-Bow Incident*, or to any other work which moves its audience through the unmerited grief or suffering of the central characters. Such tragedy may conveniently be termed Trojan Tragedy.

At the other end of the spectrum is daimonic tragedy, in which we recognize as the major force the hero's daimon, which makes him what he is, simultaneously endowing him with authentic drives and obsessing him so that he cannot do other than he does. Timon, Coriolanus and Tamburlaine are obvious examples of men whose daimon is at once their downfall and the source of all their characteristic strength: as Peter Alexander has well put it, 'what destroys the hero is what wins for him our admiration and sympathies.'[39]

Between these extremes can be placed the other kinds of tragedy I have been discussing. Revenge Tragedy is clearly daimonic, even when the figure of Revenge is externalised, and we might argue that love tragedy is similarly daimonic even when, as in the story of Tristan and Iseult, there is the immediate agency of a love potion.[40] These kinds of tragedy make it evident that your daimon—'that thy spirit which keeps thee'—is something which you have not willed—'hereditary/Rather than purchased, what he cannot change/Than what he chooses', as Lepidus says of Antony. It seems then that we should be able to anatomize both Love Tragedy and Revenge Tragedy in terms of a similar affliction by Fate. But when we contemplate a man in the grip of an obsession we can say either 'Why doesn't he fight against it?' or 'Poor fellow, he can't help himself.' When we see a man driven by the desire for vengeance our reaction is nearer to the first of these. But since on the whole we do not normally feel that lovers are doing others harm by their love, we pity them far more readily than we reproach them, and recognise their helplessness. Thus love tragedy, although obsessional, often affects us in a way not very different from Trojan tragedy.

Far the commonest kind of tragedy is the tragedy of mixed circumstance, in which the hero is brought to disaster by a combination of the operations of his daimon and unlucky external circumstance. Broadly one may say that either the circumstances conspire to force the hero to resist his daimon, and that the conflict destroys him, (e.g. *Hamlet*), or that circumstances conspire to put the hero under the power of his daimon, which drives him to acts of destructive wickedness, (e.g. *Macbeth*).

This may suggest an answer to the puzzling question of why it seems natural to say that Shakespearean tragedy is in some way nobler than the later revenge tragedies. The heroes of the Jacobean plays readily yield themselves in thrall to revenge, so that the main interest normally lies in the ingenuity of the mechanism. Many of Shakespeare's heroes on the other hand are notably hard to arouse, so that the power and nature of their daimon are only gradually revealed to the audience. Hamlet, in spite of the supernatural solicitings of the ghost, is never able to dedicate himself with a single mind to revenge. Othello is slow to be overcome even by the diabolical promptings of Iago. Macbeth is committed to a life of blood only after he has been with difficulty persuaded by the witches and his wife to kill Duncan, but he does accept the commitment and the play is in consequence closer than the others to Jacobean tragedy. *Lear* is virtually unclassifiable. It begins as a study of a man in the grip of a daimon, but then the daimons multiply. Edmund in particular pursues his own tragic trajectory.

By the time Lear's daimon has been expelled or exorcised all the material circumstances have changed, and the sublime melodrama of the final act is resolved in what is very like a Trojan mode.[41]

Shakespeare's heroes are normally conscious of a richer array of possibilities open to them, whether these are real or apparent, than the Jacobean heroes, and this implies a less rigid definition of human nature. It is almost as if the Shakespearean hero had some say in the kind of daimon that he allowed himself to be possessed by—though some daimon it must be. The tragedies of blood may well be telling a truth about man and the world he lives in, but they do not tell all the truth, since they take too little account of our intuitions of possible ways of living and our strivings to attain a different state, even to create a different self. Such intuitions may be illusory and such strivings vain, but they are an integral part of human experience. In comparison with Shakespeare the revenge tragedies appear inflexible and diagrammatic. They offer the full irony of the contrast between almost demoniacal self-assertion and abject human helplessness, but it is the exception to find in these plays, what we find in our own lives, the strenuous and painful compromise on the middle ground between the two.

If then it is accepted that the cardinal achievement of the tragic playwrights of this period was not the creation of an ideal moral world but the presentation of the realities of the moral life, it follows, I think, that Lodge and Puttenham are of little help in locating the source of tragic pleasure. In particular it is no longer possible to stipulate that the drama should demonstrate the operation of poetic justice, in the sense that actions are to attract a happy or unhappy outcome according to their desert. Indeed if we open our minds to any significant extent to the ideas of the ultimate powerlessness of humanity which we encounter so often in the tragic drama we shall be even less inclined to accept the argument that human beings must deserve their punishment before we can enjoy watching it. On the contrary we shall separate our notions of what is just (in the sense of what men feel that they are entitled to expect) and what is tragic (in the sense of what men are likely to get), and thus refuse to debar ourselves from taking a proper pleasure in any true representation of the human condition through the medium of art, even in the representation of events where injustice is apparent.[42] In a just world there would be no tragedies.

It may seem that if we enjoy the spectacle of injustice we are merely indulging the sadist in us, as we should be if we watched Grand Guignol. Yet once it is granted that what we are seeing is a representation of something universal to human life we are bound to recognize that we are watching not just the suffering of others but that of ourselves. Masochism would be as accurate a description of this as sadism. But of course 'suffering' must not be taken in a completely passive sense. Even in Trojan tragedy the characters suffer their fate in the sense of enduring or sustaining it. As Wordsworth says in *The Borderers* 'Suffering is permanent, obscure and dark,/And shares the nature of infinity.' (III. 1543–4). It shows us man at his limits. It does not seem to me to be in any way perverted to take an intense interest in what Jaspers calls 'boundary situations'. When Regan says to Lear, 'Nature in you stands on the very verge/Of her confine,' we may take her words in another sense, and agree that Lear's extremity is, precisely because he stands at the frontier of human experience, of inestimable value in defining the boundaries of human nature.

Nothing emerges from this chapter more clearly than the doubtful value of trying to arrive at any single statement of what 'pure' tragedy is. Even the characteristic sense of tragic loss and waste is double in its operation. On the one hand it implies that what has been lost is of value—in that sense it is humanly reassuring: on the other it confronts us with unpleasant and unavoidable truths about the conditions of our life. The matter may be put at its lowest and simplest by saying that tragedy does harrow us; it does evoke terror as well as pity; by presenting us with life as a mystery it does force us to conjecture about the terms on which we hold life and ultimately surrender it, so that we ask incredulously with Kent 'Is this the promised end?' and echo Edgar's reply 'Or image of that horror?' Yet what is still a mystery must allow some room for hope. What Shakespeare makes Edgar say of the terrifying fiction he enacts with the blind Gloster—'Why I do trifle thus with his despair/Is done to cure it'—could be applied to his own tragic art.

The great sweep of the tragic theatre from 1590 to 1640 presents the unceasing tension between two post-Renaissance views of man—one epitomized in Chapman's glorious 'I am a nobler substance than the stars,' the other in Sir John Davies' more sober reflections:

> I know my body's of so frail a kind
> As force without, fevers within, can kill;
> I know the heavenly nature of my mind,
> But 'tis corrupted both in wit and will.

> I know my Soul hath power to know all things,
> Yet she is blind and ignorant in all;
> I know I am one of Nature's little kings,
> Yet to the least and vilest things am thrall.

I know my life's a pain and but a span,
I know my Sense is mockt with every thing:
And, to conclude, I know myself a MAN,
Which is a proud, and yet a wretched thing.

These lines from *Nosce Teipsum* perhaps indicate why the next work I shall discuss is Book III of *Paradise Lost*.

In addition to the works cited in the notes the following have useful material on the themes of this chapter: H. R. Patch, *The tradition of the Goddess Fortuna in Medieval Philosophy and Literature*, Smith College Studies in Modern Languages (1922); Howard Baker, *Induction to Tragedy* (Northampton, Mass: 1939); W. C. Greene, *Moira: Fate, Good, and Evil in Greek Thought* (Cambridge, Mass: Harvard U.P., 1944); Robert Ornstein, *The Moral Vision of Jacobean Tragedy* (Madison: Wisconsin U.P., 1960); Nicholas Brooke, 'Marlowe as Provocative Agent in Shakespeare's Early Plays', *Sh S*, 14 (1961), 34–44; Roland M. Frye, *Shakespeare and Christian Doctrine* (Princeton, 1963), esp. pp. 157–65; Robert Heilman, *Tragedy and Melodrama: Versions of Experience* (Seattle, 1968); Wilbur Sanders, *The Dramatist and the Received Idea: Studies in the plays of Marlowe and Shakespeare* (Cambridge U.P., 1968); E. A. J. Honigmann, *Shakespeare's Seven Tragedies* (London: Macmillan, 1976); Robert G. Hunter, *Shakespeare and the Mystery of God's Judgments* (U. of Georgia P.: Athens, 1976) esp. ch. 3; Harry Levin, *Shakespeare and the Revolution of the Times: Perspectives and Commentaries* (O.U.P., 1976); Frederick Kiefer, 'Fortune and Providence in *The Mirror for Magistrates*', *SP*, 74 (1977), 146–64; Joel Altman, *The Tudor Play of Mind* (University of California Press, 1978), esp. chapters 8–10.

3

Paradise Lost Book III

I TEMPTATION

God-ward man has no 'free will', but is a captive, slave, and servant either to the will of God or to the will of Satan.—LUTHER, *De servo arbitrio*, tr. Henry Cole.

Any discussion of the theology of *Paradise Lost* encounters the difficulty of explaining the relation between freedom and obedience. If perfect freedom can be found only in the service of God, it is equally true that real obedience is impossible unless the person obeying is free to disobey. In the *Areopagitica*, where he is defending not just the right to print but the right to hold opinions differing from the prevailing orthodoxy, Milton makes this point repeatedly, often with explicit reference to the temptation and fall of Adam. But in *Paradise Lost* the assumption of Divine foreknowledge conflicts *prima facie* with that of human freedom, especially Adam's, the notion of Divine punishment conflicts with the idea of Adam's freedom also, and finally the entailing of Adam's sins on his descendants conflicts with the idea of their freedom. To mitigate this last point Milton naturally lays emphasis on man's ability to choose Christ and thus win salvation. He has then to meet the objection that if God is omniscient he knows in advance which men will choose to be saved and which will not.

In *Paradise Lost* this contention is most closely examined at the beginning of Book III, in which God 'clears his own Justice and Wisdom from all imputation, having created Man free', and later declares his intentions about the salvation or damnation of Adam's posterity. The wording of the Argument is interesting. It leaves no doubt that Milton was writing defensively at this point. The kind of attack against which he had to defend God was of a kind which is familiar enough: it is put cogently and succinctly by Shelley in his notes on *Queen Mab* (VI. 198):

> The doctrine of Necessity teaches us that in no case could any event have happened otherwise than it did happen, and that, if God is the author of good, He is also the author of evil; that, if He is entitled to our gratitude for the one, He is entitled to our hatred for the other; that, admitting the existence of this hypothetic being, He is also subjected to the

dominion of an immutable necessity. It is plain that the same arguments which prove that God is the author of food, light, and life, prove Him also to be the author of poison, darkness, and death.

If the argument begins not from the doctrine of Necessity but from the reality of human suffering, it can be presented in the words of Hume:

> [Philo:] Why is there any misery at all in the world? Not by chance surely. From some cause then. Is it from the intention of the Deity? But he is perfectly benevolent. Is it contrary to his intention? But he is almighty. Nothing can shake the solidity of this reasoning, so short, so clear, so decisive; except we assert, that these subjects exceed all human capacity, and that our common measures of truth and falsehood are not applicable to them.[1]

It is clear that Milton might have evaded a critical scrutiny of God's providence as Philo suggests, by simply affirming that God, being the First Cause, acts according to his own will and pleasure and that there are no other values in terms of which the rightness or wrongness of His actions may be assessed. He might, that is to say, have echoed Daniel's Cleopatra:

> When yet our selues must be the cause we fall,
> Although the same be first decreed on hie:
> Our errors still must beare the blame of all,
> Thus must it be; earth, aske not heauen why.

But Milton clearly wished to justify the ways of God to men in a literal sense, and it is important to recognize that he fails in his de-clared purpose unless he can satisfy his readers of God's justice in the accepted meaning of the term. A remark of Mill's is exactly to the point—'I will call no being good who is not what I mean when I apply that epithet to my fellow-creatures; and if such a being can sentence me to hell for not so calling him, to hell I will go.'[2]

The difficulty confronting Milton can thus be very simply stated. God is omniscient and omnipotent: no concessions on these points can be contemplated. With this invariable condition Milton sets out to consider the following questions. First, was Adam acting as a free agent when he fell, since God already knew that he would in fact succumb to temptation? For Milton's purposes it is of course essential that the answer to this question should be 'Yes'. Assuming that it is, we can ask secondly whether there is any defence for God's allowing Adam to fall, although He had foreseen the fall and might have prevented it, and thirdly whether Satan was acting independently and not as an instrument of divine purpose when he seduced Eve. Once again Milton must elicit affirmative answers to these questions before he can go on to ask, fourthly, whether man is now free and, fifthly, whether God is good, that is, whether judged by the standards of human reason He now deals justly with mankind. Unless we find an affirmative answer for both these final questions Milton's theodicy has obviously failed.

Lying behind all these questions and occasionally coming to the surface of the poem is the more general question of God's purposes in creating Man and the whole universe. If for 'purposes' we read 'motives' the difficulty is even plainer, since the task is now to explain what forces could conceivably influence a Being who is omnipotent, or, to put it rather differently, where such forces could have their origin, since God was Himself all that existed. When Adam asks Raphael 'what cause/ Mov'd the Creator in his holy Rest/Through all Eternitie so late to build/In *Chaos*' (VII. 90‒3),[3] the question is, as Alastair Fowler observes, one of unanswerable naïveté.[4] God, when He speaks of His own actions, necessarily repudiates any cause except His own will, and affirms unambiguously His own sole responsibility for His creation:

> My overshadowing Spirit and might with thee
> I send along, ride forth, and bid the Deep
> Within appointed bounds be Heav'n and Earth,
> Boundless the Deep, because I am who fill
> Infinitude, nor vacuous the space.
> Though I uncircumscrib'd my self retire,
> And put not forth my goodness, which is free
> To act or not, Necessitie and Chance
> Approach not mee, and what I will is Fate.   (VII. 165‒73)

With the primary condition of God's omnipotence thus prominently written in to the poem what is Milton's strategy for inducing the desired answers to the five questions which I have listed?

For a plain statement of Milton's case we need look no further than the beginning of Book X:

> [God] Assembl'd Angels, and ye Powers return'd
> From unsuccessful charge, be not dismaid,
> Nor troubl'd at these tidings from the Earth,
> Which your sincerest care could not prevent,
> Foretold so lately what would come to pass,
> When first this Tempter cross'd the Gulf from Hell
> I told ye then he should prevail and speed
> On his bad Errand, Man should be seduc't
> And flatter'd out of all, believing lies
> Against his Maker; no Decree of mine
> Concurring to necessitate his Fall,
> Or touch with lightest moment of impulse
> His free Will, to her own inclining left
> In even scale.   (34‒47)

If this can be accepted at its face value it solves all the problems. Adam and Eve were created free. They weighed God's prohibition against Satan's temptations, and chose freely to do what Satan advised. God's punishment is therefore just. But there are bound to be objections raised, which Milton must meet. In particular God knows certainly that Satan will seduce Eve and that Adam in turn will sin. How is this compatible with the repeated statements that Adam was acting freely when he fell? The necessary argument is expounded at length by God in Book III:

> Onely begotten Son, seest thou what rage
> Transports our adversarie, whom no bounds
> Prescrib'd, no barrs of Hell, nor all the chains
> Heapt on him there, nor yet the main Abyss
> Wide interrupt can hold; so bent he seems
> On desperat revenge, that shall redound
> Upon his own rebellious head. And now
> Through all restraint broke loose he wings his way
> Not farr off Heav'n, in the Precincts of light,
> Directly towards the new created World,
> And Man there plac't, with purpose to assay
> If him by force he can destroy, or worse,
> By som false guile pervert; and shall pervert;
> For man will heark'n to his glozing lyes,
> And easily transgress the sole Command,
> Sole pledge of his obedience: So will fall
> Hee and his faithless Progenie: whose fault?
> Whose but his own? ingrate, he had of mee
> All he could have; I made him just and right,
> Sufficient to have stood, though free to fall.
> Such I created all th'Ethereal Powers
> And Spirits, both them who stood & them who faild;
> Freely they stood who stood, and fell who fell.
> Not free, what proof could they have givn sincere
> Of true allegiance, constant Faith or Love,
> Where onely what they needs must do, appeard,
> Not what they would? what praise could they receive?
> What pleasure I from such obedience paid,
> When Will and Reason (Reason also is choice)
> Useless and vain, of freedom both despoild,
> Made passive both, had servd necessitie,
> Not mee. They therefore as to right belongd
> So were created, nor can justly accuse
> Thir maker, or thir making, or thir Fate;
> As if Predestination over-rul'd
> Thir will, dispos'd by absolute Decree
> Or high foreknowledge; they themselves decreed
> Thir own revolt, not I: if I foreknew,
> Foreknowledge had no influence on their fault,

Which had no less prov'd certain unforeknown.
So without least impulse or shadow of Fate,
Or aught by me immutablie foreseen,
They trespass, Authors to themselves in all
Both what they judge and what they choose; for so
I formed them free, and free they must remain,
Till they enthrall themselves: I else must change
Thir nature, and revoke the high Decree
Unchangeable, Eternal, which ordain'd
Thir freedom, they themselves ordain'd thir fall.
The first sort by thir own suggestion fell,
Self-tempted, self-deprav'd: Man falls deceiv'd
By the other first: Man therefore shall find grace,
The other none: in Mercy and Justice both,
Through Heav'n and Earth, so shall my glorie excel,
But Mercy first and last shall brightest shine.   (80–134)

This is the clearest statement in the poem. It rests on the phrase
'without . . . aught by me immutablie foreseen' (120–1). Only if
some meaning can be attached to this can we avoid the conclusion
that God had ordained Adam's fall, or, at best, had known that he
would certainly be unable to resist temptation but had nevertheless allowed him to encounter it. We need not perhaps completely
agree with Empson's comment, 'What would have happened if
Adam and Eve had irritated God by refusing to do what he foreknew is too horrible to imagine',[5] but we must at least wonder why
Milton raises the problem if he is not prepared to offer an answer
to it. What is, of course, obvious in the passage I have quoted is
God's readiness to intermingle past, present, and future tenses, so
that he can discuss man as if he had already fallen.[6] Similarly
Divine syntax permits, indeed encourages, a steady ambiguity
about whether God is discussing the fall of the angels, the fall of
man, or both at once. The effect of these devices is to take the
reader's attention at this point in the poem away from the Fall as a
prospective event which will inevitably take place at some later
point in the poem, and to encourage him to think of it as in the past
and inevitable in the sense that what has already happened cannot
be avoided. Then, of course, there is no point in asking whether it
'might have been' avoided: the obviously sensible thing to do is to
concern oneself with its present consequences.

If then Milton is able to impose the Divine perspective in this
way, it is possible to accept God's assurance that Adam was free,
and, if we accept that, there is little difficulty in agreeing also that
God was right to create Man free, following the general argument
of Raphael in Book V, especially lines 519–43.

On the general question of whether God could in any sense have prevented the Fall four points should be taken into account. First, when Raphael is sent down to earth to warn Adam and Eve God instructs him in these terms:

>   Such discourse bring on
> As may advise him of his happie state,
> Happiness in his power left free to will,
> Left to his own free Will, his Will though free,
> Yet mutable, whence warne him to beware
> He swerve not too secure: tell him withall
> His danger, and from whom, what enemie
> Late falln himself from Heaven, is plotting now
> The fall of others from like state of bliss;
> By violence, no, for that shall be withstood,
> But by deceit and lies; this let him know,
> Least wilfully transgressing he pretend
> Surprisal, unadmonisht, unforewarnd.   (v. 233–45)

But Raphael's voyage is notably ineffective in safeguarding Adam. If anything he makes it easier for Satan to seduce Eve. Secondly, according to the Argument to Book V, God's motive in sending Raphael was 'to render Man inexcusable'. Thirdly, God has already prevented His angels from arresting Satan (IV. 977–1015), but Raphael does not warn Adam and Eve explicitly that Satan is at large and has evil designs on them. Finally, evidence of rather a different kind is presented by the beginning of Book IV:

> O for that warning voice, which he who saw
> Th'*Apocalyps*, heard cry in Heav'n aloud,
> Then when the Dragon, put to second rout,
> Came furious down to be reveng'd on men,
> *Wo to the inhabitants on Earth!* that now,
> While time was, our first Parents had bin warnd
> The coming of thir secret foe, and scap'd
> Haply so scap'd his mortal snare.   (1–8)

This suggests that a timely warning might have been given.

Satan, thus operating by Divine permission, seems to be operating by Divine intention: it is hard to feel that Eve is wrong when she describes him as 'a foe by doom express assigned us'. Yet, if God is to be seen as truly just, it is essential that Satan should not appear in the poem merely as the instrument which God uses to damn mankind. In what sense then can we say that Satan is presented as a free agent? The first point to notice is that God is *ex hypothesi* in complete command of all his creation: in particular the fallen angels act against mankind only by 'the will/And high permission of all-ruling Heaven'. In Book II Belial states the position truly:

> for what can force or guile
> With him, or who deceive his mind, whose eye
> Views all things at one view? he from heav'ns highth
> All these our motions vain, sees and derides;
> Not more Almighty to resist our might
> Then wise to frustrate all our plots and wiles.   (188–93)

Abdiel in Book V insists on Satan's impotence to defy the doom of God:

> O alienate from God, O spirit accurst,
> Forsak'n of all good; I see thy fall
> Determind, and thy hapless crew involv'd
> In this perfidious fraud, contagion spred
> Both of thy crime and punishment: henceforth
> No more be troubled how to quit the yoke
> Of Gods *Messiah*: those indulgent Laws
> Will not now be voutsaf't, other Decrees
> Against thee are gon forth without recall;   (874–82)

Satan leaves Hell only by God's leave (VIII. 237) and remains at liberty only because of His intervention (IV. 977 ff.) This then is the problem which confronted Milton, that Satan had to be represented as under the control of God, deriving from Him all his power and wielding it only by His will and high permission, and at the same time as capable of interfering disastrously with His plans. The only way in which Milton can present Satan as a convincing menace to the will of God is by not indicating the precise nature of God's power over and precautions against him, and risking the obvious danger that the reader will feel unsatisfied because the relation between the central antagonists is never defined.

While the conflicts and excitements of dualism offer much more scope to the writer of epic than the austerities of Christian theology, Milton was of course bound to avoid any suspicion of constructing his poem on a dualist basis. Indeed, as we have seen, he several times states, with complete orthodoxy, the total subordination of his Satan to His God. But these explicit statements are undermined by the structure of the poem. For the first two books the driving force of the action is the will of Satan. This becomes a reality to the reader, who accepts Satan as a free agent from the outset. Thereafter however scrupulously Milton affirms God's omnipotence it is hard not to think of Satan as directly responsible for the Fall in defiance of God's designs.

Satan is thus given extraordinary prominence and power. Helen Gardner has well compared his appeal to the reader with that of Macbeth or Faustus or Beatrice-Joanna.[7] In confirmation one might note that Chaucer's *Monk's Tale*, which tells the great tragic stories

of the world, begins with the story of Lucifer. Again, when Satan
tempts Eve in Book IX what he is offering her is essentially *virtú*, in
the sense which I have described in my discussion of Marlowe. He
begins by claiming, with all the pride of the Renaissance, that he
understands 'things in their causes' (682), declares that he has
himself gone beyond his Fate and ventured higher than his Fortune
(689–90) and incites Eve to a display of 'dauntless virtue' by which
she shall attain universal knowledge and freedom from fear—'Ye
shall be as gods,/Knowing both good and evil as they know' (708–9).
In this way Milton achieves with ease his end of making Satan
credible as an independent agent, but only at the cost of identifying
him in the reader's mind with personages of great power.

The misconstructions that attend on this are too well-known to
require notice: one other consequence is perhaps less obvious, that
in order to guard against the heretical ascription to Satan of
autonomy Milton must clearly represent him as being subject to
Divine control, yet the more convincingly he does this the more
difficult it becomes for the reader to continue to believe in the free
will of Adam and Eve, since God seems to have engineered and
authorized a temptation which will, He knows, be too powerful for
them to resist. Moreover the tempter is depicted as an agency outside them acting under the control of God, while the forces of resistance are interior and God continually insists that they are not
under His control and that He has no responsibility for them.

Hence Milton's strategy must be directed initially to preventing
the reader from asking precisely how free Satan is. This is achieved
with almost excessive thoroughness in Books I and II, which determine the reader's mind on the matter before he is aware that there
is even a problem. Similarly the awkwardness of reconciling God's
foreknowledge and Man's freedom is circumvented by placing
God's account of His proceedings very early in the poem, at the
beginning of Book III, once again before the reader knows
precisely what conduct the Almighty is justifying. God's exculpa-
tion of Himself would sound rather differently at the beginning of
Book XI for instance. Thus the events of the Creation and the War
in Heaven are necessarily postponed in the poem until the massive
flashback in Books V–VIII. Book IX begins, like the *Troilus*, by
looking forward to the tragic fall, thus emphasizing its inevitability.
This book illustrates with especial clarity a point that is true of
Paradise Lost as a whole, that it impresses a modern reader as
being inverted or inside out. Milton throughout argues violently
and in detail in favour of free will (which most modern readers
would be prepared to concede as a primary fact of individual experience), but in fact proffers a Universe which proves on examination to be totally determined by the will of God (a view of the

world for which most modern readers would require a closely-argued justification).

So much for the temptation of Eve and of Adam. I am aware that I have covered no new territory, for critic after critic has recognized the fundamental importance of the three questions confronting Milton here. Rather less attention has been paid to the consequences of the Fall, but these are what we must next examine if we are to consider Milton's answer to the question, 'Does God now treat men justly?'

II DAMNATION AND SALVATION

> Ah, why should all mankind
> For one mans fault thus guiltless be condemn'd,
> If guiltless? But from mee what can proceed,
> But all corrupt, both Mind and Will deprav'd,
> Not to do onely, but to will the same
> With me; how can they acquitted stand
> In sight of God?   (x. 822–8)

Adam's reluctant admission that his sin is inevitably entailed on his descendants is a crucial step in Milton's justification of God, but is bound to provoke a further question: if men since Adam have been infected by original sin and burdened with total depravity, have they any real freedom? In a sense it is matter for scholastic dispute whether God created the Universe freely or Satan was a free agent or Adam freely chose to sin: what matters to us and what mattered to Milton is whether man is free now. It is this living question which lies behind and animates the extended discussions of election in the poem.

From the premise that God is Omnipotent and Omniscient the hard-line Calvinist or Gomarist doctrine of election emerges as a logical conclusion. To convey this as vividly as possible I quote first from the Westminster Confession and Larger Catechism:

> [Chapter ix] I. God hath indued the Will of man with that natural liberty, that is neither forced, nor by any absolute necessity of nature determined to do good or evil.
> II. Man, in his state of innocency, had freedom, and power, to will, and to do that which was good, and well-pleasing to God; but yet mutably, so that he might fall from it.

Fallen man has lost all ability to will his own spiritual good and is entirely dependent on God's aid. Only God by His grace allows man to will good, but even so man, being corrupt, wills evil also.

Chapter X deals with matters of salvation and distinguishes first of all those 'whom God hath predestined unto life'. These, and these only, are called to Grace through Christ, and this effectual call owes nothing to anything in the men themselves who are 'altogether passive therein'. Section IV describes those who are 'not elected, although they may be called by the Ministry of the Word, and may have some common operations of the Spirit'. They cannot be saved, much less men who do not even profess Christianity 'be they never so diligent to frame their lives according to the light of Nature, and the Law of that Religion, they do professe'. Chapter XI emphasizes that the elect are not infused with righteousness but are accepted as righteous by God 'not for any thing wrought in them, or done by them, but for Christs sake alone'. Even their faith 'they have, not of themselves, it is the gift of God'. Section IV of the same chapter states simply 'God did, from all eternity, decree to justify all the Elect', while the second section of chapter XVII makes it plain that the 'perseverance of the Saints depends not upon their own free-will, but upon the immutability of the Decree of Election, flowing from the free and unchangeable love of God the Father . . . and the nature of the Covenant of Grace: from which ariseth also the certainty, and infallibility thereof'.

The Larger Catechism states the same doctrine with equal force and clarity:

> Q. *Are the Elect effectually called?*
> All the Elect, and they only, are effectually called, although others may be, and often are, outwardly called by the ministry of the word, and have some common operations of the Spirit, who for their wilful neglect and contempt of the grace offered to them, being justly left in their unbelief, do never truly come to Jesus Christ.

An orthodox expansion of this position some eighty years later is found in Jonathan Edwards' sermon preached at Enfield, Connecticut in 1741 on the text from Deuteronomy 32: 35, 'Their foot shall slide in due time.'

> The observation from the words that I would now insist upon is this. —'There is nothing that keeps wicked men at any moment out of hell, but the mere pleasure of God.'—By the *mere* pleasure of God, I mean his *sovereign* pleasure, his arbitrary will, restrained by no obligation, hindered by no manner of difficulty, any more than if nothing else but God's mere will had in the least degree, or in any respect whatsoever, any hand in the preservation of wicked men one moment.

Edwards advances ten arguments in support of this position:

> 2. They *deserve* to be cast into hell; so that divine justice never stands in the way, it makes no objection against God's using his power at any

moment to destroy them. Yea, on the contrary, justice calls aloud for an infinite punishment of their sins. Divine justice says of the tree that brings forth such grapes of Sodom, 'Cut it down, why cumbereth it the ground?', Luke xiii. 7. The sword of divine justice is every moment brandished over their heads, and it is nothing but the hand of arbitrary mercy, and God's mere will, that holds it back.

3. They are already under a sentence of *condemnation* to hell. They do not only justly deserve to be cast down thither, but the sentence of the law of God, that eternal and immutable rule of righteousness that God has fixed between him and mankind, is gone out against them, and stands against them, so that they are bound over already to hell. John iii. 18, 'He that believeth not is condemned already.' So that every unconverted man properly belongs to hell; that is his place; from thence he is. John viii. 23, 'Ye are from beneath.' And thither he is bound; it is the place that justice, and God's word, and the sentence of his unchangeable law assign to him.

He concludes the first part of his sermon as follows:

> So that, thus it is that natural men are held in the hand of God, over the pit of hell; they have deserved the fiery pit, and are already sentenced to it; and God is dreadfully provoked, his anger is as great towards them as to those that are actually suffering the executions of the fierceness of his wrath in hell, and they have done nothing in the least to appease or abate that anger, neither is God in the least bound by any promise to hold them up one moment; the devil is waiting for them, hell is gaping for them, the flames gather and flash about them, and would fain lay hold on them, and swallow them up; the fire bent up in their own hearts is struggling to break out: and they have no interest in any Mediator, there are no means within reach that can be any security to them. In short, they have no refuge, nothing to take hold of; all that preserves them every moment is the mere arbitrary will, and uncovenanted, unobliged forbearance of an incensed God.

Towards the end of the sermon Edwards gives this warning:

> God seems now to be hastily gathering in his elect in all parts of the land; and probably the greater part of adult persons that ever shall be saved, will be brought in now in a little time, and that it will be as it was on the great out-pouring of the Spirit upon the Jews in the apostles' days; the election will obtain, and the rest will be blinded.

I have said that this doctrine that those who are to be saved are already chosen and those who are not are already damned is the logical extension of the given premises about the nature of God and man, but I am aware that this statement would not pass unchallenged. Consider for example God's comment on the fallen angels quoted earlier:

they themselves decreed
Thir own revolt, not I: if I foreknew,
Foreknowledge had no influence on their fault,
Which had no less prov'd certain unforeknown.   (III. 116–19)

On this passage Fowler has the following note.

> *De doctrina* i 4 shows that Milton believed in a liberal version of the
> doctrine of Predestination, but that he carefully defined predestination
> and foreknowledge in such a way as to exclude 'necessity' or deter-
> minism. See, e.g. Columbia [*Works*, ed. F. A. Patterson, (1931–8)], xiv
> 85: 'Future events which God has foreseen, will happen certainly . . .
> because the divine prescience cannot be deceived, but they will not
> happen necessarily, because prescience can have no influence on the
> object foreknown, inasmuch as it is only an intransitive action.'

It is helpful to look at these three slightly varying statements of
the position. The beginning of the quotation from the *de Doctrina*
is, as we have seen from Boethius, irrefutable, but there is a
sophistry in the second half. Milton maintains quite correctly that
it is not the act of foreknowing which necessitates, yet if the event
will certainly happen as foreknown then it will necessarily happen
as foreknown. The fact that it can be foreknown at all puts it in the
category of actions which must occur.[8]

The passage from *Paradise Lost* makes the same point and fails to
meet the same objection. God defends himself from the charge of
foreordaining by foreknowing, but in doing so concedes the more
serious, because more general, charge that the revolt of the angels
was certain to happen and therefore the angels were not free to
refrain from revolting. Their fall is a matter of 'absolute decree'
(115) rather than one of 'high foreknowledge' (116). Once more
foreknowledge enters into the argument because it is a proof of
foreordaining, though not in itself a necessitating agent.

Fowler's note then will not do as it stands. Foreknowledge cannot
be defined so as to exclude determinism, for it is itself a proof of a
determined future. If therefore God's foreknowledge in the matter
of salvation is admitted then the doctrine of predestination itself
must be admitted, and if the doctrine is held at all it can only mean
that it is already determined who shall be saved and who damned.
Thus there is no 'liberal version of the doctrine of predestination'.

But the strict doctrine immediately presents serious difficulties.
There is the obvious danger that the elect may be guilty of antinomianism: the terrifying possibilities are fully exploited in Hogg's
Confessions of a Justified Sinner. An even more worrying problem
for a religion that wished to bring the Kingdom of the Saints into
this world was that if damnation and salvation were already decided there was no incentive to virtuous behaviour. But Jonathan

Edwards' sermon was preached with a moral end, that of frightening the wicked into abandoning their wickedness, which implies that a man's conduct in this life has some bearing on his destiny in the hereafter.

Similarly the Westminster Confession, although offering no hope to those not already elected, is at pains to provide what sanctions it can against misconduct on the part of the unregenerate:

> Chapter xv   III. Although repentance is not to be rested in as any satisfaction for sin, or any cause of the pardon thereof, which is the act of God's free grace in Christ, yet is it of such necessity to all sinners, that none may expect pardon without it.
>
> Chapter xvi   VI. Yet notwithstanding, the Persons of Believers being accepted through Christ, their good works also are accepted in him, not as though they were in this life wholly unblameable and unreproveable in God's sight; but that, he looking upon them in his Son, is pleased to accept, and reward that which is sincere, although accompanied with many weaknesses and imperfections.
>
> VII. Works done by unregenerate men, although, for the matter of them, they may be things which God commends, and of good use both to themselves, and others: yet, because they proceed not from an heart purified by faith; nor are done in the right manner, according to the Word; nor, to a right end, the glory of God; they are therefore sinfull, and cannot please God, or make a man meet to receive grace from God. And yet, their neglect of them is more sinfull, and displeasing unto God.

Thus even in the more strictly guarded sanctuaries of the Calvinist faith Milton could point to certain expedient modifications of the narrow doctrine of the inutility of works.

These modifications he exploits to the full in God's central discussion of grace and salvation in Book III:

> To whom [Christ] the great Creatour thus reply'd.
> O Son, in whom my Soul hath chief delight,
> Son of my bosom, Son who art alone
> My Word, my wisdom, and effectual might,
> All hast thou spok'n as my thoughts are, all   171
> As my Eternal purpose hath decreed:
> Man shall not quite be lost, but sav'd who will,
> Yet not of will in him, but grace in me
> Freely voutsaft; once more I will renew   175
> His lapsed powers, though forfeit and enthrall'd
> By sin to foul exorbitant desires;
> Upheld by me, yet once more he shall stand
> On even ground against his mortal foe,
> By me upheld, that he may know how frail
> His fall'n condition is, and to me ow
> All his deliv'rance, and to none but me.

Some I have chosen of peculiar grace   183
Elect above the rest; so is my will:
The rest shall hear me call, and oft be warnd
Thir sinful state, and to appease betimes
Th'incensed Deitie while offerd grace
Invites; for I will cleer thir senses dark,
What may suffice, and soft'n stonie hearts
To pray, repent, and bring obedience due.
To prayer, repentance, and obedience due,
Though but endevord with sincere intent,
Mine eare shall not be slow, mine eye not shut.
And I will place within them as a guide
My Umpire *Conscience*, whom if they will hear,
Light after light well us'd they shall attain,
And to the end persisting, safe arrive.   197
This my long sufferance and my day of Grace
They who neglect and scorn, shall never taste;
But hard be hard'nd, blind be blinded more,
That they may stumble on, and deeper fall;
And none but such from mercy I exclude.   (167–202)

Especially in lines 183 to 197 Milton seems to be suggesting the
possibility of an escape from the rigidity of Calvinist doctrine, so
that the speech is much more Arminian than Gomarist in impression yet it leaves Milton uncommitted on the vital points of difference. How is this done?

The first, and obviously essential step is to abstain entirely from
all overt indication that God's foreknowledge operates here, otherwise it would be impossible, as we have seen above, to present men
as freely accepting or rejecting God's grace.[9]

The next and most important device is a verbal one. In the introduction to his edition of *Paradise Lost* Alastair Fowler lists the following qualities of God's conversation, 'The high level of abstraction: the sustained abstention from imagery, except the very
simplest and least sensuous: the calm freedom from unresolved
emotional expressions' (p. 453).[10] But if we look at the passage in
question, this is no longer true.[11] The way in which God speaks
with a double voice is plain from lines 171–5. 'All hast thou spok'n
as my thoughts are, all/As my Eternal purpose hath decreed'
sounds like the foundation for a rigid predestinarian doctrine, but
God immediately adds, 'Man shall not quite be lost, but sav'd who
will.' This suggests that He is about to lay down conditions for salvation which will ultimately depend on man's prayer, repentance
and obedience, but He at once reverts to a more orthodox Calvinist
position, saying 'Yet not of will in him, but Grace in me/Freely
voutsaft.' This doctrine is developed in the next section of the

speech, in which God states his intention that man shall know 'how frail/His fall'n condition is, and to me ow/All his deliv'rance, and to none but me'.

God next distinguishes the different destinies of men. It is easy enough to understand the first category 'chosen of peculiar grace/ Elect above the rest' by the mere will of God: these are the Saints. The last category—that of the hardened sinners (198–202)—is equally straightforward. But in between there is a third group who will eventually 'safe arrive'. The problem is to know whether they do so as a consequence of their own exertions or by the exercise of divine grace.[12]

I offer first a paraphrase of the passage (185–97) which attempts to eliminate all the metaphors replacing them by the phrases in italics. 'The rest of mankind *shall be conscious* that they are sinful and that they should placate me while there is still time; for I will ensure that their senses are sufficiently clear to understand this and *will remove their inclinations* not to pray, repent, and be obedient. If they even sincerely try to do this I *shall notice* (or, *I shall give them as much credit as if they had succeeded*). And I will ensure that they shall always know right from wrong by their Conscience. If they always do right, and thus show that they are taking advantage of my guidance, *they will advance steadily in understanding*, and, if they persist to the end, *be saved*.'

The main body of the paraphrase is straightforward enough: only the phrases I have italicized present a difficulty. In each case the difficulty is of the same kind, a metaphor which cannot be accurately reduced to a statement of doctrine. 'Hear me call' is easily interpreted as 'know that I am offering them my grace', which presumably means 'know that they have an opportunity to be saved if they wish to be saved'. This would be perfectly acceptable to an Arminian, but not to a Gomarist. 'Soften stony hearts' defies literal translation. It might mean 'dispose men to repent etc.' or 'so alter men's dispositions that they actually do repent etc'. I cannot choose between the two possible meanings of the next italicized phrase. 'Light after light well us'd they shall attain' is obviously a promise of something good to come. The light to be attained is presumably equivalent to the safe arrival of the following line, while the light that must first be correctly employed is presumably the guidance of Conscience which must be heeded and obeyed. But the phrase 'light well us'd' is simply a compact expression of the basic ambiguity. Heavenly Grace and human effort are both required for salvation: Milton is careful not to indicate what factors will determine whether a man will or will not make a sufficient effort to take advantage of the chance of salvation, whether these factors are under divine or human control, and, as I have said earlier, whether God knows which men will in fact achieve salvation in this way.

The effect of all these 'unresolved emotional expressions' is to make it impossible to decide from the speech whether the crucial element in a man's salvation is Divine grace, or whether Milton is here relaxing his puritan orthodoxy and maintaining that at the end of the day the essential distinction between the saved and the damned is not the vouchsafing of God's grace (which is available to all, whatever that means). This poised vocabulary, in which the metaphors are carefully chosen so that they imply the second while remaining formally consistent with the first interpretation, is of course a small reflection of an ambiguity which we have seen written large in the structure of the poem.

Milton's motives here are not hard to understand, for if he states clearly and without any counterbalance that man is saved or damned by the mere will of God he is confronted with the task of justifying to his readers a scheme of preordained election and reprobation which bears no relation to belief or conduct. Alternatively if men can save themselves by their own exertions it is no longer possible to sustain a belief in the omnipotence of God. Had Milton been required to adopt explicitly one or other of these doctrines as the basis of his poem, he would presumably have chosen the former.

When, later in Book III, God says to Christ

> Be thou in *Adams* room
> The Head of all mankind, though *Adams* Son.
> As in him perish all men, so in thee
> As from a second root shall be restor'd
> As many as are restor'd, without thee none.
> His crime makes guiltie all his Sons, thy merit
> Imputed shall absolve them who renounce
> Thir own *both righteous and unrighteous deeds*,
> And live in thee transplanted, and from thee
> Receive new life.   (285–94; my italics in 292)

the idea that salvation depends on the renunciation even of righteous human works can only be accommodated in a Calvinist framework of justification. Nevertheless in Book III the second view is offered with sufficient prominence to ensure that God appears to be extending a valuable concession to mankind.

The same question receives rather similar treatment in Book XII. Michael emphasizes that man must conclude that Law is insufficient to remove sin and that

> Some bloud more precious must be paid for Man,
> Just for unjust, that in such righteousness
> To them by Faith imputed, they may finde
> Justification towards God, and peace
> Of Conscience, which the Law by Ceremonies
> Cannot appease, nor Man the moral part
> Perform, and not performing cannot live.   (293–9)

Later Michael tells Adam of the coming of the Saviour:

>   thy punishment
> He shall endure by coming in the Flesh
> To a reproachful life and cursed death,
> Proclaiming Life to all who shall believe
> In his redemption, and that his obedience
> Imputed becomes theirs by Faith, his merits
> To save them, not thir own, though legal works.(404–10)

Christ will pay the ransom

>   which Man from death redeems,
> His death for Man, as many as offerd Life
> Neglect not, and the benefit imbrace
> By Faith not void of workes.   (424–7)

In the last phrase Milton once again leaves the difficult question unresolved: it appears that faith unaccompanied by good works is here being described as insufficient to procure salvation, yet if challenged on this point Milton could point to a less precise meaning of the word 'works': 'We are justified by faith without the works of the law, but not without the works of faith' (*De doctrina* i. 22; Columbia xvi. 39), a distinction which he makes also in *Paradise Lost* (xii, 306).

But even if we grant that Books III and XII can be interpreted in the light of that passage we are bound to ask eventually whether God already knows which of Adam's descendants will not take advantage of his offered grace and, if He does, as He surely must,[13] we face the problem of understanding how a God who condemns people in advance can create a world in which the human will is truly free.

III RESPONSIBILITY

Clearly one could continue pointing to places in the poem where a close examination of the varying doctrines stated or implied about the freedom of Satan, of Adam and of his descendants reveals inconsistencies or contradictions.[14] These, if noticed, may be seen as difficulties which Milton must either explain away or conceal: at the very least he must distract the reader's attention from them. I should like to conclude my observations on Milton by suggesting seven possible ways of regarding these difficult points.

(a)   They do not exist: Milton says what the Bible says and this is true. Man should heed the injunction, 'Solicit not thy thoughts with matters hid.' If there are apparent inconsistencies this is only to be expected since all the great Christian truths are paradoxes (e.g. Christ is fully man and fully God: God is One Person and Three Persons). Whenever the reader encounters a difficulty the fault is his. I do not know if it is possible to take this view of the poem, though Stanley Fish's *Surprised by Sin* (1967) is not very far away from it:[15] if it is taken it renders criticism impossible, since it accepts the poem simply because of its coincidence with another source of values.

(b)   There are difficulties in the nature of God as presented in the Bible, and we can now see them clearly. Milton is not aware of them. He writes as if there were no difficulties, and thus unwittingly makes them more obvious and more troublesome. Without knowing it he is of the devil's party.

(c)   There is a difficulty in the traditional account of the Fall. Milton sees the difficulty and his poem offers an enlightened Christian resolution of it. In the poem we have the Fall presented to us as an actuality: we see Adam and Eve in the process of deliberating and making up their minds, and can no longer doubt Man's liberty and hence his responsibility. We are equally convinced of God's Justice and His Mercy. The poem thus dramatises the present relationship between God and Man.

It is in this group that one would put many of the most persuasive of modern writers on Milton such as C. S. Lewis, Douglas Bush, J. H. Summers, Dennis Burden, and Alastair Fowler.[16] Titles such as *The Muse's Method* and *The Logical Epic* convey the approach of these critics, who show, in Fowler's words, 'a new respect for the logical structure of *Paradise Lost*. When the poem is approached by this admittedly arduous route it takes on an authentic, challenging aspect. . . . When once the fruits of this kind of criticism have been tasted . . . there can never be uncertainty about Milton's overall artistic intention. . . . It is not just that we come to be sure of Milton's moral intention, his intention to justify the ways of God, but that we come to see this intention as worked out in the structure of *Paradise Lost* and in the details of its action. Almost throughout its extent, the poem is found to be theologically informed to a remarkable degree' (Introduction pp. 33–4).

(d)   There are difficulties. Milton is aware of them. He thinks that he has surmounted them. In fact he has only made them more obvious by making God semi-human, trying to account for His actions in terms of the motives that sway mankind, and thus inviting the reader to judge Him by quasi-legal standards. If you put God into the witness-box you are inviting the reader to cross-examine Him. Inevitably God stands condemned by human systems, or at best is reduced to exculpating himself by the sterile ingenuities of the court-room, thus justifying Pope's critical comment—'In quibbles, angel and archangel join,/And God the Father turns a school-divine.' Once again Milton by totally miscalculating the direction of the reader's sympathies has strengthened the case of the devil's party. A. J. A. Waldock's *Paradise Lost and its Critics* (1947) shows how strongly this case may be argued.

(e)   There are difficulties. Milton is aware of them. He deliberately pretends to have overcome them, but he knows all the time that he is making God into a monster. He is knowingly anti-Christian. 'The poem, if read with understanding, must be read with growing horror unless you decide to reject its God. But it seems to me that C. S. Lewis was also right when he protested that this is merely the traditional Christian God. . . . The Christian God the Father, the God of Tertullian, Augustine and Aquinas, is the wickedest thing yet invented by the black heart of man. . . . If you praise [the poem] as the neo-Christians do, what you are getting from it is evil.' These quotations from *Milton's God* by William Empson summarise the conclusions he reaches after a formidable analysis of the poem's ambiguities and contradictions.

(f)   There is a difficulty. Milton was aware of it, but he had schooled his mind, like a professional pleader, to see all round a question without understanding or caring that one view might be intrinsically sounder than another, as opposed to being merely more expedient. Therefore he is not concerned with the question of whether God is in fact justified. Milton is a pamphleteer still, ready to represent with great technical skill the point of view of his party, which is, broadly, the Puritans. His poem is written to sell the public a justified God, which is a pity, since this is the most unpromising line to take, especially for a man of Milton's imaginative power and his experiences. Thus Eve, Adam and Satan are more sympathetically presented than is altogether consistent with Milton's commission to defend Divine authoritarianism.

In other words he is professionally employed to argue the case for one side, but other views, such as that Adam and Eve needed to know Good and Evil before they could be truly free,[17] and that innocence is less valuable than experience, appealed to him with great emotional and intellectual power, as we may see most obviously from the *Areopagitica*. Thus Milton is always making out a case against his own deepest intuitions, either by fudging the facts and blurring the issues to disguise an incongruity (hence the much-criticized vagueness of his diction) or by indulging in rhetoric to conceal the weak places in his argument (hence the much-criticized inflation of his diction).

(g)   The poem is of a complexity far too intricate and integral to be comprehended by describing it solely in terms of Christian ortho-doxy. In particular the literary critic requires an approach which places the difficulties not as blemishes but as essential parts of the poem. One might for example argue that Milton willingly accepts the difficulties in the Christian doctrine of an Omnipotent God be-cause he is not concerned with the literal truth of Genesis but with its potentialities as myth. It is plain that, to consider the most ob-vious instance, the figures of Sin and Death have an allegorical sig-nificance. The question is how far into the poem an allegorical interpretation can be pressed.[18] How far, in other words, should we try to take *Paradise Lost* as being a poem not about Christian belief but about human life in the world? The first step must be to eliminate a transcendant God and to treat him as a figure for 'that general law which is the origin of everything, and under which everything acts', to employ Milton's own expression from *De Doctrina Christiana*.[19] 'God' would thus be a term for the immutable and all-compelling force which is not man and for which the most compact secular expression is 'Nature'. Indeed, on this basis, every-thing in the poem, except Adam and Eve, would represent a differ-ent manifestation of Nature, Satan for example presumably standing for all those elements in the universe which induce man to act in a way contrary to his best interests.

This vague equivalence can be made rather more precise if con-siderable weight is given to the exchange between Abdiel and Satan at the end of Book V. Abdiel grounds his reprobation of Satan on God's undoubted right to do as he pleases with His Creation:

> Shalt thou give Law to God, shalt thou dispute
> With him the points of libertie, who made
> Thee what thou art, and formd the Pow'rs of Heav'n
> Such as he pleasd, and circumscrib'd thir being?   (819–22)

Satan's reply is a proud affirmation of his own independent exis-tence:

> We know no time when we were not as now;
> Know none before us, self-begot, self-rais'd
> By our own quick'ning power. . . .

5

> Our puissance is our own, our own right hand
> Shall teach us highest deeds, by proof to try
> Who is our equal: (856–8, 861–3)

At the root of the Fall of the Angels and, though not so obviously, of the fall of man lies the assertion of self-creation and the denial of any external authority. The quality which is almost invariably associated with Satan's rejection of God is 'disdain', a 'sense of injured merit', or the anger arising from offended dignity.[20] He refuses to admit that he is subservient to any powers. Once again Abdiel explains Satan's false view of the world:

> Unjustly thou deprav'st it with the name
> Of *Servitude* to serve whom God ordains,
> Or Nature; God and Nature bid the same,
> When he who rules is worthiest, and excells
> Them whom he governs. This is servitude,
> To serve th' unwise, or him who hath rebelld
> Against his worthier, as thine now serve thee,
> Thy self not free, but to thy self enthrall'd; (VI. 174–81)

Man's resistance to the temptation to suppose that he can set himself up against the power that created him must come from within. He knows that he breaks Nature's laws at his peril and if he does so will suffer. If he puts his hand in the fire it will be burned. What happens is inevitable and at the same time his own fault. God's foreknowledge, on this reading, would be a figure for the predictability of any completely determined system.

As I have suggested, the actual choice which Eve makes is hardly with any precision of language to be described as a free choice.[21] Adam similarly is not completely free since he is already deeply committed to Eve. Yet beyond any doubt their two acts of choice are the centre of the poem: in terms of the allegory this would represent the crucial importance in human life of human acts of choice, whether these are in fact free or not. But if we assume that God in the poem is in some way representative of nature, then the poem also asserts the omnipresence and inviolability of natural law.

This, I suggest, corresponds to what many readers discover in the poem—that it is dedicated to the demonstration and justification of a system of complete authority, yet nevertheless insists throughout on the reality of the freedom of the human will. At the heart of its greatness is this fundamental truth about the nature of man: it holds in tension two incompatible views of freedom, just as most of its readers do in their own lives. The various problems or difficulties or inconsistencies or paradoxes that I have mentioned are maintained in the poem not as unresolved contradictions but as metaphors for this central ambiguity. The nature of the ambiguity is closely defined by Milton's choice of fable, which focuses the reader's attention on the act of choosing, on the significance of free choice and in particular on the difficulty of explaining what a free action is. It is, for example, important for Milton's purposes to establish that acting through self-love is not freedom but bondage, that 'true Libertie . . . alwayes with right Reason dwells/Twinn'd, and from her hath no dividual being', since what takes the place of the controlling reason is not liberty but 'inordinate desires/And upstart Passions' which 'to servitude reduce/Man till then free' (XII. 83–90), and that the will of man is unconstrained by God, or nature, or Fate, or necessity, or Destinie (V. 520–34). Similarly Adam and Eve after the Fall lose the solace of individuality, which was the basis of salvation before, and learn that salvation is to be found jointly, that is, by mutual effort and comfort. At the end of the poem Raphael praises Adam for acknowledging Christ the Redeemer:

> This having learnt, thou hast attaind the summe
> Of wisdom . . . . only add
> Deeds to thy knowledge answerable, add Faith,
> Add Vertue, Patience, Temperance, add Love,
> By name to come call'd Charitie, the soul
> Of all the rest: then wilt thou not be loath
> To leave this Paradise, but shalt possess
> A Paradise within thee, happier farr.   (XII. 575 . . . 587)

This view of the difficulties has at least the merit that it treats them as an integral part of the poem and not as a series of extra-poetic hazards through which Milton has to pick his way before he can even being writing his poem. But there remains as an objection to this and to almost every other allegorical interpretation that two terms—salvation and grace—are very hard to consider as being figures for something else. It would, for example clearly be inadequate to treat salvation as standing for some kind of secular achievement: apart from anything else the nature of the success would have to be defined, and Milton gives us no materials for such a definition. If then we wish to translate salvation into secular terms we are left with some such expression as 'what a man becomes, either through his own efforts, or because of what happens ot him'. Grace would presumably correspond to 'gifts of nature' or, since it is often contrasted with human will, something like 'luck'. Both terms tend to become, like the forbidden fruit, a symbol without content.

In fact, however, 'salvation' and 'grace' are concepts which strongly resist allegorizing if the process entails emptying them of particular significance. They insist tenaciously on a specific theological meaning and a specific sense of promise, and the promise is not one that can be in any sense fulfilled in this world: I do not see how it can be interpreted in secular terms. The fact that these key expressions cannot be transposed prevents the poem from turning into an allegory like *A Tale of a Tub* in which the literal sense of the story is entirely absorbed in and eventually superseded by the figurative. This in turn means that while the poem carries a full weight of significance for men confronted with the world here and now, it is not to be demythologized into a purely secular description of human nature. Once again Milton contrives to hold in tension, but in an uneasy tension, two opposed views of man's relation with what is not man.

What then, to put the matter as bluntly as possible, are we able to infer from *Paradise Lost* about the nature and the extent of human freedom? It will be plain from what I have said that Milton presents the reader with an account of human freedom which, although stated with great emphasis and positiveness, is heavily qualified by the action of the poem. It exists within the framework and by the permission of an overriding authority, and the use a man makes of such freedom as he has may be determined by agencies outside him. Its exercise will be punished by the severest punishments which are conceivable if the consequences offend that authority: the possibility is nevertheless left open that it is only by risking such exercise that man can realize his complete nature. Hence choosing with a consciousness of irrevocable commitment is enormously important: the whole poem is directed against levity of choice. Milton, in short, like Kierkegaard, defines freedom as a kind of responsibility or burden. Whether an attribute so ambiguous and circumscribed is rightly called freedom is a question we must not expect to be able to answer simply by inspection of the poem.

Milton's achievement in the poem is not one of reconciliation or synthesis: it is to hold together in the grip of his narrative a succession of contrarieties about man, his will, the world he lives in, the laws by which he lives in the world, and his intuitions of possible better worlds. The poem insists at once on freedom as an essential human attribute and on the necessity of obedience, on the central responsibility of the individual and on the vital importance of subordinating the individual to some larger loyalty in order to give his life purpose and meaning, on the power and grandeur of the human reason and the reach of man's unconquerable mind and on the point where the questioning intellect must halt. At some point in reading the poem we are required to accept a painful truth about our own creatureship, and have to acknowledge that whether or not there is a real, living, transcendent God our only way of defining ourselves is by recognizing our relation to and dependence on something not ourselves, that freedom, once we move beyond the Satanic stage of barren self-assertion, can only mean freedom to decide for what cause we choose to give up our freedom.

Once again the familiar hint of a self-referential paradox suggests that the task of describing the operations of the human mind is not to be undertaken by human minds. If indeed the nature of man is of a complexity beyond human power to comprehend, and if Milton has undertaken the immense task of displaying the conditions upon which human existence is possible, it is hardly surprising that *Paradise Lost* leaves the reader not with a comfortable feeling of having arrived in the safe haven of a settled answer but with a sense of having shared in a journey of heroic exploration, a quest which begins again at the end of the poem.

> The World was all befor them, where to choose
> Thir place of rest, and Providence thir guide:
> They hand in hand with wandring steps and slow,
> Through *Eden* took thir solitarie way.

In addition to the works cited in the text and in the notes the following have useful material on the themes of this chapter: R. J. Zwi Werblowsky, *Lucifer and Prometheus: A Study of Milton's Satan* (London: RKP, 1952); Harry F. Robins, *If This Be Heresy: A Study of Milton and Origen*, Illinois Studies in Language and Literature, 51 (1963); Northrop Frye, *Five Essays in Milton's Epics*, (Toronto U.P., 1965); C. A. Patrides, *Milton and the Christian Tradition* (Oxford: Clarendon, 1966); W. B. Hunter, C. A. Patrides and J. H. Adamson, *Bright Essence: Studies in Milton's Theology* (University of Utah Press, 1971).

4

Retrospect One 1350–1660

After many ages persuaded of the headlong decline and impending dissolution of society, and governed by usage and the will of masters who were in their graves, the sixteenth century went forth armed for untried experience, and ready to watch with hopefulness a prospect of incalculable change.—ACTON, Inaugural lecture on the Study of History (Cambridge 1895), p. 9.

And there was one central question, which mediaeval theology had striven in vain to solve, and which now urgently demanded an answer from the wisdom of the ancients, namely, the relation of Providence to the freedom or necessity of the human will. To write the history of this question even superficially from the fourteenth century onwards, would require a whole volume. A few hints must here suffice.— BURCKHARDT, part VI.

This is the first of four intercalary chapters in which I survey the changing ideas of human freedom over the centuries and offer some conjectures about the reciprocal relation between these ideas and their expression in literature. A compendious quotation from Basil Willey is a convenient place to begin the enquiry:

In the earlier centuries of Christianity there was a general belief, common to Christians and pagans, in the malignant influence of the *stoicheia* or elements of nature, and especially of the planets—influences sometimes associated with destiny or change, or (in the Christian version) with the Prince of the Air and the other defaulting angels. In the popular imagination, too, nature—meaning the physical world, its woods, streams, mountains, caves and recesses, and its secret lore—was long held or felt to be the home of heathen deities, dethroned but not destroyed by the victorious new creed, and ever waiting on the devil's side to work havoc against God and man.[1]

This quotation presents clearly a traditional antithesis between man and nature. The forces of nature are hostile to man, oppress him and limit his actions not only physically but as the ministers of destiny: at the same time they force him to realize his humanness and to struggle for freedom.

Whitehead puts the point succinctly:

When we think of freedom, we are apt to confine ourselves to freedom of thought, freedom of the press, freedom for religious opinions. Then the limitations to freedom are conceived as wholly arising from the antagonism of our fellow men. This is a thorough mistake. The massive habits of physical nature, its iron laws, determine the scene for the sufferings of men. Birth and death, heat, cold, hunger, separation, disease, the general impracticality of purpose, all bring their quota to imprison the souls of women and of men. . . The essence of freedom is the practicability of purpose. Mankind has chiefly suffered from the frustration of its prevalent purposes, even such as belong to the very definition of its species. The literary exposition of freedom deals mainly with the frills. The Greek myth was more to the point. Prometheus did not bring to mankind freedom of the press. He procured fire.[2]

While it is not, I think, true to say that 'the notion of freedom has been eviscerated by the literary treatment devoted to it',[3] White-head makes a fair point when he observes that the idea of the cold powers of the physical world as the principal forces thwarting mankind is not one which has attracted many writers. As Willey suggests, the form which Nature was accorded in literature was very often that of a supernatural agent. In Medieval literature it is hard to escape the brooding presence of the Fates, the blind disposers of the affairs of men.[4]

It is at first sight difficult to explain how a single system could embrace the ideas of Fate and Fortune, which are apparently in-compatible, since Fortune implies a universe governed by the arbit-rary operations of chance, the 'fortuit hap' of Boethius, while Fate implies a universe governed by the necessary consequences of what 'has gone before, 'an uneschuable byndinge togidre'. But Chaucer, for example, shows in *Troilus* how they can be assimi-lated through their common quality, their inevitability. As Fortune is 'remuable' so no human actions can control her vagaries, and as she is inconsistent so, sooner or later, she will inevitably desert her favourites: Fate likewise is not to be averted.

From this perspective the most important innovation of the Re-naissance is the assertion that mankind and indeed the individual man had the power to stand against the rest of creation and impose the human will on the world. 'A new vision dawned upon men: a vision of knowledge and power, of nature mastered and con-trolled, of progress and undreamed-of glory and joy for mankind.'[5] It is notable that Pico della Mirandola not only wrote a celebrated and effective treatise denouncing astrology and rejecting the idea that planetary influences were responsible for human conduct, but also expressed the loftiest conceptions of the dignity of man in a speech which Burckhardt singles out as one of the noblest of the age:

God, he tells us, made man at the close of the creation, to know the laws of the universe, to love its beauty, to admire its greatness. He bound him to no fixed place, to no prescribed form of work, and by no iron necessity, but gave him freedom to will and to love. 'I have set thee,' says the Creator to Adam, 'in the midst of the world, that thou mayst the more easily behold and see all that is therein. I created thee a being neither heavenly nor earthly, neither mortal nor immortal only, that thou mightest be free to shape and to overcome thyself. Thou mayst sink into a beast, and be born anew to the divine likeness. The brutes bring from their mother's body what they will carry with them as long as they live; the higher spirits are from the beginning, or soon after, what they will be for ever. To thee alone is given a growth and a development depending on thine own free will. Thou bearest in thee the germs of a universal life.'[6]

It has been for many years traditional to regard 'the emergence of the individual' as the crucial feature of the Renaissance. Burckhardt, for example, tracing the development of the *uomo singolare* and the *uomo unico*, writes in large terms, such as 'At the close of the thirteenth century Italy began to swarm with individuality: the ban laid upon human personality was dissolved; and a thousand figures meet us each in its own special shape and dress' (p. 81), quotes Ghiberti as saying 'only he who has learned everything is nowhere a stranger: robbed of his fortune and without friends, he is yet the citizen of every country, and can fearlessly despise the changes of fortune',[7] and finishes his impassioned account of Alberti with the words, 'Like all the great men of the Renaissance, he said, "Men can do all things if they will."'[8] From a slightly different perspective Michelet wrote in the introduction to the seventh volume of his *Histoire de France*, 'To the discovery of the outward world the Renaissance added a still greater achievement, by first discerning and bringing to light the full, whole nature of man.' But of course the history of the Renaissance cannot be written in terms of the exceptional man. Equally important were the widely disseminated practical and technical consequences of the new ways of seeing and behaving:

The discovery of the individuum was parallel to the discovery of the nude. . . . Machiavelli's hero is the counterpart of the nudes painted by Signorelli or sketched by Leonardo: he is a scientific being.[9]

From the beginning of the sixteenth century this first form of institutional civilization, with its feudalism, its guilds, its universities, its Catholic Church, was in full decay. The new middle classes, whether scholars or traders, would have none of it. They were individualists. For them the universities were secondary, the monasteries were a nuisance, the Church was a nuisance, feudalism was a nuisance, the guilds were a nuisance. They wanted good order, and to be let alone with their individual activities.[10]

The gunned ship developed by Atlantic Europe in the course of the fourteenth and fifteenth centuries was the contrivance that made possible the European saga. It was essentially a compact device that allowed a relatively small crew to master unparalleled masses of inanimate energy for movement and destruction.[11]

Such examples could, of course, be multiplied many times. Even allowing for the natural anxiety of historians to ascribe the paternity of their special interest to Renaissance man whenever this can be done with any show of plausibility, there still remains a solid body of evidence. J. A. Mazzeo neatly summarizes the transition when he observes that Dante's three categories of sin—incontinence, force, and fraud—are to Machiavelli the three components of 'a dynamic system in terms of which life is lived'.[12] Man is 'hopelessly incontinent, infinitely desirous, endlessly ambitious', yet to survive at all he must restrain his desires. Thus force, either anarchic or legalized, must operate to check incontinence, aided by fraud, interpreted to include every kind of social convention and illusion.

The crucial distinction is between a world in which man is a small part of some non-human design and the new secular states of Italy, established and maintained by force, with no claim to divine authority, with no sanction from tradition or hereditary transmission of rulership, with none of the apparatus of government. When we see through the eyes of Machiavelli the naked mechanisms of political power, we see a state of affairs which is a purely human responsibility and which a ruler must control by human resources, guiding his actions by his understanding that men operate in their own interests. 'How we live is so far removed from how we ought to live, that he who abandons what is done for what ought to be done, will rather learn to bring about his own ruin than his preservation.'[13]

This total rejection of abstractions, of theoretical speculations about the probable nature of a part of an assumed whole, in favour of questions about the actual behaviour of men makes Machiavelli an especially appropriate figure to speak the prologue to one of Marlowe's plays. Marlowe, like most of his contemporaries, simplified and vulgarized Machiavelli's sophisticated statecraft, but perceived the essentially humanist nature of his assumptions—

> I count religion but a childish toy,
> And hold there is no sin but ignorance.
> (Prologue to *The Jew of Malta*, 14–15)

It is in Marlowe's plays that the new sense of man's power and liberty finds its most vivid expression in English, yet even his heroes overreach themselves and are shown ambiguously: their ambitions and their achievements are stupendous, but in the end their power must find its limits and their liberty prove an illusion. Tamburlaine's vaunt

> And with our own bright armour, as we march,
> We'll chase the stars from heaven, and dim their eyes
> That stand and muse at our admired arms.   (II. iii)

is at last silenced by the 'wrath and tyranny of death'.[14]

By 1600 we find widely expressed in English literature a sense that man was a free being with powers limited, if at all, not by supernatural forces but only by the nature of the world of which he formed part. It is pointless to try to offer a specific date. All we can say is that at one period most men seemed to believe in some sense in the dominance of Fortune, so that Cavendish, for example, writing his *Life of Wolsey* in 1557 could still explain events in terms of the turning of Fortune's wheel, while at a later period certain kinds of literature took their origin from an expression of man's independence of fortune. When Cornwallis, for example, writes in 1601, 'There are no mischances, there is no fortune, there is no miserie in our humaine lives, except we looke into the feeblenesse of our merits, & our Creators bountie, in other things we are deceived by imagination, the circumstances of things are more than themselves',[15] he brings to mind a large number of similar passages from the dramatists. The first is from Chapman: the point to note is that Byron is expressly defying the predictions of the magician, La Brosse, who has foretold his execution—'Spite of the stars, and all astrology,/I will not lose my head.' He repudiates La Brosse's melancholy reflections on human helplessness:

> Give me a spirit that on this life's rough sea
> Loves t'have his sails fill'd with a lusty wind,
> Even till his sail-yards tremble, his masts crack,
> And his rapt ship run on her side so low
> That she drinks water, and her keel plows air.
> There is no danger to a man that knows
> What life and death is; there's not any law
> Exceeds his knowledge; neither is it lawful
> That he should stoop to any other law.
> He goes before them and commands them all
> That to himself is a law rational.
>   (*The Conspiracy of Charles, Duke of Byron*, III. i)

Plate 3. Title page of THE CASTLE OF KNOWLEDGE (1556) by
Robert Recorde. The figure in the centre is Astronomy. *By courtesy
of Glasgow University Library*

The second quotation is from Fletcher's scornful address to astrologers:

> Man is his own Star, and the soul that can
> Render an honest, and a perfect man,
> Commands all light, all influence, all fate;
> Nothing to him falls early, or too late.
> Our Acts our Angels are, or good or ill,
> Our fatal shadows that walk by us still.
> (*Upon an Honest Man's Fortune*, 33–8)[16]

The plot of Dekker's play *Old Fortunatus*, which I have already
mentioned, is designed to show the arbitrariness of Fortune's
power, but at the end of the play the 'accursed Queen of chance'
has to concede that there is a higher deity:

> Virtue the victory! for joy of this,
> Those self-same hymns which you to Fortune sung
> Let them be now in Virtue's honour rung.   (V. ii)

No doubt the name which epitomizes for most people this view of
man as master of his own destiny is that of Francis Bacon, *novi
temporis buccinator*. He is especially convenient for my purposes,
since he is not purely a literary figure, but is a talented historian, a
celebrated scientist and a distinguished philosopher. 'Bacon, like
Moses, led us forth at last,' wrote Cowley in his ode *To the Royal
Society*.

> The orchard's open now, and free:
> Bacon has broke that scarecrow Deity [Authority];
> Come, enter, all that will,
> Behold the ripened Fruit, come gather now your fill.

A few quotations show the characteristic emphasis which he gave
to humanist ideas. Most readers will think at once of the letter to
Lord Burleigh (1592), in which Bacon declares in a phrase worthy
of one of Marlowe's heroes, 'I confess that I have as vast
contemplative ends, as I have moderate civil ends; for I have taken
all knowledge to be my province', or perhaps the words of the
Father of Salomon's House, the college of science in the ideal state
of *The New Atlantis* (?1624), 'The end of our foundation is the
knowledge of causes, and secret motions of things; and the
enlarging of the bounds of human empire, to the effecting of all
things possible.'

The general position is well conveyed in a passage from his essay
'Of Fortune':

Chiefly, the mould of a man's fortune is in his own hand. *Faber quisque fortunae suae*, saith the Poet. And the most frequent of external causes is, that the folly of one man is the fortune of another.

Bacon amplifies the point in *The Advancement of Learning*. He offers a wealth of Latin quotations to show that the notion that a man can mould his own fortunes is of respectable antiquity, but concedes that there is a lack of clear information about how to do it. 'Wherein it may appear at the first a new and unwonted argument to teach men how to raise and make their fortune; a doctrine wherein every man perchance will be ready to yield himself a disciple, till he see the difficulty.' He suggests that the quality which is most necessary to the man who wishes to prevail in fortune is the ability to look into the hearts of his fellows—

> that is, to procure good informations of particulars touching persons, their natures, their desires and ends, their customs and fashions, their helps and advantages, and whereby they chiefly stand: so again their weaknesses and disadvantages, and where they lie most open and obnoxious; their friends, factions, and dependencies; and again their opposites, enviers, competitors, their moods and times, *Sola viri molles aditus et tempora noras* [*Aen*. iv. 423]; their principles, rules, and observations, and the like: and this not only of persons, but of actions; what are on foot from time to time, and how they are conducted, favoured, opposed, and how they import, and the like. . . . We will begin, therefore, with this precept . . . that the sinews of wisdom are slowness of belief and distrust.[17]

It will be plain that the elevated sentiments of della Mirandola have been rapidly translated into the calculating scepticism of Machiavelli. 'We are much beholden to Machiavelli and others, that write what men do, and not what they ought to do.'[18]

I offer then this brief sketch of the extraordinary double impact of the central idea of the Renaissance on Britain. The excitement and buoyancy of the joyous notion of human freedom from supernatural limitations is almost instantly counterbalanced, though not overwhelmed, by a recognition that natural limitations will take the place of the supernatural, and by a sense that these may in the end prove even harder for man to bear.[19] Three passages, all extremely well known, must serve to convey this darker aspect of liberty. Epernon, in the *Tragedy of Charles, Duke of Byron*, observes the ruin of the hero and comments

> Oh of what contraries consists a man!
> Of what impossible mixtures! vice and virtue,
> Corruption, and eternnesse, at one time,
> And in one subject, let together, loose!

> We have not any strength but weakens us,
> No greatness but doth crush us into air.
> Our knowledges do light us but to err,
> Our ornaments are burthens: our delights
> Are our tormentors; fiends that, raised in fears,
> At parting shake our roofs about our ears.   (v. i)

His companion Soissons begins a similar speech with the line 'O Virtue, thou art now far worse than Fortune.'

The second passage is from Fulke Greville's *Mustapha*, and reflects the same preoccupation with the paradoxes of the human condition:

> Oh wearisome Condition of Humanity!
> Born under one law, to another bound:
> Vainely begot, and yet forbidden vanity,
> Created sicke, commanded to be sound:
> What meaneth Nature by these diverse Lawes?
> Passion and Reason, selfe-division cause.

The disintegrating effect of this anguished questioning of man's purposes and institutions is expressed, with some dramatic exaggeration, in Donne's *An Anatomie of the World*, which includes *The first Anniversary*:

> And new Philosophy calls all in doubt,
> The Element of fire is quite put out;
> The Sun is lost, and th'earth, and no mans wit
> Can well direct him where to look for it.
> And freely men confesse that this world's spent,
> When in the Planets, and the Firmamant
> They seeke so many new; they see that this
> Is crumbled out againe to his Atomies.
> 'Tis all in peeces, all cohaerence gone;
> All just supply, and all Relation:
> Prince, Subject, Father, Sonne, are things forgot,
> For every man alone thinkes he hath got
> To be a Phoenix, and that then can bee
> None of that kinde, of which he is, but hee.
> This is the worlds condition now. . . .   (205–19)[20]

It was as if at the end of the sixteenth century a mighty angel had announced with a fanfare of celestial trumpets, 'Man shall now enjoy perfect freedom', and some time later, without a fanfare, had added, 'Up to a point.' The confusion would have been less had he explained the nature of the point or the meaning of freedom.[21]

The subsequent uncertainty I see as lasting for seventy or eighty years, a period of doubt, controversy, revolution, affirmation and counter-affirmation in every sphere of English life. Looking back over more than a century Johnson wrote in his *Life of Butler*

> It is scarcely possible, in the regularity and composure of the present time, to image the tumult of absurdity and clamour of contradiction which perplexed doctrine, disordered practice, and disturbed both public and private quiet, in that age when subordination was broken, and awe was hissed away; when any unsettled innovator who could hatch a half-formed notion produced it to the public; when every man might become a preacher, and almost every preacher could collect a congregation.

The titles of books such as H. J. C. Grierson's *Cross Currents in English Literature of the Seventeenth Century, or The World, the Flesh & the Spirit, their Actions & Reactions*, V. Harris's *All Coherence Gone*, and Marjorie Nicolson's *The Breaking of the Circle* recognize the period as one of turmoil and indecision: Cowley in the Preface to his *Poems* (1656) refers to the century as 'this warlike, various and tragical age'. It is plain that many of the controversies, if not all of them, can be seen as ultimately arguments about the nature of freedom.

My chief concern at this point is to draw attention to periods about which general statements can be made: I therefore present a series of paradigms as if they represented a universal and homogeneous state. Yet if a state changes there must have been present even in the perfect paradigm the seeds of change, the processes by which it is eventually to be displaced and a new paradigm generated. In a period of stability there are the elements of later disruption: conversely in a period which, like the beginning of the seventeenth century, is characterized by its volatility, it is possible to discern those forces which were in time to encourage a less turbulent intellectual climate. In constructing this tentative map of the movement of ideas, I continually make the assumption that a major agency of change is a preceding change, however caused, in the prevalent beliefs about the nature of man and his relation to the rest of the universe, especially in the question of the freedom of the human will. Accordingly, although it is not part of my purpose to offer a demonstration or explanation of the mechanism of these changes, I point to the obvious influences of Hobbes and Locke, of Newton and his fellows, and of Milton, all operating to encourage a scepticism about the extent of human freedom.

There is increasing agreement about the importance of Hobbes. 'Hobbes was a potent influence right through from the seventeenth century to the nineteenth. . . . There ought not to be any question as to whether Hobbes was in the main stream of English political thought; it should rather be acknowledged that he dug the channel in which the main stream subsequently flowed.'[22] Hobbes looks forward to the eighteenth century not so much in his explicit determinism as in the Euclidean nature of his treatment of mind and in his discussion of human nature and actions as topics amenable to a rigorously deductive approach. The importance of Locke's account of mental processes is hardly less, especially as simplified by Condillac and Hartley. Not lightly did Keynes call the *Essay Concerning Human Understanding* 'the first modern English book', or Alfred Cobban refer to Locke as the author whose influence 'pervades the eighteenth century with an almost scriptural authority'.[23] It is worth noting that Voltaire describes Locke as the true philosopher, that is as a superb anatomist who can explain the human reason just as he can explain the operations of the human body.[24]

Newton is an even more powerful figure, especially in the experimental tradition initiated by Bacon and continued expressly by the Royal Society.[25] Robert Hooke, who was recommended to the Society by Boyle as Curator of Experiments, stated the Society's method of proceeding as follows:

> [It] will not own any hypothesis, system or doctrine of the principles of naturall philosophy, proposed or mentioned by any philosopher ancient or modern, nor the explication of any phenomena where recourse must be had to originall causes (as not being explicable by heat, cold, weight, figure, and the like, as effects produced thereby); nor dogmatically define, nor fix axioms of scientificall things, but will question and canvass all opinions, adopting nor adhering to none, till by mature debate and clear arguments chiefly such as are deduced from legitimate experiments, the truth of such arguments to be demonstrated invincibly.[26]

It might be supposed that one effect of such a view of the Universe as Newton put forward with his irresistible authority would naturally be a sense of constriction or even imprisonment, with the human mind reduced to the status of a dispassionate observer of phenomena. Yet in fact, as is well-known, the increase of systematized scientific knowledge was on the whole felt to signal an advance in the human condition, in the sense that it promised mastery over the animate and inanimate world and a development of truly rational behaviour. While making much less extreme claims for the value of autonomous man and accepting that his decisions were much more subject to external pressures, it was still possible to claim that this allowed man a different and higher kind of freedom. 'Freedom' then is still accepted as eminently desirable, but the content of the word has changed: this change is in part effected by the merging of terms, such as God, Nature, and Reason, which had in previous centuries been set in opposition.

The part played by Milton in this transference is ambiguous and hard to determine. His ringing defence of rational liberty in the *Areopagitica* is, or was, familiar to every Englishman. It is notable that he does not confine himself to the simple political issue of the merits of an unlicensed press, but deliberately grounds his case on the absolute value of free actions as such:

> If every action which is good, or evil in man at ripe years, were to be under pittance, and prescription, and compulsion, what were virtue but a name, what praise could be then due to well-doing, what gramercy to be sober, just, or continent? Many there be that complain of Divine Providence for suffering Adam to transgress; foolish tongues! when God gave him reason, he gave him freedom to choose, for reason is but choosing; he had been else a mere artificial Adam, such an Adam as he is in the motions [puppet shows].

On the other hand the many passages of *Paradise Lost* in which attempts to discover the truth of the Universe by the exercise of the intellect are scorned or rebuked are in a very different key. As I have indicated in chapter 3 I do not think that it is possible to make Milton's epic echo *Areopagitica* as an ardent affirmation of belief in the reality and intrinsic value of human liberty and human enquiry. Raphael tells Adam that his commission from God is 'to answer thy desire/Of knowledge within bounds; beyond abstain/To ask, nor let thine own inventions hope/Things not reveal'd . . .' (VII. 119–22). In Book VIII the angel replies benevolently to Adam's questions about celestial motions:

> To ask or search I blame thee not, for Heav'n
> Is as the Book of God before thee set,
> Wherein to read his wondrous Works, and learne
> His Seasons, Hours, or Days, or Months, or Yeares.   (66–9)

But the whole burden of Raphael's long speech is an attack on the entire process of astronomy as presumptuous and unpleasing to a jealous God. He concludes

> But whether thus these things, or whether not,
> Whether the Sun predominant in Heav'n
> Rise on the Earth, or Earth rise on the Sun . . .
> Sollicit not thy thoughts with matters hid,
> Leave them to God above, him serve and feare; . . .

> . . . Heav'n is for thee too high
> To know what passes there; be lowlie wise:
> Think onely what concernes thee and thy being;
> Dream not of other Worlds, what Creatures there
> Live, in what state, condition or degree,
> Contented that thus farr hath been reveal'd
> Not of Earth onely but of highest Heav'n.   (159–78)[27]

Milton insists throughout his poem that the human will is free, but he presents a physical universe which has been determined in all its parts by the pure will of God, and is not all open to human understanding.

Of course much may be said in defence of Milton's cosmology. It can, for instance, be plausibly argued that he at least offered his readers a universe with man at the centre of a defined system, as opposed to the infinite and decentralized universe implied by post-Copernican astronomy and envisaged in post-Brunonian philosophic speculation. If any readers had come to fear that they were insignificant specks of life in an infinite universe that might contain an infinity of inhabited worlds, if they echoed Pascal's 'Le silence éternel de ces espaces infinis m'effraie', if they suffered, in Koestler's striking phrase, from 'cosmic agoraphobia',[28] the poem would at least restore to them a world in which the crucial choices were human choices. To this extent the poem is an anti-Hobbes poem, since it asserts the reality and importance of free choice: nor does it limit human knowledge to what is derived from the senses.[29]

In fairness to Milton I must mention also the argument that the poem is designed to demonstrate not only man's doubleness of belief about free will in general but also man's ambivalent response to scientific advance. Just as the fruit of the tree of knowledge is double in its effects, so knowledge of the world is at once good and bad, simultaneously liberating man from centuries of darkness through 'the knowledge of causes and secret motions of things, to the effecting of all things possible' and reducing him to the status of an infinitesimal part of an enormous machine.

Even if such a line of defence is considered sufficient to save Milton's credit in the case of *Paradise Lost*, it is more difficult to evade the issues he places before us in *Paradise Regained*. There is a crucial passage in book iv, in which Christ repudiates the entire body of Classical philosophy, statesmanship and literature in so far as it offers to find in man virtue and an object of worship. At every point submission to God and to the word of God in the Scriptures is given emphatic preference. All this is very different from Marlowe[30] and from the spirit of Bacon or Hobbes. *Paradise Lost* marks the end of the burst of self-affirmation which began in 1590 or so, looking backwards to it with sympathy but also looking forward to a world of accepted authority, whether that authority proves to be the reason, or the needs of society, or Sir Isaac Newton, or the word of the Lord. The poem which created Satan and subdued him is a Janus-poem, with one face towards *Tamburlaine* and the other towards the *Essay on Man.*[31]

In addition to the works cited in the text and in the notes the following have useful material on the themes of this chapter: Erich Fromm, *Escape from Freedom* (New York: Holt, Rinehart, 1941), esp. ch. 3; *The Renaissance Philosophy of Man*, ed. Ernst Cassirer, Paul Kristeller and John Randall Jr (University of Chicago, 1948); Charles Trinkaus, 'The Problem of Free Will in Renaissance and the Reformation', *JHI*, 10 (1949), 51–62; Alexandre Koyré, *From the Closed World to the Infinite Universe*, (Baltimore: Johns Hopkins P., 1957); Michael Macklem, *The Anatomy of the World: Relations between Natural and Moral law from Donne to Pope*, (Minneapolis, 1958); Eugene M. Waith, *The Herculean Hero in Marlowe, Chapman, Shakespeare and Dryden*, (London: Chatto, 1962); Marie Boas, *The Scientific Renaissance 1450–1630*, (London: Collins, 1962); Peter Burke, *The Renaissance Sense of the Past* (London: Arnold, 1969); Charles Trinkaus, *In Our Image and Likeness: Humanity and Divinity in Italian Humanist Thought*, (London: Constable, 1970); Keith Thomas, *Religion and the Decline of Magic*, (London: Weidenfeld and Nicolson, 1971) esp. chs. 4, 10–12; Fernand Braudel, *Capitalism and Material Life 1400–1800*, tr. M. Kochan (London: Weidenfeld, 1973); Quentin Skinner, *The Foundations of Modern Political Thought*, 2 vols. (Cambridge U.P., 1978); Elizabeth L. Eisenstein, *The Printing Press as an Agent of Change: Communications and cultural transformations in early-modern Europe*, 2 vols. (Cambridge U.P., 1979), esp. ch. 3; Isaiah Berlin, 'The Originality of Machiavelli', in *Against the Current* (London: Hogarth, 1980) pp. 25–79.

5

Pope's *Essay on Man*

The World was all before them, where to choose
Thir place of rest, and Providence thir guide:
They hand in hand with wandring steps and
slow,
Through *Eden* took thir solitarie way.

Paradise Lost XII. 646-9.

I A NOTE ON *GULLIVER'S TRAVELS*

One of the simplest but most telling strokes of satire in *Gulliver's Travels* (1726) is the account in the fourth chapter of Part One of the party strife between the High-heels and the Low-heels and of the ideological dispute between the Lilliputians, who break the smaller end of their eggs before eating them, and the Big-Endians of Blefuscu. The inference to be drawn from these petty controversies is that what Europeans have always considered to be fundamental issues of principle are in fact points of little importance or complete indifference on which a man's views are determined by trivial accidents or the chances of upbringing.[1] This in turn leads to the argument that there are no absolute values in the light of which men can order their lives but that their opinions are dictated by their circumstances. Gulliver himself sets out on his voyages with certain preconceptions about the proper or 'natural' standards of human behaviour. As these are shown to be erroneous or unnecessary he is forced to discard them, eventually shedding even the idea of human nature as something pre-existent and constitutive of the right way to live. He is compelled by his experiences to become the first existential hero. Nothing can be taken for granted, not even the proper size for a man to be.

In Parts I and II Gulliver is forced to accept a role, as conquistador in Lilliput and court fool in Brobdingnag, which is largely determined by his stature. Thereafter the book deals more and more with the difficulties entailed in choosing for oneself. In Part III Gulliver moves into a mechanical world, which has absorbed Newton and looks forward to de la Mettrie. He deliberately rejects this, showing his independence of mind by holding himself aloof. The whole of the satire in chapter five is directed against those who try to substitute machinery, in the widest sense, for the operations of instinct.[2] At the end of Part III in a chapter of peculiar power Swift describes Gulliver's encounter with the Struldbruggs or Immortals. The irony operates in a complex way. When Gulliver first learns that there are men who cannot die he embarks upon a rapturous account of the completely satisfying life which must be led by those who are free from the fear of death: his hearers, who know the actual nature of the Struldbruggs, encourage Gulliver to elaborate his visions. When he has finished he is told how miserably the Immortals in fact live, and is allowed to encounter some, whom he admits to be 'the most mortifying Sight I ever beheld', adding 'I grew heartily ashamed of the pleasing Visions I had formed.' It seems at first that the reader's reaction to this should be rather like that of the Laggnuggian person of quality —'a sort of a Smile, which usually ariseth from Pity to the Ignorant'.

It is, however, important to notice that Gulliver is not convicted of a foolish notion of what life should be at its best: he is merely tricked into forgetting, like Tithonus, that immortality does not confer immunity from the operations of time. The vices and infirmities of the old continue to torture the Struldbruggs with no promise of release except in the oblivion of dotage. But the deception, although it leaves Gulliver open to raillery, does not make the ideal state he has projected any less desirable. There is nothing for Gulliver to be ashamed of in his 'Visions': what he has learned is that even if the ideal life were not unattainable because of the certainty of death it would be unattainable because of the irresistible ravages of old age. He is thus in the position of seeing what human life might be and having to acknowledge that forces beyond the control of man make it impossible to realize this ideal. The episode is not especially apposite to the rest of Part III, but it paves the way admirably for Part IV, in which Gulliver's function is that of a choosing agent.

It appears absurd to say this, since Gulliver is by birth a Yahoo and can never be otherwise:

> When I thought of my Family, my Friends, my Countrymen, or human Race in general, I considered them as they really were, *Yahoos* in Shape and Disposition, perhaps a little more civilised, and qualified with the Gift of Speech. (chapter 10)

With the gulf between a rational and an irrational way of life symbolized by a difference of species it might seem that Gulliver was quite simply doomed to be a Yahoo. Yet all the violent emotion in the book arises from his longing to transcend his nature and to be a Houyhnhnm. To be a choosing man in an unchangeable situation can clearly generate a bitterly painful anguish at the human situation which it is quite inadequate to describe simply as pessimism.

The pattern made by the four voyages is as follows. Parts I and II are static and frieze-like. The comedy is abundant but it is used to rigidify, almost to petrify. The figures have the energy and the aridity of a caricature or a drawing in a comic paper. Gulliver himself is as two-dimensional as his background.[3] The effect of ludicrous over-simplification is enhanced by the Escher-like way the two voyages complement one another. In Part III Gulliver is conscious of a growing gap between himself and the mechanical world, as symbolized by the scientists. The Part concludes with the episode of the Struldbruggs, which forces Gulliver to acknowledge the physical limitations which thwart human desires. In Part IV he is, if anything, excessively conscious of the agonies of choosing, and, at the end of his travels, his realization of the awful responsibility of choice combines with his realization of the impossibility of choosing to be other than what we must be to reduce him to a state where his sanity is in danger.

It is true that Gulliver finds some positive values, most obviously in the traditional landowner of Laputa and in the rationality of the Houyhnhnms, and that he does not approve of the rootless questioning of the Academy in Part III. These points might seem to mark him as distinctly not existentialist. The crucial difference is that Gulliver is driven away from all conventional supports and systems and notably away from any revealed or transcendental truths into a set of deliberately unstructured situations. The positive values he finds are based on human experiences and qualities.

II *ESSAY ON MAN*

It is my suggestion that Pope's *Essay on Man* (1732–4) is planned as a direct answer to the Pyrrhonism of *Gulliver*. It is not perhaps too much of a paradox to describe the poem as the last great literary work of the Middle Ages, in the sense that it attempts to persuade men to accept the comfort of an allotted place in a beneficient and well-designed Universe and offers a system of values derived from inherent and invariable features of the creation. Its interest lies in Pope's endeavours to find for the anomalous term 'man' a way of co-existing harmoniously in the poem with words of such established power as 'order', 'content' and 'submission'.

I wish to examine two points in particular—first the accusations levelled at the poem not long after its publication of being Spinozistic, that is, deterministic; secondly the many direct indications that Pope considered himself to be working in precisely the same area as Milton in *Paradise Lost*. For example, his exordium, after an allusion to the 'Garden, tempting with forbidden fruit' concludes

> Laugh where we must, be candid where we can;
> But vindicate the ways of God to Man.   (I. 15–16)[4]

Pope commented in a note, 'The last line sums up the moral and main Drift of the whole.' We may fairly regard the *Essay* as an attempt to arrive at the conclusions of *Paradise Lost* by rational argument without the aid of revelation: it offered not a secularized but a demythologized account 'of the Nature and State of Man, with respect to the UNIVERSE'. It is important to remember that Pope is not putting before us a Godless universe or one with, to use Pascal's phrase, a 'deus absconditus'. The point is made explicit in Epistle I:

> All [i.e. human tasks and pains] are but parts of one stupendous whole,
> Whose body, Nature is, and God the soul.   (267–8)

What Pope wishes to show is that the part man must play in the world is determined not by some arbitrary decree of God's but by the very nature of the Universe itself and the principles of order which sustain it. We encounter once again 'Nature' as the widest possible name for the forces which immediately shape and restrict the desires of men, but there is now a crucial difference. Whereas to Marlowe Nature manifested itself as virtú, a mysterious instinctual prompting, to Pope it was a plain, evident and consistent order of events. Remembering his epigram 'Nature, and Nature's Laws lay hid in Night./God said, *Let Newton be!* and All was *Light*', one might make a distinction between 'Nature' in Marlowe's sense and 'Nature's Laws', which at times become virtually synonymous with 'God' and 'Order'.

The basis of the argument which establishes the close relation between these three terms is simple enough, as may be seen from the following representative passages from Epistle I. We are required to grant first the principle of plenitude, 'that God could not rest in his own perfections till He had communicated as many degrees of perfection (kinds of being, each with its special powers) to the universe as possible'.[5] Thus there can be no voids in the Universe; everything possible must have been created and related in the best way possible to its neighbours. As God is supreme, all created things must show a progressive falling-off from His perfection:

> Of Systems possible, if 'tis confest
> That Wisdom infinite must form the best,
> Where all must full or not coherent be,
> And all that rises, rise in due degree;
> Then, in the scale of reas'ning life, 'tis plain
> There must be, somewhere, such a rank as Man;
> And all the question (wrangle e'er so long)
> Is only this, if God has plac'd him wrong?   (43–50)

If in fact the Universe is established on this hierarchical principle it is plain that attempts to subvert it, for instance by men who claim a higher position than has been assigned to them, put at risk the entire fabric of the world:

> In Pride, in reas'ning Pride, our error lies;
> All quit their sphere, and rush into the skies.
> Pride still is aiming at the blest abodes,
> Men would be Angels, Angels would be Gods.
> Aspiring to be Gods, if Angels fell,
> Aspiring to be Angels, Men rebel;
> And who but wishes to invert the laws
> Of ORDER, sins against th'Eternal Cause.   (123–30)

Thus it is the great chain of being which sustains all nature. It follows that the universe itself is dependent on the principle of subordination, or knowing one's place:

> See, thro' this air, this ocean, and this earth,
> All matter quick, and bursting into birth.
> Above, how high progressive life may go!
> Around, how wide! how deep extend below!
> Vast chain of being, which from God began,
> Natures aethereal, human, angel, man,
> Beast, bird, fish, insect! what no eye can see,
> No glass can reach! from Infinite to thee,
> From thee to Nothing!—On superior pow'rs
> Were we to press, inferior might on ours:
> Or in the full creation leave a void,
> Where, one step broken, the great scale's destroy'd:
> From Nature's chain whatever link you strike,
> Tenth or ten thousandth, breaks the chain alike.   (233–46)

Since disturbing any link of the chain is, in effect, to destroy the whole, the cardinal sin is presumption.

> Know thy own point: This kind, this due degree
> Of blindness, weakness, Heav'n bestows on thee.
> Submit—

The celebrated conclusion of Epistle I makes the point plainly enough:

> All Nature is but Art, unknown to thee;
> All Chance, Direction, which thou canst not see;
> All Discord, Harmony, not understood;
> All partial Evil, universal Good:
> And, spite of Pride, in erring Reason's spite,
> One truth is clear, 'Whatever IS, is RIGHT.'   (289–94)[6]

It is perfectly clear that taken literally this could be used to justify a rigidly authoritarian view of society. Similarly if Pope believed that the entire creation was a manifestation of the Divine will and believed that man's prime duty was a submissive resignation, it is hard to see how he could avoid a thoroughgoing fatalism. If, in short, God is 'the Eternal Cause' (130) there is little room for other causes, such as the human will. The general tendency is well illustrated by lines 61–8 of Epistle I:

> When the proud steed shall know why Man restrains
> His fiery course, or drives him o'er the plains;
> When the dull Ox, why now he breaks the clod,
> Is now a victim, and now Ægypt's God:
> Then shall Man's pride and dulness comprehend
> His actions', passions', being's, use and end;
> Why doing, suff'ring, check'd, impell'd; and why
> This hour a slave, the next a deity.

Passages of this kind go some way to justify the early attacks on the poem under the general epithets of 'Spinozistic' or 'Leibnizian'.

Pope, like Milton, is confronting the problem of explaining the place of Man in a Universe created by the Divine Will and sustained by immutable principles. Although Pope is not committed, as Milton was, to maintaining human free will as an essential step in the vindication of God, he cannot rest content with presenting man as merely a puppet. Thus he has next to consider what it is that makes men act. Appropriately Epistle II moves into its superb beginning with a battery of paradoxes:

> Know then thyself, presume not God to scan;
> The proper study of Mankind is Man.
> Plac'd on this isthmus of a middle state,
> A being darkly wise, and rudely great:
> With too much knowledge for the Sceptic side,
> With too much weakness for the Stoic's pride,
> He hangs between; in doubt to act, or rest,
> In doubt to deem himself a God, or Beast;

In doubt his Mind or Body to prefer,
Born but to die, and reas'ning but to err;
Alike in ignorance, his reason such,
Whether he thinks too little, or too much:
Chaos of Thought and Passion, all confus'd;
Still by himself abus'd, or disabus'd;
Created half to rise, and half to fall;
Great lord of all things, yet a prey to all;
Sole judge of Truth, in endless Error hurl'd:
The glory, jest, and riddle of the world!   (1–18)[7]

The celebrated lines that follow make the point very clearly that al
though Newton attained the power to 'unfold all Nature's law' he
was impotent to give even the simplest description of 'one move
ment of his Mind'. Pope, in an excellent philosophical tradition
then offers to be the Newton of the mind by presenting his own
account of human motives; it is an additional paradox that this
account would, if accepted as true, dissipate much of man's ignorance of his own inner life and thus remove much of the point of
Pope's earlier description of man's confused existence.

Pope first distinguishes two contrary motive forces, both of
which are essential:

Two Principles in human nature reign;
Self-love, to urge, and Reason, to restrain;
Nor this a good, nor that a bad we call,
Each works its end, to move or govern all:
And to their proper operation still,
Ascribe all Good; to their improper, Ill.
Self-love, the spring of motion, acts the soul;
Reason's comparing balance rules the whole   (53–9)

These principles are often at odds, yet are not really opposed—
'Self-love and Reason to one end aspire,/Pain their aversion, Plea
sure their desire' (87–88).[8] He then moves on to the point of
doctrine that characterizes the epistle, that of the Ruling Passion
This seems to be as much beyond human control as any Newtonian
force, and is represented as being inevitably more powerful than
Reason. In a particularly striking passage Pope compares it to a
hereditary and fatal disease:

As Man, perhaps, the moment of his breath,
Receives the lurking principle of death;
The young disease, that must subdue at length,
Grows with his growth, and strengthens with his strength:
So, cast and mingled with his very frame,
The mind's disease, its ruling Passion came.   (133–8)[8]

The argument that follows chops uneasily to and fro, especially when Pope tries to define and explain the relation between the Ruling Passion and the Reason. Having set up his ideal balance between Reason and Self-Love, he has to admit that this is overturned by the Ruling Passion. He then argues that Reason can turn the Ruling Passion to use and at the same time admits that we use our reason to serve our ruling passion.[9] The ruling passions are thus essential—'A Mightier Pow'r [than Reason] the strong direction sends' (165)—and are indeed the seat of the best qualities of man—'The surest Virtues thus from Passions shoot,/Wild Nature's vigor working at the root' (183–4), yet they are almost invariably identified with vices.[10] Pope thus brings virtue and vice perilously close together, arguing in effect that while the Ruling Passions are vices, it would be plainly unjust to condemn man from birth to a vicious life: therefore it must be true that the Ruling Passions can engender virtues, although we must nevertheless continue to acknowledge that they are themselves vicious:

> Fools! who from hence into the notion fall,
> That Vice or Virtue there is none at all.
> If white and black blend, soften, and unite
> A thousand ways, is there no black or white?
> Ask your own heart, and nothing is so plain;
> 'Tis to mistake them, costs the time and pain.   (211–16)

It is evident that in order to accomplish his vindication of Divine Providence, Pope needs to show how the Ruling Passion becomes a source of good and not simply 'the mind's disease'. To do this he widens the perspective at this point in the poem—'HEAV'N'S great view is One, and that the Whole' (238)—maintaining that Heaven can bring good out of evil. As social dependence grows out of individual weakness, so, almost *a fortiori*, individual happiness accrues in spite of individual differences. That is to say, the world being *ex hypothesi* created as it should be, the ruling passion must in fact be beneficial.

Two difficulties follow from this. The first is that whenever Pope describes anyone in the grip of a ruling passion his inveterate sense of the ridiculous in human conduct inclines him to scornful mockery; this places the Ruling Passion in a category where, like Jonson's humours, it can scarcely be regarded as other than a disabling obsession. On a deeper level there is the problem that having presented the Ruling Passion as stronger than any other force in the individual, Pope has to place the controlling and reconciling of the passions outside the individual and in the dispositions of an All-Just God, who must know what is best. Between the Ruling Passion

below and the ordaining God above there is clearly little scope for
the free will of man.

These two complications continue in the closing lines of the
Epistle:

> Behold the child, by Nature's kindly law,
> Pleas'd with a rattle, tickled with a straw:
> Some livelier play-thing gives his youth delight,
> A little louder, but as empty quite:
> Scarfs, garters, gold, amuse his riper stage;
> And beads and pray'r-books are the toys of age:
> Pleas'd with this bauble still, as that before;
> 'Till tir'd he sleeps, and Life's poor play is o'er!   (275–82)

The dismissive monosyllabic rhyming words, the deft but almost
mechanical wit, the reduction of every aim in life to a 'play-thing', a
'toy', or a 'bauble', and every pleasure in life to a stimulus that
'pleases', 'tickles' or 'amuses', all these combine to point the irony of
the phrase 'Nature's kindly law'. The lines that follow offer scant
consolation:

> Mean-while Opinion gilds with varying rays
> Those painted clouds that beautify our days;
> Each want of happiness by Hope supply'd,
> And each vacuity of sense by Pride:
> These build as fast as knowledge can destroy;
> In Folly's cup still laughs the bubble, joy.   (283–8)

We have now reached the point where knowledge destroys happiness and human life is made tolerable only through the operations
of Opinion, Hope, Pride and Folly. These abstract qualities, since
they delude man into accepting human life as more agreeable than
it is in reality, must operate outside his control, and thus constitute
yet another set of forces under whose domination he must live.

I do not see how we can read the last two passages which I have
quoted without being aware that they do not, except on a formal
level, correspond with the argument prefixed to the early editions:
'VI. *That, however, the* Ends *of* Providence *and* general Good *are
answered in our* Passions *and* Imperfections, VER. 238, &c. *How usefully these are distributed to all* Orders *of* Men, VER. 261. *In every*
state, *and every* age *of* life, VER. 271, &c.' Contrast this serene confidence with Pope's final picture of man 'Pleas'd with this bauble
still, as that before', 'Each want of happiness by Hope supply'd,/And
each vacuity of sense by Pride'. It is plain that something has not
gone according to plan here, and the discrepancy is too wide to be
concealed by the couplet that concludes the Epistle:

> See! and confess, one comfort still must rise,
> 'Tis this, Tho' Man's a fool, yet GOD IS WISE.

It is as if, throughout the Epistle, Pope had been uneasily conscious of the difficulty of accommodating his theory to life as it really was, so that at the end when the moralist dutifully proclaims that Providence turns man's deficiencies to good account the satirist cannot resist the ironic retort, 'Yes, that must be true—look how useful Ignorance is: it makes even life appear tolerable.'

There is in the second Epistle then an interesting effect of swinging debate, an impression that Pope could find no point of rest in the argument. This gives the epistle a sense of uncertainty and risk which is absent alike from the composed general laws of Epistle I and the systematic theorizing of Epistle III. The disequilibrium does much to convey Pope's intuition of the paradox of man's condition—'He hangs between; in doubt to act, or rest.'

Epistle III deals with Society. Pope has been attempting to give a coherent account of the inner impulses of Man, that is, self-love or 'what I owe to myself', and has encountered the familiar difficulty of explaining what gives the self its desires and impulses: now he turns to 'what I owe to others' and finds this rather easier to handle. He begins by returning to his earlier image of the great chain of being: the metaphor itself is sufficient to convey the ideas of dependence and connection:

> Look round our World; behold the chain of Love
> Combining all below and all above.
> See plastic Nature working to this end,
> The single atoms each to other tend,
> Attract, attracted to, the next in place
> Form'd and impell'd its neighbour to embrace.
> See Matter next, with various life endu'd,
> Press to one centre still, the gen'ral Good. . . .
> Nothing is foreign: Parts relate to whole;
> One all-extending, all-preserving Soul
> Connects each being, greatest with the least;
> Made Beast in aid of Man, and Man of Beast;
> All serv'd, all serving! nothing stands alone;
> The chain holds on, and where it ends, unknown.   (7–14, 21–6)

As one would expect, a large part of the Epistle is devoted to showing the consequences of man's position as an intermediate link in the chain:

> Know, Nature's children all divide her care;
> The fur that warms a monarch, warm'd a bear.
> While Man exclaims, 'See all things for my use!'

'See man for mine!' replies a pamper'd goose;
And just as short of Reason he must fall,
Who thinks all made for one, not one for all.   (43–8)

Once more the device of the proportion sum—God : Man :: Man : Lower Animals—is used. The implication is double. First, as we have seen in Epistle II, Man is the middle term, a crucial but ambiguous position. Secondly, as God and the beasts act out of their own nature so man has his own nature which is distinct from either. Since the whole poem is an attempt to define this 'nature' and since, if there is such a 'nature' as Pope describes, it must determine the conduct of man just as it determines the conduct of an animal, there is always a present danger of proving the Universe to be a rigid and totally determined system.[11]

> God, in the nature of each being, founds
> Its proper bliss, and sets its proper bounds;
> But as he fram'd a Whole, the Whole to bless,
> On mutual Wants built mutual Happiness:
> So from the first eternal ORDER ran,
> And creature link'd to creature, man to man.   (109–14)

In the rest of the epistle there is a slackening of poetic interest, perhaps because the ideas that Pope is handling are not new. He wishes to explain on well-worn lines the evolution of social forms, showing first how the family came into being, then the state, then the king.

> Great Nature spoke; observant Men obey'd;
> Cities were built, Societies were made: (199–200)

One reason for that couplet's dismaying limpness is the conventional sequence of unexciting ideas which it expresses. Pope follows a popular theory that kings became corrupt chiefly through superstition, but have subsequently been forced in self-defence to practise justice and benevolence (280). He suggests that since all the arguments about the divine right of kings have been settled, the modern state can be framed on the basis of a balance of interests designed to secure the general good,

> 'Till jarring int'rests of themselves create
> Th' according music of a well-mix'd State.
> Such is the World's great harmony, that springs
> From Order, Union, full Consent of things!   (293–6)[12]

Then in a celebrated passage Pope adds

> For Forms of Government let fools contest;
> Whate'er is best administer'd is best:
> For Modes of Faith, let graceless zealots fight;
> His can't be wrong whose life is in the right.   (303–6)[13]

Clearly what Pope wishes the reader to take from this Epistle is the comforting message that there is no clash between 'what I owe to myself' and 'what I owe to my fellow-men'.

> Man, like the gen'rous vine, supported lives;
> The strength he gains is from th'embrace he gives.
> On their own Axis as the Planets run,
> Yet make at once their circle round the Sun:
> So two consistent motions act the Soul;
> And one regards Itself, and one the Whole.
> Thus God and Nature link'd the gen'ral frame,
> And bade Self-love and Social be the same.   (311–18)

There are two overlapping lines of argument here. First Pope wishes to show once more the harmonizing powers of the Creator —'Th' Eternal Art educing good from ill': secondly he wishes to establish that the pattern of social conformity is part of the nature of man and thus part of the fabric of the Universe. If then there is no conflict of interest between self-love and social duty there can be no diminution of individual freedom in an act of social conformity.

Yet the general impression of the Epistle seems to me ultimately at odds with what is ordinarily understood by human freedom. Pope's world is not a world without God, since everything is ultimately attributed to Divine Providence; it is a world which God has created and adjusted in detail. Pope's method of argument depends on showing that one can see how the human situation has become what it is by a natural process of change and development. Good has thus been invariably produced from evil—the family, for example, evolved to combat individual weakness. Similarly when we look to the future we may be sure that good will come of evil, as it always has, and that selfish actions will inevitably be translated into beneficial effects. If then Pope represents God as a master clockmaker who has made and set going a superbly-regulated time-piece it is hard for him to avoid the implication that man can do nothing but tick.

> Self-love, the spring of motion, acts the soul;
> Reason's comparing balance rules the whole.   (II. 59–60)[14]

The fourth Epistle has thus to handle a number of very difficult questions. Pope has inspected the constitution of the Universe;

from this he has deduced the private and social impulses that actuate mankind. Now the principal question to be answered is, 'What should a man do to live happy in this Universe with these impulses?' The essential argument is given early in the Epistle:

> ORDER is Heav'n's first law; and this confest,
> Some are, and must be, greater than the rest,
> More rich, more wise; but who infers from hence
> That such are happier, shocks all common sense.
> Heav'n to Mankind impartial we confess,
> If all are equal in their Happiness:
> But mutual wants this Happiness increase,
> And Nature's diff'rence keeps all Nature's peace.   (49–56)

Thereafter Pope elaborates this idea. Envy consists essentially of wishing to occupy a higher place in the hierarchy. This is literally an unnatural desire since the pattern of the Universe *is* Nature. Thus the first step towards happiness must be to realize the folly of envying others, whether for riches, or success, or fame, or wisdom. Pope proposes the much more modest and conservative objects of Health, Peace, and Competence, all attributes which allow a man to dwell content in his allotted station.

> Know, all the good that individuals find,
> Or God and Nature meant to mere Mankind;
> Reason's whole pleasure, all the joys of Sense,
> Lie in three words, Health, Peace, and Competence.
> But Health consists with Temperance alone,
> And Peace, oh Virtue! Peace is all thy own.
> The good or bad the gifts of Fortune gain,
> But these less taste them, as they worse obtain.   (77–84)

'Virtue' to Pope here, as in IV. 310 and 350, seems to mean something very close to 'Benevolence' or 'Charity' a quality which is especially important because it affords a practical demonstration that actions in pursuit of private satisfaction produce public benefits.

> Self-love thus push'd to social, to divine,
> Gives thee to make thy neighbour's blessing thine.
> Is this too little for the boundless heart?
> Extend it, let thy enemies have part:
> Grasp the whole worlds of Reason, Life, and Sense,
> In one close system of Benevolence:
> Happier as kinder, in whate'er degree,
> And height of Bliss but height of Charity.   (353–60)

We now see even more clearly why 'All mankind's concern is Charity' (III. 308): the man who extends the principle sufficiently is able to experience in his own life the order and concord of the Universe, 'And Heav'n beholds its image in his breast' (IV. 372).

The need for man to find his happiness by attuning himself to the universal harmonies is at the heart of Pope's presentation of human life. Near the beginning of the fourth Epistle he wrote

> Take Nature's path, and mad Opinion's leave,
> All states can reach it, and all heads conceive;
> Obvious her goods, in no extreme they dwell,
> There needs but thinking right, and meaning well;
> And mourn our various portions as we please,
> Equal is Common Sense, and Common Ease.   (29–34)

'Take Nature's path' has been the burden of the poem. Pope now at the climax of his poem translates this wise but vague precept into human terms, celebrating the ideally happy man:

> Slave to no sect, who takes no private road,
> But looks thro' Nature, up to Nature's God;
> Pursues that Chain which links th'immense design,
> Joins heav'n and earth, and mortal and divine;
> Sees, that no being any bliss can know,
> But touches some above, and some below;
> Learns, from this union of the rising Whole,
> The first, last purpose of the human soul;
> And knows where Faith, Law, Morals, all began,
> All end, in LOVE of GOD, and LOVE of MAN.   (331–40)

All the major themes of the poem are deftly summarized in the concluding address to Bolingbroke:

> Shall then this verse to future age pretend
> Thou wert my guide, philosopher, and friend?
> That urg'd by thee, I turn'd the tuneful art
> From sounds to things, from fancy to the heart;
> For Wit's false mirror held up Nature's light;
> Shew'd erring Pride, WHATEVER IS, IS RIGHT;
> That REASON, PASSION, answer one great aim;
> That true SELF-LOVE and SOCIAL are the same;
> That VIRTUE only makes our Bliss below;
> And all our Knowledge is, OURSELVES TO KNOW.   (389–98)

Pope thus restates the major points of his argument—that God is just and must necessarily have created a just Universe, that Reason and Passion are not at war, that love of oneself and love of one's fellows are not necessarily in conflict, and that, in Pope's words, 'the *Perfection of Happiness* consists in a *Conformity* to the *Order* of *Providence* here'. We conform with this order by acting in accordance with our own nature: accordingly knowing ourselves is the first step towards happiness. Pope is thus, like Milton, claiming to instruct men in the most fundamental truths about their life on earth.

III MAN AND ORDER

What is the bearing of this analysis on the understanding and evaluation of the poem as a whole? The first step in the answer is to recognize the obvious point that the poem is very far from being consistent with an assertion of the absolute freedom of will of the individual. It is a poem designed to show the qualities and possibilities of a life of dependence and order rather than one of self-assertion and libertarianism.

At the beginning of Epistle I the reader encounters what seems to be a familiar enough cluster of ideas. God, being perfect, could only make a perfect Universe, which, being perfect, can operate in only one way, this way being essentially hierarchical. This is the burden of the simple positive enunciations as of fundamental truth in the first epistle. It is no easy matter to decide on what level Pope expects his readers to believe in the Great Chain. If literal belief is not expected and the chain is to be regarded simply as a metaphor for the taxonomy of the Universe, is 'God' similarly to be construed as a personification of Natural Law? It soon becomes evident, I think, that God is disappearing from the poem, though still formally present, and that the question Pope is really answering is 'What sort of model of the Universe should I have to construct to provide a theoretical justification for my emprical insights into the nature of man?' The ostensible syllogistic form of the poem—A. The Universe is ordered in this way. B. Man is part of the Universe. ∴ C. Man is ordered in this way—will not hold water, since the major term is little more than assertion with revelation held in reserve.[15] Pope therefore, while still retaining the form of the syllogism, does not rely on it for his most telling points. Instead he works backwards from his own knowledge and intuitions of man. As the opening of Epistle II is the intellectual centre of the poem, so it is the emotional spring.

This epistle is the most agitated in the poem, with an unremitting sense of urgency, as Pope tries to explain the origin of the Ruling Passion without lapsing into dualism. It might seem that Pope could, as Professor Priestley's account of the poem suggests he

does, find a convenient solution to his difficulties in some principle
of the reconciliation of contrarieties, by saying 'But ALL subsists by
elemental strife' (I. 169). No doubt this is, as Maynard Mack observes, a traditional element in a theodicy, and no doubt Pope, as at
the beginning of *Windsor Forest*, understands very well the poetic
and argumentative potentialities of a world where harmony is produced from confusion, but he has two particular reasons for
caution. First that the principle can be easily understood to imply
that all human actions, whatever their object, are automatically
converted to the service of some larger power: this compromises
the idea of human responsibility. Alternatively it might be understood to imply that since the Eternal Cause may be relied on to
rectify all contradictions, each man can safely give reign to his
ruling passion and live a purely selfish life: this is entirely counter
to Pope's ethical purposes.

The poem is not designed to support the theory lying behind a
policy of *laissez-faire*, that if every man pursues his own ends the
result will be a general increase in prosperity, although parts of
Epistle III might be used for this purpose.[16] But even there the real
burden is, 'All join to guard what each desires to gain' (278), that is
that even crude motives of self-interest are sufficient to generate
'Government and Laws', if only for the protection of property. But
Pope, of course, wishes to go beyond this. If 'self-love and social are
the same' it is because a man who rightly understands the nature
of the world, the human mind, and human society will recognize
that living for other people is in fact the best way to further his
own interests, for only in this way can he realize his own nature by
bringing it into harmony with the principle of dependence which
runs through the Creation.

> The gen'ral order, since the whole began,
> Is kept in nature, and is kept in man.

This is almost the reverse of *laissez-faire*.

The third and fourth Epistles represent a serious attempt to explain in purely human terms how a responsible attitude to other
people can be regarded as a fulfilling of man's true nature, not a
limitation of his freedom. Exception has been taken to Epistle IV on
the grounds that it is practical, limited and humdrum, and thus
unworthy of the great themes of the earlier Epistles, but there is
no real disharmony. Pope deplores ambition of all kinds, not because personal fame is transient but because it is essentially a
desire to assert one's self; he recommends Benevolence, or living
for others, as the prime source of Happiness, not because it is more
blessed to give than to receive, but because it is the nature of man

to find satisfaction co-operatively, as part of a total order, rather than individually, defying established patterns. The contrast is that between 'Nature's path' (IV. 29) and the 'private road' (IV. 331)

Maynard Mack has excellently characterized the way in which the central meaning of the poem is dramatized in the very texture of the verse—on the one hand a sense of 'fecundity and comprehensiveness', on the other 'an ideal order, unity, harmony and purpose'.[17] It is plain that both of these are to be found in the natural world, and that man must somehow ally himself, if he is to live a complete life, with both elements. I would simply add to Professor Mack's remarks on the surface of the poem the point that the paradox of man's intermediate position is equally expressed in the poem's structure. The architecture of the four epistles reflects a world in which parts are duly subordinated to the whole: they are orderly, proportioned, and reassuringly obvious. The single exception is the sense of unease, of hazard, in Epistle II. This disharmony makes the poem a more accurate model of the Creation—sane, stable, predictable, concordant, a perfection disturbed only by the unquiet spirit of man, 'the glory, jest, and riddle of the world', 'a being darkly wise, and rudely great', living untidily in a corner of a Palladian Universe, the grain of sand in the oyster. That is why, although passage after passage seems to commit Pope to a determinist or fatalist position the poem as a whole avoids any rigidity of this kind but conveys quite astonishingly a sense of the complexity and taxingness of being human.

6

'Human Nature seeming born again'

I WORDSWORTH. *PRELUDE* II and *EXCURSION* IV

> O William! we *receive* but what we *give*
> And in our life alone does Nature live.
> —COLERIDGE, *Dejection, An Ode* (Coleorton MS)

In Book X of *The Prelude*,[1] having narrated the political events of the period since 1789 and in part described his reaction to them, Wordsworth reconsiders the same period from the point of view of his own inner life. The successive stages are clearly set out. At the beginning of the French Revolution he was overjoyed and lived in a 'cordial transport', which survived the excesses of the early days of the Revolution—'Beneath the Evening star we saw/Dances of liberty.' But when Britain declared war on France and the French became 'oppressors in their turn' Wordsworth was roused to debate and consider general principles more ardently than before (x. 799–805). It was at this point that he was powerfully attracted by a philosophy of pure rationality, free from the accidents of human life:

> . . . The dream
> Was flattering to the young ingenuous mind
> Pleas'd with extremes, and not the least with that
> Which makes the human Reason's naked self
> The object of its fervour. What delight . . .
> [To] Build social freedom on its only basis,
> The freedom of the individual mind,
> Which, to the blind restraints of general laws
> Superior, magisterially adopts
> One guide, the light of circumstances, flash'd
> Upon an independent intellect. (815–30)[2]

Wordsworth describes how he ruthlessly rejected any side of his own nature which did not conform with the strictest principles of abstract reason:

Plate 4. Thomas Naudet. The Festival of The Supreme Being. The Festival was arranged by Robespierre in June 1794. *By courtesy of Musée Carnavalet, Paris*

> Thus I fared,
> Dragging all passions, notions, shapes of faith,
> Like culprits to the bar, suspiciously
> Calling the mind to establish in plain day
> Her titles and her honours, now believing,
> Now disbelieving, endlessly perplex'd
> With impulse, motive, right and wrong, the ground
> Of moral obligation, what the rule
> And what the sanction, till, demanding *proof*,
> And seeking it in everything, I lost
> All feeling of conviction, and, in fine,
> Sick, wearied out with contrarieties,
> Yielded up moral questions in despair.   (889–901)

Mathematics proved a poor substitute. Luckily the influence of Coleridge made itself felt at this point in the poet's life, Dorothy Wordsworth 'maintained for me a saving intercourse/With my true self',

> And lastly, Nature's Self, by human love
> Assisted, through the weary labyrinth
> Conducted me again to open day.

These passages are all familiar, and give a comparatively clear and consistent account of this period in Wordsworth's life. It is usually, and I think, rightly assumed that Wordsworth is referring specifically to the influence on him of William Godwin in 1794 and 1795, and his subsequent dejection. But the account of this unhappy episode does not find its place in Book X simply because it happens to be true: it points to a major theme of great importance in every part of the poem. My argument is first that Wordsworth's repudiation of Godwin was exactly parallel to Coleridge's rejection of Hartley[3] and 'modern Infidels', and secondly that whereas Coleridge was deeply influenced by his reading of the German philosophers, Wordsworth's conversion was, in the narrow sense of the word, more authentic.

   Godwin is sometimes seen as a crank, who objected to symphony orchestras because they depended on co-operation and thus diminished individual freedom, sometimes as a rather sinister figure, who threw his daughter in Shelley's way and then sponged on him, but he represented a set of rational and radical principles operating for the benefit of humanity at large. His visions of an ideal state for mankind were not contemptible, and for a time genuinely seemed to offer the prospect of a new and shining future: this must be said to account for his powerful appeal to the young Wordsworth and to Shelley. But consider a typical passage from the *Enquiry concerning Political Justice*:

He who regards all things past present and to come as links of an indissoluble chain, will, as often as he recollects this comprehensive view, be
superior to the tumult of passion; and will reflect upon the moral
concerns of mankind with the same clearness of perception, the same
unalterable firmness of judgement, and the same tranquillity as we are
accustomed to do upon the truths of geometry.   (2nd ed. I. 398)

It would not be surprising if Wordsworth rejected this as being
necessitarian (and thus *prima facie* fatal to morality) and unnatural
(in that it sets aside certain deep-seated human emotions),[4] but
underlying all Godwin's teaching was a view of the human consciousness which, if I am correct, disturbed Wordsworth even
more profoundly. For Godwin had maintained that 'the Characters
of Men originate in External Circumstances' and that 'Man, considered in himself, is merely a being capable of impression, a recipient of perceptions'. I shall try to show that such a view of man
was totally unacceptable to Wordsworth and that when he found
relief from mental and moral anguish in the redemptive power of
Nature he was obliged to describe the operations of this power
with great circumspection in order to avoid aligning himself once
again with Godwin's sensationism and necessitarianism.

The Prelude was given its title by Mrs Wordsworth after the
poet's death: Coleridge refers to it in *The Friend* (1808–9) as 'an
unpublished Poem on the Growth and Revolutions of an Individual
Mind'. To explain the fashioning of his own mind it was essential
for Wordsworth to consider the general question of how the
human mind or soul or personality was shaped by its experiences.
Are we free, that is, to accept or reject the effects of our environment in making us what we are? It is, of course, a version of Pope's
problem in the *Essay on Man*, but Wordsworth dispenses with
Pope's postulate of an ordered Universe and attempts to answer
the question on the basis of his own experience—'With my best
conjectures I would trace/The progress of our Being' (II. 238–9).

At the beginning of the poem Wordsworth is so eager to pay tribute to the formative powers of the natural scenery of the Lake
District that he seems virtually committed to the theory that a
man's character is purely the work of his environment:

> The mind of Man is fram'd even like the breath
> And harmony of music. There is a dark
> Invisible workmanship that reconciles
> Discordant elements, and makes them move
> In one society. Ah me! that all
> The terrors, all the early miseries
> Regrets, vexations, lassitudes, that all
> The thoughts and feelings which have been infus'd

> Into my mind, should ever have made up
> The calm existence that is mine when I
> Am worthy of myself! Praise to the end!
> Thanks likewise for the means! But I believe
> That Nature, oftentimes, when she would frame
> A favor'd Being, from his earliest dawn
> Of infancy doth open up the clouds,
> As at the touch of lightning, seeking him
> With gentlest visitation; not the less,
> Though haply aiming at the self-same end,
> Does it delight her sometimes to employ
> Severer interventions, ministry
> More palpable, and so she dealt with me.   (I. 351–71)

The use of the word 'ministry' is to be noted. Wordsworth has it again, at I. 494 for example; at I. 439 he has spoken of 'discipline'. This is echoed in I. 625–40, where he refers to 'the impressive discipline of fear'. When Wordsworth offers his conjectures of the beginning of this process, on 'those first-born affinities that fit/Our new existence to existing things' (I. 582–3), he comments

> Hard task to analyse a soul, in which,
> Not only general habits and desires,
> But each most obvious and particular thought,
> Not in a mystical and idle sense,
> But in the words of reason deeply weigh'd,
> Hath no beginning.   (II. 232–237)

Taken by itself this might suggest that Wordsworth had completely changed his theories and now maintained that no mental process had an observable external origin. But he goes on to describe how a baby 'doth gather passion from his Mother's eye!'

>   Thus, day by day,
>   Subjected to the discipline of love,
>   His organs and recipient faculties
>   Are quicken'd, are more vigorous, his mind spreads,
>   Tenacious of the forms which it receives.   (II. 250–4)

What follows must be quoted at length to show the subtle fluctuations of Wordsworth's thought:

> In one beloved presence, nay and more,
> In that most apprehensive habitude
> And those sensations which have been deriv'd
> From this beloved Presence, there exists
> A virtue which irradiates and exalts
> All objects through all intercourse of sense.

No outcast he, bewilder'd and depress'd;
Along his infant veins are interfus'd
The gravitation and the filial bond
Of nature, that connect him with the world.
Emphatically such a Being lives,
An inmate of this *active* universe;
From nature largely he receives; nor so
Is satisfied, but largely gives again,
For feeling has to him imparted strength,
And powerful in all sentiments of grief,
Of exultation, fear, and joy, his mind,
Even as an agent of the one great mind,
Creates, creator and receiver both,
Working but in alliance with the works
Which it beholds.   (II. 255–75)

Wordsworth thus suggests that 'feelings' (undifferentiated, but presumably feelings of love) are imparted to the child by his mother and these feelings as it were sensitize the *tabula rasa* of his mind, so that it becomes capable of receiving and combining sense-impressions, and of endowing external objects with a life of their own. He is thus part of the life of the universe, which he perceives, but not passively, for it is his task to animate what would otherwise be purely material.

This is a difficult passage. On the one hand Wordsworth is obviously aware of the danger of implying that Nature alone can shape the human personality. If man is to retain any dignity at all it is essential for Wordsworth to show that man in the face of Nature is 'not prostrate, overborne, as if the mind/Itself were nothing, a mean pensioner/On outward forms' (VI. 666–8). He therefore suggests a primary source of feeling in the earliest family contacts. He can then safely allow Nature to perform its ministry since it is now acting upon a sensibility which has its own independent springs of power. Man and Nature can only thus enter into a fruitful mutual relationship, which Wordsworth celebrates with great fervour.

Of course none of this is contrary to the principles of sensationism, nor is it formally incompatible with necessitarianism, but it is clear that Wordsworth, having with his usual winning candour disclaimed any ability to offer a final solution to the question, does feel that interposing this 'infant sensibility/Great birthright of our being' makes the whole problem easier to handle.

For the remainder of Book II he celebrates the beneficence of Nature's shaping hand. As he describes his own upbringing, he emphasizes that the influences that operated to form his character were all 'natural', in the sense 'not artificial', and thus have a sort of prescriptive force. The implication is that as this is the most natural way to bring up a child (that is, most consonant with the nature of man) it is therefore the best.[5] Yet if nature (=rus) in fact wholly shapes the growing boy, if all the mind does is 'lie open' to the 'influxes' of nature then the human personality becomes no more than the passive product of experience. To safeguard against this danger Wordsworth insists

> But let this, at least
> Be not forgotten, that I still retain'd
> My first creative sensibility,
> That by the regular action of the world
> My soul was unsubdu'd.   (II. 377–81)

.Wordsworth speaks of this as 'a *plastic* power', 'a *forming* hand', 'a local spirit of its own'. The danger now is precisely the opposite one, that anyone claiming to possess such a power will be told that the objects and qualities it pretends to detect in the external world are purely illusory and subjective.[6] To guard against this new peril Wordsworth insists that though the informing spirit was 'at war/ With general tendency' it was 'for the most/Subservient strictly to the external things/With which it commun'd'. In a key phrase he describes it as 'an auxiliar light', that is, it is a source of illumination, not simply a mirror. Yet it is 'auxiliar' in the sense that it operates only in collaboration with an external reality, making the sunset more splendid, the midnight storm darker, and so on. It is this happy interchange of power that Wordsworth celebrates in the rhapsodic conclusion to Book II:

> I, at this time
> Saw blessings spread around me like a sea . . .
>
> I was only then
> Contented when with bliss ineffable
> I felt the sentiment of Being spread
> O'er all that moves . . .
>
> Wonder not
> If such my transports were; for in all things now
> I saw one life, and felt that it was joy . . .
>
> in thee [the mountains and Nature]
> For this uneasy heart of ours I find
> A never-failing principle of joy,
> And purest passion.   (413–14, 418–21, 428–30, 463–6)

The point that emerges clearly from Book II is that for Wordsworth genuine happiness is impossible unless he can convince himself that he is neither a passive recipient of the mechanical operations of nature nor a deluded agent unable to achieve certain knowledge of any external reality whatsover. But if a middle position can be found, the grown man will have the unutterable bliss of being in a fruitful relationship with Nature, 'creator and receiver both'. A self fashioned in this way will out of its own re-sources be competent to withstand all subsequent urban and human pressures on it, such as might be encountered in Cam-bridge, or in London, or in revolutionary France, or in the seduc-tive but unnatural doctrines of false teachers.

> And thus
> Was founded a sure safeguard and defence
> Against the weight of meanness, selfish cares,
> Coarse manners, vulgar passions, that beat in
> On all sides from the ordinary world
> In which we traffic. Starting from this point,
> I had my face towards the truth.   (VIII. 451–7)

Gradually, Wordsworth suggests in Book IV and VIII, 'the common haunts of the green earth' are insensibly leading to a love of 'the ordinary human interests/Which they embosom'[7]:

> Then rose
> Man, inwardly contemplated, and present
> In my own being, to a loftier height;
> As of all visible natures crown; and first
> In capability of feeling what
> Was to be felt; in being rapt away
> By the divine effect of power and love,
> As, more than anything we know instinct
> With Godhead, and by reason and by will
> Acknowledging dependency sublime.   (VIII. 630–9)[8]

The mind nurtured and strengthened by Nature—'the anchor of my purest thoughts, the nurse,/The guide, the guardian of my heart, and soul/Of all my moral being'—and by human sympathies should be able to choose correctly at all times: moral behaviour and joy in the whole creation thus go very close together, so that dejection, for example, is not far from sin. If by chance the mind becomes temporarily corrupted by alien influences it can always be restored by going back to Nature. This is the theme of Books XI and XII—'Imagination, How Impaired and Restored'.

'Imagination' is the name which Wordsworth gives to the 'virtue which irradiates and exalts/All objects through all intercourse of sense', 'the first/Poetic spirit of our human life'. As I have tried to explain, its loss entails not merely a dimming of the artist's powers, but also a weakening of that balance between Man and Nature on which Wordsworth's deepest intuitions of Man's dignity rest: in VIII. 640–63 the process is described vividly, and it is clear that not just morality but even sanity is threatened. Thus any doctrine, whether it is the simple associationism of Hartley or the more complex implications of Godwinism, which denies the possibility of a reciprocal relationship between Man and the rest of the Universe threatens simultaneously a number of different but interdependent vital centres of Wordsworth's being. Recovery of imagination is not just a struggle to reacquire some useful minor talent but far more like a battle to win back a lost faith, or even a fight for liberty.

Having recovered from the perils described in the passages I' have quoted from Book X, Wordsworth learns once more that even his 'secret happiness' in Nature is subject to change:

> how could there fail to be
> Some change, if merely hence, that years of life
> Were going on, and with them loss or gain
> Inevitable, sure alternative.   (XI. 38–41)

The fluctuations between security and doubt which Wordsworth chronicles so scrupulously in *The Prelude* are not, I think, meant to be totally distinct from one another, nor is Wordsworth always concerned to analyse their origins. At this point in the poem he describes how he fell victim to the analytic Reason, 'a Bigot to a new Idolatry', liable to 'narrow estimates of things', 'bent overmuch on superficial things', forgetting 'the moral power, the affections, and the spirit of the place'. In addition there was

> another cause
> More subtle and less easily explain'd
> That almost seems inherent in the Creature,
> Sensuous and intellectual as he is,
> A twofold Frame of body and of mind;
> The state to which I now allude was one
> In which the eye was master of the heart,
> When that which is in every stage of life
> The most despotic of our senses gain'd
> Such strength in me as often held my mind
> In absolute dominion.   (XI. 166–76)

The peril is again the Godwinian combination of necessitarianism and analytic reasoning. Both must be resisted if the imagination is to survive, and once again Wordsworth succeeds in throwing off 'this degradation':

> I had felt
> Too forcibly, too early in my life,
> Visitings of imaginative power
> For this to last: I shook the habit off
> Entirely and for ever, and again
> In Nature's presence stood, as I stand now,
> *A sensitive, and a creative soul.*
> (XI. 251–7, my italics: Wordsworth (1850) italicizes *creative*)

The last line expresses precisely the 'twofold Frame' which Wordsworth must maintain if he is to preserve his composure. The
'spots of time' which he commemorates in the remainder of the
book are moments of especial power in reimposing the balance
when it is threatened: they reassure us 'that the mind/Is Lord and
master, and that the outward sense/Is but the obedient servant of
her will' (XI. 271–3). Wordsworth cherishes them accordingly: they
are, he says, 'the hiding-places of my power', a term which well
conveys the central place which his theory of the Imagination
holds in his whole conception of human life and its relation to its
environment.

It is a simple matter to pursue this theme through Book XII from
Wordsworth's initial reverence for the Power that 'holds up before
the mind . . . a temperate shew/Of objects that endure', noting his
mistrust of 'sanguine schemes,/Ambitious virtues' and 'the books/
Of modern Statists'. It will be remembered that at the end of Book
VIII Wordsworth, though attracted more and more 'by slow grada-
tions towards human kind' nevertheless declared, 'My Fellow
beings still were unto me/Far less than she [Nature] was.' Towards
the end of Book XII Wordsworth records a change of opinion

> I felt that the array
> Of outward circumstance and visible form
> Is to the pleasure of the human mind
> What passion makes it, that meanwhile the forms
> Of Nature have a passion in themselves
> That intermingles with those works of man
> To which she summons him, although the works
> Be mean, have nothing lofty of their own;   (XII. 286–93)

The thought is not completely clear here, but the passage evidently
marks a slight shift in the balance, emphasising the power of the
mind over 'outward circumstances'. Thus if for example a Lake
District leech-gatherer could find beauty in his work and if Nature
in addition sheds her own beauty on the humblest human labour
then the poet can boldly write about such men. Wordsworth
accordingly hopes

> that a work of mine,
> Proceeding from the depth of untaught things,
> Enduring and creative, might become
> A power like one of Nature's.   (XII. 309–12)

At the close of the book he characteristically takes pride in the fact that in praising his verse Coleridge had observed

> That also then *I must have exercised*
> Upon the vulgar forms of present things
> And actual world of our familiar days,
> A higher power, *have caught from them* a tone,
> An image, and a character, by books
> Not hitherto reflected.   (XII. 360–5)

The apparently contradictory phrases which I have italicized exactly typify the double role which Wordsworth requires the imagination to assume in order to defend the mind of man simultaneously against necessitarianism and solipsism. Wordsworth concludes the book by defining once more the essential qualities of the world as he saw it at this time,

> having for its base
> That whence our dignity originates,
> That which both gives it being and maintains
> A balance, an ennobling interchange
> Of action from within and from without,
> The excellence, pure spirit, and best power
> Both of the object seen, and eye that sees.   (XII. 373–9)

The concept of mutual sustainment of perceiver and perceived could hardly be more distinctly put. Book XIII at once reaffirms the importance of the idea for 'our dignity'. The superb picture of the huge sea of mist on the ascent of Snowdon leads Wordsworth to reflect on the power of Nature to dominate 'the outward face of things' and to find a counterpart to this power in 'the glorious faculty/Which higher minds bear with them as their own'.

> Willing to work and to be wrought upon,
> They need not extraordinary calls
> To rouze them, in a world of life they live,
> By sensible impressions not enthrall'd,
> But quicken'd, rouz'd, and made thereby more apt
> To hold communion with the invisible world.
> Such minds are truly from the Deity,
> For they are Powers; and hence the highest bliss
> That can be known is theirs, the consciousness

> Of whom they are habitually infused
> Through every image, and through every thought,
> And all impressions; hence religion, faith,
> And endless occupation for the soul
> Whether discursive or intuitive;
> Hence sovereignty within and peace at will
> Emotion which best foresight need not fear
> Most worthy then of trust when most intense.
> Hence chearfulness in every act of life
> Hence truth in moral judgements and delight
> That fails not in the external universe.
>   Oh! who is he that hath his whole life long
> Preserved, enlarged, this freedom in himself?
> For this alone is genuine Liberty: (XIII. 100–22)[9]

Liberty then is the sum and epitome of all the master-qualities
Wordsworth has attributed to 'higher minds'. The alternative is

> The tendency, too potent in itself,
> Of habit to enslave the mind, I mean
> Oppress it by the laws of vulgar sense,
> And substitute a universe of death,
> The falsest of all worlds, in place of that
> Which is divine and true.   (XIII. 138–43)

Wordsworth has thus laid a firm foundation in experience and in
metaphysics for his pronouncement that imagination

> Is but another name for absolute strength
> And clearest insight, amplitude of mind,
> And reason in her most exalted mood.
> This faculty hath been the moving soul
> Of our long labour. . . .   (XIII. 168–72)

Compare with this the last lines of the poem

>   . . . the mind of man becomes
> A thousand times more beautiful than the earth
> On which he dwells, above this Frame of things
> (Which, 'mid all revolution in the hopes
> And fears of men, doth still remain unchanged)
> In beauty exalted, as it is itself
> Of substance and of fabric more divine.   (XIII. 446–52)

A process has been completed. The mind of man, which at the beginning of the poem seemed little more than a blank tablet, has by
the ceremonies which Wordsworth has described been so informed and nurtured that it is now far more beautiful than the

forces which shaped it. These, however, Wordsworth of course insists, keep their own reality and are not simply a projection of the human mind.

The interest of Wordsworth's treatment of free will lies in the earnestness with which he asks himself in what ways an environment could conceivably on sensationist principles form a human personality. What sort of account would Godwin, for example, have to give of the way in which an individual receives his faculties? To avoid a simple mechanical answer, 'a universe of death', Wordsworth posits a more complex system of understanding of and response to environment. Thus the question transposes into one of perception; it is handled in the poem in terms of Wordsworth's own exposure to natural scenery. Imagination in its full exercise enables man to participate in the act of creation and thus to understand the meaning of free will in his own experience. This is of course completely in accordance with Coleridge's celebrated declaration, 'The primary Imagination I hold to be the living power and prime agent of human perception, and as a repetition in the finite mind of the eternal act of creation in the infinite I AM.'[10] The imagination is thus itself a causal progenitor, not passive, but capable of creative activity.

Readers of *Natural Supernaturalism*, M. H. Abrams' penetrating and suggestive account of the Romantic movement, will recognize how nearly the argument to this point corresponds with his account of what he calls the Politics of Vision (pp. 356–72).[11] While it is never congenial to find one's own conclusions so closely anticipated it is nevertheless encouraging to find them powerfully corroborated by an approach from a different direction. To Professor Abrams, laying as he does particular stress on *The Prelude*, the reconciliation offered by Wordsworth and, in their degree, by the other Romantic poets is an almost wholly successful one. Yet there must reside a doubt, for Wordsworth has, as we saw, only interpolated a term into the determinist account by suggesting that 'the discipline of love', which is absorbed in his mother's arms, enables the child, otherwise a 'torpid life', to operate on 'the forms which it receives'. Again Wordsworth has to admit that, even on his own theories, if the Lake District can enrich and sanctify the imagination, a savage or degraded environment could similarly brutalize it, and thus the course of a man's development would be almost wholly determined by accident of birth.[12] These are points where Wordsworth cannot afford to press the argument. In addition he is defending a compromise which, as I have shown, allows little room for manoeuvre. What is the effect of all this on the poem?

I think that it is well summed up in some lines I quoted earlier from Book II. 'The mind of man,' Wordsworth says, 'is fram'd even

like the breath/And harmony of music', a firm positive statement—
'fram'd' and 'breath' give a comforting combination of the planned
and the natural: 'harmony' suggests their compatibility. Then
Wordsworth goes on, in language which seems to me to undermine his earlier positiveness while apparently reinforcing it,

> There is a dark
> Invisible workmanship that reconciles
> Discordant elements, and makes them move
> In one society.

'Dark' and 'invisible' are the words which call attention to the fact
that the palpable events of his wholesome boyhood and the general
conclusions about the mind of man that he draws from them have
their root in a mystery to which he can offer no solution. It is in
Wordsworth's sense of 'the mystery of Man' that we must look for
the origin of many of the most noticeable and characteristic effects
of the poem, such as its simultaneous obviousness and elusiveness.
This is perhaps most easily seen in the passages where Wordsworth, after narrating an incident in apparently exhaustive detail,
confesses that his painstaking analysis has somehow failed to
identify the feature that makes it of especial importance; indeed it
is often the incident's unaccountable impression on him that has
caused it to dwell in his mind. Such expressions of an indefinable
power are among the most durable experiences of a reading of *The
Prelude*:

> Imagination! lifting up itself
> Before the eye and progress of my Song
> Like an unfather'd vapour; here that Power,
> In all the might of its endowments, came
> Athwart me; I was lost as in a cloud,
> Halted, without a struggle to break through.
> And now recovering, to my Soul I say
> I recognise thy glory; in such strength
> Of usurpation, in such visitings
> Of awful promise, when the light of sense
> Goes out in flashes that have shewn to us
> The invisible world, doth Greatness make abode,
> There harbours whether we be young or old.
> Our destiny, our nature, and our home
> Is with infinitude, and only there;
> With hope it is, hope that can never die,
> Effort, and expectation, and desire,
> And something evermore about to be.   (VI. 525–42)

I choose this passage from many[13] to illustrate how at crucial moments in the poem what the reader is most conscious of is Wordsworth's sense of a scarcely expressible truth, or at least a truth so impalpable that it can be conveyed only by some inexplicable property of language. His own account of the quality of great poetry describes the process:

> Visionary Power
> Attends upon the motions of the winds
> Embodied in the mystery of words.
> There darkness makes abode, and all the host
> Of shadowy things do work their changes there,
> As in a mansion like their proper home;
> Even forms and substances are circumfused
> By that transparent veil with light divine;
> And through the turnings intricate of Verse,
> Present themselves as objects recognis'd,
> In flashes, and with a glory scarce their own.   (v. 619–29)

In addition since it is his primary task to explain and illustrate the peculiar reciprocal relationship of man and nature, mediated by the imagination, he uses expressions which present this symbiosis to the full, often depending, as in the opening of Book XII, on images of mutual interchange. These are at times carried almost to the point of paradox, reinforcing the suggestion that at vital moments the normal careful language of the poem can no longer bear the pressure of meaning.[14]

It may, however, be objected that the whole basis of this reading of *The Prelude* is misguided since there is no need to take account of Wordsworth's theories of the imagination. If we simply accept Wordsworth's account of his upbringing, it might be said, and observe the sensibility with which he records his mundane and mystic experience alike, we can actually witness the imagination at work and need not encumber our minds with Wordsworth's rationalizings of his own instinctive powers. The answer to this is threefold. First, these rationalizings occupy a substantial part of the poem and cannot simply be ignored as an undistinguished feature of the landscape: the fluctuations between observation and introspection are the essential movements of the poem and are themselves representative of the alternating process by which the human personality is created. Secondly, Wordsworth carefully records his hopes that the very act of writing will 'fix the wavering balance of my mind' (I. 650). This may mean 'help me to decide what to make of my life', but taken in conjunction with 654–5 ('should . . . I be taught/To understand myself') it seems to refer more directly to the poet's need to clarify his own opinions on the major issues he raises, including of course the tormenting question of character and environment. Many of the strange fits of depression or disgust which are the main psychological incidents of the poem derive from Wordsworth's sense that he has failed to maintain the 'wavering balance' of views on which his theory of the imagination depended. In this sense his fight for stability is of more importance than the overtly autobiographical material. For it is, finally, this struggle for faith and purpose which must enable the reader to move from an account of the youth of a North-country poet to a general view of human experience. There is no doubt that Wordsworth wished his readers to take the widest possible application of his poems. 'There is scarcely one of my poems which does not aim to direct the attention to some moral sentiment, or to some general principle, or law of thought, or of our intellectual constitution.'[15] That this is supremely true of *The Prelude* is shown by XIII. 439–45, where, at the conclusion of his great poem, he trusts that time remains for him and Coleridge to be

> . . . joint-labourers in a work
> (Should Providence such grace to us vouchsafe)
> Of their redemption, surely yet to come.
> Prophets of Nature, we to them will speak
> A lasting inspiration, sanctified
> By reason and by truth; what we have loved,
> Others will love; and we may teach them how.

Throughout *Natural Supernaturalism*, but especially in the earlier chapters, Professor Abrams makes two points of first importance —that Wordsworth was continuously aware of the parallel between his own enterprise and that of Milton in *Paradise Lost*, and that Wordsworth was in fact offering a secular version of redemption to man, a redemption to be achieved by a true understanding of the relation between Nature and the imagination. If we pursue the correspondence with Milton we can state Wordsworth's problem in quasi-theological terms by saying that he cannot, if he is to justify God's ways to men, rest content with showing how a particular set of consolations operated in his own case, but must show that a similar grace is available to all, that man is free in a more important sense than the political, and that we can all claim 'the Godhead that is ours, as natural beings in the strength of nature'. Wordsworth at once encounters the familiar Miltonic difficulty of deciding whether such grace is resistible: where Milton was concerned not to concede any failure in God's power or knowledge, Wordsworth's chief care is to defend the autonomy of the individual.

If Man is merely a passive recipient of Nature's imprint the results will be, at best, fortuitous and may even be unsatisfactory, as we see from *Ruth* (127–56). The question of how the redemptive imagination is to be persuaded to play its part in establishing the true mutual relationship, which alone gives spiritual health, and thus preserving men from morbid dejection is most fully discussed in *The Excursion*, especially in Book IV, 'Despondency Corrected'. Towards the end of this book there is a debate about 'the Imaginative Will' (1128), which in the main follows the lines laid down in *The Prelude*, with a broadly similar form of poetic expression. The Wanderer, who speaks with the voice of the Sage, makes a number of familiar claims. 'Within the soul a faculty abides' which can, as the moon irradiates a grove of trees, create 'a calm, a beautiful, and silent fire' from all the misfortunes of human life 'and sometimes . . . from palpable oppressions of despair'. The Solitary, to whom this comfort has been extended, replies with some asperity

> 'But how begin? and whence? "The Mind is free
> Resolve," the haughty Moralist would say,
> "This single act is all that we demand."
> Alas! such wisdom bids a creature fly
> Whose very sorrow is, that time hath shorn
> His natural wings!'   (1080–5)

The Wanderer begins his reply by telling of 'the curious child' who holds a shell to his ear and hears with joy the sound of the sea:

> Even such a shell the universe itself
> Is to the ear of Faith; and there are times,
> I doubt not, when to you it doth impart
> Authentic tidings of invisible things;
> Of ebb and flow, and ever-during power;
> And central peace, subsisting at the heart
> Of endless agitation.   (1141–47)

All good things must follow from love of Nature, including love of man and love of what is right:

> Trust me, that for the instructed, time will come
> When they shall meet no object but may teach
> Some acceptable lesson to their minds
> Of human suffering, or of human joy.
> So shall they learn, while all things speak of man,
> Their duties from all forms; and general laws,
> And local accidents, shall tend alike
> To rouse, to urge; and with the will, confer
> The ability to spread the blessings wide
> Of true philanthropy.   (1235–44)

The Sage continues in language strongly reminiscent of God in Book III of *Paradise Lost:*

> The light of love
> Not failing, perseverance from their steps
> Departing not, for them shall be confirmed
> The glorious habit by which sense is made
> Subservient still to moral purposes,
> Auxiliar to divine.   (1244–49)

Even scientists will not use their eye passively, 'chained to its object in brute slavery', but as a support to 'the mind's *excursive power*'. Then the Sage attempts once more to explain how in spite of the energetic ministrations of nature man is still free:

> . . So build we up the Being that we are;
> Thus deeply drinking—in the soul of things,
> We shall be wise perforce; and, while inspired
> By choice, and conscious that the Will is free,
> Shall move unswerving, even as if impelled
> By strict necessity, along the path
> Of order and of good.   (1264–70)

The doubts and ambiguities which lie behind Wordsworth's understanding of the formation of the human personality and which in *The Prelude* contributed so powerfully to the tensions of the poem here stand nakedly and awkwardly across his path. It does not really save Wordsworth's argument to say that we are free but behave as though we were not, especially if we are to be made wise 'perforce'. The phrase 'inspired by choice', with its combination of passive participle and active noun, embodies the contradictions of Wordsworth's position. In spite of his protestations, he comes here very close to a secular version of the doctrine of irresistible grace, the 'simplicity/And beauty, and inevitable grace' of which he had spoken in Book VIII of *The Prelude* (lines 157–8). The whole passage echoes the Miltonic arguments about the extent to which salvation may be earned, and embodies their fundamental contradictions.

Milton and Wordsworth are both faced with a paradox which they cannot completely resolve. Each of them has arrived at his personal and partial solution for understanding and accepting the paradox, for living with it, as we say. Their declared intention is to make their solutions available to others through poems more or less explicitly religious: the nature of the solution will necessarily play a large part in determining the nature of the poem which presents it. In *The Excursion* the sense of personal conflict is not so strong as in *The Prelude*. At the end of the Wanderer's speech he exclaims in language which defies paraphrase yet is unmistakably encouraging in tone:

> Whate'er we see,
> Or feel, shall tend to quicken and refine;
> Shall fix, in calmer seats of moral strength,
> Earthly desires; and raise, to loftier heights
> Of divine love, our intellectual soul.[16]   (1270–4)

Although the affirmations in *The Excursion* are firm and unqualified, the right to make them seems to have earned on some other field. 'I yet despair not of our nature' Wordsworth had said in Book II of *The Prelude*: in that poem he narrated with great fidelity and patience the processes by which he was able to convince himself that man is a free agent. He was thus able to make the poem a testimony to human sovereignty, to the power of 'man's unconquerable mind', and to

> The dignity of individual Man,
> Of Man, no composition of the thought,
> Abstraction, shadow, image, but the man
> Of whom we read, the man whom we behold
> With our own eyes.   (*Prelude* XII. 83–7)

II SHELLEY. A note on *Prometheus Unbound*

In the declaratory exordium which prefaces the Declaration of Rights, we see the solemn and majestic spectacle of a Nation opening its commission, under the auspices of its Creator, to establish a Government; a scene so new, and so transcendentally unequalled by anything in the European world, that the name of Revolution is diminutive of its character, and it rises into a Regeneration of Man.—TOM PAINE, *Observations on the Declaration of Rights*.

The speed and thoroughness with which Wordsworth and Coleridge lost their early enthusiasm for the French Revolution are too well-known to require illustration, and it is a commonplace of criticism that Wordsworth's 'more than Roman confidence' in the powers of the free man was heavily qualified in his later years. One might point to the alterations in *The Prelude*, notably the inclusion of the superb panegyric on Burke, to the later versions of *The Excursion*, or to the way in which *Poems dedicated to National Independence and Liberty* were followed by *Sonnets Dedicated to Liberty and Order*. This last eminently Wordsworthian title points

to the poet's increasing awareness of the complicated relationship
between personal liberty and human responsibilities. The *Ode to
Duty* (1805, pub. 1807) shows this clearly:

> Me this unchartered freedom tires;
> I feel the weight of chance-desires . . .
> Yet not the less would I throughout
> Still act according to the voice
> Of my own wish; and feel past doubt
> That my submissiveness was choice.
>
> (37–8, 41–4)

If it is characteristic of Wordsworth that he should address a poem
to the 'Stern Daughter of the Voice of God' it is no less characteristic of Shelley that he should include with *Prometheus Unbound*
(1820) the fine *Ode to Liberty*. The question I wish to consider in
this note is how Shelley's passionate belief in liberty is to be
reconciled with his equally fervent necessitarianism.

The doubleness of thought can be seen in *Queen Mab*. Clearly
Shelley is carrying into this very early work a great deal of his
reading of the eighteenth-century *philosophes*. It is not hard to
detect echoes of Hume, Holbach and Godwin, among others. The
intellectual framework seems inescapably necessitarian, yet there
is a vision of man triumphant:

> Yes! crime and misery are in yonder earth,
>   Falsehood, mistake, and lust;
>   But the eternal world
> Contains at once the evil and the cure.
> Some eminent in virtue shall start up,
>   Even in perversest time:
> The truths of their pure lips, that never die,
> Shall bind the scorpion falsehood with a wreath
>   Of ever-living flame,
> Until the monster sting itself to death.
> How sweet a scene will earth become!
> Of purest spirits a pure dwelling-place,
> Symphonious with the planetary spheres;
> When man, with changeless Nature coalescing,
> Will undertake regeneration's work,
> When its ungenial poles no longer point
>   To the red and baleful sun
>   That faintly twinkles there.   (VI. 29–46)[17]

The vision will be made real by the dauntless heroism of men
themselves, not acting with any kind of divine aid, but in co-
operation with the invincible processes of Futurity.

The idea of the 'omnipotent hour' which is to signalize the downfall of tyranny is similarly prominent in *Hellas* (1822). Indeed Shelley's poetry on this theme is consistent from first to last: it is perhaps not too strong to say that all his major poems on man and society take over the vision and even the pattern of *Queen Mab*. He described *The Revolt of Islam* (1817) as 'an experiment upon the temper of the public mind, as to how far a thirst for a happier condition . . . of society survives, among the enlightened and refined, the tempests which have shaken the age in which we live'. The subtitle of the first version of this poem—'The Revolution of the Golden City: A Vision of the Nineteenth Century'—could stand in apposition to nearly all Shelley's major poems, but to none more appropriately than to *Prometheus Unbound* (written 1818–19). Shelley again creates a world in which the governing force is inexorable necessity, moving slowly in Time, and represented in the drama by Demogorgon; he is then confronted by the question of what virtues a man can conceivably display in a world ruled by necessity. In such a situation a man may either hope or despair. Shelley assumes that he is free to choose between these alternatives: he affirms that the chief virtue is to choose to hope, and that the great function of the poet is to give man things to hope for. How is this embodied in the work itself?

It is somewhat puzzling that there has been considerable disagreement among critics. Shelley's Preface and Mrs Shelley's lengthy Note agree with one another and with the poem:

> The prominent feature of Shelley's theory of the destiny of the human species was that evil is not inherent in the system of the creation, but an accident that might be expelled. . . . Shelley believed that mankind had only to will that there should be no evil, and there would be none. It is not my part in these Notes to notice the arguments that have been urged against this opinion, but to mention the fact that he entertained it, and was indeed attached to it with fervent enthusiasm. That man could be so perfectionized as to be able to expel evil from his own nature, and from the greater part of the creation, was the cardinal point of his system. And the subject he loved best to dwell on was the image of One warring with the Evil Principle, oppressed not only by it, but by all—even the good, who were deluded into considering evil a necessary portion of humanity; a victim full of fortitude and hope and the spirit of triumph emanating from a reliance in the ultimate omnipotence of Good. Such he had depicted in his last poem, when he made Laon the enemy and the victim of tyrants. He now took a more idealized image of the same subject.

Mrs Shelley then tells the story of Prometheus, carefully distinguishing between 'the mythological story', in which Prometheus 'bought pardon for his crime of enriching mankind with his gifts' and was set free by Hercules, nothing being said of the fate of Jupiter, and the way in which 'Shelley adapted the catastrophe of this story to his peculiar views' by making Prometheus continually defiant until 'the Primal Power of the world' has driven Jupiter from his throne. Only then is 'Humanity, typified in Prometheus' set free and united with Nature 'in perfect and happy union'.

This is plain enough: it is also plain that we have set before us in the first act precisely the sort of situation I have discussed. Jupiter, who represents every form of evil, tyranny and ignorance, seems to have the entire created world in his grasp. The sole exception is the defiant Prometheus:

> Mother, thy sons and thou
> Scorn him, without whose all-enduring will
> Beneath the fierce omnipotence of Jove,
> Both they and thou had vanished, like thin mist
> Unrolled on the morning wind. Know ye not me,
> The Titan? He who made his agony
> The barrier to your else all-conquering foe?
>
> (I. 113–19)

There is in Prometheus' first speech a point of interpretation which, though small, proves crucial for an account of the structure of the drama. Before the play opens, Prometheus has pronounced a terrible curse on Jupiter, breathing contempt and defiance. At one point in his first speech he says, 'The curse/Once breathed on thee I would recall' (I. 58–9). Some critics have interpreted 'recall' in the sense of 'revoke' and have made these lines the critical moment of the action from which all the following events flow. We have then a drama of regeneration, with a pattern not unlike that of *The Ancient Mariner*. On this reading Prometheus has degraded the nature of man by allowing himself to hate Jupiter, but when he finds it in his heart to forgive his adversary Jupiter is overthrown and Prometheus triumphs.

This reading encounters a number of difficulties. First, Shelley does not use 'recall' (= *revoke*) elsewhere. It normally means 'remember' or 'call back into mind'. Thus in this passage it is more probable that Prometheus is asking to be reminded of the precise wording of his curse, or, even stronger, is calling it back into existence. This is corroborated by the last words of his speech:

> If then my words had power,
> Though I am changed so that aught evil wish
> Is dead within; although no memory be
> Of what is hate, let them not lose it now!
> What was that curse? for ye all heard me speak.
>
> (I. 69–73)

and many other passages in Act I.[18] Secondly Prometheus in fact continues to defy Jupiter and Earth continues to show pride in him for doing so. Thirdly as Maurice Bowra has pointed out, if Jupiter in fact represents the principle of evil, it would clearly be wrong for Prometheus to forgive him. Finally at the end of the play Demogorgon has three rhymed stanzas, of which the first begins, 'This is the day, which down the void abysm/At the Earth-born's spell yawns for Heaven's despotism.' The 'Earth-born's spell' is Prometheus' curse.[19] The last stanza runs

> To suffer woes which Hope thinks infinite;
> To forgive wrongs darker than death or night;
>   To defy Power, which seems omnipotent;
> To love, and bear; to hope till Hope creates
> From its own wreck the thing it contemplates;
>   Neither to change, nor falter, nor repent;
> This, like thy glory, Titan, is to be
> Good, great and joyous, beautiful and free;
> This is alone Life, Joy, Empire, and Victory.

Demogorgon clearly attributes the downfall of Jupiter to this curse, not to its revocation: it was Prometheus' glory to suffer infinitely and not to resent that suffering, yet still to maintain his defiance of Jupiter, without changing, faltering *or repenting*. For if Prometheus is considered to have revoked his entire curse his resistance also must be considered at an end, since his curse is not simply an outburst of hatred, but an expression of defiance and confidence in the outcome. This is made particularly clear in I. 262–5.

At this point it seems reasonable to consider as corroborating evidence Shelley's statement in the Preface. He says 'But, in truth, I was averse from a catastrophe so feeble as that of reconciling the Champion with the Oppressor of mankind. The moral interest of the fable, which is so powerfully sustained by the sufferings and endurance of Prometheus, would be annihilated if we could conceive of him as unsaying his high language and quailing before his successful and perfidious adversary.'

Not only is the regenerative theory poorly supported by the text, but further difficulties appear when we apply it to the work as a whole, since, by making Prometheus' change of heart the pivot of the drama it distorts the entire action.[20] It is true that Prometheus clearly fights throughout on the side of love, whereas Jupiter's empire is founded on fear, and it is true also that Prometheus has grown in wisdom during his bondage, but this regeneration is touched on only incidentally and as something effected before the play begins, nor is there any evidence in the text that it is symbolized by the revocation of the curse or that this revocation is the cause of Jupiter's overthrow. To say then that forgiveness of

Jupiter is Prometheus's only weapon against evil or that the Titan triumphs through forgiveness and pity is to impose on the poem without justification a causal pattern.

I think there is a better case to be made out for saying that the Titan's sole weapon against tyranny is his certainty that the hour will arrive which will drag Jupiter to his doom. That this doom is to be terrible, as terrible indeed as that invoked in the curse, is inevitable, and Prometheus' recantation could have no effect on it: his task is to endure, ensuring by his defiance that the tyrant's dominion shall not be absolute. Therefore it is no unfounded paradox to say that, far from Prometheus' regeneration enabling Demogorgon to cast Jupiter from his throne, it is the inevitability of Demogorgon's overthrow of Jupiter which has enabled Prometheus to continue his resistance, and that his certain vision of the fatal hour alone enables him to pity Jupiter (I. 53). When the play opens the Titan knows that victory is already won: it is this which gives him the magnanimity of the victor, and not the magnanimity which enables him to win the victory. Effectively Prometheus is unbound from the start of the play, since he is secure in the certain knowledge that the hour of Jupiter's overthrow must come. 'I wait/Enduring thus, the retributive hour' (I. 405–6). When the hour arrives its simultaneous effects, among them the physical release of Prometheus, are presented consecutively.

I suggest that this is what Shelley meant when he described *Prometheus Unbound* as having a 'mechanism of a kind yet unattempted'. Instead of the causal machinery of the orthodox drama Shelley offers a vision of two states of mankind, given significant relationship by juxtaposition. We are shown first man constricted but defiant, and then man released:

> Thrones, altars, judgement-seats, and prisons; wherein,
> And beside which, by wretched men were borne
> Sceptres, tiaras, swords, and chains, and tomes
> Of reasoned wrong, glozed on by ignorance,
> Were like those monstrous and barbaric shapes,
> The ghosts of a no-more-remembered fame,
> Which, from their unworn obelisks, look forth
> In triumph o'er the palaces and tombs
> Of those who were their conquerors: mouldering round,
> These imaged to the pride of kings and priests
> A dark yet mighty faith, a power as wide
> As is the world it wasted, and are now
> But an astonishment; even so the tools
> And emblems of its last captivity,
> Amid the dwellings of the peopled earth,
> Stand, not o'erthrown, but unregarded now.

And those foul shapes, abhorred by god and man,—
Which, under many a name and many a form
Strange, savage, ghastly, dark and execrable,
Were Jupiter, the tyrant of the world;
And which the nations, panic-stricken, served
With blood, and hearts broken by long hope, and love
Dragged to his altars soiled and garlandless,
And slain amid men's unreclaiming tears,
Flattering the thing they feared, which fear was hate,—
Frown, mouldering fast, o'er their abandoned shrines:
The painted veil, by those who were, called life,
Which mimicked, as with colours idly spread,
All men believed or hoped, is torn aside;
The loathsome mask has fallen, the man remains
Sceptreless, free, uncircumscribed, but man
Equal, unclassed, tribeless, and nationless,
Exempt from awe, worship, degree, the king
Over himself; just, gentle, wise: but man
Passionless?—no, yet free from guilt or pain,
Which were, for his will made or suffered them,
Nor yet exempt, though ruling them like slaves,
From chance, and death, and mutability,
The clogs of that which else might oversoar
The loftiest star of unascended heaven,
Pinnacled dim in the intense inane.   (III. iv. 164–204)[21]

This leads into the rapturous vision of Act Four.

This view of the structure of *Prometheus Unbound* is confirmed at every point by Shelley's own Preface. The passage that is most immediately relevant to the concerns of this book runs as follows:

> The only imaginary being resembling in any degree Prometheus, is Satan; and Prometheus is, in my judgement, a more poetical character than Satan, because, in addition to courage, and majesty, and firm and patient opposition to omnipotent force, he is susceptible of being described as exempt from the taints of ambition, envy, revenge, and a desire for personal aggrandisement, which, in the Hero of *Paradise Lost*, interfere with the interest. The character of Satan engenders in the mind a pernicious casuistry which leads us to weigh his faults with his wrongs, and to excuse the former because the latter exceed all measure. In the minds of those who consider that magnificent fiction with a religious feeling it engenders something worse. But Prometheus is, as it were, the type of the highest perfection of moral and intellectual nature, impelled by the purest and the truest motives to the best and noblest ends.

Immediately before *Prometheus* Shelley had completed a much slighter and less ambitious piece, *Julian and Maddalo* (pub. 1824). Of the narrator, Julian, Shelley writes in his Preface, 'Julian is an Englishman of good family, passionately attached to those philosophical notions which assert the power of man over his own mind, and the immense improvements of which, by the extinction of certain moral superstitions, human society may yet be susceptible. Without concealing the evil in the world, he is for ever speculating how good may be made superior.' Julian declares

> It is our will
> That thus enchains us to permitted ill—
> We might be otherwise—we might be all
> We dream of happy, high, majestical.
> . . . .
> Those who try may find
> How strong the chains are which our spirit bind;
> Brittle perchance as straw. . . . We are assured
> Much may be conquered, much may be endured,
> Of what degrades and crushes us. We know
> That we have power over ourselves to do
> And suffer—what, we know not till we try;
> But something nobler than to live and die.   (170–3, 180–7)

In Julian Shelley accurately describes his own character, especially his own optimism. The situation in *Prometheus* is typical. Shelley symbolizes the world in terms of a universe dominated by a brutal tyrant. Only one man is still resisting. He is chained and tortured. He has no weapon but hope, but simply by refusing to despair he achieves at last for all mankind a world in which there is nothing but what is good. Shelley thus affirms simultaneously a rigid determinism and an unshakeable trust that the spirit of man is free, softening the contradiction by insisting that man, if he exerts himself sufficiently and refuses to be overborne by the press of events, will be assisted by irresistible forces to abolish, if not necessity itself, at least those manifestations of it which are most oppressive to the human spirit. That is, necessity as the inevitable march of progress is welcomed, while necessity which shows itself as oppression is to be overcome. Effectively what Shelley is doing is arguing that, if a man has an irresistible impluse to choose to be free and obeys it, this obedience is not a proof that he acts as he must, but a demonstration of his freedom.

He makes this seem plausible in two ways. First by meeting any direct request for a definition of precisely what it is that oppresses humanity by answering initially in political terms. That is to say, he would identify the constricting forces with political tyranny of any kind. If this is so, it may be Utopian, but is not necessarily ridiculous, to trust that man will eventually achieve liberty. Secondly, if pressed to say more precisely how this is to be brought about

Shelley responds by executing the opposite manoeuvre and returning the argument from the political level to one that is far removed from any very direct contact with the physical manifestations of the necessary world. There is more than a little truth in his ironic comment—'as to real flesh and blood, you know that I do not deal in those articles; you might as well go to a gin-shop for a leg of mutton, as expect anything human or earthly from me.'[22] If then Shelley is a political poet with 'a passion for reforming the world' how does he reconcile these practical ends with his reluctance to write directly about 'real flesh and blood', especially as he maintained also 'didactic poetry is my abhorrence'? In the Preface to *Prometheus Unbound* he makes his position a little clearer. He denies that he dedicates his poems 'solely to the direct enforcement of reform' or considers them 'as containing a reasoned system on the theory of human life'. He continues, 'My purpose . . . has . . . been to familiarise the highly refined imagination of the more select classes of poetical readers with *beautiful idealisms of moral excellence.*' The phrase I have italicized is directly relevant to his description of *Prometheus* as 'in the merest spirit of ideal poetry'.[23]

In his *Defence of Poetry* (1821) Shelley wrote, 'The great secret of morals is love; or a going out of our own nature, and an identification of ourselves with the beautiful which exists in thought, action or person, not our own. . . . The great instrument of the moral good is the imagination; and poetry ministers to the effect by acting on the cause.' Shelley is exploiting the well-known difficulty which confronts anyone who tries to account for the origin of his own moral principles in a way that preserves his freedom and dignity as a moral agent. In effect Shelley argues that if we do in fact choose our moral principles we must in the last analysis choose them for their beauty. Thus the poet who wishes to move the world forward need not operate at the practical level: he can change men far more effectively by putting before them at the primary level 'beautiful idealisms of moral excellence'. This is an interesting argument because it provides an analogy for Shelley's apparently contradictory beliefs about free will. Many people who reject any theories of the world as determined on the grounds that in such a world moral choices would no longer be real because no longer free would nevertheless accept that aesthetic choices are not free, in the sense that between two pictures we can have only one intuitive preference and cannot choose which we shall prefer. If we do not regard this as compromising our freedom of artistic judgement, why should we not accept the same limitation of our moral judgement, especially if, as Shelley suggests, the two are intimately related?

Applying this abstract argument to man in the early nineteenth century Shelley says that technically his age has all the knowledge it needs.[24] What is needed now is the imagination to see what to do with this knowledge. Poets, by bringing mankind into sympathy with 'hopes and fears it heeded not' are able to become the mirrors of the gigantic images which futurity casts upon the world. The precise relationship between 'unawakened earth' and 'the trumpet of a prophecy' is left in doubt. We may imagine that Shelley wishes to work on the wills of men, though not, as I have said, at the level of conscious choice, to urge them to want to bring the new world into being. Some response would be required—either political action, or if that is impossible 'To hope till Hope creates/From its own wreck the thing it contemplates': without any response the new world can never come to birth. Alternatively we may see Shelley and other poets as, so to speak, preparing man for the inevitable, even preparing the way for the inevitable: in this case no response is appropriate except, I suppose, the cultivation of a generally welcoming state of mind.

One might speculate in passing on how far this doubleness of attitude is responsible for a characteristic feature of Shelley's verse. Many critics have accused Shelley of vagueness, and have pointed to a number of local ambiguities in support of their case. Yet an inspection of Shelley's verse often suggests a different conclusion. Consider *England in 1819*:

> An old, mad blind, despised, and dying king,—
> Princes, the dregs of their dull race, who flow
> Through public scorn,—mud from a muddy spring,—
> Rulers who neither see, nor feel, nor know,
> But leech-like to their fainting country cling,
> Till they drop, blind in blood, without a blow,—
> A people starved and stabbed in the untilled field,—
> An army, which liberticide and prey
> Makes as a two-edged sword to all who wield,—
> Golden and sanguine laws which tempt and slay;
> Religion Christless, Godless—a book sealed;
> A Senate,—Time's worst statute unrepealed,—
> Are graves, from which a glorious Phantom may
> Burst, to illumine our tempestuous day.

If this sonnet can fairly be criticized as vague it is not because of the obscurity of allusions such as 'Time's worst statute' or because of its looseness of structure (in fact the massing of subjects and use of apposition give the syntax a cumulative interest) but because the last two lines leave the reader stranded between an active and a passive response. The list of evils prompts to action: the promise that they will themselves engender their own destruction inclines to resignation. Even if the fatally candid 'may' were replaced by 'shall', the ambiguity would remain.

It is a metaphysical uncertainty of this kind that seems to me to lie at the heart of the impression of vagueness in many of Shelley's major poems, not an imprecision in the use of words. Even though the uncertainty is not intellectually crippling, since it can be put in perspective by comparing our response to the poem with our response to a picture, which might involve no overt activity but yet change for ever our standards of beauty, it is nevertheless felt as a lack of sureness at the aesthetic level. What is involved is not simply a dual response to the word 'shall' but also a conflict between the total determinism of the cosmic world-view and the exhortatory tone of the language. 'Exhortatory' is too weak: the tone is evangelical, breathing rapturous enthusiasm and excitement and trust that the spirit of man will overcome all obstacles. It is an irresistible plea for generous action in a world where action is unnecessary. Thus the parts of Shelley's poems in which he characterises and denounces tyranny (typical verb 'is') are usually felt to be firmer and more precise than the parts in which he characterises and welcomes Liberty (typical verb 'shall'). Possibly the fault is our own: perhaps we should be in command of the appropriate response to prophecy. Possibly the ambiguity of the word 'prophet' is to blame.

In any case it is plain that for Shelley poets have a vital part to play in the world, that he sees, fairly consistently, how they should play it, and sees moreover, on the practical level, just what the forces of oppression are. When he claims that 'poets are the unacknowledged legislators of the world', we may perhaps demur at the choice of noun, but allow him to include poets among 'those radiant spirits, who are still/The standard-bearers in the van of Change'.[25] This is what we must bear in mind when we weigh the truth of Arnold's celebrated dismissal of Shelley as 'a beautiful and ineffectual angel, beating in the void his luminous wings in vain'.[26] Shelley appears to be in the void because he is operating directly on a very deep layer of the human personality, the unconscious level in which are embodied our highest ideals of the capacities of man. Change this, enlarge a man's conception of what human nature is by showing him the beauty of moral ideas, and you change every subsequent action. This faith is at the root of Shelley's life and of all his presentations of the visionary as hero.

III BYRON. *Manfred* and *Don Juan*

Count Maddalo is . . . a person of the most consummate genius, and capable, if he would direct his energies to such an end, of becoming the redeemer of his degraded country. But it is his weakness to be proud: he derives, from a comparison of his own extraordinary mind with the dwarfish intellects that surround him, an intense apprehension of the nothingness of human life. His passions and his powers are incomparably greater than those of other men; and, instead of the latter having been employed in curbing the former, they have mutually lent each other strength. His ambition preys upon itself, for want of objects which it can consider worthy of exertion. I say that Maddalo is proud, because I can find no other word to express the concentered and impatient feelings which consume him; but it is on his own hopes and affections only that he seems to trample.—Preface to *Julian and Maddalo: A Conversation*

Shelley's description of Maddalo is the best introduction to Byron. From his first appearance Maddalo's role in the poem is that of the unillusioned older man whose views are set in contrast to the impatient Utopianism of Julian:

> Of all that earth has been or yet may be,
> All that vain men imagine or believe,
> Or hope can paint or suffering may achieve,
> We descanted, and I (for ever still
> Is it not wise to make the best of ill?)
> Argued against despondency, but pride
> Made my companion take the darker side.
> The sense that he was greater than his kind
> Had struck, methinks, his eagle spirit blind
> By gazing on its own exceeding light.   (43–52)

He leaves the poem on the same note:

> And I remember one remark which then
> Maddalo made. He said: 'Most wretched men
> Are cradled into poetry by wrong,
> They learn in suffering what they teach in song.'   (543–6)

I want in this chapter to consider the nature of Byron's suffering and in what sense he may be said to teach. The suffering is not difficult to display: the idea of Byron as a teacher is less acceptable, in spite of his well-known comment in a letter to Murray of 1821— '[The ethical] is the highest of all poetry.' If one were asked to say what the popular notion of Byron's teaching was, a fair reply would be that just as Shelley offers us the visionary as hero, so Byron presents the rebel as hero, with all the inadequacies that such a presentation would imply.

Yet even of his early poems this would not be a complete account. His career as a poet effectively began with the first and second cantos of *Childe Harold* (1812), which was a kind of verse

journal of his travels in 1809–11, the development of the poem
being determined by the order in which the scenes described had
actually been visited. Although the identification between Byron
and his hero is fairly close in these cantos,[27] there is at least a
formal division between the Childe with his melancholy, loneliness,
boredom, disillusion and self-dramatizing introversion on the one
hand, and the outward-looking, inquiring traveller on the other. It
is plain however, that, though differentiated, they each represent
one side of the poet's nature.

It is not easy to illustrate briefly the genuine force of the more
extravagant vein of Byron's poetry, to convey the sense of overpowering and inescapable suffering that broods behind the flashy
and apparently empty rhetoric, to show what Byron meant when
he spoke of poetry as 'the lava of the imagination, whose eruption
prevents the earthquake'. Perhaps the most compact example is
Manfred (1817), published the year after Canto III of *Childe Harold.*
Manfred, living in his castle in the Higher Alps, has studied 'Philosophy and science, and the springs/Of wonder, and the wisdom of
the world'. He has acquired enormous powers, and like Faust has
spirits at his command, but since he has committed an unspecified
sin at 'an all-nameless hour', he has no happiness or rest. He orders
the spirits to appear to him, and when they do not conjures them
as follows:

> If it be so—Spirits of earth and air,
> Ye shall not thus elude me: by a power,
> Deeper than all yet urged, a tyrant-spell,
> Which had its birthplace in a star condemn'd,
> The burning wreck of a demolish'd world,
> A wandering hell in the eternal space;
> By the strong curse which is upon my soul,
> The thought which is within me and around me,
> I do compel ye to my will—Appear!   (I. i. 41–9)

They ask what he wants and he tells them that his only wish is for
forgetfulness:

Manfred	Will death bestow it on me?
Spirit	We are immortal, and do not forget;
	We are eternal; and to us the past
	Is, as the future, present. Art thou answer'd?
Manfred	Ye mock me—but the power which brought ye here
	Hath made you mine. Slaves, scoff not at my will!
	The mind, the spirit, the Promethean spark,
	The lightning of my being, is as bright,
	Pervading, and far darting as your own,
	And shall not yield to yours, though coop'd in clay!
	Answer, or I will teach you what I am. (148–58)

Plate 5. John Martin. Manfred on the Jungfrau (1837). By courtesy of Birmingham Museums and Art Gallery

Oblivion is the one thing which cannot be granted: instead Manfred is cursed in a long incantation—

> By thy delight in others' pain,
> And by thy brotherhood of Cain,
> I call upon thee! and compel
> Thyself to be thy proper Hell!   (248–51)

Thus in the first scene many of the characteristics of the Byronic hero are forcefully indicated. He has committed a mysterious and inexpiable crime, for which he suffers eternal remorse, though never precisely repenting. He is a man of immense power, he confronts a hostile destiny, he defies it in the name of human freedom, yet is doomed to misery. Oblivion offers his only hope of escape, but this is denied him. Manfred soliloquizes as follows:

> There is a power upon me which withholds,
> And makes it my fatality to live,—
> If it be life to wear within myself
> This barrenness of spirit, and to be
> My own soul's sepulchre, for I have ceased
> To justify my deeds unto myself—
> The last infirmity of evil.
> . . . .
>   Beautiful!
> How beautiful is all this visible world!
> How glorious in its action and itself!
> But we, who name ourselves its sovereigns, we,
> Half dust, half deity, alike unfit
> To sink, or soar, with our mix'd essence make
> A conflict of its elements, and breathe
> The breath of degradation and of pride,
> Contending with low wants and lofty will,
> Till our mortality predominates,
> And men are—what they name not to themselves,
> And trust not to each other.   (I. ii. 23–9, 36–47)

It is interesting to note that Pope's 'being darkly wise, and rudely great' has now become 'half dust, half deity'.

Manfred is rescued as he tries to throw himself over a precipice, and in Act II his constant burden is the impossibility of bearing the weight of self-knowledge:

> My solitude is solitude no more,
> But peopled with the Furies;—I have gnash'd
> My teeth in darkness till returning morn,
> Then cursed myself till sunset;—I have pray'd

> For madness as a blessing—'tis denied me.
> I have affronted death—but in the war
> Of elements the waters shrunk from me,
> And fatal things pass'd harmless; the cold hand
> Of an all-pitiless demon held me back,
> Back by a single hair which would not break.
> In fantasy, imagination, all
> The affluence of my soul—which one day was
> A Croesus in creation—I plunged deep,
> But, like an ebbing wave, it dash'd me back
> Into the gulf of my unfathom'd thought.
> I plunged amidst mankind—Forgetfulness
> I sought in all, save where 'tis to be found,
> And that I have to learn; my sciences,
> My long-pursued and superhuman art,
> Is mortal here: I dwell in my despair—
> And live—and live for ever.   (II. ii. 130–49)

Once again the ironic echo is of Pope—'And all our knowledge is, ourselves to know.' Whereas for Pope pride is the source of human error, it is now all that Manfred has left to sustain him. When the Witch of the Alps offers to help him if he will swear obedience to her will he indignantly refuses—

> I will not swear—Obey! and whom? the spirits
> Whose presence I command, and be the slave
> Of those who served me—Never!   (II. ii. 158–60)

When she has gone Manfred reflects as follows in a soliloquy alive with Shakespearean turns of phrase:

> We are the fools of time and terror: Days
> Steal on us, and steal from us; yet we live,
> Loathing our life, and dreading still to die.   (164–6)

He determines to call up the dead and ask them what death is. The soliloquy ends

> Yet in this hour I dread the thing I dare:
> Until this hour I never shrunk to gaze
> On spirit, good or evil—now I tremble,
> And feel a strange cold thaw upon my heart.
> But I can act even what I most abhor,
> And champion human fears.—The night approaches.   (199–204)

There follows a scene on the summit of the Jungfrau in which the Three Destinies or Fates wait for the arrival of Nemesis. They are uniformly malevolent, and exist only to make mankind wretched. Nemesis is as powerful as Shelley's Demogorgon, but her energies are devoted to strengthening the forces of tyranny:

First Destiny   Say, where hast thou been?
                My sisters and thyself are slow to-night.
Nemesis   I was detain'd repairing shatter'd thrones,
                Marrying fools, restoring dynasties,
                Avenging men upon their enemies,
                And making them repent their own revenge;
                Goading the wise to madness; from the dull
                Shaping out oracles to rule the world
                Afresh, for they were waxing out of date,
                And mortals dared to ponder for themselves,
                To weigh kings in the balance, and to speak
                Of freedom, the forbidden fruit.—Away!
                We have outstay'd the hour—mount we our clouds!
                                (II. iii. 60–72)

This completes the picture of a hostile Universe with one free man, as in *Prometheus Unbound*, but in Byron the future holds no hope;[28] only pride can lead Manfred to prefer defiance to submission. He goes to Hell and, in a scene reminiscent of Beckford's *Vathek*, confronts the destinies and their ruler Arimanes, to whom he refuses to bow down. He calls up the vision of the dead Astarte, presumably his sister, who prophesies that he will die the next day. After a number of not dissimilar scenes in which Manfred speaks of his doom—'Look on me! there is an order/Of mortals on the earth, who do become/Old in their youth, and die ere middle age'—the hour arrives when he must die. The Spirits of the Underworld come to hale him away, but Manfred defies them and refuses to obey them:

                                      Back to thy hell!
Thou hast no power upon me, *that* I feel;
Thou never shalt possess me, *that* I know:
What I have done is done; I bear within
A torture which could nothing gain from thine:
The mind which is immortal makes itself
Requital for its good or evil thoughts,—
Is its own origin of ill and end—
And its own place and time: its innate sense,
When stripp'd of this mortality, derives
No colour from the fleeting things without,
But is absorb'd in sufferance or in joy,
Born from the knowledge of its own desert.
Thou didst not tempt me, and thou couldst not tempt me;

> I have not been thy dupe, nor am thy prey—
> But was my own destroyer, and will be
> My own hereafter.—Back, ye baffled fiends!—
> The hand of death is on me—but not yours! (III. iv. 124–41)

The Demons disappear and Manfred yields up his life, saying, 'Old man! 'tis not so difficult to die.'

The implications of *Manfred* for my argument are not difficult to draw. It is clear that Manfred represents will incarnate and power unlimited. Yet given infinite potentiality all he can find to desire is oblivion. The passages I have quoted establish the utter desolation in which he lives, sustained only by indomitable pride—'The lion is alone and so am I.' He is presented by Byron without overt or implied criticism, and is only one of a large number of similar characters. For example:

> Lone, wild, and strange he stood alike exempt
> From all affection and from all contempt. (*The Corsair*)

> There was in him a vital scorn of all:
> As if the worst had fall'n which could befall,
> He stood a stranger in this breathing world,
> An erring spirit from another hurl'd;
> A thing of dark imaginings, that shaped
> By choice the perils he by chance escaped;
> But 'scaped in vain, for in their memory yet
> His mind would half exult and half regret:
> . . . .
> But haughty still, and loth himself to blame,
> He call'd on Nature's self to share the shame,
> And charged all faults upon the fleshly form
> She gave to clog the soul, and feast the worm;
> Till he at last confounded good and ill,
> And half mistook for fate the acts of will: (*Lara* I. 312–20, 331–6)

With these should be included the Childe Harold of the third and fourth cantos: the character of the Childe grows much more melancholy—in Canto III his independence, originality, boldness, and hatred of hypocrisy are almost submerged in his vanity, petulance, self-pity and arrogance, while in Canto IV the self-pity is generalized into a rather gloomy stoicism. Whereas in Canto III everything was firmly related to a central obsessive 'Childe/Byron' personality, in Canto IV the tone is shifting, now resigned, now bitter, always conscious of mutability. It is important to bear this character in mind since it establishes the closeness of the connection between the demon-haunted heroes and the poet's own situation, 'My own wretched identity' as he calls it in the *Journal of an*

Alpine Tour.[29] Scott commented in May 1816, 'Lord Byron . . . has Childe Harolded himself and Outlawed himself into too great a resemblance with the pictures of his imagination.'[30]

Little that Byron wrote after this point in his career was valued in Britain or abroad during the nineteenth century. In the twenty years after Byron's death Byronism swept the Continent, especially France: it was taken to signify 'la révolte de l'individu contre la société . . . la révolte de l'homme contre la vie'.[31] It is important to remember that those who fell under this powerful influence were responding to less than the whole of Byron's work,[32] and it is a source of some insular complacency to reflect that in Britain at least the later poems, including *Don Juan*, have been recognized as essential to an understanding of Byron. This satisfaction can be easily dispelled by looking at such an influential piece of work as Bertrand Russell's article on Byron.[33] This careless and mischievous essay virtually ignores the later Byron, treats the dramas purely as autobiography, takes no account of the complicated variations of tone in *Childe Harold,* and in effect uses Byron as a pretext for denouncing a vague idea of 'German romanticism'. The only point Russell has to make is made in two sentences—'The type of man encouraged by Romanticism, especially of the Byronic variety, is violent and anti-social, an anarchic rebel or a conquering tyrant. . . . The romantic movement is, in essence, a revolt of our solitary instincts against the difficult precepts of social co-operation.' Russell ignores the point I have been emphasizing in this chapter, that what Byron is offering us in his poems and plays so far is his consciousness of the *inadequacy* of boundless self-assertion. His heroes derive their energies from pride, from wilfulness, from defiance, but these energies are presented as ultimately destructive of the self, and thus the emotional colouring of the poems is extravagantly tragic, as if Byron had traversed in a few years the whole range of emotion from *Tamburlaine* to *'Tis Pity,* from hope to bitterness.

I have drawn attention already to one or two places where Byron explicitly dismisses ideas which Pope accepted. I might have mentioned also his rejection of the great chain of being,[34] or his rapturous acclaim of Rousseau and the destructive powers of Voltaire and Gibbon,[35] or, at a further remove, the obvious influence of Cuvier.[36] All these mark his distance from Pope. Yet for the peak of his poetic career he returned to a manner which is closer to Pope's familiar style than to that of any romantic poet. Although his frequent tributes to Pope and Dryden show that he was perfectly conscious of these affinities, *Don Juan* is not a pastiche of an Augustan poem. Byron is not reverting to an easier age for poetry: there is no way back to an Augustan security. He is using the intervening years and all the distance that lies between the *Essay on*

Man and *Manfred* as well as regarding them with detachment. That
is why in critical attempts to place the poem we find the need to
use phrases consisting of two terms in rather unexpected conjunction, of which 'Romantic irony' is the most popular.

Don Juan was begun in 1818. When Byron died in 1824 he had
completed sixteen cantos and a small fragment of the seventeenth,
publishing as he wrote. The cantos vary in length from under 700
to nearly 1800 lines: the total length is over 16,000 lines. The action
of the poem is purely episodic in the tradition of the picaresque
novel, a form which *prima facie* one would expect to be adapted to
the expression of a fairly libertarian point of view. It begins in the
1780s when the hero is a youth and follows him through his
amorous escapades in Seville, his prudent travels abroad, a ship-
wreck, and an idyllic love affair. He is sold into slavery, spends a
night in a seraglio disguised as a woman, escapes and finds himself
involved in the battle of Ismail, travels to the court of Catherine the
Great and is sent by her as an envoy to London. The remaining
cantos deal with life in the capital and at a large country-house
party, during which Juan becomes involved with a titled English-
woman. The poem is unfinished, and thus takes its place with the
other great abandoned romantic projects: this adds to the initial
difficulty of judging it.

The narrative tension is so slack that Byron has opportunity for
ample digression and comment. An industrious scholar has calculated that exactly a third of the poem as we have it consists of
material which is not narrative: in the later cantos the proportion
of digression and comment increases, at times to over a half. It
soon becomes apparent that while the successive incidents are
handled with great skill and stated with considerable weight, *Don
Juan* is not really a narrative poem, since the main centre of the
reader's interest is not the story as such—

> But what's this to the purpose? you will say.
>   Gent. reader, nothing; a mere speculation,
> For which my sole excuse is—'tis my way;
>   Sometimes *with* and sometimes without occasion,
> I write what's uppermost, without delay;
>   This narrative is not meant for narration,
> But a mere airy and fantastic basis,
> To build up common things with common places.   (XIV/7)

Byron refers to his poem sometimes as an 'epic satire' (XIV/99),
sometimes as 'a grand poetic riddle' (VIII/139), or remarks ironically
on its 'regularity of design' (I/7) and traditional form:

> My poem's epic, and is meant to be
>   Divided in twelve books; each book containing,
> With love, and war, a heavy gale at sea,
>   A list of ships, and captains, and kings reigning,
> New characters; the episodes are three:
>   A panoramic view of hell's in training,
> After the style of Virgil and of Homer,
> So that my name of Epic's no misnomer.   (ɪ/200)

The uncertain conduct of the narrative is so obvious that Byron can afford to comment on it with mock disapproval, the comments themselves constituting further digressions, as for example stanzas 41 and 42 of Canto IX. The technique is that of *A Tale of a Tub*, with its 'Digression in praise of digressions', or of *Tristram Shandy*. The narrative is not shaping the poem: thus Byron can ironically pretend in Canto XII that he has only just begun his poem and half ironically threaten to extend it to a hundred cantos (xɪɪ/54–5). All of this reinforces the impression that the poem has no predetermined length which Byron failed to reach.

  Byron's most celebrated comment on the form of his own poem runs

> Some have accused me of a strange design
>   Against the creed and morals of the land,
> And trace it in this poem every line;
>   I don't pretend that I quite understand
> My own meaning when I would be *very* fine;
>   But the fact is that I have nothing plann'd,
> Unless it were to be a moment merry,
> A ,novel word in my vocabulary.   (ɪv/5)

Such a stanza increases the difficulty of offering a critical account of *Don Juan*. It seems to admit that the poem is shapeless and not meant to be taken seriously, yet the very fact that Byron could write it shows his self-awareness and his understanding of the objections to a shapeless poem. This in turn suggests that the poem is not really unplanned after all; if so, we have to find a way of justifying these ironic apologies for its shapelessness.

  Byron's tone in the poem is admirably suited to convey this bewildering combination of looseness and control. It is very much in the assured confident vein of *The Vision of Judgement*, and almost completely free from the rhetorical extravagances of *Childe Harold*. But, like that poem, it is discursive, and Byron's language is accordingly much more relaxed than in *The Vision of Judgement*. It reproduces with some exactness the rhythms, the turns of phrase, and the carelessness of informal gentlemanly conversation. The stanza form and the digressions work to the same end, as do Byron's insolent wit and his brilliant use of deflationary rhyme.

The reader is given the impression of listening to an accomplished raconteur who is always ready to break off his story and talk of other matters, and who reveals his own opinions most clearly in these asides.

What then are these other matters and if they are of importance why are they handled as digressions from the main story? The main topics of the poem are briefly enumerated: love and friendship; the innocence of youth, which leads to reflections on old age and middle-age; war; and British society. Similarly the main targets of Byron's satire are pretentious women; contemporary poets, especially Wordsworth; the cant of sentiment, including *Childe Harold*;[37] the hypocrisy of society, especially of British society in matters of sexual morality; tyranny, and war as an instrument of tyranny.

The poem, although unfinished, gives the impression, at first and subsequent readings, of a complete and uniform work of art. Thus the obvious second question to ask is what can possibly unify a poem with so many different themes, sometimes sublime, often coarse, written neither with consistent irony nor consistent sincerity, and with a deliberately disrupted narrative line. The simplest way to describe the operation of the poem is to say that we meet with statements of four major kinds:

  (a) Statements about the fictional adventures of Juan, set in, say, 1790;
  (b) Statements about historical events of the 1790s, such as the siege of Ismail;
  (c) General statements about the human condition, offered as being true in 1820; and
  (d) Statements about Byron's own life and temperament, arising as reflections in the course of writing the poem.

I shall argue that the poem shows how Byron has progressed beyond the simple Romantic self-assertion which Russell finds so barbarous and that this new painfully acquired understanding of the human predicament finds expression in the form of the poem, notably in the way in which Byron uses the four kinds of statement which I have just distinguished.

The primary subject of the poem is love, or rather what it is like to be in love. Juan's adventures are mainly with women: Byron's comments naturally reflect this, and move from love to friendship, a topic which is to him almost of equal importance. In Canto III, for example, Juan and Haidee act freely and innocently, but in the digressions Byron expresses a much more profound knowledge than they have of the varieties of love, and regards these variations with a cynical or stoical awareness. He knows, as Juan does not, that love can turn to bitterness, or to marriage, which is almost worse (V/158), that friends turn to enemies, and that time will change everything (X/8), even the ardent passions of youth (XVI/108, 109). It is in the digressions that Byron offers his general reflections on life, casting them in the form of universal, and therefore inevitable laws governing human conduct.[38] In this way he dramatizes the situation of the innocent and ignorant individual moving at his peril among laws which he cannot know, because they are only to be discovered retrospectively and can be expressed only by someone standing outside the action. On the whole the generalizations in the digressions tend to be anti-Romantic, since by making their appeal to common experience they normally minimize the uniqueness of the events narrated.

It is not hard to show this method in operation in the poem. For a light-hearted example take IV/24-5, for an obvious one X/25, for a more bitter one XII/57-8, for a dextrous one XIV/100-2, where Byron obliquely suggests his own role as a writer who offers truth to mankind instead of fiction. One passage shows with especial clarity the ease and swiftness with which Byron moves from the prosaic details of a back-alley murder to speculations about human destiny and then back to his narrative:

> The other evening ('twas on Friday last)—
>   This is a fact and no poetic fable—
> Just as my great coat was about me cast,
>   My hat and gloves still lying on the table,
> I heard a shot—'twas eight o'clock scarce past—
>   And, running out as fast as I was able,
> I found the military commandant
> Stretch'd in the street, and able scarce to pant.
>
> Poor fellow! for some reason, surely bad,
>   They had slain him with five slugs; and left him there
> To perish on the pavement: so I had
>   Him borne into the house and up the stair,
> And stripp'd, and look'd to,—But why should I add
>   More circumstances? vain was every care;
> The man was gone: in some Italian quarrel
> Kill'd by five bullets from an old gun-barrel. . . .
>
> The scars of his old wounds were near his new,
>   Those honourable scars which brought him fame;
> And horrid was the contrast to the view—
>   But let me quit the theme; as such things claim
> Perhaps even more attention than is due
>   From me: I gazed (as oft I have gazed the same)
> To try if I could wrench aught out of death
> Which should confirm, or shake, or make a faith;

> But it was all a mystery. Here we are,
>   And there we go:—but *where*? five bits of lead,
> Or three, or two, or one, send very far!
>   And is this blood, then, form'd but to be shed?
> Can every element our elements mar?
>   And air—earth—water—fire live—and we dead?
> *We*, whose minds comprehend all things. No more;
>   But let us to the story as before.   (v/33–4, 38–9)

When Byron generalizes about love he gives full weight to the unhappiness that inevitably overwhelms the early raptures:

> The nightingale that sings with the deep thorn,
>   Which fable places in her breast of wail,
> Is lighter far of heart and voice than those
> Whose headlong passions form their proper woes.
>
> And that's the moral of this composition,
>   If people would but see its real drift: (vi/87–8)

This does not mean that you should avoid love: looking back you can see that it is better to 'sigh with your son than cough with your grandfather':

> He [Anthony] died at fifty for a queen of forty;
>   I wish their years had been fifteen and twenty,
> For then wealth, kingdoms, worlds are but a sport—I
>   Remember when, though I had no great plenty
> Of worlds to lose, yet still, to pay my court, I
>   Gave what I had—a heart; as the world went, I
> Gave what was worth a world; for worlds could never
> Restore me those pure feelings, gone for ever.   (vi/5)

This last quotation shows how powerfully the digressions are charged by the reader's consciousness that they are spoken by a Byron who has himself lived through the innocence and freedom of Juan and experienced the constraining effects of Time, especially on love and on human nature. This is most obvious in the well-known *Ubi sunt?* passage xi/76–85:

> 'Where is the world?' cries Young, at *eighty*—'Where
>   The world in which a man was born?' Alas!
> Where is the world of *eight* years past? 'Twas there—
>   I look for it—'tis gone, a globe of glass!
> Crack'd, shiver'd, vanish'd, scarcely gazed on, ere
>   A silent change dissolves the glittering mass.
> Statesmen, chiefs, orators, queens, patriots, kings,
> And dandies, all are gone on the wind's wings.

Talk not of seventy years as age; in seven
  I have seen more changes, down from monarchs to
The humblest individual under heaven,
  Than might suffice a moderate century through.
I knew that nought was lasting, but now even
  Change grows too changeable, without being new:
Nought's permanent among the human race,
Except the Whigs *not* getting into place.   (xi/76, 82)

Byron was himself, at the time of writing, approaching middle age,[39] which gives his generalizations about life a particular application to his own state. They stand in the poem not only as basic laws of human nature but as the conclusions he has reached through his own unhappy experience of love. Whether his reflections are tolerant, bitter, sardonic or simply envious, they are given an extra charge of personal feeling by their reference to the present state of the poet. Juan will eventually be 'schooled by life': Byron has already arrived at a kind of unillusioned resignation:

There still are many rainbows in your sky,
  But mine have vanish'd. All, when life is new,
Commence with feelings warm, and prospects high;
  But time strips our illusions of their hue . . .
. . . .
'All this is very fine, and may be true,'
  Said Juan, 'but I really don't see how
It betters present times with me or you.'
  'No?' quoth the other; 'yet you will allow
By setting things in their right point of view,
  Knowledge, at least, is gain'd.'   (v/21, 23)

The beginning of Canto XIV shows the whole process in brief compass—scepticism, stoicism, comment on his own style of discursive speculation (7), reflections on his own life (9), on his own writing and his own poem, on the subjects of this poem abstractly considered, and on women in general (23). Then Byron says (29), 'We left our heroes and our heroines'; after another two stanzas he moves on to a general account of Juan. There is in fact hardly a single specific incident narrated in the whole canto.

Exactly the same technique is used to handle the topic of war. Cantos VII and VIII are entirely taken up with an account of the Russian siege in 1790 of Ismail, a town on the Danube held by the Turks. Ismail was a particularly hard-won and brutal victory and

Byron spares us none of the horrors—'Sliding knee-deep in lately frozen mud/Now thaw'd into a marsh of human blood'—but characteristically places them in a wider context:

> The bayonet pierces and the sabre cleaves,
>   And human lives are lavish'd everywhere,
> As the year closing whirls the scarlet leaves
>   When the stripp'd forest bows to the bleak air,
> And groans; and thus the peopled city grieves,
>   Shorn of its best and loveliest, and left bare;
> But still it falls in vast and awful splinters,
> As oaks blown down with all their thousand winters.
>
> It is an awful topic—but 'tis not
>   My cue for any time to be terrific:
> For checker'd as is seen our human lot
>   With good, and bad, and worse, alike prolific
> Of melancholy merriment, to quote
>   Too much of one sort would be soporific;—
> Without, or with, offence to friends or foes,
> I sketch your world exactly as it goes.   (VIII/88–9)[40]

He finishes with a pious hope that the time will come when his children and his children's children will live in a world where wars are no more and will not even know what kings are:

> For I will teach, if possible, the stones
> To rise against earth's tyrants. Never let it
>   Be said that we still truckle unto thrones;—
> But ye—our children's children! think how we
> Show'd *what things were* before the world was free!
> . . . .
> And when you hear historians talk of thrones,
>   And those that sate upon them, let it be
> As we now gaze upon the mammoth's bones,
>   And wonder what old world such things could see,
> Or hieroglyphics on Egyptian stones,
>   The pleasant riddles of futurity—
> Guessing at what shall happily be hid,
> As the real purpose of a pyramid.   (VIII/135, 137)

So much for the explicit moral of the Ismail episode—'War's a brain-spattering, windpipe-slitting art,/Unless her cause by right be sanctified.' It is conveyed with great skill and bravura. But more subtle is the interweaving of the personal and the general which I have noticed earlier. In a way which has since become perfectly familiar to us but was then more of a novelty, Byron incorporates this into his description of the actual fighting. All parties operate in a state of confused ignorance:

A sad miscalculation about distance
  Made all their naval matters incorrect;
Three fireships lost their amiable existence
  Before they reach'd a spot to take effect;
The match was lit too soon, and no assistance
  Could remedy this lubberly defect;
They blew up in the middle of the river,
While, though 'twas dawn, the Turks slept fast as ever. (VII/28)

The Turkish palisades were back to front, the river approach was left unfortified, 'the Russian batteries were incomplete,/Because they were constructed in a hurry', there was a fault in the first attack, the Cossack cavalry was wiped out, and Koutoussow was rescued by pure chance. When Juan is spoken to in German by General Lascy he nods, uncomprehending, and because of this the battle goes on. Juan and Johnson do not know where they are going or why they are fighting:

Juan and Johnson join'd a certain corps,
  And fought away with might and main, not knowing
The way which they had never trod before,
  And still less guessing where they might be going;
But on they march'd, dead bodies trampling o'er,
  Firing, and thrusting, slashing, sweating, glowing,
But fighting thoughtlessly enough to win,
To their *two* selves, *one* whole bright bulletin. (VIII/19)

The wills that are driving them are not their own but those of their tyrannous and bloodthirsty rulers—

The letter of the prince to the same marshal
  Was worthy of a Spartan, had the cause
Been one to which a good heart could be partial—
  Defence of freedom, country, or of laws;
But as it was mere lust of power to o'erarch all
  With its proud brow, it merits slight applause,
Save for its style, which said, all in a trice,
'You will take Ismail at whatever price.'

'Let there be light!' said God, 'and there was light!'
  'Let there be blood!' says man, and there's a sea!
The fiat of this spoil'd child of the Night
  (For Day ne'er saw his merits) could decree
More evil in an hour, than thirty bright
  Summers could renovate, though they should be
Lovely as those which ripen'd Eden's fruit;
For war cuts up not only branch, but root. (VII/40–1)

The ignorant armies clash by night. Each is composed of individual men helpless in the power of the imperious wills that drive them forward. The narrator, who alone understands all that is happening, presents it in a way that encourages the reader to find in the confusion and the cruelty an emblem of the human lot in general.

When Byron expounds the truths to which the individual situation must conform he makes them statistical truths, for in a chancy business like war we cannot predict the fate of any specific soldier:

> History can only take things in the gross;
>   But could we know them in detail, perchance
> In balancing the profit and the loss,
>   War's merit it by no means might enhance,
> To waste so much gold for a little dross,
>   As hath been done, mere conquest to advance.
> The drying up a single tear has more
> Of honest fame, than shedding seas of gore.   (VIII/3)

A few stanzas earlier, ending Canto VII, Byron had written

> Here pause we for the present—as even then
>   That awful pause, dividing life from death,
> Struck for an instant on the hearts of men,
>   Thousands of whom were drawing their last breath!   (87)

The point is that nobody at that time knows who will be killed and who will survive:

> And then with tears, and sighs, and some slight kisses,
>   They parted for the present—these to await,
> According to the artillery's hits or misses,
>   What sages call Chance, Providence, or Fate—
> (Uncertainty is one of many blisses,
>   A mortgage on Humanity's estate)—
> While their beloved friends began to arm,
> To burn a town which never did them harm.   (VII/76)

This emphasizes the superiority of the narrator, who has the double advantage of the retrospective view[41] and an experience of life and men which enables him to formulate the general laws governing the situations in which he involves his creatures. Once again Juan typifies the free agent ('A thing of impulse and a child of song' VIII/24) at the mercy of the irresistible pressures of existence ('This o'erwhelming world, where all must err' X/52).

The third main theme, society, is similarly handled. Although the

generalizations are sometimes sombre, they are more often
flippant or cynical. Byron of course had known what it was to
offend against social proprieties, and constantly relates the
generalizations to his own case. Characters such as Lady Adeline
and the Duchess of Fitz-Fulke are hardly given even as much
reality as the women of the earlier cantos, while Juan too fades
into a narrative device. The real weight of the poem is expressed in
Byron's circumambient presence, and in the relentlessness with
which the laws of his world determine the fate of its inhabitants.
Byron's characteristic stance is that of a man who is full of
instinctive admiration for and even envy of the enthusiasms of
youth, especially ardent generous love, but can extend no hope
that they will survive.

Such considerations give substance to Byron's own account of his
poem:

> And such as they are, such my present tale is,
>   A nondescript and ever-varying rhyme,
> A versified Aurora Borealis,
>   Which flashes o'er a waste and icy clime.
> When we know what all are, we must bewail us,
>   But ne'ertheless I hope it is no crime
> To laugh at *all* things—for I wish to know
> *What*, after *all*, are *all* things—but a *show*?
>
> They accuse me—*Me*—the present writer of
>   The present poem—of—I know not what—
> A tendency to under-rate and scoff
>   At human power and virtue, and all that;
> And this they say in language rather rough.
>   Good God! I wonder what they would be at!
> I say no more than hath been said in Dante's
> Verse, and by Solomon and by Cervantes;

In similar vein Byron points to Swift, La Rochefoucauld, Rousseau
and even Socrates and Newton.

> Ecclesiastes said, 'that all is vanity'—
>   Most modern preachers say the same, or show it
> By their examples of true Christianity:
>   In short, all know, or very soon may know it;
> And in this scene of all-confess'd inanity,
>   By saint, by sage, by preacher, and by poet,
> Must I restrain me, through the fear of strife,
> From holding up the nothingness of life?　　(VII/2–3, 6)

To call the poem then a triumph of Romantic irony is not to give empty praise, if we accept that the expression means at one level a way of writing in which the poet does not conceal or remain detached from his own feelings, but is intensely aware of them and can comment on them, even on their excesses and absurdities, and at another level that the writer is similarly aware of the nobility of men's assertion of their own freedom[42] in spite of his conviction through experience that such an assertion must at last be proved futile. The aim of such writing is to arouse a complicated set of ultimately irreconcilable reactions: this aim is perfectly realised in a heterogeneous poem like *Don Juan*, whose very incompleteness, echoing the poet's death, seems more appropriate than any other ending. As one of Byron's greatest admirers wrote, 'The incomplete,/More than completion, matches the immense'.

All this is perfectly comprehended in the form of the poem; Juan's apparent freedom to wander where he will in the picaresque tradition is in fact an illusion. He is always under pressure and his wanderings are shaped by solid blocks of general law. He is formally the hero and his actions are suitably heroic, for Byron continues to recognize the value of primary emotions, and to entertain generous, if illogical hopes for human potentiality; with these he combines a recognition of the forces which effectively limit human freedom and a consequent deep scepticism about the status of the free individual. This is not now a cause of extravagant despair, for Byron regards the paradox with an almost Augustan detachment and stoicism, while making it quite plain that he has reached this position only after intensely painful personal experience.

It is this forcible fusion of incompatibilities that entitles the poem to be regarded as the best, perhaps the only, example of our literature of Romantic wit: it is Byron's unceasing attempts to discover the right attitude to adopt in the face of the paradoxes which he exposes that entitle him to be recognized as, in his own phrase, a 'Columbus of the moral seas'.

In addition to the works cited in the notes the following have useful material on the themes of this chapter: M. H. Abrams, *The Mirror and the Lamp: Romantic Theory and the Critical Tradition* (O.U.P., 1953); Carl R. Woodring, 'On Liberty in the Poetry of Wordsworth', *PMLA*, **70** (1955), 1033–48; Newton Phelps Stallknecht, *Strange Seas of Thought: Studies in William Wordsworth's Philosophy of Man and Nature* (Bloomington: 1958); Karl Kroeber, *Romantic Narrative Art* (Wisconsin U.P., 1960); Herbert S. Lindenberger, *On Wordsworth's Prelude* (Princeton: 1963); Earl R. Wasserman, 'The English Romantics: The Grounds of Knowledge', *SIR*, **4**

(1964), 17–34; Robert Langbaum, 'The Evolution of Soul in Wordsworth's Poetry', in *The Modern Spirit* (London: Chatto, 1970), pp. 18–36; Stephen Prickett, *Coleridge and Wordsworth: The Poetry of Growth,* (Cambridge U.P., 1970); Michael G. Cooke, *The Romantic Will,* (New Haven and London: Yale U.P., 1976); Richard Cronin, *Shelley's Poetic Thoughts* (London: Macmillan, 1981), esp. chs. 3 and 4.

7

Retrospect Two 1660–1830

The skin, pores, muscles, and nerves of a day-labourer, are different from those of a man of quality: so are his sentiments, actions, and manners. The different stations of life influence the whole fabric, external and internal; and these different stations arise necessarily, because uniformly, from the necessary and uniform principles of human nature. Men cannot live without society, and cannot be associated without government. Government makes a distinction of property, and establishes the different ranks of men. This produces industry, traffic, manufactures, law-suits, war, leagues, alliances, voyages, travels, cities, fleets, ports, and all those other actions and objects which cause such a diversity, and at the same time maintain such an uniformity in human life.—HUME, *A Treatise of Human Nature* (1739) II iii 1.

I see clearly that the principal ties which kept the different classes of society in a vital and harmonious dependence upon each other have, within these thirty years, either been greatly impaired or wholly dissolved. Everything has been put to market and sold for the highest price it would buy.—WORDSWORTH (1817).

Although it is clearly wrong to present the eighteenth century as a period when all men were of one mind, and although the most penetrating studies are those which discriminate most subtly between the various shades of opinion, yet some generalizations may be ventured and a brief indication given of the directions in which support for them is to be found. In my chapter on Pope the word I used most often to express the force limiting free action was 'Order'; whether our knowledge of it is based on revelation, or on faith, or on the latest discoveries and theories of science, 'ORDER is Heav'ns first law.' In general man was felt to inhabit, by right, an allotted place in a universe of measured completeness. 'The course of things goes quietly along, in its own true channel of Natural Causes and Effects.' It is no longer necessary to postulate a God, so that Naigeon, for example, can refer to Divinity as an 'unnecessary cog in the machine of the world'. What constrains man is the order of Nature, the way the world is constituted. It is notable that the literary reaction to this was seldom one of helplessness or despair: on the contrary each scientific advance

which demonstrated the logic of the universe was hailed as the
occasion for an even more optimistic version of man's place in the
creation.[1] A few quotations from various sources and periods
illustrate the point:

> The gates are now set open, and by his means we may freely enter into
> the knowledge of the hidden secrets and wonders of natural things. He
> has so clearly laid open and set before our eyes the most beautiful
> frame of the System of the World, that, if *King Alphonsus* were now
> alive, he would not complain for want of the graces either of simplicity
> or of harmony in it. Therefore we may now more nearly behold the
> beauties of Nature, and entertain ourselves with the delightful
> contemplation; and, which is the best and most valuable fruit of
> philosophy, be thence incited the more profoundly to reverence and
> adore the great MAKER and LORD of all.[2]

Thomson, continuing a much earlier tradition, observes with satisfaction the Great Chain of Being, and does not conceal its
determinist implications when he talks of the scientific reason

> up-tracing, from the dreary void,
> The chain of causes and effects to Him,
> The world-producing Essence, who alone
> Possesses being.   (*Summer* 1745–8)

But in his long poem *Liberty* he is at pains to make the goddess
Liberty say in the concluding book

> Science, my close associate, still attends
> Where'er I go. . . .
> Such the kind power whose piercing eye dissolves
> Each mental fetter and sets reason free.   (v. 400–1, 427–8)

It is plain from this passage, and from many others such as that on
Pythagoras, that Thomson is not limiting the definition of liberty to
political freedom, important though that is. He is celebrating
eighteenth-century Britain as a place where man is in the widest
sense free and science as a prime instrument in the securing of
that freedom. In Thomson's *To the Memory of Sir Isaac Newton*
(1727) he shows deep respect for 'awful Newton's'[3] economical
picture of the universe. Gratitude is his primary emotion as he uses
Newton as an example to shame the 'hopeless gloomy-minded tribe'
who contend against 'the prime endearing privilege/Of being'
and allege that the soul is nothing 'but a finer breath/Of spirits
dancing through their tubes awhile,/And then for ever lost in
vacant air'. One encounters occasional passages of Miltonic
repressiveness, such as *Liberty* III. 561–70, but on the whole

Plate 6. Etienne-Louis Boullée. Cenotaph for Newton. *By courtesy of Bibliothèque Nationale, Paris*

Thomson's presentation of the place of man in the world was reasonably optimistic, as in the celebrated lines from *Spring*, and reasonably representative of his age:

> Man superior walks
> Amid the glad creation, musing praise
> And looking lively gratitude.   (170–2)

We are in well-trodden territory when we consider the question of the embodiment in Augustan literature of this vision of the world, and even the commonplaces of the literary textbooks confirm the close correspondences. Churchill's satire *Gotham* is a convenient example of the way in which a form apparently corrosive and destructive could play its part in the maintaining of social order by constantly measuring the defective realities of human affairs against universal principles of what is stable and natural. The novel not the romance is the major form of eighteenth-century fiction, not least because it offers to reflect the world as it is, and is thus natural in another sense, while ultimately bringing the adventures of the characters into harmony with ideal and universal principles of justice and morality. In landscape poetry the emphasis falls on the tidiness and harmony of the rural world where 'order in variety we see' (*Windsor Forest*): particular scenes and detailed individual descriptions, since they tend to eccentricity, were not especially favoured, but any mode or figure that offered a general truth needed no further justification. An obvious instance of this is the botanic or classifactory description, which orders phenomena into categories.

> 'The business of the poet,' said Imlac, 'is to examine not the individual, but the species; to remark general properties and large appearances. He does not number the streaks of the tulip, or describe the different shades in the verdure of the forest. . . . He must divest himself of the prejudices of his age and country; he must consider right and wrong in their abstracted and invariable state; he must disregard present laws and opinions, and rise to general and transcendental truths, which will always be the same.'

These familiar words from the tenth chapter of *Rasselas*, like similar passages from *The Lives of the Poets* and Shaftesbury's *Characteristics* and Reynolds' *Discourses*, spring not from a misguided addiction to the wrong kind of poetry but from a seriously held view of what the universe is, of man's place in it, and of the part poetry has to play in the whole life of man.

Voltaire wrote in 1753, 'Je n'estime la poésie qu'autant qu'elle est l'ornement de la raison.' Throughout the eighteenth century,

especially in France, the most earnest inquiries into human potentialities and the most assiduous attempts to free man from bondage
to tradition or superstition go hand in hand with, and even imply, a
defining of his position in a defined universe.[4] It is not important at
this point to distinguish between those who, like William King, took
this position on broadly theological grounds, arguing that there
was a 'natural necessity' in the actions of the creator, and those
who preferred to argue from a scientific scrutiny of physical law:
'Order as a principle of Nature' emerges from either argument as
more powerful than man. There is common ground between the
mechanistic determinism of Laplace or the raw materialism of
Helvétius[5] on the one hand and the more sophisticated ideas of
Condorcet or Turgot on the other.[6]

In the *Second Sorbonnique* (1750) Turgot concedes that the
phenomena of the natural world are subject to constant laws: he
wishes to exempt man from this cyclical process by stressing the
continuity of human institutions, but the arguments he employs
are scarcely calculated to elevate one's idea of human freedom. 'All
ages are linked to each other by a series of causes and effects,
which bind the present state of the world to all those that have preceded it.' Turgot grants that progress brings misery to many,
which they can in no way avoid, but insists that it is irresistible,
which, though cheering, is not a particularly strong argument for
human freedom.[7]

Similarly Condorcet, in his *Esquisse*, represents men in general as
terms in a mathematical progression: 'perfectibility' almost becomes a non-human power determining the direction of human
development. His famous 'Calculemus' is clearly related to Laplace
and de Moivre's calculus of probabilities and is not far removed in
spirit from de la Mettrie's two books *L'Homme Machine* and
L'Homme Plante. The more determined a writer's efforts to show
the unity of the natural order and the inevitability with which good
must be engendered from self-interest the more colour he gives to
the idea of a world in which the efforts of the individual count for
little or nothing.[8] When, for example, Dean Tucker writes,
'National commerce, good morals and good government are but
part of one general scheme, in the designs of Providence',[9] when
Hume writes, 'We cannot reasonably expect that a piece of woollen
cloth will be brought to perfection in a nation, which is ignorant of
astronomy, or where ethics are neglected. . . . *Industry, knowledge,
and humanity*, are linked together by an indissoluble chain',[10] when
Winckelmann or Herder suggest that the aesthetic values of a
culture are necessarily associated with the moral values, both
pursuing the same predictable cycle of change, there is an unmis-
takable implication that some larger order determines the possi-

bilities open to man, and that human development is the result of something other than the combination of a number of individual free decisions.

When Hume described the law of association as operating like the law of gravity, 'a kind of attraction, which in the mental world will be found to have as extraordinary effects as in the natural, and to show itself in as many and various forms,' he spoke, like many men of his time, with a deliberate emphasis on the affinities between mental philosophy and natural science.[11] Burke's language is much closer to that of theology, as will appear from the following extremely well-known passages:

> We are all born in subjection . . . to one great, immutable, preexistent Law, prior to all our devices, and prior to all our contrivances, paramount to all our ideas, and all our sensations, antecedent to our very existence, by which we are knit and connected in the eternal frame of the Universe, out of which we cannot stir.[12]

> The awful Author of our being is the Author of our place in the order of existence; and . . . having disposed and marshalled us by a divine tactic, not according to our will, but according to His, he has, in and by that disposition, virtually subjected us to act the part which belongs to the place assigned us.[13]

The corollary of this emphasis on a natural order within which the individual plays a preordained and more or less passive part is the argument that the self is relatively unimportant. In his *Treatise on Human Nature*, described in a subtitle as 'an attempt to introduce the experimental method of reasoning into moral subjects', Hume not surprisingly disputes the very existence of personal identity abstracted from perception:

> There are some philosophers who imagine we are every moment intimately conscious of what we call our *self*; that we feel its existence and its continuance in existence; and are certain, beyond the evidence of a demonstration, both of its perfect identity and simplicity. The strongest sensation, the most violent passion, say they, instead of distracting us from this view, only fix it the more intensely, and make us consider their influence on *self* either by their pain or pleasure. . . . Unluckily all these positive assertions are contrary to that very experience which is pleaded for them; nor have we any idea of *self*, after the manner it is here explained. For, from what impression could this idea be derived? This question it is impossible to answer without a manifest contradiction and absurdity. . . . [Men] are nothing but a bundle or collection of different perceptions, which succeed each other with an inconceivable rapidity, and are in a perpetual flux and movement. . . . The mind is a kind of theatre, where several perceptions

successively make their appearance; pass, repass, glide away, and
mingle in an infinite variety of postures and situations. . . . The identity
which we ascribe to the mind of man is only a fictitious one, and of a
like kind with that which we ascribe to vegetable and animal bodies.[14]

Although it is easier to generalize about the eighteenth century
than about the seventeenth and it is possible to point with some
confidence to a prevalent set of ideas, this is very far from establishing any uniformity or orthodoxy. We need look no further than
the powerful ambiguous figures of Johnson and Montesquieu to
learn what wide variations are possible, even in men who seem in
many ways to be the epitome of their time. Even where we can
perceive a fair measure of agreement on man's nature, his place in
the world and the value of human institutions, a closer scrutiny
reveals that the age of stability nourished, like other ages, the
principles that were ultimately to change it.

There are many general accounts of eighteenth-century literature which trace its course from the bondage of neo-classicism to
the intoxicating freedom of the early Romantics, and there are
many general intellectual histories of the Enlightenment, several of
which present the great Romantic artists, musicians and writers as
the culmination, if not the justification, of the process. The steps on
the way are well trodden, and it seems as though, in terms of this
book, nothing more were required than to remind the reader of
the ways in which literature became progressively 'freer' from say
1740 to 1800, as the principle of order gradually lost its coercive
force over the individual man. There is a substantial truth in this
picture: indeed it could be amplified in many ways—by pointing, as
Ernest Tuveson has done, to the shift from judgement to sensibility
in the century,[15] or perhaps even more tellingly to the way in
which certain unconventional works of literature such as *Tristram
Shandy* (1760–7), Diderot's *Jacques le Fataliste* (1773) and Tieck's
Puss-in-Boots (1797) exercise their own special influence by
exploiting the paradoxes of literary illusion and manipulation as
instruments for reopening the question of the nature of free action
in general. This tends to lead writers in particular to a freer speculation about their relation to their own fictitious characters and by
an obvious transition about the nature of human freedom.[16]

To forces such as these one might briefly add four others. First,
and most important, there is a basic ambiguity in the concept of
order, most obvious when 'the traditional idea of universal Order
begins to give way to the idea of men locked in self-enclosed and
self-subsistent orders, seeming to use the same words but in fact
unable to comprehend each other's meaning'.[17] Secondly the
philosophes, while they were labouring to establish the structure of
the universe on a rational basis, and to that extent reinforcing ideas

of order, were at the same time keenly critical of existing institutions and thus helping to bring about changes in the human order.[18] The title of the second volume of Peter Gay's massive history of the Enlightenment is *The Science of Freedom*. Thirdly an optimistic theology naturally acknowledges the necessary presence of pain and evil. Similarly the principle of plenitude involves accepting things as they are, that is in all their diversity with all their imperfections. Once again the forces that appear to consolidate ideas of order have the additional result of reinforcing other ideas which have ultimately a disruptive effect. 'The philosophers of optimism were not . . . as a rule of a Romantic disposition; and what they were desirous of proving was that reality is rational through and through, that every fact of existence, however unpleasant, is grounded in some reason as clear and evident as an axiom in mathematics. But in the exigencies of their argument to this ambitious conclusion they found themselves constrained to attribute to the Divine Reason a conception of good extremely different from that which had been most current among men, and especially among philosophers.'[19]

The fourth point really incorporates all the others—the fermenting of the *Aufklärung*, which by celebrating the capacity of the human intellect to perceive a universal natural order led to a renewed confidence in the power of the individual man, particularly the human power to originate, rather than to exist passively as a tabula rasa or function as a sensitized plate exposed indifferently to external impressions. I need do no more than to point to the well-documented stages by which the scepticism of Hume was broadened by Kant to a general examination of the active agency of the mind, and by which Kant's insistence on the autonomy of the individual was in turn converted by Fichte to an insistence on the absolute primacy of the Ego:

> What I desired was this: that I myself, that of which I am conscious as my own being and person, . . . that this 'I' would be independent, would be something which exists not by another or through another, but of myself, and, as such, would be the final root of all my determinations.[20]

The power to create is obviously of paramount importance in the realm of original thought, the poets being as influential as the philosophers. Poetry, as Shelley said, 'creates anew the Universe'. Thus the Romantic dedication to the esemplastic imagination is closely related to the Romantic dedication to freedom. There is some truth even in Hazlitt's claim that 'These Titans of our days . . . have made the only incorrigible Jacobins, and their school of

Plate 7. William Hogarth. John Wilkes Esq. *By courtesy of The British Museum*

poetry is the only real school of Radical Reform'.[21] The central importance of the imagination as the means by which the human mind can transcend the mechanical limitations of the material world was clearly recognized by Mill when he wrote, 'The Germano-Coleridgean doctrine [as opposed to the ideas of Hartley and Bentham] expresses the revolt of the human mind against the philosophy of the eighteenth century.'[22]

Given these powerful internal and external forces for change it is therefore understandable that even the age of stability proved impermanent, nor is it surprising that its passing should be regarded as a triumph for the spirit of liberty over the forces of oppression. It can all be presented as a simple enough story, with 'Release from Imprisonment' as the obvious title, a dedication to Rousseau and Blake,[23] and Kant's 'Sapere aude' as the motto on the title-page. Yet those who have read the main part of this book will know that the road from the beginning of chapter five to the end of chapter six is by no means the smooth path from darkness to light which such an account would imply. The difficulty may be briefly expressed by saying that the change from Pomfret's *Choice* (1700)[24] to *Childe Harold* (1812) does not impress the reader as a change from blind misery to clear-sighted happiness, but rather the contrary. As I have said, it is plain that many writers in the eighteenth century did not receive with fatalistic despair their commitment to a totally ordered world, but welcomed the order of their universe as a warrant for a broadly hopeful view of man's nature and destiny. Why then should an equally profound conviction of cosmic determinism in the following century normally issue in an intense pessimism? To ask the question in this way is to oversimplify. I have tried to show how an Augustan view of the place of man in the world could produce not only the optimism of Pope and Condorcet but also the pessimism of Swift and Gray: what is now required is to show how a Romantic view of the world could lead not only to the ardent hopefulness of Shelley but also to the various kinds of despair that afflicted Byron.

The previous pages have moved by an indirect route from the principles of Newton to a general principle of order and shown how by slow degrees the principle was qualified and finally superseded. It is worth noting that the process seemed in retrospect to have been much less circuitous.[25] Shelley writes in the notes to *Queen Mab*, 'In fact, religion and morality, as they now stand, compose a practical code of misery and servitude: the genius of human happiness must tear every leaf from the accursed book of God ere man can read the inscription on his heart' (note on V 189), and it is clear from the context that he is thinking of religion and morality as agencies which limit 'choice and change'. Shortly

afterwards he comments, 'The consistent Newtonian is necessarily
an atheist' (note on VII. 13). Thus by a simple route the principles of
Newton restore freedom of choice to man.[26] In the Preface to
Prometheus Unbound Shelley explicitly associates this release with
the Renaissance, the Reformation and English literature in the time
of Shakespeare:

> We owe the great writers of the golden age of our literature to that
> fervid awakening of the public mind which shook to dust the oldest and
> most oppressive form of the Christian religion. We owe Milton to the
> progress and development of the same spirit: the sacred Milton was, let
> it ever be remembered, a republican, and a bold inquirer into morals
> and religion. The great writers of our own age are, we have reason to
> suppose, the companions and forerunners of some unimagined change
> in our social condition or the opinions which cement it. The cloud of
> mind is discharging its collected lightning. . . .

Again, at the end of the *Defence of Poetry* Shelley writes:

> The literature of England, an energetic development of which has ever
> preceded or accompanied a great and free development of the national
> will, has arisen as it were from a new birth. . . . We live among such
> philosophers and poets as surpass beyond comparison any who have
> appeared since the last national struggle for civil and religious liberty.[27]

I do not wish at present to dwell on the other ways in which men
felt a sense of liberation at the end of the eighteenth century and
the beginning of the nineteenth. I wish simply to draw attention to
the sense that a new age had dawned, that it was in some way the
peculiar triumph of poets and men of letters to have ushered it in,
and that on both counts there was a remarkable parallel with what
had happened in Britain two hundred years earlier.[28] Of the reality
and intensity of this feeling of newly recovered freedom there can
be no doubt. A convenient sample of the change is to compare *Don
Giovanni* with *Fidelio*. In scene five of the first act of Mozart's opera
all the characters in the quintet sing 'Viva la Libertá', but with
varying qualifications or ironic reversals of the simple sentiment.
In *Fidelio* the great cry of 'Freiheit' as the prisoners are released is
subject to no such tempering. Browning well describes in *Pauline*
the intoxicating effect of Shelley on a young and impressionable
mind:

> I was vowed to liberty,
> Men were to be as gods and earth as heaven.

Yet the ambiguity of the political situation needs no stressing.

When Napoleon at his coronation brushed aside the Pope and put the crown on his own head he symbolically proclaimed the emancipation of humanity and the supreme dominion of the individual. It was an assertion of the authority of the self worthy of Milton's Satan:

> We know no time when we were not as now;
> Know none before us, self-begot, self-raised
> By our own quickening power.

But just as Satan was corroded, in Coleridge's phrase, by 'the intense selfishness, the alcohol of egotism', so the individual man soon experienced the double power of the self. 'Self-consciousness', was rightly pointed to by Mill in his essay on Bentham as 'that daemon of the men of genius of our time, from Wordsworth to Byron, from Goethe to Chateaubriand, and to which this age owes so much of its cheerful and its mournful wisdom'.[29]

The sense of a new liberty was very rapidly disturbed though not obliterated by an equally powerful sense of disappointment, doubt and fear. The primary simple enthusiasm for liberty—'Eternal Spirit of the chainless Mind'—gave way to a secondary, or rather overlapping stage, of which the principal feature was the questioning of the adequacy of freedom as a personal or political creed.[30] In this questioning and discrediting Byron was the central figure. Like Marlowe, he wrote about men of infinite ambition and infinite power: his heroes are in one sense as free as Tamburlaine or Faustus, but like Marlowe's heroes they are fated to a tragic condition.[31] The difference is that in Byron their tragedy is not their fall and death, that is, freedom terminated by an external cause, but the fierceness of their attempts to live a free life and the anguish of their discovery that they cannot sustain its burdens, that is freedom collapsing through internal stress. 'Worse than adversity the Childe befell;/He felt the fulness of satiety.' In 1839 Mazzini described the Byronic hero as 'free, but nothing more than free'.[32]

The paradox brings to mind one of the most striking passages from Burckhardt:

If we now attempt to sum up the principal features in the Italian character of that time, as we know it from a study of the life of the upper classes, we snall obtain something like the following result. The fundamental vice of this character was at the same time a condition of its greatness, namely, excessive individualism. The individual first inwardly casts off the authority of a State which, as a fact, is in most cases tyrannical and illegitimate, and what he thinks and does is, rightly or wrongly, now called treason. The sight of victorious egotism in others drives him to defend his own right by his own arm. And, while thinking to restore his inward equilibrium, he falls, through the vengeance which he executes, into the hands of the powers of darkness. His love, too, turns mostly for satisfaction to another individuality equally developed, namely, to his neighbour's wife. In face of all objective facts, of laws and restraints of whatever kind, he retains the feeling of his own sovereignty, and in each single instance forms his decision independently, according as honour or interest, passion or calculation, revenge or renunciation, gain the upper hand in his own mind.

If therefore egotism in its wider as well as narrower sense is the root and fountain of all evil, the more highly developed Italian was for this reason more inclined to wickedness than the members of other nations of that time.

But this individual development did not come upon him through any fault of his own, but rather through an historical necessity.

This is very much in the spirit of an earlier passage:

The curtain is now and then drawn aside, and we see with frightful evidence a boundless ambition and thirst after greatness, independent of all means and consequences. . . . In more than one remarkable and dreadful undertaking the motive assigned by serious writers is the burning desire to achieve something great and memorable. This motive is not a mere extreme case of ordinary vanity, but something daemonic, *involving a surrender of the will*, the use of any means, however atrocious, and even an indifference to success itself.[33]

Burckhardt speaks of 'this age of overstrained and despairing passions and forces': after Byron the word Romanticism often, though not invariably, carries explicit associations with despair, reckless or stoic, rather as the Elizabethan hero after Marlowe is normally a tragic hero.[34] The difference between Shelley and Byron is well brought out in their contrasting treatments of one of the central Romantic myths, that of Prometheus. In *Prometheus Unbound* the Titan represents everything in the human spirit that responds instinctively to the cry 'Liberty'. All that is most generous and ardent, all that longs for freedom for oneself and for others, all that passionately holds the highest faith in the potentialities of the human spirit, Shelley comprehends with great clarity and candour in his Promethean hero. In his short poem *Prometheus* Byron addresses the Titan in terms which do something to show how a figure of such heroic energy could also function as a symbol of the hopelessness of the human condition:

> Thy Godlike crime was to be kind,
>   To render with thy precepts less
>   The sum of human wretchedness,
> And strengthen Man with his own mind; . . .

Thou art a symbol and a sign
   To Mortals of their fate and force;
Like thee, Man is in part divine,
   A troubled stream from a pure source;
And Man in portions can foresee
His own funereal destiny;
His wretchedness, and his resistance,
And his sad unallied existence:
To which his Spirit may oppose
Itself—and equal to all woes,
   And a firm will, and a deep sense,
Which even in torture can descry
   Its own concenter'd recompense,
Triumphant where it dares defy,
And making Death a Victory.   (35–9, 45–59)

Byron emphasizes not Prometheus' achievement but his helplessness, not his heroism, but his suffering. His defiance is not now his
choice, but the only attitude left to him. *The Modern Prometheus*
was the subtitle of *Frankenstein.*

In addition to the works cited in the notes the following have useful
material on the themes of this chapter: W. J. Bate, *From Classic to Romantic*
(Cambridge, Mass., 1946); A. D. McKillop, *The Background of Thomson's
'Liberty'* (Houston, 1951); Paul Hazard, *European Thought in the Eighteenth
Century: From Montesquieu to Lessing* (London, Hollis and Carter, 1954),
esp. Pt. III, 'Disaggregation'; A. Cobban, *In Search of Humanity: The Role of
the Enlightenment in Modern History* (London: Cape, 1960); G. R. Cragg, *The
Church and the Age of Reason* (Harmondsworth: Penguin, 1960) and *Reason
and Authority in the Eighteenth Century* (Cambridge U.P., 1964); P. Fussell,
The Rhetorical World of Augustan Humanism (Oxford, 1965); Hugh Honour,
Neo-Classicism (Harmondsworth: Penguin, 1968); R. W. Harris,
Romanticism and the Social Order (London: Blandford, 1969); Lillian Furst,
Romanticism in Perspective (London: Macmillan, 1969); Douglas H. White,
Pope and the Context of Controversy (Univ. of Chicago Press, 1970); Eric
Voegelin, *From Enlightenment to Revolution* ed. John H. Hallowell (Durham,
N.C.: Duke U.P., 1975) esp. chs. 1–4; Karl Kroeber and William Walling
(edd.), *Images of Romanticism: Verbal and Visual Affinities* (New Haven &
London: Yale U.P., 1978).

8

Tennyson's *In Memoriam*

Tennyson is too intimately and essentially the poet of the nineteenth century to separate himself from its leading characteristics, the progress of physical science, and a vast commercial, mechanical and industrial development. Whatever he may say or do in an occasional fit, he cannot long either cross or lose its sympathies; for while he elevates, as well as adorns it, he is flesh of its flesh and bone of its bone.
—GLADSTONE, *Gleanings from Past Years* II. 146.

I SCIENCE AND POETRY

The most cursory reader of *In Memoriam* soon understands that for Tennyson the force which most painfully threatens man's freedom is his own consciousness of the structure of the Universe as it was presented by scientific research and theory in the middle years of the nineteenth century. Nothing could contrast more sharply with the general reception of scientific teaching at the beginning of the eighteenth century, as I have described it in the preceding chapter. One naturally wonders what has become of the abounding confidence expressed in, for example, Dryden's *To Dr. Charleton* (1663), where the poet declares his pride that so many pioneers of scientific and medical discovery have been Englishmen, and rejoices that they were in the forefront of a movement which, by relying on empirical observation, would do away with man's thraldom to the dogma of Aristotelian principles, 'the longest Tyranny that ever sway'd'. The emphasis on liberation is equally evident in Akenside's *Hymn to Science* (1739). Far from being a constricting force Science, according to Akenside, is to free man from domination by his 'passions', his 'desires', and his 'heart'. By enabling man to understand his own 'means and motives' it places him in control of his actions: thus greater scientific knowledge, as well as obviously increasing human capacity ('Founders of cities, orders, laws') will also enlarge the genuine freedom of human activity ('Of wealth, power, freedom, thou the cause') and can be stopped short if at any point it threatens to undermine Faith. It is perhaps not unfair to point also to the poem's imagery—'fair effusive ray', 'dauntless steps', 'her working hand', 'Through every maze', 'Reason, the judge', 'just ascent', 'scale', 'degrees', 'every various scene', 'the daring sail', 'faithless sea', 'vain tumult', and so on. These phrases do an adequate amount of work in the poem and do not degenerate into clichés, but they are strongly conventional and indicate how little scientific knowledge was felt to disturb traditional attitudes. It was, on the contrary, expected to provide confirmation of a rational way of life.

Set against Akenside's placidity the following:

Cain	And wherefore did it [the earth] fall?
Lucifer	Ask him who fells.
Cain	But how?
Lucifer	By a most crushing and inexorable

Destruction and disorder of the elements,
Which struck a world to chaos, as a chaos
Subsiding has struck out a world: such things,
Though rare in time, are frequent in eternity.
. . . .
What ye in common have with what they [the previous
      inhabitants of Earth] had
Is life, and what ye *shall* have—death: the rest
Of your poor attributes is such as suits
Reptiles engender'd out of the subsiding
Slime of a mighty universe, crush'd into
A scarcely-yet shaped planet, peopled with
Things whose enjoyment was to be in blindness.

This is taken from Act II scene 2 of Byron's 'mystery' play, *Cain* (79 ff). In a note to the Preface Byron explains that he is adopting 'in this poem the notion of Cuvier, that the world has been destroyed several times before the creation of man'. Georges Cuvier (1769–1832) was a figure of great importance in the development of science in England and France. He was a comparative anatomist and a palaeontologist of distinction. Having noticed that different geological strata offered different species he concluded that each stratum represented an epoch that had been terminated by a cataclysm and succeeded by another epoch with changed species. In science the effect of his great prestige was to render suspect the evolutionary theories of Lamarck and, initially at least, those of progressionist geologists such as Hutton. The natural interpretation of his catastrophism was a pessimistic one, since its plain implications are that all the achievements in which mankind takes such pride are peculiar to the present epoch and will doubtless be overwhelmed and forgotten in their turn. Thus although Cuvier did much to systematize scientific research into the history of life the principle most widely associated with his work was that of irresistible and cataclysmic change.[1] The feeling of hopelessness at

the transience of human institutions which Byron expresses so
powerfully in Canto IV of *Childe Harold* is even more appropriate to
the greater cycles of cosmic alteration.

Cuvier's theories are strongly voiced also in *Don Juan*:

> But let it go:—it will one day be found
> 　With other relics of 'a former world,'
> When this world shall be *former*, underground,
> 　Thrown topsy-turvy, twisted, crisp'd, and curl'd,
> Baked, fried, or burnt, turn'd inside-out, or drown'd,
> 　Like all the worlds before, which have been hurl'd
> First out of, and then back again to chaos,
> The superstratum which will overlay us.
>
> So Cuvier says:—and then shall come again
> 　Unto the new creation, rising out
> From our old crash, some mystic, ancient strain
> 　Of things destroy'd and left in airy doubt;
> Like to the notions we now entertain
> 　Of Titans, giants, fellows of about
> Some hundred feet in height, *not* to say *miles*,
> And mammoths, and your wingéd crocodiles.　(IX/37,38)

Thus even when Byron refers to Newton and the consequences of
Newton (X/1,2) there is an obvious irony in his agreeing to suppose
that science offers 'a thing to counterbalance human woes'. Strong
though the influence of Cuvier is in the poem it engenders in Byron
not despair but a sombre scepticism about the ends of human
activity:

> 'Que sçais-je?' was the motto of Montaigne,
> 　As also of the first academicians;
> That all is dubious which man may attain,
> 　Was one of their most favourite positions.
> There's no such thing as certainty, that's plain
> 　As any of Mortality's conditions;
> So little do we know what we're about in
> This world, I doubt if doubt itself be doubting.
>
> It is a pleasant voyage perhaps to float,
> 　Like Pyrrho, on a sea of speculation;
> But what if carrying sail capsize the boat?
> 　Your wise men don't know much of navigation;
> And swimming long in the abyss of thought
> 　Is apt to tire: a calm and shallow station
> Well nigh the shore, where one stoops down and gathers
> Some pretty shell, is best for moderate bathers.　(IX/17,18)

If the history of the world according to Cuvier left man only the unattractive choice between pessimism and Pyrrhonism, it might be assumed that the scientists whose theories of an evolving universe superseded his would furnish more support for a fairly sanguine view of humanity. At first sight this is true. If the world has developed steadily then it may be supposed to be improving steadily, and, if so, scientific knowledge presents no barrier to a belief in a beneficient creator. But, of course, there are difficulties. First, the Biblical account of the Creation and the Flood can no longer be accepted as literally true: thus the work of Hutton, for example, was held to menace the foundations of religious belief. Secondly, and more seriously, Uniformitarian geological theories implied literally inconceivable spans of time and therefore contradicted all traditional accounts of human history. Thus Lyell's *Principles of Geology*,[2] the great landmark in the development of geological theory, was a double-edged weapon in the hands of those who wished to press it into the service of natural theology. If Lyell proved hard to accommodate an even more troublesome set of arguments was to follow.

II CHAMBER'S *VESTIGES*

Vestiges of the Natural History of Creation by Robert Chambers was published in 1844.[3] Chambers' object was to bring together a uniformitarian theory of terrestrial creation and progressionist theories of geological change and to argue from these in favour of a continuously evolving creation of animate matter.[4] His emphasis is thus on the regularity of the Universe, on the fact that it is governed by 'laws of infallible harmony of operation' (246). From time to time he observes, quite justly, that there is nothing in this to disturb faith in a Divine Creator: indeed some such invariable general laws are precisely what we should expect from a Deity who was not subject to caprice.

It sounds from this as though Chambers could, without too much difficulty, be received into a general tradition of natural theology which included Paley and the Bridgewater Treatises.[5] Yet the *Vestiges* was assailed as a work of deeply sceptical and anti-religious tendencies—'Prophetic of infidel times, and indicating the unsoundness of our general education, the Vestiges has started into public favour with a fair chance of poisoning the fountains of science, and sapping the foundations of religion.'[6] It is important to understand why the work aroused such hostility. I speak at this point subject to correction from those who have studied the scientific history of the period in more detail than I have, but it is my

impression that Chambers' book represents a very full and fair
statement in popular terms of the theory of evolution. It was left to
Darwin to convince the world by proposing a mechanism for the
mutation of species, which Chambers did not.[7] To the best of my
observation Darwin's work, when it was published, contradicted
very little in Chambers; it showed that some of his tentative
guesses were wrong, but on the other hand provided massive
support for his general position.[8] Thus Darwin and Chambers hang
together: Darwin did not render Chambers obsolete, while cri-
ticisms of the 'infidelity' of Chambers apply equally to the work of
Darwin. At one point indeed Darwin's doctrine of natural selection
went beyond Chambers in a direction that was felt to be danger-
ously close to a denial of God's Providence. The crucial point was
the part played by chance in the Creation.

  Chambers, as I have said, never explicitly denies or openly questions the agency of God in the Universe, but the emphasis of his
work, especially the last chapter, 'Purpose and General Condition
of the Animated Creation', is so insistently on the statistical nature
of Universal Law that the notion of Divine Providence virtually
disappears, and the reader might be excused for taking the whole
book as a satire in the vein of Samuel Butler.[9] When Chambers
examines 'the whole Uranographical arrangements' as they apply
to persons he gives 'uniformity' the sense of 'actuarial regularity',
and concludes, 'This statistical regularity in moral affairs fully
establishes their being under the presidency of law.'[10] Again:

> The indefiniteness of the potentiality of the human faculties, and the
> complexity which thus attends their relations, lead unavoidably to
> occasional error. . . . Causality and conscientiousness are, it is true,
> guides over all; but even these are only faculties of the same indeter-
> minate constitution as the rest, and partake accordingly of the same
> inequality of action. Man is therefore a piece of mechanism, which
> never can act so as to satisfy his own ideas of what he might be. (360–1)

The laws governing mankind are, like all other universal laws,
subject to local irregularities:

> We there [in the constitution of nature] see the Deity operating in the
> most august of his works by fixed laws, an arrangement which, it is
> clear, only admits of the main and primary results being good, but dis-
> regards exceptions. . . . The laws presiding over meteorology, life, and
> mind, are necessarily less definite [than the mechanical laws] as they
> have to produce a great variety of mutually related results. . . . Often
> there must be an interference of one law with another; often a law will
> chance to operate in excess, or upon a wrong object, and thus evil will
> be produced.   (369–70)

A passage from the final argument gives the method and the tone:

> Man's sense of good and evil . . . would incline him to destine the vicious
> man to destruction and save the virtuous. But the Great Ruler of Nature
> does not act on such principles. He has established laws for the opera-
> tion of inanimate matter, which are quite unswerving, so that, when we
> know them, we have only to act in a certain way with respect to them,
> in order to obtain all the benefits and avoid all the evils connected with
> them. He has likewise established moral laws in our nature, which are
> equally unswerving, (allowing for their wider range of action), and
> from obedience to which unfailing good is to be derived. But the two
> sets of laws are independent of each other. Hence it is that virtue forms
> no protection against the evils connected with the physical laws.
>
> (383)[11]

Finally

> It may be that, while we are committed to take our chance in a natural
> system of undeviating operation, and are left, with apparent ruthless-
> ness, to endure the consequences of every collision into which we
> knowingly or unknowingly come with each of its regulations, there is a
> system of Mercy or Grace behind the screen of nature, towards which
> we stand in a peculiar class of relations, which is capable of compensa-
> ting for all casualties endured here, and whose very largeness is what
> makes these casualties a matter of indifference to God.   (400–1)

If we add to these passages Chambers' suggestion that civilization
and the arts are a natural and spontaneous reaction to environment (326), his thorough-going materialism about mental processes
(341–8), and his ready admission that every kind of disease, crime,
evil and injustice can take place in 'an economy governed by
general laws' (386) it is easy to see that he writes from no very profound conviction of the special value of human activity. This is
completely confirmed by the conclusion of the *Explanations*:

> Arithmetic could state, if we knew it, the connexion between the birth
> of a babe which saw the light an hour ago, and the time when the
> elements of our astral system began to resolve themselves into those
> countless orbs, one of which is Man's, the stage of his long descended
> history, and the bounds within which all his secular phenomena must
> ever be confined. The unit of each individuality, great or humble in
> social regard, takes a fixed place in that march of life which rose
> unreckoned ages ago, and now goes on to a 'weird', which no wizard
> has pretended to know. . . . It may be, as some one has suggested, that
> there is not only a term of life to the individual, but to the species, and
> that when the proper time comes, the prolific energy being exhausted,
> man is transferred to the list of extinct forms. Strange thought, that the

beauteous phenomena of personal existence ... should be thus resolved; passing away whole 'equinoxes' into the past, as far as we
particular men are concerned, still passing further back as respects the
larger personalities called nations, and still further in inconceivable
multiplication with regard to the species—gone, lost, hushed in the
stillness of a mightier death than has hitherto been thought of! But yet
the faith may not be shaken, that that which has been endowed with
the power of godlike thought, and allowed to come into communion
with its Eternal Author, cannot be truly lost.   (186–8)

That passage, in its conscientious attempt to convert emptiness
into substance, echoes the end of the *Vestiges*:

There may yet be a faith derived from this view of nature sufficient to
sustain us under all sense of the imperfect happiness, the calamities, the
woes, and pains of this sphere of being. For let us but fully and truly
consider what a system is here laid open to view, and we cannot well
doubt that we are in the hands of One who is both able and willing to do
us the most entire justice. And in this faith we may well rest at ease,
even though life should have been to us but a protracted disease, or
though every hope we had built on the secular materials within our
reach were felt to be melting from our grasp. Thinking of all the contingencies of this world as to be in time melted into or lost in the greater
system, to which the present is only subsidiary, let us wait the end with
patience, and be of good cheer.   (402–3)

The general drift of my argument will be clear—that the *Vestiges*,
for all its careful acknowledgement of what may be achieved by
faith in a beneficent Creator, represented a Universe operating
without God's attention and by laws which could be represented as
universal only in a statistical sense. It is not putting the case too
strongly to say that what Chambers offers is 'a dreary view of the
Divine economy' in which the laws governing aggregate behaviour
are inexorable and yet the individual is still at the mercy of
chance.[12] Chambers' style is on the whole not inclined to terseness,
but three of his crisper apophthegms may summarize the genuine
challenge of his theory:

The chronology of God is not as our chronology   (373)

The first object is to ascertain truth. No truth can be derogatory to the
presumed fountain of truth (*Explanations* 139)

Man is now seen to be an enigma only as an individual; in the mass he is
a mathematical problem.   (338)

III *IN MEMORIAM*

In this section I shall look at *In Memoriam* and note a number of passages where Tennyson's arguments and Chambers' run on similar lines. *Vestiges* was available to Tennyson and he asked Moxon to buy him a copy, although he insisted that he had not read the book before he wrote the 'Evolution parts' of his poem.[13] I wish to show not that he was directly influenced by Chambers but that the poem is more easily put in perspective once we know that the anxieties that vexed the poet were not phantoms but perfectly reasonable inferences from current scientific thought and speculation. Even if Tennyson had been able to dismiss Chambers as more of a popularizer than a serious man of science he would have had to take account of work such as Lyell's, which could not be lightly set aside,[14] and it is a commonplace that the Universe which the major scientists were presenting in ever more convincing detail was not easy to reconcile with traditional belief in a divine plan.[15] In particular Tennyson was troubled by the dilemma of the isolated individual attempting to define himself in relation to a world, perhaps indeed an infinite plurality of worlds, of vast distances and enormous spans of time:

> The baby new to earth and sky,
>   What time his tender palm is prest
>   Against the circle of the breast,
> Has never thought that 'this is I:'
>
> But as he grows he gathers much,
>   And learns the use of 'I', and 'me',
>   And finds 'I am not what I see,
> And other than the things I touch.'
>
> So rounds he to a separate mind
>   From whence clear memory may begin,
>   As through the frame that binds him in
> His isolation grows defined.   (XLV)

Tennyson here starts from precisely the same premises as Wordsworth in Book II of *The Prelude* and arrives at a precisely opposite conclusion. These inconceivable dimensions menace the isolated individual in an even subtler and more disabling way than certain knowledge of human mortality:

> My own dim life should teach me this,
>   That life shall live for evermore,

Else earth is darkness at the core,
And dust and ashes all that is;
. . . .
What then were God to such as I?
  'Twere hardly worth my while to choose
  Of things all mortal, or to use
A little patience ere I die;

'Twere best at once to sink to peace,
  Like birds the charming serpent draws,
  To drop head-foremost in the jaws
Of vacant darkness and to cease.

Yet if some voice that man could trust
  Should murmur from the narrow house,
  'The cheeks drop in; the body bows;
Man dies: nor is there hope in dust:'

Might I not say? 'Yet even here,
  But for one hour, O Love, I strive
  To keep so sweet a thing alive:'
But I should turn mine ears and hear

The moanings of the homeless sea,
  The sound of streams that swift or slow
  Draw down Aeonian hills, and sow
The dust of continents to be;

And Love would answer with a sigh,
  'The sound of that forgetful shore
  Will change my sweetness more and more,
Half-dead to know that I shall die.'   (xxxiv-v)[16]

This sense of human values diminished to nothing on the massive scale of geological time persists as a resonant undertone in the poem, sometimes finding open expression, as in section CXXIII:

There rolls the deep where grew the tree.
  O earth, what changes hast thou seen!
  There where the long street roars, hath been
The stillness of the central sea.

The hills are shadows, and they flow
  From form to form, and nothing stands;
  They melt like mist, the solid lands,
Like clouds they shape themselves and go.[17]

It is plain that even if Lyell's theory of gradual change is preferred to Cuvier's more drastic version it offers little comfort to the individual, especially not to an individual who hopes to assuage his grief for his friend by assuring himself that there is some hope for man of life after death or, failing certain promise of immortality, at least that human life is not pointless. There can be nothing special about man in a world whose only principle is that of eternal mutability:

> We pass; the path that each man trod
> Is dim, or will be dim, with weeds:
> What fame is left for human deeds
> In endless age? It rests with God.   (LXXIII)

In Pope and Byron we have observed some possible attitudes towards a determined world: to a limited extent it was open to Tennyson also to regard natural change as 'eternal process moving on' (LXXXII). The type of organic evolution which was found in Lyell was essentially Lamarckian, which allows for a *nisus* or upward striving in every creature, whereas Chambers, as we have seen, although he is careful not to deny the First Cause or Eternal Author, in fact describes a world in which free will is meaningless, where 'law' is a generalization, and where the fate of the individual is a matter of pure chance. My reading of *In Memoriam* sees Tennyson confronting as his ultimate problem that of discovering a significance for human life in a world such as Chambers depicts, inflexible in its general laws but random in their individual application.

> [My soul was] whirled
> About empyreal heights of thought,
> And came on that which is, and caught
> The deep pulsations of the world,
>
> Aeonian music measuring out
> The steps of Time—the shocks of Chance—
> The blows of Death. At length my trance
> Was cancelled, stricken through with doubt.   (XCV. 37–44)

Where, in his last chapter, Chambers pointedly declines to draw out the full moral implications of his view of the cosmos, Tennyson pushes painfully forward, incidentally bringing himself rather closer than one would expect to a Darwinian position:

LV

> The wish, that of the living whole
> No life may fail beyond the grave,
> Derives it not from what we have
> The likest God within the soul?

Are God and Nature then at strife,
 That Nature lends such evil dreams?
 So careful of the type she seems,
So careless of the single life;

That I, considering everywhere
 Her secret meaning in her deeds,
 And finding that of fifty seeds
She often brings but one to bear,

I falter where I firmly trod,
 And falling with my weight of cares
 Upon the great world's altar-stairs
That slope through darkness up to God,

I stretch lame hands of faith, and grope,
 And gather dust and chaff, and call
 To what I feel is Lord of all,
And faintly trust the larger hope.

LVI

'So careful of the type?' but no.
 From scarpèd cliff and quarried stone
 She cries, 'A thousand types are gone:
I care for nothing, all shall go.

'Thou makest thine appeal to me:
 I bring to life, I bring to death:
 The spirit does but mean the breath:
I know no more.' And he, shall he,

Man, her last work, who seemed so fair,
 Such splendid purpose in his eyes,
 Who rolled the psalm to wintry skies,
Who built him fanes of fruitless prayer,

Who trusted God was love indeed
 And love Creation's final law—
 Though Nature, red in tooth and claw
With ravine, shrieked against his creed—

Who loved, who suffered countless ills,
 Who battled for the True, the Just,
 Be blown about the desert dust,
Or sealed within the iron hills?

No more? A monster then, a dream,
   A discord. Dragons of the prime,
   That tare each other in their slime,
Were mellow music matched with him.

O life as futile, then, as frail!
   O for thy voice to soothe and bless!
   What hope of answer, or redress?
Behind the veil, behind the veil.

It is possible to make out quite a strong case on general poetic grounds in favour of the 'Lyell-derived' passages which I quoted earlier. It can, for example, be fairly said that the scientific imagery opens the poem out and gives an impression of boundless space and time, first magnifying Tennyson's grief by associating it with the immensity of the Universe and ultimately solacing it by reducing the significance of human sufferings in comparison with the great span of the natural world. All this is perfectly appropriate to an elegy. But no such argument seems to me to be open for the sections I have just quoted. They are there because the questions they ask are questions that worried Tennyson: in particular the prodigality of Nature, with wastefulness and ruthlessness as its corollaries, disturbed him deeply, since it implied the insignificance of every individual and, if a long enough view was taken, of the human race as a whole.

At the end of *In Memoriam* Tennyson returns to these preoccupations. In all discussions of his use of science in the poem section CXVIII occupies a central place:

Contemplate all this work of Time,
   The giant labouring in his youth;
   Nor dream of human love and truth,
As dying Nature's earth and lime;

But trust that those we call the dead
   Are breathers of an ampler day
   For ever nobler ends. They say,   7
The solid earth whereon we tread

In tracts of fluent heat began,
   And grew to seeming-random forms,
   The seeming prey to cyclic storms,
Till at the last arose the man;   12

Who throve and branched from clime to clime,
   The herald of a higher race,
   And of himself in higher place,
If so he type this work of time

Within himself, from more to more;
  Or, crowned with attributes of woe
  Like glories, move his course, and show
That life is not as idle ore,

But iron dug from central gloom,
  And heated hot with burning fears,
  And dipt in baths of hissing tears,
And battered with the shocks of doom

To shape and use. Arise and fly
  The reeling Faun, the sensual feast;
  Move upward, working out the beast,
And let the ape and tiger die.

Two points call for comment. First, lines 7–12 are sometimes taken as a reference to Cuvier's cataclysmic theory, yet they are much closer to an evolutionary theory such as Chambers', especially in the phrases 'seeming-random forms' and 'the seeming prey'. The second point is the difficulty of discovering precisely what Tennyson is driving at in the rest of the section. I offer a paraphrase as follows: 'From one point of view man is, in the inescapable processes of time, no more than the forerunner of the higher forms which will eventually supersede him. But he has also the power to reproduce a similar progression in his own span. (The use of "man" here leads to ambiguity: Tennyson may be thinking of the lifetime of the individual or the whole history of the human species.) Alternatively, even if he is unable to make such a positive contribution to human advancement, he can at least "move his course" (another ambiguous expression, meaning either "fulfil his appointed function" or "exert himself to steer *his own* course") and demonstrate that even in sorrow life is not inert (i.e. man is not passive) and that even sorrow can be regarded as a necessary tempering process fitting man for an active life.[18] Let man then develop away from his animal ancestors into something higher.[19] ("Man" is again ambiguous here: the lines seem to apply to the gradual refining of mankind as a race, yet as an exhortation they can surely be addressed only to the individual man in a particular situation.)'

It seems that Tennyson is unwilling to allow himself to be put in the position of having to accept a syllogism of which the major premise begins 'Mankind is . . .' (such as a scientific generalization about the human race) because it might force him to acknowledge also an unacceptable conclusion beginning 'Therefore each individual man . . .'.[20] If this is so it might account for his reluctance to resolve some of the 'contradictions on the tongue' which lurk more and more thickly at the end of *In Memoriam*. Consider section CXX,for example: at first reading it is perfectly explicit.

> I trust I have not wasted breath:
>   I think we are not wholly brain,
>   Magnetic mockeries; not in vain,
> Like Paul with beasts, I fought with Death;
>
> Not only cunning casts in clay:
>   Let Science prove we are, and then
>   What matters Science unto men,
> At least to me? I would not stay.
>
> Let him, the wiser man who springs
>   Hereafter, up from childhood shape
>   His action like the greater ape,
> But I was *born* to other things.

With lines 2 and 3 commentators compare Chambers on the electrical nature of mental impulses. Some such notion was probably in Tennyson's mind especially as a speculative footnote of Chambers' on this point had been singled out for attack by *Blackwood's* in 1845: he may however equally possibly have been thinking of the use of electricity in experiments designed to generate life or of its possible function as a determinant of regular organic form.[21] Lines 1 to 5 are odd in many ways. 'I trust I have not wasted breath' may refer either to his labours in writing the poem so far or to his visit to the scenes of his youth which he has described in the preceding section or to his whole course of life: 'I think we are not wholly brain' is a general statement about the nature of man: 'not in vain . . . Death' is presumably also governed by 'I trust', while 'not only cunning casts in clay' requires us to understand 'I think we are'. The intimate connection is woven between what Tennyson must accept intellectually about the physical nature of man and his environment and what he needs to believe about the non-physical (and thus perhaps immortal) components of the human person. If Science can ever prove beyond doubt that these do not exist then they will have removed all values from human life and *a fortiori* from Science itself.[22] And then with his characteristic honesty Tennyson reflects that he should not claim to speak for mankind as a whole. Speaking for himself he must declare 'I would not stay'. Unless this is a simple threat to commit suicide[23] it is hard to say exactly what it is: it is a little reminiscent of Hardy's 'I think I am one born out of due time, who has no calling here'. The last stanza is comparatively straightforward. One day a generation will come which will determine its conduct by purely material standards and this will represent no doubt an advance in human wisdom, but

Tennyson by his nature is incapable of acting in this way. Science then, even while it insists that the human race is only part of the great progress of events seems also to be denying the values in terms of which 'progress' is significant to the poet. This is one reason why evolutionary doctrines are less conducive to optimism than one might expect.

Section CXXIV has been pointed to, by Graham Hough among others, as the real answer which Tennyson gives to the questions which he has raised. The difficulty with the section, as indeed with the poem as a whole, is the loose arrangement of the parts: sometimes Tennyson seems to have thought that juxtaposition was a form of syntax. What emerges most clearly is first the simple contrast between 'Believe no more' and 'I have felt', as if feeling were in itself a sufficient proof of the existence of 'The Power in Darkness whom we guess'; secondly the qualification of this 'in doubt and fear'; and thirdly the coming of wisdom which brings certain knowledge that there is in the world a power which cares for mankind, however mysterious its operations remain.[24] The progression from indignant assertion, through doubt and fear, to wisdom and certainty is, one may readily accept, central to the design of the poem, but when it is described as mistily as it is here it seems a disconcertingly lifeless embodiment of belief in the vitality of the human spirit.

The rest of the poem can perhaps be summed up in a phrase from section CXXVIII. Tennyson says, 'I see in part', and in the climax of his sequence of poems he tries to express honestly the scope and limitations of his vision. The staple unit of the poem—the confrontation of a doubt about the whole destiny of mankind with a trust that 'all is well'—is exploited even more emphatically, and the transition from bewilderment to affirmation is even more rapid—'I cannot guess', 'I seem . . . to feel', 'I seem to love', 'I have thee still', 'I shall not lose thee' (CXXX).[25] The Epilogue, which is an Epithalamium for the marriage of Edmund Lushington and Cecilia Tennyson, resumes many of the earlier themes. Since he is celebrating a wedding and looking forward to the birth of a child, Tennyson can legitimately confine his attention to the more progressive implications of evolutionary ideas. He is therefore able to hope that the child who is to be born will take mankind one generation nearer to 'the crowning race', which will no longer be 'half-akin to brute'. Of this higher humanity, Tennyson declares in the concluding stanzas of his poem,

> the man, that with me trod
> This planet, was a noble type
> Appearing ere the times were ripe,
> That friend of mine who lives in God,

That God, which ever lives and loves,
  One God, one law, one element,
  And one far-off divine event,
To which the whole creation moves.[26]

The last stanza is obviously crucial, but its syntax is awkward. I think it means '[Hallam is now with God], who is eternal and always loving: who is indivisible, just as there is a single controlling Law in the Universe, just as there is a homogeneous Substance of the Universe, and just as there is a single Terminus ordained by God towards which the whole of his creation is developing'. Once again the syntax is such that it is not possible to tell whether the poet is stating a fact or voicing a hope: on this eminently Tenny-sonian note of mingled affirmation and prayer the poem ends.

Throughout the poem, as I have said, what Tennyson fears is the random, capricious and unpredictable. As early as section III he makes it plain that the effect of sorrow on him is to make him fear that the Universe is planless:

O Sorrow, cruel fellowship,
  O Priestess in the vaults of Death,
  O sweet and bitter in a breath,
What whispers from thy lying lip?

'The stars,' she whispers, 'blindly run;
  A web is woven across the sky;
  From out waste places comes a cry,
And murmurs from the dying sun:

'And all the phantom, Nature, stands—
  With all the music in her tone,
  A hollow echo of my own,—
A hollow form with empty hands.'

And shall I take a thing so blind,
  Embrace her as my natural good;
  Or crush her, like a vice of blood,
Upon the threshold of the mind?

Unless man is immortal the beauty of the world is merely fantastic, 'such as lurks/In some wild Poet, when he works/Without a con-science or an aim' (XXXIV): in the poet's moods of deepest depression Time is no more than 'a maniac scattering dust,/And Life, a Fury slinging flame' (L): without Love and Faith what is Knowledge 'But some wild Pallas from the brain/Of Demons?' (CXIV). In the face of such perils he naturally trusts 'that nothing walks with aimless feet'

(LIV) and remembers most gratefully from the days when he talked with Hallam

> Large elements in order brought,
>   And tracts of calm from tempest made,
>   And world-wide fluctuation swayed
> In vassal tides that followed thought.   (CXII)

The broad movement of the poem from 'the phantom, Nature . . . a hollow form with empty hands' to 'the hands/That reach through nature, moulding men' (CXXIV) is echoed in the poem *De Profundis*, begun in 1852 on the birth of Tennyson's son Hallam. The last section ends

> Live thou! and of the grain and husk, the grape
> And ivyberry, choose; and still depart
> From death to death through life and life, and find
> Nearer and ever nearer Him, who wrought
> Not Matter, nor the finite-infinite,
> But this main-miracle, that thou art thou
> With power on thine own act and on the world.   (50–6)

The effect of the poem is to set the single will-using human creature against and superior to the process by which he was born 'out of the deep,/Where all that was to be, in all that was,/Whirled for a million aeons through the vast/Waste dawn of multitudinous-eddying light.'[27]

To conclude, in *In Memoriam* Tennyson begins by trying to console himself for Arthur Hallam's death and ends by relying on the reality of his grief to assure him that the entire Universe is not a mockery, and that the life of the individual has meaning. In section XLVII, for example, he refers, I think, directly to the passage which I have quoted from the conclusion of *Vestiges* when Chambers speaks of 'all the contingencies of this world as to be in time melted or lost in the greater system':

> That each, who seems a separate whole,
>   Should move his rounds, and fusing all
>   The skirts of self again, should fall
> Remerging in the general Soul,
>
> Is faith as vague as all unsweet:

Tennyson can protect his position only by an ordering of experiences, an ordering in which Knowledge must be made to recognize her subordinate role.

> Let her know her place;
> She is the second not the first.

Once this subordination has been established Tennyson is prepared to extend a welcome to Science.[28]

IV LATER POEMS

A rapid survey of Tennyson's later poems suggests that the elaborate defensive works which he constructed to protect his beliefs in *In Memoriam* did not give him lasting satisfaction.[29] For example, *Despair* (1881) is a dramatic monologue in Tennyson's most agitated manner spoken by a man who has tried to drown himself. Chief among the motives which he offers is the feeling of utter hopelessness at the barren world which Science is offering man, lit by 'the suns of a limitless Universe'. His family life has been spectaularly unhappy: why should he go on living?

> Why should we bear with an hour of torture, a moment of pain,
> If every man die for ever, if all his griefs are in vain,
> And the homeless planet at length will be wheeled through the
> silence of space,
> Motherless evermore of an ever-vanishing race,
> When the worm shall have writhed its last, and its last brother-worm
> will have fled
> From the dead fossil skull that is left in the
> rocks of an earth that is dead?
>
> (81–6)

These questions are those of a man who, 'crazed' by 'horrible infidel writings', is persuaded that 'the Sun and the Moon of our science are both of them turned into blood'. While Tennyson is careful to present these speculations as those of a disturbed mind he does little to indicate by making explicit his ideas about the true nature of human freedom that any more balanced conclusion might be available.[30]

When Tennyson applies 'the great law' more directly to his own situation the argument does not change. Lying behind *Vastness* (1885, revised 1889) is a death, probably still Hallam's,[31] which leads Tennyson into a familiar pattern of generalization:

> Many a hearth upon our dark globe sighs after many a vanished
> face,
> Many a planet by many a sun may roll with the dust of a vanished
> race.

> Raving politics, never at rest—as this poor earth's pale history runs,—
> What is it all but a trouble of ants in the gleam of a million million of
>   suns?[32]   (I–II)

Tennyson then lists the various activities, achievements and qualities, good or bad, to which humans attach importance:

> Stately purposes, valour in battle, glorious annals of army and
>   fleet,
> Death for the right cause, death for the wrong cause,
>   trumpets of victory, groans of defeat;   (IV)

> Trade flying over a thousand seas with her spice and her
>   vintage, her silk and her corn;
> Desolate offing, sailorless harbours, famishing populace,
>   wharves forlorn;   (VII)

> Love for the maiden, crowned with marriage, no regrets for
>   aught that has been,
> Household happiness, gracious children, debtless competence,
>   golden mean;   (XII)

He brings all these great nominal abstractions to rest as subjects of
a simple question:

> Spring and Summer and Autumn and Winter, and all these old
>   revolutions of earth;
> All new-old revolutions of Empire—change of the tide—what is all of it
>   worth?   (XV)

He amplifies the question, picking up the imagery from section II:

> What is it all, if we all of us end but in being our own corpse-coffins at
>   last,
> Swallow'd in Vastness, lost in Silence, drowned in the deeps of a
>   meaningless Past?

> What but a murmur of gnats in the gloom, or a moment's anger of bees
>   in their hive?[33]

There is a row of asterisks and then Tennyson smothers rather
than resolves his doubts in the last line of the poem—'Peace, let it
be! for I loved him, and love him for ever: the dead are not dead
but alive.' If, as seems likely, Tennyson is referring here to Hallam
we have a very close analogue, almost a précis, of the argument

which I have suggested as the major organizing principle of *In Memoriam*.[34]

This consistent mistrust of what scientific knowledge could lead to was compatible, but only just, with an appreciation of its tangible benefits, actual or prospective, as for example in his celebration of British achievements during the reign of Victoria:

> Fifty years of ever-broadening Commerce!
> Fifty years of ever-brightening Science!
> Fifty years of ever-widening Empire!
> (*On the Jubilee of Queen Victoria* (1887) 52–4)

In spite of such public declarations of confidence Tennyson never completely resolved in his poetry the dilemma with which the 'sad Astrology' of the new science confronted him. His endeavours are most fully chronicled in *In Memoriam*, where we see the poet struggling to preserve the values appropriate to a freely-willing individual—'Our wills are ours, we know not how' (Prologue 15)—in a world which is totally destructive of these values, either because it is completely determined or, more terrifying still, because it is completely at the mercy of chance happenings. It is this tripartite engagement which gives the poem its character and marks it as a document of the modern mind. Referring to the years he spent writing the poem Tennyson reflected: 'For I myself with these have grown/To something greater than before' (Epilogue 19–20). I make the obvious suggestion that this is not simply an assertion of personal maturity or a complacent expression of satisfaction at having 'closed/Grave doubts and answers here proposed', but rather as a justifiable claim to have arrived, in the course of successive statements and restatements, at a deeper understanding of the nature of the question. In this sense *In Memoriam* is a poem of discovery, an exploration, tentative, fluctuating and indirect, of a central problem of Tennyson's time. Like so many of his contemporaries he could neither find a satisfying answer nor bring himself to relinquish the quest. Yet he offered his readers a way of living with doubt and uncertainty: trust and endurance are both possible, and thus Tennyson can not dishonourably say at the end of *Locksley Hall Sixty Years After* (1886):

Follow Light, and do the Right—for man can half-control his doom.

V A NOTE ON ARNOLD

> Amongst us one,
> Who most has suffered, takes dejectedly
> His seat upon the intellectual throne;
> And all his store of sad experience he
> Lays bare of wretched days;
> Tells us his misery's birth and growth and signs,
> And how the dying spark of hope was fed,
> And how the breast was soothed, and how the head,
> And all his hourly varied anodynes.
> This for our wisest!   (*The Scholar-Gipsy* (1853) 182–91)

This rather unexpected reference to a contemporary writer is usually taken as a direct criticism of *In Memoriam*.[35] The lines are, I think, fair comment: the only problem is that they come a little oddly from a poet who is himself not notable for repressing his own misgivings about the world. In this note I suggest an affinity between Tennyson and Arnold, or rather a common element in their differing sorts of melancholy or dismay.

'Most men in a brazen prison live' wrote Arnold in *A Summer Night*, and the sense of men as the prisoners of a determined Universe is frequent in his work. Even if we do not attribute directly to Arnold the rigid stoicism of *Empedocles*, it is enough to point to *Balder Dead* with its 'Nornies' or to the careful use of Fate as a dramatic instrument in *Sohrab and Rustum*[36] or to his celebrated farewell to the author of *Obermann*:

> I go, fate drives me; but I leave
> Half of my life with you.
> We, in some unknown Power's employ,
> Move on a rigorous line;
> Can neither, when we will, enjoy,
> Nor, when we will, resign.   (131–6)

But Arnold also feels, perhaps even more acutely, the sense of life as not determined but fragmentary, directionless and chance-ordered. This is especially true of modern life: *Dover Beach* provides an invaluable conspectus of Arnold's major preoccupations and his favourite ways of expressing them. I am not thinking so much of the sea-imagery, which many critics have noticed, or of his acute sense of 'the eternal note of sadness', as of the implications of the last section of the poem. Arnold has already used the striking phrase 'the turbid ebb and flow/Of human misery', and in the concluding lines he defines in a pregnant simile his apprehension of the human condition as one of pointless random collision:

> And we are here as on a darkling plain
> Swept with confused alarms of struggle and flight,
> Where ignorant armies clash by night.

In this world from which Faith has retreated there is only one resource suggested—'Ah, love, let us be true/To one another!'.

Resignation conveys with great explicitness the qualified resolution with which Arnold is able to confront the vicissitudes of modern life:

> Yet they, believe me, who await
> No gifts from chance, have conquered fáte.
> They, winning room to see and hear,
> And to men's business not too near,
> Through clouds of individual strife
> Draw homeward to the general life. . . .
>
> Yet, Fausta, the mute turf we tread,
> The solemn hills around us spread,
> This stream which falls incessantly,
> The strange-scrawled rocks, the lonely sky,
> If I might lend their life a voice,
> Seem to bear rather than rejoice.
> And even could the intemperate prayer
> Man iterates, while these forbear,
> For movement, for an ampler sphere,
> Pierce Fate's impenetrable ear;
> Not milder is the general lot
> Because our spirits have forgot,
> In action's dizzying eddy whirled,
> The something that infects the world.   (247–52, 265–78)[37]

I have suggested elsewhere[38] that a similar sense of nineteenth-century life as random, aimless, nondescript and increasingly muddled is the principal source of disturbance in *The Scholar-Gipsy* and *Thyrsis*. It finds expression in images of disintegration, fragmentation, unindividualizing and lack of distinction.[39] Arnold uses this imagery in many connections, most interestingly to characterize the changes which are converting Britain into an urban country, merging discrete communities into a generalized industrial suburb, and confronting man with a world whose most obvious quality is its multitudinousness,[40] where poetry is seen as something which was possible in a 'jocund, youthful time' but is now drowned by 'the great town's harsh, heart-wearying roar'. The future can offer only 'baffling change' and 'tedious tossing to and fro'. Even if it is moving to some 'far-set goal'

> This and that way swings
> The flux of mortal things.   (*Westminster Abbey* 151–2)

Perhaps Arnold's most direct statement of his response to the emerging world is in *Stanzas from the Grande Chartreuse*. Admitting the attractions of a life of retirement, Arnold recognizes that this would find favour neither with the 'rigorous teachers' who moulded his mind nor with the 'sons of the world' who represent the spirit of progress: sciolists reprobate his melancholy as outmoded, yet, Arnold says, it will endure while 'the restlessness, the pain' endure.

> Years hence, perhaps, may dawn an age,
> More fortunate, alas! than we,
> Which without hardness will be sage,
> And gay without frivolity.
> Sons of the world, oh, speed those years;
> But, while we wait, allow our tears!
>
> Allow them! We admire with awe
> The exulting thunder of your race;
> You give the universe your law,
> You triumph over time and space!
> Your pride of life, your tireless powers,
> We laud them, but they are not ours.   (157–68)

This passage seems to me to lay bare the nature of Arnold's melancholy; he recognizes that, whether he wills it or not,

> A wanderer is man from his birth.
> He was born in a ship
> On the breast of the river of Time.   (*The Future* 1–3)

It is not possible to stand still, yet change is always from an organized to a less organized state, from a state in which many options are open to a state in which fewer options are open. For Arnold, as for Tennyson, the effect of this on human wills and purposes was stifling and ultimately fatal:

> For what wears out the life of mortal men?
>   'Tis that from change to change their being rolls;
> 'Tis that repeated shocks, again, again,
>   Exhaust the energy of strongest souls
>   And numb the elastic powers.
> Till having used our nerves with bliss and teen,
>   And tired upon a thousand schemes our wit,
>   To the just-pausing Genius we remit
> Our worn-out life, and are—what we have been.
>   (*Scholar-Gipsy* 142–50)

In a world of idle fluctuations 'without term or scope' man could not be represented as an integral part of a determined plan, since there will neither be evidence that such a plan exists nor any need to postulate its existence. Chance will account for evolution, just as chance will account for thermo-dynamic events, and when the chance arrives which eliminates man there will be no essential change in the nature of the Universe. If this is what Arnold and Tennyson perceived they had perhaps understood more of the drift of nineteenth-century science than is usually supposed.

At this point the argument divides. The first track is the main line, in which Arnold's prose writings take their place in a discussion of the literary works in which the main constraining force on the individual is his fellow men. The account of Tennyson and Arnold which I have just given provides also an immediate point of contact with the work of Hardy, who lies to one side of the general direction of my argument, as the terminus of a branch line, so to speak. In the following chapter I offer some account of his work, returning to the main line in chapter 10, p. 282.

In addition to the works cited in the notes the following have material relevant to the themes of this chapter: Graham Hough, 'The Natural Theology of *In Memoriam*', *RES*, **23** (1947), 244–56; Georg Roppen, *Evolution and Poetic Belief* (Oslo: 1956); Milton Millhauser, *Fire and Ice: The Influence of Science on Tennyson's Poetry*, Tennyson Society Monographs 4 (Lincoln: 1971); Susan Gliserman, 'Early Victorian Science Writers and Tennyson's *In Memoriam*: A Study in Cultural Exchange', *VS*, **18** (1975), 277–308, 437–59.

9

Hardy

I THE POEMS

There is an odd episode in Book II of *Paradise Lost*. Satan, voyaging across the abyss from Hell to the world, meets 'a vast vacuity':

> all unawares
> Fluttring his pennons vain plumb down he drops
> Ten thousand fadom deep, and to this hour
> Down had been falling, had not by ill chance
> The strong rebuff of som tumultuous cloud
> Instinct with Fire and Nitre hurried him
> As many miles aloft.   (932–8)

The implication that the fall of man would not have occurred as it did but for the intervention of sheer chance does not fit very happily into the logic of Christian epic, and the incident is not dwelt upon. In the years after Milton the idea that the entire fabric of the Universe was purely contingent received, not surprisingly, very little attention in literature, until, as we have seen, Tennyson and Arnold were confronted with the disconcerting implications of nineteenth-century scientific theories. The simplest way to show the nature of Hardy's concern with this issue is to quote a poem called *Hap*, which was written in 1866, possibly as a direct result of reading Browning's *Caliban upon Setebos* (1864):

> If but some vengeful god would call to me
> From up the sky, and laugh: 'Thou suffering thing,
> Know that thy sorrow is my ecstasy,
> That thy love's loss is my hate's profiting!'
>
> Then would I bear it, clench myself, and die,
> Steeled by the sense of ire unmerited;
> Half-eased in that a Powerfuller than I
> Had willed and meted me the tears I shed.

242

But not so. How arrives it joy lies slain,
And why unblooms the best hope ever sown?
—Crass Casualty obstructs the sun and rain,
And dicing Time for gladness casts a moan. . . .
These purblind Doomsters had as readily strown
Blisses about my pilgrimage as pain.

At once we are introduced to one of the most striking features of Hardy's presentation of human life—his complete readiness to accept the possibility that everything in the world, including the activities of men, is purely fortuitous.

I do not think that it is helpful to try to trace the origins of Hardy's view of the world. He clearly knew something of the work of Darwin, Huxley and Herbert Spencer: he had read and may have been influenced by Comte and Fourier: he is said to have a good knowledge of Mill: and a fair amount has been made of his reading of Schopenhauer and von Hartmann. The derivation of the ideas is not of the first importance. It is enough to say that the doubts which Arnold and Tennyson express about the existence and efficacy of providence are with Hardy no longer doubts. We never meet a living God in Hardy. If the world is governed at all, it is governed by a power to whom the affairs of man are of no concern.

Sometimes Hardy entertains the speculation that the directing principle is a simple mechanical determinism, and derives no comfort from it. It may be asked why Hardy finds the prospect so depressing if Pope, for example, could derive from the inexorable laws of Newtonian mechanics the foundation for a cheerful acceptance of the place of man in the creation. The essential difference, of course, is that Pope is still able to derive his Universe from a Providence which, though admittedly withdrawn and abstracted, may be understood as having furnished for man a defined place and thus a defined role. Pope therefore does not contemplate the possibility that human life is meaningless. Hardy has no such defences and asks himself constantly what values can be found in human activity in a world without God or any other sustaining power, a world which, whether determined or random, is simply 'a welter of futile doing' (*In Tenebris* III). What is impressive in Hardy is the speed with which he identifies and characterizes the possible modes of organization of such a world, and secondly the consistency with which throughout his life he assaulted the associated problems by every means in his power, at first in the novels, then in *The Dynasts*, and finally in the poems, his answers becoming increasingly explicit.

Otherwise I do not detect any significant shift of attitude during the long span of Hardy's career. I shall accordingly begin with the poems, since they present most starkly the nature of Hardy's diagnosis of the human condition. In point of date of writing they run from 1865 to 1928, though none were published until 1898. They are remarkably consistent: it would be a bold man who would undertake to demonstrate any constant direction of change or development of matter or technique. Hardy, like Browning, insisted that his poems were not to be taken as literally accurate records of his personal opinions—'. . . much is dramatic or impersonative even where not explicitly so. Moreover, that portion which may be regarded as individual comprises a series of feelings and fancies written down in widely differing moods and circumstances, and at various dates.'[1] Yet even if we heed Hardy's warning it seems to me impossible to resist deriving from his poems a single, coherent view of the world and humanity which it would be disingenuous to offer to divorce from the poet and to ascribe to a series of imaginary speakers. The poems are too short, the dramatic indications too feeble, and the consistency too remarkable for this. Consider, for example, the first of the *In Tenebris* poems:

> Wintertime nighs;
> But my bereavement-pain
> It cannot bring again:
>   Twice no one dies.
>
> Flower-petals flee;
> But, since it once hath been,
> No more that severing scene
>   Can harrow me.
>
> Birds faint in dread:
> I shall not lose old strength
> In the lone frost's black length:
>   Strength long since fled!
>
> Leaves freeze to dun;
> But friends can not turn cold
> This season as of old
>   For him with none.
>
> Tempests may scath;
> But love can not make smart
> Again this year his heart
>   Who no heart hath.
>
> Black is night's cope;
> But death will not appal
> One who, past doubtings all,
>   Waits in unhope.

I readily concede that this need not be taken as a definitive statement of Hardy's philosophy of life, and may be considered as the
expression of a mood, perhaps even a temporary one. But I cannot
see that it is more than formally possible to suppose that it is the
mood of some fictitious character, not Hardy.

The difficulty in undertaking to extract a 'harmonious philosophy'[2] from Hardy's poems is not that they contradict one
another, but that every piece seems to embody its own untrans-
latable epitome of his thought. I therefore consider first a number
of poems, not necessarily his best, which deal directly with the condition of man and offer to explain the grounds for Hardy's
'unhope'. These poems depend on a fairly consistent set of assumptions, as follows:

(a)   There is no God, or any equivalent power:

> 'O man-projected Figure, of late
> Imaged as we, thy knell who shall survive?
> Whence came it we were tempted to create
> One whom we can no longer keep alive?
>
> Framing him, jealous, fierce, at first,
> We gave him justice as the ages rolled,
> Will to bless those by circumstance accurst,
> And longsuffering, and mercies manifold.
>
> And, tricked by our own early dream
> And need of solace, we grew self-deceived,
> Our making soon our maker did we deem,
> And what we had imagined we believed.
>
> Till, in Time's stayless stealthy swing,
> Uncompromising rude reality
> Mangled the Monarch of our fashioning,
> Who quavered, sank; and now has ceased to be.
>
> So, toward our myth's oblivion,
> Darkling, and languid-lipped, we creep and grope
> Sadlier than those who wept in Babylon,
> Whose Zion was a still abiding hope.'   (*God's Funeral* VI-X)

Or, if there is a God, he is inferior to man, as in *New Year's Eve*, or
An Inquiry, or *Fragment*, or *God's Education*:

> Said I: 'We call that cruelty—
>   We, your poor mortal kind.'
> He mused. 'The thought is new to me.
> Forsooth, though I men's master be,
>   Theirs is the teaching mind!'   (*God's Education* 16–20)

If God, or some equivalent, exists anywhere in the Universe it is not as a transcendent controlling power.[3]

(b) All the Universe, including mankind, is one great machine, which is governed simply by its own state or its own inherent tendencies. Were things left at this one might suppose that Hardy implied a classical mechanical determinism. He is certainly prepared to rest the occasional poem on these foundations, but he more often personifies the inevitable course of the world as Doom, or the Doomsters, or the Immanent Will. Exactly what Hardy is able to comprehend in this term we shall see when we look at *The Dynasts*. At present it is enough to say that Hardy in his poems sometimes suggests that the Immanent Will moves along predetermined paths and sometimes that its 'designs' are simply matters of chance, 'crass casualty' or 'purposeless propension' (*A Philosophical Fantasy*).[4] It is 'the Immanent Doer That doth not know': it works 'automatically like a somnambulist, not reflectively, like a sage'.

(c) Which of these happened to be true would be of no consequence were it not that at some point in time human consciousness evolved, or appeared like a 'stray exotic germ', as Hardy says in *The Aërolite*. Until then the Universe had rubbed along very well on simple mechanical principles. But 'this disease called sense' is an unexpected by-product, and unwelcome, since it cannot co-exist happily with scientific law:

> A time there was—as one may guess
> And as, indeed, earth's testimonies tell—
> Before the birth of consciousness,
>   When all went well.
>
> None suffered sickness, love, or loss,
> None knew regret, starved hope, or heart-burnings;
> None cared whatever crash or cross
>   Brought wrack to things.
>
> If something ceased, no tongue bewailed,
> If something winced and waned, no heart was wrung;
> If brightness dimmed, and dark prevailed,
>   No sense was stung.
>
> But the disease of feeling germed,
> And primal rightness took the tinct of wrong;
> Ere nescience shall be reaffirmed
>   How long, how long?   (*Before Life and After*)[5]

(d) The Immanent Will has by definition, not the slightest interest in human concerns. 'My imagination may have often run away with me; but all the same, my sober opinion—so far as I have any definite one—of the Cause of things, has been defined in scores of places, and is that of a great many ordinary thinkers: that the said Cause is neither moral nor immoral, but *un*moral: "loveless and hateless" I have called it, "which neither good nor evil knows"—etc. No doubt people will go on thinking that I really believe the Prime Mover to be a malignant old gentleman, a sort of King of Dahomey —an idea which, so far from holding it, is to me irresistibly comic,' Hardy wrote in a letter of 19 December 1920, and it is true that he normally represents the Prime Mover, and indeed the whole of the natural world, as quite unconcerned about the affairs of men.[6] So pointedly indifferent indeed is the Immanent Will that it permits the most outrageous thwartings of human desires, even appearing to engineer coincidences and ironically painful situations out of a malicious pleasure in seeing men crossed and baffled by their own acts.[7] 'The Doomsters' become 'The Wrongers' in *After the Last Breath*.

(e) Men, in a world of this kind, have consciousness, but no power of free willing. At best they have a choice of ways to their inevitable destruction. If they struggle they regularly flounder deeper in the quicksand—so regularly that it seems inevitable—and the indifference or casual malevolence of the Immanent Will takes care that they realise that their sufferings are entailed by their own actions.[8] Yet if they remain inert they will simply drift towards death and oblivion, and thus might as well be already dead.

If then we take the world of Hardy's poems as a world a man might inhabit we see that he could live in it only as in a trap.[9] Man needs to show tenderness and compassion to vindicate his own humanity, yet the warmer his heart the more he will suffer. This is the dilemma of man in the world.[10] His burden is consciousness without knowledge: he is able to suffer and knows that he suffers —of everything else he is ignorant.

> When moiling seems at cease
>   In the vague void of night-time,
>   And heaven's wide roomage stormless
>   Between the dusk and light-time,
>   And fear at last is formless,
> We call the allurement Peace.
>
> Peace, this hid riot, Change,
>   This revel of quick-cued mumming,
>   This never truly being,
>   This evermore becoming,
>   This spinner's wheel onfleeing
> Outside perception's range.

>   ('*According to the Mighty Working*')

This ignorance is the distinguishing mark of human life from birth (*To an Unborn Pauper Child, In Childbed*) to death (*Six Boards*). Those who perceive the true nature of the world are not heeded (*Mad Judy*); and this is true of the poet himself (*In Tenebris* II).[11]

So far I have looked principally at poems in which Hardy is openly recounting and illustrating his painful conjectures about the condition of man. The poems which are not overtly speculative are completely consonant with those that are. Two master-themes are constant throughout these poems; they are, as one might expect, love and death. Love is usually, but not invariably, a source of unhappiness:[12] either it is viewed retrospectively, so that Hardy laments or notes with resignation the passage of time,[13] or presented as full of peril, 'For winning love we win the risk of losing,/And losing love is as one's life were riven' (*Revulsion*). The reader is left with the conclusion that either an active or a passive approach to love will lead to wretchedness. At worst the passive approach will be visited with regret for love let slip, which is much the preferable alternative, since to Hardy, in his poems as elsewhere, one of the supreme ironies of human existence is displayed when a person realizes too late that he has chosen wrongly in marriage.[14] 'Love is a terrible thing: sweet for a space,/And then all mourning, mourning' (*A Hurried Meeting*). Hardy's own first marriage seems to have brought him both kinds of unhappiness in succession, the regret coming after his wife's death; it is memorably recorded in the *Poems of 1912-13* and other poems of the same period.

Death as a topic appealed to Hardy in many ways. First as a source of inevitable grief, a grief which is more acute if it laments also a missed opportunity:

'O lonely workman, standing there
In a dream, why do you stare and stare
At her grave, as no other grave there were?

If your great gaunt eyes so importune
Her soul by the shine of this corpse-cold moon
Maybe you'll raise her phantom soon!'

'Why, fool, it is what I would rather see
Than all the living folk there be;
But alas, there is no such joy for me!'

'Ah—she was one you loved, no doubt,
Through good and evil, through rain and drought,
And when she passed, all your sun went out?'

'Nay: she was the woman I did not love,
Whom all the others were ranked above,
Whom during her life I thought nothing of.' (*In the Moonlight*)

Secondly because it is often an occasion of bizarre or pathetic accident, as in *Squire Hooper, Royal Sponsors, Her Second Husband, The Single Witness, After the Burial, Julie-Jane, The Three Tall Men, The Workbox* and many others. The traditional mitigations of the burden of human mortality are notably absent, man normally being presented as 'but a thing of flesh and bone/Speeding on to its cleft in the clay' (*The Dream-Follower*). Many of Hardy's most moving poems are about the passing of time, seen simply as the force that bears all men towards death, and in particular is carrying the poet irresistibly away from everything except the grave:[15]

Everybody else, then, going,
And I still left where the fair was? . . .
Much have I seen of neighbour loungers
Making a lusty showing,
Each now past all knowing.

There is an air of blankness
In the streets and the littered spaces;
Thoroughfare, steeple, bridge and highway
Wizen themselves to lankness;
Kennels dribble dankness.

Folk all fade. And whither,
As I wait alone where the fair was?
Into the clammy and numbing night-fog
Whence they entered hither.
Soon one more goes thither!   (*Exeunt Omnes*)

It would be an easy matter to multiply examples of the way in which Hardy unites in poem after poem his sense of the inevitable passing of time[16] and his apprehensions of the certainty of human suffering, and finds his only consolation in the reflection that in time the suffering must also cease. 'When a man falls he lies' (*A Sign-seeker*). Thus death can sometimes be presented as positively desirable. In *A Wasted Illness*, for example, he describes the pain and the delirium:

Through vaults of pain,
Enribbed and wrought with groins of ghastliness
I passed, and garish spectres moved my brain
To dire distress.

>   And hammerings,
> And quakes, and shoots, and stifling hotness, blent
> With webby waxing things and waning things
>   As on I went.

Eventually, when at death's door, he recovers. The poem concludes:

>   I roam anew,
> Scarce conscious of my late distress. . . . And yet
> Those backward steps to strength I cannot view
>   Without regret.

>   For that dire train
> Of waxing shapes and waning, passed before,
> And those grim chambers, must be ranged again
>   To reach that door.

It is right at this point to mention certain poems which may be held to relieve this generally bleak picture, such as *The Oxen*, *The Darkling Thrush*, part of *God's Funeral*, and *In Time of 'the Breaking of Nations'*. A recent critic, Roy Morrell, has drawn attention to their place in the body of Hardy's work, and claimed particular importance for them.[17] Yet such tentative indications of cheerfulness as are to be detected in the poems seem to be expressed in such a way that the despair is of a solider quality than the hope. Even in the poem *A Commonplace Day*, which Mr Morrell particularly commends for its positive qualities,[18] I can find only an expression of disappointment and regret.

Yet if Hardy's sanguine moments are hard to detect, we are never in doubt of his compassion for 'Poor humanity's afflicted will/ Struggling in vain with ruthless destiny'. Many of his poems, in which he is neither speculating about the Universe nor reflecting on his own life but apparently offering an impersonal account of a scene or an event, show the same misgivings about the human lot and the same pity. It is enough to look at some of his finest pieces, such as *No Buyers*, *Throwing a Tree*, *Horses Abroad*, *Silences*, *A Nightmare, and the Next Thing*, or *At a Country Fair* to see at once their close relation with the more explicitly metaphysical poems. Poem after poem gives us the characteristic sense of the patient endurance that outlasts both hope and despair. Since an end must be made somewhere I offer three lines from a poem written on Hardy's eighty-sixth birthday. They are supposed to be spoken by the World to the poet:

'I do not promise overmuch,
  Child; overmuch;
Just neutral-tinted haps and such.'

The poem has the title *He Never Expected Much.*

From the poems then it is possible to derive a coherent summary of Hardy's view of the world. Does this world-view help us to understand *The Dynasts* and his major fiction? Or, to rephrase the question slightly, do we find in the novels and in *The Dynasts* the same sense of crushing constraint as in the poems? The object of asking the question in this form is not to enable the reader to detect in the larger works something which would otherwise not have been discovered, but to direct the enquiry towards the relation between Hardy's determinism and the forms of his fiction. In other words I am asking whether the world-view which completely informs so many of the poems is in any way modified or compromised when Hardy embodies it in a full-scale representation of human life.

II *THE DYNASTS*

Your Byron publishes his *Sorrows of Lord George*, in verse and in prose, and copiously otherwise: your Bonaparte presents his *Sorrows of Napoleon* Opera, in an all-too stupendous style; with music of cannon-volleys, and murder-shrieks of a world; his stage-lights are the fires of Conflagration; his rhyme and recitative are the tramp of embattled Hosts and the sound of falling Cities.

—CARLYLE, *Sartor Resartus* II, chapter vi

The Dynasts (1903–8) is an extremely long epic-drama, mainly in verse, covering the chief events of European history from 1805 to 1815. The view of human activity which it embodies is in substantial agreement with the general position Hardy adopts in his poetry, both earlier and later. Three central features may be briefly indicated. First, throughout the drama we are in a world where human will is an illusion. Metternich's sardonic comment on Maria Louisa accords precisely with Hardy's general presentation:

Metternich   So much for form's sake! Can the river-flower
         The current drags, direct its face up-stream?
         What she must do she will; nought else at all. (269)[19]

Secondly, what drives man is not his own volition but a Universal Will which has no concern for men. Since men are ignorant of this pervading power its presence and nature are made manifest to the audience by a number of non-human Intelligences who comment on the action in various modes. They understand the operation of this Eternal Urger (118): in particular they understand that it is not hostile to mankind, but completely indifferent, indeed completely without discernible motive. The position is stated unambiguously in the Fore Scene:

Shade of the Earth	What of the Immanent Will and Its designs?
Spirit of the Years	It works unconsciously, as heretofore,
	Eternal artistries in Circumstance,
	Whose patterns, wrought by rapt aesthetic rote,
	Seem in themselves Its single listless aim,
	And not their consequence. (1)
Spirit of the Years	Nay. In the Foretime, even to the germ of Being,
	Nothing appears of shape to indicate
	That cognizance has marshalled things terrene,
	Or will (such is my thinking) in my span.
	Rather they show that, like a knitter drowsed,
	Whose fingers play in skilled unmindfulness,
	The Will has woven with an absent heed
	Since life first was; and ever will so weave. (2)
Spirit of the Years	'Tis not in me to feel with, or against,
	These flesh-hinged mannikins Its hand upwinds
	To click-clack off Its preadjusted laws;
	But only through my centuries to behold
	Their aspects, and their movements, and their mould.
Spirit of the Pities	They are shapes that bleed, mere mannikins or no,
	And each has parcel in the total Will.
Spirit of the Years	Which overrides them as a whole its parts
	In other entities. (4)

The spirits refer to this force as the Immanent Unrecking (517), the Great Unshaken (76), the Great Necessitator (118), and the Great Foresightless (521). Its works are a kind of clockwork (245).

Thirdly, the agony comes only because Mankind has consciousness and knows when it suffers:

Shade of the Earth	Yea; that they [men] feel, and puppetry remain,
	Is an owned flaw in her consistency
	Men love to dub Dame Nature—that lay-shape
	They use to hang phenomena upon—
	Whose deftest mothering in fairest spheres
	Is girt about by terms inexorable! (34)
Spirit of the Pities	But out of tune the Mode and meritless
	That quickens sense in shapes whom, thou hast said,
	Necessitation sways! A life there was
	Among these self-same frail ones—Sophocles—

Who visioned it too clearly, even the while
He dubbed the Will 'the gods'. Truly said he,
'Such gross injustice to their own creation
Burdens the time with mournfulness for us,
And for themselves with shame.'[20]—Things
   mechanized
By coils and pivots set to foreframed codes
Would, in a thorough-sphered melodic rule,
And governance of sweet consistency,
Be cessed no pain, whose burnings would abide
With That Which holds responsibility,
Or inexist.   (99)

This is not a sign of the malevolence of the Immanent Will, for consciousness is merely a casual consequence of its operation:

Spirit of the Years   The cognizance ye mourn, Life's doom to feel,
If I report it meetly, came unmeant,
Emerging with blind gropes from impercipience
By listless sequence—luckless, tragic Chance,
In your more human tongue.   (100)

Chorus (aerial music) . . . Our overseeings, our supernal state,
                              Our readings Why and Whence,
Are but the flower of Man's intelligence;
And that but an unreckoned incident
Of the all-urging Will, raptly magnipotent. (137)

Thus the Spirit of the Pities can lament 'the intolerable antilogy/Of
making figments feel' (77).

All this is familiar ground to anybody acquainted with the poems:
in *The Dynasts* the operation of the Will is expressed in more
directly physical terms, so as to dramatize the extent of human
puppethood. Hardy contrives two devices for this purpose, both
embodied principally in stage-directions, but neither of them
designed to be realized in the theatre. The first is the actual presentation of the Immanent Will as a visible agency:

Spirit of the Pities   Amid this scene of bodies substantive
(after a pause)   Strange waves I sight like winds grown visible,
Which bear men's forms on their innumerous coils,
Twining and serpentining round and through.
Also retracting threads like gossamers—
Except in being irresistible—
Which complicate with some, and balance all.

Spirit of the Years   These are the Prime Volitions,—fibrils, veins,
Will-tissues, nerves, and pulses of the Cause. (7)

This happens at crucial moments throughout the action, as for
example during the battle of Vitoria:

> *There immediately is shown visually the electric state of mind that
> animates WELLINGTON, GRAHAM, HILL, KEMPT, PICTON, COLVILLE,
> and other responsible ones on the British side; and on the French KING
> JOSEPH stationary on the hill overlooking his own centre, and surrounded
> by a numerous staff that includes his adviser MARSHAL JOURDAN, with,
> far away in the field, GAZAN, D'ERLON, REILLE, and other marshals.
> This vision, resembling as a whole the interior of a beating brain lit by
> phosphorescence, in an instant fades again back to the normal.* (368)

During the battle of Waterloo the Spirit of the Years undertakes to
show how little even Wellington is in command of his actions:

Spirit of the Years   Know'st not at this stale time
That shaken and unshaken are alike
But demonstrations from the Back of Things?
Must I again reveal It as It hauls
The halyards of the world?

> *A transparency as in earlier scenes again pervades the spectacle, and the
> ubiquitous urging of the Immanent Will becomes visualized. The web
> connecting all the apparently separate shapes includes WELLINGTON in its
> tissue with the rest, and shows him, like them, as acting while discovering
> his intention to act. By the lurid light the faces of every row, square, group,
> and column of men, French and English, wear the expression of that of
> people in a dream.* (505)

In this way Hardy gives a mechanical reality to the Will, as 'a brain-
like network of currents and ejections, twitching, interpenetrating,
entangling, and thrusting hither and thither the human forms'
(118), and a physical meaning to comments such as

Spirit of   So the Will heaves through Space, and moulds the times,
the Years   With mortals for Its fingers! We shall see
Again men's passions, virtues, visions, crimes,
 Obey resistlessly
The purposive, unmotived, dominant Thing
Which sways in brooding dark their wayfaring![21]   (191)

The second device is justly celebrated. It is that by which Hardy
elevates the point of view from which events are described until
they are robbed of any human dimension:

*The nether sky opens, and Europe is disclosed as a prone and emaciated
figure, the Alps shaping like a backbone, and the branching mountain-
chains like ribs, the peninsular plateau of Spain forming a head. Broad and
lengthy lowlands stretch from the north of France across Russia like a
grey-green garment hemmed by the Ural mountains and the glistening
Arctic Ocean.*

*The point of view then sinks downwards through space, and draws near
to the surface of the perturbed countries, where the peoples, distressed by
events which they did not cause, are seen writhing, crawling, heaving, and
vibrating in their various cities and nationalities.*   (6)

The method is used most impressively in the description of the
battle of Leipzig and the subsequent invasion of France:

(Leipzig) *So massive is the contest that we soon fail to individualize the
combatants as beings, and can only observe them as amorphous drifts,
clouds, and waves of conscious atoms, surging and rolling together; can
only particularize them by race, tribe, and language. Nationalities from the
uttermost parts of Asia here meet those from the Atlantic edge of Europe
for the first and last time. By noon the sound becomes a loud droning,
uninterrupted and breve-like, as from the pedal of an organ kept continuously down.*   (383)

DUMB SHOW
*At first nothing—not even the river itself—seems to move in the panorama.
But anon certain strange dark patches in the landscape, flexuous and
riband-shaped, are discerned to be moving slowly. Only one movable object
on earth is large enough to be conspicuous herefrom, and that is an army.
The moving shapes are armies. . . .*
*Turning now to the right, far away by Basel (beyond which the Swiss
mountains close the scene), a still larger train of war-geared humanity, two
hundred thousand strong, is discernible. It has already crossed the water,
which is much narrower here, and has advanced several miles westward,
where its ductile mass of greyness and glitter is beheld parting into six
columns, that march on in flexuous courses of varying direction. . . .*
*All these dark and grey columns, converging westward by sure degrees,
advance without opposition. They glide on as if by gravitation, in fluid
figures, dictated by the conformation of the country, like water from a
burst reservoir; mostly snake-shaped, but occasionally with batrachian and
saurian outlines. In spite of the immensity of this human mechanism on its
surface, the winter landscape wears an impassive look, as if nothing were
happening.*
Evening closes in, and the Dumb Show is obscured.   (398)

Original and brilliantly effective as these devices are, it will be seen
that the massive increase in scale does nothing to temper the bleak
philosophy of the poems. On the contrary Hardy is able to

demonstrate on a much larger canvas the richness of one of his favourite sources of irony—a man's conviction of his own powers of initiating action rendered absurd by the reader's knowledge that he is nothing but a unit in a mass of humanity which is itself without independent volition and whose fate is a matter of indifference to the rest of the Universe.

It is important to observe how rigorously this subordination is insisted on by Hardy, since it affects our whole interpretation of his purpose in the epic-drama. One might, for example, construe the entire work as a pacifist document, designed to show that 'war's a game, which, were their subjects wise,/Kings would not play at', or, to put it as Roy Morrell does, that 'there are larger aims, the aims of common humanity, which cut across national and dynastic interests'.[22]

There is no shortage of evidence for this view of war as 'the dynasts' death-game' (244). For example, the speech in which the Spirit of the Pities describes the men of the various armies 'wheeling them to and fro/In moves dissociate from their souls' demand/For dynasts' ends that few even understand' (299), Burdett's resigned conclusion that 'scarcely any goal/Is worth the reaching by so red a road' (446) and many other passages exposing the bloody folly of 'Warfare mere,/Plied by the Managed for the Managers' (515).

The view of history which Hardy presents may thus at first sight seem to be one in which the common man suffers and dies at the will of his rulers, who are themselves remote from the immediate agony of battle.[23] But the whole burden of the play is that these dynasts likewise dance to Napoleon's will. The chain of command is clearly brought out in the scene immediately following the death of Nelson:

> *Boy* I don't like Billy [Pitt]. He killed Uncle John's parrot.
> *Second Citizen* How may ye make that out, youngster?
> *Boy* Mr Pitt made the war, and the war made us want sailors; and Uncle John went for a walk down Wapping High Street to talk to the pretty ladies one evening; and there was a press all along the river that night—a regular hot one—and Uncle John was carried on board a man-of-war to fight under Nelson; and nobody minded Uncle John's parrot, and it talked itself to death. So Mr Pitt killed Uncle John's parrot; see it, sir?
> *Second Citizen* You had better have a care of this boy, friend. His brain is too precious for the common risks of Cheapside. Not but what he might as well have said Boney killed the parrot when he was about it.
> (101)

Napoleon then might appear to be free, the sole causal progenitor. After the birth of his son the Chorus of Ironic Spirits comments with assumed admiration:

The Will Itself is slave to him,
And holds it blissful to obey! . . .
The Will grew conscious at command,
And ordered issue as he planned.   (298)

But one of Hardy's purposes is to show the mockery that lies behind ambiguous statements like this. Even applied to the dominant spirit of Napoleon they are false, for he is equally a finger of the Immanent Will:

> *The unnatural light before seen usurps that of the sun, bringing into view, like breezes made visible, the films or brain-tissues of the Immanent Will, that pervade all things, ramifying through the whole army, NAPOLEON included, and moving them to Its inexplicable artistries.*

Napoleon (with sudden despondency)	That which has worked will work!—Since Lodi Bridge The force I then felt move me moves me on Whether I will or no; and oftentimes Against my better mind. . . . Why am I here? —By laws imposed on me inexorably! History makes use of me to weave her web To her long while aforetime-figured mesh And contemplated charactery: no more. (330)

Napoleon himself recognizes that he is not free:

Napoleon (gravely)	Know you, my Fair That I—ay, I—in this deserve your pity.— Some force within me, baffling mine intent, Harries me onward, whether I will or no. My star, my star is what's to blame—not I. It is unswervable! . . .
Spirit of the Years	He spoke thus at the Bridge of Lodi. Strange, He's of the few in Europe who discern The working of the Will. (179)
Napoleon (in his sleep)	Why, why should this reproach be dealt me now? Why hold me my own master, if I be Ruled by the pitiless Planet of Destiny? (468)

The final comment of the Spirit of the Years on Napoleon is designed to point to his insignificance and helplessness:

Spirit of the Years	Such men as thou, who wade across the world To make an epoch, bless, confuse, appal, Are in the elemental ages' chart

> Like meanest insects on obscurest leaves
> But incidents and grooves of Earth's unfolding;
> Or as the brazen rod that stirs the fire
> Because it must.   (521)

The effect then of settling the action in the shadow of 'a world-calamity/As dark as any in the vaults of Time' (444) is not primarily to suggest that common men should refuse to fight dynastic wars but to force the reader to the conclusion that all mankind, even the greatest ruler is in the same state of impotent suffering as the most wretched foot soldier.

This is brought out with enormous force in the short scene on Walcheren (251-3). The English army lies racked by fever on the marshy island at the mouth of the Scheldt: their harrowing lamentation is repeated by the Spirit of the Pities, to meet with the following comment by the Spirit of the Years:

> Why must ye echo as mechanic mimes
> These mortal minions' bootless cadences,
> Played on the stops of their anatomy
> As is the mewling music on the strings
> Of yonder ship-masts by the unweeting wind,
> Or the frail tune upon this withering sedge
> That holds its papery blades against the gale?
> —Men pass to dark corruption, at the best,
> Ere I can count five score: these why not now?—
> The Immanent Shaper builds Its beings so
> Whether ye sigh their sighs with them or no!
> (*The night fog enwraps the isle and the dying English army.*)

The entire scene, which forms the artistic and moral centre of the drama, is one of the great things in our literature.

Hardy's technical problem in *The Dynasts* is not so much that of convincing his audience of 'a Universal Will, of whose tissues the personages of the action form portion' (36) as that of creating (or re-creating) characters who think that they are acting of their own volition and presenting them to an audience which knows, from external sources, that they have no independent volition. J. I. M. Stewart well observes that Hardy succeeds by 'exploiting our sense of the nature of dramatic illusion, whereby there may coexist in our consciousness impressions of the free agency of the persons appearing before us and of their moving unintermittently under an exterior compulsion'.[24] Hardy himself suggested that his drama, if it was ever to be presented on the stage, would call for an automatic style, 'a monotonic delivery of speeches, with dreamy conventional gestures, something in the manner traditionally maintained by the old Christmas mummers, the curiously hypnotizing impressiveness of whose automatic style—that of persons who spoke by no will of their own—may be remembered by all who ever experienced it' (xi). It is true that every time we see a play we are watching someone pretending to be choosing his words and actions but in fact doing what the playwright and the producer have predetermined that he shall do.[25] It is true also that when a drama concerns historical personages we are able to relax our demands for a convincing portrayal of human freedom. The characters can act only as they really did act: Napoleon cannot decide not to invade Russia any more than he can win the battle of Waterloo. In these ways the freedom of the characters is already circumscribed, and the reader is in consequence already partly disposed to accept a world in which human volition is not the principal agent.

But a novel is normally expected to be a freer form, in the sense that the reader derives his pleasure from a sensation of life, not from a conventional representation of life. If this sensation of life depends on a sense of a freely-acting set of characters, how is it to be achieved by a novelist who implies that there is no such thing as a free man, much less a freely-acting character? If Hardy's novels embody the same view of the status of human actions as his poems and *The Dynasts* is it possible for them to convey also the novel's characteristic sense of significant human activity, or do they in fact offer nothing but the shallow contrivance of the puppet-show and the dry click-clack of flesh-hinged mannikins? Must we, in short, accept Forster's judgement in *Aspects of the Novel* that Hardy 'has emphasized causality more strongly than his medium permits'?

III THE NOVELS

> There seemed a finality in their decisions. But other forces and laws
> than theirs were in operation.   (*Jude the Obscure*, IV, 2)

Hardy's firm and unconcealed handling of causality in his novels has attracted the attention of every critic, usually to Hardy's disadvantage. A substantial body of critical opinion is most conveniently summarized in a quotation from Walter Allen's *The English Novel* (1954), a book which is so well-known and deservedly respected that it may almost be considered a standard history. In the course of his generally favourable remarks on Hardy Professor Allen writes:

> But Hardy's chief weakness in plot arises from his view of causality. He
> is intent to show that the stars in their courses fight against the
> aspiring, the man or woman who would rise above the common lot
> through greatness of spirit, of ambition, or passion. . . . It is silly to
> blame Hardy for the emphasis he places on coincidence; simply, he
> believed in coincidence. . . . We begin to feel that the author has aligned
> himself with the nature of things against his characters, that he is mani-
> pulating fate against them . . . We feel that . . . the issue is being
> brought about not because it is in the nature of things but because
> Hardy wishes it to be so. It is the one turn of the screw too many.
>
> (Ch. 5)[26]

This is a challenging formulation of one line of criticism of Hardy,
though its precise bearing is not easy to assess. Exception can
hardly be taken to the fact that Hardy's novels end unhappily, for
the same objection would hold good to any tragic fiction. The core
of the criticism is plainly that Hardy is manipulating causality in the
processes of the novel, deliberately contriving a story in which
characters for whom he has engaged the reader's sympathy are
displayed as powerless to avert misfortune, and that he offers this
as a sample of human experience from which his readers are
meant to conclude that humanity in general is composed of
creatures without freedom moving inevitably to unhappiness. As J.
I. M. Stewart puts it, also in the course of a generally favourable
account of the novels, 'In *Jude* we are having foisted on us as
human life a puppet show that is *not* human life.'[27] Yet clearly
neither critic wishes to maintain that any fictitious characters in
fact act independently of their creator. The point should perhaps
be rephrased to read, 'Hardy's characters do not give even the
necessary minimum of illusion that they are acting freely.' It is not
easy to say why this is felt to be a sign of inadequacy in Hardy
whereas it is not similarly objected to in, say, Sophocles. No doubt
the reason is in part that the third-person novel exposes with great
clarity the processes of fiction. A reader who is always conscious
of the writer's shaping presence is thus tempted to comments such
as, 'The Durbeyfield's horse would not have been killed by the mail
cart unless Hardy had *made* it be killed. Therefore he can't offer us
the consequences of this as an unbiased sample of human experience.' The point is made in brief compass in chapter 31 of *The
Mayor of Casterbridge*:

> New events combined to undo him. It had been a bad year for others
> besides himself, and the heavy failure of a debtor whom he had trusted
> generously completed the overthrow of his tottering credit. And now,
> in his desperation, he failed to preserve that strict correspondence
> between bulk and sample, which is the soul of commerce in grain. For

this, one of his men was mainly to blame; that worthy, in his great unwisdom, having picked over the sample of an enormous quantity of second-rate corn which Henchard had in hand, and removed the pinched, blasted, and smutted grains in great numbers. The produce, if honestly offered, would have created no scandal; but the blunder of misrepresentation, coming at such a moment, dragged Henchard's name into the ditch.

If the reader feels that the unexpected failure of the debtor is simply an underserved affliction gratuitously invented by Hardy as an additional damning circumstance, he is likely to feel also that Hardy is failing to preserve in human affairs 'that strict correspondence between bulk and sample which is the soul of commerce' between an author and his readers.

This point would presumably be developed as follows to demonstrate its injurious effect on Hardy's fiction: Hardy, as we have seen, afflicts his characters with strokes of misfortune (for example with the weather, which is so important in *The Mayor of Casterbridge*, or through unhappy coincidence), which have no relation to their decisions. Alternatively he places them in situations where they cannot make a winning move: as they will lose whatever they do, their decisions are irrelevant. In either case their destiny is pre-ordained, their reality of choice is diminished and they cease therefore to be convincing characters.

One might defend Hardy's realism either by psychological or philosophical arguments,[28] but it is perhaps more profitable to concede that he is not a realist in the sense that everything he offers his readers is based on accurate observation and description of the actual: much of the time it is not even probable. Occasionally it is scarcely possible, as for example the episode in chapter 13 of *The Woodlanders* where Giles is 'shrouding' the elm-tree in front of John South's house. It is a powerful and telling scene, but there are many difficulties in the way of taking it as a realistic account. Giles, climbing the tree in nailed boots, is using a bill-hook to lop the largest limbs from a grown tree: he does not use a rope to support or lower the boughs: if we are to take Hardy literally he cuts off the branches on which he is standing; he climbs so high that he is hidden from sight by the mist; and, after his mysterious dialogue with Grace, he descends the tree again although he has cut away his footholds.

It seems to me that here and elsewhere Hardy claims the licence which is not invariably available to a novelist but is normally conceded to a writer of romance. The territory we are in is the Black Forest, the world of *Der Freischütz* and the Grimm brothers. But in the traditional romances Fortune reigns supreme—Johannes, as it falls out, becomes king of all the country, while Honest John is unjustly cut to pieces. One way of describing Hardy's distinctive achievement is to say that he writes romances in which 'crass casualty' plays a more important part than Fortune. Particularity of characterization is an irrelevance in the romance, and thus, to come to the final point of the original argument, the lack of convincing characters would no longer be an insuperable objection.

If it is argued that this may be all very well for romance, but no tragic work can succeed without engaging the audience with the central character, the discussion can be taken back to the Aristotelian emphasis on the importance of the tragic action. Such an emphasis is reasonable in a world in which everything is pre-ordained, since in that case actions will still be real whereas the motives will be pseudo-events, that is, deliberations conducted by people under the illusion that two alternative decisions are possible. The fully-informed spectator of course knows that one outcome and one only is inevitable. Discussion of motive would thus be principally an occasion for pathos or irony. If then we try to imagine a novel written to illustrate Aristotle's ideas of tragedy it would presumably be one in which the relations between the people of the novel were of more importance than the character of any one of them.[29] It would be unlike the novel as we find it in the works of, say, Henry James, where the chief excitement lies in the sense that we are exploring complex and rewarding characters and where the novelist's skill is used to devise situations in which character is most tellingly revealed. The Aristotelian tragic novel would, we may conclude, be close to the novels of Hardy, where, as I have said, the wishes of the characters are often set at naught by events, the narrative is conducted in the third person, normally without any attempt to look through the eyes of a single character, and the plot is intricate, almost always pivoting on love and marriage and usually consisting of episodes from the lives of four or five people, whose relations are interlocked and tangled.

The object of this section has been to establish, if possible, that a generally determinist framework is not *a priori* incompatible with a work of tragic fiction. If that general position is granted, then it follows that Hardy's characteristic view of human nature does not, in so far as it involves determinism, make it automatically impossible for him to write a novel. I want now to show the particular qualities of the kind of novel that he was able to write, taking as my main example *The Mayor of Casterbridge*.

My argument will be, in brief, that Hardy in the novels barely qualifies the profound sense of human helplessness which emerges so plainly in the poems and *The Dynasts*, but that he disguises and diversifies the operations of the Immanent Will, entrusting them to constraining agencies in a way which makes for complexity of causal chains and gives an impression of many-layered experience. The characters are circumscribed thoroughly but very variously, and Hardy is careful to entertain a number of different hypotheses about the ultimate causes of things. The early poem *Nature's Questioning* compactly expresses some of the possibilities:

> . . . 'Has some Vast Imbecility,
>   Mighty to build and blend,
>   But impotent to tend,
> Framed us in jest, and left us now to hazardry?
>
> Or come we of an Automaton
>   Unconscious of our pains? . . .
>   Or are we live remains
> Of Godhead dying downwards, brain and eye now gone?
>
> Or is it that some high Plan betides,
>   As yet not understood,
>   Of Evil stormed by Good,
> We the Forlorn Hope over which Achievement strides?'
>
> Thus things around. No answerer I . . .
>   Meanwhile the winds, and rains,
>   And Earth's old glooms and pains
> Are all the same, and Life and Death are neighbours nigh.

His refusal to adopt one hypothesis to the exclusion of all others enables Hardy to conform sufficiently closely to the requirement that the novel shall be 'life-like' or 'non-diagrammatic'.

Nevertheless there is in all the novels a strong sense that the final outcome is one which lies outside the control of all the characters. In *The Mayor* Hardy brings this about in a number of ways. He uses, of course, the method of warning the reader of what lies ahead, the classical or Chaucerian use of premonition:

> Friendship between man and man; what a rugged strength there was in it, as evinced by these two. And yet the seed that was to lift the foundation of this friendship was at that moment taking root in a chink of its structure. (Ch. 15)

Hardy also deliberately demonstrates his power as author to engineer events:

> Poor Elizabeth-Jane, little thinking what her malignant star had done to blast the budding attentions she had won from Donald Farfrae, was glad to hear Lucetta's words about remaining.
> For in addition to Lucetta's house being a home, the raking view of the market-place which it afforded had as much attraction for her as for Lucetta. The *carrefour* was like the regulation Open Place in spectacular dramas, where the incidents that occur always happen to bear on the lives of the adjoining residents . . . It was the node of all orbits. (Ch. 24)

Again, in the action of the novels events bring their inevitable consequences and all human doings are part of one huge pattern, as Hardy memorably expresses it in a celebrated passage in the third chapter of *The Woodlanders*. Henchard in particular learns that nobody can escape the consequences of his own actions. In *The Mayor* Hardy conveys with exceptional force the sense of things moving to their appointed end. Not only are the parts of the book linked causally to one another—'Henchard's chiding, by be-getting in her [Elizabeth] a nervous fear of doing anything defin-able as unladylike, had operated thus curiously in keeping them unknown to each other at a critical moment. Much might have resulted from recognition . . .' (ch. 21)—so that acts are seen to bear their consequences, but the whole pattern of the book is shown to spring from one event, the sale of Henchard's wife and child. The freedom and the five guineas are enough to enable him to rise:

> 'I'd challenge England to beat me in the fodder business; and if I were a free man again, I'd be worth a thousand pound before I'd done o't. But a fellow never knows these little things till all chance of acting upon 'em is past.' (Ch. 1)

The discovery is sufficient for his fall:

> Small as the court incident had been in itself, it formed the edge or turn in the incline of Henchard's fortunes. On that day—almost at that minute—he passed the ridge of prosperity and honour, and began to descend rapidly on the other side.   (Ch. 31)

Much that happens in *The Mayor* arrives with an unexpected appropriateness, almost as if the Immanent Will had more sense of pattern than Hardy credits it with in *The Dynasts*. Henchard's selling of his family is the initial sacrifice of stability for which he tries in vain to compensate in the rest of the book, by balancing money and love. He tries continually to vary the terms of his bargain, to recover love by parting with money, but finally loses both. One point, however, should be noticed. While the whole plot is scrupulously devoted to the precipitating act and its fully-caused consequences, that act itself is deliberately shown as chance-occasioned, as far as human acts can be, or at least determined by ironic accident:

> Neither of our pedestrians [Henchard and Susan] had much heart for these things [the fairground side-shows, including 'readers of Fate'], and they looked around for a refreshment tent among the many which dotted the down. Two, which stood nearest to them in the ochreous haze of expiring sunlight, seemed almost equally inviting. One was formed of new, milk-hued canvas, and bore red flags on its summit; it announced 'Good Home-brewed Beer, Ale, and Cyder.' The other was less new; a little iron stove-pipe came out of it at the back, and in front appeared the placard, 'Good Furmity Sold Hear.' The man mentally weighed the two inscriptions, and inclined to the former tent.
>
> 'No—no—the other one,' said the woman. 'I always like furmity; and so does Elizabeth-Jane; and so will you. It is nourishing after a long hard day.'
>
> 'I've never tasted it,' said the man. However, he gave way to her representations, and they entered the furmity booth forthwith.   (Ch. 1)

Once the initial decision has been made all follows. As Jude puts it, 'Nothing can be done. Things are as they are, and will be brought to their destined issue.'

Although this rigid pattern of cause and effect is continually softened by the interposition and exploitation of chance, especially of coincidence—'He [Farfrae] might possibly have passed by without stopping at all . . . had not his advent coincided with the discussion on corn and bread; in which event this history had never been enacted' (ch. 6)—this does not mean that Hardy ultimately places his characters in a world at the mercy of hazardry, for he takes equal care to qualify the operations of chance.

For example, he demonstrates repeatedly the inconsistent way in which men regard the operation of chance in their own lives. Sometimes this is displayed in details, such as Mrs Durbeyfield's attempt to discover Tess's fate from the *Fortune-Teller*: sometimes it has more profound effects, as when Liddy and Bathsheba toss up a hymn-book to decide whether or not to send a valentine and thus bring about Boldwood's tragic embroilment. A revealing instance comes from *The Trumpet-Major*:

> Still he did not positively go towards home. At last he took a guinea from his pocket, and resolved to put the question to the hazard. 'Heads I

go; tails I don't.' The piece of gold spun in the air and came down heads.
  'No, I won't go, after all,' he said. 'I won't be steered by accidents any
more.'   (Ch. 20)

Secondly, Hardy arranges that, on the whole, the bad chances will
outnumber the good at least on this planet, though things may be
happier elsewhere. 'In the ill-judged execution of the well-judged
plan of things the call seldom produces the comer, the man to love
rarely coincides with the hour for loving . . . Out of which mala-
droit delay sprang anxieties, disappointments, shocks, catastrophes, and passing-strange destinies', he writes at the end of
chapter 5 of *Tess*: on a similar situation at the end of the fourth
chapter of *Jude* he comments, 'Somebody might have come along
that way who would have asked him his trouble, and might have
cheered him. . . . But nobody did come, because nobody does.'
None of Hardy's characters could expect much improvement in
their lot by electing to live in a random world. As Hardy puts it at
the end of the poem *Sine Prole*, modern man has been schooled to
know that although life is a lottery there are no prizes.

Though chance plays a prominent part in all the novels, and the
characters think of themselves as the victims of good or bad luck,
there is a pervasive suggestion that on a wider view its operations
should be discounted and brought into a generally determined
scheme of things: '[It] was curious—if anything should be called
curious in concatenations of phenomena wherein each is known to
have its accounting cause' (*Mayor* ch. 29). Hardy, like most people, is
not completely consistent in his view of the relation of chance and
causality. He oftens suggests that what men take to be chance is part
of the Immanent Will's inexorable design, yet this, as we have seen,
is not a preconceived plan but an arbitrary patterning. Hardy is
certainly conscious of the latent antinomy, and emphasizes now one
wing of the paradox, now the other, as serves his tactical purposes
best, the purpose often being to display the helplessness of men at
the mercy of either a casual or an inevitable set of forces.

The intermediate powers which are agents or manifestations of
the Immanent Will act in various ways, sometimes competing with
one another; what they have in commoñ is that they all operate to
subdue the human will. Hardy speaks of them as if taking it for
granted that men will not be free. For instance:

When she looked down sideways to the girl she became pretty. . . .
When she plodded on in the shade of the hedge, silently thinking, she
had the hard, half-apathetic expression of one who deems anything
possible at the hands of Time and Chance, except, perhaps, fair play.
The first phase was the work of Nature, the second probably of civilization.   (*Mayor* ch. 1)

Taken by itself this passage might suggest that Nature was essentially benign, and that what was at fault was the creation of society. Hardy certainly refers to 'those households whose crime it was to be poor' and in the later novels *Tess of the d'Urbervilles* and *Jude the Obscure* he is clearly not altogether unsympathetic to Jude's comment, 'I perceive that there is something wrong somewhere in our social formulas'. It is possible to take *Tess* as a social satire, arguing that the various manifestations of a malign or indifferent controlling power are no more than ironic parallels to the main theme, and serve to emphasize the impossibility of a working girl's resisting social pressures and conventions designed to keep her in her place. It is easy to support this view by quoting passages such as the following:

> But this encompassment of her own characterization, based on shreds of convention, peopled by phantoms and voices antipathetic to her, was a sorry and mistaken creation of Tess's fancy—a cloud of moral hobgoblins by which she was terrified without reason. It was they that were out of harmony with the actual world, not she. Walking among the sleeping birds in the hedges, watching the skipping rabbits on a moonlit warren, or standing under a pheasant-laden bough, she looked upon herself as a figure of Guilt intruding into the haunts of Innocence. But all the while she was making a distinction where there was no difference. Feeling herself in antagonism she was quite in accord. She had been made to break an accepted social law, but no law known to the environment in which she fancied herself such an anomaly. (Ch. 13)[30]

The force of these and similar passages is to make the reader reject every 'arbitrary law of society, which had no foundation in Nature' (ch. 41). Angel's 'You almost make me say that you are an unapprehending peasant woman, who have never been initiated into the proportions of social things' (ch. 35) and Hardy's dry comment 'Outside humanity, she had at present no fear' (ch. 41) operate in the same way.

Alternatively one can regard *Tess* as an example of the helplessness of all humans who happen to be born on this blighted star.[31] On this view the rigidity of social conventions is simply one of the many instruments which confine, torture and eventually destroy the individual. Ian Gregor makes the shrewd objection that Hardy seems at one point to speak well of Nature as the antithesis of Society and at another to regard Nature as 'the way things are' and thus indefensible. Professor Gregor comments, 'There is contradiction here, not complexity.'[32] I do not think that this is altogether justified: there are inconsistencies which may even amount to a contradiction, but there is a complex shifting of terms also, which is most clearly perceived if we recognize that to Tess life is unkind and from her point of view the immediate agent of the unkindness is her society, which hems her in with unnatural conventions. She is right to think this; the reader, seeing in part through her eyes, sympathizes with her. Clearly Hardy feels that a man-made set of social rules has added an unnecessary burden to her life. The contrast however is not between the wicked world of man and the benevolent world of nature, but between a society which inflicts guilt on its members and the natural world, which is morally neutral. This is the difficult lesson to learn. Tess is wrong to feel that there is some Power judging and condemning her; if there is such a Power it is indifferent. Tess's misery has been caused by her fellow-men.

At the same time Hardy characteristically presents the longer view, forcing us to recognize that society itself is part, an inevitable part, of the way things are, and that nature itself is simply as it is. We are then able to place Tess's distress at her supposed misconduct and our own indignation at the intolerance of society in the widest possible context.[33] Hardy is here forcing the reader to regard Tess's life in two ways simultaneously, aware at once of the pain of her baffled will and of a universe whose blind operations ensure that all human wills are ultimately insignificant.[34]

The shape that the Inevitable takes in Hardy is normally not simply the pressure of other men: similarly 'Nature' is rarely presented as a force of uncomplicated benevolence. The Woodlanders provides a straightforward example. Early in the book Hardy describes Mr Melbury and Grace walking through the Hintock woods in late autumn:

They went noiselessly over mats of starry moss, rustled through interspersed tracts of leaves, skirted trunks with spreading roots whose mossed rinds made them like hands wearing green gloves; elbowed old elms and ashes with great forks, in which stood pools of water that overflowed on rainy days, and ran down their stems in green cascades. On older trees still than these huge lobes of fungi grew like lungs. Here, as everywhere, the Unfulfilled Intention, which makes life what it is, was as obvious as it could be among the depraved crowds of a city slum. The leaf was deformed, the curve was crippled, the taper was interrupted; the lichen ate the vigour of the stalk, and the ivy slowly strangled to death the promising sapling. (Ch. 7)

The Unfulfilled Intention, a phrase which at once implies the existence of an immanent power and ridicules the imperfection of its achievement, is adroitly linked in this paragraph with the grotesquely deformed trees.[35] Later the image recurs:

They halted beneath a half-dead oak, hollow and disfigured with white tumours, its roots spreading out like claws grasping the ground. A chilly wind circled round them ... The vale was wrapped in a dim atmosphere of unnaturalness, and the east was like a livid curtain edged with pink. There was no sign nor sound of Fitzpiers.　　　　　　　(Ch. 29)

She continually peeped out through the lattice, but could see little. ... Above stretched an old beech, with vast arm-pits, and great pocket-holes in its sides where branches had been removed in past times; a black slug was trying to climb it. Dead boughs were scattered about like ichthyosauri in a museum, and beyond them were perishing woodbine stems resembling old ropes.

From the other window all she could see were more trees, in jackets of lichen and stockings of moss. At their roots were stemless yellow fungi like lemons and apricots, and tall fungi with more stem than stool. Next were more trees close together, wrestling for existence, their branches disfigured with wounds resulting from their mutual rubbings and blows. It was the struggle between these neighbours that she had heard in the night. Beneath them were the rotting stumps of those of the group that had been vanquished long ago, rising from their mossy setting like black teeth from green gums. Further on were other tufts of moss in islands divided by the shed leaves—variety upon variety, dark green and pale green; moss like little fir-trees, like plush, like malachite stars; like nothing on earth except moss.　　　　　(Ch. 42)

The result is a kind of Darwinian determinism: what dooms man is the kind of world he lives in:

[Sue] 'O why should Nature's law be mutual butchery?'
'Is it so, mother?' asked the boy [Time] intently.
'Yes!' said Sue.

Phillotson later comments with biting sadness, 'Cruelty is the law pervading all nature and society; and we can't get out of it if we would!' Nature, then, can hardly be called in aid to redress the wrongs of civilization. Some of the most striking passages in Hardy emphasize the part that Nature, especially the weather, plays in the chains of circumstance that bind mankind:

The farmer's income was ruled by the wheat-crop within his own horizon, and the wheat-crop by the weather. Thus, in person, he became a sort of flesh-barometer, with feelers always directed to the sky and wind around him. The local atmosphere was everything to him; the atmosphere of other countries a matter of indifference. The people, too, who were not farmers, the rural multitude, saw in the god of the

weather a more important personage than they do now. Indeed, the
feeling of the peasantry in this matter was so intense as to be almost
unrealizable in these equable days. Their impulse was well-nigh to prostrate themselves in lamentation before untimely rains and tempests,
which came as the Alastor of those households whose crime it was to be
poor.

After midsummer they watched the weather-cocks as men waiting in
antechambers watch the lackey. Sun elated them; quiet rain sobered
them; weeks of watery tempest stupefied them. That aspect of the sky
which they now regard as disagreeable they then beheld as furious.

(Ch. 26)

The image by which the farmer is transformed into a piece of
mechanism—a 'flesh-barometer'—is especially telling.[36]

To society, Nature, and the weather a fourth intermediate force
might be added, that of Love. As in the poems, so in the novels love
is an instrument of bondage:

[Lucetta] 'How many years more do you think I shall last before I get
hopelessly plain?'
. . . 'It may be five years,' [Elizabeth] said judicially. 'Or with a quiet life,
as many as ten. With no love you might calculate on ten.' (ch. 24)

though this quiet remark is perhaps more significant for the light it
throws on Elizabeth-Jane's understanding of life.

The extent to which the will may be overmastered by the attraction of the opposite sex is shown with particular clarity in the early
chapters of *Jude*, where the hero is shown to be acting 'in commonplace obedience to conjunctive orders from headquarters, unconsciously received by unfortunate men when the last intention of
their lives is to be occupied with the feminine'. He is in no intellectual doubt of Arabella's unworthiness, but his 'discriminative
power was withdrawn':

In short, as if materially, a compelling arm of extraordinary muscular
power seized hold of him—something which had nothing in common
with the spirits and influences that had moved him hitherto. This
seemed to care little for his reason and his will, nothing for his so-called
elevated intentions, and moved him along, as a violent schoolmaster a
schoolboy he has seized by the collar, in a direction which tended
towards the embrace of a woman for whom he had no respect, and
whose life had nothing in common with his own except locality.   (ch. 7)

Hardy, in his Preface, refers to *Jude* as a novel 'which attempts to
deal unaffectedly with the fret and the fever, derision and disaster,
that may press in the wake of the strongest passion known to

humanity', a description which holds good of most of his major novels.

The idea of love as a chain is, as I have mentioned earlier, the basic structural device of many of Hardy's plots. The forging of the links between characters, the incidents which lead to new connections, and the painful rupturing of existing bonds constitute the matter of the novels. Not surprisingly the short stories emphasize this patterning more clearly, even at the expense of character: *The History of the Hardcomes* is a fine example of the extraordinary power which Hardy generates in this way.

In the longer narratives character of course has a larger part to play, almost as another constraining agency, a function well illustrated in *The Mayor of Casterbridge*:

> But most probably luck had little to do with it. Character is Fate, said Novalis, and Farfrae's character was just the reverse of Henchard's, who might not inaptly be described as Faust has been described—as a vehement gloomy being, who had quitted the ways of vulgar men, without light to guide him on a better way.
>
> (Ch. 17)

On the day Browning died Hardy copied into his notebook an observation from the Preface to the second edition of *Sordello*: 'Incidents in the development of a soul—little else is worth study.' This has caused a certain confusion. It is important to recognize that the phrase meant something different to each man. Browning referred to the crucial importance of those moments of self-examination which issue in a critical step forward in self-knowledge. For Hardy it had no such inward focus, but conveyed, I think, the observer's sense of the successive stages by which a man becomes what he must become. Similarly to Hardy the notion that Character is Fate does not convey 'Our character can control (i.e. influence) our destinies', but 'The form our fate takes is that of our character, which directs us inevitably from our birth onwards' or, as Schopenhauer put it, 'No real change of character is at all possible in a world in which man is from his birth controlled by irresistible impulses.'

We must now return to the argument that Hardy so severely compromises the autonomy of his creations that he can no longer present them as convincing characters and thus the fictions cannot command the requisite assent from the reader. The minor personage of Jopp is a fair example of Hardy's strongminded manipulation of his material. He is used simply as a contrivance in the plot and an index of the depth of Henchard's fall— there is no attempt to characterize him in proportion to his importance as an agent. His actions are provided with a brief but adequate explanation in terms of an expected response to a situation, as are those of the bull in chapter 29.

Lucetta is not much more subtly presented. Like many of Hardy's outsiders, who interrupt and disrupt the lives of the Wessex people, she is treated, one is tempted to say, callously, in the sense that her actions and her eventual destiny are never allowed to be matters of concern in themselves. Just as Felice Charmond is shot when she is no longer needed for the plot, so Lucetta dies. Nor is Farfrae handled with much more sensitivity. If he emerges more powerfully it is only because he plays a more interesting part in the novel: at one point indeed it almost seems as if he is to be himself the embodiment in the novel of the accurate mechanism that shapes the consequence to the act. When he takes over Henchard's yard Hardy comments: ' . . . the scales and steelyard began to be busy where guesswork had formerly been the rule' (ch. 31). But eventually Farfrae is subdued to a subsidiary role in the plot, and at the end is shown in what is for Hardy a distinctly unsympathetic light.

With the central characters of Henchard and Elizabeth-Jane character is indeed Fate: in particular the way a man thinks about destiny is part of his destiny. The obvious point to make is that Hardy shows both of them conscious of living in a world which operates in an unknowable way. Consider the following quotation:

> He [Henchard] looked out at the night as at a fiend. Henchard, like all his kind, was superstitious, and he could not help thinking that the concatenation of events this evening had produced was the scheme of some sinister intelligence bent on punishing him. Yet they had developed naturally. If he had not revealed his past history to Elizabeth he would not have searched the drawer for papers, and so on. The mockery was, that he should have no sooner taught a girl to claim the shelter of his paternity than he discovered her to have no kinship with him.
>   This ironical sequence of things angered him like an impish trick from a fellow-creature.
>   (Ch. 19)

The phrase 'like all his kind' should not, I think, be read with contemptuous overtones, although it is difficult to avoid doing this. The real force of the passage comes from Hardy's power to analyse the situation more deeply than Henchard, who feels instinctively that he is at the mercy of some sinister or malicious force when what is really plaguing him is the inevitability with which acts produce their consequences. It is in this that the mockery and the irony lie, and it is because Henchard does not accept this simple but unpalatable truth that he thinks of himself as a victim. 'The movements of his mind seemed to tend to the thought that some power was working against him' (ch. 27).[37] Having thus briefly and austerely formulated the workings of Henchard's mind Hardy casually introduces the image that most powerfully colours the reader's response to the story of Henchard's gradual decline and humiliation:

> A stone post rose in the midst, to which the oxen had formerly been tied for baiting with dogs to make them tender before they were killed in the adjoining shambles. In a corner stood the stocks.   (Ch. 27)

For much of its course this descent is conducted steadily but inexorably. His ruin is charted in commercial terms and in terms of housing and employment. His failure to win Lucetta leads to his increasing alienation from Elizabeth-Jane. His civic power is taken from him and he makes an exhibition of himself on a Royal occasion. The sense of prolonged and inevitable sinking is powerfully conveyed, relieved by occasional passages of comparative prosperity and calm which seem designed to give what Walter Allen calls the extra 'turn of the screw'. For example, immediately before Newson's reappearance Henchard reflects on his feelings for Elizabeth. 'In truth, a great change had come over him with regard to her, and he was developing the dream of a future lit by her filial presence, as though that way alone could happiness lie' (ch. 41). At this moment there is a knock on the door. Elizabeth's true father has returned. Henchard tells him that she is dead, but does not expect his deception to last for long. He is sure that Elizabeth will be taken from him. 'The whole land ahead of him was as darkness itself; there was nothing to come, nothing to wait for. Yet in the natural course of life he might possibly have to linger on earth another thirty or forty years—scoffed at; at best pitied.' His lie holds for a time, but Newson returns again and Henchard's 'new-sprung hope' is blasted. Rather than be exposed, he leaves Casterbridge. 'I—Cain—go alone as I deserve—an outcast and a vagabond. But my punishment is *not* greater than I can bear!' (ch. 43). Newson's return from the dead, like Sergeant Troy's reappearance in *Far From The Madding Crowd*, at first seems merely a sign of Hardy's clumsy contrivance in the manipulation of his plot. Yet this artless device is not altogether without justification, for it enables Hardy to show the wayward operations of chance and our helplessness to predict or control them, together with the continuing claim that the past has on us and our powerlessness to cancel that claim.

If then we are confronted with questions such as 'Is *The Mayor of Casterbridge* a tragedy?' or 'Can we have a tragic hero whose will is powerless to avert his fate?' it is clear that the argument has, not unexpectedly, reached the same point as in our discussion of

Troilus or the *De Casibus* tragedies. Once again the reply must be first that the difficulty is that of defining tragedy: if the force of *The Mayor* is recognized as a tragic force then the definition of tragedy must be drawn so as to include it. Secondly, it is fair to repeat the observation that to anyone who believes that we in fact live in a determined world (or any world where human free will is inoperative) all tragedies, like all other forms, must necessarily represent men whose will is powerless against their circumstances.

The further question then arises 'If all men are in the same state of impotence, why is one man's life tragic yet that of someone else equally helpless is not?' It is to this problem that Hardy is addressing himself in *The Mayor*, and his chief device is, as I have hinted already, the creation of two characters who represent contrasting ways of responding to the ironies of Fate. Whereas Henchard, if he does not suppose himself the victim of especial malice or 'the visitation of the devil' concludes that he must be 'in Somebody's hand', his supposed daughter, Elizabeth-Jane, is under no illusions of either kind.

Her role in the novel is built up with some care. Early in the novel she takes part in an entertaining episode in the granary when her clothes are covered with chaff and Farfrae offers to help her:

> As Elizabeth neither assented nor dissented, Donald Farfrae began blowing her back hair, and her side hair, and her neck, and the crown of her bonnet, and the fur of her victorine, Elizabeth saying 'Oh, thank you,' at every puff. (Ch. 14)

After this scene, anticipating Lawrence in its mixture of warmth and awkwardness, Elizabeth can never seem a cold character, and Hardy can safely draw attention to her detachment.

> 'More bread-and-butter?' said Lucetta to Henchard and Farfrae equally, holding out between them a plateful of long slices. Henchard took a slice by one end and Donald by the other; each feeling certain he was the man meant; neither let go, and the slice came in two.
> 'Oh—I am so sorry!' cried Lucetta, with a nervous titter. Farfrae tried to laugh, but he was too much in love to see the incident in any but a tragic light.
> 'How ridiculous of all three of them!' said Elizabeth to herself.   (Ch. 26)

Her ability to stand aside and see the situation with an unengaged eye is characteristic of the way Elizabeth-Jane has learned to regard all human experience:

> She had learnt the lesson of renunciation, and was as familiar with the wreck of each day's wishes as with the diurnal setting of the sun. If her earthly career had taught her few book philosophies it had at least well practised her in this. Yet her experience had consisted less in a series of

pure disappointments than in a series of substitutions. Continually it had happened that what she had desired had not been granted her, and that what had been granted her she had not desired. So she viewed with an approach to equanimity the now cancelled days when Donald had been her undeclared lover, and wondered what unwished-for thing Heaven might send her in place of him. (Ch. 25)[38]

At the conclusion of the book she is awarded the prize of a happy marriage. It is instructive to scrutinize the terms in which Hardy describes her reception of happiness.

As the lively and sparkling emotions of her married life cohered into an equable serenity, the finer movements of her nature found scope in discovering to the narrow-lived ones around her the secret (as she had once learnt it) of making limited opportunities endurable; which she deemed to consist in the cunning enlargement, by a species of microscopic treatment, of those minute forms of satisfaction that offer themselves to everybody not in positive pain; which, thus handled, have much of the same inspiriting effect upon life as wider interests cursorily embraced. . . .

Her position was, indeed . . . one that . . . afforded much to be thankful for. That she was not demonstratively thankful was no fault of hers. Her experience had been of a kind to teach her, rightly or wrongly, that the doubtful honour of a brief transit through a sorry world hardly called for effusiveness, even when the path was suddenly irradiated at some half-way point by daybeams rich as hers. But her strong sense that neither she nor any human being deserved less than was given, did not blind her to the fact that there were others receiving less who had deserved much more. And in being forced to class herself among the fortunate she did not cease to wonder at the persistence of the unforeseen, when the one to whom such unbroken tranquillity had been accorded in the adult stage was she whose youth had seemed to teach that happiness was but the occasional episode in a general drama of pain.

These words end the book: it is perhaps not mistaken to see in them Hardy's own opinions of the best that can be hoped for in the way of human happiness. The phrase 'the persistence of the unforeseen' does not of course compromise Hardy's presentation of a determined Universe. The point is that events, either for good or for bad, are unforeseen by men, although they are bound to happen. The 'secret . . . of making limited opportunities endurable' involves an understanding of the constitution of the world, recognizing that what will be will be, that 'there's no joy save sorrow waived awhile', that a cessation of 'positive pain' must therefore be welcomed as a kind of happiness, and that not much more is to be looked for in life. With these sensibly frugal expectations she can hope for tranquillity because she has grasped the nature of the impersonal world she finds herself in, while Henchard batters himself to death in a vain attempt to bend the nature of things to his will, or in vain anger against a non-existent supernatural power.[39]

If then there are illustrated in the novel two ways of regarding human destiny, one leading to tolerable contentment and the other to frustration and ultimate desolation, it might seem that the burden of the book is, 'Choose the first way: shun the second.' But *ex hypothesi* human beings cannot make free choices. What good then is it to them to confront them with two possible responses? Hardy's answer must be, I think, that the first response can be made only by those who truly understand what Fate is (and thus what man is). Therefore he gives them not an exhortation to free choice but the sort of understanding of the working of the world without which it is not even possible for them to respond as Elizabeth did.

In this sense Hardy is a realist patiently schooling his readers to accept things as they are, not as men would like them to be. He is not, of course, laying claim to be a totally impartial and uncommitted recorder. Like all novelists he gives his own emphasis to his material in his choice of what to reveal to the reader at any one time. For instance, the reader shares Henchard's knowledge, not any other character's, or Hardy's.[40] For Hardy's purposes it is essential that we should see events through the eyes of a central suffering character (or sometimes a group of such characters) and should see them also from outside, like the Intelligences in *The Dynasts*, and thus realize in the fabric of his novels the truth of his definition of tragedy as 'the WORTHY encompassed by the INEVITABLE'. Although, as I say, we are often presented with events that bring suffering to worthy characters for whom our sympathies are enlisted, this does not of itself compromise Hardy's claim to be a realist, simply recording the points as they are won or lost. The life of the worthiest of men is, for Hardy, likely to be one of the common sort in which more points are lost than won, however earnestly the reader may hope for the opposite result. His tragic novels draw their power from his ability to present simultaneously the individual's sense of his will as a personal quality thwarted by circumstance, and a view of the cosmos in which individual wills are of no consequence.[41] When he offers this double perspective on human suffering we are able to receive it with the double response of pity and understanding.

Clym Yeobright's reflections on Egdon Heath are never far from Hardy's mind: 'There was something in its oppressive horizontality which too much reminded him of the arena of life; it gave him a sense of bare equality with, and no superiority to, a single living thing under the sun.' He described *Moments of Vision* (1917) in these terms: 'I do not expect much notice will be taken of these poems: they mortify the human sense of self-importance by showing, or suggesting, that human beings are of no matter or appreciable value in this nonchalant universe.' If human choices are illusory and if in addition the governing principle of the Universe, however sorely it afflicts mankind, does so as 'no aimful author' but casually and unconsciously, if, that is, the First Cause works, as Sue Bridehead thought, 'automatically like a somnambulist, and not reflectively like a sage', then if Hardy wishes to represent the human condition faithfully he will be confronted by the traditional difficulty of containing a world of random events within the necessary constraints of a work of art.

What is distinctive in Hardy is the way in which he puts before us the paradox of an artist using non-random forms to express his intuitions of a random world: it is an image of the whole paradoxical situation of humans trying to make sense of a chance-governed universe by imposing on it their own categories of order. Logically both ought to give up the vain attempt, but neither does. Therefore to agree that there is a struggle raging in Hardy's work, and no doubt generating much of the roughness and rusticity and unevenness of tone to which critics point, is not to admit that the work is thereby crucially damaged. The endeavour to express the 'intolerable antilogy of making figments feel' is what gives his poems and novels their power to hurt, as truth hurts.

The novel confronts Hardy with a particularly difficult formal problem. To exist at all it must interest the reader in the actions of human beings and convince him that they are of appreciable value. Further, if the novelist is to render truly the surface of human life, he is bound to depict characters who in the main feel themselves to be faced with real choices, however clearly a longer perspective shows them not to be so. In Hardy, the characters, though consistently represented as, to an all-seeing eye, no more than 'puppetry', are not always viewed with such a lofty regard. Especially in the later novels he is prepared, sometimes for chapters on end, to present events and people in a purely human focus, so that we accept the characters' view of the importance of their own acts of choice. 'They are shapes that bleed, mere mannikins or no.'

Again, the material that Hardy displays is not in fact gathered at random—it is a product, like almost all art, of conscious selection—and does not faithfully reproduce the randomness of human affairs. The mere fact of consecutive narration is enough to dispel the sense of randomness in occurrences. If you set down a number of dots at haphazard on a piece of paper it is always possible to connect them to make a spiral in such a way that they appear no longer random but points deliberately selected to mark out a helical pattern. Drawing the line is enough to deny the arbitrariness of the original material: similarly writing the novel is enough to impose a sense of pattern on events. This effect is heightened by Hardy's taste for the bizarre. Particularly in the short stories, he delights in relating how, even when an event occurs purely through chance, it thwarts expectation so ironically that the strongest sense is not of a casual occurrence but of a patterning, a satire of circumstance. The combinations of random incidents thus look like part of some deliberate intention even though Hardy protests that he is writing about a world without structure or design. In the famous passage from the end of *Tess*—'"Justice" was done, and the President of the Immortals, in Aeschylean phrase, had ended his sport with Tess'—the mocking inverted commas convey Hardy's opinion of society's way of dealing with a pure woman, while the sarcastic phrase 'had ended his sport' serves chiefly to impute, for rhetorical purposes, a certain gleeful malevolence ("a was a merry man') to the strictly neutral First Cause.

   Hardy's powerful sense of life's little ironies is somewhat subdued when he turns from imaginary to actual characters. In *The Dynasts* there is a stronger feeling that human affairs are purely fortuitous collisions of events: indeed part of the effect of the drama comes from the contrast between the Spirits' knowledge that what occurs is the accidental product of an absent-minded Will, and the elaborate imposed structure of situation and intelligent decision which men first invent and then call History. The characters by definition cannot be free, and by a device of a complexity normally quite foreign to the drama Hardy is able to show not merely their bondage, but the way in which the years pass, bringing changes in all human affairs and revealing the forces which persist. Here, as in the novels, there is a doubleness of view. Hardy constantly causes his reader to reflect that the unpredictability of the individual lot is always to be thought of in the context of the utter certainty with which one can pronounce on the fate of the entire population. Even a random world can be described statistically and expected to conform in the mass to inexorable laws.

   Of all the forces that operate in this way none is so constantly and vividly realized in Hardy as the pulse of time, the power that ultimately constrains all men, whether their wills are free or not, whether their actions are determined or casual. Time is at once the medium in which the Immanent Will works its eternal artistries and the current in which mankind is carried helplessly along. These two ways of regarding time are well brought out in a comment on Henchard, which is generalized into an observation on the impoverished condition of human life:

But the ingenious machinery contrived by the Gods for reducing human possibilities of amelioration to a minimum—which arranges that the wisdom to do shall come *pari passu* with the departure of zest for doing—stood in the way of all that. (Ch. 44)[12]

It is worth remarking that Tess's child is called Sorrow and Jude's child is called Time.

Understanding the extent of human subjection to time is a sign of maturity: after the death of her child Tess begins to reflect that the day of her death 'lay sly and unseen among all the other days of the year, giving no sign or sound when she annually passed over it; but not the less surely there', and Hardy comments, 'Almost at a leap Tess thus changed from simple girl to complex woman.' Similarly her awareness of time and its implications is one sign of Elizabeth-Jane's superior sense of reality. As she watches by her dying mother she learns 'to take the universe seriously':

> The silence in Casterbridge. . . was broken in Elizabeth's ear only by the time-piece in the bedroom ticking frantically against the clock on the stairs; ticking harder and harder till it seemed to clang like a gong; and all this while the subtle-souled girl asking herself why she was born, why sitting in a room, and blinking at the candle; why things around her had taken the shape they wore in preference to every other possible shape. Why they stared at her so helplessly, as if waiting for the touch of some wand that should release them from terrestrial constraint; what that chaos called consciousness, which spun in her at this moment like a top, tended to, and began in. (Ch. 18)

In 1909 Hardy published a volume of poems with the title *Time's Laughingstocks.* It included the following lines:

> Time has tired me since we met here
>   When the folk now dead were young,
> Since the viands were outset here
>   And quaint songs sung.
>
> And the worm had bored the viol
>   That used to lead the tune,
> Rust has eaten out the dial
>   That struck night's noon.
>
> Now no Christmas brings in neighbours,
>   And the New Year comes unlit;
> Where we sang the mole now labours,
>   And spiders knit.

(*The House of Hospitalities* 5–16)

Time, 'the feathered thing', which dissolves and bears away all gestures towards permanence, operates throughout the poems and the novels as the great agency of change and disintegration, and inspires Hardy's characteristic tone of regret for the mutability of human affairs and even of Nature itself. Yet from another point of view Time, like chance, is not random, but precise and infallible. It is principally by using time in this way that Hardy conveys so powerfully the inflexibility of an unstable world. However wayward the lesser devices for cancelling alternatives may be, so wayward indeed that men almost fancy that they are themselves doing the cancelling, all human possibilities are expunged by 'Time's unflinching rigour' operating 'in mindless rote'. There is one force which all men acknowledge as a remorseless constraint, 'the melancholy marching of the years' as Hardy calls it in *The Graveyard of Dead Creeds*. He is thus able to come before the readers of his poems and his novels as one who is prepared to acknowledge and face the ultimate reality, telling them 'The news that pity would not break,/Nor truth leave unaverred' (*The Unborn*).[43].

The justification of literature of this kind is not difficult to frame. In Hardy's own words

> Those [novels]. . . which impress the reader with the inevitableness of character and environment in working out destiny, whether that destiny be just or unjust, enviable or cruel, must have a sound effect, if not what is called a good effect, upon a healthy mind.[44]

In a very early poem—*She, to Him—I* (1866)—Hardy struck out one of his most memorable lines, 'Sportsman Time but rears his brood to kill.' The image of the game-birds is a pregnant one, conveying as well as his harsh honesty the sympathy that Hardy feels for mankind helpless in the toils of time, a sympathy which is sometimes forgotten. But who can forget Sue, releasing the pigeons she has had to sell but will not see killed, or Tess killing the injured pheasants whose suffering she cannot endure, or Hardy's wonderful angry pity for the blinded bird?

> So zestfully canst thou sing?
> And all this indignity,
> With God's consent, on thee!
> Blinded ere yet a-wing
> By the red-hot needle thou,
> I stand and wonder how
> So zestfully thou canst sing!

Resenting not such wrong,
Thy grievous pain forgot,
Eternal dark thy lot,
Groping thy whole life long,
After that stab of fire;
Enjailed in pitiless wire;
Resenting not such wrong!

Who hath charity? This bird.
Who suffereth long and is kind,
Is not provoked, though blind
And alive ensepulchred?
Who hopeth, endureth all things?
Who thinketh no evil, but sings?
Who is divine? This bird.

In addition to the works cited in the notes the following have material relevant to the themes of this chapter: John Holloway, *The Victorian Sage* (London: Macmillan, 1953); David J. de Laura, '"The Ache of Modernism" in Hardy's Later Novels', *ELH*, 34 (1967), 380–99; Ian Gregor, *The Great Web: the Form of Hardy's Major Fiction* (London: Faber, 1974); Laurence Lerner, *Thomas Hardy's* The Mayor of Casterbridge: *Tragedy or Social History* Text and Context series (Sussex U.P., 1975); Susan Dean, *Hardy's Poetic Vision in 'The Dynasts': The Diorama of a Dream* (Princeton U.P., 1977); C. H. Salter, *Good Little Thomas Hardy* (London: Macmillan, 1981).

10

George Eliot, Dickens, and the Victorian Novel

> And thus the evening passes, in a strain of rational good-will and cheerfulness, doing more to awaken the sympathies of every member of the party in behalf of his neighbour, and to perpetuate their good feeling during the ensuing year, than half the homilies that have ever been written, by half the Divines that have ever lived.—DICKENS, 'A Christmas Dinner' (*Sketches by Boz*)

> The great conception of universal regular sequence, without partiality and without caprice—the conception which is the most potent force at work in the modification of our faith, and the practical form given to our sentiments—could only grow out of that patient watching of external fact, and that silencing of preconceived notions, which are urged upon the mind by the problems of physical science.—GEORGE ELIOT, review of Lecky's *History* (1865).

In the next chapters I shall consider the consequences for a writer of believing, whether consciously or unconsciously, that the principal limitations of human freedom are those created by man himself. These may range in scope from the claims of a single individual, which limit the freedom of action of another person, through the ties of family and community, through the overt constraints of society, through the unconscious but unremitting pressures which Heidegger, for example, sees other men ('They') exerting on the individual, to the total physical control and mental conditioning which may be exercised by the powers of the corporate state. Of course these factors which limit freedom may also be the conditions defining its nature and boundaries. From one point of view we may consider all human institutions as instruments for expressing the proper province of freedom: they are modes of definition, by which men have tried for centuries to make actual what is perhaps impossible to put into words, the meaning of freedom.

From this point onwards, in spite of the obvious claims of dramatists such as Shaw and Ibsen, my main concern will be with the novel. Why the novel should be considered peculiarly well fitted to explore these questions will be as obvious to some readers as it is doubtful to others. Perhaps the most persuasive argument in its favour is that represented by W. J. Harvey's claim that the novel is 'the distinct art form of liberalism' in the sense that the liberal state of mind, like the novelist's 'has as its controlling centre an acknowledgement of the plenitude, diversity and individuality of human beings in society, together with a belief that such characteristics are good as ends in themselves'. One might rephrase this into the argument that the operation of other people in society is always a pressure towards conformity to a general pattern of behaviour. Since the conditions of the novelist's art ensure that he can never accept characters who become more like one another, he is always on the side of the individual against the social or political forces which diminish the importance of the individual. As a working hypothesis this seems sensible, though obvious exceptions will occur to every reader.

Against this should be set the view that the novel is the most social of literary forms, since it is the form which most fully realizes the duties of man, because it is the form which most fully places a man's actions in context and shows with the most flexibility and fullness their repercussions and effects, direct and indirect, on the world in which he lives. It might be argued, that is, that the very undertaking of writing a novel implies a certain assumption about the nature of man—that his actions are significant in relation to his society, and this in turn implies that society as such is important to man. Very few novelists, for example, however oppressive to the individual the world of their novels may be, suggest that total anarchy is a real alternative. What is tacitly recommended is some less constricting social system, which does not necessarily imply a looser social organization: one can imagine that a socialist novel, for instance, might point to the conclusion that an increase in the power of the state would be useful to control private oppression. Thus against Professor Harvey's very reasonable description of the novel as the art form of liberalism, with an overriding interest in individuality, might be set the equally reasonable description of the novel as the art form which most powerfully emphasizes the importance of the social component in human existence, echoing George Eliot's comment, 'The social factor in Psychology . . . [is] the supremely interesting element in the thinking of our time.'

It is plain that what we encounter here is a special form of the paradox which we have been meeting throughout this book, that every man has two sets of imperative duties, what he owes to himself and what he owes to others, and that these are normally in conflict. The novel in general presents and examines human behaviour as an attempt to find a compromise between these duties.

According as the first or the second is shown to be the more important so we may find more or less support for Professor Harvey's
view. It is characteristic of the novel that both sets of duties can be
represented with great comprehensiveness: the novel therefore
can be fairly described as either the most social or the most
individualistic of literary forms.

If a man is impelled both by his duty to himself and by his duty
to his fellows we may ask which of these impulses is more easily re-
concilable with the idea of man as a freely willing being, the first,
as seems initially likely, or the second, for which an equally strong
case can be made out. Alternatively we may conclude that if all
man's decisions are the outcome of two warring sets of duties, one
imposed from within and the other from without, no actions so
motivated can be called truly free. I wish therefore for the remainder of this book to consider two related questions—first, how far
the novelists provide us with crucial cases, or experiments, for the
definition of the freedom of man in society, and secondly, how far
regarding the novel since 1830 from this point of view helps us to
understand it. The simplest proposition which links these
questions is that which states that as long as writers believed that it
was an abstraction, such as Fate, or God, or Nature, which limited
human freedom, they were studying the problem at one remove
from reality. When however there arose in the novel a form which
specialized in dealing with human relationships its exponents were
able to join issue directly with the fundamental problem. Arguing
on these lines it is thus possible to maintain that the novel, for all its
apparent triviality and irrelevant personal detail and lack of
general ideas, is able to offer not just a more comprehensive but a
more accurate account of human freedom than any earlier form.

I GEORGE ELIOT

'Consequences are unpitying. Our deeds carry their terrible consequences, quite apart from any fluctuations that went before—consequences that are hardly ever confined to ourselves.'

Mr Irwine in *Adam Bede*, chapter xvi

About my first example, *The Mill on the Floss*, I have only two
points to make, both brief. The first is that in this book we have
descended the social scale. If we consider the earlier texts that I
have dealt with in chapters I–VII only *Don Juan* offers anything
even approaching the same attention to the lives of working
people, and that only in a few cantos. The theory behind the *Fall of
Princes* and similar works was that tragedy consisted in a decline
from a great estate: thus a tragedy of humble life was a

contradiction in terms. Moreover the fall of a ruler had obviously important consequences and thus the decline itself displayed sufficient magnitude ('the essential τι μέγεθος ')[2] to justify the work of art. George Eliot is aware of her originality here and is quick to defend herself. For example at the very end of the first book she writes:

> Yet at the end of a fortnight it turned out to the contrary; not because Mr. Tulliver's will was feeble, but because external fact was stronger . . . Mr. Tulliver had a destiny as well as Oedipus, and in this case he might plead, like Oedipus, that his deed was inflicted on him rather than committed by him. (Book I, ch. xiii)

A little later she comments:

> Mr. Tulliver, you perceive, though nothing more than a superior miller and maltster, was as proud and obstinate as if he had been a very lofty personage, in whom such dispositions might be a source of that conspicuous, far-echoing tragedy, which sweeps the stage in regal robes and makes the dullest chronicler sublime. The pride and obstinacy of millers, and other insignificant people, whom you pass unnoticingly on the road every day, have their tragedy too; but it is of that unwept, hidden sort, that goes on from generation to generation, and leaves no record. (Book III, ch. i)

In this passage George Eliot is clearly anticipating the charge, which was of course made, that she was trading in matters too humdrum and trivial to warrant the name of tragedy.[3] She points out that even working people have the emotions which precipitate tragedy, and takes the less obvious point that tragedy need not be a matter of a sudden downfall, but may simply consist in the whole environment 'in which all the functions of life are depressed'. This theme is resumed in the important first chapter of Book Four. George Eliot remarks on the ruined and deserted villages of the Rhone valley, 'dismal remnants of commonplace houses, which in their best days were but the sign of a sordid life'. They lack all the grandeur of the ruined castles of the Rhine—

> But these dead-tinted, hollow-eyed, angular skeletons of villages on the Rhone oppress me with the feeling that human life—very much of it—is a narrow, ugly, grovelling existence, which even calamity does not elevate, but rather tends to exhibit in all its bare vulgarity of conception; and I have a cruel conviction that the lives of these ruins are the traces of, were part of a gross sum of obscure vitality, that will be swept into the same oblivion with the generations of ants and beavers.
>
> Perhaps something akin to this oppressive feeling may have weighed upon you in watching this old-fashioned family life on the banks of the

Floss, which even sorrow hardly suffices to lift above the level of the tragi-comic. It is a sordid life, you say, this of the Tullivers and Dodsons—irradiated by no sublime principles, no romantic visions, no active, self-renouncing faith—moved by none of those wild, uncontrollable passions which create the dark shadows of misery and crime—without that primitive rough simplicity of wants, that hard, submissive, ill-paid toil, that childlike spelling-out of what nature has written, which gives its poetry to peasant life. Here one has conventional worldly notions and habits without instruction and without polish—surely the most prosaic form of human life; proud respectability in a gig of unfashionable build: worldliness without side-dishes.

At the end of the paragraph she again picks up the image of the anthill and refers to the 'emmet-like Dodsons and Tullivers'. She continues:

I share with you this sense of oppressive narrowness; but is is necessary that we should feel it, if we care to understand how it acted on the lives of Tom and Maggie—how it has acted on young natures in many generations. . . The suffering, whether of martyr or victim, which belongs to every historical advance of mankind, is represented in this way in every town, and by hundreds of obscure hearths; and we need not shrink from this comparison of small things with great.

Thus the points are established, first that it is the very 'prosaic form of human life' which constitutes part of the tragedy, that is to say the tragedy consists not in a fall from prosperity but in being born to a miserable lot in life, secondly that for the novel the central theme is not merely 'the iron hand of misfortune' but the 'oppressive narrowness' of the life bearing in on Maggie and Tom, and thirdly that this theme derives its importance not from its exceptional grandeur but from precisely the opposite, its universal applicability—'every single subject suggests a vast sum of conditions'.

In the following paragraph George Eliot, in one of her most brilliant passages explains the form which this narrowness takes: she does this by describing the dominant motives in the lives of the Dodsons, whose care for other people's opinions determines all their actions:

The religion of the Dodsons consisted in revering whatever was customary and respectable: it was necessary to be baptised, else one could not be buried in the churchyard, and to take the sacrament before death as a security against more dimly understood perils; but it was of equal necessity to have the proper pall-bearers and well-cured hams at one's funeral, and to leave an unimpeachable will. A Dodson would not be taxed with the omission of anything that was becoming, or that belonged to that eternal fitness of things which was plainly indicated in the practice of the most substantial parishioners, and in the family traditions—such as, obedience to parents, faithfulness to kindred, industry, rigid honesty, thrift, the thorough scouring of wood and copper utensils, the hoarding of coins likely to disappear from the currency, the production of first-rate commodities for the market, and the general preference for whatever was home-made. The Dodsons were a very proud race, and their pride lay in the utter frustration of all desire to tax them with a breach of traditional duty or propriety.

The Dodsons at once represent the pressure of conventional public opinion and account, by birth, for half of Maggie's nature. The other half comes from the Tullivers:

> The same sort of traditional belief ran in the Tulliver veins, but it was carried in richer blood, having elements of generous imprudence, warm affection, and hot-tempered rashness.

Thus Maggie's ancestry ensures that she shall feel to the full in her own person a deep conflict of duties. The conflict between the impulsive individual and the accepted behaviour of his society does not forfeit its tragic possibilities because the individual is humble and the society dull. George Eliot argues that the struggle and the suffering occur endlessly wherever young people 'have risen above the mental level of the generation before them, to which they have been nevertheless tied by the strongest fibres of their hearts'. It is the form which this conflict takes in the novel which constitutes my second point.

If you examine *The Mill on the Floss* and classify the characters according to the extent to which they are apparently free to determine the pattern of their own lives, an odd thing can be seen, that all the female characters have less freedom than all the men. The Dodson sisters illustrate this very clearly. They are determined by their household goods, by their husband's position in society, and by family tradition. Thus Aunt Glegg, though singularly independent through her husband's generosity and able to make small investments,[5] can only leave her money as tradition prescribes (I. xiii). Mrs Deane rises in St. Ogg's automatically because her husband makes more money (III. iii), and Mrs Tulliver sees the family's ruin solely in terms of sprigged china and spotted linen and straight-spouted teapots.

All this comes to bear on Maggie. She wishes to govern her own life and to do it on generous and expansive 'Tulliver' principles—'I was never satisfied with a *little* of anything.' That this brings her into conflict with her appointed role in society is indicated, directly and indirectly, from the beginning of the book. The seventh chapter of Book I puts the point succinctly. It begins with the description of Mrs Glegg's care not to wear clothes that were newer than the occasion demanded:

> So of her curled fronts: Mrs Glegg had doubtless the glossiest and crispest brown curls in her drawers, as well as curls in various degrees of fuzzy laxness; but to look out on the week-day world from under a crisp and glossy front, would be to introduce a most dreamlike and unpleasant confusion between the sacred and the secular. Occasionally, indeed, Mrs. Glegg wore one of her third-best fronts on a week-day visit, but not at a sister's house; especially not at Mrs. Tulliver's, who, since her marriage, had hurt her sister's feelings greatly by wearing her own hair.[6]

In direct contrast to Aunt Glegg's regard for propriety is the epsiode later in the same chapter where Maggie cuts off her own hair:

> One delicious grinding snip, and then another and another, and the hinderlocks fell heavily on the floor, and Maggie with Tom's help stood cropped in a jagged uneven manner, but with a sense of clearness and freedom, as if she had emerged from a wood into the open plain.

Maggie is represented not simply as longing to be free, but as deserving more freedom than she has. The repeated comparison between her lot and Tom's make it plain that he is freer than she is simply by virtue of being a boy.[7] In particular Maggie is cleverer than Tom:

> 'The little un takes after my side, now: she's twice as 'cute as Tom. Too 'cute for a woman, I'm afraid,' continued Mr. Tulliver, turning his head dubiously first on one side and then on the other. 'It's no mischief much while she's a little un, but an over-'cute woman's no better nor a long-tailed sheep—she'll fetch none the bigger price for that.' (I. ii)

Later Maggie asks Tom's schoolmaster

> 'Couldn't I do Euclid, and all Tom's lessons, if you were to teach me instead of him?'
> 'No; you couldn't,' said Tom, indignantly. 'Girls can't do Euclid: can they, sir?'
> 'They can pick up a little of everything, I daresay,' said Mr. Stelling. 'They've a great deal of superficial cleverness; but they couldn't go far into anything. They're quick and shallow.' (II. i)

The other half of Mr Tulliver's remark has been echoed earlier when Luke tells Maggie that Tom's rabbits are dead:

> 'Don't you fret, Miss,' said Luke soothingly, 'they're nash things, them lop-eared rabbits—they'd happen ha' died, if they'd been fed. Things out o' natur niver thrive: God A'mighty doesn't like 'em.' (I. iv)

Maggie's intelligence is thus, if anything, a disadvantage to her. When the Tullivers are ruined Tom can earn money and speculate to increase his earnings: chapter v of Book III is called 'Tom applies his knife to the oyster.' But Maggie is not allowed to help, for she lives in a world where the whole duty of woman is polishing pier-glasses and mangling sheets.[8] This is why she finds Thomas à Kempis so apposite, since he teaches her an attitude suitable to someone to whom action is denied. Philip tells her, 'It is mere cowardice to seek safety in negations,' but Maggie is doing no more than accept the passive role which is all that is permitted to her.[9] Even when she goes off with Stephen Guest she just drifts 'carried away by the tide'. She does decide to return, in obedience to the precepts of her society, only to find that this society rejects her. All she achieves in the book is nursing her father and rescuing her brother, appropriately enough in a century which had no place for women unless they were Florence Nightingale or Grace Darling.

The social pressures are exerted on men as well, but less oppressively, especially if they show entrepreneurial initiative. Mr Deane, his assistant Mr Spence with his invaluable knowledge of Swedish Bark, Tom himself, and Bob Jakin all illustrate this point: the second chapter of Book III is an especially full expression of it. The other side of the medal is seen in the disposition of Mr Tulliver. He reacts automatically, almost instinctively, to any threat to his water supply, and this robs him of the flexibility which is necessary for 'getting on', but he is at least free to ruin his family. When Mrs Tulliver tries to intervene she is powerless: she merely puts an idea into Wakem's head, which he, being a man, is able to act on.

In domestic life the pressures are different, but once again the women are the victims. The deliberate parallel between Mr Tulliver and his sister Mrs Moss on the one hand and Tom and Maggie on the other emphasises the way in which men can use women's loving hearts to subjugate them.[10]

> Mrs. Moss [snubbed by her brother] did not take her stand on the equality of the human race; she was a patient, prolific, loving-hearted women. . .
> She turned towards her brother again to say, 'Not but what I hope your boy 'ull allays be good to his sister, though there's but two of 'em, like you and me, brother.'

That arrow went straight to Mr Tulliver's heart. He had not a rapid imagination, but the thought of Maggie was very near to him, and he was not long in seeing his relation to his own sister side by side with Tom's relation to Maggie. Would the little wench ever be poorly off, and Tom rather hard upon her?   (I. viii)

The central relationship of the book is that between Tom and Maggie: he uses his position of masculine superiority to snub, bully and dominate her, and accepts this as his right. He leads her into mischief and allows her to take the consequences. Maggie is cleverer and more loving than he is, but less able to harden her heart. An occasional kind word from Tom is enough to maintain her love for him, and he is thus able to impose his will on her. 'Tom, like every one of us, was imprisoned within the limits of his own nature, and his education had simply glided over him, leaving a slight deposit of polish' (VII. iii). Maggie's freedom is thus doubly compromised by the disabilities of her sex. The final ironic reversal occurs after her return from her elopement with Stephen Guest, when she discovers that it is the women who are most censorious:

> The ladies of St. Ogg's were not beguiled by any wide speculative conceptions; but they had their favourite abstraction, called Society, which served to make their consciences perfectly easy in doing what satisfied their own egoism—thinking and speaking the worst of Maggie Tulliver, and turning their backs upon her.   (VII. iv)

The irony, of course, lies in the fact that the women, who are most rigidly imprisoned in the oppressive framework of society, are the most vindictive in pursuit of any woman who wishes to break free. Stephen is virtually exonerated.

> As for poor Mr Stephen Guest, he was rather pitiable than otherwise: a young man of five-and-twenty is not to be too severely judged in these cases—he is really very much at the mercy of a designing bold girl. . . . No good could happen to her: it was only to be hoped she would repent, and that God would have mercy on her: He had not the care of Society on His hands—as the world's wife had.   (VII, ii)

Oppression and subordination to a routine of ritual observances produces conformity and a hatred of freedom.[11]

These observations can be briefly applied to the novel as a whole. If, as I suggest, an important part of George Eliot's aim in the book is to demonstrate the narrowness of the life of Victorian women and to show how this leads to intolerance or apathy or acute unhappiness, it is plain that the profusion of domestic detail, to which some critics have objected, is easily justified, since it represents fully in the fabric of the novel the time-wasting destiny of most women. 'Being a Dodson', with all the tedious duties and petty satisfactions that this implies, is a bitterly effective metaphor for 'being a woman'.

Again, if Maggie is in some way representative of the individual whose desires for freedom are limited or frustrated by Society, it must be agreed that George Eliot depicts this conflict with great accuracy and understanding. 'To be limited by Society' means to be born among a set of people who observe a set of rules about behaviour and punish those who do not. Your role is allocated by your sex and by the status of your parents: it is the desire to enlarge this role that brings Maggie to disaster, for she finds herself limited by 'the average quality of surrounding minds'. This side of the novel is handled with unfailing strength and delicacy, and withstands comparison with anything in *Middlemarch*.

One possible line of criticism of the book as a whole is that the final catastrophe is not directly caused by or even connected with the pressures of Society. It can be argued that it is not altogether unprepared for and that the references to the river and the foreboding mentions of death by drowning are all quite adequately placed, but this suggests a conception of Destiny of a very different kind and on a very different scale from that implied when we say that Maggie rebelled against her 'destiny obscure'.

This doubleness of definition is the most obvious point of resemblance between *The Mill on the Floss* and *Tess*. In both novels the idea of a harsh or indifferent Providence is developed in parallel with the harshness or indifference of society to give a detailed picture of the human condition as one in which the very possibility of genuinely free action is cast into profound doubt. Yet even as they demonstrate the precariousness of human freedom the authors leave us in no doubt of the strength of the human need for it. That is to say, they confront their readers with the hypothesis that pressures on the individual are so overwhelming that no choices are freely made, and go some way towards providing the evidence that would persuade their readers to accept this: at the same time they give full weight to the aspiration to be free.

That is why we can call both these books 'tragic' and 'realistic' or 'honest', as well as 'positive' or some such word that does not indicate total despair of human potentialities. The combination of these qualities takes us somewhere near stoicism on the one hand and radicalism on the other, according as the emphasis falls on the need for endurance or on the possibility of change for the better. To clarify the application of this very general observation to George Eliot it is helpful to return to the idea of the double duty—to oneself and to one's fellows—with which I began this section, and to compare her practice with that of the man whom she called 'perhaps the most wonderful writer of fiction the world has ever seen'—Balzac.[12]

The difference between the two novelists may be simply expressed by saying that Balzac carefully avoids the suggestion that there are overriding powers at work in the world. Human freedom is, of course, circumscribed, but what circumscribes it is not Destiny; for Destiny is just a personification of what has to happen. Events lead directly to other events. The whole system is one of springs, levers and cogwheels with exact teeth. What supplies the motive power is money. The sense of inevitability comes because money always elevates the possessor and lack of it is always destructive, because the desire for money is therefore almost universal, and because other motives such as ambition or revenge are transmuted into financial terms such as 'longing to be rich' or 'desire to bankrupt an enemy'. These general laws function almost as scientific laws in the world of Balzac's novels and impose their own necessity on the characters.[13]

George Eliot is by no means blind to the economic facts which determine the pattern of human life. In the last chapter of Book IV of *The Mill on the Floss* she notes that

> good society, floated on gossamer wings of light irony, is of very expensive production; requiring nothing less than a wide and arduous national life condensed in unfragrant, deafening factories, cramping itself in mines, sweating at furnaces, grinding, hammering, weaving under more or less oppression of carbonic acid—or else, spread over sheepwalks, and scattered in lonely houses and huts on the clayey or chalky corn-lands, where the rainy days look dreary.

She is, however, not prepared to leave the matter at that point but directs the reader's attention to the 'solution' which even 'unspeculative minds' demand to 'life in this unpleasurable shape'. In good society 'principles and beliefs are not only of an extremly moderate kind, but are always presupposed,' whereas in 'the wide national life' most people

> require something that good society calls 'enthusiasm', something that will present motives in the entire absence of high prizes, something that will give patience and feed human love when the limbs ache with weariness, and human looks are hard upon us—something, clearly, that lies outside personal desires, that includes resignation for ourselves and active love for what is not ourselves.

That which 'presents motives in the entire absence of high prizes' is duty, a word of unlimited importance in any discussion of George Eliot. 'Taking as her text the three words which have been used so often as the inspiring trumpet-calls of man—the words *God, Immortality, Duty*—[she] pronounced, with terrible earnestness, how inconceivable was the *first*, how unbelievable the *second*, and yet how peremptory and absolute the *third*.'[14] One of the characteristic experiences of reading George Eliot is a sense of the power of duty as a motive in the lives of her characters. In particular, as I have said, the conflict of duty to others with the equally peremptory and absolute demands of one's duty to one's self is the source of the most intense moral excitement in her novels.

Inevitably this sometimes appears as a conflict between the aspirations of the individual and the pressures of a society which refuses to acknowledge those aspirations. The difficulty Maggie has in being herself is the same as Dorothea has in *Middlemarch*, 'nature having intended greatness for men'. But neither book is a feminist tract. That Maggie and Dorothea are women in a man's world does not limit the application of their plight, longing to realize themselves but limited by what others will allow them to do: 'being a woman' with all the frustrations that this implies is a bitterly effective metaphor for 'being a human'.

Nevertheless George Eliot also gives full weight to the claims of others: *Adam Bede* is a careful exposition of all that this implies, as is *Silas Marner*. *Middlemarch*, I think, takes the debate a stage further. Total liberty to follow one's inclinations, as Dorothea finds, brings no satisfaction. The solution, of course, is not to take refuge in a set of social conventions as a refuge from the burdens of freedom, as Uncle Pullet does.[15] The true alternative is 'an active love for what is not ourselves'. Towards the end of *Middlemarch* Dorothea, after a sleepless night, asks herself what she should do if she were able to forgot her own unhappiness and think of others.

It had taken long for her to come to that question, and there was light piercing into the room. She opened her curtains, and looked out towards the bit of road that lay in view, with fields beyond, outside the entrance-gates. On the road there was a man with a bundle on his back and a woman carrying her baby; in the field she could see figures moving—perhaps the shepherd with his dog. Far off in the bending sky was the pearly light; and she felt the largeness of the world and the manifold wakings of men to labour and endurance. She was a part of that involuntary, palpitating life, and could neither look out on it from her luxurious shelter as a mere spectator, nor hide her eyes in selfish complaining.

(lxxx)

II DICKENS

'A family home, however small it is, makes a man like me look lonely.'—George Rouncewell in *Bleak House* (chapter xxvii).

Dickens is an interesting author for a freedom-analysis because he clearly thought less analytically than, say, Hardy or George Eliot about the autonomy of his characters. He took over, especially from Fielding and Smollett, a tradition of story-telling and plot-constructing that was unselfconscious in the extreme.[16]

This must at once be qualified in order to make it clear that no criticism is intended. One might for example say that Mrs Gaskell was much less concerned with problems of narrative technique than Henry James without in the least implying that this issues as a defect in *Wives and Daughters*. Similarly I do not imply that Dickens' novels are impaired by his spontaneity of writing. But if freedom-analysis is to be of general use it must operate even where the author is not explicitly dealing with the nature of human freedom, and it must operate in two ways. First by making plain the assumptions about human freedom on which the writer works, and secondly by making it possible to say something of value about those works which would have passed unnoticed but for this kind of scrutiny, or to explain a difference which is perceived but can otherwise not be accounted for. This last is my initial objective in this chapter.

I propose to consider three consecutive novels written at the height of Dickens' powers—*Bleak House* (1852-3), *Hard Times* (1854), and *Little Dorrit* (1855-7). In the span of Dickens' career these are flanked on one side by *David Copperfield* (1849-50), in which after a totally successful beginning the plot picks up a new set of characters and proceeds by various routes to a much less assured conclusion, and on the other by *Great Expectations* (1860-1), Dickens' most carefully constructed novel, in which the whole weight of the plot is on the side of the proposition that events bring their inevitable consequences. My object in this brief survey is not to chart any consistent course of development but to indicate one or two signs of a changing view of the relation between man and society.

Hard Times has been written about a good deal recently, sometimes with quite exceptional respect, but it seems to me to lie open to criticism of the most obvious kind. John Holloway has rightly objected that Dickens does not offer any coherent philosophy of life as an alternative to set against mercantilism.[17] This is true, but not necessarily a criticism of the novel: Dickens could reasonably reply that his object was primarily to tell an interesting story in an interesting setting, and that the writer of fiction can operate as a social critic merely by calling attention to the existence of a situation. If industrialization as depicted impresses his readers as intolerably ugly then he has made a sufficient comment. Even if he can suggest no politically or economically practical alternative, the novel may nevertheless be completely successful within these terms.

But it seems fair to comment that *Hard Times* is not successful even on its own terms. So much is made at the outset of Utilitarianism and Manchester economic theories and the Department of Practical Art that it is disconcerting to notice how little they have to do with the book. Moreover two of the most strikingly drawn characters are kept completely aloof from the Utilitarian theme. Bounderby is a figure from the Comedy of Humours, but his humour of pretending to have started life in a state of extreme poverty has no connection with anything Dickens has to say elsewhere in the book about the effect of early upbringing on character. Mrs Sparsit, as for example in the superlative first chapter of Book Two, stands comparison with any of Dickens' comic achievements but her attitude to the operatives of Coketown owes nothing to Utilitarianism or economic theory of any kind.

There are two generally illuminating contrasts—that between Gradgrind and Sleary and that between Sissy and Bitzer, the *reductio ad absurdum* of Benthamite Man. What emerges from these contrasts is that the only reliable guide to conduct is to be found in the promptings of the untutored human heart. Even if we allow that such promptings are, in the novel, adequately distinguished from the enlightened self-interest to which they are to be preferred, is this enough? How are they to be distinguished from the simple self-assertiveness which is so repulsive in Bounderby, or the selfishness of Tom or Hartshorne, or the self-indulgence of Mrs Sparsit, or the recklessness which almost brings Louisa to ruin? It seems that Sissy Jupe alone is rightly guided by her heart, but her values are purely private and are of no relevance to the industrial conflict which runs through the book. What Dickens is protesting against most vigorously is the view of human nature which claims to be able to discuss human conduct as something predictable and calculable, ignoring its 'mystery'.

So many hundred Hands in this Mill; so many hundred horse Steam Power. It is known, to the force of a single pound weight, what the engine will do; but not all the calculators of the National Debt can tell me the capacity for good or evil, for love or hatred, for patriotism or discontent, for the decomposition of virtue into vice, or the reverse, at any single moment in the soul of one of these its quiet servants, with the composed faces and the regulated actions. There is no mystery in it; there is an unfathomable mystery in the meanest of them, for ever.—Supposing we were to reserve our arithmetic for material objects, and to govern these awful unknown quantities by other means?[18]

One may say then that in treating his fictional characters as 'awful unknown quantities' Dickens is being true to his opposition to Utilitarianism and to statistical accounts of human behaviour. But this is no compensation for the lack of direction in the novel, for the lack of any indicated standard for distinguishing between the acceptable and the unacceptable ways of obeying the dictates of the self. It is too easy to apply Stephen Blackpool's "Tes all a muddle' to the book as a whole, but not perhaps unfair to accept the complaint that Dickens' Intuitionalism is so naive that it leaves the moral bearings of his characters' actions in a state of confusion, a confusion which is not adequately dispelled by the author's evident preference for one set of characters over another. *Hard Times* most clearly illustrates the way in which a failure to suggest a solution to the problem of the authentication of values weakened Dickens' presentation of a complex moral situation: in *Bleak House* and *Little Dorrit* the problem takes a rather more elusive form.

   Little Dorrit is curiously like a reworking of *Bleak House*, as if Dickens were either dissatisfied with the earlier novel and wished to rewrite it more to his liking, or very pleased with the pattern and wished to use it again. Thus character types from *Bleak House* are repeated in *Little Dorrit*. Mr Jarndyce and Mr Meagles play the stern old man with a soft heart who furnishes the background for the book: Skimpole and Turveydrop fuse in Mr Dorrit: George Rouncewell's independence is repeated in Doyce: Bucket and Pancks are similar in character and play a similar part in the plot: Lady Dedlock and Mrs Clennam have different roles, but each guards a secret and each is made hard and bitter by it: Chadband and Casby are cut from the same pattern of sanctimonious hypocrisy. Other pairs are Ada Clare and Pet Meagles, Richard Carstone and Henry Gowan, Jo and Maggy, and the Smallweeds and the Flintwiches. Little Dorrit herself has much in common with Esther Summerson, but there is the crucial difference that she is not required to undertake any of the burden of narrative, as Esther is. Instead Arthur Clennam, who has no equivalent in *Bleak House* except the shadowy Allan Woodcourt, is introduced as the orthodox figure of the hero through whose eyes the bulk of the action is seen.[19] Incidents and institutions are similarly transmuted. The spontaneous combustion of Krook becomes the entombing of

Rigaud by the spontaneous collapse of Mrs Clennam's house: instead of Chancery we have the Marshalsea: the Coodles and Doodles of *Bleak House* are the Barnacles of *Little Dorrit*. When we examine plot we can see that both novels may be brought into a single general category, for in both the main character's true parentage is unknown until the end of the book and this buried secret generates a large part of action and an even larger part of the suspense.

So one could go on pointing to resemblances of one kind and another, but it is equally important to observe the most fundamental point of difference between the plots of the two books. While at a first reading they might seem to follow a precisely similar pattern of accident and intrigue, a closer inspection shows a remarkable difference. The plot of *Bleak House* is a tissue of coincidences, many of the most astonishing being possible only because of the dual system of narration. W. J. Harvey, in his full and sympathetic study of the novel,[20] has much to say about the way in which 'one accepts coincidence as a natural part of the *Bleak House* world'. In particular he quotes Forster's comment 'On the coincidences, resemblances, and surprises of life Dickens liked especially to dwell, and few things moved his fancy so pleasantly. The world, he would say, was so much smaller than we thought it; we were all so connected by fate without knowing it and people supposed to be far apart were so constantly elbowing each other. . . .' Harvey comments, 'This theme is heavily stressed in the opening chapters of *Little Dorrit*.'

No doubt he had in mind the second chapter, in which two speeches of Miss Wade's seem to point to some over-riding destiny framing the lives of the characters.

'In our course through life we shall meet the people who are coming to meet *us*, from many strange places and by many strange roads,' was the composed reply; 'and what it is set to us to do to them, and what it is set to them to do to us, will all be done.'

'Your pretty daughter,' she said, 'starts to think of such things. Yet,' looking full upon her, 'you may be sure that there are men and women already on their road, who have their business to do with *you*, and who will do it. Of a certainty they will do it. They may be coming hundreds, thousands, of miles over the sea there; they may be close at hand now; they may be coming, for anything you know, or anything you can do to prevent it, from the vilest sweepings of this very town.'

Yet we learn at the end of the book that these doom-laden observations are not in fact mysteriously prophetic, since Miss

Wade was in Marseilles for the express purpose of observing Pet Meagles and had presumably already hired Rigaud as her spy. This is typical of the quite extraordinary care which Dickens takes to show that many apparent coincidences are not in fact accidental.[21] He is however by no means unwilling that the reader should, for most of the book, feel that dark forces are controlling the destinies of his characters. For example, two paragraphs at the beginning of chapter xv pick up the trite imagery of Miss Wade's speeches

> Strange, if the little sick-room fire were in fact a beacon fire, summoning some one, and that the most unlikely some one in the world, to the spot that *must* be come to. Strange, if the little sick-room light were in effect a watch-light, burning in that place every night until an appointed event should be watched out! Which of the vast multitude of travellers, under the sun and the stars, climbing the dusty hills, and toiling along the weary plains, journeying by land and journeying by sea, coming and going so strangely, to meet and to act and to re-act on one another, which of the host may, with no suspicion of the journey's end, be travelling surely hither?
>
> Time shall show us. The post of honour and the post of shame, the general's station and the drummer's, a peer's statue in Westminster Abbey and a seaman's hammock in the bosom of the deep, the mitre and the workhouse, the woolsack and the gallows, the throne and the guillotine—the travellers to all are on the great high road; but it has wonderful divergences, and only Time shall show us whither each traveller is bound.

Here the empty rhetoric and the smooth clichés are clues to the function of the passage. It sounds portentous and implies the working out of some vast design, but it tells the reader nothing except that the future is the future and is not known until it happens. Dickens uses in a similar way such phrases as 'destiny's dice-box' and the 'sealed book of Fate', or ends a chapter with 'so deep a hush was on the sea, that it scarcely whispered of the time when it shall give up its dead'. These seem to portend the revelation of some singular and sinister patterning of human affairs, but are in fact, as far as I can see, no more than decorative flourishes. Sometimes Dickens is actively misleading, as when he writes of ' that beginning of the destined interweaving of their stories [Arthur and Amy's]'. The reader learns later that their stories had in fact come together many years before: Dickens, having as good as stated that Little Dorrit has come into Mrs Clennam's employment by sheer chance, later goes out of his way to emphasize that Mrs Clennam had found her and patronized her in full knowledge of who she was.[22] The coincidence which seems so unlikely to have occurred by chance that it must be part of some unapprehended large design, has in fact no such implication, since it is seen in the event not to be a coincidence at all. If therefore *Little Dorrit* is in any sense a determinist novel it is not because it shows human life as enmeshed by a net of astonishing but mysteriously pre-ordained coincidences, in spite of Dickens' conventional gestures towards such a positon. In fact ironic anticipation is seen to operate in a very different and much subtler way in the superb scene where Mr Merdle visits the Sparklers. (The chapter is called 'The Evening of a Long Day'.)

But if the novel is not determinist in this sense, it may yet be so in less obvious ways. One might, for instance, plausibly argue that it is the work of Dickens in which environment is most powerfully shown to determine character. Miss Wade would be an obvious example: Henry Gowan is an equally clear case, as are Tip and Fanny Dorrit.[23] Yet it is clear that Dickens sets the novel with counter-examples which are of greater weight, of which Little Dorrit herself is the most telling

> What her pitiful look saw, at that early time, in her father, in her sister, in her brother, in the jail; how much, or how little of the wretched truth it pleased God to make visible to her; lies hidden with many mysteries. It is enough that she was inspired to be something which was not what the rest were, and to be that something, different and laborious, for the sake of the rest. Inspired? Yes. Shall we speak of the inspiration of a poet or a priest, and not of the heart impelled by love and self-devotion to the lowliest work in the lowliest way of life!
>
> With no earthly friend to help her, or so much as to see her, but the one so strangely assorted; with no knowledge even of the common daily tone and habits of the common members of the free community who are not shut up in prisons; born and bred, in a social condition, false even with a reference to the falsest condition outside the walls; drinking from infancy of a well whose waters had their own peculiar stain, their own unwholesome and unnatural taste; the Child of the Marshalsea began her womanly life.   (Book I, chapter vii)

Nothing is plainer than the implication in the rest of the book that there is some quality in Little Dorrit that enables her to resist even these overwhelming forces. Similarly Arthur is able to survive life with Mrs Clennam and is not embittered or hardened by the treatment which she describes (Book II, chapter xxxi). Conversely Dickens will not admit that wickedness can be excused as a product of hard circumstances. When the men in the Break of Day inn at Chalons are discussing Rigaud, the landlady dismisses him as 'a wicked wretch'.

'Stay, madame! Let us see,' returned the Swiss, argumentatively turning his cigar between his lips. 'It may have been his unfortunate destiny. He may have been the child of circumstances. It is always possible that he had, and has, good in him if one did but know how to find it out. Philosophical philanthropy teaches—'

. . . 'Hold there, you and your philanthropy,' cried the smiling landlady, nodding her head more than ever. 'Listen then. I am a woman, I. I know nothing of philosophical philanthropy. But I know what I have seen, and what I have looked in the face, in this world here, where I find myself. And I tell you this, my friend, that there are people. . . who have no good in them—none. That there are people whom it is necessary to detest without compromise. That there are people who must be dealt with as enemies of the human race. That there are people who have no human heart, and who must be crushed like savage beasts and cleared out of the way. They are but few, I hope; but I have seen. . . that there are such people. . . .'

The landlady's lively speech was received with greater favour at the Break of Day, than it would have elicited from certain amiable white-washers of the class she so unreasonably objected to, nearer Great Britain.   (Book I, chapter xi)

While this indicates that Dickens entertained such firm ideas about the persistence of character that he could hardly avoid admitting that some people are born irremediably wicked (and therefore presumably cannot be blamed for their wickedness), this is not, of course, a consequence of the argument which he allows to obtrude in the novel. Instead he directs attention to the implication that people exist and their characters are formed independently of their immediate environment.

If we ask then what other forces are shown in *Little Dorrit* as determining a man's character the answer is most clearly given in the words of Lionel Trilling:

Little Dorrit is about society. . . . It is about society in relation to the individual human will. . . . The subject of *Little Dorrit* is borne in upon us by the informing symbol, or emblem, of the book, which is the prison. . . . Symbolic or emblematic devices are used by Dickens to one degree or another in several of the novels of his late period, but nowhere to such good effect as in *Little Dorrit*. . . . . This is because the prison is an actuality before it is ever a symbol; its connexion with the will is real, it is the practical instrument for the negation of man's will which the will of society has contrived.[24]

All this seems to me undeniably true, and Mr Trilling's introduction admirably follows home his initial points. Taking a slightly different line one might observe that the entire shape of the novel is indicated by Dickens' division of it into two books, the first entitled 'Poverty', the second 'Riches'. The first is dominated by the

Marshalsea, here functioning not as a symbol of oppression but simply as a building: in the second, Mr Dorrit is free, he is rich, he is 'in society', but, as John Butt and Kathleen Tillotson rightly observe, 'Gaining wealth, Mr Dorrit escapes only from one prison into another: the prison of society—with Mr Merdle's butler and Mrs General as half-comic jailers.'[25] This seems to me to state the most important fact about the book, that the main symbolic function of the Marshalsea is as an ironic parallel to the pressures of society. Mr Trilling's placing of *Little Dorrit* in the great tradition of Romantic anti-prison literature, a tradition which I explore further in a later chapter, thus seems to me less accurate than his alternative suggestion that prison had come to stand 'for the ineluctable condition of life in society' (Introduction, vii)

Throughout the second book of *Little Dorrit* the reflection that the Dorrits are no freer than they were is not allowed to be long absent from the reader. In particular the character of William Dorrit is presented with great fullness. In both halves of the novel he shows Dickens' quite extraordinary gifts for depicting selfishness that stops far short of wickedness. Mr Dorrit has grown so accustomed to closing his eyes to disagreeable truths in the Marshalsea that it is very hard to say what he honestly believes. It is altogether appropriate that when he dies in his splendid palace he should feel that he had returned to the Marshalsea. This part of the novel is worked out in Dickens' most powerful manner, that is to say with unmatched vigour and verbal invention. Dickens also provides his usual abundance of supporting material which bears out the theme of imprisonment, sometimes literally, more often metaphorically—Miss Wade and Mrs Clennam are confined by their own implacable natures, Affery Flintwich is virtually a prisoner, Ephraim Flintwich was a keeper of lunatics, Rigaud is a jail-bird, the inhabitants of Bleeding Heart Yard are in thrall to their landlord, the Barnacles encrust and weigh down the whole country—all these correspondences are carefully worked out. Would it, then, be true to say that *Little Dorrit* is a determinist novel because of the pervasive implication that human life is essentially a state of imprisonment of one kind or another?

I think that this is in general a fair description, but calls for considerable qualification. In particular the ending implies that it is possible to find a modified contentment by retiring into private life, and that this is a choice open to many people, though not to all. The effect of this implication on *Little Dorrit* is readily seen by considering two linked general propositions about Dickens' novels; the first is that the only positively good way of life that he puts forward anywhere in his novels is that of domestic tranquillity, the second is that he represents this kind of happiness as to be had only by a deliberate act of withdrawal from every other sphere of human activity.

The argument for these propositions begins most easily from *Great Expectations*. In chapter xxv Pip visits Mr Jaggers' clerk, Wemmick, at his house in Walworth:

> Wemmick's house was a little wooden cottage in the midst of plots of garden, and the top of it was cut out and painted like a battery mounted with guns.
>
> 'My own doing,' said Wemmick. 'Looks pretty, don't it?'
>
> I highly commended it. I think it was the smallest house I ever saw; with the queerest gothic windows (by far the greater part of them sham), and a gothic door, almost too small to get in at. . . . The bridge was a plank, and it crossed a chasm about four feet wide and two deep. . . . Then he conducted me to a bower about a dozen yards off, but which was approached by such ingenious twists of path that it took quite a long time to get at; and in this retreat our glasses were already set forth. Our punch was cooling in an ornamental lake, on whose margin the bower was raised. This piece of water (with an island in the middle that might have been the salad for supper) was of a circular form, and he had constructed a fountain in it, which, when you set a little mill going and took out a cork of a pipe, played to that powerful extent that it made the back of your hand quite wet.

Wemmick introduces Pip to his father:

> 'This is a fine place of my son's, sir,' cried the old man. . . 'This is a pretty pleasure-ground, sir. This spot and these beautiful works upon it ought to be kept together by the Nation, after my son's time, for the people's enjoyment.'

Pip asks whether Mr Jaggers admires the Castle:

> 'Never seen it,' said Wemmick. 'Never heard of it. Never seen the Aged. Never heard of him. No; the office is one thing, and private life is another. When I go to the office, I leave the Castle behind me and when I come into the Castle, I leave the office behind me. If it's not in any way disagreeable to you, you'll oblige me by doing the same. I don't wish it professionally spoken about'

Pip stays the night and walks back into the City with Wemmick. 'By degrees, Wemmick got dryer and harder as we went along, and his mouth tightened into a post-office again.' This might all be taken as a harmless eccentricity on Wemmick's part, but it is to be noted that when Pip wishes to help Herbert Pocket and approaches Wemmick in Mr Jaggers' office for assistance Wemmick tells him that he might as well pitch his money into the Thames as give it to a friend:

'Then is it your opinion,' I inquired, with some little indignation, 'that a man should never—'

'—Invest portable property in a friend?' said Wemmick. 'Certainly he should not. Unless he wants to get rid of the friend—and then it becomes a question how much portable property it may be worth to get rid of him.'

'And that,' said I, 'is your deliberate opinion, Mr Wemmick?'

'That,' he returned, 'is my deliberate opinion in this office.'

'Ah!' said I, pressing him, for I thought I saw him near a loophole here; 'but would that be your opinion at Walworth?'

'Mr Pip,' he replied with gravity, 'Walworth is one place, and this office is another. Much as the Aged is one person, and Mr Jaggers is another. They must not be confounded together. My Walworth sentiments must be taken at Walworth; none but my official sentiments can be taken in this office.'

'Very well,' said I, much relieved, 'then I shall look you up at Walworth, you may depend upon it.'

'Mr Pip,' he returned, 'you will be welcome there, in a private and personal capacity.' (chapter xxxvi)

Accordingly Pip visits Wemmick at Walworth. Once again they pass an agreeable evening:

I felt as snugly cut off from the rest of Walworth as if the moat were thirty feet wide by as many deep. Nothing disturbed the tranquillity of the castle. . . . We ate the whole of the toast, and drank tea in proportion, and it was delightful to see how warm and greasy we all got after it. (chapter xxxvii)

The point of the visit is that, taken on his home ground, Wemmick heartily approves of Pip's plan to help Herbert and promises his assistance. In the event he is able to devise and execute a thoroughly successful scheme, which Pip later considers 'the only good thing I had done'. The implication is clear—that 'public' life is governed by a set of rules and calculations which are arbitary and unfeeling and therefore inhuman: private life on the other hand fosters not simply contentment and placidity but all the unselfish virtues.

Such contrasts run through the novels, showing themselves now in scenes of domestic harmony, now in Dickens' consistent contempt for every kind of public activity. If a man chooses a profession he cannot choose well. It is not the conventional message that riches do not bring happiness, though *Great Expectations* and *Our Mutual Friend* show this clearly enough. Nor is it simply a rejection of birth as an index of merit, as in *Nicholas Nickleby* and *Bleak House*. It is rather that every form of public activity is based on unsound principles and every man who engages in it is corrupted by them. One need think only of Dickens' disdain for politics (as in

Pickwick Papers, Bleak House, Gregsbury in *Nicholas Nickleby, David Copperfield, Little Dorrit* and *Our Mutual Friend*), for Society (*Little Dorrit* and *Our Mutual Friend*), for reform, whether through government or through charity (as in *Hard Times, Oliver Twist, Edwin Drood, David Copperfield,* and *Bleak House*), for education (*Nicholas Nickleby, David Copperfield, Dombey and Son*), for religion (*Bleak House* and *Edwin Drood*), for the law (*Pickwick Papers, Old Curiosity Shop, David Copperfield, Bleak House, Little Dorrit*) or for commercial success.

The last point may seem debatable to the reader who remembers the Cheeryble brothers, Fezziwig, the ironmaster in *Bleak House* or Clarrikers in *Great Expectations,* but these are isolated exceptions to the general indictment which Dickens presents in *Martin Chuzzlewit, Dombey and Son,* and *Hard Times,* an indictment whose general tenor is summarized in chapter xiii of *Little Dorrit*:

> 'I like business,' said Pancks, getting on a little faster. 'What's a man made for?'
>
> 'For nothing else?' said Clennam.
>
> Pancks put the counter question, 'What else?' It packed up, in the smallest compass, a weight that had rested on Clennam's life; and he made no answer.
>
> 'That's what I ask our weekly tenants,' said Pancks. 'Some of 'em will pull long faces to me, and say, Poor as you see us, master, we're always grinding, drudging, toiling, every minute we're awake. I say to them, What else are you made for? It shuts them up. They haven't a word to answer. What else are you made for? That clinches it.'
>
> 'Ah dear, dear, dear!' sighed Clennam.
>
> 'Here am I,' said Pancks, pursuing his argument with the weekly tenant. 'What else do you suppose I think I am made for? Nothing. Rattle me out of bed early, set me going, give me as short a time as you like to bolt my meals in, and keep me at it. Keep me always at it, and I'll keep you always at it, you keep somebody else always at it. There you are with the Whole Duty of Man in a commercial country.'

The general nature of Dickens' contempt is seen in the set pieces such as Mrs Leo Hunter's party in *Pickwick,* or the American scene in *Martin Chuzzlewit,* or the Great Patriotic Conference in chapter xii of the second book of *Little Dorrit* in which 'Bar', 'Bishop' and 'Physician' are given no other names, or the entertainments of the Veneerings and the Podsnaps in *Our Mutual Friend*: in all of these there is a uniform assumption that the public figures are corrupt or hypocritical or, at best, ridiculous. If they have any pretension to culture, these are hollow.[26]

It is difficult to know how seriously to take this. If we think of the drama, a department of life which we know to have been close to Dickens' heart, we find that when he mentions it in his novels he never goes beyond the simple travesty of the *Sketches by Boz*. He never suggests that there is more to the theatre than can be expressed by pointing to the incongruity between the lofty station and emotions of the characters and the physical reality of the performance. ('On our arrival in Denmark, we found the king and queen of that country elevated in two arm-chairs on a kitchen-table, hoiding a court.') Thus we have the presentation of actors in *Nicholas Nickleby*, *Little Dorrit* and *Great Expectations* which makes their professional activities into an absurd game, however amiable their private lives. A similar reductive impulse seems to animate Dickens' consistent belittling of public life: he is not fired by a powerful conviction of its wickedness or rottenness, but does not choose to show any but its ridiculous side. If a public appearance has elements of the conventional it is always possible to find in those elements a source of comedy. Dr Parker Peps and Mr Pilkins in the first chapter of *Dombey*, the Scots doctor in chapter xi of *Bleak House* and the surgeon in chapter xiii of *Little Dorrit* show how superficially Dickens handled medical men, for instance. He seems unable to resist the invitation: there is a kind of reflex action by which any professional man, however competent, becomes a sort of humours character, exhibiting the failings traditionally associated with his trade. As there is virtually nothing to counterbalance this, the general impression of the novels is that of a world in which a man can find no vocation which will allow him to preserve his self-respect.[27]

It may seem that this could equally well be expressed as a merit in Dickens, rather than as the weakness it appears in my phrasing of it. One might, for instance, say that throughout his work Dickens is on the side of the humble, the oppressed, and the unambitious against the Establishment, and against those who wish to reduce human life to a matter of statistics and economic theory, that he champions 'human creativity' against 'the technologico-Benthamite world' (the phrases are Dr Leavis's). That is, one could offer, as a microcosm of his work, *The Chimes*, where the economist Filer and Alderman Cute and Sir Joseph Bowley, the Poor Man's Friend, are set in their callousness and sanctimoniousness against the simple virtues of Toby Veck, Richard and Meg, and Will Fern. There is much truth in this view of Dickens, and it is one of the immediately appealing features of his novels. But if we think of the alternatives to the Establishment which he leaves open it is plain that they are few. The commonest pattern of a Dickens novel is that of a young man growing up to make a choice of life. Being young he is naturally oppressed by existing institutions, and the novel thus naturally rejects them, but what else is there in the novels for the hero to choose?

Some people can be lovable, good-hearted eccentrics—Tony Weller, Dick Swiveller, Newman Noggs, Captain Cuttle, Mr Micawber, Mr Snagsby, Flora Finching: these are the most memorably Dickensian characters in the novels, yet as the description 'eccentric' suggests, they do not represent a generally practicable way of life, and this is shown by the condescending amusement with which the hero regards them. Another group are shown as honest unpretentious fellows doing a sound job of work—men such as Mark Tapley, Bucket, John Browdie, George Rouncewell, Pancks, Doyce, and Wemmick—and are valued because of their usefulness. They play an essentially subsidiary and adjutory role in the plot: the hero is grateful to them, but there is seldom any suggestion that he should adopt a similar career.[28] It is true that Martin Chuzzlewit determines to be like Mark Tapley in cheerfulness and resolution, but it is clear throughout the book that in terms of a choice of life Mark has nothing to offer him. It is partly of course a matter of class: with the third category of admirable characters this is even plainer. I refer to the large group of noble characters which includes Tom Pinch, Little Nell, Smike, Jo, Stephen Blackpool and Rachel, Sissy Jupe, Maggy, John Chivery, Joe Gargery, 'Rumpty' Wilfer, Mrs Higden and Jenny Wren. These are distinguished by their humility or meekness, wonderfully exhibiting the single virtue proper to their sphere, and often deriving their extraordinary pathos from the disparity between their goodness and their state in the world. But is never suggested that it is possible to choose to be like them.

A choice must however in time be made: child-heroes have to grow up. It is remarkable how many of the novels end with the hero and the heroine proposing to retire into domestic obscurity and a satisfying *égoisme à deux*. Mr Pickwick, Mr Brownlow, Mr Garland, Mr Jarndyce and Mr Meagles show the kind of contentment that can be achieved by a retired gentleman with no other ambition than to avoid public life. They represent, in their elderly way, the only sort of happiness that is shown as proper for heroes and heroines, a more affluent version of a buttery evening with the Wemmicks at the Castle or with the Plornishes at Happy Cottage. The Christmas Books show the idea of retreat from the world carried almost to the point of caricature.[29] This can hardly be an accident: it seems plain that Dickens knew perfectly well what he was doing in celebrating unpretentious domestic happiness. Christmas is a time which tests the satisfaction of other kinds of achievement fairly exhaustively and Dickens has every right to use it in this way. Similarly he has every right to put forward the happiness that comes from a loving family as the most desirable and durable of all kinds of happiness. But his constant devotion to this scheme has two consequences for his novels.

First, if it is true that happiness comes only from the family, and if, as Dickens implies, any sort of public life whatever is incompatible with self-respect, the action of his novels, though apparently that of a man, usually a young man, coming to grips with the world, is in fact one of disengagement. Any larger issues or wider loyalties or loftier ambition are in the novel only to be grown out of and discarded. The action of the book is one of retreat, not of achievement. This is not of itself objectionable, but it is hard to put out of one's mind Ruskin's references to British domestic painting as 'The Art of the Nest': 'To be quite comfortable in your nest, you must not care too much for what is going on outside. . . . As there is in the spirit of domesticity always a sanctified littleness, there may also be a sanctified selfishness, and a very fearful one.'[30]

A second consequence is that the novels tend to fall into a pattern. At the end of the book what is waiting for the hero and heroine is the opportunity to vanish from view. The hero may have to earn his living—if so it will probably be as a partner in a small but honest firm[31]—but essentially the highest reward available is the same as Arthur Clennam's:

> Little Dorrit and her husband walked out of the church alone. They paused for a moment on the steps of the portico . . . and then went down. Went down, into a modest life of usefulness and happiness. . . . They went quietly down into the roaring streets, inseparable and blessed; and as they passed along in sunshine and shade, the noisy and the eager, and the arrogant and the froward and the vain, fretted, and chafed, and made their usual uproar. (Book II, chapter xxxiv)[32]

The pattern is, as I have tried to show, not a simple one to handle, because of the constant danger that the only way of life endorsed in the novel will be a negative one. The powerful clarity of design in *Dombey and Son* enables Dickens to overcome the danger. In *Great Expectations* he controls his material with such skill that Pip's visit to Wemmick really appears, in spite of Pip's youthful condescension, as his most genuinely valuable experience in the novel. Again in *Little Dorrit* he uses the Marshalsea with great dexterity to suggest that Arthur and Amy are in the end making a positive escape rather than a negative withdrawal. These three novels seem to me to be his great successes: they show that at his best Dickens can convince the reader that his main characters have freely and rightly chosen an adequate way of life.

Yet if we set aside our immediate pleasure in Dickens' realizations of domestic contentment and our immediate distaste for the

shams of public life as Dickens presents it, we can ask finally wha
sort of view of human freedom lies behind the novels, successfu
and unsuccessful alike. It is not, I think, a very cheerful one, simpl
because it is so limited. Dickens has a great gift for showing th
ordinary man—Will Fern or Stephen Blackpool—standing up to h
social superiors who wish to repress him: indeed his majo
achievement as a social novelist was to induce his middle-clas
readers to identify with working-class radicals. It seems therefor
absurd to say that he offers a poor and attentuated kind c
freedom. But, as I have tried to show in this chapter, Dicker
presented his readers with a version of Victorian England in whic
a young man growing up and meditating like Rasselas on the choic
of life finds only one path that he can decently and respectabl
tread: without any kind of direct oppression the structure c
society confronts him with Hobson's choice, which is no choice a
all. In this sense I think it is fair to describe Dickens as a socia
determinist. If the world offers you only one kind of real prize tha
is the prize at which you must necessarily aim: thus the world i
which you live determines what kind of hero you can be, an
a *fortiori* what sort of hero the novelist of real life can plausibl
create. Thus the kind of novels Dickens wrote depended ultimatel
on his view of the choices available to individuals in Victoria
Britain.

It is at this point that I must differ from Dr Leavis's account c
Little Dorrit. It is a magnificent exercise in encomium, and a
equally splendid demonstration of a wholly sympathetic reading c
a great novel. Dr Leavis rightly draws attention to the book
'urgently personal criticism of life in Arnold's sense—that entaile
in the inescapable and unrelenting questions: "What shall I dc
What can I do? What are the possibilities of life—for me, and, mor
generally, in the very nature of life? What are the conditions c
happiness? What is life for?"' (pp. 285-6). I diverge from Leavi
only in that part of his conclusion which is represented by th
following quotation: 'To insist that the psyche, the individual life,
both of its nature creative and in its individuality inherently soci
is to insist that all human creativity is, in one way or anothe
collaborative. . . . Dickens insists to this effect both implicitly ar
consciously' (p. 355).

I do not find that Dickens suggests any way in which the individu
could freely *become* part of his society, either because he was unab
to imagine what such a process would be like or because he felt th
no such way in fact existed. He gives us a penetrating picture of
number of societies, but seldom represents a community. The exce
tions are large lower-class families or family enterprises —th
Peggottys, Sleary's Horse Riding, Jarleys Waxworks, Todgerses

Martin Chuzzlewit, Fagin's boys in *Oliver Twist*, the Kenwigses and especially the Crummleses in *Nicholas Nickleby*. No doubt these are all 'on the side of life' and can be fairly put forward as evidence of Dickens' insistence on collaborative creativity, and they certainly function in their respective novels as examples of warmth and human fellowship deliberately contrasted with the chill relationships of formal or acquisitive societies, but they are not available to the hero as a permanent solution to the inescapable and unrelenting questions.

> 'Won't you stop to say something to Mrs Crummles?' asked the manager, following him down to the door.
> 'I couldn't stop if it were to prolong my life a score of years,' rejoined Nicholas. 'Here, take my hand, and with it my hearty thanks.—Oh that I should have been fooling here!'
> Accompanying these words with an impatient stamp upon the ground, he tore himself from the manager's detaining grasp, and darting rapidly down the street was out of sight in an instant.
> 'Dear me, dear me,' said Mr Crummles, looking wistfully towards the point at which he had just disappeared; 'if he only acted like that, what a deal of money he'd draw! He should have kept upon this circuit; he'd have been very useful to me. But he don't know what's good for him. He is an impetuous youth. Young men are rash, very rash.'
>
> (*Nicholas Nickleby*, chapter xxx)

On the face of it the Dickens hero is freer than George Eliot's characters, less formidably burdened with notions of duty and social responsibility. Yet Dickens confronts us unavoidably with the paradox that freedom of choice *per se* is valuable only if it can be exercised on ends depicted as worth choosing. Once something is found worth choosing a commitment to it must be made. Freedom is thereby lost, and replaced by a sense of calling. The criticism is not that the characters in Dickens do not work—some of them are very obviously industrious—but that he does not seem to understand what is meant by choosing to dedicate oneself to a way of life. When Bacon says in the Preface to the *Elements of Common Law*, 'I hold every man a debtor to his profession', or Ruskin says, 'A cobbler is not a man who makes shoes, but a man who keeps Christendom shod', or Yeats records in *Autobiographies*, 'I remind myself that I am an artist's son and must take some work as the whole end of life and not think as others do of becoming well-off and living pleasantly', they are expressing a concept of commitment to a life's work which is nowhere apparent in Dickens' novels and seems alien to the whole current of his habits of thought about art and life. George Eliot, on the other hand, everywhere endorses the passage she quotes from Riehl: 'The ardent pursuit of a fixed practical calling can alone satisfy the active man.'[33]

The difference may be compactly illustrated by a comparison of Dickens' easy caricature of Evangelism in the persons of Stiggins and the preacher in Little Bethel in *The Old Curiosity Shop* (ch. xli) with George Eliot's picture of Amos Barton. He is shown as under-bred and humanly deficient, yet because he is dedicated to his calling he never loses George Eliot's respect or the reader's. Alter-natively one might state the difference equally summarily but less unfavourably to Dickens by saying that his perpetual strength lay in his ability to grasp and present the truth of Burns's famous affirmation:

> To make a happy fire-side clime
>   To weans and wife—
> That's the true pathos and sublime
>   Of human life.

George Eliot's strength lay in her ability to see its inadequacy as a complete account of human objectives. 'The first condition of human goodness is something to love; the second, something to reverence.' Consequently she offers in her novels a wider range of possible ways of living than are available to the characters of Dickens.

III THE PRESSURES OF SOCIETY

> The chariot of civilisation, like that of the Idol of Juggernaut, is hardly interrupted even by these martyrs' hearts, less easily crushed than others; though its wheels are checked for a moment, it quickly break them and passes on its triumphal course.—BALZAC, *Père Goriot.*

> Je ne propose rien, je ne suppose rien, je n'impose rien . . . j'expose.– ZOLA.

I have dealt with the two special cases of *The Mill on the Floss* and *Little Dorrit* because they seem to me to show in the most direct way what can be uncovered by asking certain questions about a novel. In each case what emerges most strongly is the writer's sense that it is impossible to discuss a man's freedom of action in the nineteenth century without considering his relation to the conventional organization of the world in which he finds himself living—in a word, Society. 'There is no private life which has not been determined by a wider public life' (*Felix Holt*, chapter iii).

It is tempting to suggest that this is generally true of novelists in the period, but it is beyond my present compass to present a suffi-ciently wide selection of texts to test this hypothesis. The most can do is indicate briefly some other notable writers in the period whose works depend on the tension between a man's duty to himself and his duty to society, and who imply that, in general, society is the most important force which limits (and by limiting defines) human freedom.

I have already mentioned Balzac; clearly the next stage in an argument such as I have outlined would begin with Balzac and move to Zola, looking at Stendhal and Flaubert en route. It is not, I think, necessary to take too literally the account which Zola gives in the first chapter of *Le Roman Expérimental* (1880) of the methods of the realistic novelist. He suggests that the novelist is 'half observer, half experimenter'. The observer furnishes the facts:

> Then the experimentalist appears and introduces an experiment, that is to say, sets his characters going in a certain story so as to show that the succession of facts will be such as the requirements of the determinism of the phenomena under examination call for. . . . The problem is to know what such a passion, acting in such a surrounding and under such circumstances, would produce from the point of view of an individual and of society; and an experimental novel, *Cousine Bette*, for example, is simply the report of the experiment that the novelist conducts before the eyes of the public. In fact the whole operation consists in taking facts from nature, then in studying the mechanism of these facts, acting upon them, by the modification of circumstances and surroundings, without deviating from the laws of nature. Finally, you possess knowledge of the man, scientific knowledge of him, with his individual and social relations.

He continues the scientific analogy in chapter ii:

> We have just seen the great importance that Claude Bernard attaches to the study of 'intra-organic' environment, an element which has to be taken into account if one wishes to discover the determinism of events in living beings. Well now, in the study of a family, or group of living beings, I believe that the social environment has a similar capital importance. . . . Man is not alone but exists in society, in a social environment, and so far as we novelists are concerned, this environment is constantly modifying events. That is just where our real task lies, in studying the interaction of society on the individual and of the individual on society. For the physiologist, environment—whether external or internal—is purely chemical and physical, which makes it easy for him to determine its laws. On the other hand, we are in no position to prove that the *social* environment is only chemical and physical. It is that, certainly, or at any rate it is made with all its variations by a group of living beings who are themselves entirely subject to the physical and chemical laws that govern dead and living matter. Once we grasp this, we see that social environment will be affected by our manipulation of all those human phenomena we learn to control. And in this direction lies all that

constitutes the experimental novel; mastery of the mechanism of human events: demonstration of the way in which intellectual and sensory processes, as explained to us by physiology, are conditioned by heredity and environment; and finally portrayal of the human being in the environment which he himself has made and alters daily, and in the midst of which he in his turn undergoes continual transformation. And thus it is that we look to physiology for guidance, taking the isolated individual from the physiologist's hands in order to carry research further by solving scientifically the problem of how men behave once they become members of society.

Clearly, if we took these quotations at their face value, we should have to conclude that every item of human behaviour was simply the reaction of a given temperament with its environment, and the chief inventive talent of a novelist was the ability to devise a conclusive series of reactions.[34] Instinctively one rejects this notion of the novel, yet Zola goes some way towards justifying it by his own practice. For example, he plays down the individual character, particularly in his later novels, putting in its place the group. This is in accordance with what we learn from science, that life is larger than the individual in the sense that it is the species which survives, not the individual member of it.[35] Again, Zola is keenly conscious of the power of capital, and uses the capitalist system, in *Germinal* especially, almost as a symbol of the sum of forces that determine human conduct.[36] Finally, we may consider the title of his great work, *Histoire naturelle et sociale d'une famille sous le second Empire*; the twenty volumes that he devotes to the fortunes of the Rougon-Macquart family may make some claim to be a 'natural history', and it is a title that is more easily granted to the series as a whole than to any single book. As far as I know there is no critical work on the theory of the serial novel or the series of separate stories all dealing with the same character. Yet obviously some special kind of reality attaches to a fictional character who appears in more than one novel. Balzac had exploited this in the *Comédie Humaine*, but it was left to Zola to employ it systematically. The effect is ultimately to diminish the impression that a given character is acting freely by accounting much more fully than is possible in a single novel for his antecedents and for the accumulated circumstances that have led him to act in a particular way. Nana's odd combination of impulsiveness and cupidity seems less astonishing and far more like a fatal hereditary endowment when we have read *L'Assommoir*. Thus in each novel the particular constraints on the individual are those imposed by characters and forces which lie beyond the confines of the book, and the great chain of novels becomes itself a symbol of a heavy and ineluctable system of causality.[37]

It is important not to lose sight of the wide variety of situations which may be classified under the general description of man against society. At one extreme we may be considering purely private pressures, either the simple tie of blood, as chronicled in many novels whose burden is best expressed in a line from Arnold Wesker's *Roots*: 'The apple don't fall far from the tree—that it don't', or the overt coercion by parents of the will of a child as in Samuel Butler's *The Way of All Flesh* (1903) or in the family politics of the novels of Ivy Compton-Burnett. At the other we may be referring to the direct constraints which social, political or economic forces impose on man in general, especially when these are seen as part of a large working-out of laws of human development or patterns of change which are more powerful than the decisions of any individual, as in the novels of Dreiser, or Norris, or Upton Sinclair. In *The Jungle*, for example, the environment is a prison, built and policed by economic necessity. *Sybil* offers a good illustration of the range of novels of this kind. Not only does Disraeli, in a celebrated passage, suggest that the Queen rules over two nations, so that a child born into the poorer nation is always and inescapably a citizen of an underdeveloped and exploited country, but he also presents very vividly the power of the sheer pressure of other people:

'I have been persuaded of late that there is something going on in this country of more efficacy; a remedial power, as I believe, and irresistible; but whether remedial or not, at any rate a power that will mar all or cure all. You apprehend me? I speak of the annual arrival of more than three hundred thousand strangers in this island. How will you feed them? How will you clothe them? How will you house them? They have given up butcher's meat; must they give up bread? And as for raiment and shelter, the rags of the kingdom are exhausted, and your sinks and cellars already swarm like rabbit warrens. . . . 'Tis the most solemn thing since the deluge. What kingdom can stand against it? Why, go to your history, you're a scholar, and see the fall of the great Roman empire; what was that? Every now and then, there came two or three hundred thousand strangers out of the forests, and crossed the mountains and rivers. They come to us every year, and in greater numbers. What are your invasions of the barbarous nations, your Goths and Visigoths, your Lombards and Huns, to our Population Returns!'   (Book II, chapter xvi)

In Britain in the nineteenth century the most interesting novels fall in the middle ground, and are not so much novels of social protest as novels of social movement. Every major novelist from Dickens to Gissing adopted as part of the economy of his novels the class-structure of Victorian society, indeed many of the greatest novels are directly about the social classes and their effect on the individual. It is perhaps going too far to say that all the major novels show a young person learning by experience at what point in the social system he can find his place, and that this is usually demonstrated by marriage,[38] but a brief review of the period will show how many novels in fact fit into the general pattern marked out by *Pendennis*, *Great Expectations*, *Evan Harrington* (or *He Would be a Gentleman*), and Lytton's *Kenelm Chillingly* (1873). The one essential handbook for the study of the Victorian novel is *The Book of Snobs*.

Here we reach a situation which strains to the utmost our ability to give any content whatever to the idea of freedom. What is perfectly clear is that Thackeray, the most conscious and subtlest practitioner, Dickens, Meredith, Trollope, the most comprehensive example, Mrs Gaskell, George Eliot, and literally hundreds of lesser Victorian novelists simply accept as the basic fact of their novel the class system of England (suitably modified north of the border as they accept the laws of gravity or the wickedness of murder. Class and class-consciousness are the medium in which all the characters move and by virtue of which they are able to move. It is the water in which they swim. It constitutes the fabric of the novels, and, what is even more important, represents people as being on different levels and hence as having energy, whereas if all the characters were on the same level they would be in a state of maximum social entropy. Their being higher or lower than one another gives gradient, and since there is gradient there can be movement up and down. The existence of a social system is thus of vital importance as a source of motives for the characters. To put the hero of a Victorian novel into a world with no 'up' and 'down' is it is to disorient him completely. From this point of view the class system is the origin and sustaining condition of activity. Yet, as we see in *Vanity Fair*, for example, or even more clearly in *The Newcomes*, it can easily be depicted with such fulness and shown to affect the actions of the characters so regularly and so radically that they are almost deprived of the power to frame their own lives.

It is pointless to ask whether the class system is a reality or an illusion, just as it is pointless to ask whether the colour bar is 'real' or not. Both things exist in the minds of those who believe that they exist, and if they exist at all, even in one person's mind, they affect that person and everyone who wishes to have dealings with him. When the belief is virtually universal nobody can escape the effects, and these are undeniably real. These effects are what the Victorian novelists and many Victorian dramatists show us in abundant detail. The question with which they confront us is this:

How can we say that the class-structure limited the freedom of the individual, as seems the natural thing to say, when it is in fact the main source of incentive for the individual? When an event provides an individual with a powerful motive to do a particular thing should this properly be regarded as in some way limiting his freedom since it makes him want to act in one way to the exclusion of others? Is the water a limitation on a fish's freedom?

The system of classes in nineteenth-century Britain is a good example of the way in which the same institution can simultaneously incite one particular set of actions and inhibit others, and can thus be regarded as that which on the one hand limits freedom and on the other as that which defines it, so giving it content and value. Clearly the opinion of one's fellow men in general comes into the same category, their approval being something a man will work for a lifetime to win, their disapproval sufficient to prohibit and eventually destroy a whole range of human impulses. Not surprisingly many great works of literature turn on the conflict that arises when an individual is unable or unwilling to accept the opinions of the society in which he lives. The clearest examples are to be found in Ibsen's 'dramas of ethical motivation.' *An Enemy of the People* or *The Lady from the Sea* provide useful material for analysis since they both, at different levels, emphasize the responsibility of choice.[39] The issue is intensified by the influence of Kierkegaard and his insistence on the individual's duty to be true to himself and to resist patterns of life imposed by others.

What I have discussed in this chapter represents only a fraction of the ways in which writers, especially in the nineteenth century, saw man's freedom as principally limited by the other people in the world. If this is to attach too broad and general meaning to society, one might point to less contentious examples in the novels of Wells and Bennett or in George Moore's *Esther Waters* (1894). About my final example there will be no dispute, Arthur Morrison's *A Child of the Jago* (1896). The old Jago is a particularly poor and vicious district of the East End of London. The child who is born there can never, Morrison suggests, be free, not because of Fate or the Laws of Nature or the Immanent Will, but simply because English society is so constituted that the Jago is allowed to exist, and the Jago is so constituted that escape is impossible. The people of the Jago imprison one another. Mr Weech for his own ends prevents Dicky Perrott, the child of the book's title, from keeping honest work. The young boy who nearly breaks free is shackled again.

> Dicky's intellectuals began to arrange themselves. Plainly Mr. Weech's philosophy was right after all. He was of the Jago, and he must prey on the outer world, as all the Jago did; not stray foolishly off the regular

track in chase of visions, and fall headlong. Father Sturt was a creature of another mould. Who was he, Dicky Perrott, that he should break away from the Jago habit, and strain after another nature? What could come of it but defeat and bitterness? As old Beveridge had said, the Jago had got him. Why should he fight against the inevitable, and bruise himself? The ways out of the Jago old Beveridge had told him, years ago. Gaol, the gallows, and the High Mob. There was his chance, his aspiration, his goal: the High Mob. To dream of oil-shops or regular wages was foolishness. His bed was made in the Jago, and he must lie on it. His hope in life, if he might have a hope at all, was to be of the High Mob. Spare nobody, stop at nothing, do his devilmost: old Beveridge had said that years ago. The task was before him, and he must not balk at it. As for gaol and the gallows, well! There they were, and he could not help it; ill ways out of the Jago, both, but still—ways out.

He rubbed his face carefully with his sleeve, put away his foolish ambitions, and went forth with a brave heart: to accomplish his destiny, for well or ill,—a Jago rat.   (chapter xxi)

With that superlative example I conclude this brief survey of a few of the works of literature dealing with the situation where a man's freedom is seen as limited or defined simply by the fact that he must share the world with other people, and is expected to honour the conventions which the people among whom he is born have devised to control the behaviour of one man relative to another. The writers whose work I have been discussing do not suggest that all social pressures are necessarily vicious—they may be accepted as part of the way things are and therefore part of what the novelist of the real world must write about: alternatively even if a novelist exposes inexcusable social abuses it does not follow that he advocates the abolition of or even any fundamental change in the social system.

Yet if we reduce the basic assumptions of these writers to a neutral slogan such as 'Social Pressures Limit Human Freedom' it is plain that this can be construed as an indictment of society. Such an indictment might, however, lead to either of two opposed courses of action. On the one hand one might conclude that it is necessary to reject all social relationships and all values derived from society as unauthentic: this would lead at the extreme to a view of human life such as I describe in chapter xii. Alternatively it could be argued that the pressures which bear hardest on the individual are the product of a social and economic system whose obvious defect is its lack of control, the blind tyranny of what Kingsley in *Alton Locke* calls 'the great King Laisser Faire'. In that case one way of protecting the individual is to control the system by strengthening the authority of government. This would lead at the extreme to a view of human life such as I describe in chapter xiii.

In addition to the works cited in the notes the following have material relevant to the themes of this chapter: John Holloway, *The Victorian Sage* (London: Macmillan, 1953); George Levine, 'Determinism and Responsibility in the Works of George Eliot', *PMLA*, **77** (1962), 268–79; Bernard J. Paris, *Experiments in Life: George Eliot's Quest for Values* (Detroit: Wayne State U.P., 1965); Jerome B. Schneewind, 'Moral Problems and Moral Philosophy in the Victorian Period', *VS*, supplement to 9 (1965), 29–46; John Lucas, *The Melancholy Man: A Study of Dickens's Novels*, (London: Methuen, 1970); Alexander Welsh, *The City of Dickens* (Oxford: Clarendon 1971); Michael Goldberg, 'From Bentham to Carlyle: Dickens' Political Development', *JHI*, **33** (1972), 61–76; N. N. Feltes, 'Community and the Limits of Liability in Two Mid-Victorian Novels', *VS*, **17** (1973–4) 355–69; Felicia Bonaparte, *Will and Destiny: Morality and Tragedy in George Eliot's Novels* (N.Y.U.P., 1975); Walter M. Kendrick, 'Balzac and British Realism: Mid-Victorian Theories of the Novel', *VS*, **20** (1976), 5–24; Jeannette King, *Tragedy in the Victorian Novel* (Cambridge U.P., 1978) esp. chaps. 3, 4, 5.

11

Retrospect Three 1830–1890

Modern times find themselves with an immense system of institutions, established facts, accredited dogmas, customs, rules, which have come to them from times not modern. In this system their life has to be carried forward; yet they have a sense that this system is not of their own creation, that it by no means corresponds exactly with the wants of their actual life, that, for them, it is customary, not rational. The awakening of this sense is the awakening of the modern spirit. . . . Dissolvents of the old European system of dominant ideas and facts we must all be, all of us who have any power of working.—ARNOLD, 'Heinrich Heine' from *Essays in Criticism*, First series (1865).

The railway lines from Redhill to Dorking, from East Grinstead to Three Bridges, and from Redhill far on the way to Brighton, are visible from this point; the wreaths of white smoke that float above the deep foliage of the Weald marking the progress of the trains across the old country of the Iguanodon and the Plesiosaurus.—*Murray's Handbook for Surrey* (1865).

One way in which the nineteenth century differed from most of its predecessors is that until the beginning of that century the world seemed to most men to be inhabited or controlled by active forces which were not human. These forces might be called variously the gods, or God, or Fortune, or Fate, or Nature, or an Invisible Presence, or the Infernal Powers. They existed and man acted only within the limits they permitted him. Though man was thus subordinate to a more powerful external agency he was not alone in the universe. To this point in the argument it has been possible, by a violent simplification of the issues, to consider, at least as a hypothesis, that at any one time one power generally was recognized as chiefly limiting the freedom of men. Thus the Fates (or Fortune) in the time of Chaucer, Nature for Marlowe, the Gods for Webster, God for Milton, and a principle of natural order for Pope. But by the end of the eighteenth century no single power was regarded as necessarily exercising a universal constraint, and it was thus possible for men to differ widely about what actually limited their freedom and how painfully. Wordsworth, Shelley and Byron, for instance, though contemporaries, show no measure of agreement. For Wordsworth an unspecifiable power that is not man is still available to him through the natural world, shaping him from his earliest days and imposing on him the need, if he is ever to be fully human, to become so in conjunction and harmony with the forces of nature. To Shelley Tyranny, man's inhumanity to his own kind, would probably have seemed a more immediate constraint, while Byron's position may be briefly characterized by Arnold's description of the heroes of his poems—'not so much in collision with outward things as breaking on some rock of revolt and misery in the depths of their own nature'.

I am not concerned here to argue for the precise details. The point to which I wish to give particular emphasis is a similarity between the periods 1590–1620 and 1790–1820. We have there, I think, a striking pattern repeated—the same sudden surge of belief in the freedom and power of the individual, followed in each case very rapidly by doubts, mistrust of the new liberty and disillusion. I want now to suggest further that just as the earlier part of the seventeenth century was a time of great confusion and controversy, so the age succeeding that of the great Romantics has been one of shifting loyalties and divided aims, the instability deriving from the same uncertainty about the nature and extent of human liberty. If with Byron and Shelley we reach a point where Man can be thought of as quite alone in the universe, or at least as the highest form of existence, it might seem that we have reached the point where we can at last say that man is free. Yet, as I have indicated, the news that God was dead produced a curiously divided response. 'While in our inquiries into Greek and medieval art I was able to describe in general terms what all men did or felt, I find now many characters in many men. . . . We need not, therefore,' as Ruskin said, 'expect to find any single poet or painter representing the entire group of powers, weaknesses, and inconsistent instincts which govern or confuse our modern life.'[1] I think that it is necessary to distinguish at least four main lines of thought in the nineteenth century.[2]

I.   First, it was possible for some to preserve a simple faith in the reality and the value of human freedom, assenting wholeheartedly, for example, to all the implications of Byron's very early translation of Horace's *Justum et tenacem propositi virum* (*Odes* III. iii):

> The man of firm and noble soul
> No factious clamours can control;
> No threat'ning tyrant's darkling brow
>   Can swerve him from his just intent:
> Gales the warring waves which plough,
>   By Auster on the billows spent,
> To curb the Adriatic main,
> Would awe his fix'd, determined mind in vain.

Ay, and the red right arm of Jove,
Hurtling his lightnings from above,
With all his terrors there unfurl'd,
  He would unmoved, unawed, behold.
The flames of an expiring world,
  Again in crashing chaos roll'd,
In vast promiscuous ruin hurl'd,
Might light his glorious funeral pile:
Still dauntless 'midst the wreck of earth he'd smile.

The developments of this way of regarding the power of the human will are not difficult to trace. They range from poems such as Ella Wheeler Wilcox's *Winds of Fate*

One ship drives east, and another drives west,
  With the self-same winds that blow,
'Tis the set of the sails and not the gales
  Which tells us the way to go. . .

to rather more convincing versions of the same idea such as Longfellow's *The Two Rivers*. The tone is sometimes one of exhortation, as in Adelaide Anne Procter's *Now*:

Rise! for the day is passing,
  And you lie dreaming on;
The others have buckled their armour,
  And forth to the fight are gone:
A place in the ranks awaits you,
  Each man has some part to play;
The Past and the Future are nothing,
  In the face of the stern To-day.

or Longfellow's *A Psalm of Life*:

Life is real! Life is earnest!
  And the grave is not its goal;
Dust thou art, to dust returnest,
  Was not spoken of the soul. . . .
Lives of great men all remind us
  We can make our lives sublime,
And, departing, leave behind us
  Footprints on the sands of time. . . .
Let us, then, be up and doing,
  With a heart for any fate;
Still achieving, still pursuing,
  Learn to labour and to wait.

sometimes one of defiance, as in Henley's *Invictus*:

Out of the night that covers me,
  Black as the pit from pole to pole,
I thank whatever gods may be
  For my unconquerable soul.

In the fell clutch of circumstance
  I have not winced nor cried aloud.
Under the bludgeonings of chance
  My head is bloody, but unbowed.

Beyond this place of wrath and tears
  Looms but the Horror of a shade,
And yet the menace of the years
  Finds, and shall find, me unafraid.

It matters not how strait the gate,
  How charged with punishments the scroll,
I am the master of my fate:
  I am the captain of my soul.

The simple notion of men as free agents in a world with no super-natural constraints is not one which animates many major works of literature.[3] Perhaps only Browning begins from this uncompli-cated, but not necessarily optimistic, assumption that man is essentially a deliberating and deciding animal, that his motives are interior but can be made available for inspection, and that in the end a man is to be judged for what he decides to do, not pitied as a victim of circumstance. Blougram's previous history is of no concern to the reader, the Pope takes account of Guido's wicked-ness, not his misfortune, and so on. With this important exception the writers who work from simple assumptions about the nature and extent of human freedom are not the major writers. It is not hard to detect in the following extract from the *Art Journal* the superficiality of the connection the writer makes between liberty and the artistic life of the country:

> This school of pictorial art is emphatically English . . . because we in England are daily making to ourselves a contemporary history . . . Britain is a land of action and of progress, trade, commerce, growing wealth, steadfast yet ever changeful liberty; a land and a people wherein a contemporary Art may grow and live, because in this actual present hour we act heroically, suffer manfully and do those deeds which in pictures and by poems, deserve to be recorded.[4]

II. The reasons for the weakening of this primary faith in the sufficient powers of the individual are manifold, but two are of particular importance. First stands the obvious truth that it is not possible for all men to be free and that one man's freedom will only be exercised at the cost of someone else's. This hard necessity was made immediately and inescapably manifest by the sheer physical pressures of city life. As Alexander Welsh rightly observes, 'In the nineteenth century, as this or that condition of the city is seen, however dimly, to have some physical or quasi-physical cause, the possibility of choice diminishes. Individual moral choice seems hopelessly interwoven and dependent on other choices, many of them not moral at all.'[5] From Malthus in the 1790s to Huxley in the 1890s the inexorably increasing weight of numbers is the great immovable obstacle in the way of all schemes for the improvement of the human condition.

The characteristics of Victorian city life are recorded in innumerable places—in the Blue Books and statistical accounts of the time, in the descriptions and analyses of the journalists and essayists, whether impartial, like Mayhew, or angry, like Ruskin, and not least memorably in the works of the novelists. Dickens expresses superbly not just the squalor and misery but the ruthlessness of the unplanned city, of the 'labyrinth of narrow courts upon courts, and close streets upon streets, which had come into existence piecemeal, every piece in a violent hurry for some one man's purpose, and the whole an unnatural family, shouldering, and trampling, and pressing one another to death'.[6]

At the same time it was becoming more common to question the value of individual freedom as an end in itself, as it had indeed been questioned earlier in the century, not least searchingly by those, such as Hegel, who had experienced it most strongly. On a personal level we find Byron as early as September 1816 lamenting the burden of 'my own wretched identity'.[7] I have tried in chapter six to trace the violence with which Byron confronted the contradictions in his own thought. It is worth noting that Carlyle in *Signs of the Times* observed that Byron was already beginning to go out of vogue in 1829. Similarly in *Sartor Resartus* (1833–4) the reader is advised to turn from Byron and self to Goethe and sanity —'Close thy Byron: open thy Goethe.' Alongside those who believed whole-heartedly in the value of personal freedom there existed many others who doubted and repudiated the principle. Whitman's 'Spontaneous Me' is answered by Rimbaud's 'Je est un autre'.[8] Mill can lay down as an axiom in his *Principles of Political Economy* (1848), 'After the means of subsistence are assured, the next in strength of the personal wants of human beings is liberty.' But Ruskin stated equally forcefully in *Fors Clavigera*, 'My own teaching has been, and is, that Liberty, whether in the body, soul, or political state of man, is only another word for Death, and the final issue of Death, putrefaction.'[9] Nor is this simply Ruskin in his eccentric old age. Compare with the passage from the *Art Journal* the chapter 'Of modern landscape' in *Modern Painters*, in which Ruskin traces the connection between the age he lives in and the leading doctrines of its artistic life:

> Whereas all the pleasure of the medieval was in *stability*, *definiteness*, and *luminousness*, we are expected to rejoice in darkness and triumph in mutability; to lay the foundation of happiness in things which momentarily change or fade; and to expect the utmost satisfaction and instruction from what it is impossible to arrest and difficult to comprehend.

Ruskin notices how in painters this takes the form of an excessive interest in clouds and mist and comments:

> Much of the instinct . . . partially developed in painting may be now seen throughout every mode of exertion of mind—the easily encouraged doubt, easily excited curiosity, habitual agitation, and delight in the changing and the marvellous, as opposed to the old quiet serenity of social custom and religious faith.

He comments, 'The next thing that will strike us, after this love of clouds, is the love of liberty.' This, it is true, leads to a love of mountain scenery, but a love without awe—'our modern society in general goes to the mountains not to fast, but to feast, and leaves their glaciers covered with chicken-bones and egg-shells.' This in turn leads to a 'general profanity of temper in regarding all the rest of nature', and this conduces to 'a strong tendency to deny the sacred element of colour'.

> These, I believe, are the principal points which would strike us instantly, if we were to be brought suddenly into an exhibition of modern landscapes out of a room filled with medieval work. It is evident that there are both evil and good in this change; but how much evil or how much good, we can only estimate by considering . . . what are the real roots of the habits of mind which have caused them.

The route that Ruskin follows is idiosyncratic in the extreme, but his conclusion that the distinctive temper of the nineteenth century was intimately connected with prevalent ideas about human liberty and that this connection had brought losses as well as gains is reasonable and was accepted by more and more people as the century advanced.

The central chapter of Arnold's *Culture and Anarchy* (1869) is called 'Doing as One Likes'. Familiar though it is, it must be quoted, since it shows with unsurpassed clarity the extent of the reaction against assertive liberalism:

> When I began to speak of culture, I insisted on our bondage to machinery, on our proneness to value machinery as an end in itself, without looking beyond it to the end for which alone, in truth, it is valuable. Freedom, I said, was one of those things which we thus worshipped in itself, without enough regarding the ends for which freedom is to be desired. In our common notions and talk about freedom, we eminently show our idolatry of machinery. . . .
>
> For a long time, as I have said, the strong feudal habits of subordination and deference continued to tell upon the working class. The modern spirit has now almost entirely dissolved those habits, and the anarchical tendency of our worship of freedom in and for itself, of our superstitious faith, as I say, in machinery, is becoming very manifest.

The double nature of the uneasiness is clear. It was compounded partly of the fear that human freedom in itself was deficient and required some external correlative to complete it and partly of the fear that some dominant power, new or revived, would yet impose unavoidable limitations on the scope of the human will.

III. It was possible to consider man's relations with his fellow men as the set of constraints that most obviously and painfully limited his freedom: they might alternatively be seen as the determining external impulses which alone could give his freedom content and meaning. Carlyle, for example, showed how a concept such as 'Social Responsibility' might be employed to give purpose to and amplify the concept of freedom, even in the close contacts of urban life—'It is in society that man first feels what he is; first becomes what he can be. In Society an altogether new set of spiritual activities are evolved in him, and the old immeasurably quickened and strengthened.'[10]

It is not surprising that one of the major enterprises of the century was the attempt first to understand and control the forces governing social behaviour, and then, in Kropotkin's phrase, 'to deduce the laws of moral science from the social needs and habits of mankind'. The extent to which this line of thought could be taken is shown by various works of social philosophy of the period, such as Robert Owen's *The Book of the New Moral World* (Parts I–VII, 1842–4), described as an 'attempt to analyse the laws of nature and to build upon them a social theory',[11] or Herbert Spencer's *Social Statics: or, the Conditions Essential to Human Happiness Specified, and the First of These Developed* (1851), or Bagehot's *Physics and Politics* (1872) in which he tried to apply scientific principles to the development of political institutions. One might mention also Spencer's *The Data of Ethics* (1879), and

T. H. Huxley's *Science and Morals* (1886), which continue, though at a far remove, in the spirit of Bentham's Table of the Springs of Action, Fourier's 'Infinitesimal Calculus of the Sympathies',[12] and Quetelet's study of 'moral statistics' in *Sur l'homme* (1835).

It is easy to see how the scientific study of man in society leads to the aggregating of human happenings and thus to a statistical view of mankind as a whole. This in turn generates statements of rules of behaviour for the total population which individuals are power-less to overthrow. The obvious possibility is that of re-establishing a non-human constraining power. Here the statistical or 'scientific' view of mankind as a whole comes very close to the so-called 'romantic' or 'organic' view of those who saw the individual as 'a mere cell in the collective organism of humanity'. The actual forces at work on the organism and *a fortiori* on its constituent cells have been given various names, ranging from Comte's Great Being to Spencer's Unknown Reality and Frazer's 'masked wizard of history', from tightly formulated concepts such as Spengler's pre-destined cultural life-cycles to much looser notions such as the Spirit of the Age or Carlyle's 'Tree Igdrasil' that 'buds and withers by its own laws,—too deep for our scanning' and 'that has its roots down in the Kingdoms of Hela and Death, and whose boughs overspread the highest Heaven!' They all imply that mankind as a whole is moving at the command of some larger force—perhaps to a foreseen end, perhaps in irresistible cycles of perpetual change. Human history is, according to this conception of man, not the product of a series of human decisions but the tracing out of non-human patterns, according to the mighty working. The concept of the nation-state is particularly crucial here, since it suggests the argument that the life of the individual is given meaning only by his membership of a sovereign state and is therefore inevitably involved in the varying fortunes of his country, these fortunes being beyond human control and thus presumably in more powerful hands. I examine the implications of this argument more fully in chapter 13.

For many members of both groups, the scientific and the organic, the category of development provided the basic means of understanding reality and human history. Historical events were without individual character, but were to be seen as part of the stream of history. Presumably it was arguments of this kind, encouraged as they doubtless were by current ideas of evolution, that enabled proponents of both doctrines to offer a generally opti-mistic presentation of their conclusions. If the determinist implica-tions could be played down, the belief that human affairs and the destinies of nations were ultimately controlled by some invisible genius of history could obviously be cheering:

It shall be clearly seen that, from the beginning there has been no discrepancy, no incongruity, no disorder, no interruption, no inter-
ference; but that all the events which surround us, even to the furthest
limits of the material creation, are but different parts of a single
scheme, which is permeated by one glorious principle of universal and
undeviating regularity.[13]

Such a belief might be allied with a faith in the beneficent powers
of technological invention, like that of Lancelot Smith in Kingsley's
Yeast—'The spinning-jenny and the railroad, Cunard's liners and
the electric telegraph, are to me, if not to you, signs that we are, on
some points at least, in harmony with the universe' (chapter 5), or
that of the writer of a guide-book to Folkestone in the 1850s—
'Steam will prove a universal peace-maker. The natives of all
countries will cease to regard each other as enemies. Man will meet
man as his brother. *War will cease.* Similar reflections to these will
naturally suggest themselves to the visitors while lounging on the
Pier.'[14] Comte's progressivism, with its account of successive stages
in man's development, the theological being superseded by the
metaphysical, which gives way in turn to the positivist, suggests
also some power which inevitably assures the due transitions from
one mode to the next. Any account of human development which
sees mankind as necessarily becoming more perfect is likely to consider the individual life as a constituent part of some larger
organism and to that extent not free.

IV. If these determinist elements are specified the invitation to
subordinate the single life to the larger design may obviously meet
with a much less welcoming response: the fourth group which I
distinguish includes those who saw, or feared, that the mighty
working was not that of some vast beneficent superintending
power but a set of inexorable natural laws. 'Tell us not that the
world is governed by universal law; the news is not comfortable,
but simply horrible.'[15] Leaving aside the obvious examples from the
world of philosophy, I may mention Clough, Fitzgerald, John
Davidson, Housman and James Thomson: I am thinking in particular of the splendid description of Durer's *Melencolia* at the end of
The City of Dreadful Night, an eloquent depiction of a universe
which has not been explained, but rather drained of meaning by
the questioning intellect of the Renaissance.[16] If the growth of
scientific knowledge determined ever more rigidly the unavertable
ends of all physical activity, it seemed to many inquirers that
Nature once more had the final say, but Nature in no kindly
shape.[17]

The idea of the nineteenth century as 'the first age in which the
accumulation of scientific knowledge was more important than

law, religion, art and letters in determining the direction of ideas and the attitude of the public at large towards accepted values'[18] is a commonplace, but it is worth emphasizing how far-reaching the implications were of adopting a thoroughgoing scientific approach to all human experience. If 'it is wrong everywhere and for anyone, to believe anything upon insufficient evidence'[19] man has no special claim for exemption. An obvious example of the process is the application of the theories of evolution. The extension to the human race was made very rapidly, so that *The Origin of Species* (1859) was followed by T. H. Huxley's *Man's Place in Nature* (1863), Lyell's *Geological Evidence of the Antiquity of Man* (1863), Tylor's *Researches into the Early History of Mankind* (1865), Ernst Haeckel's *The History of Creation* (1868) and Darwin's *The Descent of Man* (1871). It was in the course of a review of this last book that Huxley wrote, 'In a dozen years the *Origin of Species* has worked as complete a revolution in Biological Science as the *Principia* did in Astronomy.'[20] The view of the world which followed from this is well depicted in his 'A Liberal Education' from *Lay Sermons*:

> The chess-board is the world; the pieces are the phenomena of the universe; the rules of the game are what we call the laws of Nature. The player on the other side is hidden from us. We know that his play is always fair, just, and patient. But also we know, to our cost, that he never overlooks a mistake, or makes the smallest allowance for ignorance.

Huxley's not unpleasing picture of life as a demanding game to be played according to defined rules is somewhat disturbed if we ask how free men are to choose their own moves and look for the answer in a celebrated passage at the end of his Belfast address to the British Association in 1874:

> It is quite true that, to the best of my judgement, the argumentation which applies to brutes holds equally good of men; and, therefore, that all states of consciousness in us, as in them, are immediately caused by molecular changes of the brain substance. It seems to me that in men, as in brutes, there is no proof that any state of consciousness is the cause of change in the motion of the matter of the organism. If these positions are well based, it follows that our mental conditions are simply the symbols in consciousness of the changes which take place automatically in the organism; and that, to take an extreme illustration, the feeling we call volition is not the cause of a voluntary act, but the symbol of that state of the brain which is the immediate cause of that act. We are conscious automata, endowed with free will in the only intelligible sense of that much-abused term—inasmuch as in many respects we are able to do as we like—but none the less parts of the great

series of causes and effects which, in unbroken continuity, composes that which is, and has been, and shall be—the sum of existence.

The general position may be summed up in a single quotation: one of the great anthropologists of the century, E. B. Tylor, wrote in *Primitive Culture* (1871):

> Our thoughts, wills and actions accord with laws as definite as those which govern the motion of waves, the combination of acids and bases, and the growth of plants and animals.

One might mention here scientists like Darwin's cousin, Francis Galton, who tried to account for human destinies in terms of an 'inner force',[21] and then look forward to the work of the behaviourists, but I am more concerned at this point to consider the general implications of scientific theory for the status of mankind. I drew attention in the chapter on Tennyson to the way in which the geologist and the biologist discredited the idea of special creation, called in question the validity of ethical systems and cast doubt on the value of imaginative literature. In 1820 Peacock had concluded his *Four Ages of Poetry* with a reference to the

> mathematicians, astronomers, chemists, moralists, metaphysicians, historians, politicians, and political economists, who have built into the upper air of intelligence a pyramid, from the summit of which they see the modern Parnassus far beneath them, and, knowing how small a place it offers in the comprehensiveness of their prospect, smile at the little ambition and the circumscribed perceptions with which the drivellers and mountebanks upon it are contending for the poetical palm and the critical chair.

As I have mentioned in chapter 8, the diminished state of poetry similarly troubled Tennyson. In the first stanzas of his short poem *Parnassus* (1889) he asks the Muses, as poets have traditionally asked, to raise him to the top of Parnassus so that his voice may go on sounding for ever and ever through the world. The second stanza runs

> What be those two shapes high over the sacred fountain,
> Taller than all the Muses, and huger than all the mountain?
> On those two known peaks they stand ever spreading and heightening;
> Poet, that evergreen laurel is blasted by more than lightning!
> Look, in their deep double shadow the crowned ones all disappearing!
> Sing like a bird and be happy, nor hope for a deathless hearing!
> 'Sounding for ever and ever?' pass on! the sight confuses—
> These are Astronomy and Geology, terrible Muses!

Daunting though the Victorians found the discoveries of the geologists and astronomers, nothing seems to have offered such irrefutable warrant for a fatalist view of the human lot as the laws of thermodynamics. The plain implication of the first law is that in every mechanical process, and indeed in every form of activity a certain amount of the energy involved will be converted into heat, which is the least defined form of energy. The second law, if generally true, describes the Universe in which energy once dissipated in the form of heat cannot be recovered except at the cost of an even greater quantity of energy of some higher kind. It seems to follow that the whole process of the Universe is one of gradual degeneration from an earlier state when all matter was charged with potentially useful energy to an ultimate state in which all energy has been converted to heat, everything is the same temperature, and no life or identifiable motion exists. Whether we call this a condition of maximum entropy, or the heat-death of the Universe, or a state of total randomness is not of any importance. The point is that if we have this view of the world we must see it as a clock that is running down; indeed we may think of the gradual increase in entropy as itself a kind of measurement of time.

Anyone who understood the laws of thermodynamics in this sense, and such interpretations were not uncommon in the nineteenth century,[22] would have strong grounds for a pessimistic view of all human activity. For the picture that represents the span of the Universe is of two forces at work. First, through living matter, which implies organization, and is most clearly exemplified by purposeful communities of creatures, determining and controlling their own environment, there appears to be a steady progress in redeeming Earth from the primal Chaos. At the same time a slower, but surer, tendency of the kind I have described irresistibly draws everything including living matter to a state of total disorganization. The history of the Universe is thus a chronicle of inevitable decay, terminating at the point when nothing is available except general information in a statistical form.

It is but a short step to the use of this picture of the physical world as a metaphor for any kind of human behaviour which, while it may in fact impose some kind of organization on matter, is short-sighted, careless, heedless, or reckless of its consequences for society. We use 'disorderly' quite correctly for any conduct which offends against our sense of organization or fitness for purpose. Hence we have a complex of ideas in which randomness or lack of particularized information, purposeless human activity, and the passing of time are intimately linked, and stand as symbols for one another. Thus emotions such as regret for lost youth or vexation at the sort of unintelligent human behaviour that resulted in

the great urban slums of Victorian Britain are but different faces of
the same coin. Either emotion can be transposed into grief that in
time the entire fabric of the Universe will be without energy or
movement or meaning: either emotion thus offers an immediate
route to a pessimism of the most thorough-going kind, especially
difficult to combat because it is justified by an apparently irrefrag-
able chain of scientific reasoning.

A precisely similar complex of ideas finds linked expression in
many of Arnold's poems. *The Future* is one of many obvious
examples: Arnold says that as the world grows older

                                          Our minds
          Are confused as the cries which we hear
          Changing and shot as the sights which we see.
          And we say that repose has fled
          For ever the course of the river of Time.
          That cities will crowd to its edge
          In a blacker, incessanter line;
          That the din will be more on its banks,
          Denser the trade on its stream,
          Flatter the plain where it flows,
          Fiercer the sun overhead.   (55–65)

The beginning of *Consolation* is in a similar vein:

              Mist clogs the sunshine.
              Smoky dwarf houses
              Hem me round everywhere;
              A vague dejection
              Weighs down my soul.

The use of a model of this kind serves also to place Arnold's ideas of
artistic creation as one of the few modes of human activity which,
with only a minimal dissipation of energy as heat, really do impose
an organization on the world and thus apparently arrest the
resistless flux of time. 'These fragments I have shored against my
ruins.' This is why Arnold's most poignant moments of desolation
occur when he feels that human beings cannot, by their nature,
communicate even through art, but are eternally separated by the
'unplumbed, salt, estranging sea'.

As I said in the chapter on Tennyson and Arnold, what is really
interesting is not the reaction of writers to crudely materialistic
accounts of mental activity, such as Vogt's 'The brain secretes
thought, just as the liver secretes bile', but their attempts to understand the implications for mankind as a whole of a way of describing the world which left no room for anything beyond the

observable facts.[23] Many an earnest thinker of the nineteenth century must have echoed Ruskin's cry of 1851—'If only the Geologists
would let me alone, I could do very well, but those dreadful
Hammers! I hear the clink of them at the end of every cadence of
the Bible phrases.'[24] Humanists found it equally difficult to maintain an uncomplicated faith in the liberty and efficacy of man's
will.[25] While the idealist created massive abstractions in the grip of
which the individual was helpless, the empiricist came to doubt all
but mechanical phenomena and to see men as governed by physical laws, whether immediate or ultimate.[26] As usual Shaw over-
states the case, but there is no better brief account of the baleful
effects of scientific advance, what he calls 'the doltish materialism
of the laboratories', than his section 'The Wicked Half Century' in
the preface to *Heartbreak House*:

> For half a century before the war [i.e. 1860–1914] civilization had been
> going to the devil very precipitately under the influence of a pseudo-
> science as disastrous as the blackest Calvinism. Calvinism taught that as
> we are predestinately saved or damned, nothing that we do can alter
> our destiny. Still, as Calvinism gave the individual no clue as to whether
> he had drawn a lucky number or an unlucky one, it left him a fairly
> strong interest in encouraging his hopes of salvation and allaying his
> fear of damnation by behaving as one of the elect might be expected to
> behave rather than as one of the reprobate. But in the middle of the XIX
> century naturalists and physicists assured the world, in the name of
> Science, that salvation and damnation are all nonsense, and that pre-
> destination is the central truth of religion, inasmuch as human beings
> are produced by their environment, their sins and good deeds being
> only a series of chemical and mechanical reactions over which they
> have no control. Such figments as mind, choice, purpose, conscience,
> will, and so forth, are, they taught, mere illusions, produced because
> they are useful in the continual struggle of the human machine to
> maintain its environment in a favorable condition, a process inciden-
> tally involving the ruthless destruction or subjection of its competitors
> for the supply (assumed to be limited) of subsistence available. We
> taught Prussia this religion; and Prussia bettered our instruction so
> effectively that we presently found ourselves confronted with the
> necessity of destroying Prussia to prevent Prussia destroying us. And
> that has just ended in each destroying the other to an extent doubtfully
> reparable in our time. . . .
>   When the new departure in scientific doctrine which is associated
> with the name of the great naturalist Charles Darwin began, it was not
> only a reaction against a barbarous pseudo-evangelical teleology
> intolerably obstructive to all scientific progress, but was accompanied,
> as it happened, by discoveries of extraordinary interest in physics,
> chemistry, and that lifeless method of evolution which its investigators
> called Natural Selection. Howbeit, there was only one result possible in
> the ethical sphere, and that was the banishment of conscience from

human affairs, or, as Samuel Butler vehemently put it, 'of mind from the universe'.

The nineteenth century defies any summary, but if we had to choose a single symbol for the intricate web of processes at work the least inadequate might be found in the third act of *Siegfried*. Throughout *The Ring* Wotan has confronted the same intractable problem as Milton's God, how to give earthly men their freedom while at the same time ensuring that they do not defy the divine intentions. After Siegfried has killed the dragon and taken possession of the ring which is the token of supremacy, Wotan attempts to bar his path with his spear, another instrument of majesty, which had at a touch brought Siegfried's father to his death. Siegfried shatters the spear with one blow of his sword and passes on to meet his destiny. Wotan turns away and plays no further part in the action. At the end of *Gotterdämmerung* the divine order is destroyed by fire and flood: Siegfried is already dead, killed by his fellow men.

In addition to the works cited in the notes the following have material relevant to the themes of this chapter: W. L. Burn, *The Age of Equipoise* (London: Unwin, 1964); F. E. Manuel, *Shapes of Philosophical History* (London: Allen and Unwin, 1965); R. H. Super, *The Time-Spirit of Matthew Arnold* (Ann Arbor: U. of Michigan P., 1970); Jerome Beaty, 'All Victoria's Horses and All Victoria's Men', *New Literary History*, 1 (1970), 271–92; David J. DeLaura, 'Matthew Arnold and the Nightmare of History', in *Victorian Poetry*, ed. M. Bradbury and D. Palmer (London: Arnold, 1972); J. A. Rogers, 'Darwinism and Social Darwinism', *JHI*, 33 (1972), 265–80; Peter Conrad, *The Victorian Treasure-House* (London: Collins, 1973); H. Y. Vanderpool ed., *Darwin and Darwinism: Revolutionary Insights concerning Man, Nature, Religion and Society* (Toronto and London: D. C. Heath, 1973); Alexander Welsh, 'Theories of Science and Romance 1820–1920', *VS*, 17 (1973), 135–54; Owen Chadwick, *The Secularization of the European Mind in the Nineteenth Century* (Cambridge U.P., 1975), esp. chapters 7–10; Michael Timko, 'The Victorianism of Victorian Literature', *New Literary History* 6 (1975), 607–27; Maurice Larkin, *Man and Society in Nineteenth-Century Realism: Determinism and Literature* (London: Macmillan, 1977).

12

Wilde and the Modern Theatre

I *THE PICTURE OF DORIAN GRAY*

All art is at once surface and symbol.
Those who go beneath the surface do so at their peril.

No artist has ethical sympathies. An ethical sympathy in an artist is an
unpardonable mannerism of style.

These pairs of sentences occur in the sequence of aphorisms which
Oscar Wilde set as a preface to *The Picture of Dorian Gray* (1891).
Their expected stresses and cadences lead the casual reader to
classify them in the familiar category of the provocative epigram
which reduces morality to an impurity of artistic technique. Yet on
a closer inspection it is plain that they offer divergent accounts of
the relation between life and art. To decide which pair bears
Wilde's endorsement we must read the book. No doubt it seems
solemnly wrong-headed to be debating the truth-value of epigrams,
and no doubt Wilde elsewhere in his work shows his scorn for
those who do so, but the paradox of *Dorian Gray* is that epigrams
are like art because both are dangerous, only epigrams are dangerous when they are taken seriously and art is dangerous when it
is not.

The character who speaks with the epigrammatist's voice in the
book is Lord Henry Wotton. He smokes 'heavy opium-tainted
cigarettes', he has a 'romantic olive-coloured face and worn expression', a 'low languid voice', 'dark crescent-shaped eyebrows' and
'cool, white, flower-like hands'. He is allowed remarks such as 'Conscience and cowardice are really the same things, Basil. Conscience
is the trade-name of the firm. That is all'. He seems to fill in every
respect the part of the dandy, the detached flaneur who refuses to
admit that the ideals which the other characters pursue so
earnestly are ultimately of more importance than elegance of dress
or neatness of phrasing. Normally the challenge which the dandy
presents to current moral standards is declined: the central characters in Wilde's plays, for example, simply go on living by conventions which Pinero or Henry Arthur Jones would find perfectly
acceptable. Like Wilde, the dandy discovers that a wittily phrased

remark will never be taken seriously and may therefore be made with impunity.

It seems at first as though Lord Henry Wotton had been cast from the same mould as Lord Goring, Lord Darlington and other flippant peers. Early in the book he observes:

> Now, the value of an idea has nothing whatsoever to do with the sincerity of the man who expresses it. Indeed, the probabilities are that the more insincere the man is, the more purely intellectual will the idea be, as in that case it will not be coloured by either his wants, his desires, or his prejudices.   (I/9)[1]

His listener ignores the remark, which seems no more than the dandy's frivolous defence of his own frivolity.[2] Yet in the following chapter Lord Henry takes a similar idea and expounds it at length. It still has the same ring of wilful paradox, but Dorian Gray, the beautiful young man to whom Lord Henry is now speaking, attends to the argument:

> [Lord Henry] 'All influence is immoral—immoral from the scientific point of view.'
> [Dorian] 'Why?'
> 'Because to influence a person is to give him one's own soul. He does not think his natural thoughts, or burn with his natural passions. His virtues are not real to him. His sins, if there are such things as sins, are borrowed. He becomes an echo of someone else's music, an actor of a part that has not been written for him. The aim of life is self-development. To realise one's nature perfectly—that is what each of us is here for. People are afraid of themselves, nowadays. They have forgotten the highest of all duties, the duty that one owes to one's self. Of course they are charitable. They feed the hungry, and clothe the beggar. But their own souls starve, and are naked. Courage has gone out of our race. Perhaps we never really had it. The terror of society, which is the basis of morals, the terror of God, which is the secret of religion—these are the two things that govern us. And yet . . . I believe that if one man were to live out his life fully and completely, were to give form to every feeling, expression to every thought, reality to every dream—I believe that the world would gain such a fresh impulse of joy that we would forget all the maladies of mediævalism, and return to the Hellenic ideal—to something finer, richer, than the Hellenic ideal, it may be. But the bravest man amongst us is afraid of himself. The mutilation of the savage has its tragic survival in the self-denial that mars our lives. We are punished for our refusals. Every impulse that we strive to strangle broods in the mind, and poisons us. The body sins once, and has done with its sin, for action is a mode of purification. Nothing remains then but the recollection of a pleasure, or the luxury of a regret. The only

way to get rid of a temptation is to yield to it. Resist it, and your soul grows sick with longing for the things it has forbidden to itself, with desire for what its monstrous laws have made monstrous and unlawful. It has been said that the great events of the world take place in the brain. It is in the brain, and the brain only, that the great sins of the world take place also. You, Mr. Gray, you yourself, with your rose-red youth and your rose-white boyhood, you have had passions that have made you afraid, thoughts that have filled you with terror, day-dreams and sleeping dreams whose mere memory might stain your cheek with shame—'

'Stop!' faltered Dorian Gray, 'stop! you bewilder me. I don't know what to say. There is some answer to you, but I cannot find it.'   (II/17–18)

This emphasis on the duty that one owes to oneself is the key to the book and to many other books written in the last eighty years, especially if we amplify it by a passage from Wilde's letters (487–8) —'A man whose desire is to be something separate from himself, to be a Member of Parliament, or a successful grocer, or a prominent solicitor, or a judge, or something equally tedious, invariably succeeds in being what he wants to be. That is his punishment. Those who want a mask have to wear it.'[3] It is interesting to note Wilde's sense of the pressure that 'They' exert on the individual and his condemnation of yielding to this pressure as an act of *mauvaise foi*, but of more immediate importance is the function in the novel of Lord Henry's speech. The ideas that 'the aim of life is self-development' and that the supreme value lies in the one man living 'out his life fully and completely' bring logically with them the further idea that this can be done only by defying conventional morality, which would convert a man into 'an echo of someone else's music'. Sin is thus the only way 'to realise one's nature perfectly' and the only token of freedom.

In another long speech shortly afterwards Lord Henry impresses on Dorian the value of youth and the horrors of old age. At a critical moment he links this with his earlier exhortations to follow 'the impulse' wherever it leads:

Ah! realize your youth while you have it. Don't squander the gold of your days, listening to the tedious, trying to improve the hopeless failure, or giving away your life to the ignorant, the common, and the vulgar. These are the sickly aims, the false ideals, of our age. Live! Live the wonderful life that is in you! Let nothing be lost upon you. Be always searching for new sensations. Be afraid of nothing.   (II/22)

Wilde's description of the way in which this speech is received is a fine illustration of his method:

Dorian Gray listened, open-eyed and wondering. The spray of lilac fell from his hand upon the gravel. A furry bee came and buzzed round it for a moment. Then it began to scramble all over the oval stellated globe of the tiny blossoms. He watched it with that strange interest in trivial things that we try to develop when things of high import make us afraid, or when we are stirred by some new emotion for which we cannot find expression, or when some thought that terrifies us lays sudden siege to the brain and calls on us to yield. After a time the bee flew away. He saw it creeping into the stained trumpet of a Tyrian convolvulus. The flower seemed to quiver, and then swayed gently to and fro.

Lord Henry, unlike his fellow dandies, is not without effect on his hearers. He impregnates Dorian with the idea that a morality derived from other people is 'monstrous', that self-denial is a kind of mutilation, and that old age brings only the memory of 'the exquisite temptations that we had not the courage to yield to'. Dorian lives the life that Lord Henry recommends, accepting the argument that self-restraint is a form of cowardice and that the only consequences of an action are physical. At this point Wilde introduces the central device of his plot. Dorian discovers that his life of sin and debauchery does not affect his appearance at all: instead a portrait of him, painted when he was at the height of his youth and beauty, steadily becomes more heavily marked by age and corruption. Jacob Korg has suggested that Wilde is working here in the fruitful *fin-de-siècle* tradition of stories about the *doppelgänger*, such as *Dr Jekyll and Mr Hyde*.[4] In the course of a survey of nineteenth-century thought in which he relates the work of Taine and F. H. Bradley to ideas about the nature of schizophrenia Korg concludes that *Dorian Gray* is an attempt to present the sense of the fluidity of personal identity. Thus he sees the notion of the double self as a device to prevent the self from vanishing under the pressure of personal introspection. 'The monstrous notion of a double is a product of the rage of Caliban. It was the last, desperate holding operation of the romantic ego, individualism in another, heretical form.' This seems to me a fair account of most of the works Korg deals with, but not true of *Dorian Gray*. The picture is not a double, or a genuine alter ego, but a scapegoat, an invention for satisfying the condition in the question. 'If the physical consequences to himself of his actions can be escaped, is there any reason why a man should not do precisely what he pleases, thus acting from his authentic self and not as a vehicle for the moral ideas of other people?' Professor Korg makes it instrumental, and suggests that once a double self has been created the next step is to postulate multiple selves which rapidly become so numerous that there is no self at all: thus the personality disintegrates.

I do not dispute the disintegration of personality. Where I differ from Professor Korg is over the question of agency. In my view the agency of Dorian's degeneration is the doctrine which Lord Henry implants. Freed from the natural consequences of his actions, Dorian tries to live an entirely selfish life. I borrow Professor Korg's words once more to describe what happens:

> Though yielding to the senses means adopting the identity of an animal, Dorian feels that this alienation is preferable to the deforming effects of the self-denial imposed by the tightly-knit world of conventional life. What he wants is a world where obligations, memory, habit, custom, and all the strands that bind the personality together have been cast aside. . . . Dorian goes [to the opium-den] because he finds that the isolated pleasures of 'the new Hedonism' cannot form a satisfying reality, and that he must turn to experiences of violence and disgust to gain a sense of actuality.

On his way to the opium-den Dorian repeats to himself the words that Lord Henry had said on the first day that they had met—'With hideous iteration the bitter lips of Dorian Gray shaped and reshaped those subtle words'—until they reconcile him to his sordid surroundings:

> Ugliness that had once been hateful to him [Dorian] because it made things real, became dear to him now for that very reason. Ugliness was the one reality. The coarse brawl, the loathsome den, the crude violence of disordered life, the very vileness of thief and outcast, were more vivid, in their intense actuality of impression, than all the gracious shapes of Art, the dreamy shadows of Song.   (XVI/186)

This inversion of values is a necessary consequence of abandoning accepted standards of behaviour: in order to demonstrate one's freedom to the full one must not simply ignore but positively defy established ways of living. This accounts for the repeated hints of corruption and perversion in the book. In *De Profundis* (164) Wilde refers to 'the note of doom that like a purple thread runs through . . . *Dorian Gray*'.[5] The sense that he is exploring the dark side of the mind helps to reconcile the reader to the novel's most obvious awkwardness, the magical agency of the portrait, which, but for the general suggestion of sinister distortion, would be hard to accommodate to the careful detailing of London life.

At length Dorian, by now a murderer, finds the picture that bears his guilt an intolerable burden. 'It had been like conscience to him. Yes, it had been conscious. He would destroy it.' Determined to obliterate even this transferred consequence of his profligate life he takes up a knife. 'It was bright, and glistened. As it had killed the painter, so it would kill the painter's work, and all that that meant. It would kill the past, and when that was dead he would be free.' He stabs the picture, a horrible cry is heard, and the servants eventually force their way into the room. The book ends:

> When they entered they found hanging upon the wall a splendid por-
> trait of their master as they had last seen him, in all the wonder of his
> exquisite youth and beauty. Lying on the floor was a dead man, in
> evening dress, with a knife in his heart. He was withered, wrinkled, and
> loathsome of visage. It was not till they had examined the rings that
> they recognized who it was.

Dorian Gray discovers at last that complete freedom cannot be found by rejecting morality, by avoiding the consequences of one's acts and by destroying the past. Such freedom has only one issue.

Four points remain to be made. First, on a general level, the novel is technically one of the great achievements of the nineteenth century in the realm of prose fiction. It has no superfluities. Even Lord Henry's more obtrusive epigrams have their place in the scheme since nobody takes them seriously and he deduces from this that what is artistically presented can have no practical effect. He tells Dorian, 'Art has no influence upon action. It annihilates the desire to act. It is superbly sterile.' From this erroneous belief all the multiplying ironies of the book take their origin. Just as Lord Henry is shown to be wrong to insist on the inefficacy of art, so he is wrong to suppose that Dorian will pay no attention when he is told, for example, 'Good resolutions are useless attempts to interfere with scientific laws. Their origin is pure vanity. . . . They are simply cheques that men draw on a bank where they have no account.' Every episode in the book is designed to show the contamination of a man who repudiates society in the name of authenticity and tries to live as a pure uncontaminated individual. The quality of the writing, except for some melodramatic lines of dialogue, is extraordinarily consistent. The images in the descriptive passages seem now perhaps a little obvious—'The moon hung low in the sky like a yellow skull'—but Wilde places them with great sureness. The final impression is not of self-indulgent over-writing but of cleanness and certainty.

The irony extends to the second point, for, in spite of Lord Henry's and Wilde's own assertions of the ethical neutrality of art the book invites a surprisingly forthright moral construction. Sin in the name of freedom brings not freedom but death. This is firm and clear enough. Yet the novel is not a tract. I do not think that we need to make use of our knowledge of Wilde's career to perceive that Dorian is not presented merely as a vain young man who is

fool enough to take literally the casuistry of a cynical friend. What
is said about the hypocrisy of a conformist morality is in part true
and is felt to be so. Dorian is not wholly mistaken to despise the
values he is expected to receive from others and to hate the social
code that led his grandfather to have his father done away with.
His suffering is not just the convenient retribution traditionally
visited on those who break the rules, but springs from a genuine
agony of the human condition. Although Wilde shows no sign of
approving of Dorian's solution he is candid in his presentation of
the painful difficulty of reconciling what a man owes to society
with what he knows he owes to himself. The novel is a parable, but
an honest parable.

Thirdly, the most important single action of Dorian's life is his
sudden and brutal rejection of a poor young actress, Sibyl Vane,
who is in love with him. During their last interview (VII/85‒88) she
tells him that since she has known what it is to love in real life she
is no longer able to act the part of Juliet with any conviction. 'I
might mimic a passion that I do not feel, but I cannot mimic one
that burns me like fire.' Dorian despises her for this, saying 'How
little you can know of love, if you say it mars your art! Without
your art you are nothing.' He leaves her and she kills herself in despair. Lord Henry's consolation to Dorian is 'You must think of that
lonely death in the tawdry dressing-room simply as a strange lurid
fragment from some Jacobean tragedy, as a wonderful scene from
Webster, or Ford, or Cyril Tourneur. . . . Mourn for Ophelia, if you
like. Put ashes on your head because Cordelia was strangled. Cry
out against Heaven because the daughter of Brabantio died. But
don't waste your tears over Sibyl Vane., She was less real that they
are.' As I have said, the relation between art and life is a pervasive
topic in the novel: it is disastrous to suppose that they are completely insulated from one another, but it is equally fatal to fail to
distinguish rightly between them.

This brings me to my final point, a consideration of chapter XI. It
is here that we can see most clearly the cardinal place of *Dorian
Gray* in a major modern literary tradition. No doubt when I suggested earlier that the novel was without superfluities there were
those who considered that this chapter constituted an obvious re-
futing case. At the end of chapter X Lord Henry sends Dorian 'a
book bound in yellow paper, the cover slightly torn and the edges
soiled'. Dorian becomes absorbed by it. 'Cloudless, and pierced by
one solitary star, a copper-green sky gleamed through the
windows. He read on by its wan light till he could read no more.'
Wilde gives a full description of the atmosphere of the book. The
most telling sentences are: 'It was a poisonous book. The heavy
odour of incense seemed to cling about its pages and to trouble the

brain.' The book is *A Rebours* (published in 1884) and Wilde devotes the whole of chapter XI to an account of the fascination which it exercises over Dorian. Lord Henry had already persuaded Dorian that happiness could come only from indulging his desires: Huysmans' book completes the work by irrevocably inclining Dorian to 'the worship of the senses', to the new Hedonism whose aim 'was to be experience itself, and not the fruits of experience'. Thus Dorian spends his days and nights in 'action and experiment', exploring the mysteries of the senses. He studies perfumes—'musk that troubled the brain', 'champak that stained the imagination', 'spikenard that sickens', and 'hovenia that makes men mad': he develops a taste for 'the harsh intervals and shrill discords of barbaric music' and forms a collection of strange instruments, *juruparis*, flutes of human bones, the *teponaztli*: he takes up the study of jewels—chrysoberyl, cymophane, peridot and spinel—and stories about the great jewels of the past—'Marco Polo had seen the inhabitants of Zipangu place rose-coloured pearls in the mouths of the dead . . . Edward II gave to Piers Gaveston a suit of red-gold armour studded with jacinths, a collar of gold roses set with turquoise-stones, and a skull-cap *parsemé* with pearls': 'then he turned his attention to embroideries' and Wilde gives a similar echoing catalogue of great garments and tapestries of past years and fine textiles and vestments of the present—'the Dacca gauzes, that from their transparency are known in the East as "woven air", and "running water", and "evening dew".'

I have tried to represent briefly the profuse and carefully-wrought descriptions which Wilde gives of Dorian's quest for aesthetic pleasure and the way in which he offers his readers a sense of physical delight in the exotic names and evocative associations of material objects. This is not just fine writing or learning ostentatiously displayed, but a necessary part of his complex purpose. He states fully and fairly the rewards of a life of sensual gratification: on the other hand he records accurately the beginning of the process by which ugliness becomes for Dorian 'the one reality'. 'He would often adopt certain modes of thought that he knew to be really alien to his nature, abandon himself to their subtle influences.' 'He felt a curious delight in the thought that Art, like Nature, has her monsters, things of bestial shape and with hideous voices.' 'He used to wonder at the shallow psychology of those who conceive the Ego in man as a thing simple, permanent, reliable, and of one essence. To him, man was a being with myriad lives and myriad sensations, a complex multiform creature that bore within itself strange legacies of thought and passion, and whose very flesh was tainted with the monstrous maladies of the dead.' He becomes fascinated by the portraits of his ancestors,

especially those about whom 'strange stories' were told. He traces
his literary ancestry also. 'There were times when it appeared to
Dorian Gray that the whole of history was merely the record of his
own life . . . as it had been in his brain and in his passions. He felt
that he had known them all, those strange terrible figures that had
passed across the stage of the world and made sin so marvellous
and evil so full of subtlety.'[6] This brings him back directly to *A
Rebours*, particularly to the chapter in which des Esseintes identifies himself with the more corrupt Roman emperors. 'Over and
over again Dorian used to read this fantastic chapter, and the two
chapters immediately following, in which, as in some curious
tapestries or cunningly-wrought enamels, were pictured the awful
and beautiful forms of those whom Vice and Blood and Weariness
had made monstrous or mad.' Another catalogue follows,
abominable crimes chronicled in glittering prose. The chapter concludes with the following paragraph:

> There was a horrible fascination in them all. He saw them at night, and
> they troubled his imagination in the day. The Renaissance knew of
> strange manners of poisoning—poisoning by a helmet and a lighted
> torch, by an embroidered glove and a jewelled fan, by a gilded
> pomander and by an amber chain. Dorian Gray had been poisoned by a
> book. There were moments when he looked on evil simply as a mode
> through which he could realize his conception of the beautiful.
>
> (XI/146)

The part played by *A Rebours* in *Dorian Gray* is plain. A fantasy of
sensual indulgence is presented and accepted as a manual of moral
behaviour: the confusion of ethical and aesthetic values is the
centre of the novel. Dorian's apparently harmless delight in the
senses leads by clear steps to a fascination with evil and perversion. This is decadence and is shown for what it is. The whole of
Dorian Gray, but especially the treatment of Huysmans, is designed
to show the shallowness of such epigrams as 'All art is quite
useless' and 'Art never expresses anything but itself' and 'There is
no such thing as a moral or an immoral book. Books are well
written, or badly written. That is all.'
In *De Profundis* Wilde stated clearly his consciousness of his significance in his own time:

> I was a man who stood in symbolic relations to the art and culture of
> my age. I had realized this for myself at the very dawn of my manhood,
> and had forced my age to realize it afterwards. Few men hold such a
> position in their own lifetime, and have it so acknowledged. . . . With
> me it was different. I felt it myself, and made others feel it. Byron was a
> symbolic figure, but his relations were to the passion of his age and its

weariness of passion. Mine were to something more noble, more permanent, of more vital issue, of larger scope. The gods had given me almost everything.   (151)

Yet in the following paragraph, charting the course of his own downfall, he says 'Tired of being on the heights, I deliberately went to the depths in the search for new sensation.'

The central part played in *Dorian Gray* by the extended exploration of the paradoxes of *A Rebours* is no accident. Wilde is consciously relating his book to Huysmans and through him to the Baudelaire of *Les Fleurs du Mal* and thus to one of the great forms of modern literature—the study of the man who, for the sake of freedom, is compelled to do what his nature abhors.[7] My thesis in the remainder of this chapter will be that this intolerable situation, and the various possible ways of escaping from it, constitute one of the major preoccupations of the novelists and dramatists of our own time.

II A NOTE ON GIDE AND GENET

Michel, the central character of Gide's *L'Immoraliste* (1902), is a young man who marries a girl called Marceline although he does not love her. They travel for his health to Biskra, where he meets Arab boys who restore his love of life. As he becomes stronger he persuades himself of his need to cast aside moral standards: when Marceline protests he replies, 'C'est ce qu'il faut.' He plunges into a subterranean world of disorder and excess, requiring ever more violent amusements, which outrage social proprieties. 'Pour un peu je n'eusse vu dans l'honnêteté que restrictions, conventions ou peur.' Marceline has a miscarriage, and dies through Michel's agency. Michel does not find happiness when he is free. At the end of the book he is stagnating in Biskra 'comme mort'.

In *Les Nourritures Terrestres* (1897) Gide had diagnosed in the human condition the central difficulty of remaining uncommitted (*disponible*): the theme is taken up again at the beginning of Michel's narrative in *L'Immoraliste*—'J'ai besoin de parler, vous dis-je. Savoir se libérer n'est rien: l'ardu, c'est savoir être libre.' It has often been observed that the values of this book derive from Gide's opposition between health and vitality (which is virtuous) and ill-health (which is to be despised). The sickly Marceline, to whom Michel's duty lies, is powerless to compete with the vigorous Arab boys. It is thus necessary for Michel to set aside the claims of convention in favour of the claims of life and to become the amoral man of the book's title, rejecting a code of behaviour that rests on 'la notion du permis et du defendu, dans ce qu'elle a de plus arbitraire'.[8] He has to discover an authentic human experience, and realizes the difficulties he will encounter:

> Il me semblait alors que j'étais né pour une sorte inconnue de trouvailles; et je me passionais étrangement dans ma recherche ténébreuse, pour laquelle je sais que le chercheur devait abjurer et repousser de lui culture, décence et morale.

In the last section of the book he tells those who have listened to his story:

> Il me semble parfois que ma vraie vie n'a pas encore commencé. Arrachez-moi d'ici à présent, et donnez-moi des raisons d'être. Moi je ne sais plus en trouver. Je me suis délivré, c'est possible; mais qu'importe? je souffre de cette liberté sans emploi. . . . Arrachez-moi d'ici; je ne puis le faire moi-même. Quelque chose en ma volonté s'est brisée.

The problem of freedom was one which haunted Gide: in one of his greatest works, *Les Caves du Vatican*, a young man, Lafcadio, is driven to unmotivated murder by the need to assert his autonomy. The narrowness of the line between the *acte gratuit* and an insane obsession is exposed even more starkly in Genet's *Querelle de Brest*. The sailor Georges Querelle finds release only by yielding to a compulsion to murder, theft, perversion and betrayal. Because loyalty to one's friends is a virtue he allows his friend Jonas to be hanged for a murder he has committed himself and betrays his friend Gil to the police for a similar offence. Genet comments: 'Please be liberal in your judgment of the attitude we choose to adopt . . . in that it may lead us to discover the given psychological world which upholds the liberty of choice.' Immediately afterwards he has a similar parenthesis—'(Querelle, let us note, very clearly discerned the mechanism by which he would eventually achieve success, since he was, and knew himself to be, at the very heart of liberty of choice)'.[9] The irony of the situation is that in the name of liberty Querelle finds himself in the same sort of bondage to the practices of an inverted morality as the Marquis de Sade, who justified his indulgences on the determinist ground that he was 'only a piece of mechanism that Nature moves as she wills'.

Genet, in *Querelle* and elsewhere,[10] embodies in a human situation the metaphysical difficulty of defining a free action if 'action' presupposes a motive force. One set of compulsions is rejected with contempt, only to be changed for another set: if the first set is more 'natural' then freedom must be asserted by

12

choosing 'unnatural' conduct. 'Crime' and 'abnormality' are merely categories invented by other people to stop you doing what you want to do. But the arduous task, as Gide observed, is not simply to make a single free gesture but to continue free. The possible ways of escaping from this situation, all equally desperate, find their fullest expression in the modern drama.

III THE THEATRE OF THE PERVERSE WILL

> Every man is capable of showing his contempt for the cruelty and stupidity of the Universe by making his own life a poem of incoherence and stupidity.

This pronouncement by Alfred Jarry (1873–1907) is not a great deal more ridiculous than most manifestos. It is easy to see how it can be used to justify not only the Theatre of the Absurd but also the Theatre of Cruelty, and I shall not argue the case in detail. The quickest way to make the point is by direct quotation from Antonin Artaud (1896–1948). It is necessary to begin by making it clear that by Theatre of Cruelty, a phrase which he coined himself, Artaud does not mean a Grand Guignol theatre relying exclusively on realistic presentation of torture and physical pain:

> In fact, cruelty is not synonymous with bloodshed, martyred flesh, or crucified enemies. Associating cruelty and torture is only one minor aspect of the problem. Practising cruelty involves a higher determination to which the executioner-tormentor is also subject and which he must be *resolved* to endure when the time comes. Above all, cruelty is very lucid, a kind of strict control and submission to necessity.
>
> ('Letters of Cruelty: *First Letter*', pp. 79–80)[11]

> I use the word cruelty . . . in the sense of the inescapably necessary pain without which life could not continue.   (ibid., *Second Letter*, p. 80)

Possibly 'Theatre of Physical Sensation'[12] or 'Theatre of Suffering' would be a less tendentious title. Whatever it is called, two facts are plain—first that Artaud's conception of theatre depends on freeing the drama from conventional moral and social values, and secondly that his theories, taken in their widest application, have been of profound influence on the theatre of our time.

The force and incoherence of Artaud's ideas are both impressively displayed in 'Theatre and the Plague'. The essay begins with a vivid description of the plague in which every mental and physical symptom is detailed with admiration. At the point when the reader is bewildered and sickened Artaud makes his typical thrust:

> The scum of the populace, immunised so it seems by their frantic greed, enter the open houses and help themselves to riches they know will serve no purpose or profit. At this point, theatre establishes itself. Theatre, that is to say that momentary pointlessness which drives them to useless acts without immediate profit.   (15)

This astonishing collocation is maintained throughout the essay:

> There is something both victorious and vengeful in theatre just as in the plague. . . .   (18)

> If fundamental theatre is like the plague, this is not because it is contagious, but because like the plague it is a revelation, urging forward the exteriorisation of a latent undercurrent of cruelty through which all the perversity of which the mind is capable, whether in a person or a nation, becomes localised.   (21)

The value of this 'perversity' lies, not unexpectedly, in its power to strip away the deadening masks which we wear through convention:

> And finally from a human viewpoint we can see that theatre action is as beneficial as the plague, impelling us to see ourselves as we are, making the masks fall and divulging our world's lies, aimlessness, meanness, and even two-facedness. It shakes off stifling material dullness which even overcomes the senses' clearest testimony, and collectively reveals their dark powers and hidden strength to men, urging them to take a nobler, more heroic stand in the face of destiny than they would have assumed without it.   (22)

The drama of the past, being dead, can only reinforce dead ideas: hence the necessity to break away from 'the conformity that makes us confuse the sublime, the concepts, and the objects with the forms they have acquired in our minds through the ages—our affected, snobbish, aesthetic mentality the public no longer understands' (57). The quotation is from an essay firmly entitled 'No More Masterpieces' in which Artaud sums up his view of traditional culture—'There are too many signs that everything which used to sustain our lives no longer does so and we are all mad, desperate and sick' (58).

Thus when Artaud comes to write his two Manifestos of the Theatre of Cruelty he offers what is by now a reasonably familiar account of what it will achieve. 'Repudiating psychological man with his clear-cut personality and feelings, it will appeal to the whole man, not social man submissive to the law, warped by religions and precepts' (*Second Manifesto*, p. 82). So far all is more or less of a piece. The difficulty comes when we ask precisely what plays will show all this happening. Can we, in other words, test Artaud's theories by going to the Theatre of Cruelty and observing it in operation as he claims? It must be admitted that he is not profuse with evidence. If we except his general commendation of the Eastern Theatre, there is very little except *'Tis Pity She's a Whore*[13] and an impressive list of projects, including

> One of the Marquis de Sade's tales, its eroticism transposed, allegorically represented and cloaked in the sense of a violent externalisation of cruelty, masking the remainder.   (*First Manifesto*, 77–8)[14]

The audience, who are to be liberated by the new theatre, find themselves operated on like helpless but unanaesthetized patients:

> The secret is to irritate those pressure points as if the muscles were flayed.
> The rest is achieved by screams.   ('An Affective Athleticism' 94–5)

Much more might be said here: in particular it would be illuminating to look more closely at actual examples of the Theatre of Cruelty.[15] For the moment I simply point to the *prima facie* contradiction that the attempt to break free from the deadening effect of traditional social and artistic pressures entails accepting in their place an equally dominant, if more spectacular, set of physical compulsions.

I shall treat the Theatre of the Absurd as fundamentally different in method from the Theatre of Cruelty, while emphasizing their common purpose.[16] The whole tenor of Artaud's theatre is away from verbal to physical qualities. Since his end is to create an atmosphere partaking equally of the tribal ritual and the torture chamber, words are used primarily as objects for assaulting the audience or instruments for operating on them: the play itself is rarely of great literary interest. The audience is the enemy. The Theatre of the Absurd, though its designs on the audience are equally aggressive, is marked by a strong linguistic bias and a continual reference to conventional literary modes. It is as if the same problem confronted both sets of playwrights—to depict on the stage a man acting freely: whereas the creators of the Theatre of Cruelty offer the pointlessly and sickeningly brutal act as their instance of free behaviour, with the results which I have just described, the dramatists of the Absurd explore the alternative line of taking the typical free act to be that of saying something which is not governed by the normal laws of discourse. The result is a disintegration not simply of language but of logic and personality.

Ionesco's 'anti-play' *La Cantatrice Chauve* (produced 1950) displays in the most obvious way the breaking down of language. Its concluding scene begins with an exchange of banal or nonsensical observations, such as,

M Martin	Le plafond est en haut, le plancher est en bas.
Mme Smith	Quand je dis oui, c'est un façon de parler.

The remarks gradually depend more and more on rhymes, puns and assonances until M Smith cries 'A bas le cirage!' After this the speeches of the characters are even more firmly determined by the sound of the words. One speech of M Smith is 'Kakatoes' repeated ten times, Mme Smith replies 'Quelle cacade' repeated nine times, and M Martin comments 'Quelle cascade de cacades' repeated eight times. The characters pick up syllables from one another and volley them angrily back until the following fierce exchange takes place:

M Smith	Le pape dérape! Le pape n'a pas de soupape. La soupape a un pape.
Mme Martin	Bazar, Balzac, Bazaine!
M Martin	Bizarre, beaux-arts, baisers!
M Smith	A, e, i. o, u, a, e, i, o, u, a, e, i, o, u, i!
M Martin	B, c, d, f, g, l, m, n, p, r, s, t, v, w, x, z!
M Martin	De l'ail a l'eau, du lait a l'ail!
Mme Smith (*imitant le train*)	Teuff, teuff, teuff, teuff, teuff, teuff, teuff, teuff, teuff, teuff, teuff.

The same thing happens at the end of *Les Chaises*. The Orator can only emit 'des râles, des gémissements, des sons gutturaux de muet.'—'He, Mme, mm. mm. Ju, gou, hou, hou. Heu, heu, gu, gou, gueue.' All he can write on a blackboard is 'ANGEPAIN' followed by 'NNAA NNM NWNWNW V':[17] This is a clear and literal collapse of words.

The breakdown of logic is equally common, as in sentences like 'C'est une précaution inutile, mais absolument nécessaire', or in M. Smith's description of his clock—'Elle marche mal. Elle a l'esprit de contradiction. Elle indique toujours le contraire de l'heure qu'il est.' In *La Leçon* vast stretches of the instructor's addresses to his pupil are deliberate derangements of sense. A compact example is 'Attention, car les ressemblances sont grandes. Ce sont des ressemblances identiques.'

Personality is similarly fragile. The Instructor and the pupil in *La Leçon* speak one another's lines. In *La Cantatrice Chauve* M and Mme Martin visit the Smiths together. When they are left alone they at once devote their time to establishing that they have met before and that they are in fact married to each other. The maid comments, aside, 'Malgré les coïncidences extraordinaires qui semblent être des preuves définitives, Donald et Elisabeth . . . ne sont pas Donald et Elisabeth. Il a beau croire il est Donald, elle a beau se croire Elisabeth. Il a beau croire qu'elle est Elisabeth. Elle a beau croire qu'il est Donald: ils se trompent amèrement. Mais qui est le véritable Donald? Quelle est la véritable Elisabeth? Qui donc a interêt a faire durer cette confusion? Je n'en sais rien. Ne tâchons pas de le savoir. Laissons les choses comme elles sont.' Similarly M and Mme Smith discuss a family of which all the members are called Bobby Watson.

All these 'absurdities' can be brought under one heading—the deliberate confounding of the audience's expectations that the world of the play will conform to the general pattern of behaviour which may safely be taken for granted in the world outside the play. Physical laws are set aside, as mushrooms, coffee cups, chairs, furniture or noses multiply without explanation. The expected consequence of a remark or of an action is averted or delayed until we cannot tell whether it is a consequence or not. The normal assumptions about what constitutes a rational response to a situation are shown to be no more than assumptions which the play has falsified. The conventions of logical discourse are replaced by arbitrary associations. Meaning vanishes until words are no more than sounds. At length we are unable to predict the consequences of any event. In scene VIII of *La Cantatrice Chauve* M Smith argues that when the doorbell rings there is always someone there, Mme Smith that the ringing of the doorbell shows that nobody is there. The fireman satisfies both of them by saying, 'Vous avez un peu raison tous les deux. Lorsqu'on sonne à la porte, des fois il y a quelqu'un, d'autres fois il n'y a personne. . . . Les choses sont simples, en réalité.' The notion of life as a consistent correlation between events is undermined. The result is a *dépaysement*, at first comic, later psychologically disturbing and shocking.[18]

IV A NOTE ON BECKETT

> The situation is that of him who is helpless, cannot act, in the end
> cannot paint, since he is obliged to paint. The act is of him who,
> helpless, unable to act, acts, in the event paints, since he is obliged to
> paint.
> *D.*—Why is he obliged to paint?
> *B.*—I don't know.
> *D.*—Why is he helpless to paint?
> *B.*—Because there is nothing to paint and nothing to paint with.—
> BECKETT, *Third Dialogue*

It will be plain that the basic procedure of this chapter is to show
that in certain central texts in the literature of our time the
severing of the conventional bonds between an individual and his
society leads not to freedom but to a different kind of imprisonment. The most ostentatiously anti-conventional of modern
novelists, William Burroughs, is in the end reduced, as has been
well observed, to treating the body as 'a corpse full of cravings',
and to searching in vain for a self-abolishing language and even a
self-abolishing literary structure.[19] Other examples abound, but the
clearest and most interesting is Samuel Beckett. It is a commonplace of criticism that his plays, never crowded with circumstantial
detail, have become progressively starker and sparer, until the
later pieces stand like a sardonic commentary on the human condition, friendless, plotless, motionless and eventually wordless.[20]

One of Beckett's most telling plays is *Happy Days*, first performed
in 1961.[21] There are two characters, Winnie and Willie; neither can
move very much and Willie can hardly speak. When the play opens
Winnie is buried to the waist in a heap of earth, while Willie is lying
behind it out of sight. The stage direction calls for the 'maximum of
simplicity and symmetry'. The action is, necessarily, circumscribed, and derives its power from its limitations as the audience
watches the enormous expenditure of effort by Winnie for the
most trivial ends. At one point, for example, she wishes to use a
magnifying glass to read the writing on a toothbrush handle. The
stage direction reads:

> WINNIE *lays down glass and brush, takes handkerchief from bodice, takes
> off and polishes spectacles, puts on spectacles, looks for glass, takes up
> and polishes glass, lays down glass, looks for brush, takes up brush and
> wipes handle, lays down brush, puts handkerchief back in bodice, looks for
> glass, takes up glass, looks for brush, takes up brush and examines handle
> through glass.*   (pp. 15–16)

As Winnie's monologue develops, the point is made more and more strongly that there is no activity except a pointless routine, which is nevertheless necessary to fill the vast empty stretches of human life:

> *Winnie*   Is not that so, Willie, that even words fail, at times? (*Pause. Back front*) What is one to do then, until they come again? Brush and comb the hair, if it has not been done, or if there is some doubt, trim the nails if they are in need of trimming, these things tide one over (*Pause.*) That is what I mean. (*Pause*) That is all I mean (*Pause*)   (p. 20)[22]

Clearly in a world of this kind the satisfactions will not be of a very high order:

> *Winnie*   Raise a finger, dear, will you please, if you are not quite sense-less. (*Pause*) Do that for me, Willie please, just the little finger, if you are still conscious. (*Pause. Joyful*) Oh all five, you are a darling today, now I may continue with an easy mind.   (p. 29)

The stage direction for the opening of the second scene is as follows:

> *Scene as before.* WINNIE *embedded up to neck, hat on head, eyes closed. Her head, which she can no longer turn, nor bow, nor raise, faces front motionless throughout act. Movements of eyes as indicated.*   (p. 37)

As in all Beckett's work, an increasingly oppressive physical constriction is the dramatic sign of a limitation of human possibilities. Far from bringing freedom, isolation becomes itself a more painful kind of imprisonment. The phrase 'solitary confinement' expresses the temper of almost all Beckett's plays. The novels may seem to offer a much richer field of experience, but in all of them what predominates is a similar sense that they deal only with men who cannot make effective contact with other men.[23] The best that can be offered is a grim unreasoning private obstinacy, as at the end of *The Unnameable*—'Perhaps [the words] have carried me to the threshold of my story, that would surprise me, if it opens it will be I, it will be the silence where I am. I don't know. I'll never know, in the silence you don't know, you must go on, I can't go on, I'll go on.'

In addition to the works referred to in the notes see Richard Ellmann, *Golden Codgers* (O.U.P., 1973), essays 3, 4, and 5, pp. 39–100; J. H. Matthews, *Theatre in Dada and Surrealism* (Syracuse P., 1974), pp. 17–43, 133–54.

13

Fictions of the Prison State

Clive Barry's short novel *Crumb Borne* (1965) is set in a prison camp. The nationality of the prisoners is not specified, neither is that of the guards. The prisoners know one another only by names such as the Hut Leader and the Professor. The novel is in part about the oppression of the prisoners by the guards, but is more deeply concerned with the enclosed system of society devised by the prisoners themselves:

> Like a heap of oysters on a rock, they were not really trying to con-
> struct anything. Each was merely competing for security of position.
> Any prisoner preferring not to be in the heap was excused from com-
> petition, but he thereby lost the protection of neighbours.   (5)[1]

This society is essentially competitive and hierarchical, ferocity at the centre breeding fear at the circumference.

> There was one prisoner however who failed utterly in penetrating
> society. Since his dealings with others were shamelessly accommoda-
> ting, he was soon squeezed to the bottom of society where, for his
> meanness of enterprise, he was given the nickname of Frugal.   (5)

The main interest of the novel lies in the prisoners' way of dealing with Frugal: the situation is thus essentially a political one. A dialogue between the Professor and the Hut Leader makes the point economically:

> [*Professor*] 'It is no good saying that Frugal would object to being elimin-
> ated.'
> [*Leader*] 'You mean it would be a sort of privilege for him?'
> 'No one would want to prolong the agony of prison life.'
> 'Oh, I see, Professor'. . . .
> 'For his own benefit, Frugal has got to be shaken up.'
> 'Very well, Professor. What is it you want to do?'
> 'But I don't want to do what I want. Can't you see? That is the whole
> point. Frugal wants to be taught a lesson.'
> 'Hmm.'   (21)

In this microcosm of the State, political processes are exaggerated, and the dangers of any system of government accentuated:

> Security was dangerous. The prisoners' weaknesses were aggravated by the sanctuary they were in. Not healed by it. Starvation itself among free men would have been a spur to greater effort. In the compound it only made them shuffle.
> The barbed-wire could be blamed for everything. Its protection increased the prisoner's vulnerability. Every scratch became a festering sore. Every carbuncle a feverish colony. Every conversation a mental abrasion. The prisoners were being protected to death.   (97)

The result is an enforced conformity, indeed an anonymity. The prisoners recover their identity momentarily when they are called by their names at roll-call and then at once return to the world of nicknames, 'sucked along in the slipstream of ministerial powers' (86).

It is Frugal's insistence on retaining his individuality that makes him difficult to fit into the system of prison life:

> The Hut Leader scowled at a thistle which was somewhat apart from the others. It was an inconceivably distorted specimen. Its leaves had been twisted into probing antennae. Its stem was unravelled pithless fibre.
> The Hut Leader always said he hated thistles. This one somehow reminded him of Frugal. He thrust his knee into the tangle of wiry cellulose and ground it savagely into the earth. But it recoiled into an erect attitude after each grinding. The damned thing seemed imperishable.   (81)

Eventually the Hut Leader tells Frugal, 'If you won't be like everyone else, Frugal, you won't be allowed to live in the hut. You've got to develop some moral responsibility.' Frugal replies, 'All right. I accept that.' 'Well, for God's sake give yourself a character the others can deal with.' 'No. I mean the part about not living in the hut.' 'You must bear in mind,' the Leader says, 'that almost no one could survive outside the hut.' 'Being almost no one is my business,' Frugal replies. In an entirely convincing ending he not only leaves the hut but also escapes from the prison camp. 'A wisp of a man he was, scarcely able to stand against the wind, yet prison society had never really touched him' (128).

I

In our time the destiny of man presents its meaning in political terms.
                                                    —THOMAS MANN

What in this century do men feel as the chief limitation on their freedom? To answer this question we must, if Mann is correct, discuss freedom in its political aspect even though this entails considering texts which are not of the same commanding stature as those dealt with in earlier periods. There is a series of novels and a small group of plays which treat directly of the relation of the individual man and the modern State, or indirectly with the same theme expressed in terms of the individual in prison, in the army, in a court of law or a similar institution which symbolizes the State in its constrictive aspect.

The theme of the individual resisting tyranny is not new. *Prometheus Unbound*, *The Prisoner of Chillon* and *Fidelio* are obvious examples. But they all assume that the tyranny is exercised by a despot who can be overthrown. The prisoners will emerge into the sunshine, there will be a great cry of 'Freiheit' and under popular rule everyone will live happily for ever. The question asked by the writers I consider in this chapter is 'But what happens when the individual is oppressed by popular rule, when the tyranny is the tyranny of the majority?'

As well as *Crumb Borne* the novels I have in mind include *Darkness at Noon*, *Brave New World*, *1984*, *Animal Farm*, *Catch-22*, *The Fixer*, *Fahrenheit 451*, *We*, *Bend Sinister*, *Invitation to a Beheading*, *The Comedians*, *The Birthday King*, and *That Hideous Strength*. These seem to me to constitute a sufficiently distinct group. What they have in common is a consideration of the situation of an individual in a society or organization which claims supreme sovereignty in the name of the State, not of a single tyrant, and exacts total obedience from its members. The constraint exercised on the individual may take the form of physical oppression, or it may be a smothering of the opinions of the single man in the opinions of the majority. Godwin's *Caleb Williams* (1794), for example, was designed to show 'the tyranny and perfidiousness exercised by the powerful members of the community against those who are less privileged than themselves'. The systematic hunting-down of Caleb Williams, though not by all the agencies of the State yet by a powerful adversary backed by the law and the forces of the law, is closely in line with later writings on the subject. *Les Misérables* similarly illustrates the way in which a 'grand roman social', initially of the kind I described at the end of the previous chapter, somewhat changes its character when the hero offends against the law of the land. The real responsibility for the oppression of the individual still lies with those who accept a society in which theft is the only alternative to starvation, but the instruments of punishment are those set up by law and thus the hero is physically confined by the agency of the State.

Against this situation, where the conflict between the individual and the State is in a sense accidental, set the position of Stephen Blackpool in *Hard Times*. He refuses for personal reasons to join the union, and his fellow workers reject him from their companionship. The delegate Slackbridge reassures the men that they are acting rightly:

> Was it not the sacred duty of the men of Coketown, with forefathers before them, an admiring world in company with them, and a posterity to come after them, to hurl out traitors from the tents they had pitched in a sacred and a God-like cause? The winds of heaven answered Yes, and bore Yes, east, west, north and south. And consequently three cheers for the United Aggregate Tribunal!
>
> Slackbridge acted as fugleman, and gave the time. The multitude of doubtful faces (a little conscience-stricken) brightened at the sound, and took it up. Private feeling must yield to the common cause. Hurrah! The roof yet vibrated with the cheering, when the assembly dispersed.
>
> (II, ch. iv 'Men and Brothers')

Dickens describes the way in which Stephen's fellow-workers send him to Coventry, refusing to speak to him or look at him, refusing even to walk on the same side of the street. The effect on Stephen is severe and immediate—'It was even harder than he could have believed possible, to separate in his own conscience his abandonment by all his fellows from a baseless sense of shame and disgrace.' Stephen loses his job, is suspected of robbery and becomes a hunted man. But it is in this subsidiary incident of the clash with the Union that Dickens most firmly touches on the features that recur in the novel of political freedom.

I wish to represent original writers as engaged in a continuing debate on these matters, which are of universal importance. To do this it is necessary to set up, however inexpertly and crudely, two divergent patterns of opinion about the relation of the individual and the State: a few leading quotations must suffice. The first is the tradition going back to Locke in which primacy is given to the rights of the individual. Men in the natural state had 'perfect freedom to order their actions, and dispose of their possessions and persons as they think fit, within the bounds of the law of nature, without asking leave or depending upon the will of any other man'. 'Man being born, . . . with a title to perfect freedom and uncontrolled enjoyment of all the rights and privileges of the law of nature . . . no one can be put out of this estate and subjected to the political power of another, without his own consent.' Locke has then to face the first question that confronts a political theorist and explain why any man should obey another man or set of men. To answer this he supposes, like many others, that for the safe-guarding of life, health, liberty and possessions and the arbitration of disputes a Social Contract has been drawn up and agreed. This supposition is not altogether essential to his theory, but is rather a convenient metaphor for expressing it. By this fictional contract the State is created; to the State men commit a limited power, retaining in everything else their own natural rights. This limits their obligation to the State in two ways. The sovereign power can be deposed if it fails to perform the function for which it was appointed: this is a crucial point of difference between Locke's version of the Social Contract and Hobbes's.[2] Secondly men's natural rights are not affected by the Social Contract, nor are their natural duties. 'The keeping of faith belongs to men as men, and not as members of society.' Thus the idea of an overriding loyalty to the nation-state is quite alien to Locke: on the contrary he insists that the sovereign power is itself subject to the law of nature. From all this it is plain that to Locke there is nothing in the least sacrosanct about the State. It is a convenient arrangement and no more. No attempt to pretend otherwise will prevent an oppressed people from discarding an unjust sovereign power. 'Cry up their governors as much as you will for sons of Jupiter, let them be sacred and divine, descended or authorized from Heaven, the same will happen.'

These familiar quotations are echoed in the following centuries by others which are perhaps less familiar but show the unmistak-able impress of Locke's teaching.

Jefferson, for example, says succinctly, 'That government is best which governs least':[3] the corollary is well expressed by Sir Philip Francis when he points out the need for constant vigilance to prevent the powers of government from being misapplied:

> The government of England is a government of law. We betray our-selves, we contradict the spirit of our laws, and we shake the whole system of English jurisprudence, whenever we entrust a discretionary power over the life, liberty, or fortune of the subject, to any man, or set of men, whatsoever, upon a presumption that it will not be abused.

In Europe Constant in particular argued the case against the absolute power of the State with candour and persuasiveness—'It is not the arm that is unjust but the weapon that is too heavy—some weights are too heavy for the human hand,' while in Britain Herbert Spencer commented with characteristic force, 'Let men learn that a legislature is *not* "our God upon earth", though, by the authority they ascribe to it and the things they expect of it, they would seem to think that it is. Let them learn rather that it is an institution serving a purely temporary purpose, whose power, when not stolen, is, at the best, borrowed.' The line of argument that government is an evil tolerated only for its utility and should therefore be kept to a minimum is most briefly expressed by Shaw when he says, 'What we want to know is how little government we can get along with without being murdered in our beds',[4] and is most fully displayed by John Stuart Mill. The celebrated passages from his essay *On Liberty* (1859) are almost too well-known to quote, yet they cannot be omitted from any work that offers to discuss the meaning of freedom:

> If all mankind minus one, were of one opinion, and only one person were of the contrary opinion, mankind would be no more justified in silencing that one person, than he if had the power, would be justified in silencing mankind.

> Such are the differences among human beings in their sources of plea-sure, their susceptibilities of pain, and the operation on them of different physical and moral agencies, that unless there is a corres-ponding diversity in their modes of life, they neither obtain their fair share of happiness, nor grow up to the mental, moral and aesthetic stature of which they are capable.

> Mankind are greater gainers by suffering each other to live as seems good to themselves, than by compelling each to live as seems good to the rest.

> The individual is not accountable to society for his actions, in so far as these concern the interests of no person but himself.

These and other passages are rightly regarded as expressing with unsurpassed clarity a position which is central to any discussion of freedom.

Since the time of Locke many people have welcomed the con-tinuing growth of representative institutions, feeling that demo-cratic party government, however great its obvious disadvantages, at least offered a guarantee of political liberty. But, as Burke had seen, if power resides with society as a whole it can exert unprece-dently great force on a single dissenter. Mill broadens the argu-ment to consider the issues at stake when the enemy of freedom is not an absolute monarch or an oppressive aristocracy but what he calls 'the tyranny of the majority', and attempts to answer the crucial question of how the dissenting individual is to be safe-guarded against the oppression of his fellows:

> Bentham . . . not content with enthroning the majority as sovereign . . . exhausted all the resources of ingenuity in devising means for riveting the yoke of public opinion closer and closer round the necks of all public functionaries, and excluding every possibility of the exercise of the slightest or most temporary influence either by a minority, or by the functionary's own notions of right. Surely when any power has been made the strongest power, enough has been done for it; care is thenceforth wanted rather to prevent that strongest power from swallowing up all others. Wherever all the forces of society act in one single direction, the just claims of the individual human being are in extreme peril.   ('Bentham')

> The majority have not yet learnt to feel the power of the government their power, or its opinions their opinions. When they do so, individual liberty will probably be as much exposed to invasion from the government, as it already is from public opinion.[5]   (*On Liberty* chapter i)

The whole point of *On Liberty* is to demonstrate the dangers of a 'collective mediocrity'[6] which might suppress opposition either directly through the machinery of the state or by establishing a 'collective opinion' which eventually obliterates all alternative ideas, 'the tyranny of the prevailing opinion and feeling', but this does not affect my argument. Whether the oppressing force is organized under the forms of government or not it is still the tyranny of the majority, not of a small group, and the individual is confronted not with a situation which he can evade or depart from but with a total environment attempting to exact conformity.

In some ways *On Liberty* reads like a final elucidation of the problem, at least for nineteenth-century Europe, but Mill's arguments were by no means universally accepted. Those who resisted them did so for various motives: three main schools of opponent may be distinguished. The first were those who adopted a rival view of the *raison d'être* of the state. In *Leviathan* Hobbes had expressed very forcibly the idea that the contract by which a sovereign was given authority was a binding contract which required men to surrender all their rights to a common authority for the sake of protection. Thus he can write 'No Law can be Unjust. The Law is made by the Soveraign Power, and all that is done by such Power, is warranted, and owned by every one of the people; and that which every man will have so, no man can say is unjust.' But he goes on to qualify this by saying, 'A Law that is not Needfull . . . is not Good. A Law may be conceived to be Good, when it is for the benefit of the Soveraign; though it be not neces-

sary for the People; but it is not so.' There are signs here of a
relenting in the iron hand with which Hobbes pictures the
sovereign grasping the throat of his subjects, but they are faint. On
the whole the tenor of *Leviathan* must be taken as asserting as a
theoretical position the absolute authority of government, not with
a view to recommending systematic oppression of the subject but
with a view to establishing unshakeably the legal rights of a
supreme power, the alternative being anarchy, and as consistently
justifying this by asserting the identity of the people with the
government.[7]

An even more important body of opinion in opposition to Mill derived its arguments ultimately from Locke himself, whose theories
of education emphasized the importance to man of his environment and implied that he could be made better: Helvétius added 'by
legislation' and thus became 'the founding father of modern
governmentalism'. This line of thought, since it held out hope of
creating a better world, appealed to many thinkers of the Enlightenment. It is anti-populist, in that it assumes a class of
educators, yet it depends on some powerful source of authority,
such as the democratic state, for the enforcement of the necessary
educative legislation.

The third school of thought is that originating with Rousseau. I
must admit that in spite of many attempts and much expert help,
and in spite even of Professor Starobinski's luminous study,[8] I am
unable to extract from Rousseau's writings any coherent account of
the nature and purposes of the state. At first it seems as though he
were following Hobbes fairly closely. When he writes that the only
valid contract is 'the complete submission of each member with all
his rights to the whole community', and adds, 'for since all make this
complete submission, the conditions are the same for all, and consequently none can have any interest in making them hard for the
others', he does not seem very far removed from Hobbes's 'It is in
the Lawes of a Commonwealth, as in the Lawes of Gaming: whatsoever the Gamesters all agree on, is Injustice to none of them' (ch.
xxx). From this position however Rousseau arrives at his famous
idea of the General Will, which is a disinterested desire on the part
of all to promote the good of all. This endows Society with a positive
moral purpose and for the first time gives prominent expression to
the idea that Society should be not, as Locke thought, a device to
allow individuals enough peace to look after their own moral life
but the active instrument of the improvement, by force if necessary, of the individuals who compose it. For Rousseau the creation
of the State involves not simply the surrender of private rights for
the sake of communal benefits but a surrendering of the individual's purposes (that is, his motives for willing) to the General Will.

This doctrine was to receive a fuller, but perhaps not substantially clearer, expression from Hegel. In his *Phenomenology of the Spirit* he writes of his conviction of the inadequacy of the notion of individual freedom. 'All determinate elements disappear in the loss which the self experiences in its absolute freedom; its negation is meaningless death, the sheer horror of the negative.' A purely subjective notion of freedom to perform actions with no other object than to gratify the ego is quite incommensurate with our ideas of Righteousness. Hegel objected to 'the atomistic principle, which insists on the sway of individual wills, maintaining that all government should emanate from their express power, and have their express sanction'. The larger purpose which is needed by man is to be found in the State. The State expresses itself in its laws and institutions and is the embodiment of Social Righteousness. It is 'the actually existing, realised moral life. For it is the Unity of the universal essential Will with that of the individual; and this is "Morality"'. It is 'the idea of Spirit in the external manifestation of human Will and its Freedom'. It is 'the ethical Universe'. Thus true freedom for men consists in acting in conformity with the precepts of Social Righteousness, and 'nothing short of the State is the actualization of freedom'.

As the middle term between man and the preordained design the nation-state can claim, or rather its representatives can claim on its behalf, almost supernatural authority over its subjects and almost supernatural sanction for its behaviour: as Hegel put it, 'The existence of the State is the movement of God in the world. It is the absolute power on earth; it is its own end and object.' These claims may be as general as Mussolini's glorification of the State as 'self-conscious ethical substance'[9] or as particular as the assertion that a specific role in the world has been allotted to individual nations, sometimes to Britain:

> For England too (equally with any Judah whatsoever) has a History that is Divine; an Eternal Providence presiding over every step of it . . .; guiding England forward to *its* goal and work, which too has been considerable in the world![10]

more often to the United States:

> The *untransacted* destiny of the American people is to subdue the continent—to rush over this vast field to the Pacific Ocean.[11]

> Our manifest destiny to overspread the continent allotted by Providence for the free development of our yearly multiplying millions.[12]

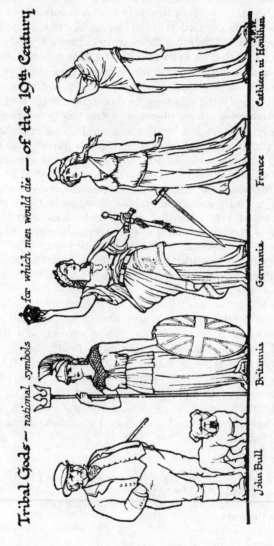

Tribal Gods — national symbols for which men would die — of the 19th Century

John Bull   Britannia   Germania   France   Cathleen ni Houlihan

Plate 8. Tribal Gods of the 19th Century, illustration by
J F Horrabin from THE OUTLINE OF HISTORY (1920) by H G Wells.
By courtesy of Cassell Ltd

To what new fates, my country, far
 And unforeseen of foe and friend,
Beneath what unexpected star,
 Compelled to what unchosen end?

Across the sea that knows no beach
 The Admiral of nations guides
Thy blind obedient keels to reach
 The harbor where thy future rides! . . .

There is a hand that bends our deeds
 To mightier issues than we planned,
Each son that triumphs, each that bleeds,
 My country, serves its dark command.

I do not know beneath what sky
 Nor on what seas shall be thy fate;
I only know it shall be high,
 I only know it shall be great.[13]

There is a mysterious cycle in human events. To some generations much is given. Of other generations much is expected. This generation of Americans has a rendez-vous with destiny.[14]

Even from this drastically simplified presentation it is plain that the doctrine of the State as the 'ultimate end which has ultimate rights against the individual' can readily be used to justify a complete supersession of the individual will and conscience by the State, the abrogation of individual rights wherever these might conflict with the purposes of the State, and the erection of the nation-State into an entity above law and morality in its dealing with other states.[15] The English Idealists developed Hegel's theories: F. H. Bradley, for example, wrote, 'What we call an individual man is what he is because of and by virtue of community, and communities are not mere names but something real.' 'A man's life with its moral duties is in the main filled up by his station in that system of wholes which the State is, and . . . this partly by its laws and institutions, and still more by its spirit, gives him the life which he does live and ought to live.' Bernard Bosanquet in *The Philosophical Theory of the State* (1899) goes still further, referring to the State as 'the guardian of our whole moral world, and not a factor within our organized moral world', exempting the State from all moral judgements, and declaring that 'more of the State . . . and not less, is required within communities'. 'Whatever loyalties [to other associations] may exist in the mind, the State will undoubtedly, when need arises, of which it through constitutional methods is the sole judge, prohibit and prevent the expression, in external acts, of any loyalty but that to the community which it represents. Absoluteness in this sense is inherent in the State.' The burden of Bosanquet's argument can be summarised in a sentence from his Preface—'The deepest and loftiest achievements of men do not belong to the particular human being in his repellent isolation.'

Although Hegel's reverence for the State lends itself readily to debasement of this kind it might equally well point the way, as he doubtless intended, to a dedicated and altruistic society. Having quoted Bosanquet at some length it is only fair to offer a more sympathetic version of the idealist case. A reading of *Culture and Anarchy* is helpful here. I think that Arnold had Macaulay[16] and Bright in mind rather than Mill, but what he says is a direct reply to Mill's arguments:[17]

> Freedom, I said, was one of those things which we thus worshipped in itself, without enough regarding the ends for which freedom is to be desired. . . . We have not the notion, so familiar on the Continent and to antiquity, of *the State*—the nation in its collective and corporate character, entrusted with stringent powers for the general advantage, and controlling individual wills in the name of an interest wider than that of individuals. . . . Now if culture, which simply means trying to perfect oneself, and one's mind as part of oneself, brings us light, and if light shows us that there is nothing so very blessed in merely doing as one likes, that the worship of the mere freedom to do as one likes is worship of machinery, that the really blessed thing is to like what right reason ordains, and to follow her authority, then we have got a practical benefit out of culture. We have got a much-wanted principle, a principle of authority, to counteract the tendency to anarchy which seems to be threatening us. . . .
>
> We want an authority, and we find nothing but jealous classes, checks, and a deadlock; culture suggests the idea of *the State*. We find no basis for a firm State-power in our ordinary selves; culture suggests one to us in our *best self*.   ('Doing as One Likes')

I have multiplied these examples and juxtaposed them without any special regard for chronology to make the central point that by the nineteenth century there was a radical conflict of opinion, represented on the one hand by Emerson's 'Society everywhere is in conspiracy against the manhood of every one of its members' and 'Whoso would be a man must be a nonconformist', and on the other by Ruskin's 'Government and co-operation are in all things and eternally the laws of life. Anarchy and competition eternally and in all things the laws of death'.[18] Arnold's title, *Culture and Anarchy*, thus poses, though with very different emphasis, precisely the same alternatives as Herbert Spencer's *The Man versus the State* (1884). For most men the problem was not to choose one extreme or the other but, recognizing the force of the arguments on both sides, to discover some middle ground. Arnold rightly observes that an increase of liberty will not, of itself, bring increased happiness and will, after a point, bring anarchy. Spencer makes the equally obvious point that an increase of constraint does not bring happiness either. Both ways seem to leave man in painful bondage. Thus as well as asking 'Which way does happiness lie?' the Victorians were also asking 'Which way does freedom lie?' As Carlyle put it in *Past and Present*, 'How, in conjunction with inevitable Democracy, indispensable Sovereignty is to exist: certainly it is the hugest question ever heretofore propounded to mankind! The solution of which is work for long years and centuries.' In the remainder of this chapter I shall discuss the way the battle has gone in the twentieth century.

Perhaps the simplest and most striking index of the change of opinion in Britain and elsewhere is provided by a passage from Mill's *On Liberty*. On the subject of education he writes

> If the government would make up its mind to require for every child a good education, it might save itself the trouble of providing one. It might leave to parents to obtain the education where and how they pleased, and content itself with helping to pay the school fees of the poorer classes of children, and defraying the entire school expenses of those who have no one else to pay for them. The objections which are urged with reason against State education do not apply to the enforcement of education by the State, but to the State's taking upon itself to direct that education; which is a totally different thing. That the whole or any large part of the education of the people should be in State hands, I go as far as any one in deprecating. All that has been said of the importance of individuality of character, and diversity in opinions and modes of conduct, involves, as of the same unspeakable importance, diversity of education. A general State education is a mere contrivance for moulding people to be exactly like one another: and as the mould in which it casts them is that which pleases the predominant power in the government, whether this be a monarch, a priesthood, an aristocracy, or the majority of the existing generation; in proportion as it is efficient and successful, it establishes a despotism over the mind, leading by natural tendency to one over the body. An education established and controlled by the State should only exist, if it exist at all, as one among many competing experiments, carried on for the purpose of example and stimulus, to keep the others up to a certain standard of excellence.
>
> (ch. 5)

Mill's views on education were, as he implies, advanced for his day, yet now how many people who read his measured condemnation of State education will not dismiss him as a misguided reactionary clinging to the outmoded notion of parental responsibility. This is a measure of the running of the tide.[19]

II

I have been attempting to illustrate by selective quotation two ways of defining liberty—'positive' and 'negative' liberty as they are sometimes rather misleadingly called. The deficiencies of negative liberty have often been noticed, especially in its extreme forms. Most of the novels that I have mentioned in chapter 10 could be interpreted as pointing to the helplessness of the individual when he is left at the mercy of unchecked social and economic forces, as implying the need for intervention by some larger organization and thus as critical of the whole concept of negative liberty. The novels I consider in the rest of this chapter take the complementary point of view: they are to be read as in part a critique of the 'positive' doctrines of liberty that now prevail, making their case by the classic method of a *reductio* designed to show that positive liberty is in its turn capable of being perverted into a denial of freedom. The novelists are taking part, consciously or unconsciously, in an established conflict and proceed by depicting an extreme condition. To do this they adopt various devices—some novels are set in prisons, the place where the State most plainly limits the freedom of the individual: some are set in the services during the war, the time when the claims of the State are pitched at their highest: some look forward to an imagined point when changes that are now only beginning have been completed.

Of this last group Zamiatin's *We* (1924) is an early, influential, and rightly celebrated example. Aldous Huxley's *Brave New World* (1932) makes many of the same points with greater comic force.[20] The opening sentences set the tone with characteristic directness:

> A squat grey building of only thirty-four stories. Over the main entrance the words, CENTRAL LONDON HATCHERY AND CONDITIONING CENTRE, and, in a shield, the World State's motto, COMMUNITY, IDENTITY, STABILITY.

Huxley's first task is to describe the sort of world which one would logically expect if the Utilitarian view of happiness as the Sovereign Good were allowed to stand as a complete description of human purposes and an extreme version of the idealist view of the State were invoked as justifying the total subjugation of the individual life. Artificial insemination, incubation, embryonic control and sleep teaching produce children already adapted to the needs of the State and conditioned to embrace the State's purposes as their own:

> 'Till at last the child's mind *is* these suggestions, and the sum of the suggestions *is* the child's mind. And not the child's mind only. The adult's mind too—all his life long. The mind that judges and desires and decides—made up of these suggestions. But all these suggestions are *our* suggestions!' The Director almost shouted in his triumph. 'Suggestions from the State.' (II)

Throughout their adult life the people are subjected to propaganda from the College of Emotional Engineering: the object is to merge the identity of the individual in the corporate order ('I drink to the Greater Being') and to deter any attempt to disturb the prevailing system:

> [*The Director*] 'Consider the matter dispassionately, Mr Foster, and you will see that no offence is so heinous as unorthodoxy of behaviour. Murder kills only the individual—and, after all, what is an individual? . . . Unorthodoxy threatens more than the life of a mere individual; it strikes at Society itself.' (X)

Stability is the aim of the State—it has assumed absolute world-sovereignty in order to assure itself of retaining absolute world-sovereignty—and uniformity is its instrument. Knowledge of the past is discouraged, the literature of the past is suppressed, and original work that might be subversive does not receive the necessary *imprimatur*. Naturally the values of individual freedom are presented only to be derided:

> 'Sleep teaching was actually prohibited in England. There was something called liberalism. Parliament, if you know what that was, passed a law against it. The records survive. Speeches about liberty of the subject. Liberty to be inefficient and miserable. Freedom to be a round peg in a square hole.' (III)

The framing and presenting of the new World-State is the most ingenious and memorable feature of the book. Huxley presents in concrete form the question that lies behind all Utilitarian theories of government—'If the aim of man is happiness and the State guarantees to make you happy by removing some desires and gratifying others, why bother about personal freedom?' He answers this question in two ways, first by presenting a world in which only easily gratified desires remain and convincing the reader that this world, with its childish amusements such as Centrifugal Bumble-puppy, is not adequate for grown men: secondly by subjecting the ideal state to the test of different sets of values, particularly those of an Alpha citizen who has not been thoroughly conditioned, those of a Savage who has been brought up in a primitive community, and those in surviving copies of literary works (Shakespeare, Newman and Maine-de Biran). In each case the sense is that there is a fuller version of experience available than the official one:

> He [Bernard] laughed, 'Yes, "Everybody's happy nowadays." We begin giving the children that at five. But wouldn't you like to be free to be happy in some other way, Lenina? In your own way, for example; not in everybody else's way.'
> 'I don't know what you mean,' she repeated. (VI)

The point is made with particular clarity at the end of chapter XVII:

> 'But I don't want comfort. I want God, I want poetry, I want real danger, I want freedom, I want goodness. I want sin.'
> 'In fact,' said Mustapha Mond, 'you're claiming the right to be unhappy.'
> 'All right, then,' said the Savage defiantly, 'I'm claiming the right to be unhappy.'
> 'Not to mention the right to grow old and ugly and impotent; the right to have syphilis and cancer; the right to have too little to eat; the right to be lousy; the right to live in constant apprehension of what may happen tomorrow; the right to catch typhoid; the right to be tortured by unspeakable pains of every kind.'
> There was a long silence.
> 'I claim them all,' said the Savage at last.
> Mustapha Mond shrugged his shoulders. 'You're welcome,' he said.

This is the burden of the book—that freedom, if it is to mean anything at all, must mean more than the ability to find approved satisfactions for authorized wants. Huxley argues that to make this ability the end of political activity cannot be justified nor can any view of the state that encourages or permits men to do so. It is beside the point to claim that no philosopher has ever framed an ideal state such as Huxley envisages: the novel's argument is complete if we accept that the World Controller could justify every article of his policy and practice by quoting Rousseau, Fichte, Hegel, T. H. Green even, Bradley or Bosanquet, with supplementary assistance from Kant, Comte and Marx. The principle once conceded it is too late to be scrupulous about the practical measures. It is pointless to swallow the General Will and strain at Bokanovsky's Process. The reader is satisfied that the Idealist State claims too much.

George Orwell's *1984* (1949) is in the same tradition of political satire. Orwell's primary concern is not to predict the course of human development but to record as forcefully as possible the dangerous symptoms which he had already observed in Russia, America, Nazi Germany and above all in Britain. To do this he extrapolated and exaggerated them, foreshortening the whole to bring it within the probable lifetime of most of his readers. *1984* is not about the future of the world: it is about the world we are living in. To treat it as merely allegorical or prophetic is to weaken Orwell's insistence that all the horrors of which he writes are not abstractions or imaginings but are already in the world.

The detail with which Orwell realizes the all-pervading state is what makes the book terrifying. On the level of what he calls 'the physical texture of life' it owes a great deal to memories of Britain during the war—the shabby buildings, the inadequate rations, the loose Victory cigarettes, the broken lifts, the gritty soap, the blunt razor blades, the saccharine tablets, the sense that aesthetic pleasure of any kind was unpatriotic if not treasonable. Ideologically it combines memories of the war with memories of the Communist Party:

> The Ministry of Truth . . . was startlingly different from any other object in sight. It was an enormous pyramidal structure of glittering white concrete, soaring up, terrace after terrace, 300 metres into the air. From where Winston stood it was just possible to read, picked out on its white face in elegant lettering, the three slogans of the Party:
>
>
>
> WAR IS PEACE
> FREEDOM IS SLAVERY
> IGNORANCE IS STRENGTH
>
>

The novel is set in 'London, chief city of Airstrip One, itself the third most populous of the provinces of Oceania'. Oceania is one-third of the world, the other parts being Eurasia and Eastasia. 'In one combination or another, these three super-states are permanently at war, and have been so for the past twenty-five years.' The war, which is presented by the rulers as a major ideological conflict, is largely a sham, since in fact 'the conditions of life in all three super-states are very much the same. In Oceania the prevailing philosophy is called Ingsoc, in Eurasia it is called neo-Bolshevism, and in Eastasia it is called by a Chinese name usually translated as Death-Worship, but perhaps better rendered as Obliteration of the Self. . . . Everywhere there is the pyramidal structure, the same worship of a semi-divine leader, the same economy existing by and for continuous warfare.' 'The rulers of such a state are absolute, as the Pharaohs or the Caesars could not be. They are obliged to prevent their followers from starving to death in numbers large enough to be inconvenient, and they are obliged to remain at the same low level of military technique as their rivals; but once that minimum is achieved, they can twist reality into whatever shape they choose.' The Party's apparatus for shaping opinion is described with careful detail: members of the general public are never allowed to learn the true facts, while members of the Party are required to develop the technique of *doublethink*.[21]

> A Party member is expected to have no private emotions and no res-pites from enthusiasm. He is supposed to live in a continuous frenzy of hatred of foreign enemies and internal traitors, triumph over victories, and self-abasement before the power and wisdom of the Party.... Oceanic society rests ultimately on the belief that Big Brother is omni-potent and the Party is infallible, but since in reality Big Brother is not omnipotent and the Party is not infallible, there is need for an unweary-ing, moment-to-moment flexibility in the treatment of facts.

The Party thus maintains its power partly by control over the minds of its members[22] and partly by physical coercion. 'This day-to-day falsification of the past, carried out by the Ministry of Truth, is as necessary to the stability of the régime as the work of repression and espionage carried out by the Ministry of Love.' When the Thought-Police or the telescreens discover disloyal thoughts or actions the offender is handed over to the Ministry of Love, whose operations are also described in detail. Its means are violence, torture and degradation. The systematic distortion of fact, the corruption of language and logic, the propaganda against imaginary enemy states and internal traitors, and the ruthless torture and extermination are in combination sufficient to secure the Party almost total domination over the lives of the people of Oceania.

An exception is the hero of the novel, Winston Smith,[23] who begins to question the ways of the régime, to understand them and ultimately to resist them. He reflects that

> In the end the Party would announce that two and two made five, and you would have to believe it. It was inevitable that they should make that claim sooner or later: the logic of their position demanded it. Not merely the validity of experience, but the very existence of external reality, was tacitly denied by their philosophy. The heresy of heresies was common sense.

In his private diary he writes, '*Freedom is the freedom to say that two plus two make four. If that is granted, all else follows.*' He works for the Ministry of Truth, at 'Reality control', rewriting history to accord with the Party's current needs: unlike the other citizens of Oceania he knows how consistently the facts are falsified. He writes in his diary *'I understand HOW: I do not understand WHY.'* This is where *1984* goes beyond Orwell's earlier book *Animal Farm*, a bluntly satirical account of the processes by which a democratic revolution may be converted to a tyranny, for the story of *1984* is largely the story of how Winston comes to learn the reasons for the actions of the leaders of the Party. As well as keeping his diary, which is a crime, he falls in love with another Party member called Julia. They join the Brotherhood, a secret organization dedicated to overthrowing the régime, but discover that everything that they have been doing is known to the Party. Julia is dragged away and Winston is taken to the Ministry of Love, where his chief interrogator is a senior party member called O'Brien, whom Winston had once trusted. In their longest confrontation O'Brien speaks candidly to Winston about the Party's purposes. First he explains why the Party exacts total obedience:

> Did I not tell you just now that we are different from the persecutors of the past? We are not content with negative obedience, nor even with the most abject submission. When finally you surrender to us, it must be of your own free will. We do not destroy the heretic because he resists us: so long as he resists us we never destroy him. We convert him, we capture his inner mind, we reshape him. We burn all evil and all illusion out of him; we bring him over to our side, not in appearance, but genuinely, heart and soul. We make him one of ourselves before we kill him. It is intolerable to us that an erroneous thought should exist anywhere in the world, however secret and powerless it may be. Even in the instant of death we cannot permit any deviation.

He goes on

> What happens to you here is for ever. Understand that in advance. We shall crush you down to the point from which there is no coming back. Things will happen to you from which you could not recover, if you lived a thousand years. Never again will you be capable of ordinary human feeling. Everything will be dead inside you. Never again will you be capable of love, or friendship, or joy of living, or laughter, or curiosity, or courage, or integrity. You will be hollow. We shall squeeze you empty, and then we shall fill you with ourselves.

This speech is set in a context of brutal and unremitting torture. The implication is plain that in the last analysis the source of sovereign authority is physical force. O'Brien asks Winston, by this

time emaciated and battered, if he can conjecture the reason why
the Party should want power of this kind:

> 'You are ruling over us for our own good,' he said feebly. 'You believe
> that human beings are not fit to govern themselves, and therefore—'
> He started and almost cried out. A pang of pain had shot through his
> body. O'Brien had pushed the lever of the dial up to thirty-five.
> 'That was stupid, Winston, stupid!' he said. 'You should know better
> than to say a thing like that.'
> He pulled the lever back and continued:
> 'Now I will tell you the answer to my question. It is this. The Party
> seeks power entirely for its own sake. We are not interested in the good
> of others; we are interested solely in power. Not wealth or luxury or
> long life or happiness: only power, pure power.'

In the speeches which are crucial to the argument of the book
O'Brien makes it plain that 'power is not a means, it is an end', and
then proceeds to define the nature of power:

> 'The real power, the power we have to fight for night and day, is not
> power over things, but over men.' He paused, and for a moment
> assumed again his air of a schoolmaster questioning a promising pupil:
> 'How does one man assert his power over another, Winston?'
> Winston thought. 'By making him suffer,' he said.
> 'Exactly. By making him suffer. Obedience is not enough. Unless he is
> suffering, how can you be sure that he is obeying your will and not his
> own? Power is in inflicting pain and humiliation. Power is in tearing
> human minds to pieces and putting them together again in new shapes
> of your own choosing. Do you begin to see, then, what kind of world we
> are creating? It is the exact opposite of the stupid hedonistic Utopias
> that the old reformers imagined. A world of fear and treachery and
> torment, a world of trampling and being trampled upon, a world which
> will grow not less but *more* merciless as it refines itself. Progress in our
> world will be progress towards more pain. . . . All competing pleasures
> will be destroyed. But always—do not forget this, Winston—always
> there will be the intoxication of power, constantly increasing and
> constantly growing subtler. Always, at every moment, there will be the
> thrill of victory, the sensation of trampling on an enemy who is helpless.
> If you want a picture of the future, imagine a boot stamping on a human
> face— for ever. . . . Always we shall have the heretic here at our mercy,
> screaming with pain, broken up, contemptible—and in the end utterly
> penitent, saved from himself, crawling to our feet of his own accord.
> That is the world that we are preparing, Winston. A world of victory
> after victory, triumph after triumph after triumph: an endless pressing,
> pressing, pressing upon the nerve of power. You are beginning, I can
> see, to realize what that world will be like. But in the end you will do
> more than understand it. You will accept it, welcome it, become part of
> it.'

In the rest of the novel O'Brien's prophecy comes true. He arranges a final bizarre torture which breaks Winston's last resistance, and Winston, as empty as O'Brien has predicted, learns to love Big Brother. This part of the novel is well handled, and effectively sets acute personal suffering against the philosophical ideal of 'the absorption of the individual into the State', but it comes as something of an anti-climax after the *coup de théâtre* in which O'Brien reveals that the activities of the Ministry of Love are not the unavoidable accompaniments of tyranny but the whole purpose of its existence.

To a large extent *1984* is a physical novel—tyranny is pain and also discomfort, while the positive values are agreeable physical sensations, such as sex, the smell of coffee, handling a glass paperweight, writing on smooth creamy paper—but its political and philosophical implications are clear, perhaps too clear.[24] In general terms the quotation in the Appendix of the first few sentences of the Declaration of Independence establishes Orwell's position. In more particular terms he incorporates into Part Two his own version of twentieth-century history:

> In each variant of Socialism that appeared from about 1900 onwards the aim of establishing liberty and equality was more and more openly abandoned. . . . By the fourth decade of the twentieth century all the main currents of political thought were authoritarian. . . . The new aristocracy was made up for the most part of bureaucrats, scientists, technicians, trade-union organizers, publicity experts, sociologists, teachers, journalists, and professional politicians. . . . By comparison with that existing today, all the tyrannies of the past were half-hearted and inefficient.

The differences between Huxley and Orwell are plain, but they both follow Zamiatin in presenting a completely managed society, in which direction is carried out in the name of the State. It is an error to set aside what they say on the grounds that they are referring to a future which may never happen. Orwell, with a darker set of experiences than Huxley, has presented even more sombrely the dangers of authoritarianism. That he used the form of fantasy-fiction should not be made an excuse for refusing to consider whether he is in the right when he suggests that in fact the principal limitation of individual freedom in our time is the growing power of the State.[25]

III

Darkness at Noon (1940) by Arthur Koestler has been extraordinarily effective in establishing a pattern of the totalitarian mind, not least through its obvious influence on *Animal Farm* and *1984*, an influence which has not as far as I know been worked out in detail, but which will immediately present itself to anyone who reads Koestler's book and Orwell's in succession. *Darkness at Noon* is not a fantasy: it is set in a real state in the recent past. The central figure, Rubashov, is, Koestler tells us, a synthesis 'of a number of men who were victims of the so-called Moscow Trials'. He is a senior Communist, a veteran of the Revolution, who has suffered for the Party in foreign prisons, yet has twice been forced to make an admission of ideological error. One night he is arrested and taken to prison. The novel's first sentence is 'The cell door slammed behind Rubashov'.[26] He never leaves the prison again: the matter of the novel is his thoughts and memories in his cell, his entries in his diary, his surreptitious communication with other prisoners, and most important his repeated interrogations, first by the sympathetic Ivanov, later by his rigid successor Gletkin. The interrogation is not to establish his guilt or innocence but to persuade him to confess to a series of colourful crimes so that the Party can stage a public trial. The instruments of persuasion are not primarily physical, although the conditions of interrogation are made deliberately unpleasant.

Ivanov puts the case to Rubashov: 'I know that you are convinced that you won't capitulate. Answer me only one thing: *if* you became convinced of the logical necessity and the objective right-ness of capitulating—would you do it then?' (134). Thereafter he and Gletkin try to persuade Rubashov that, since a public recantation would be in the interests of the party, it is his duty to confess even though he knows the charges to be untrue. As Gletkin says, 'Truth is what is useful to humanity, falsehood what is harmful.' (201). Rubashov's early services to the party have often involved accepting and acting on this principle. He remembers the words he used himself on one occasion when it was necessary to justify Russian policy:

> The Party can never be mistaken. . . . You and I can make a mistake. Not the Party. The Party, comrade, is more than you and I and a thousand others like you and me. The Party is the embodiment of the revolu-tionary idea in history. History knows no scruples and no hesitation. Inert and unerring, she flows towards her goal. At every bend in her course she leaves the mud which she carries and the corpses of the drowned. History knows her way. She makes no mistakes. He who has not absolute faith in History does not belong in the Party's ranks.
>
> (43–4)

Thus he finds it hard to resist when Ivanov urges against him the classic arguments in favour of a collective morality:

> There are only two conceptions of human ethics, and they are at opposite poles. One of them is Christian and humane, declares the individual to be sacrosanct, and asserts that the rules of arithmetic are not to be applied to human units. The other starts from the basic principle that a collective aim justifies all means, and not only allows, but demands, that the individual should in every way be subordinated and sacrificed to the community—which may dispose of it as an experimentation rabbit or a sacrificial lamb. . . . Whoever is burdened with power and responsibility finds out on the first occasion that he has to choose; and he is fatally driven to the second alternative.   (142)

The logic of the interrogators is clear and, granted their premises, compelling: in the end Rubashov accepts their case, because in a sense they are right. He has come to question the basic values of the Party: logically he is guilty of the crimes of which he is accused. He signs the confession, is tried publicly and shot.

The strength of the novel lies partly in the careful and economical detail with which Koestler creates Rubashov's constricted life in his cell, and partly in the weight with which he states the positions of both sides of the debate. As in *1984*, the Party triumphs over the individual, but in Koestler's novel as in Orwell's the predominant impression is that authoritarian values stand condemned. Rubashov's arguments about the state of Russia, his reflections on the course of the Revolution, and his general case for the primacy of the individual remain unrefuted in the novel. A few quotations will give the main lines:

> A hundred and fifty years ago, the day of the storming of the Bastille, the European swing, after long inaction, again started to move. It had pushed off from tyranny with gusto: with an apparently uncheckable impetus, it had swung up towards the blue sky of freedom. For a hundred years it had risen higher and higher into the spheres of liberalism and democracy. But, see, gradually the pace slowed down, the swing neared the summit and turning-point of its course; then, after a second of immobility, it started the movement backwards, with ever-increasing speed. With the same impetus as on the way up, the swing carried its passengers back from freedom to tyranny again.   (151)

> [Rubashov] 'Our Press and our schools cultivate Chauvinism, militarism, dogmatism, conformism and ignorance. The arbitrary power of the Government is unlimited, and unexampled in history; freedom of the Press, of opinion and of movement are as thoroughly exterminated as though the proclamation of the Rights of Man had never been. . .'
> 'Well, and what of it?' said Ivanov happily. 'Don't you find it wonderful?'   (144)

> At bottom all this jugglery with 'revolutionary philosophy' was merely a
> means to consolidate the dictatorship, which, though so depressing a
> phenomenon, yet seemed to represent a historical necessity.   (160)

This is perhaps no more than an indictment of a specific regime,
but there are many indications that Koestler has in mind the
general question of loyalty to an absolute power. He quotes Saint-
Just's aphorism 'Nobody can rule guiltlessly' and Dietrich von
Nieheim on the perils of schism: he refers deliberately to Hegel:
finally he offers, at the end of the book, Rubashov's analysis of the
logic of a world in which individual wills are absorbed in a larger
purpose:

> The Party denied the free will of the individual—and at the same time it
> exacted his willing self-sacrifice. It denied his capacity to choose
> between two alternatives—and at the same time it demanded that he
> should constantly choose the right one. It denied his power to distin-
> guish good and evil—and at the same time it spoke pathetically of guilt
> and treachery. The individual stood under the sign of economic fatality,
> a wheel in a clockwork which had been wound up for all eternity and
> could not be stopped or influenced—and the Party demanded that the
> wheel should revolt against the clockwork and change its course. There
> was somewhere an error in the calculation; the equation did not work
> out.   (227)

Koestler is recognizably working in the same field as Zamiatin
and Orwell and Huxley, but his novel is more closely directed at the
realities of political history. At times he calls in question the very
existence of any abstract science of politics. One quotation,
referring to the Leader of the Party, makes this point very clearly:

> It is said that No. 1 has Machiavelli's *Prince* lying permanently by his
> bedside. So he should: since then, nothing really important has been
> said about the rules of political ethics. We were the first to replace the
> nineteenth century's liberal ethics of 'fair play' by the revolutionary
> ethics of the twentieth century.   (91)

Rubashov goes on to say that 'politics can be reasonably fair in the
breathing spaces of history; at its critical turning points there is no
other rule possible than the old one, that the end justifies the
means'. The means must of course include execution and imprisonment. What gives *Darkness at Noon* its force and tightness is
Koestler's spare but terrible description of what it is like to be
confined. The prison operates both as a figure for the enclosed
world of Communism and as a real demonstration of the
repressive powers of the State.

Plate 9. Lenin mural in Moscow. Photograph by Burt Glinn. *By courtesy of Magnum Photos Inc, New York*

13

Bernard Malamud uses incarceration in a similar way in *The Fixer* (1966), set in Kiev before the Revolution. The main character, Yakov Bok, is a poor Jewish fixer or handyman, who is accused of the ritual murder of a Christian boy. The evidence against him is slight, but anti-Semitic feeling is strong. He is committed to prison to await indictment. At first he expects to be brought to trial soon and is anxious about the result, but the formal charge is not delivered, and as the months pass it is plain that what he has to endure is the agony of waiting. At one point he is given hope by a sympathetic Investigating Magistrate named Bibikov:

> [*Bibikov*] Partly it is our situation in this unfortunate country that causes me doubt. Russia is such a complex, long-suffering, ignorant, torn and helpless nation. In one sense we are all prisoners here. . . . There is so much to be done that demands the full capacities of our hearts and souls, but, truly, where shall we begin? Perhaps I will begin with you? Keep it in mind, Yakov Shepsovitch, that if your life is without value, so is mine. If the law does not protect you, it will not, in the end, protect me.   (V/5)

There is an immediate sequel to this:

> One night a distant moaning broke into his sleep. He awoke and heard nothing. The fixer beat on the wall with his heavy shoe but there was no response. He dreamed he heard footsteps in the corridor, then a smothered cry awakened him again, terrified. Something's wrong, he thought, I must hide. A cell door clanged and there were steps of more than one man in the corridor. Yakov waited tensely in the pitch gloom, about to cry out if his door moved, but the steps went past his cell. The heavy door at the end of the corridor thumped shut, a key turned in the lock, and that was the end of the noise. In the terrible silence that followed, he could not get back to sleep. He beat on the wall with both broken shoes, shouting until he was hoarse, but could rouse no response. The next morning he was not brought food. They are leaving me to die, he thought. But at noon, a drunken guard came in with his soup and bread, muttering to himself. He spilled half the soup over Yakov before the prisoner could grab the bowl. . . . [*The guard forgets to fasten the cell door.*] . . . He [*Yakov*] looked cautiously to the left and right, then peered through the peephole into the other prisoner's cell. A bearded man, swinging gently, hung from a leather belt tied to the middle bar of the open window, a fallen stool nearby. He was staring down where his pince-nez lay smashed on the floor under his small dangling feet.
> It took the fixer an age to admit it was Bibikov.   (V/6)

Thereafter the power of the State is devoted to fabricating sufficient evidence to bring Yakov to trial. The Prosecuting Attorney attempts to persuade him to confess his guilt: 'I shall also cite testimony . . . by certain religious figures, scientists of Jewish history and theology, and alienists who are authorities on the Jewish mind. We have already gathered more than thirty reliable witnesses. His Majesty has read all the relevant testimony' (VI/8). Yakov continues to affirm his innocence, and the other arm of the State, represented by the prison authorities, tries to break his spirit by the rigours of imprisonment. In the stifling heat of summer and the piercing cold of winter he remains in solitary confinement. He has too little to eat: he is stripped and searched several times a day: he has no books or tools:

> Yakov spent hours pacing in the cell. He walked to Siberia and back. Six or eight times a day he read the prison regulations. Sometimes he sat at the shaky table. He could eat at the table but there was nothing else to do at it that he could think of. If he only had some paper and pencil he might write something down. With a knife he could whittle a piece of firewood, but who would give him a knife? He blew on his hands constantly. He feared he might go crazy doing nothing. . . . Once . . . the fixer quickly piled up the loose wood at the wall and climbed to the top of the pile to see if he could look out the window into the prison yard. He thought the prisoners might be there on their promenade. He wondered whether any of those he knew were still in prison, or had they got out. But he could not reach the window bars with his hands and all he saw out of it was a piece of leaden sky.   (VI/4)

He is often seriously ill. After a time he is chained to the wall of his cell by day and sleeps on bare boards with his feet pinioned at night.

> Time blew like a steppe wind into an empty future. There was no end, no event, indictment, trial. The waiting withered him. He was worn thin by the struggle to wait, by the knowledge of his innocence against the fact of his imprisonment; that nothing had been done in a whole year to free him. He was stricken to be so absolutely alone. Oppressed by the heat, eaten by damp cold, eroded by the expectation of an indictment that never came, were his grey bones visible through his skin? . . . Nothing changed but his age.   (VII/3)

Two linked themes receive expression in this part of the novel —the systematic destruction of an individual by an organization and the persecution of the Jewish minority in Russia. The indifference of authority and the tyranny of the majority are in the end the same thing. Yakov is not a clever man, and Malamud does not step outside his limited vocabulary. The result is a meditation (though this is too grand a word), an enforced pondering of the meaning of freedom by a man whose situation will not allow him to accept any metaphysical idea of what it is to be free: 'In chains all that was left of freedom was life, just existence; but to exist without choice was the same as death' (VIII/1). He arrives at length at an understanding of what has happened to him:

> He is enraged by what has happened—is happening to him—a whole society has set itself against Yakov Bok, a poor man with a few grains of education, but in any case innocent of the crime they accuse him of. What a strange and extraordinary thing for someone like himself, a fixer by trade, who had never in his life done a thing to them but live for a few months in a forbidden district, to have as his sworn and bitter enemies the Russian State, through its officials and Tsar, for no better reason than that he was born a Jew, therefore their appointed enemy, though the truth of it is he is in his heart no one's enemy but his own.
>
> Where's reason? Where's justice? What does Spinoza say—that it's the purpose of the state to preserve a man's peace and security so he can do his day's work. To help him live out his few poor years, against circumstance, sickness, the frights of the universe. So at least don't make it any worse than it is. But the Russian State denies Yakov Bok the most elemental justice, and to show its fear and contempt of humankind has chained him to the wall like an animal.   (VIII/2)

But his understanding of his own situation is not much help to him: all he can do is suffer and endure. At one point he is offered a pardon, but 'Yakov said he wanted a fair trial, not a pardon'. At last he receives the indictment, and a lawyer, Ostrovsky, comes to advise him. He is an educated man and places the case in the context of the political situation of Russia in general and Kiev in particular. The imperial absolutists and the reactionary groups known as the Black Hundreds wish to divert popular discontent into anti-Semitic outbreaks. Hence their persecution of the fixer. 'One man is all they need so long as they can hold him up as an example of Jewish bloodthirst and criminality. To prove a point it's best to have a victim.' Yakov's case seems desperate, yet Ostrovsky feels that he has a chance:

> Freedom exists in the cracks of the state. Even in Russia a little justice can be found. It's a strange world. On the one hand we have the strictest autocracy; on the other we are approaching anarchy; in between courts exist and justice is possible. The law lives in the minds of men.   (IX/3)

In fact, after two and a half years in prison Yakov is brought to trial. The book ends as he is being driven through hostile crowds along the streets of Kiev to the courthouse.

Malamud, as I have said, is scrupulously careful not to romanticize the fixer, or to suggest that he is an exceptionally clever man. But under the relentless pressures of confinement he is driven to beat his brains to understand why he is persecuted, why he has to resist, and why he longs for freedom. His conclusions may be represented by three quotations:

> Ostrovsky had reminded him that there was much more wrong with Russia than its anti-Semitism. Those who persecute the innocent were themselves never free.
> (IX/4)

> Afterwards he thought, Where there's no fight for it there's no freedom. What is it Spinoza says? If the state acts in ways that are abhorrent to human nature it's the lesser evil to destroy it. Death to the anti-Semites! Long live revolution! Long live liberty!
> (IX/6)

> So I learned a little, he thought, I learned this but what good will it do me? Will it open the prison doors? Will it allow me to go out and take up my poor life again? Will it free me a little once I am free? Or have I only learned to know what my condition is—that the ocean is salty as you are drowning, and though you knew it you are drowned? Still, it was better than not knowing. A man had to learn, it was his nature.
> (IX/4)

The Fixer deliberately reduces to the smallest possible compass the argument about the State and the individual. The structure is correspondingly simple. As in *Darkness at Noon* the entire mass of the book rests on the protagonist. What is opposed to him is the system. Other characters may be given verisimilitude or even some distinguishing features, but their real function is to represent an unindividualized majority exerting pressure on the solitary prisoner. In both books what is truly set against the single man is not a number of other men but the four walls of his cell. The weight of the book thus necessarily falls on the thoughts, reveries and memories of the central character. He is driven to consider what it is that makes him a person and that gives him a unique value which he must protect against the organized power of his fellow-citizens. The arguments of Locke and Mill become the tormented gropings of a man alone in a cell. The doctrines of Rousseau and Hegel and Bosanquet are condensed into the prison regulations:

> Obey all rules and regulations without question. If the prisoner is insubordinate or insulting to a guard or prison official, or he attempts in any way to breach the security of this prison, he will be executed on the spot.
> (VI/2)

Most of the other novels that I have encountered operate in a similar way. Nabokov's *Bend Sinister* is a clear example. If we include stories of actual authoritarian regimes, then Graham Greene's *The Comedians* and Gabriel Fielding's *The Birthday King*

might be seen as falling into the same pattern. In both imprisonment as a metaphor and a reality plays its vital part in establishing
the character of absolutism in Haiti and Germany respectively.
This would no doubt be the place to consider Russian literature
from Dostoievsky's *House of the Dead* (1861) down to contemporary novels of prison life in the Soviet Union. On this I am not
competent to offer an opinion: from translations it seems to fit well
enough into the general framework I have indicated.

The Fixer suggests a final set of novels of an associated kind,
those that deal with the law. The law may be employed as the
instrument of oppression, that is to give a colour of legitimacy to
the arbitrary acts of the State, or it may simply exist as a structure
of regulations limiting the freedom of citizens. More commonly it
appears as a source of delay and bewilderment, a shifting and
unpredictable web of rules and decrees that enmeshes the
unhappy individual. Kafka is of course the master here, but
Nabokov's *Invitation to a Beheading* should perhaps be mentioned
also.[27] It is true that for the most part novels of this kind suggest
that the world they represent is distorted, unstable and liable to
slide into fantasy, but they also suggest that at their heart is a real
conflict between an individual and a system which ignores or
despises individuals. Indeed the implication that even the code of
law is fluid and unpredictable brings an extra quality of nightmare
to the ordeal of the single man.

On the whole imaginative writers show little respect for the State
in its legal embodiment: they are not much more in awe of the
nation in arms.

IV

The state of war shows the omnipotence of the State in its individuality;
country and fatherland are then the power which convicts of nullity the
independence of individuals.—HEGEL

The appropriate and conscious employment of war as a political means
has always led to happy results.—GENERAL F. VON BERNHARDI, *Germany and
the Next War* (1912)

The novel of war is not new: there are many novels, about which I
shall say a brief word later, which deal with the dedicated soldier
fighting for his country, but more to my present purposes are
those novels in which there is a clash of interest between the
individual and the military power of the State. A simple example is
Jaroslav Hašek's *The Good Soldier Schweik* (1921-3), in which two

traditions converge. It takes its place in the line of picaresque narratives such as Nashe's *Unfortunate Traveller*, and *Simplicissimus*, in which a footloose character becomes involved in the wars of his betters. He naturally considers his own affairs and his own safety more important than the issues at stake in the war, and is thus an unenthusiastic spectator or participant. *Schweik*, however, deals with a soldier who is the subject of a State committed to total war; it therefore represents also a second tradition, that in which we find such books as de Vigny's *Servitude et grandeur militaires* and Erckmann-Chatrian's *Histoire d'un conscrit de 1813*. Here the State demands total obedience in the deadly engagements of the Napoleonic wars: this obedience the individual fighting man eventually accords, even though what is asked of him nearly destroys him. It was not until the first German War that a State again made such overwhelming demands on its citizens: on one side this is reflected in many of the poets and in a series of novels and autobiographies such as *Memoirs of a Fox-hunting Man*, *Death of a Hero* (Richard Aldington), *Combed Out* (F. A. Voigt), *A Private of the Guards* (Stephen Graham), and *Goodbye to all that* (R. Graves)—on the other variously in *All Quiet on the Western Front* and in *Schweik*. All these deal with the attempts of the fighting soldier to withstand the enormous pressures designed to mould him into a dedicated and unthinking part of the military machine: they question, more or less explicitly, the right of any State to make demands of this kind of its citizens. *Schweik* is particularly relevant to my inquiry here because it incorporates the older tradition of the picaro pursuing his own personal ends deaf to the thunder of military imperatives.[28] The comic possibilities of this are deftly exploited, but the physical horrors of war are presented with equal force, especially in Book III, which deals with the battle against Russia in Carpathia and Ruthenia.

The whole valley had been gouged and scooped out and the trampled state of the ground made it look as if hosts of gigantic moles had been toiling there. At the edges of the shell holes there were tattered shreds of Austrian uniforms which had been uncovered by downpours of rain. Behind Nagy-Czaba, on a charred old fir tree, in the tangle of the branches, hung the boot of an Austrian infantryman, with a piece of shinbone left in it. The forests without foliage or pine needles, the trees without tops and the isolated farms riddled with shot bore witness to the havoc which had been wrought by the artillery fire.

The train moved slowly forward along embankments which had been newly built, so that the whole battalion was able to feast its eyes on the joys of war, and by scanning the military cemeteries with their white crosses, which formed gleaming patches on the devastated hillsides, they had an opportunity of preparing their minds gradually but surely for the field of glory which terminated with an Austrian military cap, caked with mire and dangling on a white cross.   (III/3)

The second German War also produced a crop of novels of a similar kind. For my purposes I shall notice only the Gunner Asch novels by H. H. Kirst and *Catch-22* by Joseph Heller. Kirst's novels are not of the first literary importance: they are interesting because they attempt to give some insight into the world of a soldier in the army of a totalitarian régime that is fighting for its life. The technique they use to do this is not essentially different from Heller's. *Catch-22* (1961) presents a series of incidents in one wing of the U.S. Air Force during the later stages of the war in Europe. The wing is based on the Mediterranean island of Pianosa and carries out bombing missions over German-occupied Italy and France. The officers and men spend their leave in Rome. The central contrast of the book is between the organized sham of the Air Force and the reality of death and love.

> All over the world, boys on every side of the bomb line were laying down their lives for what they had been told was their country, and no one seemed to mind, least of all the boys who were laying down their young lives. There was no end in sight.   (Chapter 2)

That is the reality. This is the letter which the Colonel sends to the relations of the men who have died:

> Dear Mrs., Mr., Miss, or Mr. and Mrs. Daneeka:
> Words cannot express the deep personal grief I experienced when your husband, son, father or brother was killed, wounded, or reported missing in action.   (31)

The Air Force is a sham masquerading as a manifestation of a righteous national purpose; in fact in Heller's war the only motive force is the ambition or greed of men in power. They allege the country's need to cover their own activities and to compel others to obey them. From the start the novel promotes an investigation of the meaning of words such as loyalty or patriotism, sometimes in general terms:

> [*Old Italian*] 'Imagine a man his age risking what little life he has left for something so absurd as a country.'
>   Nately was instantly up in arms again. 'There is nothing so absurd about risking your life for your country!' he declared.
>   'Isn't there?' asked the old man. 'What is a country? A country is a piece of land surrounded on all sides by boundaries, usually unnatural.

Englishmen are dying for England, Americans are dying for America, Germans are dying for Germany, Russians are dying for Russia. There are now fifty or sixty countries fighting in this war. Surely so many countries can't *all* be worth dying for.'   (23)

more often with specific reference to the United States:

Dunbar sat up like a shot. 'That's it,' he cried excitedly. 'There was something missing—all the time I knew there was something missing— and now I know what it is.' He banged his fist down into his palm. 'No patriotism,' he declared.

'You're right,' Yossarian shouted back. 'You're right, you're right, you're right. The hot dog, the Brooklyn Dodgers, Mom's apple pie. That's what everyone's fighting for. But who's fighting for the decent folk? Who's fighting for more votes for the decent folk? There's no patriotism, that's what it is. And no matriotism, either.'   (1)

The novel takes a number of officers and shows how each of them is exposed to the deforming pressures of the military machine or, more accurately, of those whose rank allows them to manipulate the machine. Some of these are simple—

He [General Dreedle] had no taste for sham, tact or pretension, and his credo as a professional soldier was unified and concise: he believed that the young men who took orders from him should be willing to give up their lives for the ideals, aspirations and idiosyncrasies of the old men he took orders from. The officers and enlisted men in his command had identity for him only as military quantities. All he asked was that they do their work; beyond that, they were free to do whatever they pleased. They were free, as Colonel Cathcart was free, to force their men to fly sixty missions if they chose. . . .   (21)

some more devious—

Without realizing how it had come about, the combat men in the squadron discovered themselves dominated by the administrators appointed to serve them. . . . When they voiced objection, Captain Black replied that people who were loyal would not mind signing all the loyalty oaths they had to. To anyone who questioned the effectiveness of the loyalty oaths, he replied that people who really did owe allegience to their country would be proud to pledge it as often as he forced them to. . . . The more loyalty oaths a person signed, the more loyal he was; to Captain Black it was as simple as that, and he had Corporal Kolodny sign hundreds with his name each day so that he could always prove he was more loyal than anyone else.   (11)

All authority in the end depends upon a rigid set of regulations, but as these can always be set aside if they operate in favour of the individual and against the system, they too are a sham:

> There was only one catch and that was Catch-22, which specified that a concern for one's own safety in the face of dangers that were real and immediate was the process of a rational mind. Orr was crazy and could be grounded. All he had to do was to ask; and as soon as he did, he would no longer be crazy and would have to fly more missions. Orr would be crazy to fly more missions and sane if he didn't, but if he was sane he had to fly them. If he flew them he was crazy and didn't have to; but if he didn't want to he was sane and had to.   (5)

Heller's basic comic device is to bring into collision the conventional assumptions of dedicated unquestioning obedience and the natural reactions of men who are afraid:

> Havermeyer was a lead bombardier who never missed. Yossarian was a lead bombardier who had been demoted because he no longer gave a damn whether he missed or not. He had decided to live forever or die in the attempt, and his only mission each time he went up was to come down alive.   (3)

Thus cowardice is a sign of intelligence and lack of fear a sign of stupidity—'Aarfy was a dedicated fraternity man who loved cheerleading and class reunions and did not have brains enough to be afraid.' The central character, Yossarian, exploits the paradoxical logic of this situation throughout the book, especially in his conversations with a conscientious officer called Clevinger:

> [*Yossarian*] 'It doesn't make a damned bit of difference *who* wins the war to someone who's dead.'
> . . . [*Clevinger*] 'I can't think of another attitude that could be depended upon to give greater comfort to the enemy.'
> 'The enemy,' retorted Yossarian with weighted precision, 'is anybody who's going to get you killed, no matter *which* side he's on, and that includes Colonel Cathcart.'   (12)

One important passage of dialogue occurs early in the book:

> [*Yossarian*] 'I don't want to be in the war any more.'
> 'Would you like to see our country lose?' Major Major asked.
> 'We won't lose. We've got more men, more money, and more material. There are ten million men in uniform who could replace me. Some people are getting killed and a lot more are making money and having fun. Let somebody else get killed.'
> 'But suppose everybody on our side felt that way.'
> 'Then I'd certainly be a damned fool to feel any other way. Wouldn't I?'   (9)

The last lines are repeated at the end of the novel (chapter 42): they constitute the simplest refutation in the novel of the attempts made by Major Danby and Major Major, two earnest officers, to persuade the others to accept orders cheerfully and willingly:

> [*Major Danby*] 'Look, fellows, we've got to have some confidence in the people above us who issue our orders. They know what they're doing.'
> 'The hell they do,' said Dunbar. (29)

The distinction in *Catch-22* is not between an impersonal system and the people it crushes, but between those who use the system and those who are caught in it. Heller cannot therefore make a simple plea for the freedom of the individual, for the men who are exploiting others are free. He has to make a distinction between those who wish to be free in order to contract out altogether and those who wish to be free in order to profit from the organization. It follows that the only people who will continue to proclaim belief in the values of the system are those who wish to go on using it for their own ends and those innocent victims who have not yet realized what is happening. The novel is narrated from the point of view of a group of men who become steadily more aware of the truth. One by one they are killed until only Yossarian is left. When he refuses to be put upon any longer his colonels assume that since he wishes to be free he must wish to join them in duping others. Yossarian eventually rejects the colonel's plans and is told that they intend to court martial him:

> 'They will also find you guilty,' Major Danby recited, 'of rape, extensive black-market operations, acts of sabotage and the sale of military secrets to the enemy.'
> [*Yossarian*] 'How will they prove any of that? I never did a single one of those things.'
> 'But they have witnesses who will swear you did. They can get all the witnesses they need simply by persuading them that destroying you is for the good of the country. And in a way, it *would* be for the good of the country.' (42)

There seems to be no choice: either a man is a fool and believes in the reality of the national purpose, or he sees the vacuousness of this idea and uses it to exploit fools. In a carefully contrived ending, however, Yossarian learns that one of his friends, an apparently guileless man, has escaped to neutral territory: he decides to do the same. This is presumably a figure for some sort of action by which an individual can avoid the collective pressures. Just before Yossarian leaves he says,

'When I look up, I see people cashing in. I don't see heaven or saints or angels. I see people cashing in on every decent impulse and every human tragedy.'

'But you must try not to think of that,' Major Danby insisted. . . . 'You must think only of the welfare of your country and the dignity of man.'

'Yeah,' said Yossarian.   (42)

The points of comparison between *Schweik* and *Catch-22* do not need labouring. The most obvious features are the counterpointing of comedy and horror, the use of keenness and officiousness as the mark of the fool, and in particular the way in which the ludicrious inefficiency of a nation in arms is made to expose the fallibility of the organized State: this does not make it any less dangerous to the individual, but undermines its claims to be an absolute. In both novels this is most effectively brought out at a briefing which would be farcically funny except that it will certainly lead to men being killed unnecessarily.

Catch-22 is set at a period when the war is apparently as good as won, which enables Heller to avoid the difficult question of the citizen's obligation to the State if he admits that it is engaged in a just or necessary war. This is not perhaps surprising, since war propounds to the libertarian the most difficult of problems—if his country is fighting another country whose victory will entail a total loss of liberty does this in any way affect the individual's right to pursue ends not sanctioned by the State? If it seems reasonable that in time of war the State may demand any sacrifice from its citizens, including giving up their lives, is there any logical reason why the State should not make similar demands whenever it considers its stability imperilled, or, as in *1984*, manufacture a threat to its own stability whenever it wishes to oppress its citizens? The crucial question is whether the citizen may decide for himself what his obligation to the State is or whether the obligation, whatever its nature, includes an acknowledgement that the State shall be the ultimate judge of what it can itself demand.

V

1914–1918: A SES GLORIEUX ENFANTS MORTS POUR LA PATRIE

1939–1945: AUX VICTIMES DE LA GUERRE
                              —Two War Memorials at Valençay

All the books I have mentioned so far are broadly speaking on the side of the individual against the State. Before I discuss the particular direction of their attack it is right to acknowledge the objection that this general point emerges only because I have deliberately limited my consideration to books that illustrate it. I am bound to admit that the objection is of some force, although the novels that I have mentioned do not stand alone. I might for example have pointed to plays as diverse as *The Sign of the Cross*, *The Insect Play*, Frisch's *Andorra*, Havel's *The Memorandum*, and Heller's *We Bombed in New Haven*, or films such as *Metropolis*, *Round-Up*, *Intolerance*, *King Rat*, *Modern Times*, *Alphaville*, or *Canal*. It is more to the point to see whether there is any substantial body of counter examples, that is literary works which emphasize and justify the claims of the State against those of the individual. Are there in short any works which accept the challenge of Palinurus— 'Fraternity is the State's bribe to the individual; it is the one virtue which can bring courage to members of a materialist society. All State propaganda exalts comradeship for it is this gregarious herd-sense and herd-smell which keep people from thinking and so reconcile them to the destruction of their private lives. A problem for government writers or for the war artists in their war cemeteries: how to convert Fraternity into an aesthetic emotion?'[29]

These are not as numerous as one might expect, if works of Government propaganda are set aside. One might mention first Utopian novels, like those of Wells, but they are by their nature set in the future and describe an ideal reconciliation between the claims of the individual and those of the State. Novels of the present are concerned with actual imperfections. Secondly there are many novels, poems or plays about warfare, in which the individual submerges his own identity in that of the state because his country is in conflict with another country. In traditional spy stories and war stories the one quality required of the hero is unflinching loyalty to his own rulers: the measure of his heroism is indeed the extent to which he is able to subdue his own inclinations to the needs of his country. There is thus a substantial body of literature in which the highest human quality is represented as a willing patriotism. The interesting point is that against this body of literature, if not actually parasitic upon it, is an equally substantial body of anti-patriotic writing. Newbolt and Kipling are almost the necessary pre-condition of Owen and Sassoon: Richard Hannay and Bulldog Drummond acknowledge a simple loyalty which Len Deighton makes fun of and Eric Ambler more subtly questions: Le Carré denies the assumptions of Le Queux: the straightforward pieties of Ian Hay or Alistair MacLean are derided in *Schweik* and *Catch-22*: Biggles and *Journey's End* lead to *Goshawk Squadron*.

I am not denying the existence or the possibility of modern literary works animated by the same uncomplicated and unselfish love of country as Canto Six of *The Lay of the Last Minstrel* or

Where the Rainbow Ends. I simply offer such evidence as I have encountered for the hypothesis that where writers of our time see a
constraining force on the individual that force is very frequently
represented as some hostile manifestation of majority opinion
having as its ultimate sanction not social disapproval but the
authorised coercive powers of the State. It is not necessary to make
the point in detail for all the novels. The fates of their heroes are
various—the Savage commits suicide, Winston Smith is tortured
into conformity, Rubashov is executed, Yakov Bok wins a trial,
Frugal and Yossarian escape, Cincinnatus C. asserts his own will
and the apparatus of the State vanishes, K. was apparently to die
worn out by his struggle, and so on—but the pattern of the novels
is similar. The hero, simply because he is the reality in the novel,
calls into question the abstraction that seeks to absorb him. This is
done in different ways. Huxley, for example, points out the
inherent dangers in a State designed to eliminate personal motives
even though it is controlled by a man of benevolent tendencies.
Even a good State, that is, when its power is absolute, corrupts its
citizens. When the citizen has no desires apart from those the State
implants the result is not, as Hegel and Rousseau hoped, a higher
kind of freedom but a permanent state of slavery.

Alternatively the emphasis may come on the various ways in
which the machinery of the State may be used, and in the last
resort will be used, to crush the individual. The implication is that
the idealist philosophy of government is out of touch with reality
and the splendid notion of the consentient State is only a facade
concealing a prison. However plausible the protestations of its
apologists, authority ultimately depends on power, not on consent.
'Covenants, without the sword, are but Words, and of no strength
to secure a man at all.'[30] Since this is so if we want to know why
men obey the government we will go not to T. H. Green but to the
only writer who has told the truth about sovereignty, Machiavelli.
'We are much beholden to Machiavel and others, that write what
men do, and not what they ought to do.'[31]

When Machiavelli says, 'It must be understood that a prince . . .
cannot observe all those things which are considered good in men,
being often obliged, in order to maintain the State,[32] to act against
faith, against charity, against humanity, and against religion,' or 'It
is necessary for a prince, who wishes to maintain himself, to learn
how not to be good . . .' or, 'Where the very safety of the country
depends upon the resolution to be taken, no considerations of
justice, humanity, or cruelty nor of glory or of shame, should be
allowed to prevail,' we are not very far away from Bosanquet's idea
that 'the State is the guardian of our whole moral world and not a
factor in our organised moral world . . . it is hard to see how the

State can commit theft or murder in the sense in which these are moral offences', or from Hegel's 'The relation between States is a relation between autonomous entities which make mutual stipulations but which at the same time are superior to these stipulations.' If any serious attempt is made in these novels to present the idealist theories it is by people who are using them deliberately to claim power for themselves or to confuse those who are against them: a Machiavellian Prince would find Hegel a very serviceable instrument of *frode*.

It is notable that hardly any novelists attack idealist theories on the grounds which, for example, Locke suggested, that the State is too limited a concept: that is, if we are unselfish at all it is by virtue of our common humanity, not by virtue of all being English.[33] Instead they resist Hegelian and similar theories on the simple ground that they set up the State as a monster which will devour the individual. This is perhaps inevitable. The novelists operate by placing a single character in a situation where his potentialities for action are cruelly limited. He can do nothing: the action of the book must take place in his mind. His mind is assaulted in its turn, as the representatives of orthodoxy attempt to coerce him into conformity. By definition these people are not individualized, except in so far as their claim to act in the name of the State is shown to be false and their various personal motives for desiring power are alluded to in passing. But the strategy of the books is to set one fully individualized character whose physical sufferings emphasize his humanity, against a series of figures representing the régime who are deliberately depersonalized and therefore less than human. The ordinary processes of reading a novel are enough to engage our sympathies very powerfully with the isolated character.

Just as war confronts the libertarian with difficult questions these authors pose to the authoritarian in turn the case of the police state. What is to prevent its power from becoming absolute? Arnold, as we have seen, makes elegant fun of the vulgar liberal objective of 'doing as one likes', but his contempt is harder to justify if the only alternative is 'doing what somebody else thinks is good for you'.

The various ways in which a State may oppress its citizens or fail to relieve their wants can be justified, and normally are justified, by reference to a theory of what the State is and why its authority is to be accepted. But any theory of this kind must proceed from some assumptions about the nature of man and must include at least one assumption, explicit or suppressed, about the nature of the human will. This suggests that one way of testing political theories is by observing how consistently their consequences square with their assumptions, or one may state the problem conversely as follows: 'If I make certain assumptions about the freedom of the will and follow them out consistently, do they indicate one specific pattern of human organization?'

If we consider the question historically we notice that while since, say, 1350, it has been increasingly common to regard the will of man as if it were completely free, there has been at the same time a tendency to vest more and more power not in the individual but in the institutions of society. Not surprisingly therefore one of the first things we notice when we look at the writings of political philosophers is the difficulty of correlating free will with liberatarianism, or determinism with authoritarianism. Consider for example the ambiguity of a statement such as 'All men are naturally selfish' or Hobbes' argument that men are moved by Appetites and Aversions. On the one hand it is an assertion that each man is out for himself, which suggests that men are best suited by a loose framework of government, permitting the most intense kind of individualism. On the other hand it is an assertion that every man's actions are not free but are motivated solely by self-interest, which implies in turn that if all men respond as they must they can be controlled by anyone who is in a position to apply the proper stimulus and the way lies open for a completely conditioned society. So that one might move from the initial statement towards a variety of different, indeed opposed, political systems. Can one proceed indifferently from any theory of the will to any theory of the State?

I may perhaps at this point resist the temptation to display the argument in full, and content myself with the simple assertion that a single remark of Sir William Temple's provides the readiest path to a general answer. In his *Essay upon the Original and Nature of Government* he writes, 'Nor do I know, if men are like Sheep, why they need any government: Or if they are like wolves, how can they suffer it.'[34] The implications of this remark are that the more docile and predictable mankind is the less need there is of powerful authority, while the more independent men are the greater need for some restraining power. Wolves need more government than sheep. If this is right we should expect to find a strong correlation between philosophical determinism and political libertarianism on the one hand, and between free will and authoritariansim on the other. This is the opposite of what at first seems natural, yet the facts go some way to confirm it.

Two sets of examples may help to establish the pattern. On the one hand we have Hegel's glorification of the State, especially of the Prussian State, in the name of human freedom. The State, he says, is 'the embodiment of rational freedom realizing and recognizing itself in an objective form', and again, 'The State is the Idea of Spirit in the external manifestation of human will and its freedom.' The paradox is especially hard to resolve here, because once you erect the idea of a state with purposes of its own, it is natural to ask where the State derives these purposes from. To answer this one must evolve a philosophy of history in which nations are borne forward or round and round or up and down by irresistible tides. Hence the needs of States are expressed in terms such as 'Manifest Destiny' or 'the iron necessity of German history'. It is clear that to call this 'a higher kind of freedom' is at best a hopeful aspiration and at worst downright chicanery. Henry D. Aiken comments, 'Hegel's philosophy of freedom thus exhibits that paradoxical combination of outward subservience or even servility towards the State and inner spiritual freedom which is so frequently to be found among German intellectuals. Similar traits may also be discerned in such other representatives of Germany's golden age as Leibniz, Goethe, and even Kant.'[35] On this point Isaiah Berlin in his inaugural lecture 'Two Concepts of Liberty' writes, 'Kant tells us that when "the individual has entirely abandoned his wild, lawless freedom, to find it again, unimpaired, in a state of dependence according to law", that alone is true freedom, "for this dependence is the work of my own will acting as a lawgiver". Liberty, so far from being incompatible with authority, becomes virtually identical with it. This is the thought and language of all the declarations of the rights of man in the eighteenth century.'[36]

Rousseau is certainly at times ready to proclaim the freedom of the will and at others to welcome the power of the State, joyfully acknowledging that the laws of liberty might prove to be more austere than the yoke of tyranny. Fichte similarly begins with an assertion of the absolute primacy of the individual Ego, which leads him finally to his *Addresses to the German Nation*. 'To compel man to adopt the right form of government, to impose Right on them by force, is not only the right, but the sacred duty of every man who has both the insight and the power to do so.' One might point to a similar combination of ideas in Plato, in the seventeenth-century Puritans in England and America, and in Machiavelli. The point may be briefly expressed by saying that to Machiavelli the extraordinary care that a ruler must take to provide himself with a strong machinery of government is only necessary because men are essentially wolves rather than sheep.

The clearest examples of those who hold a precisely opposite view are the British philosophers of the late eighteenth century, on whom Basil Willey comments, 'It may seem strange, though it is an evident characteristic of this period, that belief in Necessity should have been part of the creed of those who were the most ardent exponents of political, intellectual, and religious Liberty. . . . Priestley, like Hartley before him and Godwin after him, knows how to turn his necessity to glorious gain. . . .'[37] Bentham and Godwin proclaim as strenuously as Priestley the combination of an unflinching necessitarianism and an unflinching hatred of authoritarianism which we have already noticed in Shelley, although Bentham is not hostile to absolute power when it is in the hands of those he approves of.[38] Godwin wrote 'We should not forget that government is, abstractly taken, an evil, a usurpation upon the private judgement and individual conscience of mankind', continuing, in words that owe everything to Locke, 'Society and government are different in themselves, and have different origins. Society is produced by our wants, and government by our wickedness. Society is in every state a blessing; government even in its best state but a necessary evil.'[39] Priestley had earlier written, 'It is an universal maxim, that the more liberty is given to every thing which is in a state of growth, the more perfect it will become,' and again, 'The hand of power . . . on the side of any set of principles cannot but be a suspicious circumstance.'[40]

Earlier and later the picture is even less clear. Pope makes it reasonably easy to see how the postulate of the more or less firmly determined world permits one to suppose that men's natural activities are beneficial—'True SELF-LOVE and SOCIAL are the same'—and therefore need not be restrained by a powerful central authority. No doubt Pope derives something of this from Spinoza, but it is perhaps not straining the point to indicate a similar process at work in Locke, whose unoppressive version of the Social Contract seems to have its roots in his equally reassuring view of the human will.

In the nineteenth century one may, as I have said, see the Philosophical Radicals in general as the most powerful voices of liberalism, while they still hold to an almost Benthamite determinism. Mill, although a celebrated passage in the *Autobiography* tells us of his unwillingness to accept the consequences of the doctrine of Philosophical Necessity, seems to have had little positive belief in free will,[41] but this did not prevent him from being the century's most eloquent defender of individual liberties. Similarly Herbert Spencer, although he saw man's life as ultimately determined by enormous irresistible evolutionary forces such as the pressures of increasing population, was nevertheless vigilant to maintain the rights of the individual against the encroaching State.[42]

In sum then my conclusion is that a particular doctrine of the will does not positively entail any given view of the nature of the State, but that in the past there has been some correlation between a belief in the freedom of the will and a belief in the need for strong and pervasive government, and a corresponding correlation between determinism and an assertion of the importance of keeping the operations of the State to a minimum. This perhaps unexpected conclusion is not merely a version of the dilemma or paradox which we have encountered at every turn in our consideration of the freedom of the will: it has now, I think, a keener edge, since it poses problems of practical conduct. To this point it has been possible to regard the whole discussion as simply the presentation of an entertaining anomaly, like the 'class of classes' puzzle, a sort of optical illusion of the mind, and to treat it as yet another instance of the peculiar constitution of humanity. But now we are dealing with ideas that, as Heine said, may destroy civilisation.

The philosophers whose theories I have referred to in this chapter are deeply conscious of the complexity of the ideas of rights and political obligations. Accordingly their works are fluid, qualified, balanced, subtle and rich, or contradictory, evasive, nebulous, dishonest, shifty, unreliable, and ambiguous, according to the reader's view, but the message from the original writers is simple and consistent—'Beware of Leviathan—he crushes.' The ideal of the corporate or garrison State as the embodiment of individual purposes has been, if the writers of novels are a true index, totally discredited by the examples since 1900 of nation-states acting with lethal irresponsibility towards other states and with brutal insensitivity to their own members. It has seemed particularly important to maintain belief in the free will of the individual in order to strengthen the arguments for resisting or diminishing the coercive powers of the State. But it does not appear from the brief survey in this chapter that this has proved an important or effective move in the past. But now circumstances have changed and the problem demands a more immediate answer. The urgent questions today are these. Is it true to say that a necessitarian has no logical grounds for complaining if his personal freedom is infringed, or indeed abolished, by external agencies, of which the State constitutes the leading case? And if so, and it were agreed that totalitarian régimes are to be resisted by every means, would this constitute a valid reason for rejecting a determinist account of man?

In addition to the works cited in the notes the following have material relevant to the themes of this chapter: Oscar Wilde, *The Soul of Man under Socialism* (1891); H. J. Laski, *Liberty in the Modern State* (Harmondsworth:

Penguin, 1937); Charles Morgan, *Liberties of the Mind* (London: Macmillan, 1951); Aldous Huxley, *Brave New World Revisited* (1959); F. A. Hayek, *The Constitution of Liberty* (1960); John Plamenatz, *Man and Society*, 2 vols. (London: Longmans, 1963); J. G. A. Pocock, *The Machiavellian Moment: Florentine Political Thought and the Atlantic Republican Tradition* (Princeton U.P., 1975) esp. Part III; Isaiah Berlin, *Against the Current* (London: Hogarth, 1979), esp. pp. 25–79, 333–55; see also Introduction, note 41.

14

Retrospect Four 1890–1980

On or about December 1910 human character changed.—VIRGINIA WOOLF, 'Mr Bennett and Mrs Brown'.

There seemed a strangeness in the air,
Vermilion light on the land's lean face;
I heard a Voice from I knew not where:—
'The Great Adjustment is taking place!'
—THOMAS HARDY, 'There Seemed a Strangeness'.

When we look at our own century even such tentative identifications of a single dominant constraining power as I have been offering become almost impossible. Naturally many of the preoccupations of the previous century persist. One might point in particular to the literature which directly examines the role of political and economic institutions, either as instruments for coercing individuals or as a means of freeing the individual from the pressures of his society. Thus alongside novels which demonstrate the power of the state to crush its citizens we have also books about oppressive urban and industrial conditions, often with the implication that some institution, presumably deriving its powers from the state, is needed to protect the individual from the unchecked forces at work in his society.

Very often the social novelist writes almost with the detachment of a sociologist or social psychologist, describing human beings in the power of non-human forces, sometimes as crudely expressed as Dreiser's 'chemisms', sometimes taking the form of the inscrutable laws by which some fall, some rise. The American novelists from E. W. Howe onwards are especially strong here. Stephen Crane's *Maggie* is a brief and painful example of an individual helpless to escape from the wretched urban world in which she lives: Frank Norris's *The Octopus* is an extended account of the way in which economic pressures acquire the status of cosmic energies, and 'forces, conditions, laws of supply and demand' are simply part of the 'colossal indifference' of nature and its 'vast trend toward appointed goals'.

Nature was, then, a gigantic engine, a vast cyclopean power, huge, terrible, a leviathan with a heart of steel, knowing no compunction, no forgiveness, no tolerance; crushing out the human atom standing in its way with nirvanic calm, the agony of destruction sending never a jar, never the faintest tremor through all that prodigious mechanism of wheels and cogs.   (II. 8)

He seemed for one instant to touch the explanation of existence. Men were nothing, mere animalcules, mere ephemerides that fluttered and fell and were forgotten between dawn and dusk. . . . Men were naught, death was naught, life was naught; FORCE only existed—FORCE that brought men into the world, FORCE that crowded them out of it to make way for the succeeding generation, FORCE that made the wheat grow, FORCE that garnered it from the soil to give place to the succeeding crop.

It was the mystery of creation, the stupendous miracle of re-creation; the vast rhythm of the seasons, measured, alternative, the sun and the stars keeping time as the eternal symphony of reproduction swung in its tremendous cadences like the colossal pendulum of an almighty machine—primordial energy flung out from the hand of the Lord God himself, immortal, calm, infinitely strong.   (II. 9)

Even from writers of this kind, committed to the cause of advancing human liberty, a frequent response has been the wry acknowledgement that no simple way exists of 'setting mankind free', especially if doing so entails defining or illustrating a free action. In fiction the results of this acknowledgement are profound. If a man is moulded, defined and located not simply by birth and fortune but by the pressure of his fellowmen, by the part 'They' expect him to play, it is not surprising that the novel and the drama are deficient in contemporary heroes. Instead of a hero we have a passive figure who explores society without changing it, or is simply operated on by it. The novelist, as Zola said, 'must kill the hero'. When Lukacs describes the novel as 'peculiarly the resolution of the problem of the individual in an open society', it is possible to apply his words to the novel of our time only by attaching a rather special sense to 'resolution': the problem is indeed embodied in the very structure of many modern novels, but it would be naive to suppose that a situation of such complexity is resolved as soon as it is objectified in a work of art.

Outside this loose tradition of social realism the landmarks are few and confusing. It is perhaps helpful to think of an opposition at the beginning of the century between dedicated optimists like Wells with a boundless faith in the power of science to improve life and those who agree with Conrad, 'If you believe in improvement you must weep, for the attained perfection must end in cold, darkness and silence,'[1] but I do not think that it is possible to point to a dominant mode of thought, unless indeed it is the growing conviction that no mode of thought or behaviour has intrinsic superiority to any other. A few miscellaneous quotations from writers of widely differing casts of mind may suggest the varied sources from which such a conviction draws strength:

> Every one of those impressions [of external objects] is the impression of the individual in his isolation, each mind keeping as a solitary prisoner its own dream of a world. PATER

> Modern thought is distinguished from ancient by its cultivation of the 'relative' spirit in place of the 'absolute'. . . . To the modern spirit nothing is or can rightly be known, except relatively and under conditions. PATER

> In life there is really no great or small thing. All things are of equal value and of equal size. WILDE

> [A pragmatist] turns away from abstraction and insufficiency, from verbal solutions, from bad *a priori* reasons, from fixed principles, closed systems and pretended absolutes and origins. He turns towards *facts*, towards *action* and towards *power*. WILLIAM JAMES

> Patchouli! Well, why not Patchouli? Is there any 'reason in nature' why we should write exclusively about the natural blush, if the delicately acquired blush of rouge has any attraction for us? Both exist; both, I think, are charming in their way; and the latter as a subject has, at all events, more novelty. If you prefer your 'new mown hay' in the hayfield, and I, it may be, in a scent bottle, why may not my individual caprice be allowed to find expression as well as yours? . . . . There is no necessary difference in artistic value between a good poem about a flower in the hedge, and a good poem about the scent in a sachet. ARTHUR SYMONS

> There are no categories of images, noble or gross or vulgar, eccentric or natural. The intuition that grasps them has no preferences or *partis pris*. Therefore the analogical style is absolute master of all matter and its intense life. MARINETTI (Futurist Manifesto)

> Everything, from one point of view, is subjective; and everything, from another point of view, is objective; and there is no *absolute* point of view from which a decision may be pronounced. T. S. ELIOT (on F. H. Bradley)

> The work of art is never beautiful by degrees, objectively, for everyone. Criticism is therefore useless; it exists only subjectively, for each person. . . . Thus DADA was born from a need for independence, for mistrust before community of ideas. Those who belong with us retain their liberty. We recognize no theory. TRISTAN TZARA (Dada manifesto, 1918)

> [Things or objects are] nothing but an average stability of certain events in a set of agitations. WHITEHEAD

> Really any plot or situation would do. Because everything's implicit in anything. The whole book could be written about a walk from

Piccadilly Circus to Charing Cross . . . . ALDOUS HUXLEY (*Point Counter Point*).

In atonal music, however, which stems from 'totalities', intervals alone are relevant. Musical expression is no longer achieved through the use of major and minor keys and of specific instruments with a *single* timbre: it is founded on the totality of intervals and timbres, and this is best and most clearly realised by using one single, tempered instrument. JOSEF MATTHIAS HAUER

In the world everything is as it is and happens as it does happen. *In* it there is no value. WITTGENSTEIN

In logic there are no morals. Everyone is at liberty to build up his own logic, i.e. his own form of language, as he wishes. CARNAP

The poet's task is the protracted, arduous and calculated disorganization of all the senses. This will make him sick, criminal and accursed, all in the highest degree, but it will also make him supreme in wisdom. SARTRE

Freedom of choice is absolute. VOGUE (1976)

Everyone is talented. LAZLO MOHOLY-NAGY

Remarks such as this last lead naturally to the commendation of the art of children and primitive peoples—'Their spontaneous expressions spring from an inner sense of what is right, as yet unshaken by outside pressure.' Similarly Jaspers puts forward Strindberg and Van Gogh as examples of the way in which insanity can reveal a level of truth inaccessible to sane men. The insights of the unbalanced genius are sometimes credited to madness in general:

> Madness has in our age become some sort of lost truth. . . . Madness . . . is a way of seizing *in extremis* the racinating groundwork of truth that underlies our more specific realization of what we are about. The truth of madness is what madness is.[2]

It is easy to say simply that the twentieth century is an unstructured time and that this is not surprisingly reflected in the problems of structure which beset and obsess the twentieth-century writer, but the paradox lies deeper than this. It is true that from one point of view the dominant mode at present is one of unexamined faith in the autonomy of man, in the equal value of every act, in a world of self-subsistent units of being, and that this faith is carried almost to the point of solipsism. Yet this is evidently not a complete statement of the case, for there has never yet been a time when liberty, in Mill's sense, was as tightly circumscribed as it is now for all classes by laws, taxes and the procedural apparatus of government.[3] There are moreover in most countries powerful forces, organized or diffused, which are successfully effecting a steady movement towards collectivism. This is comparatively recent. 'Until August, 1914, a sensible, law-abiding Englishman could pass through life and hardly notice the existence of the state, beyond the post-office and the policeman.'[4]

These powerful contrary forces have been generated in our century by the central facts of modern society. In particular social pressures, the sheer mass of other people, are variously transmitted and transformed, as I have tried to show in the three preceding chapters (11–13). The sense of a man's fellow-citizens as an obstructive and almost irresistible force is pervasive in novels of every kind:

> It occurred to him that a man's last and best friends might be his flowers. They grudged nothing; they gave you results.
>
> Yes, and how little in the way of results could most poor, flustered conventional lives show? Just pathetic rushings to and fro after the passing of that state of semi-savagery and vague rebelliousness which is childhood. Getting up in the morning and going to bed, catching trains, eating indifferent food, responding rather blindly to the sex urge, squabbling with other individual men or groups of men over twopence on the wage-sheet, going with crowds of other human cattle to some cheap holiday resort and finding the same stale crowds there. Never to be alone, or to produce anything of significance, save perhaps a few children who would repeat the same obscure slave's march.
>
> The social system! Citizenship! Boodle!
>
> And it seemed to Sorrell as he sat there in the green corner of his own contriving that the intelligent rebel, the grim lone fighter was the man to be envied. Not all men could be rebels, ploughers of lonely furrows. Nor had he any quarrel with the inevitableness of the crowd; it was just frog's spawn glued together. And becoming more and more so.
>
> Poor people! Townsmen.[5]

Living in a society of this kind can limit men's freedom in many ways, some willingly accepted as part of the social compact, others uncovenanted and oppressive. It is not hard to see how reaction against such unwelcome limitations produces the two different extreme forces which we are considering.

First, the pressures of majority or received opinion, although not given the force and sanction of an organized legal code, operate to prevent the individual from having a mind of his own: his decisions are derivative, not authentic.[6] The desire to escape from this leads to an attempt to establish activities, purposes and satisfactions that are independent of other people: as we have seen, this entails a refusal to accept current *mores* precisely because they are current. In the extreme condition the only proof of identity is a deliberate antinomianism, so that if a society values serious, kindly and natural activities it becomes necessary to behave absurdly, cruelly or perversely.

The opposite process is equally easy to understand, since the other uncovenanted effect of living in a society is that, left to itself, a society changes in ways which injure individuals.[7] Prices fluctuate as demand varies, and some people become richer while others are on the border of starvation. Freedom is limited by the apparently inescapable laws of economics. Hence there is a demand for help for the oppressed, for economic planning, for restraint of trade, for control of the organs of opinion, for stronger government, for nationalization of the commanding heights of the economy, in short for a larger managing unit which will control everybody.[8] As the novels I have looked at in chapter 13 remind us, the danger is that effective power will pass into the hands of a very few men, whose motives for action may be corrupt, and who can justify every action, however unscrupulous, as essential for the safety of the state. In the extreme condition the freedom of living men is sacrificed to the well-being of a nonentity.

> Above all to feel for the State the kind of reverence, for the law the sort of respect, that is appropriate to persons, is an emotional unreason, the very essence of superstition. To worship the State is to indulge in idolatory. To personify the State is to pervert it, so that it tends to the destruction of society, not to its preservation.[9]

What is more puzzling is that the assertion of extreme relativism and the impulse towards total collectivism, though they seem to derive from opposed premises, are often found simultaneously at work in societies and individuals. To understand how this can be it is perhaps simplest to presume a chain of loosely associated propositions as follows: 'I am an individual and have a right to complete freedom to realize my individuality. Since no opinions are intrinsically superior to any others, my opinions are as good as anybody else's. It is the great discovery of our time that there are no absolute values, only relative ones. In a world without transcendent values, the values of human actions must be derived from men themselves. Whatever values are based on men are good. But if you wish to argue that some men are superior to others you have to use criteria of superiority which are derived from some source other than man. Therefore it is necessary to maintain that all men are equal. The doctrine that all men are equal is good, and so is any political system based on this doctrine, especially if it emphasizes human solidarity. All forms of collectivism are good and all other political systems are bad.' This is not intended to represent a logical argument but to suggest a set of intermediate ideas which would make it possible to understand how someone could entertain simultaneously the first and last sentences of the sequence.

There is of course an additional, and more direct, connection between relativism and totalitarianism. One of the effects of relativism is instability. Instead of referring questions of conduct to a constant body of opinion grounded in a belief in permanent values, there is continual recourse to an appeal to immediate and tangible consequences. In politics, for example, expediency, often on a very short view, takes the place of a consistent adherence to a political policy or set of principles. In morality the question asked is not 'Is it right?' but 'Will it pay?' The point is that the answers to such questions are by definition variable, often changing from day to day, and thus ultimately destructive of all principle. Yet the strongest argument for preferring democratic or liberal governments to dictatorships relies on establishing that they are in principle better, certainly not that they are more efficient. Limit the discussion to questions of effectiveness and you are meeting totalitarianism on its own ground.[10]

Nor is this a purely political experience. It includes also the practice of literary critics. Whenever a critic takes the inviting path of critical relativism, saying that various dissimilar authors are all 'good of their kind' he is contributing to the same outcome. The commonest form of critical evasion lies in an unwillingess to look for answers to questions of the form, 'The technical reasons for the success of such and such a text are easily established, but what else is there about the text that makes it of importance? *Why* is it great? What has it to offer of permanent value?' Yet not to ask questions such as these is by implication to accept that they are either unimportant or unanswerable. In either case the result is to move the critic towards an *ad hoc* relativism ('Does it work?') and away from any principles by which literary values can be established. Eliminating consideration of subject is a crucial stage in the movement towards artistic anarchy. And the man who accepts anarchy is, as I have suggested, poorly placed to resist the movement, in the name of efficiency, towards the imposition of uniformity.

If we now consider the matter in terms of literary art, it is plain that preoccupation with the individual as such sooner or later leads a writer to confront the problem of assigning values to a completely free action. Failure in this has the effect, which may well be unintentional, of recommending by implication those actions which are admittedly not free, in the sense that they are undertaken in the interests of or even at the direction of some larger unit, and thus ultimately reinforces the general tendency to increase the power of the state. This paradox by which individualism conduces to its opposite is expressed also in structural terms:

a work dealing with the individual in isolation may have one fully-realized character, as in Beckett, but by definition can have no more than one.[11] When more characters are introduced their relationship is unsatisfactory, as in Adamov and Artaud and Albee, or incomprehensible, as in Jarry and Ionesco, issuing as violence in the first case and frustrated by total inability to make contact in the second. The choice is between the Theatre of Cruelty and the Theatre of Inertia, both, as far as the central character is concerned, branches of the Theatre of Bewilderment. If these in fact represent the logical terminus of individualism it is not surprising that the conclusion drawn from these works is that individualism issues in nothing and a more powerful social structure is called for.

It is worth noting that the writer of plays or novels of this kind is confronted with the same technical problem as the man writing about the power of the state, that the human interest of the work is limited to a single character. From this point of view they are at the same dead-end. There is not much to choose between a cell and a dustbin. For the novelist or the dramatist the most fruitful assumption is that man is most himself when he is relating freely to his society, neither introverted nor incarcerated.

It is at this point in our exploration of 'les chemins de la liberté' that an understanding of Sartre would prove most helpful, drawing together many of the different lines of enquiry, philosophical, literary, political and linguistic. Iris Murdoch says, I think with good reason, 'To understand Jean-Paul Sartre is to understand something important about the present time. As philosopher, as politician, and as novelist Sartre is profoundly and self-consciously contemporary; he has the style of the age. The landscape of his activity exhibits to us the development of this style as a natural growth out of the European tradition of thought on ethics, metaphysics and politics. Connexions which elsewhere are subterranean stand clearly traced out in the prolific lucidity of Sartre's work.' This is the beginning of Miss Murdoch's brief introduction to Sartre (1953). 'Lucidity' is not, as the rest of her book shows, precisely the word for Sartre, but in her admirable analysis of his sleight of hand with the idea of freedom (pp. 74–7) she establishes clearly the point that Sartre embodies with particular vividness confusions that are to be found elsewhere: he parades these confusions so insistently that it is hard not to feel that he does so as part of a deliberate strategy.

On the particular question of human freedom Sartre seems to me typical of his time in his desire for the best of both worlds, to be able to insist with Mathieu 'There is no within. There is nothing. I am nothing. I am free' and at the same time to insist that individual choices are 'choices for humanity'. He is like Mathieu poised between Daniel's offer of a life conditioned by an *acte gratuit* and Brunet's unreflecting commitment to Communism. The insistence on the positionlessness of the self, on its existence as a naked capacity for action, on its nature as nothing in particular, coupled with its timelessness, in the sense that every act of a man is quite unconnected with anything that has happened previously and is directed wholly towards the future instead of being determined by the past, this insistence certainly allows Sartre to set the self as free agent in powerful opposition to *le visqueux* and all the false natures that are fashioned for us by 'others', but only at the cost of adopting positions such as, 'A man exists as *nothingness*: if he becomes something specific he is no longer free.' This seems to me to take Wilde's ironic *reductio* of Huysmans and put it forward as a serious account of human experience. That which is shown to be positionless and timeless runs the risk of being also considered pointless. As Tolstoy put it, 'A being uninfluenced by the external world, standing outside of time and independent of causes would not be a human being at all.'[12]

Most men today, I think, consider that they have free will, recognize that the exercise of the will as an end in itself is insufficient, and therefore use their freedom to commit themselves in various ways that limit their freedom. This last act is in turn variously circumscribed, notably by social environment and political necessity, so that it is difficult to decide with any confidence the extent to which such social and political limitations amount to a positive diminution of the freedom of the individual's will as opposed to a disagreeable but unavoidable restriction of the scope of his actions. Although these restraints are different in kind from those I have examined in earlier centuries in that they vary from place to place and do not necessarily suppose any universal and inevitable constraining principle, it is notable that both of them tend to assimilate with science, as in the disciplines of social science and political science,[13] and to move towards the formulation of general laws of human acivity. Such laws could obviously be felt to indicate intrinsic limitations of our condition, behaviourism and Marxism being clear examples. Although Sartre never ceases to worry at the problem and continually stresses its importance, he does not seem to me to advance our understanding of it, but the contradictions which he is prepared to accept are so flagrant and so worrying that he compels his readers to return again and again to this most bewildering and fundamental of epistemological dilemmas. Human thought on questions of freedom has seldom been clear and almost never totally consistent. Not only the nature of freedom but also the nature of whatever was thought to limit

freedom has normally presented itself to mankind in forms packed
with internal contradictions, but in looking over the literature of
the last six centuries I am conscious in no other period of the same
desperate confusion as is prevalent today.[14]

In many people, especially perhaps in young people, it takes the
form of two simultaneous demands—one for unlimited personal
freedom, the other for an increase in the power and scope of the
state and the agencies of the state. Each of these seems to me to
rest on a wilful misunderstanding of what it entails. The point is
economically brought out by Durkheim in his diagnostic account of
the modern state, which, he writes in *Suicide,*

> makes a sickly effort to extend itself over all sorts of things which do
> not belong to it, or which it grasps only by doing them violence. . . . On
> the other hand, individuals are no longer subject to any other collective
> control but the State's, since it is the sole organized collectivity. . . . For
> most of their lives nothing about them draws them out of themselves
> and imposes restraint on them. Thus they inevitably lapse into egosim
> or anarchy. . . . While the State becomes inflated and hypertrophied in
> order to obtain a firm enough grip on individuals, but without suc-
> ceeding, the latter, without mutual relationships, tumble over one
> another like so many liquid molecules, encountering no central energy
> to retain, fix and organize them.[15]

It is remarkable that those who denounce existing institutions
and practices in the name of personal freedom can at the same
time contemplate with equanimity, indeed with enthusiasm, a
steady increase in the power of the corporate state. To give up all
other liberties in the name of existentialist freedom is to exchange
the substance for the shadow. 'A noble hart may haiff nane
ease,/Na ellys nocht that may him plese,/ Gyff fredome failythe',
wrote Barbour in the fourteenth century, and 'Sweet indeed is the
name of liberty and the thing itself a value beyond all inestimable
treasure', said Peter Wentworth in the sixteenth century, and
'Where Liberty dwells, there is my country', said Milton in the
seventeenth century. Presumably freedom from tyranny as
Barbour and Wentworth and Milton understood it, as Shelley, de
Tocqueville and Mill understood it, is a condition of happiness
which is not valued until it is irrecoverably lost. As I have said
earlier in this section, literature depends on a way of life which
recognizes the rights of the self and the rights of others: it can
flourish only in a society which will guarantee both of these
things.[16] If our society will not do so, it must be changed. And if
anybody suggests that it is presumptuous to demand a different
society so that we may have a different literature I reply that there

are many worse reasons for changing society. What in the world are societies for if not to enrich the lives of us all?

If it is illogical to accept simultaneously as ideals a complete personal freedom and a high level of authoritarian government, is it any more logical to reject them both? Lord Henry Wotton and Gletkin cannot both be right about the nature of freedom, but can they both be wrong? Does repudiating one mean that we must agree with the other? Is it inconsistent to deplore Sartre's or Genet's account of the free act and yet to insist on the importance of personal freedom? If it is so difficult to give any content to the notion of a free action how can anyone be certain that political liberty is genuinely desirable? Can we distinguish between the kind of sensible pluralism that tolerance enjoins and the undiscriminating relativism that leads to anarchy? We are now once more outside the realm of literature and confronted with a different face of the problem with which this book began. What I hope is now clearer is the consequence in human terms of taking particular positions in the argument. Many of the literary works that I have dealt with have shown under examination the contradictory nature of the writer's assumptions or the undesirable and unacknowledged consequences that flow from these assumptions. Are there any tenable positions left?

In addition to the works cited in the notes the following have useful material on the themes of this chapter: S. Freud, *Civilization and its Discontents* (London: Hogarth Press, 1930); Fritz Stern, *The Politics of Cultural Despair: a study in the rise of Germanic ideology* (Berkeley: California U.P., 1961); Victor H. Brombert, *The Intellectual Hero: Studies in the French novel, 1880–1955* (London: Faber, 1962); Barbara Tuchman, *The Proud Tower: a portrait of the world before the war, 1890–1914* (London: Hamilton, 1966); H. Stuart Hughes, *Consciousness and Society: the Reorientation of European Social Thought 1890–1930* (London: MacGibbon and Kee, 1967) esp. chaps. 1, 2, 9; Louis Kampf, *On Modernism: The Prospects for Literature and Freedom* (Boston, Mass: M.I.T. Press, 1967) esp. chap. 6; Samuel Hynes, *The Edwardian Turn of Mind* (London: O.U.P., 1968); Alasdair MacIntyre, *Against the Self-Images of the Age* (London: Duckworth, 1971); Richard Ellmann, *Golden Codgers* (O.U.P., 1973) pp. 113–31; Lucien Goldmann, *The Philosophy of the Enlightenment* trs. H. Maas (London: R.K.P., 1973), esp. chap. 3; Malcolm Bradbury and James McFarlane (edd.) *Modernism 1890–1930* (Harmondsworth: Penguin, 1976); Gerald N. Izenberg, *The Existentialist Critique of Freud: The Crisis of Autonomy* (Princeton U.P., 1976).

15

'This is as far as we go'

And being now at some pause, looking back into that I have passed through, this writing seemeth to me, *si numquam fallit imago,* (as far as a man can judge of his own work,) not much better than that noise or sound which musicians make while they are tuning their instruments: which is nothing pleasant to hear, but yet is the cause why the music is sweeter afterwards: so have I been content to tune the instruments of the Muses, that they may play that have better hands—BACON, *The Advancement of Learning*

I

Whether I have in any measure carried out the promises of my introductory chapter I must leave the reader to judge. One claim will not, I am confident, be disputed, that the subject of freedom is a warren of contradictions and paradoxes, which intense study does nothing to resolve, although it can perhaps make their nature and their peculiar painfulness more apparent. In Book II of *Paradise Lost* Milton observes that the more sedate of the Fallen Angels, sitting on a hill apart, found it at once their recreation and their torment to debate philosophical questions, and that they

> reason'd high
> Of Providence, Foreknowledge, Will and Fate,
> Fixt Fate, free will, foreknowledge absolute,
> And found no end, in wandring mazes lost.   (558–561)

Not the least of the pains of fallen man is a similar compulsion to examine the nature of his own compulsions, the mind continually attempting to understand the origins of its own undertakings and to frame its conclusions in language that does not continually degenerate into 'wandring mazes' of self-referential paradox.

The vocabulary of the debate has a similarly diabolical practice of changing its form in unexpected ways. Thus the harmless word ἰδιώτης 'a citizen who holds himself aloof from public life or who acts from private motives' becomes 'idiot' and implies a lack of all the qualities that make a man truly rational: while the powerful word 'authentic' comes from αὐθεντεῖν, which means among other things 'to be a murderer'. Occasionally a special irony seems to attach to a semantic change, as for example when the Greek word for 'choice' becomes 'heresy, that doctrine which it is forbidden to choose'. The inconsistency of human treatment of this area of experience is well shown in a group of phrases: 'accident', which should mean 'any chance occurrence' now means predominantly 'a disaster' especially in the strange expression 'a fatal accident', whereas 'act of God' now implies 'some experience, usually unpleasant, which has come about purely by chance'; 'happening' is a cant word for 'a prearranged event', rather like 'occasion'; although 'chance' is the common word for 'an opportunity for a person to decide to do something', its synonym 'lot' has become 'destiny'.

That these vagaries are not without their significance may appear from one of the oddest sets—that of 'necessity', 'liberty' and 'freedom'. Ανάγκη and 'necessitudo' mean not just 'necessity' but also 'a blood-relationship', a fact that brings to mind Hugh Kingsmill's remark that friends are God's way of making up for relatives. In contrast 'liber' means not just 'free' but 'dear or beloved': it is especially strange that 'freo' in Anglo-Saxon has the same pair of meanings.

Small wonder that the traveller in this jungle echoes Isaiah Berlin's plea (see p. 19) for 'a set of new conceptual tools, a break with traditional terminology'. It may seem unnecessary to make this point at a time when there is a substantial measure of agreement among philosophers about the conditions that justify calling an act free. These broadly require that the agent should be adequately informed (that is, that he should understand the nature of the act and of possible alternatives), that he should not be acting under external duress, and that he should arrive at his decision after a sufficient period of deliberation (driving into a lamp-post to avoid running over a dog, for example, may be a voluntary decision but need not be considered free, since the act was too hurried to be a deliberate one). If these conditions are observed it is argued that an agent will normally be prepared to justify his action and accept responsibility for it, that is, he will have a sufficient feeling of autonomy to adopt the act as his own. This then is the free action, or as near as we are going to get to a free action. If we ask for more we are pitching our demands for freedom at an impossibly high level.

Before we consider these conditions it is necessary to point out that choice is not in itself a guarantee of freedom. In one of Zeno's paradoxes it appears that if we can arrive at sufficiently small intervals of time there is no difference between an arrow in motion and an arrow at rest. We can only assume that the former is operating under some force as the result of a past happening

14

which, if nothing hinders, will take it to a different place by the next interval of time. It is perhaps not unfair to express the human situation similarly by describing all sentient human beings as in motion, that is, charged with that which will take them to the place they have to go to next. If there were no time, there need be no choices, that is, one could simply exist; but inevitably we find ourselves confronted each instant by a decision to make. Time forces what is into being at the cost of an infinitude of cancelled possibilities. As Wordsworth put it in Book VI of *The Excursion*:

> Time flies; it is his melancholy task
> To bring, and bear away, delusive hopes,
> And reproduce the troubles he destroys. (515–517)

The passing of time is the cancelling of possibilities. Time is a subtracting machine. For time-borne creatures choice is compulsory. The very fact of having to make a decision is enough to limit our freedom, and the fact of choice is not in itself a guarantee of free action. In the old conundrum about whether you should rescue your child or your mother from a burning building the very fact of not being able to do both is a limitation on your freedom. The point is even clearer if you consider a choice between two intensely disagreeable alternatives, row in the galleys or be whipped, kill someone or be killed yourself, submit to blackmail or go to prison. It is like being given the choice of being shot by a black man or a white man; it is the fact that one way or another you are going to be shot that limits your freedom: the area where you have choice is insignificant in comparison, though within that area it is a real choice. Thus if you have to make a choice you are no longer free: you can no longer elect not to choose. The fact that there is a choice is not a guarantee that there is also an exercise of freedom in a significant area. The conviction 'There are a number of choices open to me from time to time' does not lead to the conclusion 'I am free', still less to the conclusion 'Man is free'. As Housman puts it, no doubt with a deliberate echo of Fitzgerald:

> To stand up straight and tread the turning mill,
> To lie flat and know nothing and be still,
> Are the two trades of man; and which is worse
> I know not, but I know that both are ill.

Choice implies freedom if it offers a choice between different termini, but not if it offers only a choice of routes to the same terminus.

To return to the conditions of a free act, it is clear that 'duress' is not a simple term. If we take it merely to mean a gun in the back there is no difficulty in finding actions free from duress. But are we not equally acting under duress if we have been conditioned to behave in only one way? And can we, to take the matter a step further, fairly distinguish between conditioning and upbringing? If not, are we obliged to admit that every decision we take on a point of principle is made under a subtle kind of duress? This is a convenient place to consider in more detail Professor Ayer's successive treatments of determinism, each discussion modifying its predecessor in an important point.[1] The crucial turn of the argument in 'Freedom and Necessity' comes on page 278, where he says

> It is not, I think, causality that freedom is to be contrasted with, but constraint. And while it is true that being constrained to do an action entails being caused to do it, I shall try to show that the converse does not hold. I shall try to show that from the fact that my action is causally determined it does not necessarily follow that I am constrained to do it: and this is equivalent to saying that it does not necessarily follow that I am not free.

His argument falls into two wings. First, in terms that immediately recall T.H. Huxley[2] he denies the reality of the concept of cause and effect, replacing it by the phrase 'invariable concomitance'. Thus instead of saying 'A causes B' we should have to say 'B is the "invariable concomitant" of A', or that A and B are, as Ayer puts it on page 283, 'factually correlated'. But this does not affect the issue. 'An act and its consequence' will do just as well as 'cause and effect' provided that it is agreed that a given act will always have the same consequences. If B invariably follows A and this pattern obtains throughout the universe, then where can the sequence of events be said to be undetermined, and how can human free will have any sphere in which to operate?[3] The alternative is to suppose that B is not an invariable but only an occasional concomitant of A, and that there is no anterior event which determines whether it shall happen or not (for if there were such an event then the occurrence of B would be necessitated). In other words we must assume that B is a causal progenitor. Thus taken literally Ayer's term 'invariable concomitance' excludes the freedom of the will, while if we interpret it loosely it leaves us a choice between a determined and a random universe but gives no assurance that either will allow for the exercise of free will.

The second wing of Ayer's argument is that even if we agree that the postulate of determinism is valid we are not therefore bound to admit any diminution of human freedom, for, he says, 'It is not when my action has any cause at all, but only when it has a special sort of cause, that it is reckoned not to be free' (281). The 'special sort of cause' he has in mind here is one of physical or obsessional constraint, for only this kind of constraint really denies freedom. But, he continues, this is not what he means when he says 'cause'. Therefore 'cause' and 'constraint' are two different things. Although this particular argument has obvious weaknesses—in *The Concept of a Person* Ayer hints that he is no longer prepared to rely on it—it still rests with the necessitarian to show that determinism does 'constrain' in a real sense.

The argument that it does is clearly set out, by Shelley for example, and may be summarized as follows:

1. What a man does in a given situation is always what he thinks best having regard to the circumstances, provided that such a course of action is within his power, i.e. he *cannot* do other than what he thinks best. In other words he necessarily follows that course of action for which the motives appear strongest, for if two (or more) courses of action were equally attractive then the man, like Buridan's scrupulous ass, would be unable to act at all, since he could not prefer one to the other until they had ceased to be equally attractive. Only one course of action is therefore open to him and, since there is only one course open, this he is constrained to take.

2. The motives that will present themselves are already determined in precisely the same way as the rest of the Universe has been determined by its past. Moreover the relative strengths with which these motives will present themselves to the chooser are similarly determined by heredity and by environment.

3. Thus only one course of action is possible, the man's discovery of that course of action is inevitable, and his taking that course of action when it is discovered is mandatory. We may express this in the terminology that Ayer uses in *Man as a Subject for Science:*

A motive (S) which can be satisfied only by an action (A) must always be so satisfied unless (a) the action is not possible or (b) there is a stronger motive (S_a) not compatible with (S).

In that case (S_a) will be satisfied by performing (A_a), subject to provisos (a) and (b) above.

And so on. Until we reach the conclusion that the strongest set of compatible motives ($S_x + S_y$) must be satisfied.

Once this set has been discovered the necessary actions ($A_x + A_y$) are mandatory.

When Ayer says, 'I should have acted otherwise if I had so chosen' (282) it is clear that he could have chosen otherwise only if there had entered into his decision some factor not previously present. To suppose otherwise is to suppose that a man can prefer one course of action to another for no reason. Unless we are prepared to make this assumption we are confronted still with the cruel antinomy:

> A free man is one who does what he most wants to do.
> An unfree man is one who does what he has to do.
> Every man has to do what he most wants to do.

The challenge then is to provide some substantial context for the notion of freedom. At present I do not see that much progress is being made in this direction. Whether we regard freedom as a quality of actions or of the state of a person, the argument turns back on itself in a familiar fashion.

From what has been said above, it seems that a 'free' action should be an unmotivated action, on the grounds that all principles of choice are in some degree constraining and that all rational choice is by definition motivated. If this is accepted for the moment, what sort of actions would qualify as free actions? They might be of two kinds, either a yielding to the physical impulses of the moment (that is, man is free in the sense that a weathercock is freely suspended), or a choosing what there is no impulse to choose (that is, man is free as a lunatic is free).[4] Neither of these is very attractive as a paradigm of a free act. Anybody who has read *The Rainbow* will recognize and, I imagine, repudiate the first kind.[5]. The theme of the chapter on Wilde was the difficulty of discovering any act that adequately exemplifies the second kind and yet is not hopelessly trivial (like scratching one's nose when it doesn't itch) or masochistic (like cutting off one's ear) or destructive (like breaking a window which you would just as soon not have broken) or perverse (like doing something which revolts you). There is also the obvious objection that if you deliberately commit such an act in order to show that your will is free the act itself has clearly been motivated by an anterior consideration, whereas if you commit the act involuntarily then it is valueless as evidence of the freedom of the will. I cannot escape the conclusion that the only kind of choosing that needs to be taken seriously in the argument is the kind that there is no turning back from.[6] The alternative ('I'll accept but I don't have to go if I'm not feeling like it') is not choice but pseudo-choice: its exercise is not freedom but pseudo-freedom. To commit yourself is the only free act, but you can only perform it by being no longer free to uncommit yourself, not only deliberately abrogating freedom to do otherwise at the moment, but also accepting that the decision will entail that certain options will be closed in the future. This kind of free act is thus the willing assumption of a continuing responsibility.

The position is equally paradoxical if we consider the free actions of an intelligent individual through his lifetime. If we imagine a man assiduous to explore and understand his own personality, to discover principles of conduct and abide by them, to be consistent in his dealings, to become, as we say, an integrated personality, es-chewing eccentricity, fantasy, perverseness and caprice, always trying to be worthy of himself, it is plain that he has in one sense a sadly impoverished freedom. He is so far a prisoner of his own definition of his own nature that he is very seldom in a position to make a choice except on the basis of principles to which he is already committed. An increase in definition entails a diminution in freedom.

Once again, but for different reasons, an attempt to illustrate the nature of a free action has apparently led to a situation of attenuated freedom. Is the difficulty removed if we speak instead of a person being in a free state? A free state is presumably one in which a person is not influenced by any external considerations whatever. The condition would be one of total inactivity: to ensure that it was distinct from one of utter insensibility we should have to specify that it was such that the individual must also be able to respond to various motives and act in accordance with them. To give the state any permanence we should also, I think, have to specify that it is recoverable after action. This would give us a view of human nature as alternately committed and uncommitted: committed while acting and while existing under constraint, uncommitted, but not insentient, between actions. Objectively regarded this gives us a 'billiards ball' picture of man—at rest only until prodded in one direction by something not himself, once impelled travelling by a set path which he does not determine, coming to rest again and then theoretically capable of moving in any direction but in fact only going where he is pushed. But sub-jectively regarded the problem is more interesting. We ask in effect whether a billiards ball would be right to feel free at any point during a game, or, alternatively, whether it would make sense for a billiards ball to claim to perceive itself freer when at rest than when moving. 'Freedom in action' is a contradiction in terms, since action implies commitment to a specific course. If freedom is rightly applied to billiards balls at all it must apply to a state. The question is whether a state of inactivity in a man is in any way more valuable than it is in a billiards ball.

There is an initial difficulty in defining 'a state of inactivity'. It must be something more positive than death and sleep, yet less active than sitting motionless and thinking. What we must try to define is a state of 'wise passivity', a state suspended from activity and from the concerns of the world, in which a man contemplates inwardly, and this, I think, has to mean that he can contemplate literally nothing but his own selfhood and his own freedom. So that 'freedom' would mean something like 'the state in which the only activity is the contemplation of freedom'. This deliberately enclosed definition is designed to emphasize at once the paradox and the oriental circularity of the whole idea. To Western man this self-regarding may seem a mode of life which is hard to justify. Yet if it is the only alternative to a life of action, of itching and scratching, of striving, and of ambition it is an area worth preservation. It is not a Promethean kind of freedom, but quite the reverse: it is a private inviolable core: it is simply the self in a state of purity. If you can understand this and achieve the state then you are free, and therefore freedom is real. If you cannot then freedom is to be found nowhere else.

This suggests for 'freedom' a definition such as 'the state you are in when you have so far disencumbered yourself from all mundane concerns that you are nothing but "human"—no more specific label (name, nationality, political party) can be attached to you because you have no specific commitment, that is, you are impersonally human'. This sounds not implausible, but I find it hard to conceive what the state in question would actually be like, presumably one of inertia, of unearthly detachment, a trance-like condition very far indeed from what is normally understood by freedom. By that definition one could be just as free in a prison cell as anywhere else, freer in fact because there would be fewer distractions. Yet I do not think many people would be prepared to accept this argument from a tyrant who proposed to lock them up but assured them that it would not impair their inner liberty.

The awkwardness of making freedom an attribute either of an action or of a state is so evident that it is tempting to use some unfocused expression such as equilibrium. Choosing one way or the other in a situation would be voluntarily losing one's equilibrium. Freedom would therefore consist in control of one's equilibrium, which control would include the ability to forfeit it at an appropriate point: freedom would indeed be worthless without such an ability. Once again we arrive at the situation where the value of freedom depends on the willingness to surrender it.

To summarize: existing means existing in time, and existing in time means not only being continually forced to make decisions but also carrying with you the freight of previous decisions. Like the arrow, as soon as you are no longer charged with force from a past impulse you are permanently at rest, or dead. The parallel is with a man driving a car at very high speed. He is faced with a series of choices which cannot be evaded while the car is moving. (In fact he will of course, if he is driving well, be reducing all the time the alternatives before him by eliminating possible bad choices, his objective being to constrain himself to drive well. This is a fair reflection of many of our activities. We try to eliminate the burden of having constantly to make conscious choices, for example by making some actions habitual, and we try to eliminate dangerous possibilities, like a motorist driving in such a way that the only options he leaves open to himself are safe ones.) From this the conclusions to be drawn are first that a pure state of abstracted freedom is not possible for living man, secondly that the fact of choice is not in itself a token of freedom, and the necessity of choosing may be felt as a peculiarly painful loss of freedom, and thirdly, as is almost self-evident, that all the important choices that we make are acts of commitment: even where the fact of choice itself is not felt as a burden the consequences of these crucial choices are normally to eliminate a large number of future alternatives. 'Exercising freedom' in this sense means 'willingly accepting a commitment'.

For the moment I leave these attempts to conjecture what might be an adequate description of the attributes of a free man and turn to some current accounts of the universe as a whole, with a view to discovering whether they make any provision for the existence of freely willing creatures, assuming that we can attach some sufficient meaning to 'freely willing'.

II

With Earth's first Clay They did the last Man's knead,
And then of the Last Harvest sow'd the Seed:
  Yea, the first Morning of Creation wrote
What the Last Dawn of Reckoning shall read.—FITZGERALD, *Rubaiyát*, 53.

In the Introduction I quoted the most celebrated of all statements of a determinist position, that of Laplace. It will be remembered that in this statement Laplace wishes to emphasize the inevitability with which one state of the universe succeeds another, all the elements of the later state being already present in the earlier. Laplace is not, on my reading of the passage, saying that the universe is governed by scientific law, that a characteristic of scientific laws is that they enable predictions to be made, and that their truth or falsity can be established by testing the accuracy of their predictions. He invokes his supreme intelligence as a rhetorical device, a vivid presentation of the point that all the material that determines future states of the system is already present. One unfortunate consequence of this way of expressing things is that determinism and predictability have been closely linked. As A. J. Ayer, writing in 1963, says

> Nowadays [the doctrine of determinism] most commonly takes the form of maintaining that every event is theoretically predictable.[7]

Two possible fallacies are encouraged by stating the case in this way—first, the argument that events are not in fact predictable and therefore determinism is false, and secondly the argument that events are not even theoretically predictable and therefore the will is free.

C. S. Peirce, the American scientist and philosopher, is sometimes credited with being the first modern writer to draw attention to the impossibility of measuring physical objects precisely enough to make predictions of the order of accuracy required.[8] It does not seem to me that this is an argument of great force, any more than it would be to argue that Laplace's intelligence could not really predict the future because by the time he had gathered all the necessary information the system would have changed.

Something like the same assumption seems to underlie the arguments of those who found their case on the uncertainty of modern quantum theory. As Ayer has pointed out 'The thesis of determinism has lived very largely on the credit of classical mechanics.'[9] For example, behind Shelley's insistence that we know of no instance of an 'infraction of nature's laws'[10] stand Holbach and the secular Calvinism of Laplace, and behind them again the line stretches from de la Mettrie to Huygens, all attempting to elucidate the implications for mankind of the simple Newtonian propositions that no object could initiate its own motion or, once it was moving, alter its own speed or course. It is often suggested that atomic physics, since at times its phenomena seem to defy the laws of classical mechanics, forces us to reject a necessitarian view of the world. Werner Heisenberg writes, for example, 'With the mathematical formulation of quantum-theoretical laws pure determinism had to be abandoned.'[11] What Heisenberg has in mind is the Principle of Uncertainty, which lays down the conditions under which it is possible to ascertain accurately the momentum and the position of an atomic particle, the uncertainty lying in the fact that an accurate measurement of both properties simultaneously is not possible. Susan Stebbing comments on this

> Once the Principle of Uncertainty is accepted—and it must be accepted —then we must admit that it is not possible even in principle, to know the initial conditions in the case of quantum phenomena. Hence unless he confines himself to non-quantum phenomena, Laplace's Supreme Intelligence is not able to begin his calculations, since he cannot know precisely the initial conditions.[12]

Once again the attack seems to me to be wrongly directed. Laplace's supreme intelligence is *ex hypothesi* not restricted by human or physical limitations. If we are prepared to allow him the impossible ability to predict the total state of the world at time A_1 simply from an inspection of it at time A and a knowledge of the laws of nature, why should we hesitate to allow him equally the ability to ascertain the total state of the system even down to the position and momentum of each atomic particle.

If determinism is to be shown to be false it must, I think, be done not by personal attacks on Laplace's imaginary spirit, but by examining the notion of law and law-like behaviour. For example,, when we descend into the world of the sub-atomic particle has the expression 'law-like' any meaning? A clear statement comes from Ernst Cassirer. He describes Bohr's theory of the path of the electrons about their nucleus as follows:

> The electron can move only in certain designated circles whose radii are in proportion to the squares and whose frequencies are in proportion to the cubes of the quantum numbers; further it was shown that the electron can be raised from an inner to an outer orbit upon absorption of energy, and that it can fall from an outer to an inner orbit by energy emission. But to the question as to the *why?* of these two processes the theory lacks an answer.[13]

Now if Bohr has here given us an accurate account of atomic structure and behaviour, and this only a physicist can decide, then we live not in a determined but in an indeterminate universe. I am aware that much work has been done and is continuing either to disprove Bohr's work or to discover a cause for the jumping of the electrons. I have particularly in mind Professor David Bohm's theory that at sub-quantum level we have 'particle-like concentrations' that are 'always forming and dissolving'. It is important to note that Bohm's theory, although it accounts for many of the features of quantum mechanics by assuming a sub-quantum level, nevertheless postulates on this lower level some kind of random motion, derived for example from random fluctuations in the ψ-field itself or from 'direct interaction with new kinds of entities existing on this lower level'.[14]

If we accept Bohr's theory as being a complete description of atomic structure then we have here an example of a causal progenitor. Likewise if we accept Bohm's. There is no point here in distinguishing between microscopic and macroscopic events, since the minutest change of a single particle might conceivably have infinite consequences in the macrocosm.[15] Moreover if it is true to say that all scientific laws which describe large physical objects are in fact statistical in that they aggregate enormous numbers of happenings at molecular level no single one of which must conform to the general pattern, then the laws of physical behaviour can, strictly speaking, be expressed only as probabilities, however strong.[16] Any account of the change in the universe between Time A and Time A_1, would thus be at best provisional, not infallible, since the very laws whose constant operation must be presumed would be simply statements of probability. Notice that this has no direct relevance to the question of human free will; it merely alters our idea of the extent to which our universe is determined, that area which is not determined being governed by chance.

These are arguments of considerable force, and one might add to them by pointing to other areas of experience where events of crucial importance must, at least in the present state of scientific knowledge, be described as 'uncaused'. I have in mind such cases as the apparently spontaneous, though statistically regular, breaking up of radio-active material or the equally unpredictable, but equally critical, mutations on which evolution depends.[17]

A different objection seems to me to apply to J. R. Lucas's somewhat similar case. In *The Freedom of the Will* (1970) Lucas sets out to examine the case for physical determinism, which he identifies with total predictability. He argues that this would demand a language which offered a complete description of a system and its processes. But, he continues, Gödel has shown that any such language must contain at least one proposition that is undecidable in the language. Therefore any such language must be incomplete and no total prediction is possible. Once again we meet with an attempt to show that prediction as such is not feasible. At this point Lucas takes it as self-evident that if physical determinism cannot be established the only alternative is the traditional notion of human freedom. No doubt arguments like Peirce's and Heisenberg's and Lucas's have done much to weaken the credibility of classical determinism, but I must repeat that none of them constitutes a conclusive argument in favour of the existence of human free will; indeed they are more consonant with a world ruled by chance. It may well be true that in an indeterminate world there are very strong reasons for making every effort to devise some model of the universe that allows for human autonomy, but success cannot be taken for granted. Freedom cannot be smuggled in through gaps in scientific knowledge. The arguments I have been discussing imply that if the causal chain is broken it is broken at a point outside the will of man, that is, instead of Beggar-my-Neighbour we are playing Snakes and Ladders, not Contract Bridge. I turn now to examine briefly what is entailed in living in an indeterminist world.

III

The conception of chance enters into the very first steps of scientific activity in virtue of the fact that no observation is absolutely correct. I think chance is a more fundamental conception than causality; for whether, in a concrete case, a cause-effect relation holds or not can only be judged by applying the laws of chance to the observation.—MAX BORN

I have observed that whereas many writers have taken human free will for granted and many others, with resignation or even with a certain relief, have accepted a determined world, it is comparatively rare in literature to find an author who portrays his characters at the mercy of accident, or who seriously entertains the possibility that we live in an undetermined world. There is something repugnant in the notion that all human achievement is ultimately the product of random forces. In Einstein's phrase 'Der Herr Gott Würfelt nicht' ('The Lord God does not roll dice'), or as Jacques Monod puts it

> The probabilist ideas of modern science are plainly even more offensive than were the mechanistic theories of the early 19th century. . . . That man [might] be the sum product of a number of precariously preserved random events, how believe this, how face it otherwise than by testing it against biological man, at least against his works? How could pure chance ever have written the *Odyssey*, *Andromaque*, or the *St Matthew Passion*?[18]

Yet if the picture of the world which modern scientists almost unanimously endorse is correct, it seems sensible at least to review an indeterminist world and see what its implications are for mankind. We have then to examine a world where everything is a matter of chance, regularized into probabilities that have the force of certainties when the numbers involved are sufficiently large.

Once we cease to invoke the completeness and closure conditions which were taken for granted in classical physics, all choices become in effect choices of probabilities. As Bishop Butler put it in 1736 'Probability is the very guide in life',[19] to be echoed more than a century later by Clerk Maxwell:

> The true logic for this world is the Calculus of Probabilities, the only mathematics for practical men.[20]

Karl Popper writes, 'Indeterminism, which up to 1927 had been equated with obscurantism, became the ruling fashion. . . . I am an indeterminist—like Peirce, Compton, and most other contemporary physicists.'[21] If we accept this as a fair description of the general state of scientific opinion today, I think we must also accept the need to take account of it in our assessment of many questions of human behaviour, including problems of the will. Some philosophers, including of course Popper himself, have made notable contributions to this work,[22] but as recently as 1970 Patrick Suppes could justifiably write:

I have not read one action theorist who discussed what the theory of action would be like if matters of randomness entered into actions; for example, if causes were identified only probabilistically.[23]

Suppes' conclusions, as far as they bear on this particular argument, may be summarized in two quotations:

In principle an unaccounted probabilistic remainder cannot be eliminated.

From a general conceptual standpoint, the theory of stochastic processes can be looked upon as the theory of Causality investigated within a setting that is neither purely random, in the sense of probabilistically independent events, nor purely deterministic.[24]

The important point to notice about all these probabilist worlds, like Popper's and Monod's and Suppes's, is that the mere fact of introducing uncertainty into a determined Universe does nothing to establish the validity of a belief in free will. Monod's book ends

The ancient covenant is in pieces; man knows at last that he is alone in the universe's unfeeling immensity, out of which he emerged only by chance. His destiny is nowhere spelled out, nor is his duty. The kingdom above [i.e. objective knowledge] or the darkness below: it is for him to choose.[25]

When he expresses the modern dilemma in these striking terms Monod makes two linked assumptions—first, that men are freely willing creatures who are able to make real choices: secondly, that from a universe such as the scientists assure us we inhabit there are derivable human values strong enough to give meaning to the act of choice. If, to apply a widely-circulated phrase of Popper's, 'Indeterminism is not enough', can we find a way of advancing beyond indeterminism without making either of Monod's assumptions?

Imagine then a world in which the whole business of the

Universe proceeds in a lawlike manner (though with certain occasional random variations, some at least of which are likely to be of more than trivial effect), and there is no reason to suppose that the human will is exempt from the general laws (though human beings may from time to time perform actions to which they can assign no cause). In a world such as this what might be put forward as the strongest reasons against concluding that all human values are ephemeral and all human actions pointless and consequently relapsing into fatalism?

First, that in a random universe there would always be something to hope for, some unpredictable turn of events for the better, such as would not be possible in a determined world. Imagine a party of people stranded on a desert island. If they admitted that they could not possibly be rescued they would have nothing to look forward to but death, and if they looked at the map they would see that they could not be rescued, and so they do not look at the map. In a determined world, ignorance is a condition of survival. Yet if the people on the island knew that, in spite of the incontrovertible evidence of the map, from time to time and quite unpredictably boats departed from established routes and might turn up anywhere then hope might take the place of ignorance. The combination of destiny and hazard does much to make life tolerable.

Secondly, there are, even in such a world, real pleasures available. The fact that they are not permanent does not make them unpleasant.[26] The present can be enjoyed or, at worst, endured, and there is hope that the future will bring more pleasure than suffering. Such a set of beliefs would allow a modified Epicureanism, close to what is often called Stoicism:

"Αφοβον ὁ Θεός.
'Αναίσθητον ὁ Θάνατος.
Τὸ ἀγαθὸν εὔκτητον.
Τὸ δεινὸν ἐυεκχαρτέρητον.

('We need not fear God: We shall not feel Death: Good can be attained: Evil can be endured.')

Thirdly, even if we believe with Democritus that 'everything existing in the Universe is the creature of chance and necessity' or with Russell that 'Man is the product of causes that had no prevision of the end they were achieving; that his origin, his growth, his hopes and fears, his loves and his beliefs are but the outcome of accidental collocations of atoms'[27] we need not, I think, conclude that all human activity is 'a welter of futile doing'. It is no doubt true, to continue to quote Hardy, that 'if way to a better there be, it exacts a full look at the worst', yet man may legitimately take pride in the fact that, even if Russell is right, from an amoral universe a moral creature has evolved, capable of at least trying to comprehend ethical ideas and use them as principles of conduct. Again it would be wrong to state this in heroic terms. Arnold at one point refers to 'the struggle that keeps alive, if it does not save the soul',[28] but he does not suggest that there is any prospect of actually bringing the struggle to a decisive end. Conrad's magnificent *Victory* ends in something very like defeat: what makes Conrad the pre-eminent novelist of our century is his power to present without cynicism his unillusioned recognition of the ambiguous nature of human achievement.

These considerations, few and meagre though they are, are the strongest basis I can suggest for human life in a world such as I have postulated. They would not perhaps be sufficient to persuade a man of melancholy temperament that life in such a world was worth living. In what way, he might well ask, do men in a random world differ from the widows in the *Knight's Tale* as they complain bitterly:

> Thanked be Fortune and hire false wheel,
> That noon estaat assureth to be weel.   (925–6)

Yet removing the random element scarcely improves matters. If we allow that the world is controlled by an omnipotent power we may resign ourselves to its will, like the Clerk:

> [God] suffreth us, as for oure excercise,
> With sharpe scourges of adversitee
> Ful ofte to be bete in sondry wise;
> Nat for to knowe oure wyl, for certes he,
> Er we were born, knew al oure freletee;
> And for oure beste is al his governaunce.
> Lat us thanne lyve in vertuous suffraunce.   (1156–62)

Or if we believe in a determined world we may say with Theseus:

> Thanne is it wysdom, as it thynketh me,
> To maken vertu of necessitee,
> And take it weel that we may nat eschue,
> And namely that to us alle is due.   (3041–4)

But if, like most people, we feel that none of these ministers sufficiently to our dignity, it is natural to see with how little disturbance we may introduce into the world some small scope for human decisions that shall be neither obligatory nor haphazard.

At the conclusion of the chapter on Hardy (p. 275) I drew attention to the passage in the *Mayor of Casterbridge* where Elizabeth-Jane is shown carefully exploiting 'the secret (as she had once learnt it) of making limited opportunities endurable; which she deemed to consist in the cunning enlargement, by a species of microscopic treatment, of those minute forms of satisfaction that offer themselves to everybody not in positive pain' (XLV). The problem is to decide whether, in an undetermined world, there would be some scope for man in general to effect a similar cautious expansion of such pleasures as happen to come his way. Machiavelli begins the twenty-fifth chapter of *The Prince* from a similar position:

> It is not unknown to me how many have been and are of opinion that worldly events are so governed by fortune and by God, that men cannot by their prudence change them, and that on the contrary there is no remedy whatever, and for this they may judge it to be useless to toil much about them, but let things be ruled by chance. This opinion has been more held in our day, from the great changes that have been seen, and are daily seen, beyond every human conjecture. When I think about them, at times I am partly inclined to share this opinion.

He continues 'Nevertheless, that our free will may not be altogether extinguished, I think it may be true that fortune is the ruler of half our actions, but that she allows the other half or thereabouts to be governed by us.'[29] In an indeterminist world the characteristic intelligent human activity would presumably be that of identifying and seizing favourable 'occasions'. The task is to suggest the smallest possible human intervention which would enable man to take advantage of spontaneous changes in his environment, at once denying the sufficiency of a simple behaviourist response and eschewing the postulate of a complex choosing mechanism in man, with all the contradictions that any attempt to explain the operation of such a mechanism leads to. Take a very simple account, such as Locke's, of the process of deciding:

> The mind having in most cases, as is evident in experience, a power to suspend the execution and satisfaction of any of its desires, and so all, one after another, is at liberty to consider the objects of them, examine them on all sides, and weigh them with others. In this lies the liberty man has; and from the not using of it right comes all that variety of mistakes, errors, and faults which we run into in the conduct of our lives, and our endeavours after happiness; whilst we precipitate the determination of our wills, and engage too soon, before due examination. To prevent this, we have a power to suspend the prosecution of this or that desire, as everyone daily may experiment in himself. This seems to me the source of all liberty; in this seems to consist that which

is (as I think improperly) called *free-will*. For, during this suspension of
any desire, before the will be determined to action, and the action
(which follows that determination) done, we have opportunity to
examine, view, and judge of the good or evil of what we are going to do;
and when, upon due examination, we have judged, we have done our
duty, all that we can, or ought to do, in pursuit of our happiness; and it
is not a fault, but a perfection of our nature, to desire, will, and act
according to the last result of a fair examination.[30]

Provided we credit the mind with the power to forbear from
immediate action we need not even go so far as Locke in crediting
it with the ability to initiate decisions. In a random world merely
refraining from an instant response may give sufficient time for
chance to change the situation to our advantage. The crucial
element is that of deliberation. We might argue then that simply
because man is self-conscious he is not obliged, as many other
creatures are, to respond automatically to a stimulus. He must act
in one way or another, as we have seen, but he can shorten or
prolong the time of deliberation and thus take advantage of chance
dispositions of the state of affairs by guessing whether instant or
delayed action is likely to produce the richer set of options. Once
again time is crucial.[31]

The obvious analogy once more is with biological processes. The
question there is how 'higher' forms can conceivably have evolved
purely by chance. Darwin and modern biologists offer a highly
plausible hypothesis by which accidental variations, if beneficial,
become part of the phylum.[32] Thus without any outside inter-
ference we see more organized forms arising from more primitive.
If we credit humans with no more than the power either to act at
once or to refrain from acting until they see whether the next set
of circumstances offers a better selection of probabilities, we can
show, by a parallel argument, how this limited attribute could
enable them to improve their lot in a world of chance and ultimately evolve the whole complexity of human structures.[33] The
degree of control men are granted is by definition extremely
limited. Those areas of the system where men can exercise the
faculty we call choosing are very small indeed: the rest of the
system is beyond human reach and is not necessarily going to take
us where we want to go. We are living in, at best, an indifferent
universe and there is no inevitable progress. We can use our
occasional opportunities of choice to commit ourselves to whatever
we think will further human development, whether it is the family,
a calling, a cultural tradition, or a nation-state, but we should
expect nothing but gradual and piecemeal improvement.

Naturally the process would be much more rapid if we were

prepared to take a further step and allow also that humans can
actively encourage the emergence of chance effects, some of which
will probably be to their advantage. That is, we suppose that man is
governed by the same laws as all other creatures, except that
whereas the rest of the world has to wait for an uncaused event to
occur at random, like a plant-breeder passively hoping for an
attractive mutation, man can on his own initiative randomize a
situation, either externally (as by premium bonds, roulette wheels,
drugs, or alcohol), or internally by such devices as Edward de
Bono's 'lateral thinking', or the 'ideas session' in an advertising
agency where ideas are bandied about so quickly and with so little
restraint that they almost well up from the subconscious, the
object being to tap an original line of thought. Other examples
might be scientific discovery, according to Koestler's view, or
popular ideas of artistic creation, with considerable support from
major Romantic critics.[34] Unintelligently used this power to
introduce an element of chance into affairs might diminish
freedom, as for example a girl tossing a coin to decide whether or
not to accept a proposal. Intelligently used it can increase options, a
man either in effect betting that the second situation will be more
attractive to him than the first, or expecting that he will be able to
choose between the first and second situation (necessarily, of
course, choosing the more attractive). There are thus two cases to
consider. In the first man has the option of delaying a decision in
the hope that the situation will change to his advantage, in the
second that of inducing mutations in the hope that one will be
favourable. Although these do not increase or confer freedom,
they do at least give a man who understands his expectations from
chance occurrences a number of opportunities which are denied
to the rest of creation.

  I am deliberately not pitching my claims for human powers very
high at this point, suggesting merely that it might be possible to
argue that there is some scope, however marginal, for intelligent
human initiative in an indeterminist world, but none, as far as I can
see, in a completely determined world. This limited degree of
control of environment which I postulate is essentially experimental, and represents human development as a continual process
of trial and error. It is rather like Popper's view of the physical
world as an open system with human life evolving by a process of
error-elimination, except that I cannot find room in Popper's
account for any authentic human enterprise. I have tried to allow
for this in the most economical way; my model represents human
consciousness as operating rather like Maxwell's demon opening
and closing his shutter to select the beneficial and reject the dis-
advantageous manifestations of random activity, or like the thrifty

Dutch in Goldsmith's poem *The Traveller* gradually and painfully converting the barren ocean to productive land:

> To men of other minds my fancy flies,
> Embosomed in the deep where Holland lies.
> Methinks her patient sons before me stand,
> Where the broad ocean leans against the land,
> And, sedulous to stop the coming tide,
> Lift the tall rampire's artificial pride.
> Onward, methinks, and diligently slow,
> The firm-connected bulwark seems to grow;
> Spreads its long arms amidst the watery roar,
> Scoops out an empire and usurps the shore;
> While the pent ocean, rising o'er the pile,
> Sees an amphibious world beneath him smile:
> The slow canal, the yellow-blossomed vale,
> The willow-tufted bank, the gliding sail,
> The crowded mart, the cultivated plain,
> A new creation rescued from his reign.   (281–96)

IV

With her anchor at the bow and clothed in canvas to her very trucks, my command seemed to stand as motionless as a model ship set on the gleams and shadows of polished marble. It was impossible to distinguish land from water in the enigmatical tranquillity of the immense forces of the world. A sudden impatience possessed me.

'Won't she answer the helm at all?' I said irritably to the man whose strong brown hands grasping the spokes of the wheel stood out lighted on the darkness; like a symbol of mankind's claim to the direction of its own fate.—CONRAD, *The Shadow-Line.*

Even if we grant a randomizing power as well as a deliberating power, this merely shifts the argument to the question of what determines whether or not in any given case a man makes use of such powers as he has. It is tempting to look for an answer in some such description of a free act as I gave on p. 413, which emphasizes the characteristic willing surrender of freedom and commitment to a course of action. On this view freedom is necessarily anterior to action, resides in the moment of indecision, and is experienced as a control of equilibrium. It is thus like youth, something which must eventually be set aside in favour of maturity, or, more accurately, like money, a thing quite useless in itself, and desirable only because you can dispose of it in exchange for something else. Similarly freedom, simply as a state of possible action, is nothing in itself: it is valuable because it implies freedom to do something. The thing once done, you are committed to it and no longer free. But this is not necessarily a matter for regret. You have purchased something.

Thus to say 'I am free' is almost a contradiction in terms. It is equivalent to saying 'I have no characteristics yet', or 'I am null', or even 'I am not', or 'I am undecided'. It is incomplete as it stands, and cannot be completed until some specific characteristic can be predicated, by which time you are no longer free but identified with a particular course of action.

This line of argument, attractive though it is, must be pursued with caution, since there is an obvious risk of emptying the idea of freedom of all content whatsoever, both before and after decisions; this would be tantamount to admitting that since freedom is only a means to an end it is no longer necessary if the desirable end can be obtained otherwise.[35] To believe in the intrinsic value of freedom would thus be no more than to subscribe to an ancestral superstition.

Once again we are faced with the problem of establishing the value of freedom in general terms. It is simple enough to take the first step by displaying the obvious contrast between the man who is in control of his own life and a system which allows no independent activity whatsoever, yet the argument never rests here. Literary history, even in a rapid survey of a few selected texts, embodies the dialectic of the debate. Thus we can demonstrate the difference between on the one hand the world of Chaucer or Lydgate, where men laboured under the domination of planetary influences or fictitious entities, both used, no doubt, as emblems of inexorable disposing forces, and on the other the heroes of Marlowe or Chapman, boldly defying all physical and mental constraints in the name of individual autonomy. Yet almost simultaneously with the acknowledgement of the power and inspiration of this proud claim came the questioning. Men began to ask, like Monsieur in *Bussy d'Ambois*, whether there was at work in the world a force which necessarily limited the scope of a man however triumphant and successful, and if so whether this force was an integral part of his own character or some external agency. Milton's heroic attempt to defend the liberty of the human will in a universe completely controlled by God was the logical terminus of the argument. The fiercely independent *uomo unico* of the Renaissance did not survive the combined weight of Milton, Cromwell, Hobbes and Newton. By the time of Pope we find a prolonged period of stability, in which man is indeed constrained by the essential order of things, but not irksomely.

Perhaps, however, it is not possible for men to rest long content in a world based on deference and subordination, and once more a single heroic figure emerged, that of Prometheus, embodying the need for human freedom and the faith that it could be attained which were the great dynamic principles of Romantic political and philosophical thought. (It is notable that Day One of Month One of Comte's Positivist Calendar was called Prometheus.) But, as the later parts of this book have tried to show, the recreation of Renaissance man in terms of Titanic myth was not of long duration. Even in Book VI of *The Excursion* the Solitary is speculating whether the whole Promethean legend may not be an allegory of

> Poor humanity's afflicted will
> Struggling in vain with ruthless destiny,

and Byron, as we have seen, encourages an equal scepticism about the efficacy of defiant assertion as a way of life. (It is notable that while the Positivist Library for the Nineteenth Century included select works of Byron, *Don Juan* was particularly to be suppressed.) Once more we find man constrained by the essential order of things, but now not agreeably: Tennyson memorably recorded his distress at the implications for man of modern science, while Hardy went so far as to represent humanity as a whole as subject to the dictates of an Immanent Will which was at best neutral, at worst ironically malevolent. But such speculations, involving abstract thought, have never been general.

Far more common have been those sensations of lack of freedom which derive from the deliberate or unconscious acts of other men, either manifested as the physical or social pressures which are so powerful in the works of Dickens and George Eliot, or as codes of correct behaviour which provoke transgression as the only way to demonstrate independence, or as organized national power. Even more compelling than these, however, is our understanding that the real limitation on unbridled liberty is not the force that other people exert against ourselves but our recognition of our own responsibilities to others—in Coleridge's marvellous line, 'Duty, chosen laws controlling choice'. It is this that submerges again the figure of Prometheus, indispensable to the human spirit but inadequate to the conditions of human life.

For the second step we have now all learned to take in a discussion of freedom is to move away from any general defence of unbridled personal liberty. Perhaps we have learned from Byron or Wilde that freedom may be an almost unendurable burden— 'Liberty is a different kind of pain from prison' as Eliot says in *The Family Reunion*. Perhaps we have been thoroughly schooled by Arnold and Ruskin in the social and cultural catastrophes brought

about by 'Doing as One Likes', and willingly accept a fixed place in
an ordered world, whether the order is that of Pope or that of
Wordsworth. Perhaps we have been struck by the moral force of
Bradley's rhetorical question 'Is there any "perfect freedom" that
does not mean "service"?' If we consider that the domestic seclu-
sion with which Dickens rewards his favourite characters does not
constitute an adequate kind of service, we may be led further to
thinking, like George Eliot, in terms of calling, a devoting to the
community of whatever gifts we have. Thus, we accept a progressively more heavily qualified version of liberty, and become progressively more feebly equipped to resist the final qualification
when we are invited to discard altogether the outmoded notion of
individual liberty in favour of a more responsible dedication to a
larger unit. As we have seen in our chapter on the state, there is no
simple reply to the demand that every man should leave his own
selfish pursuits and devote himself to a life of patriotism or altruistic service of the welfare of mankind as a whole, especially if the
most powerful content we can give the concept of freedom is
something like 'a state of being undecided for an appreciable space
of time followed by an action that ensures that you are no longer
free'. Obviously a strong, or Promethean, definition of free will
would be easier to defend. The weak definition which I tentatively
propose, though better than nothing, is much harder to deploy
against tyranny. I am not thinking here primarily in terms of
physical oppression but rather of mental control or conditioning:
bodily constraint is unnecessary if the mind is subdued.[36]

It is not only when I consider the claims of the nation-state that I
am particularly conscious of this hollowness in the presentation of
the case for individual liberty, but also when I try to frame an
answer to B. F. Skinner's *Beyond Freedom and Dignity*. Skinner's
case is built on the classical materialist position: 'A small part of the
universe is enclosed within a human skin. It would be foolish to
deny the existence of that private world, but it is also foolish to
assert that because it is private it is of a different nature from the
world outside.' (p. 186) He arrives at a familiar reductionist
definition of the self: 'A self is a repertoire of behaviour
appropriate to a given set of contingencies.' Thus he can argue that
appropriate manipulation of the contingencies will elicit specific
patterns of desirable behaviour from others and so refashion their
selves. The awkward places that Skinner's argument leads him into
are plain enough, but he is nevertheless a fair-minded and
intelligent behaviourist who states his case in reasonable though
disingenuous terms and must be answered. For if we cannot
explain what is wrong with Skinner's proposals to conduct
everybody by the appropriate Owenite paths to the Golden Age I

do not see how we can explain why more obvious political tyranny over mind and body is wrong.[37]

I will restate the problem in the terms which I have used earlier in this chapter. I postulated a world in which unanticipated possibilities welled up spontaneously, but could not be *willed*. Man can either reject them or allow them to survive. A man who is reviewing a rich selection of courses of action which have occurred to him and assessing them and their probable outcomes as accurately as it is given to him to do by the most rigorous standards which have presented themselves to him, and is conscious of himself as doing this, is engaged in a satisfying human activity. It is natural to say that this activity of assessing, deliberating and deciding is the characteristic activity of man, and that it cannot be interfered with except by denaturing him. But the standards by which he is judging are those built in or programmed in. The scrupulousness of the judging is similarly innate or acquired. Is there any way of distinguishing between the man who does what he has been brought up from infancy to consider right, that is, what we should call a man of principle, and the man whom the state or Skinner's controllers have conditioned from infancy to act in a particular way, that is, what we should call an unfortunate victim of brainwashing? Is one free and the other not? If they are both equally the product of their upbringing, why do we feel that there need be no infringement of human liberty in the normal educative processes of school and family life but that the conditioning forces of a totalitarian state are an intolerable oppression?

It is at this point that I find myself reluctantly unable to accept the arguments of Frithjof Bergmann, whose book *On Being Free* (University of Notre Dame Press: 1977) is an enterprising attempt to grapple with the central problems. He rightly lays great stress on education, and reaches the conclusion that freedom as such is not the aim of education, nor is it in general a helpful concept. What matters is that men should 'identify' with their actions by accepting them as their own. 'Those who accept anything real as part of their "true" self are free if they identify with the cause of their action' (p. 238). This is a persuasive line of argument, tenaciously pursued, but I do not see how it meets questions of indoctrination. Huxley's epsilons, a contented slave, a guard at a concentration camp who has been brought up with no other set of values, all these would no doubt accept their actions as their own, for this is precisely what their masters have trained them to do. But this does not mean that they are free. Winston Smith genuinely believed that he had learned to love Big Brother.

The question that confronts us is this. When the Director in *Brave New World* says, 'At last the child's mind *is* these suggestions,

Plate 10. Giovanni Batista Piranesi. Carceri d'Invenzione. *By courtesy of the British Architectural Library, Royal Institute of British Architects, London*

and the sum of these suggestions *is* the child's mind. And not the child's mind only. The adult's mind too—all his life long. The mind that judges and desires and decides—made up of these suggestions. But all these suggestions are *our* suggestions! . . . Suggestions from the State', or the Benefactor in *We* says, 'I ask you: what have men, from their swaddling clothes days, been praying for, dreaming about, tormenting themselves for? Why, to have someone tell them, once and for all, just what happiness is—and then weld them to this happiness with chains',[38] can we repudiate their conditioning by arguments that do not apply equally to all the experiences that during a lifetime mould a person's thinking? Is education, in short, a liberating force or the reverse?

Acquiring knowledge, techniques, intellectual processes and methods of discovery and analysis is liberating in two ways—it shows a man what sort of things are available for choosing and it equips him to earn money and thus be in a position to take advantage of the choices that are available. But at the same time education is, as Burke so often insists, filling him with ideals, with standards for choosing by, with, so to speak, habits of thought, which are in themselves no doubt excellent, but which strongly determine his choices. It is not by accident that reformers begin with education: they know that the subtlest and strongest compulsions are those that come from within, from those predispositions which the young mind observes and imitates in those it admires, from those habitual prejudices and predilections which were insinuated into our minds so long ago that they seem to be part of the very constitution of thought or of moral instinct. We call them principles, exempt them from question, and do not remember that we have ever been without them.

How to make a sound distinction between permissible education and illegitimate conditioning is a notorious question in political theory. Two main lines of argument are fairly well charted. The first begins from Ferdinand Tönnies' contrasted terms *Gemeinschaft* and *Gesellschaft*; usually translated as 'community' and 'society', a community representing an unorganized group which has evolved on a basis of natural friendship, while a society is a deliberately organized association brought together by a rational calculation of the advantages of concerted action or the dangers of isolation. Tönnies' distinction is used to great effect by John Macmurray.[39] In his essay 'Freedom in the Personal Nexus'[40] he writes 'Real freedom depends upon the character of the nexus of personal relations in which we are involved . . . I believe that if we consider the problem as it appears in the nexus of direct personal relationships, we are attacking it at ground level; we are laying bare its foundations' (p. 181).[41] Macmurray discusses the problem with great patience and insight: his conclusions may be summarized in two quotations.

> The ultimate fact upon which all society rests is the fact that the behaviour of each of us conditions the behaviour of the rest and is therefore a determinant of their freedom (p. 186).

> We have thus reached the point at which we can say that freedom can only be maintained in this nexus of human relationship by maintaining the primacy of the personal nexus of community over the functional nexus of organized society. If this is secured, then no doubt a well-organized society will provide greater freedom for its members than an ill-ordered society. But the most perfect organizing of society, if it involves the primacy of the State, as the authority of organized society, must result not in the extension but the obliteration of freedom (p. 192).

If we accept this distinction between a community, essentially a group of equals held together by friendship, and a society, essentially an organization of people held together by self-interest and fear, we can see that members of a community have a set of responsibilities towards one another which carry reciprocal rights. Thus, considering the family as a community, parents have a responsibility to bring up and educate their children: they have also the right to do it. If a parent teaches a young child to be kind to his sister this is not an infringement of the child's liberty, as it would be if the state taught him to adore Big Brother. Within a community people have a right to offer their idea of human nature to those who need to be given the material for forming their own idea. Even within a community this is ideally done from a basis of equality: in a family, where strict equality is not possible, it is generally agreed that there are limits to a parent's right to impose his ideals on his children, simply because, although younger and less experienced, they are individuals, and are entitled to respect as persons.[42]

If Macmurray's distinction is accepted it simplifies the problem a little, since we can reject the label 'conditioning' for the kind of loving exercise of responsibility that takes place in a family, or the free interchange of ideas and willing amalgamation of beliefs that characterize a friendship between equals. It may be retorted that in making a distinction between two kinds of conditioning and pronouncing one kind essential to our growth as human beings and the other destructive of it, I am doing no more than taking the idealist version of the state and limiting it to a personal or domestic context. Once it is admitted that anyone at all has a right to shape our ideas it is difficult to deny that this right is equally possessed by everyone who wishes to change our ideas for the better; there is no reason in theory why the sphere of each community should not be enlarged until the entire state is one community, which no doubt is what an idealist would wish to see. But love, which is the basis of a community, cannot be universally dispensed: Johnson refers in *The Vanity of Human Wishes* to 'Love, which scarce collective man can fill'. Lacking this sanction, the bonds between members of a state are not of a sort to confer the right to shape another person's way of life. In the absence of such a right tolerance is the proper relation.[43]

If we pursue this line of argument, the strongest conclusion that we can reach is that members of a community, such as a family, acting through love, have the right and the duty to do what they think best for other members of the community, especially younger ones, whereas societies, and *a fortiori* states, have only contractual rights, based ultimately on fear or self-interest. If we add the further distinction, or assertion, that a society exists to secure or extend the freedom of action of its members at the expense of those who are not members, while a community exists to make the freedom worth having and exercising, we have perhaps gone as far as we can in the direction of repudiating one kind of upbringing and justifying the other.

The second line of argument against conditioning follows on from this. An affectionate parent is always trying to enrich his children's experience and to refine their powers of discrimination, widening and enlarging the field in which these powers are exercised. This is precisely the opposite of the action of a totalitarian state, which aims to reduce the importance of these activities and make them automatic, and uniform. The implications of this are well brought out in the celebrated passage on education from Mill's *On Liberty*, which I quoted at length in chapter 13. The crucial point is Mill's insistence on 'the importance of individuality of character and diversity in opinions and modes of conduct', introducing as it does the principle that the individual represents the reality, the state an abstraction, and that diversity represents a good in itself. As Constant put it in a celebrated passage

One must not build upon an abstract idea, in the illusory belief that it can increase the sum of individual liberty. . . . There is a part of human life which necessarily remains individual and independent, and has the right to stand outside all social control. Where the independent life of the individual begins, the jurisdiction of the sovereign ends. Rousseau failed to see this elementary truth, and the result of his error is that *Du Contrat Social*, so often invoked in favour of liberty, is the most formidable ally of all despotisms.[44]

The first voice to be silenced by those who seek to impose and secure a closed society will always be that of the man who teaches other people about the existence of alternatives to the official system of values. While the existence of an alternative system of education is not in itself a guarantee of freedom, since it might offer parents only a choice between two equally unacceptable institutions, the abolition of independent schools in any country would be a crucial step in removing from parents the possibility of remaining in control of their children's education. The prohibition of any schools except those directed by the government is an assertion of the rights of the state at the expense of the rights of individuals which constitutes a final, because irreversible, step towards a totalitarian society. It is not just that if non-conforming schools may be proscribed in the name of state solidarity so can all other dissident associations, but that the ultimate effect of prohibiting alternative systems of education will be the imposition of uniform patterns of teaching and thinking. That is why, as Mill rightly saw, academic freedom is the central keep of the battle for liberty and why ensuring the survival of independent schools is not a question of preserving a few obsolete institutions as conferrers of status and privilege but a decisive test of political understanding and will.

It is of course de Tocqueville who most forcefully reminds us that the rights of the individual, tenuous as they are, must be guarded not just against hereditary power or the naked oppression of a dictator but even more carefully against the undifferentiated popular mass of a democracy. In particular he perceives, like Burke, the possibility of a despotism which will operate with unprecedented thoroughness precisely because it does so in the name of the people as a whole:

> It would seem that, if despotism were to be established amongst the democratic nations of our days, it might assume a different character; it would be more extensive and more mild; it would degrade men without tormenting them. . . .
>
> Above this race of men stands an immense and tutelary power, which takes upon itself alone to secure their gratifications, and to watch over their fate. That power is absolute, minute, regular, provident, and mild. It would be like the authority of a parent, if, like that authority, its object was to prepare men for manhood; but it seeks, on the contrary, to keep them in perpetual childhood: it is well content that the people should rejoice, provided they think of nothing but rejoicing. For their happiness such a government willingly labors, but it chooses to be the sole agent and the only arbiter of that happiness; it provides for their security, foresees and supplies their necessities, facilitates their pleasures, manages their principal concerns, directs their industry,

regulates the descent of property, and subdivides their inheritances: what remains, but to spare them all the care of thinking and all the trouble of living?

Thus, it every day renders the exercise of the free agency of man less useful and less frequent; it circumscribes the will within a narrower range, and gradually robs a man of all the uses of himself. The principle of equality has prepared men for these things; it has predisposed men to endure them, and oftentimes to look on them as benefits.

After having thus successively taken each member of the community in its powerful grasp, and fashioned him at will, the supreme power then extends its arm over the whole community. It covers the surface of society with a network of small complicated rules, minute and uniform, through which the most original minds and the most energetic characters cannot penetrate, to rise above the crowd. The will of man is not shattered, but softened, bent, and guided; men are seldom forced by it to act, but they are constantly restrained from acting: such a power does not destroy, but it prevents existence; it does not tyrannize, but it compresses, enervates, extinguishes, and stupefies a people, till each nation is reduced to be nothing better than a flock of timid and industrious animals, of which the government is the shepherd. . . .

Our contemporaries are constantly excited by two conflicting passions; they want to be led, and they wish to remain free: as they cannot destroy either the one or the other of these contrary propensities, they strive to satisfy them both at once. They devise a sole, tutelary, and all-powerful form of government, but elected by the people. They combine the principle of centralization and that of popular sovereignty; this gives them a respite: they console themselves for being in tutelage by the reflection that they have chosen their own guardians. Every man allows himself to be put in leading-strings, because he sees that it is not a person or a class of persons but the people at large, who hold the end of his chain.

By this system, the people shake off their state of dependence just long enough to select their master, and then relapse into it again. A great many persons at the present day are quite contented with this sort of compromise between administrative despotism and the sovereignty of the people; and they think they have done enough for the protection of individual freedom when they have surrendered it to the power of the nation at large. This does not satisfy me: the nature of him I am to obey signifies less to me than the fact of extorted obedience.[45]

The complementary argument is very clearly put by Kierkegaard, emphasizing not only the dangers of the taking over of Christianity by the state but even more the unique value of the individual:

The point of Christianity is that man is spirit, and spirit is self-differentiation. Christianity's infinitely exalted thought is that every Christian becomes one by different ways and different modes—always diversity, which is precisely what God wills, he who (hater of all mere aping, which is absence of spirit) is inexhaustible in differentiating. So the state took over Christianity, and the point in being a Christian became the greatest possible factory-made uniformity. It is, incidentally, a strange thing that the God of Christianity and the state have in a way one thought in common: both wish to have complete oversight—this is indeed the task of governors. But God, as infinite concretion, has oversight with infinite ease, he is not afraid that he may lose the oversight when he permits differentiation; no, his majestic certainty that he can keep the oversight is expressed precisely by his willing differentiation everywhere. The state, which is not quite certain, wishes to have the greatest possible uniformity—for the sake of oversight.[46]

This seems irresistible, yet if we try to secularize Kierkegaard and to generalize his remarks so that they apply to all the relations between the citizen and the state we meet at the outset with the awkward task of explaining that the kind of utter nakedness of the individual that Kierkegaard insists on in the religious context is not what we have in mind. 'The common sense of modern man is being compelled to recognize that the most important moral acts, those which control the issues of happiness and security, and have power by their effects to destroy or preserve, are acts transacted in groups, by group decision, by impersonal command and obedience.'[47] Some measure of co-operative endeavour, it must be allowed, is an essential part of every man's development: the problem of course is to demonstrate that this compulsory sacrifice of individual rights, as Nozick for example would regard it, can logically be limited at all once it has been permitted.[48]

To summarize again. (1) Our understanding of reality is ultimately actuarial: the limits imposed by reality, though inflexible in the aggregate, are not absolute. (2) The only freedom we can claim as a right is the freedom to assume our proper responsibilities. We have sets of duties: if these are assumed by anyone else or any organization we are personally diminished. What we may usefully take from Kierkegaard is the error of attempting to shed responsibility and the iniquity of supposing that the state can assume it as a surrogate. The totalitarian state aims at the minimum of freedom and the minimum of responsibility for each citizen. The open society must offer the maximum of responsibility and hence the maximum of freedom. The paradigm of the responsible man is Collingwood in de Vigny's *Servitude et grandeur militaires* (3) There is no inevitable current of progress, only points, as in a railway system, where an individual can perhaps take advantage of randomly generated possibilities. (4) These 'responsibility-points' have to be recognized and responded to. Somebody must teach each person how to do this. The only people with any right to undertake this are fellow-members of a community.

On this argument maximizing the number of 'responsibility-points' must be taken as a good in itself, whereas all a state can do by coercion is to reduce the occurrence of unexpected events. If a diverse society is more likely to engender accidents, to recognize them when they appear and to be able to take advantage of them, one should on the balance of probabilities, prefer a pluralist society, that is a society in which the state is not omnipotent, in which free association is encouraged, and in which communities of various sizes provide a context for the development of individuals. The virtues of a society of this kind have often been described. Robert Nisbet's *The Social Philosophers* and *Twilight of Authority* for example are clear and straightforward expositions.[49] Like Macmurray, Nisbet writes eloquently and movingly about the ideals of community and diversity, but these generous aspirations for the future liberty of mankind depend on two things. First, on being able to make the necessary fine distinction between tolerance, which recognizes and values for themselves the intrinsic qualities of different ways of life, and a relativism which denies that any qualities whatsoever are either intrinsic or valuable. As Wordsworth well remarked, 'Latitudinarianism is the parhelion [mock sun] of liberty of conscience, and will ever successfully lay claim to a divided worship.'[50] The second necessary assumption is that of the reality of the free exercise of the human will, for, as Sir Isaiah Berlin has demonstrated, you cannot defend one kind of liberty without being prepared to defend the other.[51] If we propose to distinguish between the legitimate processes of education and the abhorrent processes of conditioning on the grounds that only the former is calculated to produce a diverse population of freely-choosing individuals we have first to address ourselves to the problem of establishing that it is in fact possible for a man to make free choices. If we are sceptical about the existence of free will, or doubtful how to explain why it is of any importance, or at best able to supply only a weak definition of its scope, how are we to resist those who with the arrogance of a dictator or the inexorable bene-volence of Professor Skinner assure us that we shall all be much happier and much more truly human with no freedom whatso-ever? If one of Skinner's controllers tells you that we live in a world where everything is determined and therefore human rights and liberties are purely illusory, it is to his major premise that the argument must be directed: similarly if it is maintained that we live in a random world and therefore qualities such as diversity are purely accidental and have no value in themselves. If Monod and Popper rest ultimately in a world where chance performs its eternal ministry of evolutionary change, what reply do they make to the man with the machine-gun who tells them that he is the next stage in the development of man and they are about to become extinct? To quote Popper once more, 'Indeterminism is not enough'.

It may seem illogical to keep worrying away at this intractable problem, when it would be much easier to rest in the sombre consolations of determinism or the headier expectations of indeterminism, but, as I have tried to show, there is an immediate practical motive for attempting to establish with accuracy the nature, the extent and the value of human freedom.

V

Every great poet, every poet who has extensively or permanently influenced mankind, has been a great thinker;—has had a philosophy though perhaps he did not call it by that name; has had his mind full of thoughts derived not merely from passive sensibility, but from trains of reflection, from observation, analysis, and generalization.—MILL, *Early Essays*.

What is the bearing on literature of this long discussion of conditioning? Part of Skinner's case is that for many years men have been beguiled by what he calls 'the literature of dignity and freedom' into resisting the rational proposals of those who wish to bring about cultural advances. 'A person who possesses a "philosophy of freedom" is one who has been changed in certain ways by the literature of freedom' (p. 193). Skinner admits (p. 36) that 'the literature of freedom has made an essential contribution to the elimination of many aversive practices in government, religion, education, family life and the production of goods' but argues that 'it has been forced to brand all control as wrong and to misrepresent many of the advantages to be gained from a social environment. It is unprepared for the next step, which is not to free men from control but to analyse and change the kinds of control to which they are exposed' (p. 47). Similarly 'what we may call the literature of dignity is concerned with preserving due credit [for autonomous man]. . . . The literature thus stands in the way of further human achievements' (p. 62). Finally 'Life, liberty, and the pursuit of happiness are basic rights. But they are the rights of the individual and were listed as such at a time when the literatures of freedom and dignity were concerned with the aggrandizement of the individual. They have only a minor bearing on the survival of a culture. . . . The literatures of freedom and dignity have made the mistake of supposing that they are suppressing control rather than correcting it. The reciprocal control through which a culture evolves is then disturbed. . . . This could be a lethal cultural mutation. . . . If [our culture] continues to take freedom and dignity, rather than its own survival, as its principal value, then it is possible that some other culture will make a greater contribution to the future' (176–8).[52] Skinner not only misrepresents the effect of literature in the past, but is unconvincing when he turns to the future, not least because he nowhere shows why the 'survival of a culture' is either a sufficient end in itself or an adequate motive for human action. If the idea of a culture means anything at all it must suggest not just survival, but that which makes survival worth the struggle, some values which give meaning to existence beyond the provision of bare animal necessities and physical comforts. 'It is true, of course, that survival is the necessary condition for everything else, but it is only a *condition* of what has value, and may have no value on its own account. Survival, in the world that modern science and technique have produced, demands a great deal of government. But what is to give value to survival must come mainly from sources that lie outside government.'[53] It is here that Skinner underestimates, or rather ignores, the contribution which writers are making and still have to make.

One literary activity I should have thought would be recognized as beneficial even in Skinner's terms. I refer to the power of art in general, but especially literature, to shape and articulate a culture, showing why it is worth preserving. 'The Poet binds together by passion and knowledge the vast empire of human society,' as Wordsworth put it in the *Preface*. The other characteristic achievements of writers are more disruptive, and thus earn Skinner's disapproval. For writers can and do present pictures of contrasting ways of life and the good and bad results of various types of commitment—to one's self, to one woman, to the family, the group, the profession, one's class, one's country, to mankind, to a principle—all shown at the level of experience and encouraging independent choice. I leave on one side the argument, ultimately derived from Kant by way of Schiller, that real freedom can exist only in 'play', particularly in disinterested aesthetic contemplation, an activity which, it could be maintained, reunites the scattered or alienated elements of the human psyche in an inner harmony and balance.[54] As I have suggested, the processes of fiction take us very quickly into the heart of questions about free action and the government of the world: for example, are coincidences in a novel evidence of randomness or of non-randomness? Finally many writers today are directly interested in the nature of freedom itself and the conditions under which it can be exercised. They are thus continuing one of the most important debates about the nature of man.

The main lines of the debate are reasonably clear if we consider only those participants who have written in Europe from the translators of Boethius onwards—Calvin, Machiavelli, Hobbes, Descartes, Newton, Leibniz, Spinoza, Locke, Hume, Hartley, Rousseau, Kant, Hegel, Malthus, Lyell, Darwin, Kierkegaard, Marx, Gauss, Freud, Nietzsche, Einstein. My whole argument is that this debate has not been, as this selection of names would suggest, a series of exchanges between philosophers, theologians, political theorists and scientists, but that poets and novelists have carried an equal voice in it. 'Poets, not otherwise than philosophers, painters, sculptors, and musicians, are, in one sense, the creators, and in another, the creations, of their age.'[55] I have tried to show what part the great writers of our literature have played, not least by their insight into the human consequences of adopting each of the various possible positions. This insight is, of course, conveyed under the conditions of their art and by the peculiar means of their art, that is, in general, obliquely and by implication, rather than by the direct articulation of a series of propositions. By asking what assumptions about the freedom of the will are necessary for a full reading of a given text I have tried to provide a way of talking about literary texts both as independent works of art and as contributions to the general discussion. Each of the works I have examined has a right to be considered in both ways. To insist on limiting ourselves to one way only is to accept too low a standing for literature.

In the world in which we and our children will find ourselves living there will perhaps be no very obvious sources of pride or consolation. A world of statistical regularities where men cut the same sort of figure on a graph as the spinning of a coin is not one to fire the imagination. 'All religions, nearly all philosophies, and even a part of science testify to the unwearying, heroic effort of mankind desperately denying its own contingency.'[56] Yet it appears unlikely that the physicists will soon provide mankind with any more sympathetic model of the universe. Any literature that helps men to understand and live in the world as it is will be justified by its honesty. That is, we need not expect every great work of literature to bring us something for our comfort. If a Greek tragedy for example, or *King Lear* gives an honest account of the human condition there is no need to insist that rightly viewed it is really quite optimistic. Human nature can stand a great deal of truth. Of a world of contingencies perhaps the clearest reflection is given by the serious novel, that is one which offers us likely situations governed by fairly well-grounded economic, social and political expectations, responded to by characters with strong enough propensities for the reader to recognize whether a given response is probable (in character) or aberrant (out of keeping). Although this sounds rather an arid and theoretical basis for a novel it is not very far in spirit from the accounts of their own practice given by Balzac, George Eliot, Zola, Hardy, and Conrad. Such works, as Boswell said of Johnson's essays, contain 'bark and steel for the mind'. But human nature is so constituted that man needs to hope, not only that things will by chance work out well for him, but also that he will perhaps be able eventually to make them work out well for himself. Literature that encourages such hopes, even if they are groundless, is not without its value, at certain times and for certain needs—'And they shall be accounted poet-kings/Who simply tell the most heart-easing things.'[57] Yet as it is in the nature of hope to meet with disappointment, perhaps those who do not hope are in the end less distressed than those who do. In any case, age ensures that fewer and fewer things are left to hope for, and at that point the literature of honesty often comes to seem more substantial than the literature of hope.

Is it even possible to be honest about freedom? Or must we acknowledge that the problem can be neither shelved nor solved, or at least that all the possible resolutions entail if not an open contradiction at least a suppressed inconsistency, such as saying 'I believe men have free will. I realize that it is impossible to define a free action or a free state satisfactorily but if you let the paradoxes of free will alone they'll let you alone' or 'I don't believe in free will. I believe we are in a determined (or random) universe but there's no difficulty in acting *as if* we were free'? Should we not then have to acknowledge also that the best we can expect to find in literature are the shadows of our own bewilderment and the reflection of our compromises?

There are two objections to this. First, neither attitude provides any argument against the man, whether he is called dictator or controller or friend of the people, who offers to imprison you and re-programme you and your children until you have learned to love your chains. Neither blind faith nor pretence will help much then. The preferable course is to bring the debate into the open, strip away the sham arguments and start trying to decide what we mean by personal freedom and why we value it. We are not to pretend to a certainty that we do not possess, but equally we are not to let the case go by default because it is difficult and exhausting. If there is any hope of arriving at a view of the world which allows some scope for human autonomy, simple political expediency, if no higher motive, suggests that we should bring all our

15*

resources to bear on the search for it. And if at the end of the day we have to recognize that personal freedom is an illusion and that our objections to conditioning have no logical foundation, then this will be yet another bitter truth which the literature of honesty will have to prepare us to accept.

Secondly, I admit that in the life of day to day it does not make very much difference whether the question 'Is my will free?' crosses our minds or not. The cabbage and the cow, the soldier and the shepherd can continue to perform their functions without introspection and without speculating about the motives of others. But if we wish to live with an understanding of ourselves and of our fellow-men we must from time to time pause and consider whether we move under our own direction or at the bidding of forces we did not originate and cannot control. Even a provisional solution may serve if it is the best we can devise after the most thorough examination we can conduct. 'An unexamined life is not worth living.' To help us in this endeavour I do not think we can find a more penetrating analysis of the nature of freedom and of the whole nature of man than in the great imaginative writers. They are great precisely because they teach us about mankind.

> For books are not absolutely dead things, but do contain a potency of life in them to be as active as that soul was whose progeny they are; nay, they do preserve as in a vial the purest efficacy and extraction of that living intellect that bred them.

In addition to the works cited in the notes the following have useful material on the themes of this chapter: Sidney Hook (ed.) *Determinism and Freedom in the Age of Modern Science* (New York U. P., 1958); A. I. Melden, *Free Action* (London: Routledge, 1961); Steven M. Cahn, *Fate, Logic and Time* (New Haven and London: Yale U. P., 1967); R. L. Franklin, *Freewill and Determinism: a study of rival conceptions of man* (London: Routledge, 1968); A. Koestler and J. R. Smythies (edd.) *Beyond reductionism: new perspectives in the life sciences*, Alpbach symposium 1968 (London: Hutchinson, 1969); K. G. Denbigh, *An Inventive Universe* (London: Hutchinson, 1975) esp. chaps. 4 and 5; Joseph M. Boyle Jr., Germain Grisez, and Olaf Tollefsen, *Free Choice: a Self-referential Argument* (London: U. of Notre Dame P., 1976); Myles Brand (ed.) *The Nature of Causation* (U. of Illinois P., 1976) esp. pp. 1–44, and bibliography pp. 369–387.

Notes

Introduction

[1] Jerome B. Schneewind, 'Moral Problems and Moral Philosophy in the Victorian Period', *VS*, supplement to vol. 9 (1965), 29-46.

[2] J. A. Mazzeo, *Renaissance and Revolution: The Remaking of European Thought* (London: Secker, 1967), p. 68.

[3] *Don Juan*, III/90.

[4] J. S. Mill, *Early Essays*, p. 260.

[5] Arnold, 'Maurice de Guérin', *Essays in Criticism* (first series). Cf. '. . . the grand business of modern poetry,—a moral interpretation, from an independent point of view, of man and the world' ('On the Study of Celtic Literature', *Complete Prose Works*, ed. R. H. Super (Ann Arbor: University of Michigan Press), III. 380.)

[6] *The Advancement of Learning*, Bk. I.

[7] Shelley, *A Defence of Poetry*, ed. H. F. B. Brett-Smith, Percy Reprints 3 (Oxford: Blackwell, 1937), p. 51.

[8] Wordsworth, *The Prelude* (1805), XII. 301-2.

[9] Boswell, *Life of Johnson*, ed. Hill, rev. Powell, III. 291 (15 April 1778).

[10] Ibid. II. 82 (16 October 1769).

[11] *Leviathan*, Part II, ch. 21.

[12] *Liberty in the Modern State*, 2nd ed. (Harmondsworth: Penguin, 1937), ch. 1, p. 49.

[13] D. D. Raphael, *Problems of Political Philosophy* (London: Macmillan, 1970), ch. 5, p. 115.

[14] *A Careful and Strict Enquiry into the Modern Prevailing Notions of that Freedom of Will which is supposed to be Essential to Moral Agency* etc. (1754), sect. I. Cf. Kant: 'What else then is the freedom of the will but autonomy, that is, the property which the will has of being a law unto itself?' (*Grundlegung* Akademie ed., p. 449); see also Fichte p. 211.

[15] Defined by Henry Sidgwick as a 'conflict of opposite inconceivabilities' (*History of Ethics*, ch. IV, § 18).

[16] Jacob Burckhardt, *The Civilization of the Renaissance in Italy*, tr. S.G.C. Middlemore, 2nd ed. (Oxford: Phaidon, 1945), Pt. VI, p. 308.

[17] Bk. I, ch. 1, § 15 (ed. C. A. Patrides (London: Macmillan, 1971), p. 116). The reference to the Preface is to p. 70 of this edition.

[18] Milton similarly repudiates 'that power/Which erring men call Chance' (*Comus* 587-8) and associates Chance with Chaos (*P.L.* II. 907-10). Note also *Pardoner's Tale* 590-628, where hazardrye is reproved, especially in rulers.

[19] The term is used by C. D. Broad in *Determinism, Indeterminism and Libertarianism* (1934).

[20] *Logic*, Bk. III, ch. 5, § 2. Elsewhere in the *Logic* Mill writes, 'The universe, so far as known to us, is so constituted, that whatever is true in any one case, is true in all cases of a certain description; the only difficulty is to find what description.'

[21] *Théorie analytique des probabilités*, 3rd ed. (Paris, 1820).

[22] L. S. Stebbing heads ch. X of *Philosophy and the Physicists* (1937), 'For of thorns men do not gather figs, nor of a bramble bush gather they grapes.' Cf. *Boece* I metrum 6.

[23] William James, 'The Dilemma of Determinism', in *The Will to Believe*, etc. (New York, 1909) p. 150.

[24] Cf. Heisenberg on Descartes: 'He was the first to attempt the development of the mechanics not only of the celestial vault, but also of the soul, of organic as well as inorganic nature: for him physiology was no less a *mechanical science* than was astronomy. Nature can only be explained by itself, and its laws are identical with those of mechanics.' *Das Naturbild der Heutigen Physik*, trans. Arnold J. Pomerans (London: Hutchinson, 1958), p. 127. Heisenberg is briefly characterizing the line of philosopher-scientists stemming from Newton and including Gassendi, Boyle, Descartes, Locke, d'Alembert, de la Mettrie and Ostwald.

[25] Epilogue to *War and Peace*, tr. Rosemary Edmonds (Harmondsworth: Penguin, 1957), Pt. Two, 10-11, p. 1440.

[26] *Beyond Freedom and Dignity* (Harmondsworth: Penguin, 1973), p. 206.

[27] *Two Cheers for Democracy* (London: Arnold, 1951), p. 78. Cf. C. A. Campbell: 'The act of decision is felt to be a genuinely creative act, originated by the self *ad hoc*, and by the self alone.' *In Defence of Free Will* (London: Allen & Unwin, 1967), p. 44. For the opposed argument, where necessity is made an essential condition of the existence of personal character, see Hume, *A Treatise of Human Nature*, Bk. II, Pt. III, ch. 2. For Skinner on the self see ch. 15 p. 428.

[28] *The Human Situation* (London: Arnold, 1937), ch. 2.

[29] Epilogue to *War and Peace* (see n. 25) sec. 9, p. 1436, p. 1431.

[30] 'Liberal Legislation and Freedom of Contract', *Works*, ed. R. L. Nettleship (London: Longmans, 1888), III. 370-2. Cf. Charles Taylor, 'What's Wrong with Negative Liberty' in *The Idea of Freedom* ed. Alan Ryan (O.U.P.: 1979) pp. 175-193.

[31] *Writer and Critic*, tr. Arthur Kohn (London: Merlin, 1970), p. 112.

[32] *Ethics*, III, prop. 2n.

[33] *The English Moralists* (London: Methuen, 1965), p. 15. Cf. Hans Vaihinger, *The Philosophy of 'As If'*, tr. C. K. Ogden, 2nd ed. (London: RKP, 1935), esp. Pt. I, ch. 9, 'Practical (Ethical) Fictions'. Writers of such varied views as Kant, Bain, Bertrand Russell and Gilbert Ryle, to name only a few, have propounded strategies for disposing of the problem, either as a metaphysical topic or as a concern in daily living. A. J. Ayer (*Central Questions*, 1973) suggests that all we mean by 'an alternative course of action' is an 'acceptable fiction that such a course existed'.

[34] *Humane Nature* 1.

[35] Cf. Tolstoy: 'Wealth and poverty, fame and obscurity, power and subjection, strength and weakness, health and disease, culture and ignorance, work and leisure, repletion and hunger, virtue and vice are only greater or lesser degrees of freedom.' Epilogue to *War and Peace* (see n. 25), sect. 8, p. 1428.

[36] *In Defence of Free Will* (see n. 27), p. 18.

[37] Quoted by Macneile Dixon, (see n. 28) p. 277. Note that in the *Critique of Pure Reason* Kant linked freedom with God and immortality as the three central problems of philosophy.

[38] Epilogue to *War and Peace* (see n. 25), sect. 8, pp. 1426-7.

[39] 'The Roots of Liberty', in *Freedom Its Meaning*, ed. R. N. Anshen, (London: Allen & Unwin, 1942), p. 73.

[40] Bacon, *The Advancement of Learning*.

[41] I do not know any historian who has worked from precisely this point of view: Lord Acton's *The History of Freedom and other Essays* (London: Macmillan, 1907) is a history of political and religious liberties. Maurice Cranston in his extremely helpful book, *Freedom: A New Analysis* (London: Longmans, 1953; rev. 1967) mentions Richard Peters' project for a political history which would provide a history of thought about freedom and constraint. Note also Henry Buckle's unfinished *History of Civilisation in England* (1857-61), and Erich Fromm, *Escape from Freedom* (New York: Holt, Rinehart, 1941). Mortimer J. Adler, *The Idea of Freedom: A Dialectical Examination of the Conceptions of Freedom* (Garden City N.Y.: Doubleday, 1958) is an exceptionally thorough and useful classification of schools of thought. See also pp. 393-94.

[42] See n. 1.

[43] F. E. Manuel, *Shapes of Philosophical History* (London: Allen & Unwin, 1965); John Passmore, *The Perfectibility of Man* (London: Duckworth, 1970).

Chapter One: Chaucer

[1] All quotations from Chaucer are taken from *Works*, ed. F. N. Robinson, 2nd ed. (London: O.U.P., 1966).

[2] For other examples see W. C. Curry, *Chaucer and the Medieval Sciences* (1926, 2nd ed., 1960). See also T. O. Wedel, *The Medieval Attitude towards Astrology* (Yale Studies in English, 1920); D. C. Allen, *The Star-Crossed Renaissance* (Durham, N.C., 1941).

[3] 'The Knight: The First Mover in Chaucer's Human Comedy', *UTQ*, 31 (1962), 299-315. See also William Frost, 'An interpretation of Chaucer's *Knight's Tale*', *RES*, 25 (1949), 289-304.

[4] *The Knight's Tale* (Cambridge: C.U.P., 1966), p. 189.

[5] W. C. Curry, 'Destiny in *Troilus*', *PMLA*, 45 (1930), 129-68. See also H. R. Patch, 'Troilus on Predestination', *JEGP*, 17 (1918), 399-422, 'Chaucer and Lady Fortune', *MLR*, 22 (1927), 377-88, and 'Troilus on Determinism', *Speculum*, 6 (1931), 225-43; Morton W. Bloomfield, 'Distance and Predestination in *Troilus and Criseyde*', *PMLA*, 72 (1957), 14-26; Chauncey Wood, *Chaucer and the Country of the Stars* (Princeton: Princeton U.P., 1970).

[6] III. 624-630 is a clear example of this. Chaucer attributes to a conjunction of the moon, Saturn and Jove a sudden downpour of 'smoky reyn' which would otherwise seem a suspiciously convenient coincidence.

[7] For the full implications of this see *Boece* V prosa 3.

[8] Similarly when Troilus is waiting for Criseyde's return Chaucer continually draws attention to the passage of time, thus reminding the reader also of the approaching doom of Troy.

[9] Cf. *Boece*, Book V prosa 3 (150-172).

[10] *Not* here is either *not* ('do not say so' or 'say that she did not') or a contraction of *ne wot* ('do not know') as for instance at v. 1167. It is usually taken as the former, but the editors of the Globe edition print *n'ot*. The difference in meaning is slight but important: on the whole I prefer *ne wot* as more consistent with Chaucer's deliberate impartiality.

[11] Robinson, p. 384: the words in italics are Chaucer's gloss.

[12] For the first view see, for example, D. W. Robertson Jr, 'Chaucerian Tragedy', *ELH*, 19 (1952), 1-37 (cf. Neuse on *Knight's Tale*): for an example of the second view see Murray F. Markland, '*Troilus and Criseyde*: the Inviolability of the Ending', *MLQ*, 31 (1970) 147-59 (e.g. 'The narrator is a man whose point of view amused Chaucer and is supposed to amuse us').

[13] *Chapters on Chaucer* (Baltimore: Johns Hopkins U.P., 1951), p. 140.

[14] 'The majority [of critics] assert the compatibility of the Epilog', according to Sanford B. Meech, *Design in Chaucer's* Troilus, (Syracuse U.P.: 1959) p. 138: Meech lists these critics on p. 455. For a summary of opinion see James D. Gordon, 'Chaucer's Retraction: a Review of Opinion', *Studies in Medieval Literature: In Honor of Professor Albert Croll Baugh* (Philadelphia U.P.: 1961), pp. 81-96. The rejection of the Epilogue is made more attractive by *Parson's Tale* 1084-6: if the Epilogue were an integral part of *Troilus* there would be no need for Chaucer to ask pardon for the poem as an 'enditynge of worldly vanitees'.

[15] A. C. Spearing, *Chaucer: Troilus and Criseyde* (London: Arnold, 1976); E. T. Donaldson, 'The Ending of Chaucer's *Troilus*', in *Early English and Norse Studies* ed. A. Brown and P. Foote (London: Methuen, 1963); C. Muscatine, *Chaucer and the French Tradition* (Cambridge: C.U.P. 1957).

[16] Notice in particular *Troilus* I. 232-59, where Chaucer expressly commends love as natural, irresistible, comforting and conducive to virtuous behaviour, and advises his readers to follow Troilus' example by yielding to Love.

[17] The end of the fourth chapter of *The Allegory of Love* (Oxford: Clarendon, 1936) is given to a discussion of *Troilus*.

[18] *Medieval Sciences* (see n. 2), esp. pp. 241-9.

[19] *The Man of Law's Tale* 1132-4.

[20] For an extended description of 'fals Fortune . . . ever laughynge/With oon eye, and that other wepynge', see *The Book of the Duchess* 618-49 and *Merchant's Tale* 2057-64.

[21] From one point of view nothing shows more clearly Pandarus' utter failure to understand the nature of Troilus' love than his artless remark that 'in the dees right as ther fallen chaunces,/Right so in love ther come and gon plesaunces' (IV. 1098-9), but he is unwittingly expressing the nature of the forces at work in the poem.

Chapter Two: Tragedy

[1] The Monk's definition comes from Boethius, *De Consolatione* II prosa 2: see pp. 42-3.

[2] Defending poetry and the theatre in about 1580 Thomas Lodge maintained that the writers of Greek tragedy 'did set forth the sower fortune of many exiles, the miserable fal of haples princes, the reuinous decay of many countryes' ([*Defence of Poetry*], in *Elizabethan Critical Essays*, ed. Gregory Smith, I. 80).

[3] *Endeavors of Art: a study of form in Elizabethan Drama*, (Madison: Wisconsin U.P., 1954) pp. 112-28.

[4] Note that it persists as late as the eighteenth century: Ned Ward's version of Clarendon (1713) has moral comments in bad verse which are very much in the spirit of *Mirror for Magistrates*.

[5] There is the further implication that no man can control his destiny and it is thus folly to plan for happiness in this world. At this point the lesson is reinforced by the powerful medieval ascetic tradition of *contemptus mundi*.

[6] See especially 3279-86, where even the man 'stable and parfit in Crist Iesu' is subject to 'Fortune's doubilnesse'.

[7] Cf. William Baldwin's Address to the Reader, in which he says that the *Fall of Princes* has been brought up to date by including the stories 'chiefly of suche as Fortune had dalyed with here in this ylande: whiche might be as a myrrour for al men as well noble as others, to shewe the slyppery deceytes of the waueryng lady, and the due reward of all kinde of vices'.

[8] As witness for example the celebrated play by T. Preston, of which the running title is *A Comedie of King Cambises* while the title page reads *A Lamentable Tragedie mixed full of pleasant mirth*. Again, R. Edwards' *Damon and Pithias* is described in the Prologue as 'a tragical comedy', a just name for 'matter, mix'd with mirth and care'. In a similar vein, but too well known to need quoting here are Sidney's attack on 'mongrel tragi-comedy' and Polonius' encomium of the players.

[9] Cf. Sidney's description of the effects of 'high and excellent Tragedy' in *An Apology for Poetry* (c.1583, published 1595) in Gregory Smith (see n. 2), I. 177-8. Note also *Women Beware Women*, IV. i. 206 ff., where the point is made that great men are more conspicuous in wickedness and therefore in corrupting example.

[10] Cf. 'The Wirdes, that we clepen Destine', *Legend of Good Women*, IX. 2580.

[11] See G. K. Hunter, 'Seneca and the Elizabethans', *Sh S*, 20 (1967), 17-24.

[12] 'I doubt whether there bee any amonge all the Catalogue of Heathen wryters, that with more grauity of Philosophicall sentences, more waightynes of sappy words, or greater authority of sound matter beateth down sinne, loose lyfe, dissolute dealinge, and unbrydled sensuality: or that more sensibly, pithily, and bytingly layeth down the guerdon of filthy lust, cloaked dissimulation and odious treachery: which is the dryft, whereunto he leueleth the whole yssue of ech one of his Tragedies.'

[13] *The Overreacher: A Study of Christopher Marlowe* (Cambridge, Mass: Harvard U.P., 1952), published in Britain as *Christopher Marlowe: The Overreacher* (1954).

[14] Cf. Caxton, 'The foure elements menace alle men that thanke not God'.

[15] Note that physicians were traditionally realists and atheists (W. R. Elton, *King Lear and the Gods*, (San Marino, Calif., 1966), p. 224n.) See also J. Parr, *Tamburlaine's Malady, and other essays on astrology in Elizabethan Drama* (Alabama, 1953).

[16] Note also from the same scene Leicester's 'Too true it is, *Quem dies vidit veniens superbum,/Hunc dies vidit fugiens jacentem*', and Baldock's 'To die, sweet Spencer, therefore live we all;/Spencer, all live to die, and rise to fall'. The Latin tag is from Seneca's *Thyestes*. In the closing speeches of Ben Jonson's moral tragedy *Sejanus* there is an unexpected emphasis on the part played by Fortune in the plot and in men's lives: the play concludes with the couplet, 'For whom the morning saw so great and high,/Thus low and little, 'fore the even doth lie'.

[17] For a penetrating analysis of Faustus' last speech see J. P. Brockbank, *Marlowe: Dr Faustus* (Studies in English Literature series: London, 1962).

[18] In the closing scene of the play Virtue vanquishes both Vice and Fortune. This appears to have been one of the scenes written specially for a performance at court in the presence of the Queen in 1599. Note that in Chapman's *Bussy d'Ambois* (1607) Monsieur is already advising Guise that Fortune is hostile to 'the restless state/Of virtue, now thrown into all man's hate' (v. ii. 53).

[19] Note that the Duc de Guise was explicitly associated with Machiavelli in the Prologue to *The Jew of Malta*, lines 1-4.

[20] *The Medieval Heritage of Elizabethan Tragedy* (Oxford, 1956). See also A. P. Rossiter, *English Drama from Early Times to the Elizabethans* (London, 1950); *Angel with Horns and Other Shakespeare Lectures* (London: Longmans, 1961).

[21] The important parts of it apply also to the tragedy of Pyramus and Thisbe in *A Midsummer Night's Dream*.

[22] Chaucer, for example, tells the story in *Legend of Good Women*, Cleopatra's constancy being the central point: she is a martyr who dies for love. Lydgate mentions the story as too well known to be repeated in *Fall of Princes*.

[23] Maynard Mack in his illuminating essay 'The Jacobean Shakespeare', in *Jacobean Theatre*, Stratford-upon-Avon Studies 1 (London: Arnold, 1960), pp. 10-41, gives a different interpretation of this crucial scene (p. 27).

[24] *Shakespeare's Doctrine of Nature: A Study of* King Lear (London: Faber, 1949), p. 40.

[25] For a commentary on some of the implications of this passage see Hardin Craig, 'The Shackling of Accidents: A Study of Elizabethan Tragedy', *PQ,* 19 (1940), 1-19.

[26] Musidorus in Sidney's *Arcadia.*

[27] *Knight's Tale* 515-6.

[28] Andreas Capellanus. See C. S. Lewis, *The Allegory of Love* (1936) chap. I, iii; also N. K. Coghill in *Patterns of Love*, ed. Lawlor (see p. 46).

[29] Hardy, *The Ballad of Love's Skeleton (Collected Poems,* p. 884).

[30] Cf. Leontes' 'It is a bawdy planet, that will strike/Where 'tis predominant.'

[31] Cf. *Measure for Measure*, where the Duke plays a not dissimilar part.

[32] Many interpretations of *Winter's Tale* find reason for cheerfulness in the images of natural rebirth and seasonal renewal in the later acts (e.g. 'Thou met'st with things dying, I with things new-born.') No doubt there is a distinct lightening of tone in the theatre once the action shifts to Bohemia. But it would be wrong to suppose that the cyclical movement of the seasons is entirely a symbol of new life. The whole point of Horace's 'Diffugere nives . . .' (*Odes* IV. vii) is that the revolving year will make good change and loss in the natural world, but when men die they are nothing but dust and a shadow. Perdita will grow old in turn. Cf. Andrew Young's fine poem *Autumn.*

[33] See also Thierry in Beaumont and Fletcher's *Thierry and Theodoret:*

> How! my subjects?
> What do you make of me? Oh Heaven! my subjects?
> How base should I esteem the name of prince,
> If that poor dust were anything before
> The whirlwind of my absolute command!
> Let 'em be happy, and rest so contented,
> They pay the tribute of their hearts and knees
> To such a prince, that not alone has power
> To keep his own, but to increase it. . . . (II. i)

[34] E.g. Hippolito in *The Revenger's Tragedy:* 'Brother, I do applaud thy constant vengeance—The quaintness of thy malice—above thought' and Vendice's description of the prospect of revenge as 'sweet, delectable, rare, happy, ravishing!' (III. iv).

[35] *Volpone* III. i. 11-13. In the tragedies Revenge is sometimes externalized as an independent character, and sometimes operates more like a Jonsonian humour.

[36] Cf. Lussurioso at the end of *The Revenger's Tragedy:* 'Farewell to all;/He that climbs highest has the greatest fall./My tongue is out of office.'

[37] Cf. 'Man's understanding/Is riper at his fall than all his lifetime.' (*Women Beware Women* v. ii. 150).

[38] A striking but not uncommon image. Note that Pericles speaks of himself as 'A man whom both the waters and the wind/In that vast tennis-court [i.e. the sea] have made the ball/For them to play on' (II. i. 64). William Lathum in *Phyala Lachrymarum etc.* (1634) has a poem which opens with an extended comparison of the world to a Tennis-court: 'All manner chance are Rackets, wherewithall/They bandie men like balls, from wall to wall.' See also the quotation from Naunton on p. 53.

[39] Peter Alexander, *A Shakespeare Primer,* (London: Nisbet, 1951), p. 109. For earlier senses of 'daimon' see Plato (e.g. *Republic* x. 620E) and Plutarch, *Moralia*, de defectu oraculorum (tr. Philemon Holland, 1603).

[40] Note that in *Tristan* the lovers drink a love-potion supposing it to be poison: in fact it brings death to both of them.

[41] Cf. '"Run, Run, O Run": Drama and Melodrama in *King Lear*', *English,* 28 (1979), 109-15.

[42] Cf. Arnold's *Mycerinus*, where the doomed ruler says that men see the gods as they really are 'When, on the strenuous just man, Heaven bestows,/Crown of his struggling life, an unjust close' (29-30).

Chapter Three: Milton

[1] Hume, *Dialogues concerning Natural Religion*, Part X (Edinburgh: Blackwood, 1907), p. 140.

[2] Mill is dealing with Mansel's *The Limits of Religious Thought* (1858).

[3] All quotations from Milton are taken from *Poetical Works*, ed. H. C. Beeching, 2nd ed. (O.U.P., 1946).

[4] *Paradise Lost*, ed. Alastair Fowler, (Longman Annotated English Poets: London, 1971), p. 362.

[5] William Empson, *Milton's God* (London: Chatto, 1961), p. 177.

[6] Cf. *P.L.* III. 77-9: 'Him God beholding from his prospect high,/Wherein past, present, future he beholds,/Thus to his onely Son foreseeing spake.'

[7] 'Milton's "Satan" and the Theme of Damnation in Elizabethan Tragedy', *ES*, 1 (1948), 46-66.

[8] The problem is a familiar one in the form 'If A knows that B will do Y, is B free (e.g. to do Z)?' 'A knows' means (a) that A can say and already be right in saying that B will do Y unless something happens to prevent it, and (b) that A can say and already be right in saying that nothing will happen to prevent it. If (a) and (b) are not true, then A does not know: he guesses. If (a) and (b) are true they exclude any action on B's part that would stop him from doing Y (e.g. deciding to do Z). Milton is obviously aware of the difficulty. While the suggestion that God is free from temporal distinctions may lead the reader not to apply the full rigour of the argument to Divine foreknowledge, the same mitigating device is not available for Adam, who is given foresight (XI. 368) and thus brings to premature birth the incidents from the future of mankind which he sees but is powerless to avert (XI. 763-76).

[9] See Arthur Barker, *Milton and the Puritan Dilemma*, (University of Toronto, 1942), pp. 313 ff.

[10] Stanley E. Fish, *Surprised by Sin* (London: Macmillan, 1967) makes this point repeatedly in ch. 2, 'The Milk of the Pure Word' (pp. 57-91). Fish's whole defence of God rests on His naked presentation of reality. Cf. also Irene Samuel, 'The Dialogue in Heaven: A Reconsideration of *P.L.* III. 1-417', *PMLA*, 72 (1957), 601-11: e.g. 'The omniscient voice of the omnipotent moral law speaks simply what is. Here is no orator using rhetoric to persuade, but the nature of things expounding itself in order to present fact and principle unadorned.'

[11] There are other unresolved expressions in Bk. III. See, for instance, lines 95-6, where God says of Adam, 'So will fall/Hee and his faithless Progenie.' Fowler takes this to mean 'He, faithless, and all his progeny', but it can be at least as plausibly interpreted as 'He and all of his equally faithless descendants' or 'He and such of his descendants as prove to be without faith'.

[12] Fowler (op. cit.) in his note on this passage suggests that these are 'parallel causes'. This is not easily understood. Can either operate without the other? If only one of them can, the other is unnecessary. If neither of them can, then they are not parallel but linked in a causal chain. If both of them can operate independently they are in effect alternative, not parallel, paths to salvation. Leon Howard, ('"The Invention" of Milton's "Great Argument": A Study of the Logic of "God's Ways to Men"', *HLQ*, 9 (1945), 149-73), argues that Milton bases his poem on Ramist ideas of cause and that it is wrong to approach it with modern assumptions about causation. He makes the interesting point that with the rise of Newtonian physics we are accustomed to require a stricter chain of causality than the Ramists or the Puritans and may thus misunderstand the poem. It would, however, be equally true to say that we are now in a better position to assess it, since we can see the defects in the Ramist treatment of cause and can see also how the need to conceal these defects as far as possible helped to shape the poem.

[13] Fowler (op.cit. p. 98) quotes *De doctrina*: 'So extensive is the prescience of God, that he knows beforehand the thoughts and actions of free agents as yet unborn, and many ages before those thoughts or actions have their origin.' See Rom. 8: 29-30: 'For whom he did foreknow he also did predestinate to be conformed to the image of his Son, that he might be the first-born among many brethren.

Moreover whom he did predestinate, them he also called: and whom he called, them he also justified: and whom he justified, them he also glorified.' (cf. 9: 11, 15).

[14] See for example A. O. Lovejoy, 'Milton's Dialogue on Astronomy', in *Reason and the Imagination*, ed. J. A. Mazzeo (Columbia U.P., 1962).

[15] This is not to suggest that Professor Fish arrives at his final position without a careful exploration of the poem. The subtitle of his book is *The Reader in Paradise Lost*, and he gives Milton credit for extreme subtlety of organization.

[16] Lewis, *A Preface to Paradise Lost*, (O.U.P., 1942); Bush, *Paradise Lost in Our Time* (Cornell U.P., 1945); Summers, *The Muse's Method: An Introduction to Paradise Lost*, (Harvard, 1962); Burden, *The Logical Epic: A Study of the Argument of Paradise Lost*, (London: RKP, 1967); Fowler, op. cit. n. 4.

[17] Cf. *P.L.* IX. 773-5, where Eve says immediately before the Fall, 'What fear I then, rather what know to feare/Under this ignorance of Good and Evil,/Of God or Death, of Law or Penaltie?' Basil Willey, *The Seventeenth Century Background*, (London, 1934), pp. 240-63, has a thorough discussion of this difficult point.

[18] Cf. Augustine: 'Quidquid in sermone divino neque ad morum honestatem neque ad fidei veritatem proprie referri potest figuratum esse cognoscas.' See Willey, op. cit. pp. 57-75.

[19] I. 2.

[20] E.g. *P.L.* I. 98, IV. 50, IV. 82, V. 663.

[21] It is free in the sense that it concerns 'a matter in itself indifferent', since the actual eating of the fruit is not an action of any intrinsic importance. On the other hand the motives that are operating at the moment of choice are her memory of the Divine injunction prompting her in one direction and the desires that Satan has implanted in her in the other. As God knows, the latter will prove stronger than the former. Again we are told that when Eve had plucked the fruit

> Greedily she ingorg'd without restraint,
> And knew not eating Death: Satiate at length,
> And hight'nd as with Wine, jocond and boon,
> Thus to her self she pleasingly began.
>
> (IX. 791-4)

That is, the crucial choice is made in ignorance. She does not know that she will be punished by being made mortal. Indeed she might have supposed not unreasonably that if God set such store by man's complete freedom there could be no punishment for disobedience. If Adam and Eve had been told clearly all the consequences of eating the fruit they could still have decided no less freely to eat or to forbear.

Chapter Four: 1350–1660

[1] *The English Moralists*, (London: Chatto, 1964), p. 36. See also S. G. F. Brandon, *Man and his Destiny in the Ancient Religions*, (Manchester U.P., 1965) and *History, Time and Deity* (Manchester U.P., 1962). I have as far as possible in these intercalary chapters made use of uncontroversial standard histories.

[2] A. N. Whitehead, *Adventures of Ideas*, (1933; rpt. Harmondsworth: Penguin, 1942), pp. 69-70. Chapter IV, 'Aspects of Freedom', is a valuable general survey.

[3] Idem. ibid. p. 69.

[4] It is important to make it quite clear that we are not dealing here with uniform patterns of thought. Gower, for example, in his *Confessio Amantis* (1386-90) has the following striking praise of human power:

> The man is overal
> His oghne cause of wel and wo.
> That we fortune clepen so
> Out of the man himself it groweth;
> And who that other wise troweth,
> Behold the people of I[s]rael:
> For evere whil thei deden wel,
> Fortune was hem debonaire,
> And whan thei deden the contraire,
> Fortune was contrariende.   (Prologue 546-55)

Yet within a few lines we find:

For every worldes thing is vein,
And evere goth the whiel aboute,
And evere stant a man in doute,
Fortune stant no while stille,
So hath ther noman al his wille.   (560-4)

Cf. *Vox Clamantis*, II.

[5] Willey, *Moralists*, p. 124.

[6] Jacob Burckhardt, *The Civilization of the Renaissance*, trans. S. G. C. Middlemore, 2nd ed. (Oxford: Phaidon, 1945), pp. 215-16. For Pico della Mirandola's attack on astrology see p. 319. His nephew Gianfrancesco also wrote a treatise against astrology dedicated to Leo X, who had as a child been told by Marsilio Ficino that his horoscope indicated that he would one day be Pope.

[7] This is in fact a quotation from Vitruvius, *Architecture*, VI. 2.

[8] J. R. Hale, *England and the Italian Renaissance*, 2nd ed., (London: Arrow, 1963), esp. ch. VI, gives many more examples of this common view of the Renaissance.

[9] Mario Praz, *Machiavelli and the Elizabethans*, British Academy lecture (London, 1928).

[10] Whitehead, *Adventures of Ideas*, p. 63.

[11] Carlo M. Cipolla, *European Culture and Overseas Expansion*, (Harmondsworth: Penguin, 1970), pp. 101-2. Cipolla also quotes the revealing phrase '*Stadtluft machts frei*' or 'The air of the town makes one a free man' (p. 13).

[12] *Renaissance and Revolution: the Remaking of European Thought*, (London: Secker, 1967) pp. 71-2.

[13] *The Prince*, trans. L. Ricci, rev. E. Vincent, (O.U.P. World's Classics, 1935), p. 68 (ch. XV).

[14] For Nature and the powers above her see Tourneur's *Atheist's Tragedy*, v. i. D'Amville thinks that gold is greater than the stars, but he learns through the death of his sons that Nature is greater than gold, and that there is a power superior even to Nature. Once again the doctor is the agency of instruction.

[15] 'Of Feare' in the *Second Part of Essayes* (1601). See also his *Discourses vpon Seneca the Tragedian* (1601), esp. Sig E recto, which contains the characteristic phrase, 'Euery man his owne fortune.' For a rather different account see Ralegh, *The History of the World*, Bk. I, ch. 1, § 15; ch. 2, § 6: also Patrides' introduction to his edition of Ralegh, sect. vi.

[16] See Eugene M. Waith, *Ideas of Greatness*, Ideas and Forms in English Literature series, (London: RKP 1971). Chapter III is particularly helpful on heroism in Chapman and Beaumont and Fletcher.

[17] *The Advancement of Learning*, Bk. II. Cf. the essays *Of Negotiating* and *Of Envy*.

[18] Cf. Blake's description of Bacon's Essays as 'Good Advice for Satan's Kingdom' (Annotations to Bacon's Essays, title-page).

[19] See Hardin Craig, *The Enchanted Glass: The Elizabethan Mind in Literature*, (New York: O.U.P., 1936); F. P. Wilson, *Elizabethan and Jacobean*, (O.U.P., 1945); Robert S. Kinsman ed., *The Darker Vision of the Renaissance* (U. California P.: 1974). For an approach from a different direction see Joel Hurstfield, 'The Paradox of Liberty in Shakespeare's England', *E & S*, 25 (1972), 57-82.

[20] Cf. Ben Jonson, *Discoveries*: 'Now things daily fall: wits grow downe-ward and *Eloquence* grows back-ward.' Donne, sermon XXXVI (1640 ed.) refers to 'the age and impotency of the world' and the increasing signs of its degeneration. See C. A. Patrides, *Milton and the Christian Tradition* (Oxford: Clarendon, 1966), ch. iv.

[21] Lionel Trilling, *Sincerity and Authenticity* (O.U.P., 1974), p. 19, puts the matter in equally strong terms, maintaining that 'in the late sixteenth and early seventeenth centuries, something like a mutation in human nature took place', See also pp. 23-5.

[22] C. B. Macpherson (ed.) *Leviathan* (Harmondsworth: Penguin, 1968), Introduction, p. 24. Cf. also Cowley, *Pindaric Ode to Mr Hobbes* (1656); D. G. James, *The Life of Reason* (London: Longmans, 1949), pp. 1-62; for an account of Hobbes' influence in his own lifetime see Quentin Skinner, 'The Ideological Context of Hobbes's Political Thought', *Historical Journal*, 9 (1966), 286-317; for determinism see e.g. *Leviathan*, ch. xxi (Macpherson 263); for his insistence on a rigorously reductive approach to human affairs see e.g. *Leviathan*, ch. xii (Macpherson 168-83).

[23] J. M. Keynes, *Essays in Biography* (London, 1951), v; Cobban, *Edmund Burke and the Revolt against the Eighteenth Century*, 2nd ed., (London: Allen & Unwin, 1960), p. 16. Note that it is Locke's political thought which is primarily referred to here.

[24] 'Anybody who has read Locke is bound to find Plato merely a fine talker and nothing else. From the point of view of philosophy a chapter from Locke or [Samuel] Clarke is, compared with the babble of antiquity, what Newton's *Optics* are compared with those of Descartes.'

[25] See Whitehead, *Adventures of Ideas*, p. 113: 'Newton finally launched modern science on its triumphant career. If success be a guarantee of truth, no other system of thought has enjoyed a tithe of such success since mankind started on its job of thinking. Within three hundred years it has transformed human life, in its intimate thoughts, its technologies, its social behaviour, and its ambitions.' See also E. J. Dijksterhuis, *The Mechanization of the World Picture* (O.U.P., 1967), and A. J. Meadows, *The High Firmament* (Leicester U.P., 1969).

[26] Cf. Thomas Sprat, *History of the Royal Society*, 2nd ed., (1702): 'From the time in which the Real Philosophy has appear'd . . . the cours of things goes quietly along, in its own true channel of Natural Causes and Effects. For this we are beholden to Experiments.'

[27] See A. O. Lovejoy, op. cit. (ch. 3, n. 14). With this passage, and with Adam's reply—'To know/That which before us lies in daily life,/Is the prime Wisdom'— Willey (*English Moralists* p. 202) well compares Locke, *Human Understanding* Introd. §5. §4 is an even closer parallel: 'This inquiry . . . may be of use to prevail with the busy mind of man to be more cautious in meddling with things exceeding its comprehension; to stop when it is at the utmost end of its tether; and to sit down in a quiet ignorance of those things which, upon examination, are found to be beyond the reach of our capacities.'

[28] *The Sleepwalkers: A History of Man's Changing Vision of the Universe* (London: Hutchinson, 1959) pt. III, §2.

[29] Cf. Marjorie Nicolson, 'Milton and Hobbes', *SP*, 23 (1926), 405-33.

[30] Note that Mountfort produced a pantomime of *Faustus* in 1685—'With the Humours of Harlequin and Scaramouche.' Halifax, in *The Character of a Trimmer* gives a vivid portrait of an absolute Prince, which reads almost like a caricature of a Marlovian hero. It concludes, 'By aiming to be more than a man, he falleth lower than the meanest of them, a mistaken creature, swelled with panegyrics and flattered out of his senses, and not only an encumbrance but a common nuisance to mankind, a hardened and unrelenting soul. Like some creatures that grow fat with poisons, he groweth great by other men's miseries; an ambitious ape of the divine greatness, an unruly giant that would storm even Heaven itself, but that his scaling ladders are not long enough; in short, a wild and devouring creature in rich trappings, and with all his pride no more than a whip in God Almighty's hand, to be thrown into the fire when the world hath been sufficiently scourged with it' (*Works*, ed. J. P. Kenyon, (Harmondsworth: Penguin, 1969), p. 64). The *Character* was published in 1684. It is interesting to note that the Don Juan character, notorious for his profligacy, disdain for human law, materialism, and insistence on his own virtu, was prominent in the European drama from 1605 onwards, but not apparently much after 1675.

[31] 'The temple of Janus with his two controversial faces might now not unsignificantly be set open'—*Areopagitica*. Marjorie Nicolson (*Breaking of the Circle*, p. 188) well observed: 'Like his own Archangel, Milton stood "betwixt the world destroyed and world restored".'

Chapter Five: Pope

[1] Cf. Pascal: 'You can hardly find an example of Justice or Injustice that does not change its nature when it changes its situation. Three degrees of latitude are enough to overturn the basis of law, and truth is decided by a line of longitude. Truly an accommodating sort of Justice which stops short at a river or a mountain. What is truth on this side of the Pyrenees is heresy on the other.'

[2] Cf. the general line Swift takes in *A Discourse concerning the Mechanical Operation of the Spirit*.

[3] It comes as a surprise when the Lilliputians observe that Gulliver is twelve times as tall as they are and therefore give him 1728 times as much food: the figure one expects is 144.

[4] References are to *An Essay on Man*, ed. Maynard Mack, Twickenham edition, vol. III.i, (London: Methuen, 1950). In his authoritative and illuminating introduction

(pp. xii-xiv, xxvi-xxxi) Professor Mack deals firmly and cogently with the objection that the *Essay* need not be taken seriously because it is not Pope's work at all but Bolingbroke's ideas hitched into verse by a poet incapable of thinking for himself. His conclusion is that the Bolingbroke influence cannot be proved in any detail, that Pope in fact differs from Bolingbroke at many crucial points, and that Bolingbroke probably did no more than suggest the area and some of the plan of the argument and encourage Pope to write the poem. D. G. James, *Life of Reason* (ch. 4, n. 22), pp. 190-2, gives a broadly similar account of Bolingbroke's contribution, making the point that 'it was on the conversations, not on the Essays, that Pope chiefly drew for the *Essay on Man*'. See also Miriam Leranbaum, *Alexander Pope's 'OPUS MAGNUM' 1729-1744* (Oxford: Clarendon 1977), esp. ch. II.

[5] See Mack, Introduction xxxiii; A. O. Lovejoy, *The Great Chain of Being*, (Harvard U. P., 1936); Douglas H. White, *Pope and the Context of Controversy: The Manipulation of Ideas in An Essay on Man*, (Chicago U.P., 1970), chs. I-II; Locke (*Essay concerning Human Understanding*, III. vi. 12) gives a clear and entertaining account of the great chain.

[6] Note the formal ambiguity of the final sentence. It can obviously mean, 'Everything that exists has been created for the best in the end', or, equally possibly, 'The only standard for right and wrong is to see what has actually been created: whatever exists has shown, simply by existing that it has a right to exist, and that we can define 'rightness' by observing what is actually the case.' Cf. Benjamin Whichcote: 'Right and Just is determined, not by the Arbitrary pleasure of him that has Power over us; but by the Nature and Reason of Things.'

[7] Cf. the passage from Greville's *Mustapha* quoted in the preceding chapter, p. 132; Pascal (*Pensées* 258): 'For in fact what is man among natural things? A Nothing in comparison with the Infinite, an All in comparison with the Nothing: a mean between nothing and everything. Because he is at an infinite distance from a full knowledge of these, the end of things and their birth are for ever shut from him as the darkest of secrets; he is equally without the power of seeing the Nothing from which he was made, and the Infinite to which he goes in his destruction.' The idea was later widely diffused, e.g. 'Midway from nothing to the Deity' (Young).

[8] Cf. Halifax, *Miscellaneous Thoughts and Reflections*: 'Self-love rightly defined is far from being a fault. A man that loveth himself right will do everything else right' (Kenyon, p. 243). This idea was also a commonplace in the eighteenth century. Cf. Douglas White, (see n. 5) ch. VII.

[9] For a rather different version of the 'springs of action' see *Moral Essays* I. 35-50. For a good account of the extent to which Pope was breaking new ground in his theory of the ruling passion see Bertrand A. Goldgar, 'Pope's Theory of the Passions: The Background of Epistle II of *An Essay on Man*', *PQ*, 41 (1962), 730-43.

[10] Lines 185-94 offer, as examples of ruling passions, spleen, obstinacy, hate, fear, anger, avarice, sloth, lust, envy, pride and shame; Pope, that is, includes all the deadly sins except gluttony.

[11] Pope must always have had in his mind Rochester's *Satire against Mankind* as one extreme of humanistic thought: he cannot afford to allow his own attempts to explain human conduct and development without recourse to revelation to take him to the position Rochester adopts, where instinct is the only impulse and the most powerful instinct is fear.

[12] Cf. Pope's comment in his Note on the Design: 'If I could flatter myself that this Essay has any merit, it is in steering betwixt the extremes of doctrines seemingly opposite, in passing over terms utterly unintelligible, and in forming a *temperate* yet not *inconsistent*, and a *short* yet not *imperfect* system of Ethics.'

[13] A note of Pope's has been preserved which amplifies this passage: 'The author of these lines was far from meaning that no one Form of Government is, in itself, better [than] another . . . but that no form of Government, however excellent or preferable in itself, can be sufficient to make a People happy, unless it be administered with Integrity. On ye contrary, the Best sort of Governmt, when ye Form of it is preserved, and ye *administration* corrupt, is most dangerous' (see Twickenham ed., p. 124).

[14] Cf. *Moral Essays*, III. 161-70, where Pope again introduces the idea of the Ruling Passions and says that they are distributed and governed by the same Almighty Power that 'gives th'eternal wheels to know their rounds'. No doubt this refers

immediately to the orbits of the planets, but it also evokes a picture of the Universe as what Cowley called in the *Davideis* 'Great Natures well-set Clock'. For a good clear account of the 'clockwork' hypothesis see Robert Boyle, 'A Free Enquiry into the Vulgarly Received Notion of Nature', in *Robert Boyle on Natural Philosophy*, ed. M. B. Hall (Bloomington: Indiana U.P., 1965), pp. 150-3. The image was a popular one: we find it in Malynes (applied to commercial relationships), in Hooke (applied to moss and mushrooms), in Blackmore's *Creation*, and as late as Clough's *The New Sinai*.

[15] In a useful article—'Pope and the Great Chain of Being', in *Essays . . . presented to A. S. P. Woodhouse*, ed. M. MacLure and F. W. Watt (Toronto U.P., 1964), pp. 213-28 —F. E. L. Priestley makes the point that one reason why Pope was so impressed by Newton is that he provided empirical evidence for the coherent planning of the Universe: Pope was able to use this as the basis of his argument without relying on an *a priori* notion of Divine perfection and natural plentitude. The point is well taken, if rather strongly stated. In the poem Pope seems equally prepared to welcome support both from Newton and from the principle of plenitude. It is worth remembering that Kant, in his early writings, thought highly of Pope and preferred his version of plenitude to Leibniz's.

[16] For the distinction between Pope's position and the superficially similar arguments of Mandeville see Martin Price, *To the Palace of Wisdom: Studies in Order and Energy from Dryden to Blake* (New York: Doubleday, 1964), chs. IV and V.

[17] For a more detailed account of the language of the poem see Reuben A. Brower, *Alexander Pope: The Poetry of Allusion*, (1959: rpt. O.U.P., 1968) ch. VII, pt. 2, pp. 206-39;

Chapter Six: The Romantic Poets

[1] All references to *The Prelude* are to the text of 1805.

[2] Whereas Burke (*French Revolution*) had argued emphatically that 'prejudice is of ready application in the emergency; it previously engages the mind in a steady course of wisdom and virtue, and does not leave the man hesitating in the moment of decision, sceptical, puzzled, and unresolved. Prejudice renders a man's virtue his habit; and not a series of unconnected acts. Through just prejudice, his duty becomes part of his nature,' Godwin maintained that 'the true dignity of human reason is, as much as we are able, to go beyond [general rules, prejudices, habits of mind], to have our faculties in act upon every occasion that occurs, and to conduct ourselves accordingly' (*Political Justice*).

[3] In *Religious Musings* (1794-6) Coleridge had hailed Hartley, together with Milton, Newton and Joseph Priestley, as a 'Coadjutor of God', 'he of mortal kind/Wisest, he first who marked the ideal tribes/Up the fine fibres through the sentient brain' (368-70). On 16 March 1801 Coleridge wrote to Poole:

> The interval since my last letter has been filled up by me in the most intense Study. If I do not greatly delude myself, I have not only completely extricated the notions of Time, and Space; but have overthrown the doctrine of Association, as taught by Hartley, and with it all the irreligious metaphysics of modern Infidels—especially, the doctrine of Necessity. (Cf. ch. 7, n. 11.)

[4] Godwin himself later modified his extreme views and candidly admitted that they were mistaken.

[5] Contrast this with the unnatural 'Child, no Child' of v. 290-349, who is a paragon of virtue and learning but ignores the more appropriate playthings of the countryside.

[6] The ardour with which Wordsworth and Coleridge insisted on the distinction between Fancy and Imagination is perhaps difficult to understand. *Prelude* VIII. 510-605 helps to explain it. Wordsworth speaks of the 'first poetic Faculty/Of plain imagination and severe', and then in an extended passage of some humour proceeds to distinguish this from 'a wilfulness of fancy and conceit'. The first is based on the realities of the external world, the second endows scenes and objects with attributes not theirs, in short with 'fictions'. 'Thus sometimes were the shapes/Of wilful fancy grafted upon feelings/Of the imagination.' It is necessary for Wordsworth to separate this 'adulterate Power' from the higher faculty of imagination in order to justify his belief that the imagination is not a purely subjective faculty but represents a genuine *reciprocal* relationship between man and Nature. Wordsworth finally congratulates himself on not falling victim to the

'vagaries' of Fancy: this, he says, was because 'I had forms distinct/To steady me' and 'I still/At all times had a real solid world/Of images about me.' The reiterated distinction is clearly an essential strategy to preserve both the objective reality of the external world and the 'plastic power' of the human imagination: human free will becomes meaningless if the first is sacrificed, impossible if the second. (For a clear short account of these themes in the epistemological speculation of Wordsworth's time see John Plamenatz, *Man and Society* (London: Longmans, 1969), II. 133.)

[7] VIII. 166-8, cf. 'My present Theme/Is to retrace the way that led me on/Through Nature to the love of Human Kind' (VIII. 585-7). Nevertheless, and in spite of *Excursion* IV. 1197, city life remains suspect, not just for the obvious reasons, but also for its lack of contact with reality (VIII. 604-5). Friends unlucky enough to have been brought up in London may escape permanent damage if they acknowledge the countryside as their proper home. (See II. 466-79). Cf. n. 12.

[8] With this cf. the 1850 text, which carefully qualifies the praise of man.

[9] Cf. Coleridge, *The Destiny of Nations* (c. 1796):

> For what is Freedom, but the unfettered use
> Of all the powers which God for use had given?
> But chiefly this, him First, him Last to view
> Through meaner powers and secondary things
> Effulgent, as through clouds that veil his blaze.
> For all that meets the bodily sense I deem
> Symbolical, one mighty alphabet
> For infant minds.

[10] *Biographia Literaria* XIII. Note that Coleridge describes the secondary imagination as 'essentially *vital*, even as all objects (*as* objects) are essentially fixed and dead'.

[11] London: O.U.P., 1971.

[12] Later in his life Wordsworth was prepared to argue that those who had been brought up in cities were unable to appreciate or benefit from subsequent acquaintance with the grander parts of the English countryside. See his letter to the *Morning Post* in 1844 objecting to the Kendal and Windermere Railway: '. . . Rocks and mountains, torrents and widespread waters, and all those features of Nature which go to the composition of such scenes as this part of England is distinguished for, cannot, in their finer relations to the human mind, be comprehended, or even very imperfectly conceived, without processes of culture or opportunities of observation in some degree habitual.'

[13] E.g. 'a dim and undetermined sense/Of unknown modes of being' (I. 419-20); 'the soul,/Remembering how she felt, but what she felt/Remembering not, retains an obscure sense/Of possible sublimity' /II. 334-7); 'that universal power/And fitness in the latent qualities/And essences of things' (II. 343-5); '[I] had glimmering views/How Life pervades the undecaying mind' (IV. 154-5).

[14] See the illuminating chapter on 'The Adequacy of Language' in David Perkins, *Wordsworth and the Poetry of Sincerity* (Cambridge, Mass: Belknap, 1964), pp. 84-107.

[15] Letter to Lady Beaumont 21 May 1807: *Wordsworth's Literary Criticism*, ed. Nowell Smith (London, 1905), p. 51.

[16] Judson S. Lyon, The Excursion: *A Study* (Yale, 1950) says that *Excursion* IV. 1207-74 was one of the earliest parts of the poem to be completed.

[17] Cf. the end of section V; also VI. 197-8, 226-38, and VII. 1-48, where the Great Chain of Being is deliberately secularized and God is rationalized away in the manner of Volney, e.g. *Ruins*, ch. XXII, sects. 8, 13.

[18] E.g. 131, 137, 180, 190. Prometheus talks of 'these unrepentant pains' (427). See also Shelley's *To the Lord Chancellor* (1817), 'I curse thee—though I hate thee not' (61).

[19] Cf. I. 180-4, where Earth refers to 'Thy curse, the which . . . my innumerable seas . . . preserve, a treasured spell'.

[20] Note that Richard Holmes, taking the 'revocation' view, finds Acts III and IV unnecessary and a failure: the first two acts, relying on the Aeschylean scheme, are much stronger. See *Shelley: the Pursuit* (New York: Dutton, 1975).

[21] Note that Asia's description of the human condition (II. iv. 101-5)—

> Evil, the immedicable plague, which, while
> Man looks on his creation like a God
> And sees that it is glorious, drives him on,
> The wreck of his own will, the scorn of earth,
> The outcast, the abandoned, the alone—

is now restated in altered terms—'Sceptreless, free, uncircumscribed etc.'. The state of man has not really changed, but if he is free it can now be regarded positively.

[22] Letter of 22 October 1821. Cf. Mrs Shelley's Note on *The Witch of Atlas*.

[23] Letter to Medwin, 20 July 1820.

[24] Some attention has been given recently to Shelley's choice as his hero of a Titan who gave man knowledge and fire, taken to symbolize the technological achievements of modern man. On this see E. A. Havelock, *Prometheus* (Seattle: Washington U.P., 1968), esp. I. 2, 'The Firegiver'.

[25] *Oedipus Tyrannus, or Swellfoot the Tyrant* II. ii. 95-6.

[26] Cf. the similar comments by Arnold on Shelley in 'Maurice de Guérin' in *Essays in Criticism*, first series (1865).

[27] In an early draft the hero's name was Childe Burun.

[28] A telling example of the difference between Byron's imagination and Shelley's is provided by setting against the passage from the end of Act III of *Prometheus Unbound* (see p. 178-9) a very different vision of the future, Byron's *Darkness*, in which mankind is exterminated. It concludes:

> The world was void,
> The populous and the powerful was a lump,
> Seasonless, herbless, treeless, manless, lifeless,
> A lump of death—a chaos of hard clay.
> The rivers, lakes, and ocean all stood still,
> And nothing stirr'd within their silent depths;
> Ships sailorless lay rotting on the sea,
> And their masts fell down piecemeal: as they dropp'd
> They slept on the abyss without a surge—
> The waves were dead; the tides were in their grave,
> The moon, their mistress, had expired before;
> The winds were wither'd in the stagnant air,
> And the clouds perish'd; Darkness had no need
> Of aid from them—She was the Universe.

[29] September 1816.

[30] Maginn (*Blackwoods*, 15, p. 765) characteristically expresses a common view: 'Lord Byron—light lie the stones upon his bones—fed us full of horrors. We had dark-eyed fellows, with bushy eyebrows, white foreheads, gloomy cogitations, deep amorosities, and a decided penchant for cutting throats, and easing honest wayfarers of the contents of their purses. These neat gentlemen were served up to us in all possible varieties. Even Don Juan was but a Childe Harold doing vagaries, like John Kemble acting Mirabel.'

[31] E. Estève, *Byron et le romantisme français* (1907), p. 32.

[32] A few perceptive readers, including Leigh Hunt, Swinburne, Ruskin, Hugo, Stendhal, de Vigny, Goethe and Grillparzer found something to admire in *Don Juan*.

[33] 'Byron and the Modern World', *JHI*, 1 (1940), 24-37.

[34] 'I can see/Nothing to loathe in nature, save to be/A link reluctant in a fleshly chain,/Class'd among creatures, when the soul can flee' (*Childe Harold* III/72). Cf. n. 17. Cf. also Rochester (*Epistle . . . to Ephelia*), 'In my dear self, I centre everything.' Rochester is the clearest link between Marlowe and Byron.

[35] *Childe Harold* III/99-107: Gibbon and Voltaire are expressly called 'Titan-like' in their scepticism and defiance of established authority.

[36] See Byron's Note to the Preface to *Cain: A Mystery* (1821).

[37] 'Does the cant of sentiment still continue in England? Childe Harold called it forth; but my Juan was well calculated to cast it into shade, and had that merit, if it had no other' (Byron to Lady Blessington, 1823).

[38] See *Don Juan* XV/25-6. Note that Byron begins his poem with a quotation from Horace, 'Difficile est proprie communia dicere.' Cf. 'I therefore deal in generalities' (XIV/80).

[39] Among many references to this, see I/213-20, X/27, XII/1-2. Note that Byron spoke of making Juan grown more 'gâté and blasé as he grew older': many critics have pointed out that Juan would presumably become very hard to distinguish from Byron himself.

[40] Cf. VIII/123-5.

[41] Note that Juan's adventures are placed thirty years earlier than the writing of the poem: by the time Byron sets down the events the world is wiser and he can place Juan's experiences in their historical context. At the same time he can charge them with emotion generated by more recent happenings, in particular by the Napoleonic wars and their aftermath: Elizabeth Boyd (*Byron's* Don Juan, 1945) points to the influence of a series of letters in the *Times* (1812-13) describing the horrors of the French wars, especially Leipzig.

[42] E.g. V/110, 128; XI/90.

Chapter Seven: 1660–1830

[1] See William Powell Jones, *The Rhetoric of Science: A Study of Scientific Ideas and Imagery in Eighteenth-Century English Poetry* (London: Routledge, 1966). For a good account of some reservations about scientific method see R. F. Jones, 'The Background of the Attack on Science in the Age of Pope', in *Pope and his Contemporaries: Essays presented to George Sherburn*, ed. Clifford and Landa (O.U.P., 1949).

[2] Roger Cotes, Preface to 2nd ed. of Newton's *Principia* (1713). Cf. the Rev. William Derham's reference to 'Newtonian Angels' in his *Astro-Theology, or A Demonstration of the Being and Attributes of God, from a survey of the Heavens* (1715).

[3] *Spring* 208.

[4] Note that the preamble to the Declaration of Independence refers explicitly to 'the laws of Nature and of Nature's God'.

[5] 'Littérateur et philosophe sensualiste' (Larousse).

[6] See Leonora Cohen Rosenfield, *From Beast-Machine to Man-Machine: Animal Soul in French Letters from Descartes to La Mettrie* (New York: 1941).

[7] Peter Gay, *The Enlightenment: an Interpretation*, (London: Weidenfeld, 1967-70), II. 109n., comments on Turgot's *Plan du Second Discours* that it is 'a tribute to man's sense of mastery over the world', but it is not clear to me how Turgot's 'famous Law of the three stages of mental development', if it is in fact a law, is compatible with mastery over the world.

[8] See R. H. Tawney, *Religion and the Rise of Capitalism* 2nd ed., (London: 1937), 'What set the tone of social thought in the eighteenth century was partly the new Political Arithmetic, which had come to maturity at the Restoration, and which, as was to be expected in the first great age of English natural science—the age of Newton, of Halley, and of the Royal Society—drew its inspiration, not from religion or morals, but from mathematics and physics' (Chapter III, iii, p. 151). Cf. also Richard Mead's mathematical model of the action of poisons in *A Mechanical Account of Poisons* (1702). Note that until about 1660 there was virtually no mathematics of probability and little understanding of actuarial calculations: see Ian Hacking. *The Emergence of Probability* (C.U.P. 1975). Note also the theories of e.g. Joseph Black that man can be regarded as operating on the same heat-cycle as a steam-engine: work and energy begin to lose their human connotations and to become book-keeping concepts.

[9] Quoted by Tawney as previous note, p. 153.

[10] 'Of Refinement in the Arts', *Works* (1882) III. 301-2. Cf. Adam Smith's hand of Jupiter or 'invisible hand' a phrase used earlier by Fontenelle. For further examples see Norman Hampson, *The Enlightenment* (Harmondsworth: Penguin, 1968), ch. III.

[11] E.g. Beccaria was referred to as 'Newtoncino'. Helvétius described himself as the Newton of legislation, and so did Bentham. Michael Macklem, *The Anatomy of the World* (see p. 137), Appendix II, has an interesting collection of examples of the use of the law of gravity as a figure of moral order. Note that Hartley set out to apply to the mind 'the method of analysis and synthesis recommended and followed by Sir

Isaac Newton', but declared that he was not at all aware that the doctrine of necessity 'followed from that of association, for several years after I had begun my enquiries; nor did I admit it at last without the greatest reluctance' (*Observations on Man* iv).

[12] *Impeachment of Warren Hastings* (1788).

[13] *Works*, ed. Rivington vi. 205-6.

[14] *Treatise of Human Nature* (1739), i. iv. 6. But note the Appendix, where Hume candidly admits, 'Upon a more strict review of the section concerning *personal identity*, I find myself involved in such a labyrinth that, I must confess, I neither know how to correct my former opinions, nor how to render them consistent,' and goes on to declare that he is quite unable to construct any satisfactory theory of the self.

[15] 'Locke and Sterne', in *Reason and the Imagination*, ed. J. A. Mazzeo (Columbia U.P.: 1962). Cf. Northrop Frye, 'Towards defining an Age of Sensibility', *ELH*, 23 (1956), 144-52.

[16] Cf. also *Don Juan* and the *Nachtwachen* of Bonaventura. The mode of operation of these and similar works of this and subsequent periods is well brought out in chapter VII of D. C. Muecke's *The Compass of Irony* (London: Methuen, 1969). There are obvious affinities with the works of Nabokov and Borges. On the particular nature of German Romanticism see Rene Wellek, 'German and English Romanticism: A Confrontation', *SIR*, 4 (1964), 33-56. For Sterne see Francis Doherty, 'Sterne and Hume: A Bicentenary Essay', *E & S*, 22 (1969), 71-87.

[17] Martin Price, Preface to *To the Palace of Wisdom* (ch. 5, n. 16), an illuminating account of literary form and the movement of ideas.

[18] 'If one looks at all closely at the middle of our century, the events that occupy us, our customs, our achievements and even our topics of conversation, it is difficult not to recognize that a very remarkable change in our ideas is taking place, one of such rapidity that it seems to promise a greater change still to come' d'Alembert (1759).

[19] A. O. Lovejoy, 'Optimism and Romanticism', *PMLA*, 42 (1925), 921-45, where the argument is set out in detail.

[20] *The Vocation of Man*, ed. R. M. Chisholm (New York: Liberal Arts Press, 1956), p. 27.

[21] *Lectures on the Age of Elizabeth*.

[22] *Dissertations and Discussions* (1867), i, 403. For a brief but penetrating account of the relation between literary, philosophical and political change see M. H. Abrams, *Natural Supernaturalism*, ch. VI, esp. sect iii.

[23] For Blake on the imagination see prose note in Rossetti MS on the design for *A Vision of the Last Judgment*, e.g.: 'The world of Imagination is the world of Eternity. . . . All Things are comprehended in their Eternal Forms in the divine body of the Saviour, the True Vine of Eternity, The Human Imagination, who appear'd to Me as Coming to Judgment among his Saints & throwing off the Temporal that the Eternal might be Establish'd,' and 'I know of no other Christianity than the liberty of both body and mind to exercise the Divine arts of Imagination.' Notice how Blake totally inverts Milton, almost as a matter of policy.

[24] See Johnson, *Life of Pomfret*: 'His *Choice* exhibits a system of life adapted to common notions, and equal to common expectations; such a state as affords plenty and tranquillity, without exclusion of intellectual pleasures. Perhaps no composition in our language has been oftener perused than Pomfret's *Choice*.'

[25] Marjorie Nicolson (*The Breaking of the Circle*, rev. ed., 1960) is able to present an extremely persuasive picture of the initial aspirations of the Renaissance working fruitfully in the expansionist scientists of the seventeenth century. See in particular her quotations from Henry Power's conclusion to his *Experimental Philosophy* (1664). In effect she regards the ferment introduced into the national life as leading directly to Romanticism. I think that there is some truth in this, but that the process was arrested for well over a century; the agencies which checked the working are of course by no means easy to isolate.

[26] Of exactly similar tenor is Priestley's remark: 'It was ill policy in Leo the X to patronize polite literature. He was cherishing an enemy in disguise. And the English hierarchy (if there be anything unsound in its constitution) has equal reason to tremble even at an air pump, or an electrical machine.' Preface to first volume on Air, quoted Anne Holt, *Joseph Priestley*, p. 98. Cf. Voltaire, *Moeurs de Nations* IV: 'On

peut dire que le Pape Leon Xme. en encourageant les Etudes donna les armes contre lui-même.' Quoted in Blake's notes on Reynolds' *Discourses* VII. Cf. 'Such is the end of Epicurean or Newtonian philosophy; it is Atheism' (ibid.).

[27] Note that in the Preface to *The Revolt of Islam* (1818) Shelley acknowledges that 'gloom and misanthropy have become the characteristics of the age in which we live' and that 'this influence has tainted the literature of the age with the hopelessness of the minds from which it flows'. Nevertheless he is able to affirm his trust that a 'slow, gradual, silent change' will lead to a general 'revival of the public hope'. Cf. also his letter to Charles Ollier of 15 October 1819, (*Letters*, ed. Jones II 127) in which he makes a direct connection between 'the great events of our age' and the 'tone of sentiment, imagery, and expression which all the best writers have in common'.

[28] Cf. Wordsworth, *Excursion* VII, where the Wanderer talks of the Elizabethan, Sir Alfred Erthing:

> The courteous Knight, whose bones are here interred,
> Lived in an age conspicuous as our own
> For strife and ferment in the minds of men;
> Whence alteration in the forms of things,
> Various and vast. A memorable age!

Cf. also Swinburne, *Christopher Marlowe*—'Soul nearest ours of all, that wert most far,/Most far off in the abysm of time. . .'.

[29] *London and Westminster Review* (1838).

[30] The contributory effect of the course of the French Revolution is well-known, especially from *The Prelude*. Coleridge's *France: An Ode* (1798) is an even more striking example:

> When France in wrath her giant-limbs upreared,
>   And with that oath, which smote air, earth, and sea,
>   Stamped her strong foot and said she would be free,
> Bear witness for me how I hoped and feared!   (22-5)

The poem goes on to show his total disillusionment with the later behaviour of the revolutionaries:

> The Sensual and the Dark rebel in vain,
>   Slaves by their own compulsion! In mad game
>   They burst their manacles and wear the name
> Of Freedom, graven on a heavier chain!   (85-8)

Note that in the eighteenth century the prisoners in the gaols of Genoa had one word stamped on their fetters—*Libertà*.

[31] Note that Goethe's *Faust* is an exact, perhaps a deliberate, echoing of the master-theme of two centuries previously. The difference is that Goethe's Faust is free from damnation as long as he never says, 'Stay thou art so fair', that is, as long as he is prepared to accept a life of continuous effort and change.

[32] See *Childe Harold* I/4; cf. I/6. For Mazzini see *Byron: the Critical Heritage*, ed. Andrew Rutherford (London: RKP, 1970), p. 333.

[33] Burckhardt, ed. cit., p. 279 and p. 93 (my italics).

[34] This statement must be heavily qualified, especially in view of M. H. Abrams' powerful analysis in *Natural Supernaturalism* of the way in which Wordsworth and Shelley embodied in their poetry a comprehensive vision of man attaining blessedness on earth within the span of a single lifetime. He rightly points to their use of the word 'Joy' to describe this supreme state, yet it is not clear to me that their confidence was of long duration or that they transmitted it to any of their successors except, in a much altered way, to Browning.

Chapter Eight: Tennyson

[1] Cf. *Faerie Queene* VII, where Nature overcomes Mutability, but only at the cost of declaring that Mutability is itself a principle of Nature. This concession throws doubt on Nature's victory, since it implies not only that Mutability is natural but that Nature itself is mutable.

[2] *Principles of Geology, being an Attempt to Explain the Former Changes of the Earth's Surface by reference to Causes now in Operation,* 3 vols. (London: 1830-3).

[3] It was frequently reprinted, reaching ten editions by 1853. Except where indicated I quote from the fourth edition (London: 1845) and from Chambers' lengthy *Explanations* (1845), in which he gives his replies to critics of the earlier editions. The first edition has been reprinted in the Victorian Library of Leicester University Press (1969) with an introduction by Gavin de Beer. For a good account see Milton Millhauser, *Just before Darwin: Robert Chambers and Vestiges* (Wesleyan U.P., 1959).

[4] 'The book, as far as I am aware, is the first attempt to connect the natural sciences into a history of creation.' (Note Conclusory to 1st ed.) 'What Robert aimed at was nothing less than a readable synthesis from nebula to man' (Gavin de Beer, introduction to Victorian Library ed., p. 25).

[5] W. R. Rutland, 'Tennyson and the Theory of Evolution', *E & S*, 26 (1940), 7-29, appositely quotes from William Whewell's third Bridgewater Treatise (1833) on the uniformity of natural law.

[6] *North British Review*, 3 (1845), 471, in the course of a review extending to some thirty-five pages. Chambers' reply is in the following volume.

[7] It should be made quite clear at this point that *In Memoriam* was published nine years before *The Origin of Species* and eight years before Darwin and Wallace's joint communication to the Linnaean Society. Yet it is evident that Tennyson did not, as is sometimes said, anticipate Darwin. There is nothing in *In Memoriam* to show that Tennyson had any notion of the mechanism of natural selection which is central to Darwin's account of evolution. Many passages in the poem which seem Darwinian in fact refer to the theory that the embryo recapitulates successively the various forms of life in the order in which they occurred. The two poles between which Victorian thought on evolution moved are well illustrated by two quotations from Darwin: 'And as natural selection works solely by and for the good of each being, all corporeal and mental endowments will tend to progress towards perfection.' (last sentence of *Origin of Species*) 'But then the horrid doubt always arises whether the convictions of a man's mind, which has developed from the mind of the lower animals, are of any value. Would anyone trust the convictions of a monkey's mind?'

[8] Note e.g. *Vestiges*, p. 241, which is purely conjectural, yet very close to Darwin's position. Darwin (*Historical Sketch*) spoke highly of *Vestiges*, as did Lyell (*Antiquity of Man*): Huxley appears to have repented of his unfavourable review of the 1853 ed. For a brief summary of Chambers' effect and reception see de Beer's Introduction (as in n. 3).

[9] E.g. 'That God created animated beings, as well as the terraqueous theatre of their being, is a fact so powerfully evidenced, and so universally received, that I at once take it for granted' (157). Chambers goes on, however, to argue that it is reasonably certain that God did not personally create all the rocks and stars, but created the laws under which they evolved. 'What is to hinder our supposing that the organic creation is also a result of natural laws, which are in like manner an expression of his will?' (158). The obvious conclusion is drawn in *Explanations* 149: 'Should it [the origin of the organic kingdom] ever be cleared up in a way that leaves no doubt of a natural origin of plants and animals, there must be a complete revolution in the view which is generally taken of our relation to the Father of our being.'

[10] Note that in *Explanations* (25) Chambers puts forward Quetelet's *Sur l'homme et le développement de ses facultés, ou essai de physique sociale* (Paris: 1835) as an example of the reduction of human affairs to statistical laws.

[11] The first edition contained an even more strikingly phrased passage: 'It is clear, moreover, from the whole scope of the natural laws, that the individual, as far as the present sphere of being is concerned, is to the Author of Nature a consideration of inferior moment. Everywhere we see the arrangements for the species perfect; the individual is left, as it were, to take his chance amidst the *mêlée* of the various laws affecting him. If he be found inferiorly endowed, or ill befalls him, there was at least no partiality against him. The system has the fairness of a lottery, in which everyone has the like chance of drawing the prize' (377).

[12] E.g. 'While it is absolutely impossible to predict of any one Frenchman that during next year he will commit a crime, it is quite certain that about one in every six hundred and fifty of the French people will do so, because in past years the propor-

tion has generally been about that amount, the tendencies to crime in relation to the temptations being everywhere invariable over a sufficiently wide range of time.'

[13] For details see John Killham, *Tennyson and* The Princess: *Reflections of an Age* (London: Athlone, 1958), ch. X: the book is far wider in its scope than the title suggests, and is still the best general introduction to Tennyson's ideas. Killham reprints the extended review of *Vestiges* in *The Examiner* (9 November 1844) and draws attention to Tennyson's probable use of Chambers in *The Princess* (1847) and *Maud* (1855). Christopher Ricks indicates a number of places in *In Memoriam* where it is likely that Tennyson had Chambers in mind (*The Poems of Tennyson*, Longmans Annotated Poets (London: 1969), from which all Tennyson quotations are taken).

[14] Note that in his 'Uniformitarian' theory Lyell is taking up the work of Hutton, who saw Earth history as an infinitely repeating cycle, to which he perceived 'no sign of a start, no sign of an end'. See also M. J. S. Rudwick, 'The strategy of Lyell's *Principles of Geology*', *Isis*, 61 (1970), 5-33.

[15] See C. C. Gillispie, *Genesis and Geology: A Study in the Relations of Scientific Thought, Natural Theology, and Social Opinion in Great Britain, 1790-1850*, (Cambridge, Mass: 1951). See also *In Memoriam* XXI. 17-20, where Tennyson imagines his own age being described as 'A time to sicken and to swoon,/When Science reaches forth her arms/To feel from world to world, and charms/Her secret from the latest moon'. If any specific allusion is intended here, it may be to the photographing of the moon in 1840 by Draper.

[16] Cf. 'The washing down of detached matter from elevated grounds, which we see rivers constantly engaged in at the present time, and which is daily shallowing the seas adjacent to their mouths, only proceeded on a greater scale in earlier epochs' (*Vestiges*, p. 148).

[17] For a close discussion of this passage see Walker Gibson, 'Behind the Veil: A Distinction Between Poetic and Scientific Language in Tennyson, Lyell, and Darwin', *VS*, 2 (1958), 60-8.

[18] John D. Jump, 'Tennyson's Religious Faith and Doubt', in *Tennyson*, ed. D. J. Palmer, Writers and their Background (London: Bell, 1973), pp. 89-114, rightly draws attention to the language of the sixth stanza. Although it is full of powerfully active images, these are all processes which man must suffer, not initiate.

[19] Cf. 'For his successful progress man has been largely indebted to those qualities he shares with the ape and the tiger' (T. H. Huxley).

[20] Cf. Tennyson's epigram, 'Man is as mortal as men . . .' (Ricks, p. 1226).

[21] Killham (op. cit.) quotes *Vestiges*, 1st ed., p. 333. There is an even more striking passage on the following page, e.g. 'The brain of a newly-killed animal being taken out, and replaced by a substance which produces electric action, the operation of digestion, *which had been interrupted by the death of the animal*, was resumed, shewing the absolute identity of the brain with a galvanic battery' (my italics). This passage was quoted at length in the *Examiner* review. Notice also Tennyson's reference in the poem to 'this electric force, that keeps/A thousand pulses dancing'. Chambers (*Explanations* 104-5) quotes from Leithead's *Electricity* (1837) to show the possibility of electricity's imparting regular form to bodies. The full title of Leithead's book is *Electricity: its nature, operation and importance in the phenomena of the Universe*.

[22] There is here an ironic echo, possibly intentional, of CXIV: 'Who loves not Knowledge? Who shall rail/Against her beauty? May she mix/With men and prosper! Who shall fix/Her pillars? Let her work prevail.' The stanza is taken from *Hail Briton!* (1831-3).

[23] Ricks (p. 1362) quotes from MS a couplet omitted from the final version of *Locksley Hall Sixty Years After*: 'Prove that all the race will perish wholly, worst and best,/Give me chloroform, set me free of it—without pain—and let me rest', and comments that Hallam Tennyson (*Memoir* II. 35) tells of a man chloroforming himself: '"That's what I should do," my father said, "if I thought there was no future life".'

[24] This is effected in the line 'But that blind clamour made me wise'. The 'blind clamour' is presumably that of lines 11-12—the sound of the land crumbling incessantly into the ocean—which at first seems, like the discoveries of the geologists, to prompt to loss of faith in God but in time brings wisdom and a confidence that God exists and cares for men: the mechanism is not specified.

[25] Tennyson does not often find difficulty in framing an appropriate resolution, e.g. in CVIII, 'I will not shut me from my kind'; 'I will not eat my heart alone'; 'I'll rather take what fruit may be/Of Sorrow.'

[26] The idea that higher types than man may be produced in the course of evolutionary change is pervasive in *Vestiges* e.g.: '[Man] is only a new guest, who has entered and sat down at a feast where other guests were before him, and which goes on and on continually: may there not be other guests to come and take their places at this perennial banquet of the High and Bountiful Master?' (p. 397); 'Is our race but the initial of the grand crowning type? Are there yet to be species superior to us in organization, purer in feeling, more powerful in device and act, and who shall take a rule over us!' (1st ed., p. 276).

[27] There is a similar movement at the climax of the *Ode on Wellington*:

> For though the Giant Ages heave the hill
> And break the shore, and evermore
> Make and break, and work their will;
> Though world on world in myriad myriads roll
> Round us, each with different powers,
> And other forms of life than ours,
> What know we greater than the soul?
> On God and Godlike men we build our trust.   (259-66)

[28] Cf. George Eliot: 'And I think we must not take every great physicist—or other "ist"—for an apostle, but be ready to suspect him of some crudity concerning relations that lie outside his special studies, if his exposition strands us on results that seem to stultify the most ardent, massive experience of mankind, and hem up the best part of our feelings in stagnation' (letter to Mrs Ponsonby 30 January 1875 (Cross III. 253), quoted by B. Willey, *Nineteenth Century Studies*). It is worth noting that Karl Jaspers was opposed to Darwin on the grounds that his work 'implies the destruction of all authentic life'.

[29] Tennyson said, 'It's too hopeful, this poem [*In Memoriam*], more than I am myself' (Ricks, p. 859, reporting J. Knowles, 1893).

[30] See *Lucretius* (1868): 'The Gods, the Gods!/If all be atoms, how should then the Gods/Being atomic not be dissoluble,/Not follow the great law?' (113-16, cf. 242 ff.).

[31] But perhaps that of Tennyson's brother Charles, who died in 1879.

[32] While the idea of the plurality of worlds had been part of the common currency of astronomical speculation since the sixteenth century and the word 'suns' is found occasionally in the eighteenth century (e.g. in Blackmore and Erasmus Darwin), the consistent use of the plural form is almost like Tennyson's signature to a poem with a scientific subject: it implies the whole body of reluctant and fearful recognition that astronomy and geology have destroyed the certainties of the old heliocentric universe. See, among other examples, the 'rejected' stanzas of *The Palace of Art* (see Ricks 412 n.); *The Golden Year* MS (see Ricks, pp. 716-17 n.)—'complicated clockwork of the suns'; *In Memoriam* CXVII; *De Profundis*—'numerable—innumerable/Sun, sun, and sun'; *Maud* I. iv, viii; Epigram XXII; *The Epilogue* to *The Charge of the Heavy Brigade*—'the vast sun-clusters' gathered blaze'; *God and the Universe*; *Locksley Hall Sixty Years After* (see pp. 195-207). Similarly in *Speak to the Lord* Tennyson refers to 'the million of million decillions of worlds'. Cf. Chambers, *Vestiges*: 'The thing to be accounted for is not merely the origination of organic being upon this little planet, third of a series which is but one of hundreds of thousands of series, the whole of which again form but one portion of an apparently infinite globe-peopled space, where all seems analogous' (p. 165). Chambers is here arguing directly against 'the doctrine of special exercise'.

[33] Cf. *In Memoriam* L, 'men the flies of latter spring'; *Locksley Hall Sixty Years After* 'What are men . . .? Insects of an hour' (201-2).

[34] I am pleased to find close confirmation of this view in John Jump's essay (see n. 18).

[35] Arnold is reported as saying that he had Goethe in mind: Quiller-Couch suggests Carlyle (*OSA*, p. 471): J. C. Maxwell proposed Leopardi (*RES*, 6 (1955), 182-3). The point is discussed in *The Poems of Matthew Arnold*, ed. Kenneth Allott, Longmans Annotated Poets (London: 1965), p. 341 n. All Arnold quotations are taken from this edition.

[36] E.g. lines 387-97, 708-25.

[37] Arnold frequently uses the word 'eddying' to express aimless, pointless motion, e.g. 'Most men eddy about/Here and there' (*Rugby Chapel* 60-1); 'Eddying at large in blind uncertainty' (*The Buried Life* 43).

[38] In *The Major Victorian Poets: Reconsiderations*, ed. Isobel Armstrong (London: RKP, 1969), pp. 199-224. See also ch. 11, pp. 329-30.

[39] What Arnold fears is obviously something like Kant's abderitism, but even more like Durkheim's *anomie*, the sort of formlessness that infects individuals and societies.

[40] Notice the key chapter II, 'Doing As One Likes' in *Culture and Anarchy*: what Arnold is opposed to is 'random and ill-regulated action', and one of his strongest adjectives of disapproval is 'multitudinous'. Cf. Kierkegaard: 'No single individual ... will be able to arrest the abstract process of levelling. ... No society or association can arrest that abstract power, simply because association is itself in the service of the levelling process. ... The abstract levelling process, that self-combustion of the human race, produced by the friction which arises when the individual ceases to exist as singled out by religion, is bound to continue, like a trade wind and consume everything' (*The Present Age* (1846)).

Chapter Nine: Hardy

[1] Preface to *Poems of the Past and the Present* (1902).

[2] The phrase is taken from the Introductory Note to *Winter Words* (1928). Note also the letter of 19 December 1920, where Hardy complains, 'It is my misfortune that people will treat all my mood-dictated writing as a single scientific theory', and the poem *So Various*, in which Hardy describes all his different selves.

[3] Cf. *A Plaint to Man, The Blow, God-Forgotten, A Philosophical Fantasy, By the Earth's Corpse, New Year's Eve* and *An Inquiry*. Note also the celebrated passage at the end of *The Return of the Native* (vi. i), where Hardy speaks of 'the generous endeavour' of men to construct a decent God.

[4] E.g. 'What bond-servants of Chance/We are all' (*Ditty*); 'Strange-pipped dice my hand has thrown me' (*Green Slates*); 'And the die thrown/By them heedlessly there' ('*By the Runic Stone*').

[5] Cf. *New Year's Eve, The Aërolite*, and the passage quoted from Hardy's pocket-book for 9 May 1881 in *The Life of Thomas Hardy 1840−1928* by Florence Emily Hardy (London: Macmillan, 1965), pp. 148−9.

[6] Cf. *The Bedridden Peasant to an Unknowing God*:

> For, say one puts a child to nurse,
>   He eyes it now and then
> To know if better it is, or worse,
>   And if it mourn, and when.
>
> But Thou, Lord, giv'st us men our day
>   In helpless bondage thus
> To Time and Chance, and seem'st straightway
>   To think no more of us!   (5−12)

[7] Note particularly *The Convergence of the Twain*, the set of fifteen poems called *Satires of Circumstance*, the book of poems called *Time's Laughingstocks*, and the book of short stories called *Life's Little Ironies*.

[8] For a crude version of this see *A Necessitarian's Epitaph*.

[9] Cf. the early sonnet *Discouragement*.

[10] Cf. *Life* (n. 5), p. 218.

[11] In the first part of this poem Hardy probably has Browning in mind.

[12] Exceptions are *A Jog-Trot Pair*, '*When I set out for Lyonnesse*', *Lines to a Movement in Mozart's E-Flat Symphony* and a few poems in which he writes about his parents' courtship and marriage.

[13] This is hardly surprising since Hardy was 58 when he published *Wessex Poems*, his first book of verse.

[14] For examples from novels and stories see section III of this chapter. Among poems may be noted *The Curate's Kindness, Four Footprints, The Fiddler, The Christening, The Newcomer's Wife, Her Secret, A Conversation at Dawn, At Mayfair Lodgings, The Telegram, The Moth-Signal, The Two Wives, 'I Knew a Lady', The Ivy-Wife, The Division,* and *The Contretemps.* The wrong marriage is the theme of many of the *Satires of Circumstance:* other examples abound of 'hearts thwartly smitten'.

[15] Hardy is not often struck by the immense spans of geological time, as Tennyson was. *The Clasped Skeletons* is an exception: see also *Transformations* and the trilobite incident in the novel *A Pair of Blue Eyes.*

[16] For Hardy's varied treatments of Time within this general scheme see *Logs on a Hearth, The Five Students, The Felled Elm and She, A Wet Night, A House with a History, An Anniversary, Old Furniture, The Rambler, The Garden Seat, Night in the Old Home, Wessex Heights, The Little Old Table,* and *The Photograph.*

[17] *Thomas Hardy: The Will and the Way* (O.U.P.: 1965), pp. 120‾37.

[18] Op. cit. p.134.

[19] References are to page numbers in the Macmillan edition (London: 1923).

[20] *Trachiniae* 1266‾72.

[21] For an example of the mechanism by which the Immanent Will traces out its designs see the poem *The Pedigree* (1916), where the emphasis is on the determining influences of heredity.

[22] Op. cit. p. 86.

[23] Hardy's cinematic technique is most effective in making this point: in Part II Act IV, for example, he cuts from the field of Talavera, where 'hurt and slain/Opposed, opposers in a common plight/Are scorched together on the dusk champaign', to the Prince of Wales' splendid birthday party in the Pavilion at Brighton.

[24] *Eight Modern Writers,* Oxford History of English Literature vol. XII, (O.U.P.: 1963) p. 69.

[25] There is the additional point that when a drama is, like *The Dynasts,* designed to be read rather than acted, the author may expect the reader to be more conscious of the conventions that govern the representation of character.

[26] I should make it plain that Allen gives clear examples of the sort of coincidences he has in mind, and is careful not to attach too much importance to Hardy's 'botches' in fashioning his plot.

[27] *Eight Modern Writers* (see n. 24), p. 45.

[28] Cf. notebook entry 16 January 1918: 'As to pessimism. My motto is, first correctly diagnose the complaint—in this case human ills—and ascertain the cause: then set about finding the remedy if one exists. The motto or practice of the optimists is: Blind the eyes to the real malady, and use empirical panaceas to suppress the symptoms' (*Life,* p. 383). See also the Apology to *Late Lyrics and Earlier* (1922).

[29] Cf. Hardy's note, July, 1881: 'The uncommonness must be in the events, not in the characters' (*Life,* p. 150).

[30] Cf. *Woodlanders,* ch. 41: 'Gazing, in her enforced idleness, from the one window of the single room, [Grace] could see various small members of the animal community that lived unmolested there—creatures of hair, fluff, and scale; the toothed kind and the billed kind; underground creatures jointed and ringed—circumambulating the hut, under the impression that, Giles having gone away, nobody was there; and eyeing it inquisitively with a view to winter quarters. Watching these neighbours, who knew neither law nor sin, distracted her a little from her trouble.' Here too the emphasis is on the artificiality of human morality, but the natural world is no kinder to Giles or Grace.

[31] Tess's description of the world to her young brother Abraham (ch. 4). He replies, ' 'Tis very unlucky that we didn't pitch on a sound one, when there were so many more of 'em!'

[32] I. Gregor and B. Nicholas, *The Moral and the Story* (London: Faber, 1962) p. 144.

[33] There is an interesting brief episode in *Tess* (ch. 49), where Angel Clare, journeying by mule through the interior of South America, meets a 'large-minded stranger' to whom he tells the sorrowful facts of his marriage. 'The stranger had sojourned in many more lands and among many more peoples than Angel; to his cosmopolitan mind such deviations from the social norm, so immense to domesticity, were no more than are the irregularities of vale and mountain-chain to the whole terrestrial curve. He viewed the matter in quite a different light from

Angel; thought that what Tess had been was of no importance beside what she would be, and plainly told Clare that he was wrong in coming away from her. The next day they were drenched in a thunder-storm, Angel's companion was struck down with fever, and died by the week's end. Clare waited a few hours to bury him, and then went on his way.'

The extended perspective of the stranger is to be compared with that of the Spirits in *The Dynasts* or with Hardy's poem *At A Lunar Eclipse*.

[34] A remark such as Tess's 'Once a victim, always a victim—that's the law' (ch. 47) obviously operates simultaneously on both levels and does something to unite them. Similarly the actual physical miseries of Flintcomb-Ash cannot be separated from the larger miseries of the cosmos: 'After this season of congealed dampness came a spell of dry frost, when strange birds from behind the North Pole began to arrive silently on the upland of Flintcomb-Ash; gaunt spectral creatures with tragical eyes—eyes which had witnessed scenes of cataclysmal horror in inaccessible polar regions of a magnitude such as no human being had ever conceived, in curdling temperatures that no man could endure' (ch. 43).

[35] Cf. the poem *In a Wood* (1887:1896).

[36] Note Hardy's use of the weather, here and elsewhere, to show man at the mercy of the non-human. Cf. also his comment on 'the curious mechanical regularity of country people in the face of hopelessness' (*Woodlanders*, ch. 17).

[37] Cf. *Jude*, part VI, ch. 3, where Hardy credits Sue with ideas very like his own 'in the days when her intellect scintillated like a star. . . . But affliction makes opposing forces loom anthropomorphous; and those ideas were now exchanged for a sense of Jude and herself fleeing from a persecutor.

'We must conform!' she said mournfully. 'All the ancient wrath of the Power above us has been vented on us, His poor creatures, and we must submit. There is no choice. We must. It is no use fighting against God!'

'It is only against man and senseless circumstance,' said Jude.

'True!' she murmured. 'What have I been thinking of! I am getting as superstitious as a savage!'

[38] Cf. 'Like all people who have known rough times, light-heartedness seemed to her [Elizabeth-Jane] too irrational and inconsequent to be indulged in except as a reckless dram now and then; for she had been too early habituated to anxious reasoning to drop the habit suddenly. . . . Her triumph was tempered by circumspection; she had still that field-mouse fear of the coulter of destiny despite fair promise, which is common among the thoughtful who have suffered early from poverty and oppression' (ch. 14).

[39] For a rather different version of Hardy's objectives at the end of the book see Robert C. Schweik, 'Character and Fate in *The Mayor of Casterbridge*', *NCF*, 21 (1966), 249–62.

[40] The reader, like Henchard, is deceived about Elizabeth-Jane's parentage. When Lucetta and Farfrae marry secretly at Port Bredy the reader is not a party to their plans and, like Henchard, is surprised and shocked by the news.

[41] It is, of course, important for Hardy to give the sense that he knows, although his characters cannot, exactly what are the large forces, social or economic, which determine so much of their lives. It is thus a sound move for him to set his novels some way in the past: this enables him to place the action in the context of major social changes or fundamental developments in agriculture, which were matters of recorded fact when he wrote but which he can represent as unperceived by his characters while they were happening. He can thus play in his own fictions a role analogous to that of the Spirit of the Years in *The Dynasts* (cf. ch. 6, n. 41).

[42] Cf. *Tess*: 'But it had not been in Tess's power—nor is it in anybody's power—to feel the whole truth of golden opinions while it is possible to profit by them. She—and how many more—might have ironically said to God with Saint Augustine: "Thou hast counselled a better course than Thou hast permitted".' (ch. 15).

[43] Cf. 'Tell me now, Angel, do you think we shall meet again after we are dead? I want to know.' He kissed her to avoid a reply at such a time' (*Tess*, ch. 58). Like Angel, Hardy is not prepared to say what he does not believe even to give comfort. 'Thus things around. No answerer I.' Of the last two poems in *Winter Words* (1928), Hardy's last collected volume, one ends 'Yes. We are getting to the end of dreams!' and the other is called *He Resolves to Say No More*.

[44] 'The Profitable Reading of Fiction' (1888).

Chapter Ten: George Eliot and Dickens

[1] *Character and the Novel*, (London: Chatto, 1965), p. 24.

[2] *The Mill on the Floss* ch. x.

[3] Most notably by Ruskin: '. . . In the railway novel, interest is obtained with the vulgar reader for the vilest character, because the author describes carefully to his recognition the blotches, burrs and pimples in which the paltry nature resembles his own. *The Mill on the Floss* is perhaps the most striking instance extant of this study of cutaneous disease. There is not a single person in the book of the smallest importance to anybody in the world but themselves, or whose qualities deserved so much as a line of printer's type in their description. . . . [Maggie and Tom are commonplace] while the rest of the characters are simply the sweepings-out of a Pentonville omnibus.

And it is very necessary that we should distinguish this essentially Cockney litera-ture, developed only in the London suburbs, and feeding the demand of the rows of similar brick houses, which branch in devouring cancer round every manufac-turing town—from the really romantic literature of France. George Sand is often immoral; but she is always beautiful. . . . But in the English Cockney schoôl, which consummates itself in George Eliot, the personages are picked up from behind the counter and out of the gutter; and the landscape, by excursion train to Gravesend, with return ticket for the City-road' (*NC*, October 1881).

[4] Cf. '. . . We do not expect people to be deeply moved by what is not unusual. That element of tragedy which lies in the very fact of frequency, has not yet wrought itself into the coarse emotion of mankind; and perhaps our frames could hardly bear much of it.' (*Middlemarch*, ch. xx) See also her review of Wilhelm Riehl's *Die Bürgerliche Gesellschaft* in *Westminster Review*, **66** (1856), reprinted in *Essays of George Eliot*, ed. T. Pinney (London: RKP, 1963): the whole essay is of first im-portance for an understanding of George Eliot's idea of the novel as natural history.

[5] Note that Mrs Glegg's attention to 'men's business' is disapproved of. Mrs Pullet says, 'I think it 'ud be a deal more becoming o' Jane if she'd have that pier-glass rubbed oftener—there was ever so many spots on it last week—instead o' dictating to folks as have more comings in than she ever had, and telling 'em what they've to do with their money. But Jane and me were allays contrairy: she *would* have striped things, and I like spots' (I. ix).

[6] For more about the Dodson sense of propriety especially in details of dress and household management see I. xii and xiii. For more about the indicative status of household possessions see III. iii.

[7] E.g. 'I've got a great deal more money than you, because I'm a boy. I always have half-sovereigns and sovereigns for my Christmas boxes, because I shall be a man, and you have only five-shilling pieces, because you're only a girl' (I. v).

[8] Cf. Tom's comment when Maggie tries to contribute to the family funds by plain sewing: 'I don't like *my* sister to do such things; *I'll* take care that the debts are paid, without your lowering yourself in that way' (IV. iii).

[9] Cf. [Philip] 'She [i.e. Maggie] ought not to take herself quite away from me.'
'Not if I were free,' said Maggie; 'but I am not—I must submit' (V. i).

[10] Cf. *Felix Holt* ch. 39, e.g. 'He will make her fond of him, and afraid of him . . . A women's love is always freezing into fear . . . God was cruel when he made women. (Mrs. Transome).

[11] George Eliot is very fair here. In VII, iii she represents Aunt Glegg as refusing to listen to the gossip against Maggie, thus demonstrating the positive as well as the negative results of the Dodson way of life.

[12] *The Leader* 21 July 1855 reviewing 'Wilhelm Meister' (Pinney 146). Note that she was nauseated by his studies of 'unmitigated vice'. Cf. also Henry James, *Views and Reviews* (1908): 'The portions of the story [*Mill on the Floss*] which bear upon the Dodson family are in their way not unworthy of Balzac. . . . We are reminded of him by the attempt to classify the Dodsons socially in a scientific manner, and to accumu-late small examples of their idiosyncrasies' (pp. 31-2). Cf. 'Character is based on physio-logical organisation'; 'My writing is simply a set of experiments in life' (G. E. to Dr J. F. Payne 25 Jan. 1876). Balzac himself drew a parallel between what he was doing in *The Human Comedy* and the work of the celebrated zoologist Geoffroy St Hilaire.

[13] [Vautrin] 'Paris, you see, is like a forest in the New World, where you have to deal with a score of varieties of savages—Illinois and Hurons, who live on the proceeds of

their social hunting. You are a hunter of millions; you set your snares; you use lures and nets; there are many ways of hunting. Some hunt heiresses; others a legacy; some fish for souls, yet others sell their clients, bound hand and foot. Everyone who comes back from the chase with his game bag well filled meets with a warm welcome in good society.' In Gautier's phrase Balzac created 'le héros métallique'. Marx, according to his son-in-law, wanted to write a review of *The Human Comedy* when he had finished with economics.

[14] F. W. H. Myers, *Essays Classical and Modern* (1883), p. 268.

[15] 'Uncle Pullet had a programme for all great social occasions [such as being asked to play his musical snuff-box], and in this way fenced himself in from much painful confusion and perplexing freedom of will' (ɪ. ix).

[16] Fielding was of course aware of the problems of fictional narrative, but his practical solution to them was so complete and apparently effortless that Smollett, for example, worries about them much less, while Dickens hardly worries about them at all except as technical questions to which he must find an economical answer.

[17] '*Hard Times*: A History and a Criticism', in *Dickens and the Twentieth Century* ed. J. Gross and G. Pearson, (London: RKP, 1962).

[18] Bk. I. ch. 11: note the revealing opposition of 'patriotism' and 'discontent'.

[19] This rather suggests that Dickens was on the whole dissatisfied technically with *Bleak House*, but did not feel that he had said all he wanted to about the characters—or perhaps that he was conscious that everything in *Bleak House* was first-rate except the system of putting it before the reader. Even the third-person chapters are over-written. If this is so it is understandable that a lot of the effervescence of the first attempt should have vanished and that *Little Dorrit* should be a more sober book.

[20] 'Chance and Design in *Bleak House*' in Gross and Pearson (see n. 17).

[21] The only important features which are left to be understood as coincidences are (i) that Miss Wade, who hired Rigaud, should meet at Marseilles Arthur Clennam, whose mother Blandois was later to attempt to blackmail, and (ii) that Clennam, being doubly connected with Rigaud in this way, should employ Cavaletto, who also knows Rigaud. There is the minor and entirely appropriate coincidence that Fanny Dorrit should chance to meet Edmund Sparkler again when she is rich. It is also a coincidence that the Dorrits should meet the Gowans in Switzerland, but this perhaps shows that they are now in a small select world whose members must be constantly encountering one another, and signifies little more than their happening to be guests at the same dinner party.

[22] Presumably the reason that Frederick Dorrit is shown as feeble-witted is that if he were in his senses he would not allow Little Dorrit to work for Mrs Clennam, knowing what he does of her.

[23] Fanny says, 'I am impatient of our situation. I don't like our situation, and very little would induce me to change it. Other girls, differently reared and differently circumstanced altogether, might wonder at what I say or may do. Let them. They are driven by their lives and characters; I am driven by mine' (Book II, ch. xiv).

[24] Introduction to *Little Dorrit* in the New Oxford Illustrated Dickens (1953), pp. v-vi.

[25] *Dickens at Work* (London: Methuen, 1968), ch. IX (p. 233).

[26] I have not space to discuss Dickens' views of art or the position of the artist in society. Two quotations must serve to illustrate the poles of the argument:
(i) 'What Dickens hated in the Calvinistic commercialism of the early and middle Victorian age . . . he sums up now in its hatred of art. That he should do so is eloquent of the place he gave to art in human life and of the conception of art that informs his practice (it seems to be essentially Blake's).' F. R. and Q. D. Leavis, *Dickens the Novelist* (London: Chatto, 1970), ch. v on *Little Dorrit* (by F.R.L.).
(ii) 'When Dickens introduced in his stories a character whom he intensely disliked he chose an artistic profession for him. Henry Gowan in *Little Dorrit* is a painter. Pecksniff is an architect. Skimpole is a musician. There is real hatred in his treatment of them.' G. B. Shaw, Foreword to the Novel Library edition of *Great Expectations* (London: Hamish Hamilton, 1947), p. xi.

[27] An exception might be made for the police force, for which Dickens normally had a very high regard.

[28] Doyce is an exception here. F. R. Leavis (see n. 26) has argued powerfully for his importance as a representative figure in *Little Dorrit*, yet what stays in the mind

about Doyce is his isolation. If Leavis is right to say that he is intended to represent a positive alternative way of life, it must also be said that he does not operate effectively in this capacity in the action of the novel.

[29] E.g. *Christmas Carol*, Stave Two: 'But now a knocking at the door was heard, and such a rush immediately ensued, that she, with laughing face and plundered dress, was borne towards it, the centre of a flushed and boisterous group, just in time to greet the father, who came home attended by a man laden with Christmas toys and presents. Then the shouting and the struggling, and the onslaught that was made on the defenceless porter! The scaling him, with chairs for ladders, to dive into his pockets, despoil him of brown-paper parcels, hold on tight by his cravat, hug him round the neck, pommel his back, and kick his legs in irrepressible affection! The shouts of wonder and delight with which the development of every package was received! The terrible announcement that the baby had been taken in the act of putting a doll's frying-pan into his mouth, and was more than suspected of having swallowed a fictitious turkey glued on a wooden platter! The immense relief of finding this a false alarm! The joy, and gratitude, and ecstasy! They are all indescribable alike.' Cf. the description of Christmas at Bob Cratchit's and at Scrooge's nephew's in Stave Three. See also *The Chimes* (Second Quarter and Fourth Quarter), the description of the Tetterby family at the beginning of chapter ii of *The Haunted Man*, and the account of Benjamin Britain's inn in Part Three of *The Battle of Life*, Note that the sub-title of *The Cricket on the Hearth* was *A Fairy-Tale of Home*.

[30] *Modern Art* (1867), 7-8.

[31] E.g. Nicholas Nickleby with the Cheerybles, Clennam in partnership with Doyce, and Pip with Clarrikers—'I must not leave it to be supposed that we were ever a great House, or that we made mints of money. We were not in a grand way of business, but we had a good name, and worked for our profits, and did very well' (ch. lviii).

[32] Cf. Esther's 'little house' at the end of *Bleak House*, or the account of the way in which Mr Brownlow, at the end of *Oliver Twist* 'linked together a little society, whose condition approached as nearly to one of perfect happiness as can ever be known in this changing world.' Earlier in the same book Harry Maylie says to Rose, 'There are smiling fields and waving trees in England's richest county; and by one village church—mine, Rose, my own!—there stands a rustic dwelling which you can make me prouder of, than all the hopes I have renounced, measured a thousand-fold. This is *my* rank and station now, and here I lay it down' (li). All readers will have noticed the simpering archness of Dickens' account of John and Bella Rokesmith's cottage at Blackheath (*OMF* Bk IV, ch. 5).

[33] See note 4 (Pinney 298). Cf. Max Weber, *The Protestant Ethic and the Spirit of Capitalism* tr. Talcott Parsons (London: Unwin, 1970), p. 80.

[34] Shaw makes much the same sort of point in the Preface to *Major Barbara*, discussing the character of Bill Walker: 'The point which I, as a professor of natural psychology, desire to demonstrate, is that Bill, without any change in his character or circumstances whatsoever, will react one way to one sort of treatment and another way to another' (xxiii).

[35] Cf. Prince Peter Kropotkin: 'By showing that the 'struggle for existence' must be conceived, not merely in its restricted sense of a struggle between individuals for the means of subsistence, but in its wider sense of adaptation of all individuals of the species for the survival of the species, as well as for the greatest possible sum of life and happiness for each and all, it [the philosophy of evolution] permitted us to deduce the laws of moral science from the social needs and habits of mankind.' 'The Scientific Bases of Anarchy', *NC*, February 1887.

[36] At this point much might be said, if space allowed, about the simplified versions of economic doctrines current in the nineteenth century, and the way in which they suggested that irresistible forces were at work in human affairs, thus simultaneously encouraging economic fatalism and excusing economic selfishness—e.g. 'It is curious to observe how, through the wise and beneficent arrangement of Providence, men thus do the greatest service to the public, when they are thinking of nothing but their own gain' (*Easy Lessons on Money Matters for the Use of Young People*, 12th ed., 1850, quoted by Maynard Keynes). The British writer who most forcefully expressed the power of money was Shaw, e.g. in the Preface to *Major Barbara* he refers to money as 'the most important thing in the world'. 'Money is the

counter that enables life to be distributed socially: it *is* life as truly as gold coins and bank notes are money. The first duty of every citizen is to insist on having money on reasonable terms. . . . The evil to be attacked is not sin, suffering, greed, priestcraft etc. . . . nor any of the other consequences of poverty, but just poverty itself.' Here Shaw is echoing, perhaps consciously, George Jacob Holyoake's epigram, 'The first duty of the industrious poor is not to be poor.'

[37] An observation by Georges Poulet—'In each event of the *Comédie humaine* one can immediately distinguish the time of a force which precedes all the "times" in the novel and determines them. Whereas, on the contrary, with Flaubert each moment of life is perceived as the extremity of an infinite series of effects' (*Studies in Time*, 1956, p. 32)—suggests, though somewhat cryptically, the importance to Balzac's novels of their place in a series, and lends some colour to the theory that the characteristic literary form of our time is the novel sequence. After Balzac one thinks at once of Trollope, Zola and Proust, but there are innumerable other examples at all levels of literature, including Galsworthy, Hugh Walpole, Arnold Bennett, R. H. Mottram, L. H. Myers, Musil, Mauriac, Mann, Ford Madox Ford, Mazo de la Roche, Grassic Gibbon, Guy McCrone, John Buchan, Evelyn Waugh, Laurence Durrell, Octavio de Faria, Upton Sinclair, Sartre, Mervyn Peake, Anthony Powell, C. P. Snow, J. I. M. Stewart, Simon Raven and Dornford Yates.

[38] 'The issue shan't be marriage, my dear sister,' the Major said resolutely. 'We're not going to have a Pendennis, the head of the house, marry a strolling mountebank from a booth. No, no, we won't marry into Greenwich Fair, ma'am' (*Pendennis*, ch. vii).

'I *will* see her,' said Arthur. 'I'll ask her to marry me, once more. I will. No one shall prevent me.'

'What, a woman who spells affection with one f? Nonsense, sir. Be a man and remember that your mother is a lady' (ch. xiii).

[39] See Shaw, Preface to *Plays Unpleasant*, xxiii, for an account of the way in which Ibsen works out, even more thoroughly than Zola, the family and personal history of his characters.

Chapter Eleven: 1830–1890

[1] *Modern Painters*, vol. iii (1856).

[2] There are in addition some remarkable aberrations, such as the extraordinary passage in Tupper's *Of Subjection* in which he sets out the classic eighteenth-century doctrine of subordination, complete with religious sanctions and the great chain of being. (*Proverbial Philosophy*, first series).

[3] It was, of course, much commoner elsewhere: a good example is Samuel Smiles' *Life and Labour* (1887), esp. ch. i. See also his *Self-Help* (1859), *Character* (1871), *Thrift* (1875), and *Duty* (1880).

[4] *The Art Journal* (1862), discussing the paintings of Henry Nelson O'Neil.

[5] *The City of Dickens* (Oxford: Clarendon, 1971), p. 15.

[6] *Hard Times*, I. 10.

[7] *Journal of an Alpine Tour*.

[8] For a thorough exposition of the implications of Rimbaud's paradox see M. H. Abrams, *Natural Supernaturalism*, pp. 415-18.

[9] Letter LVII. Cf. passages from Ruskin quoted in Introduction, pp. 14-15 and ch. 13, p. 362.

[10] *Characteristics* (1831) in *Critical and Miscellaneous Essays*.

[11] Note that Owen had no belief in the freedom of the will: the parallel with B. F. Skinner is instructive (see ch. 15, n. 37).

[12] Note that Fourier regarded passional attraction as being the personal equivalent of gravity: on this basis the way would be clear for a truly objective study of human relationships which would remove it from the sphere of the 'uncertain sciences'. Cf. Goethe and the doctrine of elective affinities in *Die Wahlverwandtschaften* esp. part I, ch. iv.

[13] Buckle, *History of Civilization in England*, II. 472.

[14] Quoted in Edith Olivier, *Country Moods and Tenses* (1941), p. 47.

[15] Charles Kingsley, 'The Meteor Shower' in *The Water of Life and other Sermons* (1890), p. 180.

[16] For Thomson's relation to certain of his European contemporaries see Robert Martin Adams, *Nil* (1966), esp. ch. ix.

[17] A good example is to be found in Winwood Reade's *The Outcasts* (1875), in which there is an account of a young man named Arthur Elliott, who loses his faith as a result of reading the *Essay on Population* and *The Origin of Species*. 'He dressed always in black, and said that he was in mourning for mankind. The works of Malthus and Darwin, bound in sombre covers, were placed on a table in his room: the first was lettered outside, *The Book of Doubt*, and the second *The Book of Despair*.'

[18] E. L. Woodward, *The Age of Reform 1815-1870* (O.U.P., 1938), p. 543.

[19] W. K. Clifford, 'The Ethics of Belief', *The Contemporary Review*, 29 (1877), 289-309, reprinted in *Lectures and Essays*, ed. L. Stephen and F. Pollock (1879).

[20] Cf. Swinburne: 'What Newton's might could not make clear/Hath Darwin's might not made?' (*The Commonweal*, stanza xxv)

[21] Note that John Linsie, *Listener*, 70 (1963), suggests that Galton may have been working obliquely, and that his real, though unconscious, objective was to provide an acceptable way of discussing not hereditary endowments but the social realities which in fact determined a man's place in the world (p. 418).

[22] Note that Carnot announced the second law of thermodynamics as early as 1824, the year in which Beethoven's ninth symphony was first performed. For a general account of the arguments about the laws and the later extensions of them see Erwin N. Hiebert, 'The Uses and Abuses of Thermodynamics in Religion', *Daedalus*, 95 (1966), 1046-80: section VII on Wilhelm Ostwald is of particular interest. See also P. M. Heimann, 'The Unseen Universe: Physics and the Philosophy of Nature in Victorian Britain', *British Journal for the History of Science*, 6 (1972), 73-9.

[23] The dilemma is memorably epitomised in Darwin's reflection that the world as a whole 'cannot conceivably be the outcome of chance, yet it seems equally impossible to explain individual beings or types as products of planning or design'.

[24] Letter to Henry Acland, 24 May 1851.

[25] On this point and on the themes of this chapter in general see Jerome B. Schneewind's invaluable study, *Sidgwick's Ethics and Victorian Moral Philosophy* (Oxford, 1977), esp. ch. 6.

[26] For a full and subtle account of the processes I have ruthlessly compressed here see Maurice Mandelbaum, *History, Man and Reason* (Johns Hopkins, 1971), esp. part II, chs. 2-7.

Chapter Twelve: Wilde and the Modern Theatre

[1] Later in the book the narrator comments, 'Is insincerity such a terrible thing? I think not. It is merely a method by which we can multiply our personalities' (XI/142). References are by chapter and page number in the edition by Isobel Murray, Oxford English Novels (Oxford, 1974).

[2] Cf. 'To be good is to be in harmony with one's self,' [Lord Henry] replied, touching the thin stem of his glass with his pale, fine-pointed fingers. 'Discord is to be forced to be in harmony with others. One's own life—that is the important thing. As for the lives of one's neighbours, if one wishes to be a prig or a Puritan, one can flaunt one's moral views about them, but they are not one's concern. Besides, Individualism has really the higher aim. Modern morality consists in accepting the standard of one's age. I consider that for any man of culture to accept the standard of his age is a form of the grossest immorality.'

'But, surely, if one lives merely for one's self, Harry, one pays a terrible price for doing so?' suggested the painter.

'Yes, we are overcharged for everything nowadays.' (VI/78)

For Wilde on Individualism see *The Soul of Man under Socialism* (1891).

[3] *Letters* ed. Hart-Davis 487-8. Cf. 'Most people are other people. Their thoughts are someone else's opinions, their lives a mimicry, their passions a quotation' (*De Profundis*, Penguin English Library p. 169).

[4] In his very interesting article 'The Rage of Caliban', *UTQ*, 37 (1967), 75-89.

[5] *De Profundis and Other Writings* (see n. 3), p. 164.

[6] About this whole section of the book there is more than a faint suggestion of *The Fall of the House of Usher*, especially the character of Roderick.

[7] The speaker of the first part of Dostoievsky's *Letters from the Underworld*, for all his baffling alternations of sanity and madness, sincerity and irony, nevertheless realizes the central dilemma with extreme force. At the same time his desperate attempts to find a level tone of voice show the unbearable nature of his position: it is not one in which a man can rest quiet. Even if it could be proved that human behaviour was totally determined a man 'would once more, out of sheer ingratitude, attempt the perpetration of something which would enable him to insist upon himself; and if he could not effect this, he would then proceed to introduce chaos and disruption into everything, and to devise enormities of all kinds, for the sole purpose, as before, of asserting his personality'. And if all this in turn could be predicted and prevented 'well, in that case, I believe, man would *purposely* become a lunatic, in order to become devoid of reason, and therefore able to insist upon himself' (Everyman's Library, tr. C. J. Hogarth), p. 37. Cf. also Paul Bourget's novel *Le Disciple* (1889), which suggests another link with Taine.

[8] *Feuillets* (*Works* VI, 368).

[9] *Querelle of Brest*, tr. Gregory Streatham (London, 1969), pp. 320, 321-2.

[10] Cf. the similar situation of the young men in *Notre-Dame-des-Fleurs*.

[11] References are to *The Theatre and its Double*, tr. Victor Corti, Signature 4 (London: Calder 1970).

[12] Cf. Theatre is the only place in the world, the last group means we still possess of directly affecting the anatomy, and in neurotic, basely sensual periods like the one in which we are immersed, of attacking that base sensuality through physical means it cannot withstand.

  Snakes do not react to music because of the mental ideas it produces in them, but because they are long, they lie coiled on the ground and their bodies are in contact with the ground along almost their entire length. And the musical vibrations communicated to the ground affect them as a very subtle, very long massage. Well I propose to treat the audience just like those charmed snakes and to bring them back to the subtlest ideas through their anatomies ('No More Masterpieces': p. 61).

[13] Cf. 'As soon as the curtain goes up on Ford's *'Tis Pity She's a Whore* to our great surprise we see before us a man launched on a most arrogant defense of incest, exerting all his youthful, conscious strength both in proclaiming and justifying it. . . . If one is looking for an example of total freedom in rebellion, Ford's *'Tis Pity* offers us this poetic example coupled with a picture of ultimate danger' ("Theatre and the Plague": pp. 19-20).

[14] It is worth noting that Artaud announces bravely, 'The first Theatre of Cruelty show will be entitled: THE CONQUEST OF MEXICO.' There follows a detailed description of the show, which reads like a direct specification of Peter Shaffer's *Royal Hunt of the Sun*.

[15] Possible plays for a Theatre of Cruelty might be Artaud's *The Cenci*, David Rudkin's *Afore Night Come*, and Arrabal's *The Two Executioners*. It is tempting to dismiss the Arrabal play as simply a piece of Grand Guignol: the perversity of Françoise's actions and presumed motives is all that elevates it, if that is the right term. From descriptions Shuji Terayama's version of Swift's *Directions to Servants* (London, 1978) seems to have been a clear example.

[16] Some modern critics, including Martin Esslin, use 'Theatre of the Absurd' as a term for virtually all contemporary playwrights, from Jarry, Apollinaire, Vitrac and Artaud to Beckett and Albee. It seems to me helpful to make what distinctions one can even though the borderlines are far from clear.

[17] There are many other examples of the same device, e.g. the dialogue between Amédée II and Madeleine II in the second act of *Amédée*, cf. Tristan Tzara's early Dada plays about the adventures of M Antipyrene.

[18] Much of what I have said in this paragraph would be equally true of earlier nonsense writers such as Carroll and Lear. What is distinctive in the absurdist playwrights is the aggressive use made of the discontinuities; disorientation rather than amusement is the effect looked for. (This goes some way towards justifying Martin Esslin's association of the Theatre of the Absurd with the Theatre of Cruelty). There is perhaps a stronger resemblance to Blake's *Island in the Moon*, where we find the same combination of nonsense, a kind of obstinate pretence at rationality, and the unexpectedly shocking (by virtue of being physically repugnant or painful).

[19] See Frank Kermode, *The Sense of an Ending* (O.U.P., 1967), p. 117. Note that *The Soft Machine*, the title of one of Burroughs' books, refers to the human body, a pointed reversion to de la Mettrie, cf. Zola's *La Bête Humaine*.

[20] E.g., *Breath, Embers, Eh Joe, Act Without Words*. One of Beckett's later works, *Lessness*, has the French title *Sans*. For Beckett's style cf. Mrs Rooney in *All that Fall*: 'Do you find anything . . . bizarre about my way of speaking? (*Pause*.) I do not mean the voice. (*Pause*.) No, I mean the words. (*Pause. More to herself*.) I use none but the simplest words, I hope, and yet I sometimes find my way of speaking very . . . bizarre.'

Later in the play her husband says to her, 'Do you know, Maddy, sometimes one would think you were struggling with a dead language.' She replies, 'Yes indeed, Dan, I know full well what you mean, I often have that feeling, it is unspeakably excruciating.'

[21] References are to *Happy Days* (London: Faber, 1966). The ironic title is borrowed from H. L. Mencken's entertaining account of his childhood in Baltimore.

[22] For Beckett time is 'a passion without form or stations'.
Cf. (*Long silence*.)

    Vladimir   That passed the time.
    Estragon   It would have passed in any case.
    Vladimir   Yes, but not so rapidly.   (*Waiting for Godot*)
and
    Henry   Keep it going, Ada. Every syllable is a second gained.   (*Embers*)

[23] Cf. Hugh Kenner's comment on the narrative of *Watt*: 'So many trivia are entoiled in such uncertainty that the author cannot make with any confidence the simplest narrative gesture.'

Chapter Thirteen: Fictions of the Prison State

[1] Page references are to the Penguin edition (Harmondsworth: 1970).

[2] When Hobbes says that 'The Obligation of Subjects to the Soveraign, is understood to last as long, and no longer, than the power lasteth, by which he is able to protect them' (ch. 21/p. 272) he is thinking not so much of the subject's right to rebel as of his right to consider the contract with the sovereign power void in certain exceptional circumstances, e.g. if the Monarch dies without heirs. However he seems to consider 'violent death . . . by Intestine Discord [i.e. civil war]' as one of the possible circumstances. References are to *Leviathan* ed. Macpherson (see ch. 4. n. 22).

[3] Cf. Emerson: 'The less government we have, the better—the fewer laws, the less confided power. The antidote to this abuse of formal Government is the influence of private character, the growth of the Individual' ('On Self-Reliance').

[4] Preface to *The Apple Cart* (1930), p. xvi.

[5] Mill no doubt has in mind de Tocqueville's gloomy account of the operations of democracy in the United States. Cf. Flaubert: 'It will no longer be a despot that oppresses the individual but the masses. I shall return to the Bedouins who are free.'

[6] 'The general tendency of things throughout the world is to render mediocrity the ascendant power among mankind' (*On Liberty*, III). Cf. Arnold: '. . . Littleness united is become invincible' (*Empedocles* II. 93-4). See also his letter to Clough of 23 Sept. 1849: 'These are damned times—everything is against one . . . the absence of great *natures*, the unavoidable contact with millions of small ones, . . . our own selves, and the sickening consciousness of our difficulties.'

[7] Cf. '. . . A subject may be put to death, by the command of the Soveraign Power; and yet neither doe the other wrong. . . . For though the action be against the law of Nature, as being contrary to Equitie, (as was the killing of *Uriah*, by *David*;) yet it was not an injurie to *Uriah*; but to *God*. Not to *Uriah*, because the right to doe what he pleased, was given him by *Uriah* himself' (*Leviathan*, part II, ch. 21, p. 265).

[8] Jean Starobinski, *Jean-Jacques Rousseau: la transparence et l'obstacle* (NRF/ Gallimard, 1971).

[9] Cf. 'Man is only free in and through the whole; the whole can only be a sovereign State which tolerates no discussion and no control' (Mussolini).

[10] Carlyle, 'Shooting Niagara: and After?' *Macmillan's Magazine*, 16 (1867).

[11] William Gilpin (1846). Cf. 'A whole bunch of people made into one crawling beast. ... It was westering and westering.'—an early pioneer quoted by W. H. Goetzmann, 'The West and the American Age of Exploration', *Arizona and the West* 2 (1960), 265-75.

[12] John O'Sullivan in *U.S. Magazine and Democratic Review*, 17 (1845), 5. See also Ernest Lee Tuveson, *Redeemer Nation: The Idea of America's Millennial Role* (Chicago U.P., 1968). For the phrase 'manifest destiny' see Edward Dicey, 'Mr Gladstone and our Empire', *The Nineteenth Century*, 1 (1877), 292-308: '[Englishmen] are bound by a manifest destiny to found empires abroad, or, in other words, to make themselves the dominant race in the foreign countries to which they wander.'

[13] Richard Hovey (1864-1900), *Unmanifest Destiny* (1898).

[14] F. D. Roosevelt, renomination speech, 1936.

[15] See K. R. Popper, *The Open Society and its Enemies*, 5th ed. (London: Routledge, 1966), II, 1-80.

[16] E.g. 'Buildings for state purposes the state must erect. And here we think that, in general, the state ought to stop' (Review of Southey's *Sir Thomas More*).

[17] Mill is not completely at odds with Arnold. He envisages a State authority to ensure that all land is used to best advantage: he is prepared to contemplate at least a temporary governing elite: he agrees that a 'culture' is a whole and organic way of life which persists in spite of political change (but in Mill, as in Burke, the implication is that the national character is more important than the apparatus of government): he even shares, rather surprisingly, Arnold's admiration for Humboldt. For a criticism on similar lines of the inadequacy of Mill's concept of freedom and of related views in our own time see B. Croce, 'The Roots of Liberty' in *Freedom Its Meaning*, ed. R. N. Anshen (London: 1942), esp. pp. 66, 72. Cf. C. L. Ten, 'Mill and Liberty', *JHI*, 29 (1968), 45-68; also Charles Taylor (Introd. n. 30).

[18] Emerson, *Essays* 'Self-reliance' (cf. n. 3); Ruskin, *Modern Painters* V. Cf. Carlyle: 'Gurth [the swineherd] is now "emancipated" long since; has what we call "Liberty". Liberty, I am told is a divine thing. Liberty, when it becomes the "Liberty to die by starvation" [as the modern worker has], is not so divine!' *Past and Present* (1843), III, xiii.

[19] Note that even Isaiah Berlin argues that Mill's ideal is to be set aside, in part because it conflicts with 'the ideal of social solidarity' (*Four Essays on Liberty*, liv).

[20] The book was said by Huxley to be a satirical attack on H. G. Wells' *Men Like Gods* (1923). Wells greatly admired Winwood Reade, whose *The Martyrdom of Man* (1872) looked forward to a time when mankind should have shaken off the fetters of religion, and science would lead the way to the perfect state when all men would 'think, feel, and act as one'. See the excellent survey in chapter 13 of John Passmore, *The Perfectibility of Man* (1970).

[21] Defined as 'the power of holding two contradictory beliefs in one's mind simultaneously, and accepting both of them. The Party intellectual knows in which direction his memories must be altered; he therefore knows that he is playing tricks with reality; but by the exercise of *doublethink* he also satisfies himself that reality is not violated.'

[22] One of Orwell's more telling inventions is that of *Newspeak*, the official language designed to make disloyal thoughts impossible to express—'every year fewer and fewer words and the range of consciousness a little smaller.' The language is described at length in an appendix to *1984*. Cf. Thucydides: 'Words changed their ordinary meanings during the war and were construed in new senses'; Wittgenstein: 'To imagine a language is to imagine a form of life.' Wilde: 'One of the results of the extraordinary tyranny of authority is that words are absolutely distorted from their proper and simple meaning, and are used to express the obverse of their right signification.'

[23] Possibly so named in memory of Lancelot Smith, the hero of Kingsley's social novel *Yeast*.

[24] Thus Nabokov can dismiss G. H. Orwell (*sic*) as 'a popular purveyor of illustrated ideas and publicistic fiction' (Foreword to *Invitation to a Beheading*).

[25] One might mention here all the totalitarian states which appear in science fiction. See Mark R. Hillegas, *The Future as Nightmare: H. G. Wells and the Anti-Utopians* (O.U.P.: 1968).

[26] I quote from the Penguin edition (Harmondsworth: 1946), translated from the German by Daphne Hardy. All references are to this edition.

[27] Cf. the short story 'Cloud, Castle, Lake' (1937) in *Nabokov's Dozen*, which is a compact example of the pressure of the State on the individual. The distinction between kinds of freedom is deftly made in another story in the same collection, 'Scenes from the Life of a Double Monster'. The hero is a Siamese twin. His brother, who is permanently linked to him, is not felt as a limitation on his freedom, rather as an extension of his personality. But his twenty-year captivity and exhibition as a travelling freak is felt as an intolerable infringement of liberty.

[28] Schweik always professes a patriotism and a military enthusiasm of the most thoroughgoing kind, which should not perhaps be taken at its face value.

[29] [Cyril Connolly], *The Unquiet Grave* (London: Arrow, 1961), p. 38.

[30] *Leviathan* ch. 17/85.

[31] Bacon, *Advancement of Learning* Bk. II. Cf. Machiavelli: 'How we live is so far removed from how we ought to live, that he who abandons what is done for what ought to be done, will rather learn to bring about his own ruin than his preservation' (*The Prince*, XV).

[32] See J. A. Mazzeo, *Renaissance and Revolution* (London: Secker, 1967), p. 118. Mazzeo's point is that it is inaccurate to translate *lo stato* as 'the State': it is rather the ruler's fundamental prerogative, his *imperium*.

[33] There is an exception in *Catch-22*. Yossarian's friend Dunbar is an interesting character, who at one point in the novel protests against a particular bombing mission simply on the grounds of its inhumanity to the Italian villagers. He thus attacks the doctrine of the nation-state because of its limited scope: if a man owes loyalty to something larger than himself it cannot be to anything smaller than the whole of humanity, and he has no obligation to behave brutally to one section of it in the interests of another section. Patriotism is not enough. However, the idea is not followed up and Dunbar is 'disappeared'.

[34] *Works* (1751), I, p. 99: quoted *Leviathan*, ed. Macpherson, p. 61.

[35] *The Age of Ideology* (New York, 1956), p. 80.

[36] *Four Essays on Liberty* (Oxford, 1969), p. 148. One can find passages in Kant which could be used on the other side of the argument, e.g. 'Every man is to be respected as an absolute end in himself; and it is a crime against the dignity that belongs to him to use him as a mere means to some external purpose'; 'Nobody may compel me to be happy in his own way. Paternalism is the greatest despotism imaginable.'

[37] *The Eighteenth Century Background* (London: Chatto, 1940), p. 178.

[38] See Gertrude Himmelfarb, *Victorian Minds* (London: Weidenfeld, 1968).

[39] *An Enquiry concerning Political Justice* (1793).

[40] *Essay on the First Principles of Government*, (1768).

[41] See e.g. *Logic* VI. iv. 2.

[42] For a brief account of the effect of the theories of thermodynamics on Spencer see P. B. Medawar, *The Art of the Soluble* (London: Methuen, 1967), pp. 39-58.

Chapter Fourteen: 1890-1980

[1] Letter to R. B. Cunninghame-Graham, 14 January 1898. Cf. 'There is a—let us say—a machine. It evolved itself (I am severely scientific) out of a chaos of scraps of iron and behold!—it knits. I am horrified at the horrible work and stand appalled . . . And the most withering thing is that the infamous thing has made itself; made itself without thought, without conscience, without foresight, without eyes, without heart. It is a tragic accident—and it has happened. You can't interfere with it. . . . It knits us in and it knits us out. It has knitted time, space, pain, death, corruption, despair and all the illusions—and nothing matters. I'll admit however that to look at the remorseless process is sometimes amusing.' (Letter of 20 December 1897). Cf. the opening of *The Dynasts*.

[2] David Cooper, introduction to Michel Foucault, *Madness and Civilization* (New York: Random House, 1965), quoted by Lionel Trilling, *Sincerity and Authenticity*, revised ed. (Oxford, 1974), p. 170.

[3] In particular the areas in which freedom of choice may be exercised are becoming steadily more trivial, while the major decisions, such as what currency a citizen may deal in, what his wages shall be, how much of his earnings he will be allowed to

spend, and where his children shall be educated, have all, like freedom to travel without a passport, been taken out of the hands of individuals.

[4] A.J.P. Taylor, *English History 1914-1945* (Oxford, 1965), opening sentence. No doubt there is an element of exaggeration here—Lloyd George's 1909 budget, for example, raised income tax from 1s. to 1s. 2d.—but the obligations imposed by the State, such as jury-duty and the completion of census returns, were far from severe.

[5] Warwick Deeping, *Sorrell and Son* (1925), ch. 37, §2.

[6] For a comprehensive treatment of these issues see Trilling (n. 2) esp. chs. 4 and 5. See also ch. 12, n. 3.

[7] Cf. David Riesman, *Individualism Reconsidered* (1954), e.g. 'To the degree that capitalist individualism has fostered an ethic of callousness, the result has been to undermine all forms of individualism, good and bad.' (p. 15). See also R. H. Tawney, *Religion and the Rise of Capitalism*, iii iii.

[8] Cf. 'Les fléaux physiques et les calamités de la nature humaine ont rendu la société nécessaire. La société a ajouté aux malheurs de le nature. Les inconvénients de la société ont amené la nécessité du gouvernement, et le gouvernement ajoute aux malheurs de la société. Voilà l'histoire de la nature humaine.' (Chamfort).

[9] John Macmurray, *Persons in Relation* (London: Faber, 1961), p. 198. Cf. Bertrand Russell, *Authority and the Individual* Reith lectures 1948-9 (London, 1949), p. 117.

[10] Cf. Ruskin: 'Men in the present century understand the word Useful in a strange way . . . as if houses and lands, and food and raiment were alone Useful, and as if Sight, Thought, and Admiration were all profitless, so that men insolently call themselves Utilitarians who would turn, if they had their way, themselves and all their race into vegetables.' (*Modern Painters* II).

[11] E.g. 'Murphy's mind pictured itself as a large hollow sphere, hermetically closed to the universe without. This was not an impoverishment, for it excluded nothing that it did not itself contain. Nothing ever had been, was or would be in the universe outside it but was already present as virtual or actual, or virtual rising into actual, or actual falling into virtual, in the universe inside it.' (Beckett, *Murphy* ch. 6).

[12] Epilogue to *War and Peace* (see Introd. n. 25) Part Two, section 10, p. 1437.

[13] According to Shaw, Sidney and Beatrice Webb substituted the term Political Science for Political Economy (Appendix to *Intelligent Woman's Guide*).

[14] Cf. Virginia Woolf: 'Our age is meagre to the verge of destitution . . . It is an age of fragments . . . Much of what is best in contemporary work has the appearance of being noted under pressure, taken down in a bleak shorthand which preserves with astonishing brilliance the movements and expressions of the figures as they pass across the screen. But the flash is soon over, and there remains with us a profound dissatisfaction.'

[15] *Suicide: a Study in Sociology*, tr. J. A. Spaulding and G. Simpson (Glencoe, Illinois: Free Press, 1951), p. 389.

[16] Cf. E. M. Forster '. . . the doctrine of *Laisser-faire* is the only one that seems to work in the world of the spirit.' ('The Challenge of our Time' in *Two Cheers for Democracy* (1951)).

Chapter Fifteen: Conclusion

[1] 'Freedom and Necessity' in *Philosophical Essays* (London, 1954), pp. 271-84; 'Fatalism' in *The Concept of a Person* (London, 1963), pp. 235-68; *Man as a Subject for Science* Comte Memorial Lecture 6, (London: Athlone, 1964)—it is interesting to note that although Ayer derives his title from *Crotchet Castle* Shelley had earlier referred to the human mind as 'a legitimate object of science' in the discussion of necessity in the Notes to *Queen Mab*; 'Chance', *Scientific American*, 213 (1965), 44-54; 'The Freedom of the Will' in *The Central Questions of Philosophy* (London: Weidenfeld, 1973), pp. 227-32.

[2] Cf. Huxley's Sunday evening address 'On the Physical Basis of Life' delivered in Edinburgh in 1868, revised and reprinted in *Lay Sermons, Addresses, and Reviews* (1870), 132-61.

[3] Cf. Hume, *An Enquiry concerning Human Understanding*, sect. VIII, pt.1.

[4] Cf. Hume: 'It is commonly allowed that madmen have no liberty. But, were we to judge by their actions, these have less regularity and constancy than the actions of

wise men, and consequently are further removed from necessity. Our way of thinking in this particular is, therefore, absolutely inconsistent; but is a natural consequence of these confused ideas and undefined terms, which we so commonly make use of in our reasonings, especially on the present subject.' *A Treatise of Human Nature*, Bk. II, Pt. 3, sect. 1.

5 The characters in this novel have virtually no will: they are almost totally subject to inexplicable waves of emotion, such as sexual antagonism or the impulse to sexual submission. These emotions alternate rapidly and violently and determine the character's behaviour in the immediate situation, but apparently without leading them to any strategy for mitigating the violence of the attacks. This is the famous Lawrentian flux and reflux. Qualities thus take on a life of their own—'There came a wanness between them'—so that these emotions have the energy that we expect of characters in a novel, while the people become simply the receptacles for the emotions. One interesting point is that these inert creatures, helpless in the grip of surging emotional impulses, can in a way be regarded as acting with the utmost degree of freedom. They are guided by no moral principles, nor by any very well defined social code, and they never feel the need to do anything to make anybody else happy. Lawrence in the end forces us to ask what we mean by a free action. Cf. Lawrence's letter to Edward Garnett (5 June 1914): 'In Turgenev, and in Tolstoy, and in Dostoevsky, the moral scheme into which all the characters fit—and it is nearly the same scheme—is, whatever the extraordinariness of the characters themselves, dull, old, dead..... You mustn't look in my novel for the old stable *ego* of the character. There is another *ego*, according to whose action the individual is unrecognizable....'

6 Cf. Kierkegaard: 'In all truly serious business, the law of either—or prevails. Either I am the man whose serious business this is, I am called to it and am willing to take a decisive risk; or, if this be not the case, then the seriousness of the business demands that I do not meddle with it at all. Nothing is more detestable and mean, and nothing discloses and effects a deeper demoralization than this lackadaisical wishing to enter "somewhat" into matters which demand an *aut—aut, aut Caesar aut nihil.*' ('What says the Fire Marshal,' *The Present Moment* VI, 5, tr. Lee M. Hollander); cf. Browning, *Bishop Blougram's Apology* 275-300.

7 'Fatalism' (See n. 1). Note that Ayer himself (p. 261) is not in favour of couching the argument in terms of prediction.

8 See Karl R. Popper, 'Of Clouds and Clocks' in *Objective Knowledge* (Oxford: 1972), pp. 212-13.

9 'Fatalism' (see n. 1), p. 262.

10 Notes to *Queen Mab* VII 135, 136.

11 *Das Naturbild der Heutigen Physik* (see Introduction, n. 24), p. 39.

12 L. Susan Stebbing, *Philosophy and the Physicists* (Harmondsworth: Penguin, 1937) p. 138.

13 *Determinism and Indeterminism in Modern Physics* tr. O. Theodor Benfey (Yale: 1956), p. 207.

14 *Causality and Chance in Modern Physics* (London: 1957).

15 Cf. Heisenberg, *Das Naturbild*, p. 42

16 Cf. Harold Jeffreys, *The Theory of Probability* (Oxford: 1961).

17 See Jacques Monod, *Chance and Necessity: an essay on the natural philosophy of modern biology* tr. A. Wainhouse (N.Y: Knopf, 1971) esp. p. 116, where Monod makes the point with great emphasis that the basic living property is not a tendency to evolve but molecular invariance. Evolution comes only from mistakes, apparently uncaused, in reproduction, DNA accepting the original and the misprint. Some misprints are in fact improvements and thus help the species to evolve, but this does not affect the central point that they are reproductive errors. Cf. however P.B. Medawar, *The Art of the Soluble* (London: Methuen, 1967) where he makes the point that chemical polymorphism is the general rule. 'The *product* of evolution is itself a population' with its own built-in *in*equalities. 'It is the population as a whole that breeds true, not its individual members' (p. 103).

18 *From Biology to Ethics* Salk Institute Occasional Papers I (San Diego: 1969), p. 19.

19 *The Analogy of Religion*, Introduction, sect. III (end). Butler is following John Willeims here: see Ian Hacking, *The Emergence of Probability* (Cambridge U.P., 1975), pp. 11, 82.

[20] Quoted by Macneile Dixon, *The Human Situation*, p. 305. Cf. Laplace: 'The most important questions of life are, for the most part, really only problems of probability.' *Théorie analytique des probabilités.*

[21] 'Of Clouds and Clocks' (see n. 8), pp. 214-15.

[22] E.g. D. Føllesdal, 'Quantification into causal context' in *Boston Studies in Philosophy of Science* ed. R. S. Cohen and M. W. Wartofsky (New York: 1965) II, 263–74; J. R. Lucas, *The Concept of Probability* (Oxford: 1970); H. O. A. Wold (ed.) *Model building in the Human Sciences* Entretiens de Monaco (1966), pp. 265-95.

[23] *A Probabilistic Theory of Causality* Acta Philosophica Fennica Fasc. XXIV (Amsterdam: North-Holland Publishing, 1970), p. 91.

[24] Ibid. pp. 91,94. In his conclusion Suppes throws out the idea, 'In my own view, many of the traditional dilemmas about free will are now replaced by dilemmas about information and how information is introduced into a causal system.' He promises to examine the question in some future works. Meanwhile the *Probabilistic Theory*, although I have had to take its mathematics largely on trust, seems to me to be a particularly interesting contribution to the discussion and a welcome attempt to bring various disciplines to bear on a common problem.

[25] *Chance and Necessity* (see n. 17), p. 180.

[26] Cf. Hardy's poem *Great Things*, which ends: 'Will these be always great things,/Great things to me?. . . /Let it befall that One will call,/"Soul, I have need of thee."/What then? Joy-jaunts, impassioned flings,/Love, and its ecstasy,/Will always have been great things,/Great things to me!'

[27] 'A Free Man's Worship' in *Mysticism and Logic* (Harmondsworth: Penguin, 1953), p. 51.

[28] Professor Nichol, quoted by Arnold in 'Byron', *Essays in Criticism*, 2nd series.

[29] *The Prince*, tr. L. Ricci, rev. E. Vincent (Oxford: World's Classics, 1935), p. 110. The remainder of the chapter casts some doubt on this sanguine estimate. It appears that Machiavelli has very little belief that any man is adaptable enough to hit consistently on the successful course of action, 'for if one could change one's nature with time and circumstances, fortune would never change'. He concludes with the surprising observation that if one must have a predisposition towards one type of policy 'I certainly think that it is better to be impetuous than cautious' (114).

[30] *Essay Concerning Human Understanding* 4th ed., Bk. II, ch. xxi, sect. 47.

[31] Cf. Whitehead: 'It is impossible to meditate on time and the mystery of the creative passage of nature without an overwhelming emotion at the limitations of human intelligence.' Quoted by G. J. Whitrow, *The Nature of Time* (Harmondsworth: Penguin, 1975), p. 144.

[32] See Alister Hardy, *The Living Stream: A Restatement of Evolution Theory and Its Relation to the Spirit of Man* (London: Collins, 1965).

[33] To continue the crude analogy from p. 417 it is as if the game were now not Snakes and Ladders but Vingt-et-un, where each player can exercise one simple option if he thinks that it will improve his chances.

[34] Poetry might be regarded as a randomizing agent on the grounds that it sets up unpredictable associations between words: cruder examples are action paintings, aleatory music, improvised drama and cut-up novels. I emphasize the restricted scope of the process which I am postulating here. From one point of view the tragedy of the Romantics was to suppose that the limited activity of deliberately injecting some random elements into a situation was the same as the free exercise of the power of fashioning circumstances to the will of the individual.

[35] Cf. Lord Acton: 'Liberty is not a means to a higher political end. It is itself the highest political end.'

[36] I have not come across this difficult area more fully and sensibly explored in a specifically literary context than it is in Charles Morgan's *Liberties of the Mind* (London: Macmillan, 1951).

[37] For the parallel between Skinner and Owen see Owen's *A New View of Society: Essays on the Formation of Character*, e.g.: 'Any general character, from the best to the worst, from the most ignorant to the most enlightened, may be given to any community, even to the world at large, by the application of proper means; which means are to a great extent at the command and under the control of those who have influence in the affairs of men. . . . That this principle is true to the utmost limit of the terms, is evident from the experience of all past ages, and from every existing fact,' (First Essay, 1812). See also J. Butt, I. Donnachie and J. R. Hume,

'Robert Owen of New Lanark,'*Industrial Archaeology*, 8 (1971): 'He backed up a system of supervision by overseers and spinning masters with his "silent monitor". This was a four-sided wooden block, designed to hang on the machine and coloured white, yellow, blue and black. The colour of the side showing to the front represented "the conduct of the individual during the preceding day"; white was excellent, and black the opposite. "Books of character" were kept up to date by the supervisors and regularly inspected by Owen.' One of the most prominent buildings in New Lanark was the New Institution for the Formation of Character.

[38] *Brave New World*, ch. 2; *We* tr. Bernard Guerney, 36th entry.

[39] *The Form of the Personal*, 2 vols. (London: Faber, I *The Self as Agent*, 1957: II *Persons in Relation*, 1961) esp. II, chs. 2, 6 and 9.

[40] In *Freedom Its Meaning*, ed. R. N. Anshen (London: Allen and Unwin, 1942).

[41] Cf. Macmurray (see n. 40) 'Only persons can limit the freedom of persons.' (p. 184); Johnson: 'They make a rout about *universal* liberty, without considering that all that is to be valued, or indeed can be enjoyed by individuals, is *private* liberty.' *Life*, ed. Hill, II 60 (May 1768).

[42] Although the principle is awkward to formulate, the extreme cases are not hard to decide. A comparison of *Mansfield Park* and *1984* illustrates clearly the difference between benevolent and malign forms of education of the young. *The Prime of Miss Jean Brodie* is less easily dealt with. Jean Brodie is within her rights to try to put 'old heads on young shoulders' and even to say, 'Give me a girl at an impressionable age and she is mine for life', because she is moulding her pupils' minds through love. This is not an easy decision for the reader to make, but I think that Miss Brodie is, as presented, just in the right. But she is wrong to try to impose her political ideas on them, especially totalitarian ideas, since she has ceased to treat them as persons. Thus although the political charges against her are a substitute for personal charges, there is an ironic justice in the fact that they are the charges that finally remove her from Marcia Blaine.

[43] Cf. E. M. Forster: ' "Love is what is needed" we chant, and then sit back and the world goes on as before. The fact is we can only love what we know personally. And we cannot know much. In public affairs, in the rebuilding of civilization, something much less dramatic and emotional is needed, namely, tolerance. . . . If you don't like people, put up with them as well as you can. Don't try to love them: you can't, you'll only strain yourself. But try to tolerate them. On the basis of that tolerance a civilised future may be built' ('Tolerance' in *Two Cheers for Democracy* (London: 1951), pp. 56-7.) Cf. Hazlitt on Bentham in *The Spirit of the Age*: 'The heart hovers and fixes nearer home.'

[44] Constant, *Cours de Politique Constitutionelle* (1818-20).

[45] *Democracy in America*, tr. Henry Reeve, Pt. 2, Bk. IV, ch. 6.

[46] *The Last Years: Journals 1853-5*, ed. and trans. R. Gregor Smith (London: Collins, 1968), p. 245 [*XI A 112*].

[47] E. A. Havelock, *Prometheus* (Seattle and London: U. of Washington P., 1968) p. 94.

[48] Robert Nozick, *Anarchy, State, and Utopia* (Oxford: Blackwell, 1974), esp. ch. 3.

[49] *The Social Philosophers* (London: Heinemann, 1974) esp. section 6; *Twilight of Authority* (London: Heinemann, 1976).

[50] *Postscript* (1835).

[51] 'Two concepts of Liberty' in *Four Essays on Liberty* (Oxford: 1969) pp. 118-172; see also Berlin's Introduction.

[52] See Intro, n. 26. In fairness to Professor Skinner I should point out that some of the passages quoted are taken from the brief summaries at the end of each chapter: the case is less crudely set out in the text.

[53] Bertrand Russell, *Authority and the Individual* Reith Lectures 1948-49 (London: 1949), p. 118.

[54] Cf. Partick Gardiner, 'Freedom as an Aesthetic Idea' in *The Idea of Freedom: Essays in honour of Isaiah Berlin* ed. Alan Ryan (Oxford: 1979), pp. 27-39.

[55] Preface to *Prometheus Unbound*.

[56] *Chance and Necessity* (see n. 17), p. 44.

[57] Keats, *Sleep and Poetry* 267-8; cf. '. . . . the great end/Of Poesy, that it should be a friend/To soothe the cares and lift the thoughts of man.' (ibid. 245-7).

Index

Numerals in bold type indicate the more important entries. *q* before a page number indicates a reference including a direct quotation. *n* following a page number indicates that the reference is to a note, (e.g. 457*n*22 refers to note 22 on p.457)